Plymouth University
Charles Seale-Hayne Library
Subject to status this item may be renewed
via your Primo account

http://primo.plymouth.ac.uk
Tel: (01752) 588588

Tourism and Geopolitics:

Issues and Concepts from Central and Eastern Europe

_____

Tourism and Geopolitics:

Issues and Concepts from Central and Eastern Europe

_____

Edited by

Derek Hall

Seabank Associates

CABI is a trading name of CAB International

CABI	CABI
Nosworthy Way	745 Atlantic Avenue
Wallingford	8th Floor
Oxfordshire OX10 8DE	Boston, MA 02111
UK	USA
Tel: +44 (0)1491 832111	Tel: +1 (617)682-9015
Fax: +44 (0)1491 833508	E-mail: cabi-nao@cabi.org
E-mail: info@cabi.org	
Website: www.cabi.org	

A catalogue record for this book is available from the British Library, London, UK.

Library of Congress Cataloging-in-Publication Data

Names: Hall, Derek R., editor.
Title: Tourism and geopolitics : issues and concepts from Central and Eastern
   Europe / edited by Derek Hall, Seabank Associates.
Description: Wallingford, Oxfordshire, UK ; Boston, MA, USA : CABI is a
   trading name of CAB International, CABI, [2017] | Includes bibliographical
   references and index.
Identifiers: LCCN 2016035553 (print) | LCCN 2016051943 (ebook) | ISBN
   9781780647616 (hbk : alk. paper) | ISBN 9781780647623 (ePDF) | ISBN
   9781780647630 (ePub)
Subjects: LCSH: Tourism--Political aspects--Europe, Central. |
   Tourism--Political aspects--Europe, Eastern. | Geopolitics--Europe,
   Central. | Geopolitics--Europe, Eastern.
Classification: LCC G155.E85 T66 2017 (print) | LCC G155.E85 (ebook) | DDC
   338.4/79143--dc23
LC record available at https://lccn.loc.gov/2016035553

ISBN-13: 978 1 78064 761 6

Commissioning editor: Claire Parfitt
Editorial assistant: Emma McCann
Production editor: James Bishop

Typeset by SPi, Pondicherry, India
Printed and bound in the UK by CPI Group (UK) Ltd, Croydon, CRO 4YY.

Contents

Figures

Tables

Boxes

Abbreviations

ABTA	Association of British Travel Agents
AITO	Association of Independent Tour Operators
ASSR	Autonomous Soviet Socialist Republic
ASW	Anti-submarine warfare
B3P	Balkan Peace Park Partnership
BfN	German Federal Agency for Nature Conservation
BGN	Bulgarian *leva* (currency)
BiH	Bosnia and Herzegovina
BUND	Friends of the Earth, Germany
CBC	Cross-Border Cooperation (Programme)
CBD	Convention on Biological Diversity
CEE	Central and Eastern Europe
CIC	International Council for Game and Wildlife Conservation
CIS	Commonwealth of Independent States
CMEA	Council for Mutual Economic Aid (COMECON)
COP	Conference of the parties
CPSU	Communist Party of the Soviet Union
DBU	German Federal Environment Foundation
DPRK	Democratic People's Republic of Korea (North Korea)
€	Euro
EAEU	Eurasian Economic Union (also EEU or EAU)
EBRD	European Bank for Reconstruction and Development
ECNC	European Centre for Nature Conservation
ECoC	European Capital of Culture
EEA	European Economic Area
EEG	Evolutionary economic geography
EES	Eurasian Economic Space
ENoM	European Night of Museums
ENoMiR	European Night of Museums in Romania
ENPI	European Neighbourhood and Partnership Instrument
ERDF	European Regional Development Fund
ETC	European Travel Commission, European Territorial Cooperation
EU	European Union

EULEX	European Union Rule of Law Mission
FAO	Food and Agriculture Organization of the United Nations
FBiH	Federation of Bosnia and Herzegovina
FCO	(UK) Foreign and Commonwealth Office
FDI	Foreign direct investment
FEZ	Free economic zone
FIFA	*Fédération Internationale de Football Association*
FTD	Facilitated Transit Document
FYROM	Former Yugoslav Republic of Macedonia
GDP	Gross domestic product
GfK	Growth from Knowledge
GIZ	German Society for International Cooperation
IATA	International Air Transport Association
ICJ	International Court of Justice
ICO	International Civilian Office
ICOM	International Council of Museums
IFI	International financial institution
IICCMER	*Institutul de Investigare a Crimelor Comunismului şi Memoria Exilului Românesc* (Institute for the Investigation of Communist Crimes and the Memory of the Romanian Exile)
IMF	International Monetary Fund
IOC	International Olympic Committee
IPA	Instrument for Pre-Accession Assistance
ISIS	Islamic State of Iraq and Syria
IUCN	International Union for the Conservation of Nature
KFOR	NATO Kosovo Force
KiViN	Russian 'Cheerful and Resourceful Club', youth wing
KLA	Kosovo Liberation Army (*UÇK*)
LBT	Local border traffic
LCC	Low-cost carrier
LNG	Liquefied natural gas
LOT	Polish Airlines (*Polskie Linie Lotnicze*)
MAP	(NATO) Membership Application Plan
MES	Macedonian Ecological Society
MFA	(Russian) Ministry of Foreign Affairs
MMA	Monitor, mentor and advise
MOTKR/MTKR	Ministry of Tourism of the Kaliningrad Region
MSEs	Mega sport events
NATO	North Atlantic Treaty Organization
NEMO	Network of European Museum Organisations
NGO	Non-governmental organisation
NLP	National Liberal Party
OHR	Office of the High Representative
OLI	Ownership–location–internalisation
OMA	Oradea Metropolitan Area
ONT	*Oficiul Naţional de Turism*
OSCE	Organization for Security and Cooperation in Europe
OUN	Organization of Ukrainian Nationalists
PAN	Protected area network
PHARE	Poland and Hungary: Assistance for Restructuring their Economies
PPNEA	Preservation of Natural Environment in Albania
R2P	Responsibility to Protect

REC	Regional Environmental Center for Central and Eastern Europe
RF	Russian Federation
RNMR	National Network of Romanian Museums (*Reţeaua Naţională a Muzeelor din România*)
RS	Republika Srpska
RSFSR	Russian Soviet Federative Socialist Republic
SAPs	Structural adjustment programmes
SAS	Scandinavian Airline System
SEZ	Special economic zone
SMEs	Small and medium-size enterprises
SNV	Netherlands Development Organisation (*Stichting Nederlandse Vrijwilligers*/Foundation of Netherlands Volunteers)
SPAI or SPACI	Stability Pact Anti-Corruption Initiative
SWOT	Strengths, weaknesses, opportunities, threats
TACIS	Technical Assistance to the Commonwealth of Independent States and Georgia
TBPA	Transboundary protected area
TNC	Transnational corporation
UAE	United Arab Emirates
UÇK	*Ushtria Çlirimitare e Kosovës* (KLA)
UEFA	Union of European Football Associations
UK	United Kingdom of Great Britain and Northern Ireland
UNDP	United Nations Development Programme
UNEP	United Nations Environment Programme
UNESCO	United Nations Educational, Scientific and Cultural Organization
UNESCO-BRESCE	UNESCO Regional Office for Science and Culture in Europe
UNMIK	United Nations Mission in Kosovo
UNSC	United Nations Security Council
UNWTO	United Nations World Tourism Organization
USA	United States of America
USD	United States dollar
USN	United States Navy
USSR	Union of Soviet Socialist Republics (Soviet Union)
WDA	Warsaw Destination Alliance
WTO	World Tourism Organization (UNWTO)/World Trade Organization
WTTC	World Travel and Tourism Council
WWF	World Wide Fund for Nature

Contributors

John Berryman teaches International Relations in the **Department of Politics, School of Social Sciences, History and Philosophy, Birkbeck College, University of London, Malet Street, London WC1E 7HX, UK**, and is Associate Professor of International Studies at Ithaca College, New York (London Division). His research focuses on Russian foreign and security policy and he has held a British Council Award for research in Russia. He also has a research interest in sea power, and has been awarded the Julian Corbett Prize in Modern Naval History by the Institute of Historical Research, University of London. He is a member of the International Institute for Strategic Studies and the Royal Institute of International Affairs.
E-mail: johnberryman@blueyonder.co.uk

Frances Brown is a freelance editor and consultant. She is the former editor of *Tourism Management* and of *Space Policy*. Her authored books include *Tourism: Blessing or Blight?*
Seabank Associates, Maidens, Ayrshire K26 9NN, Scotland, UK.
E-mail: fbrown@seabankscotland.co.uk

Ana Maria Crăciun is a PhD candidate in the **Department of Human and Economic Geography, Faculty of Geography, University of Bucharest, B-dul N. Bălcescu no 1, Bucharest 010041, Romania**. She is currently completing her thesis on tourist interpretation and the role it plays in understanding the relationship between place, identity and society. She is mainly interested in the interpretation of communist heritage, with a special focus on Romanian particularities.
E-mail: anaa.craciun@gmail.com

Dr **Marta Derek** is a geographer, an Assistant Professor in the **Faculty of Geography and Regional Studies, University of Warsaw, 30 Krakowskie Przedmieście str., 00-927 Warsaw, Poland**. Her research and teaching interests include tourism and local development, tourism planning and development, and tourism and regeneration, with a focus on urban areas. Her current research projects focus on tourism and leisure in urban brownfields and the ecosystem services concept in tourism and recreation.
E-mail: m.derek@uw.edu.pl

Dr **Pavlo Doan** graduated from the Taras Shevchenko National University of Kyiv in 2012 in Human Geography and Tourism, and obtained his PhD in Human Geography with a thesis on local tourist systems in 2015. His research areas cover: tourism, human geography, sustainable development, tourism administration and regional studies. As well as being on the geography staff at Taras Shevchenko, he is also co-owner of a Kyiv tour operating company.
Department of Regional Geography and Tourism, Faculty of Geography, Taras Shevchenko National University, ulitsa Vladimirskaya, 60, Kyiv, Ukraine 01601.
E-mail: doan.pavel@gmail.com

Dr **Sylwia Dołzbłasz** is a geographer and economist. Currently, she holds the position of Assistant Professor in the **Department of Spatial Management, Institute of Geography and Regional Development, University of Wrocław, ul. Kuźnicza 49–55, 50-138 Wrocław, Poland**, working as a researcher and lecturer. She has a strong background in political geography and regional development. Her latest research focuses on borders, border areas and transborder interactions.

E-mail: sylwia.dolzblasz@uwr.edu.pl

Dr **Daniela Dumbrăveanu** is an Associate Professor in the **Department of Human and Economic Geography, Faculty of Geography, University of Bucharest, B-dul N. Bălcescu no 1, Bucharest 010041, Romania**. Her research interests in human geography are particularly focused on tourism and geography of health. Tourist regional development, identity, destination identity, the communist past interpreted by museums, Romanian health-care system development and medical personnel migration are among her ongoing topics of interest. She is a member of the editorial team of *Human Geographies – Journal of Studies and Research in Human Geography*.

E-mail: daniela.dumbraveanu@geo.unibuc.ro

Alexandru Gavriş is a lecturer in Economic Geography in the **Faculty of Business and Tourism, Bucharest University of Economic Studies, Calea Dorobanţi 15–17, Sector 1 Bucharest 010552, Romania**. His research covers methodologies applied to Bucharest city, which he has analysed through many perspectives, ranging from risk hazards to tourism.

E-mail: alexandru.gavris@rei.ase.ro

C. Michael Hall is a Professor in the **Department of Management, Marketing and Entrepreneurship** at the **University of Canterbury, Private Bag 4800, Christchurch, New Zealand 8140**; Docent, Department of Geography, University of Oulu, Finland, and a Visiting Professor, Linnaeus University School of Business and Economics, Kalmar, Sweden. He has published widely on tourism, regional development and environmental change.

E-mail: michael.hall@canterbury.ac.nz

Derek Hall latterly held a personal chair in regional development at the Scottish Rural University College, and is currently a visiting senior research fellow at Plymouth University, UK. As a geographer/anthropologist, he has pursued interests in Central and Eastern Europe since the 1960s. **Seabank Associates, Maidens, Ayrshire K26 9NN, Scotland, UK.**

E-mail: derekhall@seabankscotland.co.uk

Kevin Hannam is Professor of Tourism in **The Business School, Edinburgh Napier University, 29 Buccleuch Place, Edinburgh EH8 9JS, Scotland, UK,** and a research affiliate at the University of Johannesburg, South Africa. He is a founding co-editor of the journals *Mobilities* and *Applied Mobilities* (Routledge), co-author of the books *Understanding Tourism* (Sage) and *Tourism and India* (Routledge) and co-editor of the *Routledge Handbook of Mobilities Research and Moral Encounters in Tourism* (Ashgate).

E-mail: k.hannam@napier.ac.uk

Hana Horáková is an Associate Professor of Social Anthropology in the **Department of International Relations and European Studies, Metropolitan University Prague, Prokopova 100/16, 130 00 Praha 3, Czech Republic**. She holds a PhD in African Studies from the Institute of the Near East and Africa, Charles University, Prague. She is President of the Czech Association for African Studies. Her research interests include anthropology of tourism and rural studies, anthropology of sub-Saharan Africa focusing on the politics of identity and nationalism, and theories of culture. She has published, edited and co-edited several books and other texts in the fields of social anthropology and African studies.

E-mail: hana.horakova@mup.cz

Ioan Ianoş is a full Professor in the **Faculty of Geography, University of Bucharest, B-dul N. Bălcescu no 1, Bucharest 010041, Romania,** where his research focus has evolved through the years. His interests target urban studies, local and regional development, the dynamics of settlement systems and spatial planning. Ioan has written over 230 papers (academic papers, book chapters, books) and has been the director of about 80 research grants. Currently, he is the director of the Interdisciplinary Centre for Advanced Research on Territorial Dynamics (CICADIT).

E-mail: ianos50@yahoo.com

Dr **Stanislav Ivanov** is a Professor in Tourism Economics and Vice Rector (Research), **Varna University of Management, 13 Oborishte str., 9000 Varna, Bulgaria**. He is editor-in-chief of the *European Journal of Tourism Research* (http://ejtr.vumk.eu) and CEO of the consulting agency Zangador (http://www.zangador.eu). His research interests include hotel chains, destination marketing, tourism and economic growth, political issues in tourism and special interest tourism.
E-mail: stanislav.ivanov@vumk.eu

Dr **Maya Ivanova** is an Assistant Professor in Tourism at **Varna University of Management, 13 Oborishte str., 9000 Varna, Bulgaria**, editorial assistant for the *European Journal of Tourism Research* (http://ejtr.vumk.eu), a certified IATA instructor, and CEO at the consulting agency Zangador (http://www.zangador.eu). Her research interests include tour operators, airlines and hotel chains.
E-mail: maya.ivanova@vumk.eu

Prof Dr **Peter Jordan** is a cultural and tourism geographer, atlas editor and toponymist with a regional focus on south-east Europe and the Adriatic space; teaching at the universities of Vienna, Klagenfurt (Austria) and Cluj-Napoca (Romania). A former director of the Austrian Institute of East and Southeast European Studies in Vienna and editor of the *Atlas of Eastern and Southeastern Europe (1989–2014)*, he is co-editor of the toponymic book series *Name & Place*, managing editor of the Communications of the Austrian Geographical Society, chair of the Austrian Board on Geographical Names, convenor of the UNGEGN Working Group on Exonyms and vice-chair of the Joint ICA/IGU Commission on Toponymy, and has published 344 scientific books and articles.
Austrian Academy of Sciences, Institute of Urban and Regional Research, Postgasse 7/4/2, 1010 Vienna, Austria.
E-mail: peter.jordan@oeaw.ac.at

Dr **Viktoriia Kiptenko** is an Associate Professor at the **Department of Regional Geography and Tourism, Faculty of Geography, Taras Shevchenko National University, ulitsa Vladimirskaya, 60, Kyiv, Ukraine 01601**. Her main teaching areas are research methods in tourism, tourism management, tourism policy and spatial planning for tourism, geography of information society, geospatial governance and geoglobalistics. Viktoriia is the author and co-author of over 70 published works, including textbooks.
E-mail: vika@goal.com.ua

Dr **Elena Kropinova**, a geographer, is Associate Professor in the **Department of Services and Tourism, Institute of Recreation, Tourism and Physical Education, Immanuel Kant Baltic Federal University of Russia, ul. Aleksandra Nevskogo, 14–β, Kaliningrad, Russia, 236041**. She has coordinated projects of INTERREG III B and ENPI CBC 2007–2013 programmes. She has also been head of the Ministry for Tourism of the Kaliningrad Region and is currently Vice-Director of Research for the Museum of the World Ocean in Kaliningrad.
E-mail: ekropinova@kantiana.ru; e.kropinova@world-ocean.ru

Dr **Jussi Laine** is Assistant Professor at the **Karelian Institute, University of Eastern Finland, Yliopistokatu 2, Aurora, PO Box 111, FI-80101 Joensuu, Finland**. Currently, he also serves as the Executive Secretary and Treasurer of the Association for Borderlands Studies and as the Project Manager of the EU FP7 project EUBORDERSCAPES. His research interests include geopolitics and particularly border studies, within which he seeks to understand better the multifaceted nature of borders, and in particular the actual and potential role of civil society in transgressing them.
E-mail: jussi.laine@uef.fi

Dr **Erika Nagy**, geographer, is a senior research fellow at the **Centre for Economic and Regional Studies, Hungarian Academy of Sciences, Békéscsaba, 7621 Pécs, Papnövelde u. 22, Hungary**, and is a senior lecturer at the University of Szeged. Her research interests lie in retail restructuring and the reorganisation of consumption spaces in CEE, and gentrification and suburbanisation processes in post-socialist contexts, peripheralisation and marginalisation of/in rural spaces and urban planning.
E-mail: nagye@rkk.hu

Dr **Piotr Niewiadomski** is an economic geographer interested in the worldwide development of the tourism production system, the influence of tourism on economic development in host territories and economic, environmental and sociocultural sustainability in tourism. He is now Lecturer in Human Geography in the **School of Geosciences, University of Aberdeen, St Mary's Building, Elphinstone Road, Aberdeen AB24 3UF, Scotland, UK.**
E-mail: p.niewiadomski@abdn.ac.uk

Dr **Rahman Nurković** is a full Professor in the **Department of Geography, Faculty of Science, University of Sarajevo, Zmaja od Bosne 33–35, 71000 Sarajevo, Bosnia and Herzegovina**, where he is also editor-in-chief of the journal *Geografski Pregled* and Project Leader of the Bosnia and Herzegovina CEEPUS III network – GEOREGNET 2013. He has published on many aspects of the geography of Bosnia and Herzegovina.
E-mail: rahmannurkovic@hotmail.com

Edyta Pijet-Migoń is a geographer, lecturer in the **Institute of Tourism, Wrocław School of Banking, Fabryczna Str 29–31, 53-609 Wrocław, Poland**, with special interest in the role of aviation in tourism, business tourism and geoheritage. She has more than 10 years of working experience as an airline representative and business travel advisor. In her doctoral thesis, she examined changes in passenger air transport in Poland after accession to the European Union.
E-mail: edyta.migon@wsb.wroclaw.pl

Dr **Alexander Sebentsov** is a researcher at the **Laboratory for Geopolitical Studies, Institute of Geography, Russian Academy of Sciences, 29 Staromonetny pereulok, Moscow, Russia**. His research interests lie in the field of political geography and geopolitics, economic geography and regional development. His current research projects are focused on regional development, everyday life and cross-border cooperation in the Russian borderlands.
E-mail: asebentsov@gmail.com

Neil Taylor is the former Director of Regent Holidays in Bristol, UK, and since retiring from that post has written extensively about the Baltic countries, in particular Estonia. He regularly leads groups there and lectures on Baltic cruises. He is the author of the *Bradt Guide to Estonia*.
Independent Travel Consultant, London and Bristol, UK, and Tallinn, Estonia.
E-mail: neiltaylor90@hotmail.com

Dr **Piotr Trzepacz** is an Assistant Professor in the **Department of GIS, Cartography and Remote Sensing, Institute of Geography and Spatial Management, Jagiellonian University, ul. Gronostajowa 7, 30-387 Kraków, Poland**. He is the author of the *Football Map of Krakow*, based on public mural graffiti. His research interests include urban studies, the geography of football and the geography of air transport.
E-mail: piotr.trzepacz@uj.edu.pl

Dr **Anca Tudoricu** is a teaching assistant in the **Department of Human and Economic Geography, Faculty of Geography, University of Bucharest, B-dul N. Bălcescu no 1, Bucharest 010041, Romania**. Her main research interests are event tourism, heritage interpretation and destination identity. Most of her work focuses on cultural events, particularly festivals.
E-mail: anca.tudoricu@ g.unibuc.ro

Antonio Violante is a Professor in the **Department of Cultural Heritage and Environment, University of Milan, Via Festa del Perdono 7, 20122 Milan, Italy**. He lived for several years in Seoul and Belgrade, working in Italian embassies' cultural offices and as a Professor in local universities. He now teaches historical, economic and political geography. His regional areas of interest include East Asia and the Balkan countries.
E-mail: antonio.violante1@unimi.it

Dr **Maria Zotova** is a researcher at the **Laboratory for Geopolitical Studies, Institute of Geography, Russian Academy of Sciences, 29 Staromonetny pereulok, Moscow, Russia**. Her research interests lie in the field of urban geography, urbanism, the development of networks, strategic planning, city marketing and development of the border regions.
E-mail: schagron@gmail.com

Acknowledgements

As a not-for-profit organisation, CAB International retains all the advantages and foibles of an organisation providing supportive personal contact and encouragement. Claire Parfitt and Emma McCann have carried out these roles in the true CABI tradition. The anonymous reviewers of my original book proposal must also be thanked for their fulsome support. But above all, the book's copy editor, Chris McEnnerney, has helped to correct, disambiguate and clarify the editor's (and others') oversights in a highly assiduous manner, for which I and the other contributors should be extremely grateful.

Warmest thanks are, of course, extended to all the contributors to this volume. Their earnest endeavour, ready response to my sometimes unrealistic demands, sustained support and enthusiasm have been greatly appreciated. We have shared many fruitful learning experiences.

There were times in the book's evolution when it almost felt like an incestuous, or at least family, affair. For, in addition to the 20 contributors from the 'region' under discussion, three of the 'Western' authors have spouses/partners from Central and Eastern Europe. I do not, but the staff of the then Portsmouth Polytechnic are to be acknowledged for their role in dragging me and a dozen or so other hapless undergraduate students on an overland expedition to Turkey during the revolutionary summer of 1968, across faraway lands of which I then knew virtually nothing. The rest was not history, more geography and anthropology in fact. And the role of Alan Burnett in stimulating the editor's early interest in 'Eastern Europe' is recorded with gratitude.

As ever, the editor takes responsibility for any errors or oversights that may follow, however unintentional. Every endeavour has been made to ascertain copyright ownership of the images used in this volume.

As always, I am indebted to the support and wisdom, both professional and personal, of Frances Brown, a former editor of the journal *Tourism Management*, who, during the production of this volume, was honoured by the International Academy of Astronautics with a well-deserved lifetime achievements award for her editorial skills and expertise.

We have lift-off.

Maidens, Scotland, UK
May and August 2016

Preface

When I first travelled in the countries of Central and Eastern Europe in the heady 1960s, English was not an overly useful language to possess. German, certainly; Russian, if necessary; French in Romania and Bulgaria; Italian in Dalmatia and Albania: languages of imperial heritage.

Much has changed; or has it? There exists a language extinction crisis. Of the world's 7000 languages, just 10 are spoken by half the globe's population. While there are clear benefits from a shared communication medium, there are also spectres of such commonality being abused on an Orwellian scale.

In Chapter 2, Michael Hall points to the geopolitics of academic publishing, and how the medium of English has come to dominate both publishing and the academic careers of non-native English speakers. (Does the French literature concur?) But, perhaps wisely, he does not offer suggestions for ways around this. I would proffer the opinion that there are at least three areas that require action:

1. The apparent trend in native English-speaking countries of reducing foreign language instruction and learning needs to be reversed. Native English speakers need to break out of the downward spiral of monolingualism – not least to be able to understand and respect other cultures better. Without such a facility, we are reduced as human beings.
2. Scholars can assist this process by seeking out the better non-English language journals and books, and by reading, promoting and citing them in their work, with more (appropriate) non-English language citations brought into mainstream English language publications.
3. TNCs (transnational corporations) that dominate English-language publishing – ironically, the largest is headquartered in a non-native English-speaking country – should be more language inclusive, not just in abstracts.

Such thoughts may be hopelessly naïve and far too late. But a useful (interim?) model is the *Journal of Alpine Research/Revue de géographie alpine,* a multidisciplinary online journal that publishes articles in two languages, '... one of which must be one of the alpine languages (French, Italian, German) or Spanish, the other being in English. The objective of this bilingualism is to encourage the exchange and diffusion of ideas' (https://rga.revues.org/?lang=en).

Is this an unrealistic model for those journals with high submission levels and/or constrained print page budgets?

Of course, given increasing academic global mobility (Scott, 2015; van der Wender, 2015), the requirement for a *lingua franca* is manifest. And with dominant Silicon Valley-sourced communications technology facilitating interaction, American English, for the moment, is the obvious medium, not merely for scholarly interchange.

As regards the current volume, the contributors represent the native speakers of 11 languages other than English. Would we otherwise have been able to communicate and collaborate if not through my own native tongue? For this I am sincerely grateful.

And, of course, this volume itself cannot be exempt from the reality of academic English language hegemony. I have been keenly aware of the role the editor has been privileged to play while imposing his agenda on the contributors through 'revising' their English, 'editing' their content and pronouncing on each chapter's quality, relevance and structure.

Native English speakers' monolingualism is often accompanied by a cavalier approach taken to the use of accents and diacritics. A few years ago, I was strolling with an acquaintance in the clichéd home/bunker of English reaction, 'Royal' Tunbridge Wells. 'Why,' he asked, 'do so many people now call their cars Shkodas and not Skodas?'

Throughout this volume, the names of countries and capital (and some major) cities are presented in the form commonly used in the English-speaking world. Thus, for example, Estonia rather than Eesti, Kosovo (albeit not universally accepted as an independent country) instead of the Albanian Kosova/Kosovë, Vienna rather than Wien, Belgrade not Beograd (but Kyiv rather than the more familiar Russianised Kiev).

With Central and Eastern Europe's complicated history of shifting boundaries, population migrations and changing hegemonies, many cities, towns, villages and hamlets often have more than one version of their name, in some cases perhaps three or four. To avoid this semantic/toponymic minefield and to maintain some semblance of consistency throughout this volume, place names other than those of capital cities are normally rendered in the form currently used in the country within which they reside. Thus, for example, Kraków rather than the anglicised Cracow (a strangely ugly form for such a beautiful city). In those languages where proper nouns decline, I have tried to use the version more widely recognised outside of the country. Thus, Durrës rather than Durrësi, Shkodra rather than Skhkodër. Inevitably, there will be some grammatical inconsistency in such usage. All names locally rendered in Cyrillic (or indeed any other non-Roman alphabet) are here transliterated in Romanised form. This, of course, is not without its problems.

In most cases, the English language translations of quotations from survey and interview respondents (usually indicated in italics) and from non-English language published sources have been made by the chapter authors.

Finally, I would like to share the fact that I have been sustained, despite my own patchy linguistic abilities, by the (fictional) writings of Diego Marani (2000/2011, 2002/2012, 2004/2016), an erstwhile Policy Officer in the External Action Service of the European Union responsible for multilingualism. Marani's second novel in his trilogy, *The Last of the Vostyachs*, is a satire of bias and prejudice in academic and philological research ...

References

Marani, D. (2000) *Nuova Grammatica Finlandese*. Bompiani, Milan. [(2011) *New Finnish Grammar* (trans. Landry, J.). Daedelus, Sawtry, UK.]

Marani, D. (2002) *L'Ultimo dei Vostiachi*. Bompiani, Milan. [(2012) *The Last of the Vostyachs* (trans. Landry, J.). Daedelus, Sawtry, UK.]

Marani, D. (2004) *L'Interprete*. Bompiani, Milan. [(2016) *The Interpreter* (trans. Landry, J.). Daedelus, Sawtry, UK.]

Scott, P. (2015) Dynamics of academic mobility: hegemonic internationalisation or fluid globalisation? *European Review* 23(S1), S55–S69.

van der Wender, M. (2015) International academic mobility: towards a concentration of the minds in Europe. *European Review* 23(S1), S70–S88.

Part I:

Introduction and Overviews

_____

1 Bringing Geopolitics to Tourism

Derek Hall*

Seabank Associates, Maidens, Ayrshire, UK

1.1 Tourism as (part of) Transnational Neoliberal Hegemony

The study of both tourism and geopolitics is subject to conflicting interpretations, contrasting methodologies and diverse theorisations. To set and exemplify the conjoining of these two arenas within the dynamic context of Central and Eastern Europe (CEE) summons all manner of possibilities and challenges.

Through a critical lens, or series of lenses, this volume explores and evaluates some of the issues and concepts relating to the tourism–geopolitics nexus, raising questions concerning the engagement of both areas of study and offering a springboard for the pursuit of further research agendas. Although this exercise is undertaken with particular reference to the countries and peoples of CEE, the conceptual frameworks, arguments and conclusions that follow often possess far wider relevance.

The main sections of the book pursue the overlapping and interrelated themes of: reconfiguring conceptions and reality, where tourism is set within evaluations of traditional geopolitical issues; tourism and transnationalism, theorising and evaluating the (extra)territorial power exerted by tourism- and leisure-related transnational corporations; borderlands, notably examining the transformation of border areas

and the tensions between dynamic, high-level (geo)political relations and local tourism-related cross-border quotidian activities; identity and image, exploring tourism's post-communist and post-conflict contributions to changing local and national self-perceptions and to overcoming the tensions of contested heritage; and mobilities, theorising and exemplifying the tourism-related processes of human movement and their interactions.

Tourism may be viewed in source countries as representing values of freedom and democracy, if only for some. It may be employed as a symbol of escape from the mundanity of the quotidian. Yet tourism is deeply embedded in politics (and, indeed, politics in tourism) at all levels. Tourism contributes significantly to global ordering (Franklin, 2004; Tribe, 2008) and embraces both the symbolism and reality of 'neoliberal hegemony' (Box 1.1). As such, it has become an obvious target for expressions of opposition to what, until recently, has been an almost exclusive 'Western' developed world project of hedonistic cultural imperialism.

In his observations on capitalist transitions in CEE, Smith (2002: 667) argued that stabilisation – an obvious prerequisite for tourism development – alongside the path to 'democracy' and to neoliberal capitalism, had resulted from the imposition of a 'new hegemony'. Neoliberal

---

*E-mail: derekhall@seabankscotland.co.uk

Box 1.1. A short history of neoliberalism

Subject to a number of critiques in this volume, neoliberalism was a concept first expressed publicly in Paris in 1938, and subsequently defined by Friedrich Hayek (1944) and Ludwig von Mies (1945). Outwardly 'economic', it asserts fundamental (geo)political and moral implications and impacts.

Neoliberalism sees competition as the defining characteristic of human relations, conceiving citizens as 'consumers'. It contends that 'the market' delivers benefits that cannot be achieved by planning. Attempts to limit competition are seen as contrary to liberty; tax and regulation must be minimised, public services privatised. The organisation of labour and collective bargaining are portrayed as market distortions that impede the natural order of winners and losers. Inequality is seen as a virtuous reward for utility and the wealth generation that 'trickles down' to enrich all. Efforts to create a more equal society are counterproductive and morally corrosive.

Hayek's 1947 organisation, the Mont Pelerin Society, was supported by wealthy sponsors and their foundations to disseminate the doctrine of neoliberalism.

Such wealthy backers would subsequently fund a series of 'think tanks' – Centre for Policy Studies, Adam Smith Institute, Institute of Economic Affairs, Cato Institute, Heritage Foundation, American Enterprise Institute.

They also financed academic positions and departments, notably at the universities of Chicago and Virginia (USA).

Hayek's view that governments should regulate competition to prevent monopolies from forming became overtaken by a more 'strident' form of neoliberalism, championed by such Americans as Milton Friedman, believing monopoly power should be seen as a reward for efficiency.

From the 1950s until the 1970s, neoliberalism appeared to be in abeyance, just too extreme for the West European post-war consensus (excluding Franco's Spain and Salazar's Portugal). This was, of course, just at a time when communism was consolidating its hold in CEE.

From the 1970s, elements of neoliberalism, especially its prescriptions for monetary policy, began creeping (back) into trans-Atlantic mainstream debate.

With the accession of Reagan and Thatcher, the rest of the neoliberal canon soon followed: tax cuts for the rich, the diminution of trade union power, deregulation, privatisation, outsourcing and competition in public services. Corporate greed, 'jackpot capitalists' (Peston, 2008), ruthlessly achieved and defended monopolies, and predatory business practices were the result.

Through the IMF, the World Bank, the Maastricht Treaty and the World Trade Organization (the 'Washington Consensus'),[1] neoliberal policies were imposed – often without democratic consent – on much of the world, not least CEE from 1989, while 'jackpot oligarchs', having profited hugely from rapid insider privatisations, siphoned off large amounts of capital to safe (offshore) havens.

(From Hayek, 1944; von Mies, 1945; Monbiot, 2016a,b; Peston, 2008; Romano, 2014; Sayer, 2014; Verhaeghe, 2014.)

---

policies attained global reach as developing countries were urged to adopt such strategies by international financial institutions (IFIs): what Friedman (2000) referred to as the 'golden straitjacket'.

As crude figures alone testify, tourism has become an inextricable part of neoliberal hegemony by virtue of its ability to pioneer economic structures, employment practices, inward investment, corporate insinuation and significant mobility flows to reconstruct the role and value of particular urban and rural spaces, pursuits and structures (see, for example, Smith, 1997; Giampiccoli, 2007).

In the wake of the fall of communism, Allcock and Przcławski (1990) argued that academics from CEE societies could offer independent analysis divergent from both Marxist precepts and 'Western' thinking: a Third Way. Such perspectives could have provided alternatives to their western counterparts.

> However, the dynamics of the momentous change that swept Eastern Europe in the early 1990s did not allow for such cross-fertilisation as the 'East' either bought into the 'market' (or was 'brought' into the 'market') without pause for such 'cross-civilisational' conversations.
> (Higgins-Desbiolles, 2006: 1203)

1.2   Tourism and Geopolitics

A growing number of studies (e.g. Weaver, 2010) have articulated the ways in which (international) tourism is an implicitly geopolitical activity: it relies on working relationships between blocs', countries' and regions' administrations. Tourism stakeholders anticipate such relationships to be sustained over coming decades, to the extent that the World Tourism Organization (WTO) predicts over two billion international tourism movements by 2030 (UNWTO, 2014b). Complementing such mobility is the facilitating of cross-border flows of the capital, commodities, labour and skills required to sustain the (international) tourism process (Reiser, 2003; Hannam, 2013) (for example, see Chapter 9).

Tourism is also subject to the outcomes of geopolitical activity. The spatial consequences of international relations at supranational and national levels can impact substantially on activity at subnational levels, both at tourism destinations (e.g. Chapters 5 and 6) and at international borders (e.g. Chapters 12–15). What a number of chapters in this volume reveal is that local tourism-related responses to such impacts will usually be place and context related, and thus articulate those differentiated local conditions (Niewiadomski, 2013). This is what Hazbun (2004), among others, refers to as reterritorialisation: the increased relevance of location and characteristics of place.

Yet 'tourism spaces primarily are articulated to serve the interests of non-locals (i.e. tourists, foreign investors, organisations)' (Saarinen and Rogerson, 2014: 25), and while the needs and aspirations of locals and non-locals may not be necessarily contradictory, critical issues can be raised that reflect potential contestation and unequal power relationships (this issue is raised in Chapter 8, for example).

Although back in 1975 Turner and Ash could declare that the study of tourism had not embraced a political dimension, much has changed in 40 years. And since the 'cultural turn' in the social sciences, a growth of critical studies in tourism and of critical geopolitics has brought new methodological insights and cross-fertilisations into areas of research that had previously remained largely positivist and relatively isolated. Hannam *et al.* (2014), for example, have pointed to the ways in which a critical, political mobilities paradigm has repositioned tourism studies more centrally within the social sciences (see Chapter 25).

Despite a wealth of 'critical' geopolitics texts (e.g. Dittmer and Sharp, 2014; Dodds *et al.*,

2014; Kuus, 2014) – a trend noted by van der Wusten (2015) – an interest in this area has yet to be widely grasped within the tourism academy (exceptions include Shin, 2004; Bianchi, 2007; Savelli, 2012; Hannam, 2013; Rowen, 2016). Reasons for and implications of this are developed further in Chapter 2.

First employed in 1899 (Ó Tuathail, 1999), 'geopolitics' is 'a slippery term' (Dodds, 2014: 1). Indeed, so slippery that it was shunned for almost half a century after World War II, its conception of competition for, and political dominance of, territory having become associated with Nazism, *lebensraum*, global aggression and genocide. As implicitly state-centric and a largely abstract construct of global power and spatial determinism, the simplistic and often static nature of geopolitical constructs, while generating numerous critiques, only gradually re-emerged as an adjunct to neoconservative Cold War thinking (see Chapter 3).

As the term returned to mainstream popular usage, 'to infer a hard-headed approach to the world in general' (Dodds, 2014: 1), 'geopolitics' became so widely applied in popular discourse as to retain little specific meaning (e.g. Lacoste, 2006; Gianfranco, 2009; Jean, 2012; Zoppo and Zorgbibe, 2013; Verluise, 2014). But within the 'cultural turn' of academic geography, it was being subject to a wholesale reappraisal.[2] What, in the 1980s, became known as 'critical geopolitics' sought to interrogate existing structures of power and knowledge,

> ... to grapple with the culture that produces imperial attempts at domination in distant places ... to expose the complicity of geopolitics with domination and imperialism.
>
> (Dalby, 2008: 413)

Critical geopolitics sought to distance itself both from the earlier 'neoclassical' geopolitics (Megoran, 2010) – which promoted essentially imperialist ways of thinking about the effects of geography on international relations – and from 'popular' geopolitics.

In contrast to a history of 'big men' (Sharp, 2000: 363) that has tended to characterise the study of (neo)classical geopolitics (see Chapter 3), the formulation of critical geopolitics was to offer a Foucauldian approach that could unravel and deconstruct '... geographical and related disguises, dissimulations, and rationalizations of power' (Dalby, 1994: 595).

Although criticised as being 'anti-geopolitics', 'anti-cartographic' and 'anti-environmental' (Haverluk *et al.*, 2014), critical geopolitics has provided a much-needed and necessary critique of classical geopolitics (Kelly, 2006). But the two are not mutually exclusive. Thus, for example, a long-time proponent of closer ties between geopolitics and international relations has argued, cognisant of the critical geopolitics debates, that

> ... the continuing importance of the geopolitical spatial context to the study of international relations .... is based not on an earlier approach based on geographic determinism, but rather *possibilism* ... and ... the need to appreciate both a locational view and the perceptual/symbolic/constructed view of space and place, and to do so within an increasingly globalized, interdependent, and transnational world system.
>
> (Starr, 2013: 433)

While both classical geopolitics and early tourism studies may have focused on a macroscale of activity, critical geopolitics and critical studies in tourism are more concerned with interrogating and understanding the apparently mundane, the quotidian; issues that directly affect people's everyday lives. The genesis of these two strands, however, has been somewhat different. In the case of tourism, gendered approaches were evident in the literature from the mid-1990s (Kinnaird and Hall, 1994; Swain, 1995), pre-dating self-ascribed 'critical studies' in the subject by a decade (Ateljevic *et al.*, 2007; Pritchard *et al.*, 2007). By contrast, 'critical geopolitics' itself has been criticised for lacking a gendered awareness: a shortcoming that echoes both classical geopolitics and international relations theory (Kofman and Peake, 1990; Staeheli, 1994). Hyndman (2004: 312), for example, argued that critical geopolitics had largely failed to 'articulate other, more embodied ways of seeing'.

The aim of a feminist geopolitics (Dowler and Sharp, 2001; Hyndman, 2001, 2004; Dixon and Marston, 2011; Gilmartin and Kofman, 2013), therefore, has been to render critical geopolitics more gendered and racialised, with particular application to issues of security and mobility at a number of different scales, while refocusing on the mundane, everyday reproductions of geopolitical power (Massaro and Williams, 2013).

Cutting across these domains of geopolitics, the term 'microgeopolitics' has been deployed:

- within classical geopolitical discourse, in relation to small/lower-scale geopolitical events or activities (e.g. Tolipov, 2011; Dwyer, 2014); and
- in the context of critical and especially feminist geopolitics, to refer to the personal level of interaction and its consequences (e.g. Fyfe, 1997; Pain and Smith, 2008; Pain, 2009; Oswin and Olund, 2010; Harker and Martin, 2012).

In this second context, 'intimacy-geopolitics' is an area of study that has emerged from feminist engagement, and has gained increasing attention (Pain and Staeheli, 2014); it offers much potential for the critical study of tourism.

The interrogation of relations between intimacy and geopolitics, within a critical geopolitics paradigm, transcends boundaries between global/local, familial/state and personal/political (Pratt, 2012; Cowen and Story, 2013). The proponents of intimacy-geopolitics view intimacy as being wrapped up in national and global geopolitical processes: international events, policies and territorial claims; that geopolitics is created by and consists of relations and practices of intimacy (Bhattacharyya, 2008; Hyndman, 2010; Pratt and Rosner, 2012).

Within this view, all forms of violent oppression are seen as working through intimate emotional and psychological registers as a means of exerting control. This is often linked to wider social norms, obligations and customs, and to economic relations (Hays-Mitchell, 2005). In this way, violence is seen to play a key role in the oppression and insecurities that disproportionately affect socially, economically and politically marginalised people and places (Koopman, 2011).

These ideas clearly possess much relevance for critical tourism studies, but have thus far enjoyed limited application (e.g. Dowler, 2013).

1.3 Tourism as 'Soft Power'? High Geopolitics, Low Political Profile

One key theme of this volume is that tourism, and implicitly international tourism, can be conceptualised and operationalised as a geopolitical instrument. One such conception of tourism is through its supposed attribute of 'soft power' (Nye, 1990, 2004; Melissen, 2005; Davis Cross and Melissen, 2013). But soft power for whom? And with what consequences for tourists and host societies?

Co-conspiring with place branding, tourism's 'soft power' can both support and be a component of 'public diplomacy' (e.g. Ociepka, 2014), a subset of nation branding that focuses on the political brand of a nation (Fan, 2008).

Hollinshead and Hou describe nation branding as:

> ... that mix of political and aspirational activities through which institutions and interest groups variously collaborate and contend to solidify particular visions of their supposed culture, heritage, and nature for not only distant/external others but for their own proximal/internal selves.
>
> (Hollinshead and Hou, 2012: 227)

In such ways, tourism becomes imbued with propaganda value: its symbols and artefacts gather meaning and implication, its stakeholders – tourists, tourism employees, destination residents and host environments – become (often unwitting) actors in the game of image projection, a pursuit that increasingly has become played out in virtual space, away from the altogether less presentable realities of destinations' quotidian (as expressed in Chapter 20).

The role of cultural heritage can be important in (re-)establishing the soft power presence of former hegemonic powers and/or in emphasising contemporary cleavages between cultural groups. In south-eastern Europe, Turkish cultural organisations have been extending the country's 'soft power' role in funding the restoration and upkeep of Ottoman heritage sites and artefacts. Yet such sites can also be the source of contested and dissonant heritage (for example, see Chapters 17 and 18). Turkish tourists and businesses are also increasing their presence in the region, in the latter case notably in relation to new highway construction (Chapter 23), thereby helping to consolidate the country's geopolitical role.

A high-profile contemporary harnessing of apparent soft power is the desire to host (and perform well in) tourist-rich 'mega sport events' (MSEs) such as athletics, soccer and other large-scale sports tournaments (for example, hosting the 2018 FIFA World Cup tournament: see Chapters 14 and 15; also UNWTO, 2014a). Although Grix and Houlihan (2014) recognised only a limited literature to be available on both the conceptual and operationalising aspects of this area of research, since the staging of the 2008 Olympic Games in Beijing there has been a growing literature addressing issues linking soft power and national image (e.g. Chen *et al.*, 2013; Song and Deng, 2014; Giulianotti, 2015).

Yet the efficacy of such supposed soft power has been seriously questioned. Manzenreiter (2010) argued that while, as a symbol of modernity and mass organisation, the 2008 Games appeared to be successful in inspiring the Chinese domestic audience, the filter of western media exerted a considerable constraining effect on the Games' positive external impacts: what Giulianotti (2015) refers to as 'soft disempowerment'.

The roles of corporate sponsorship and private financing of Olympic Games were accelerated considerably when Los Angeles was the only candidate willing to host the 1984 Summer Games. Such 'celebration capitalism' (Boykoff, 2013) would profoundly remould the political economy of MSEs for subsequent host cities and countries where significant efforts have been made to boost competitive soft power and to devise development and legacy strategies to assist sport in shaping national image (Preuss, 2007; Mangan and Dyreson, 2013). By contrast, major cultural events, such as European City of Culture conferment or the management of European Museums Night, can offer opportunities for both (international) prestige and (domestic) reflection and reappraisal at local and personal levels (see Chapter 19).

As objects of tourist consumption, the heritage, artefacts and practices of geopolitically powerful institutions such as those of organised religion, royalty, and supranational bodies such as the IOC (International Olympic Committee) and FIFA (*Fédération Internationale de Football Association*) represent an important link in the nexus between tourism and geopolitics, and as such require stronger critical conceptualisation.

With leisure-related mega-events usually being accommodated in complex and often contested urban settings, recent attention has been drawn to the security practices accompanying such

> global occasions of enormous importance and implication ... [effecting] seismic change on the cities and nations that host them.
>
> (Fussey and Klauser, 2015: 195)

The need for assurance of stringent security is fundamental to the soft power benefits to be derived from such events (Giulianotti and Klauser, 2010, 2012; Houlihan and Giulianotti, 2012). A focus placed on the 'securitising' of event-hosting city sectors sets it firmly within the growing field of critical urban geopolitics (e.g. Coaffee, 2013, 2015), embracing aspects of urban renewal related to 'new Olympic topographies' (Pavoni, 2011).

As alluded to above, tourism's soft power role can be something of a blunt instrument, not least because of the many imperfections and inconsistences associated with the perceptions, reporting and popular imagery of tourism-related development activity. Closely related but potentially more direct than soft power, tourism's propaganda value operates in complementary directions. It can act to disseminate the cultural values of tourist-generating countries within host societies, often to the further benefit of source countries' political and/or economic interests. But also, more explicitly, tourism can be employed to present an outwardly positive face to the world of a destination country or region that might in other respects be less acceptable, but then can capitalise on certain aspects of that enhanced, perhaps falsified destination image. This may be expressed most explicitly in destinations governed by 'totalitarian' regimes (e.g. Kwek *et al.*, 2014), but can be implicit in any commercial (place) branding exercise.

In a critique of the concept of soft power, Fan (2008) argues that, similarly to tourism, the nature of soft power is largely uncontrollable and unpredictable, rendering it less efficacious than its proponents might suggest. Indeed, the example of some aspects of tourist behaviour and its negative reflection on the country of origin has been the source of much debate both in the academic literature and the popular press. Guo and Zhang (2008), for example, have argued that the 'uncivil behaviours' of Chinese outbound tourists have become 'the bottleneck to hamper national soft power upgrade' (see also Loi and Pearce, 2015). The UK Foreign and Commonwealth Office's annual *British Behaviour Abroad Report* told us that more than 5400 British nationals were detained by police overseas between April 2013 and March 2014, not necessarily to the advantage of any UK national image (UKFCO, 2014; Austin, 2015). Such image 'leakages' also reduce the credibility of conceptions of tourism as encouraging peace and (international) harmony (Chapters 17 and 18): 'soft incredulity'.

The image of a nation is so complex and fluid that it defies the clarity implied in such a term as brand image (Ren and Blichfeldt, 2010). Further, for those countries that have undergone dramatic changes in their political, economic and social systems, such as those addressed in this volume, external images tend to lag behind reality (Fan, 2010). Although, it could be said that such perceptions themselves fail to keep up with the reality of such destination image formation agents as travellers' blogs and website presentations (see Chapter 20).

Branding and re-imaging may be especially important for countries that have experienced crisis – whether it be natural disaster, war or economic depression (Insch and Avraham, 2014) – for communities seeking (wider) recognition at a higher level than that which exists, such as with Kosovo seeking wider recognition as an independent country (Chapter 18) or 'stateless nations' such as Kurds or Roma seeking international representation (Barany 1998; Tahiri, 2007).

Fan (2010) has contended that empirical studies of 'nation' branding are simply exercises aimed at boosting exports or incoming tourism. As Kaneva and Popescu put it:

> ... nation branding proponents explain global relations of power through the metaphor of market competition and argue that nation branding offers a market-friendly approach to governance that transcends politics.
> (Kaneva and Popescu, 2011: 192)

Yet the nation branding campaigns pursued by most countries featured in this volume have held far greater importance than simply as tools for attracting tourism and investment (see Chapter 3). They have reflected processes contributing to the articulation of the meaning of nationhood after communism and/or after conflict, and thereby to a reconceptualisation of the local and regional geographies of Europe (Dzenovska, 2005; Kaneva and Popescu, 2011: 203). Such reconceptualisations should embrace greater cultural sensitivity and higher levels of reflection than are currently evident (Ren and Gyimóthy, 2013: 17), as emphasised by some CEE political leaderships' positions in relation to Middle

Eastern migrant/refugee mobilities into Europe (see the Introduction to Part VI).

1.4 Playing Geopolitics with Tourism

Within the tourism performance, the interaction between stakeholders – tourist and tour company, tourist and host residents/employees, tourist and host environment, tourism corporations and host governance, tourism's role in balance of payments exchanges, tourism's enmeshing within multiple international mobilities – constitute fundamental dimensions of connectivity. Such connectivity – the mobilities and interactions associated with tourism-related processes – can be subverted swiftly by overtly political, perhaps geopolitical, acts and declarations, reflecting hegemonic influence and power at a number of levels. As is well documented, many regional tourism organisations are weak in the face of the power of tour companies' and airlines' ability to transfer their business rapidly from one destination to another (e.g. Farmaki, 2015; see also Chapter 22), thereby mimicking the behaviour of transnational manufacturing corporations.

Sharpley *et al.* (1996) illustrated how government travel advisories, such as those from the US State Department and the UK Foreign and Commonwealth Office (which can seem to be conservative, overly cautious and occasionally arbitrary), can exert significant power in portraying a dominant Western world view of specific countries, regions and localities, and even ethnic or religious groupings. Such power can result in profound impacts on tourists' patterns of travel, and thus on certain tourism destinations, particularly of less developed nations, and on the economic and social opportunities of those working and living in them.

Tourism destinations squeezed between the hegemonies of Western neoliberalism and nihilistic international terrorism now include a number of Mediterranean and Middle Eastern locations. For example, shortly following an armed attack against tourists in Sousse, Tunisia, in June 2015, in which 30 Britons died, the UK government warned all its citizens – tourists, businesspeople and residents alike – to leave Tunisia, as intelligence concerning evidence of likely further terrorist acts had been received. As tourism represents a significant element of Tunisian foreign income, this act was condemned as playing into the hands of the terrorists by devastating the Tunisian tourism industry (Morris and Calder, 2015) and national economy. Within days of the attack, the first UK travel operator had removed Tunisia from its summer 2016 programmes (Calder, 2015). But a failing economy, it was argued, would simply create a recruiting pool for terrorists (Rawlinson, 2015; Sengupta, 2015).

1.5 What Follows

Although a limited number of English-language volumes on the relationship between tourism and politics/power have been published over the years (e.g. Burns and Novelli, 2007; Hazbun, 2008; Su and Teo, 2009; Butler and Suntikul, 2010; MacLeod and Carrier, 2010), no published collection (in English) expresses the thematic and regional focus of the current volume.[3] The following chapters present contributors who offer a diversity of theoretical and disciplinary approaches to the still largely uncharted, potentially extensive, territory of tourism and geopolitics.

As an experimental plunge, unashamedly embracing both 'critical' and '(neo)classical' approaches to experiences from CEE, this volume:

- explores the relationships between tourism and interpretations of geopolitics and their conceptual underpinnings;
- raises key issues arising from the tourism, geopolitics and related literatures that are relevant both to CEE and to a wider context;
- teases out themes from within CEE that have hitherto been little explored or poorly conceptualised in the tourism literature.

The issues raised and methodological approaches and analytical tools employed represent a diversity that may express some conceptual tensions. Certain chapters emphasise the empirical while others are more specifically theorised. Collectively, they present a substantial body of work and contribution to the field(s) of tourism and geopolitics. It is hoped the collection will present some exciting challenges for the reader.

Following the initial introductory and overview section, the volume's five central sections are each preceded by a context-setting introduction by the editor. Within each of the sections, contributions are made from both new and established voices from CEE (and elsewhere). In addition to tourism academics, the book draws on geographers, social anthropologists, political scientists and tourism practitioners.

In the remaining two chapters of Part I, Michael Hall in Chapter 2 offers a succinct appraisal of the current state and future potential of conceptualising tourism and geopolitics, and in Chapter 3 the geopolitical and tourism heritage of CEE is explored and the region's post-communist reorientation is evaluated.

Endnotes

[1] Shorthand for 'not only the US government, but all those institutions and networks of opinion leaders centred in the world's de facto capital – the IMF, the World Bank, think-tanks, politically sophisticated investment bankers, and worldly finance ministers … who meet each other in Washington and collectively define the conventional wisdom of the moment' (Thomas, 1999: 225).
[2] None the less, by the turn of the century Peter Taylor (2000) could note that geopolitics remained as the least problematised aspect of geographical knowledge.
[3] Hoerner (2008) is an early, if undemanding, exploration of the nexus.

References

Allcock, J.B. and Przcławski, K. (1990) Introduction. *Annals of Tourism Research* 17(1), 1–6.
Ateljevic, I., Pritchard, A. and Morgan, N. (eds) (2007) *The Critical Turn in Tourism: Innovative Methodologies.* Elsevier, Oxford, UK.
Austin, H. (2015) 11 British nationals arrested in Inner Mongolia. *The Independent* [London] 15 July, p. 5.
Barany, Z. (1998) Ethnic mobilization and the state: the Roma in Eastern Europe. *Ethnic and Racial Studies* 21(2), 308–327.
Bhattacharyya, G.S. (2008) *Dangerous Brown Men; Exploiting Sex, Violence and Feminism in the 'War on Terror'.* Zed, London.
Bianchi, R. (2007) Tourism and the globalisation of fear: analysing the politics of risk and (in)security in global travel. *Tourism and Hospitality Research* 7, 64–74.
Boykoff, J. (2013) *Celebration Capital and the Olympics.* Routledge, London.
Burns, P.M. and Novelli, M. (eds) (2007) *Tourism and Politics: Global Frameworks and Local Realities.* Elsevier, Amsterdam.
Butler, R. and Suntikul, W. (eds) (2010) *Tourism and Political Change.* Goodfellow, Oxford, UK.
Calder, S. (2015) Access all areas for terrorists in Tunisia? *The Independent Traveller* [London], 18 July, p. 3.
Chen, K.H., Du, S.Q., Chen, X.R. and Xue, D.M. (2013) The building of Chinese competitive sports soft power under the background of globalization. (In Chinese with an English summary.) *Journal of Physical Education* (Guangzhou) 20(4), 42–46.
Coaffee, J. (2013) Policy transfer, legacy and major sporting events: lessons for London 2012 and beyond. *International Journal of Sports Policy and Politics* 5, 295–312.
Coaffee, J. (2015) The uneven geographies of the Olympic carceral: from exceptionalism to normalisation. *Geographical Journal* 181(3), 199–211.
Cowen, D. and Story, B. (2013) Intimacy and the everyday. In: Dodds, K., Kuus, M. and Sharp, J. (eds) *The Ashgate Research Companion to Critical Geopolitics.* Ashgate, Aldershot, UK, pp. 341–358.
Dalby, S. (1994) Gender and critical geopolitics: reading security discourse in the new world disorder. *Environment and Planning D: Society and Space* 12, 595–612.
Dalby, S. (2008) Imperialism, domination, culture: the continued relevance of critical geopolitics. *Geopolitics* 13(3), 413–436.
Davis Cross, M.K. and Melissen, J. (2013) *European Public Diplomacy: Soft Power at Work.* Palgrave Macmillan, Basingstoke, UK.
Dittmer, J. and Sharp, J. (2014) *Geopolitics: An Introductory Reader.* Routledge, London.
Dixon, D.P. and Marston, S.A. (2011) Introduction: feminist engagements with geopolitics. *Gender, Place & Culture* 18(4), 445–453.

Dodds, K. (2014) *Geopolitics: A Very Short Introduction*, 2nd edn. Oxford University Press, Oxford, UK.

Dodds, K., Kuus, M. and Sharp, J. (eds) (2014) *The Ashgate Research Companion to Critical Geopolitics*. Ashgate, Aldershot, UK.

Dowler, L. (2013) Waging hospitality: feminist geopolitics and tourism in West Belfast, Northern Ireland. *Geopolitics* 18(4), 779–799.

Dowler, L. and Sharp, J. (2001) A feminist geopolitics? *Space and Polity* 5(3), 165–176.

Dwyer, M.B. (2014) Micro-geopolitics: capitalising security in Laos's Golden Triangle. *Geopolitics* 19(2), 377–405.

Dzenovska, D. (2005) Remaking the nation of Latvia: anthropological perspectives on nation branding. *Place Branding and Public Diplomacy* 19(2), 173–186.

Fan, Y. (2008) Soft power: power of attraction or confusion? *Place Branding and Public Diplomacy* 4(2), 147–158.

Fan, Y. (2010) Branding the nation: towards a better understanding. *Place Branding and Public Diplomacy* 6(2), 97–103.

Farmaki, A. (2015) Regional network governance and sustainable tourism. *Tourism Geographies* 17(3), 385–407.

Franklin, A. (2004) Tourism as an ordering: towards a new ontology of tourism. *Tourist Studies* 4(3), 277–301.

Friedman, T. (2000) *The Lexus and the Olive Tree*. Harper Collins, London.

Fussey, P. and Klauser, F. (2015) Securitisation and the mega-event: an editorial introduction. *Geographical Journal* 181(3), 194–198.

Fyfe, N.R. (1997) Commentary on policing space. *Urban Geography* 18(5), 389–391.

Giampiccoli, A. (2007) Hegemony, globalisation and tourism policies in developing countries. In: Reisinger, Y. and Turner, L.W. (eds) *Cross-cultural Behaviour in Tourism: Concepts and Analysis*. Elsevier, Amsterdam, pp. 175–191.

Gianfranco, L. (2009) *Scenari Geopolitici* [*The Geopolitical Scene*]. UTET Università, Milan, Italy (in Italian).

Gilmartin, M. and Kofman, E. (2013) Critically feminist geopolitics. In: Staeheli, L., Kofman, E. and Peake, L. (eds) *Mapping Women, Making Politics: Feminist Perspectives on Political Geography*. Routledge, London, pp. 113–126.

Giulianotti, R. (2015) The Beijing 2008 Olympics: examining the interrelations of China, globalization and soft power. *European Review* 23(2), 286–296.

Giulianotti, R. and Klauser, F. (2010) Security, governance and sport mega-events: toward an interdisciplinary research agenda. *Journal of Sport and Social Issues* 34(1), 49–61.

Giulianotti, R. and Klauser, F. (2012) Sport mega-events and 'terrorism': a critical analysis. *International Review for the Sociology of Sport* 47(3), 307–323.

Grix, J. and Houlihan, B. (2014) Sports mega-events as part of a nation's soft power strategy: the cases of Germany (2006) and the UK (2012). *British Journal of Politics and International Relations* 16(4), 572–596.

Guo, L.-F. and Zhang, S. (2008) A study on outbound tourism ethics of Chinese citizens and 'soft power' upgrade. *Tourism Tribune* 12. Available at: www.en.cnki.com.cn (accessed 10 June 2015).

Hannam, K. (2013) 'Shangri-La' and the new 'Great Game': exploring tourism geopolitics between China and India. *Tourism Planning and Development* 10(2), 178–186.

Hannam, K., Butler, G. and Paris, C.M. (2014) Developments and key issues in tourism mobilities. *Annals of Tourism Research* 44, 171–185.

Harker, C. and Martin, L. (2012) Familial relations: spaces, subjects and politics. *Environment and Planning A* 44, 768–775.

Haverluk, T.W., Beauchemin, K.M. and Mueller, B.A. (2014) The three critical flaws of critical geopolitics: towards a neo-classical geopolitics. *Geopolitics* 19(1), 19–39.

Hayek, F.A. (1944) *The Road to Serfdom*. Routledge, London.

Hays-Mitchell, M. (2005) Women's struggles for sustainable peace in post-conflict Peru: a feminist analysis of violence and change. In: Nelson, L. and Seager, J. (eds) *A Companion to Feminist Geography*. Blackwell, Oxford, UK, pp. 590–606.

Hazbun, W. (2004) Globalisation, reterritorialisation and the political economy of tourism development in the Middle East. *Geopolitics* 9(2), 310–341.

Hazbun, W. (2008) *Beaches, Ruins, Resorts: The Politics of Tourism in the Arab World*. University of Minnesota Press, Minneapolis, Minnesota.

Higgins-Desbiolles, F. (2006) More than an 'industry': the forgotten power of tourism as a social force. *Tourism Management* 27(6), 1192–1208.

Hoerner, J.-M. (2008) *Géopolitique du Tourisme* [*Geopolitics of Tourism*]. Armand Colin, Paris, (in French).

Hollinshead, K. and Hou, C.X. (2012) The seductions of 'soft power': the call for multifronted research into the articulative reach of tourism in China. *Journal of China Tourism Research* 8(3), 227–247.

Houlihan, B. and Giulianotti, R. (2012) Politics and the London 2012 Olympics: the (in)security Games. *International Affairs* 88, 701–717.

Hyndman, J. (2001) Towards a feminist geopolitics. *Canadian Geographer* 45(2), 210–222.

Hyndman, J. (2004) Mind the gap: bridging feminist and political geography through geopolitics. *Political Geography* 23(3), 307–322.

Hyndman, J. (2010) The question of 'the political' in critical geopolitics: querying the 'child soldier' in the 'war on terror'. *Political Geography* 29, 247–255.

Insch, A. and Avraham, E. (2014) Managing the reputation of places in crisis. *Place Branding and Public Diplomacy* 10(3), 171–173.

Jean, C. (2012) *Geopolitica del Mondo Contemporaneo* [*Geopolitics of the Contemporary World*]. Manuali Laterza, Milan, Italy (in Italian).

Kaneva, N. and Popescu, D. (2011) National identity lite: nation branding in post-communist Romania and Bulgaria. *International Journal of Cultural Studies* 14(2), 191–207.

Kelly, P. (2006) A critique of critical geopolitics. *Geopolitics* 11(1), 24–53.

Kinnaird, V.H. and Hall, D.R. (eds) (1994) *Tourism: A Gender Analysis*. Wiley, Chichester, UK.

Kofman, E. and Peake, L. (1990) Into the 1990s: a gendered agenda for political geography. *Political Geography Quarterly* 9, 313–336.

Koopman, S. (2011) Alter-geopolitics: other securities are happening. *Geoforum* 42, 274–284.

Kuus, M. (2014) *Geopolitics and Expertise: Knowledge and Authority in European Diplomacy*. Wiley Blackwell, Oxford, UK.

Kwek, A., Wang, Y. and Weaver, D.B. (2014) Retail tours in China for overseas Chinese: soft power or hard sell? *Annals of Tourism Research* 44(1), 36–52.

Lacoste, Y. (2006) *Géopolitique, la Longue Histoire d'Aujourd'hui* [*Geopolitics, the Long History of Today*]. Larousse, Paris, (in French).

Loi, K.I. and Pearce, P.L. (2015) Exploring perceived tensions arising from tourist behaviors in a Chinese context. *Journal of Travel and Tourism Marketing* 32(1-2), 65–79.

MacLeod, D.V.L. and Carrier, J.G. (2010) *Tourism, Power and Culture: Anthropological Insights*. Channel View, Bristol, UK.

Mangan, J.A. and Dyreson, M. (2013) *Olympic Legacies: Intended and Unintended: Political, Cultural, Economic, and Educational*. Routledge, Abingdon, UK.

Manzenreiter, W. (2010) The Beijing games in the western imagination of China: the weak power of soft power. *Journal of Sport & Social Issues* 34(1), 29–48.

Massaro, V.A. and Williams, J. (2013) Feminist geopolitics. *Geography Compass* 7(8), 567–577.

Megoran, N. (2010) Neoclassical geopolitics. *Political Geography* 29, 187–189.

Melissen, J. (ed.) (2005) *The New Public Diplomacy: Soft Power in International Relations*. Palgrave Macmillan, Basingstoke, UK.

Monbiot, G. (2016a) *How Did We Get Into This Mess?* Verso, London.

Monbiot, G. (2016b) The zombie doctrine. *The Guardian* [London], 16 April, pp. 19–20.

Morris, N. and Calder, S. (2015) Foreign Office advice for Britons to leave Tunisia causes diplomatic row and angers holidaymakers. *The Independent* [London], 11 July, p. 13.

Niewiadomski, P. (2016) The globalisation of the hotel industry and the variety of emerging capitalisms in Central and Eastern Europe. *European Urban and Regional Studies* 23(3), 267–288.

Nye, J.S. (1990) Soft power. *Foreign Policy* 80 (Autumn), 153–171.

Nye, J. (ed.) (2004) *Soft Power: The Means to Success in World Politics*. Public Affairs, New York.

Ó Tuathail, G. (1999) Understanding critical geopolitics: geopolitics and risk society. *Journal of Strategic Studies* 22(2–3), 107–124.

Ociepka, B. (2014) *Public Diplomacy in the European Union: Models for Poland*. Polish Institute of International Affairs (PISM), Policy Paper 5, Warsaw.

Oswin, N. and Olund, E. (2010) Governing intimacy. *Environment and Planning D: Society and Space* 28(1), 60–67.

Pain, R. (2009) Globalized fear? Towards an emotional geopolitics. *Progress in Human Geography* 33(4), 466–486.

Pain, R. and Smith, S. (eds) (2008) *Fear: Critical Geopolitics and Everyday Life*. Ashgate, Aldershot, UK.

Pain, R. and Staeheli, L. (2014) Introduction: intimacy-geopolitics and violence. *Area* 46(4), 344–347.

Pavoni, A. (2011) Turning the city: Johannesburg and the 2010 World Cup. *Brazilian Journal of Urban Management* 3, 191–209.

Peston, R. (2008) *Who Runs Britain?* Hodder and Stoughton, London.

Pratt, C. (2012) *Families Apart: Migrant Mothers and the Conflicts of Labour and Love*. University of Minnesota Press, Minneapolis, Minnesota.

Pratt, G. and Rosner, V. (2012) Introduction: the global and the intimate. In: Pratt, G. and Rosner, V. (eds) *The Global and the Intimate: Feminism in Our Time*. Columbia University Press, New York, pp. 1–27.

Preuss, H. (2007) The conceptualisation and measurement of mega sport event legacies. *Journal of Sport & Tourism* 12(3–4), 207–228.

Pritchard, A., Morgan, N., Ateljevic, I. and Harris, C. (eds) (2007) *Tourism and Gender: Embodiment, Sensuality and Experience*. CAB International, Wallingford, UK.

Rawlinson, K. (2015) Change Tunisia travel warning, officials urge Foreign Office. *The Independent* [London], 20 July, p. 8.

Reiser, D. (2003) Globalisation: an old phenomenon that needs to be rediscovered for tourism? *Tourism and Hospitality Research* 4, 306–320.

Ren, C. and Blichfeldt, B. (2010) One clear image? Challenging simplicity in place branding. *Scandinavian Journal of Hospitality and Tourism* 11(4), 416–434.

Ren, C. and Gyimóthy, S. (2013) Transforming and contesting nation branding strategies: Denmark at the Expo 2010. *Place Branding and Public Diplomacy* 9(1), 17–29.

Romano, S. (2014) *The Political and Social Construction of Poverty: Central and Eastern European Countries in Transition*. Policy Press, Bristol, UK.

Rowen, I. (2016) The geopolitics of tourism: mobilities, territory, and protest in China, Taiwan, and Hong Kong. *Annals of the American Association of Geographers* 106(2), 385–393.

Saarinen, J. and Rogerson, C.M. (2014) Tourism and the Millennium Development Goals: perspectives beyond 2015. *Tourism Geographies* 16(1), 23–30.

Savelli, N. (2012) Tourism geopolitics in the 'back of beyond': the territorial development of Valgaudemar. *Journal of Alpine Research/Revue de géographie alpine* 100(2), 2–11.

Sayer, A. (2014) *Why We Can't Afford the Rich*. Policy Press, Bristol, UK.

Sengupta, K. (2015) Travel warning could push us into recession, Tunisians claim. *The Independent* [London], 21 July, p. 12.

Sharp, J. (2000) Remasculinising geo-politics? Comments on Gearoid O'Tuathail's critical geopolitics. *Political Geography* 19, 361–364.

Sharpley, R., Sharpley, J. and Adams, J. (1996) Travel advice or trade embargo? The impacts and implications of official travel advice. *Tourism Management* 17(1), 1–7.

Shin, Y-S. (2004) Tourism development in North Korea: economical and geopolitical perspective. *Anatolia* 15(2), 150–163.

Smith, A. (2002) Imagining geographies of the 'new Europe': geo-economic power and the new European architecture of integration. *Political Geography* 21, 647–670.

Smith, M.E. (1997) Hegemony and elite capital: the tools of tourism. In: Chambers, E. (ed.) *Tourism and Culture: An Applied Perspective*. State University of New York Press, Albany, New York, pp. 199–223.

Song, Z.P. and Deng, X.H. (2014) Strategies for sport to promote China's national image from the perspective of globalization. (In Chinese with English summary.) *Journal of Physical Education* (Guangzhou) 21(5), 21–24.

Staeheli, L. (1994) Empowering political struggle: spaces and scales of resistance. *Political Geography* 13(5), 387–391.

Starr, H. (2013) On geopolitics: spaces and places. *International Studies Quarterly* 57(3), 433–439.

Su, X. and Teo, P. (2009) *The Politics of Heritage Tourism in China: A View from Lijiang*. Routledge, London.

Swain, M.B. (ed.) (1995) Gender in tourism. *Annals of Tourism Research* 22(2), theme issue.

Tahiri, H. (2007) *The Structure of Kurdish Society and the Struggle for a Kurdish State*. Mazda, Santa Anna, California.

Taylor, P. (2000) Critical geopolitics. In: Johnston, R.J., Gregory, D., Pratt, G. and Watts, M. (eds) *Dictionary of Human Geography*. Blackwell, Oxford, UK, pp. 125–126.

Thomas, C. (1999) Where is the world now? *Review of International Studies* 25, 225–244.

Tolipov, F. (2011) Micro-geopolitics of Central Asia: an Uzbekistan perspective. *Strategic Analysis* 35(4), 629–639.

Tribe, J. (2008) Tourism: a critical business. *Journal of Travel Research* 46(3), 245–255.

UKFCO (United Kingdom Foreign and Commonwealth Office) (2014) *British Behaviour Abroad Report*. Foreign and Commonwealth Office, London.

UNWTO (United Nations World Tourism Organization) (2014a) *Ministerial Meeting on Mega Events for Sustainable Tourism Development 16 June 2014 – 17 June 2014 Sochi, Russia*. UNWTO, Madrid.

UNWTO (2014b) *Tourism Highlights 2014*. UNWTO, Madrid.

van der Wusten, H. (2015) Imagined communities and practiced geopolitics. *Hungarian Geographical Bulletin* 64(4), 281–291.

Verhaeghe, P. (2014) *What About Me? The Struggle for Identity in a Market-based Society* (trans. Hedley-Prole, J.). Scribe Publications, Melbourne, Australia.

Verluise, P. (2014) *The Geopolitics of the EU Borders: Where Should Expansion Stop?* ESKA, Paris.

von Mies, L. (1945) *Bureaucracy*. Yale University Press, New Haven, Connecticut.

Weaver, D.B. (2010) Geopolitical dimensions of sustainable tourism. *Tourism Recreation Research* 35(1), 47–53.

Zoppo, C.E. and Zorgbibe, C. (2013) *On Geopolitics: Classical and Nuclear*. Martinus Nijhoff, Dordrecht, the Netherlands.

2 Tourism and Geopolitics: The Political Imaginary of Territory, Tourism and Space

C. Michael Hall*

University of Canterbury, Christchurch, New Zealand

2.1 Introduction

Geopolitics is a term with multiple layers and meanings (Hepple, 1986). In its 'traditional' form, geopolitics is best understood as the struggle for political dominance of space (Kearns, 2009). For many years, this was seen primarily in terms of global and international space whereby state actors sought to contest for control of territory, particularly with reference to the geographical assumptions and understandings that influenced world politics (Murphy *et al.*, 2004), while particular arrangements of space and specific locations in space also influenced the nature of political contests. Over time, such geopolitical contestation also came to be understood as an area for substate and even private actors. Dalby, for example, picks up on this theme, suggesting,

> It is about the spaces of politics, the geographies of rule, authority and frequently violence. It is nearly always about attempts to make, organize, dominate and control particular spaces,
> (Dalby, 2013: 38)

before going on to note that this is not just an act of explicit diplomacy or war, but is also now related to the spaces of the global neoliberal economy (Panitch and Gindin, 2012; see also Sheppard, 2002).

This broadening of the notion of geopolitics resonates well with recent scholarship that suggests that geopolitics not only is concerned with the control or occupation of space and territory by state and other political actors but also is about the political consequences of the different modes of knowledge and ways of representing the world (Mamadouh, 1998, 1999; Robinson, 2003; Dalby, 2008; Megoran, 2008; Sidaway, 2008; Pain, 2009; Dodds *et al.*, 2013), including our understanding of the everyday (Dittmer and Gray, 2010). Power and Campbell (2010) suggest that this notion of critical geopolitics encompasses a diverse range of academic challenges to the conventional ways in which political space is written, read and practised. Ó Tuathail similarly regards critical geopolitics as a gathering place for various critiques of the multiple geopolitical discourses and practices that characterise modernity:

> It is merely the starting point for a different form of geopolitics, one hopefully burdened less by nationalism and chauvinistic universals and more committed to cosmopolitan justice and self-critical analysis.
> (Ó Tuathail, 2010: 316)

Nevertheless, several themes emerge, including the importance of 'textuality' and the cultural in geopolitics; the displacement of state-centric readings of world politics to incorporate the

*E-mail: michael.hall@canterbury.ac.nz

'messy practices' of the modern inter- and intra-state system – a '"geopolitical social" which both crosses and crafts traditional borders of internal and external to the national state' (Cowen and Smith, 2009: 22); and the relations of power and gender in geopolitical thinking and discourse (Sharp, 2000; Ó Tuathail, 2010).

Power and Campbell (2010) note that critical geopolitical thinking in both geography and international relations has been influenced strongly by post-structural philosophies, and particularly the work of Michel Foucault and Jacques Derrida. This therefore has strong parallels to academic trends elsewhere in the social sciences, including tourism studies (Davis, 2001; Gale, 2012). Nevertheless, the broader influence of critical geopolitics is recognised as being relatively limited (Jones and Sage, 2010) even though it is 'engaged in the analysis of a range of enduring global challenges like environmental catastrophe, new modes of war, persistent global inequalities, imperial desires and reductive representations' (Power and Campbell, 2010: 245).

This chapter provides a brief overview of the main themes in research on tourism and geopolitics. It is divided, somewhat artificially, into two main sections. The first deals primarily with 'traditional', more state-centric, approaches to geopolitics, while the second examines the post-structuralist and cultural turn of critical geopolitics. The conclusion highlights potential future areas for development.

2.2   Geopolitics and Tourism

Geopolitics has not been a significant theme in tourism studies, although research in the area has increased in recent years. Often, such work is coming from outside what may be considered as mainstream tourism research, and it is instead researchers on geopolitics using tourism or its elements as a way of framing geopolitical issues that dominate the wider literature. Unfortunately, in many cases, tourism researchers also use the term 'geopolitics' as a shorthand means to refer to tourism and political territory or politics and tourism as a development tool in general without any seeming explicit connection to the various theoretical themes that exist in the geopolitical literature (e.g. Raymond, 2004; Hillali, 2007; Hoerner, 2007; Sarrasin, 2007; Dehoorne et al.,

2014). Nevertheless, even though geopolitics has a wide range of meanings, it is certainly not devoid of theory (see Ó Tuathail, 1994; Gray, 1999; Dahlman and Brunn, 2003; Beeson, 2009; Kaplan, 2009, for a number of useful overviews).

Early writings that connected geopolitics and tourism usually identified tourism as an indication of state activity (see also the framework proposed by Weaver (2010)), often in colonial or post-colonial situations (Doumenge, 1990), or with the possibility of tourist flows and tourism development improving state relations (Molinaro, 2002; Shin, 2004; Coles and Hall, 2005; Daher, 2007; Jordan, 2011; Chiang, 2012; Connell, 2015), especially in cross-border regions (Kandler, 2000; Duffy, 2001; Fabrizio, 2001; Gheorghe and Alexandru, 2001; Lichtenberger, 2002; Olson, 2002; Sparke et al., 2004; Chiang, 2012) or contested territories (Smiraglia, 1994; Kandler, 2000; Daher, 2007; Isaac et al., 2016). The latter themes are particularly important for European writing on tourism and geopolitics in the 1990s and early 2000s.

The work of Sparke et al. (2004) was a notable transition from much of the previous writing in tourism and geopolitics as the paper used the example of the Indonesia–Malaysia–Singapore Growth Triangle to illustrate the complex geographies of power that subverted efforts to read cross-border regionalisation as a straightforward geographical corollary of 'globalisation'. Rather than the region being treated as a complementary transborder assemblage of land, labour and capital along the lines of European work in cross-border regions, the authors suggested the area should be regarded

> as a palimpsest in which the imagined geographies of cross-border development and the economic geographies of their uneven spatial fixing on the ground are mediated by complex cultural and political geographies.
> (Sparke et al., 2004: 485)

As such, the paper highlights how the geographies of capital (including its uneven development and its links to the geoeconomics of intraregional competition), land (including post-colonial relations across the region, the geopolitics of land reclamation and the enclaved landscapes of tourism) and labour (including the divergent itineraries of migrant workers) overlay and complicate each other, and therefore problematise the more simplistic narratives of the Growth Triangle as an embodiment of contemporary global processes.

It is interesting to note that the paper had much more impact on geography and regional readings of the complexity of geopolitics in border regions (e.g. Sparke, 2006; Arnold and Pickles, 2011; Su, 2013; Zimmerbauer, 2013; Ormond, 2014; Sigler, 2014) than on tourism in the context of such areas (Hampton, 2010). In one sense this is surprising, given that the legality and regulation of the mobility of people across borders and its effects on de-territorialisation and re-territorialisation are issues that resonate strongly in the contemporary political setting (Hazbun, 2004, 2008; Chiang, 2012). Rowen (2016) extends these perspectives by showing that embodied, everyday practices such as tourism cannot be divorced from state-scale geopolitics. He uses the example of tourism flows in the Chinese region to show that at the same time that tourism is used to project Chinese state authority over Taiwan and consolidate control over Tibet and Xinjiang, it has also triggered popular protest in Hong Kong (including the pro-democracy Umbrella Movement and its aftermath) and international protest over the territorially contested South China Sea.

With respect to some of the more traditional aspects of geopolitics whereby the territorialisation of space becomes an expression of state power, tourism has an important role as an economic expression of permanent occupation under international law, with occupation also often influencing later patterns of tourism (Timothy, 2002; Gelbman and Timothy, 2010; Gosar, 2014; Hannam, 2013). Tourism has been regarded as significant for geopolitical as well as economic development reasons in disputed territories such as the Arctic, Antarctic or the Spratley and Paracel Islands in the South China Sea (Hall, 1994; Timothy, 2002). For example, cruise ship access in the Arctic has become part of the territorial disputes over national versus international waters (Blunden, 2012; Østreng et al., 2013; Kristoffersen, 2014; Huijbens and Alessio, 2015), while tourism is an action to indicate economic activity and human settlement in the terrestrial Arctic (Hall and Saarinen, 2010a,b,c; Horejsova and Paris, 2013; Müller, 2015).

In the case of the Antarctic, significant contestation exists between various cities for the opportunity to host research facilities or to act as tourist transiting stations, with the activities of such cities important in reinforcing Antarctic and Southern Ocean claims and capacities to act as a port of control (Bertram et al., 2007; Hall, 2015). For example, in the case of rival Antarctic Peninsula 'gateways', Ushuaia (Argentina) and Punta Arenas (Chile):

> They participate in the structuring of a multifaceted Antarctic frontier conquest: military, scientific, ecological and tourist. The bridgehead is a key concept to rethink the territorial structuring and control of conquest frontier. If we recall proximity and connection as minimal criteria to define a gateway, political control and territorial reference tend to reinforce the gateway as the main bridgehead place of the conquest frontier.
>
> (Guyot, 2013: 11)

The geopolitics of tourism at both a national and local state level has been explored by Xue et al. (2015) with respect to tourism in China, where they examined the displacement of people by tourism developments. They note the ubiquity of tourism development-induced displacement and resettlement in emerging economies and colonial/post-colonial societies, particularly with respect to indigenous peoples and national parks and/or tourism development projects (Brockington and Igoe, 2006; Agrawal and Redford, 2009; Attanapola and Lund, 2013). However, such processes may also occur in developed countries, especially where state intervention is part of processes of tourism-led gentrification (Gotham, 2005; Herrera et al., 2007). In such cases, poorer elements of society may be displaced as a result of policy and regulatory change, even if they have been living in a location for many years. Interestingly, the effects of such displacement has been noted for many years but have never usually been framed in terms of geopolitics, although there are clearly processes of re-territorialisation taking place as community social, political and economic structures change. One area where this has come to the fore is with respect to Klein's (2007) notion of disaster capitalism.

Post-disaster urban regeneration tends to occur in a more unstable context than mainstream regeneration (Amore and Hall, 2016b). Importantly, the phenomenon of regeneration as a process of urban restructuring is an expression of the second circuit of capital (Harvey, 1978), also referred to as 'fictitious capital' (Becker *et al.*, 2010), which is constituted by real estate, its financial conduits, state regulation of space, and by those social groups that invest in real estate so as to maximise capitalised land rent. The post-disaster regeneration underpinning the phenomenology of disaster capitalism (Klein, 2007) – as demonstrated in post-9/11 New York (Gotham and Greenberg, 2008, 2014); post-Katrina New Orleans (Johnson, 2011; Gotham and Greenberg, 2014); post-Van earthquake in Turkcy (Saraçoğlu and Demirtaş-Milz, 2014) and post-earthquake Christchurch in New Zealand – also serves to maintain core land rent values (Amore and Hall, 2016b). Mainstream forms of urban regeneration tend to be situated within general market discourse, while regeneration in cities following disasters is used by the state to justify market-directed strategies as a solution to fix the dysfunctional climate of 'uncertainty' quickly (Porter, 2009).

Nevertheless, even here, substantial similarities occur, with event-led regeneration in particular being used to create a climate of crisis in which normal planning and decision making are often suspended in order to achieve event deadlines (Hall, 2006), although it should be emphasised that non-event-led tourism regeneration is also often justified within discourses of economic, employment and even aesthetic crisis (Smyth, 2005; Porter, 2009). While the post-disaster regeneration literature is clearly connected to an understanding of the significance of the role of the state as an agent of meta-governance (Amore and Hall, 2016a), it is also clearly tied to critiques of the neoliberal project (Panitch and Gindin, 2012) and therefore provides a potential bridge between state-centric and critical geopolitical accounts of tourism.

2.3   Tourism and the Critical Turn in Geopolitics

Arguably, the first tourism-related work to engage explicitly in a substantial fashion with critical geopolitics was Saldanha's (2002) work on identity, spatiality and post-colonial resistance in Goa, India. Her work on the interplay of the different spatialities of tourism was linked to the multiple constructions of 'Goa' and 'Goan identity'.

The theme of identity in relation to geopolitics and tourism has since become a significant area of research with respect to contemporary mobilities and border crossing (Zhang, 2013), diaspora and intergenerational change (Ho, 2013), as well as the use of tourism by the state as a means to encourage the formation or reinforcement of particular identities (Gagnon, 2007; Ho, 2013). Attanapola and Lund (2013), for example, provide an examination of the case of the Veddas in Sri Lanka. They note that, traditionally, the identity of indigenous people was defined in relation to closeness to nature and the use of natural resources, including fauna and flora. In the contemporary setting, however, such identity formation has been placed under pressure from development programmes, neoliberal policies and increasing market economy. Therefore, identity for the Veddas is being redefined and renegotiated within a new socio-economic and geopolitical context characterised by limited access to traditional land as a result of development projects, lack of education, unemployment and an increasing demand for indigenous tourism. Attanapola and Lund (2013) conclude that, in such circumstances, the redefinition of the Veddas identity is being pursued via two survival strategies: tourist development and 're-indigenization', and integration into mainstream Sinhalese society.

The promotion of identity may also be used to portray different notions of security to the outside world, including the tourist, thereby seeking to separate on-the-ground realities from the images that the tourist receives. Ojeda (2013) focused on the coupling of war and tourism in the portrayal of security by Colombia and its role in hegemonic state formation and the everyday and highly uneven geographies of (in)security. Interestingly, the interplay between war, tourism and securitisation, as well as dispossession, has been picked up by several other studies, although none of these has appeared in a tourism journal (Hyndman and Amarasingam, 2014; Hyndman, 2015; Rocheleau, 2015).

Also related to critical geopolitical perspectives on security and tourism was Dowler's (2013) study of hospitality in West Belfast in Northern Island, in which she noted that for many years areas of West Belfast were perceived as no-go areas, places where the police had lost jurisdiction, and the media designated these neighbourhoods as 'terrorist enclaves'. She noted that the signing of the Peace Accords provided an opportunity for these marginalised areas to be transformed into places of hospitality for tourists curious about the heritage of 'the troubles'. Dowler (2013) highlighted the interdependent relationship between hospitality and the development of a post-war confidence for a community that had long been stigmatised, by applying feminist theories of hospitality to issues of inclusiveness. In so doing, she highlighted the 'politics of hospitality' as well as reframing understandings of security in the Northern Irish context.

The theme of hospitality has also been picked up elsewhere in critical geopolitics. For example, Fregonese and Ramadan (2015) argue that rather than being neutral sites of leisure and tourism, and hospitality mediated by financial exchange, hotels need to be researched as geopolitical sites. For them, the spaces of hotels, from conference rooms to reception halls, from hotel bars to corridors and private rooms, are connected to wider architectures and issues of security, war- and peacemaking. In illustrating their case, they present six themes: hotels as projections of soft power; soft targets for political violence; strategic infrastructures in conflict; hosts for war reporters; providers of emergency hospitality and care; and infrastructures of peace building. They conclude that the potential of hotels as a geopolitical space of hospitality emerges from their selective openness and closure to their surroundings, and their flexible material infrastructures that can facilitate and mediate geopolitical processes.

While some of the themes identified by Fregonese and Ramadan (2015) undoubtedly resonate with the role of tourism as a geopolitical subject, it is surprising that the wider context of tourism and hospitality has not been picked up by the authors. For example, Craggs (2014) highlights the centrality of hospitality to post-colonial Commonwealth diplomacy and identifies four contributions that a focus on hospitality can make to our understandings of geopolitics more broadly. First, the role of the welcome, hospitality and the host in staging political relations, and to the value of attending to hospitality. Second, the role of welcoming performances in a range of geopolitical contexts. Third, the importance of different sets of spaces – bars, clubs, hotels and tourist sites – that form an integral, but often overlooked, component of

political practice. To which this author would also add events and gateways (airports, ports). Fourth, the significance of entangled ethical-political and economic elements of hospitality practice.

The focus on hospitality as performance that is inherent in the work of Craggs (2014) and Fregonese and Ramadan (2015) provides an interesting counterpoint to the work in tourism of the significance of the hosting of events as a mechanism of cultural diplomacy and international relations. This is particularly evident in the way in which atmosphere and national stories are communicated at hallmark events, especially in opening and closing ceremonies (Pujik, 1999; Silk, 2002; Heinz Housel, 2007; Brady, 2009; Luo et al., 2010; Traganou, 2010; Giulianotti, 2015).

Tourism and hospitality has emerged as an important theme in critical geopolitics, although it has not had a significant influence on the literature that appears in tourism journals or on those that work in tourism and hospitality departments. However, some connections are beginning to emerge in areas such as the role of the visual in geopolitics (e.g. Shapiro, 2008) and the commoditisation of nature and the so-called 'green economy' in tourism (Hall, 2014). Nevertheless, the reasons for such connectivity may lie as much with a narrowness of reading and definition of the political in tourism studies as it does with the potential explanatory utility of critical geopolitics.

2.4 Conclusions and Directions

Paasi (2006) uses the term 'geopolitical remote sensing' (a term originated by the author) to describe the need to contextualise more fully the concepts and practices in human geographic research and to examine more closely the role played by internationalising (and English language-dominated) publishing markets in the review and publication of papers that increasingly cross the borders of linguistic contexts. Focusing on the geopolitics of academic publishing highlights 'the uneven geographies of international journal publishing spaces' (Paasi, 2005: 769) that are shaped by different national and institutional research agendas, as well as language, that lead to the peripheralisation of non-English publications (and hence ideas) in the 'international' discourse of tourism (and geography) (Hall, 2013).

Although the hegemony of the centre in the knowledge production process has long been acknowledged (Canagarajah, 1996), the English language has become part of the 'ideological complex' that produces and maintains the increasing hegemony of the English-speaking academy (Tietze and Dick, 2013). This indicates a major problem for some linguistically defined bodies of tourism, and other knowledge, at a time when there are demands from policy makers and university administrations to figure in international subject and university rankings. As Hall commented:

> No matter how important local and national knowledge is within a specific spatial context, unless it is conveyed in English it has little chance to enter the global marketplace and be reproduced and recirculated. Somewhat ironically, given the desire to give voice to local and indigenous perspectives, unless that voice can be spoken in English it is likely not to be heard.
>
> (Hall, 2013: 608)

These issues are significant for the relationships between geopolitics and tourism because they reflect the ways in which research debates are shaped by geopolitical forces, in the form of the state and the academic publishing and education industries, as well as the need to challenge the conventional ways in which the political space of tourism is written, read and practised. Tourism, on the whole, is not only poorly engaged with the political dimensions of its subject, but with the wider political literature as well (Hall, 1994; Jenkins et al., 2014).

The potential significance of geopolitics for tourism is therefore perhaps doubly cursed as it lies at the intersections of political geography and international relations, two subjects that have had only marginal influence on tourism studies. Nevertheless, some of the themes identified in this chapter are clearly of increasing significance for tourism studies and demonstrate some of the potential insights that a geopolitical perspective may bring to research activities. At the macro level, the role of the state clearly remains of significance to tourism. However, the micro-level geopolitical dimensions of displacement, hospitality, mobilities and border crossing clearly offer insights into the political imaginary of territory, tourism and space.

Indeed, this chapter has been completed at a time when Europe is convulsed by border crossings of displaced and mobile persons who are faced with different levels of state and personal hospitality/hostility. This situation brings into sharp focus the binaries of tourist and refugee, and hospitality and hostility, and clearly highlights the continued relevance of geopolitical perspectives in a mobile world.

References

Agrawal, A. and Redford, K. (2009) Conservation and displacement: an overview. *Conservation and Society* 7(1), 1–10.

Amore, A. and Hall, C.M. (2016a) From governance to meta-governance in tourism? Re-incorporating politics, interests and values in the analysis of tourism governance. *Tourism Recreation Research* 41(2), 109–122.

Amore, A. and Hall, C.M. (2016b) 'Regeneration is the focus now': anchor projects and delivering a new CBD for Christchurch. In: Hall, C.M., Malinen, S., Vosslamber, R. and Wordsworth, R. (eds) *Business and Post-Disaster Management: Business, Organisational and Consumer Resilience and the Christchurch Earthquakes*. Routledge, Abingdon, UK, pp. 181–199.

Arnold, D. and Pickles, J. (2011) Global work, surplus labor, and the precarious economies of the border. *Antipode* 43(5), 1598–1624.

Attanapola, C.T. and Lund, R. (2013) Contested identities of indigenous people: indigenization or integration of the Veddas in Sri Lanka. *Singapore Journal of Tropical Geography* 34(2), 172–187.

Becker, J., Jäger, J., Leubolt, B. and Weissenbacher, R. (2010) Peripheral financialization and vulnerability to crisis: a regulationist perspective. *Competition & Change* 14(3–4), 225–247.

Beeson, M. (2009) Geopolitics and the making of regions: the fall and rise of East Asia. *Political Studies* 57(3), 498–516.

Bertram, E., Muir, S. and Stonehouse, B. (2007) Gateway ports in the development of Antarctic tourism. In: Snyder, J. and Stonehouse, B. (eds) *Prospects for Polar Tourism*. CAB International, Wallingford, UK, pp. 123–146.

Blunden, M. (2012) Geopolitics and the Northern Sea Route. *International Affairs* 88, 115–129.

Brady, A.M. (2009) The Beijing Olympics as a campaign of mass distraction. *The China Quarterly* 197, 1–24.

Brockington, D. and Igoe, J. (2006) Eviction for conservation: a global overview. *Conservation and Society* 4(3), 424–470.

Canagarajah, A.S. (1996) 'Nondiscursive' requirements in academic publishing, material resources of periphery scholars, and the politics of knowledge production. *Written Communication* 13, 435–472.

Chiang, M.-H. (2012) Tourism development across the Taiwan Strait. *East Asia* 29(3), 235–253.

Coles, T. and Hall, D. (2005) Tourism and European Union enlargement. Plus ça change? *International Journal of Tourism Research* 7(2), 51–61.

Connell, J. (2015) Shining light on the darkness. Placing tourists within North Korean tourism. Comment on: Desiring the dark: 'A taste for the unusual' in North Korean tourism? *Current Issues in Tourism*, DOI: 10.1080/13683500.2015.1032896.

Cowen, D. and Smith, N. (2009) After geopolitics? From the geopolitical social to geoeconomics. *Antipode* 41, 22–48.

Craggs, R. (2014) Hospitality in geopolitics and the making of Commonwealth international relations. *Geoforum* 52, 90–100.

Daher, R. (ed.) (2007) *Tourism in the Middle East: Continuity, Change, and Transformation*. Channel View, Clevedon, UK.

Dahlman, C. and Brunn, S. (2003) Reading geopolitics beyond the state: organisational discourse in response to 11 September. *Geopolitics* 8(3), 253–280.

Dalby, S. (2008) Imperialism, domination, culture: the continued relevance of critical geopolitics. *Geopolitics* 13, 413–436.

Dalby, S. (2013) The geopolitics of climate change. *Political Geography* 37, 38–47.

Davis, J.B. (2001) Commentary: tourism research and social theory – expanding the focus. *Tourism Geographies* 3(2), 125–134.

Dehoorne, O., Depault, K., Ma, S-Q. and Cao, H. (2014) International tourism: geopolitical dimensions of a global phenomenon. In: Cao, B.-Y., Ma, S-Q. and Cao, H. (eds) *Ecosystem Assessment and Fuzzy Systems Management*. Springer, Dordrecht, the Netherlands, pp. 389–396.

Dittmer, J. and Gray, N. (2010) Popular geopolitics 2.0: towards new methodologies of the everyday. *Geography Compass* 4(11), 1664–1677.

Dodds, K., Kuus, M. and Sharp, J. (eds) (2013) *The Ashgate Research Companion to Critical Geopolitics*. Ashgate, Farnham, UK.

Doumenge, F. (1990) La dynamique geopolitique du Pacifique Sud (1965–1990). [The geopolitical dynamics of the South Pacific (1965–1990).] *Cahiers d'Outre-Mer* 43(170), 113–188 (in French).

Dowler, L. (2013) Waging hospitality: feminist geopolitics and tourism in West Belfast Northern Ireland. *Geopolitics* 18(4), 779–799.

Duffy, R. (2001) Peace parks: the paradox of globalisation. *Geopolitics* 6(2), 1–26.

Fabrizio, E. (2001) Geopolitični pomen Vzhodne Evrope za Evropsko zvezo (EU) in Italijo. [Geopolitical importance of Eastern Europe for the European Union (EU) and Italy.] *Acta Geographica Slovenica* 34(1), 91–103 (in Slovenian).

Fregonese, S. and Ramadan, A. (2015) Hotel geopolitics: a research agenda. *Geopolitics* 20(4), 793–813.

Gagnon, S. (2007) L'intervention de l'état québécois dans le tourisme entre 1920 et 1940 ou la mise en scène géopolitique de l'identité canadienne française. [The intervention of the Quebec state in tourism between 1920 and 1940 or the geopolitical staging of French Canadian identity.] *Herodote* 127, 151–166, 201, 205 (in French).

Gale, T. (2012) Tourism geographies and post-structuralism. In: Wilson, J. (ed.) *The Routledge Handbook of Tourism Geographies*. Routledge, London, pp. 37–45.

Gelbman, A. and Timothy, D.J. (2010) From hostile boundaries to tourist attractions. *Current Issues in Tourism* 13(3), 239–259.

Gheorghe, M. and Alexandru, I. (2001) Geopolitique regionale et evolution du tourisme international en Roumanie. [Regional geopolitics and evolution of international tourism in Romania.] *Acta Geographica Slovenica* 34(1), 177–188.

Giulianotti, R. (2015) The Beijing 2008 Olympics: examining the interrelations of China, globalization, and soft power. *European Review* 23(2), 286–296.

Gosar, A. (2014) The development of tourism in Istria. *International Journal of Euro-Mediterranean Studies* 7(2), 155–174.

Gotham, K.F. (2005) Tourism gentrification: the case of New Orleans' Vieux Carre (French Quarter). *Urban Studies* 42(7), 1099–1121.

Gotham, K.F. and Greenberg, M. (2008) From 9/11 to 8/29: post-disaster recovery and rebuilding in New York and New Orleans. *Social Forces* 87, 1039–1062.

Gotham, K.F. and Greenberg, M. (2014) *Crisis Cities: Disaster and Redevelopment in New York and New Orleans.* Oxford University Press, Oxford, UK.

Gray, C.S. (1999) Inescapable geography. *The Journal of Strategic Studies* 22(2–3), 161–177.

Guyot, S. (2013) La construcción territorial de cabezas de puente antárticas rivales: Ushuaia (Argentina) y Punta Arenas (Chile). [The territorial construction of Antarctic bridge rivals: Ushuaia (Argentina) and Punta Arenas (Chile).] *Revista Transporte y Territorio* 9, 11–38 (in Spanish).

Hall, C.M. (1994) *Tourism and Politics.* Wiley, Chichester, UK.

Hall, C.M. (2006) Urban entrepreneurship, corporate interests and sports mega-events: the thin policies of competitiveness within the hard outcomes of neoliberalism. *Sociological Review Monograph, Sports Mega-events: Social Scientific Analyses of a Global Phenomenon* 54(S2), 59–70.

Hall, C.M. (2013) Framing tourism geography: notes from the underground. *Annals of Tourism Research* 43, 601–623.

Hall, C.M. (2014) You can check out any time you like but you can never leave: can ethical consumption in tourism ever be sustainable? In: Weeden, C. and Boluk, K. (eds) *Managing Ethical Consumption in Tourism: Compromise and Tension.* Routledge, Abingdon, UK, pp. 32–56.

Hall, C.M. (2015) Polar gateway cities: issues and challenges. *Polar Journal* 5(2), 257–277.

Hall, C.M. and Saarinen, J. (2010a) Polar tourism: definitions and dimensions. *Scandinavian Journal of Hospitality and Tourism* 10(4), 448–467.

Hall, C.M. and Saarinen, J. (eds) (2010b) *Tourism and Change in Polar Regions: Climate, Environment and Experience.* Routledge, Abingdon, UK.

Hall, C.M. and Saarinen, J. (eds) (2010c) Tourism and change in polar regions: Introduction – definitions, locations, places and dimensions. In: Hall, C.M. and Saarinen, J. (eds) *Tourism and Change in Polar Regions: Climate, Environment and Experience.* Routledge, Abingdon, UK, pp. 1–41.

Hampton, M.P. (2010) Enclaves and ethnic ties: the local impacts of Singaporean cross-border tourism in Malaysia and Indonesia. *Singapore Journal of Tropical Geography* 31(2), 239–252.

Hannam, K. (2013) 'Shangri-La' and the new 'Great Game': exploring tourism geopolitics between China and India. *Tourism Planning and Development* 10(2), 178–186.

Harvey, D. (1978) The urban process under capitalism: a framework for analysis. *International Journal of Urban and Regional Research* 2, 101–131.

Hazbun, W. (2004) Globalisation, reterritorialisation and the political economy of tourism development in the Middle East. *Geopolitics* 9(2), 310–341.

Hazbun, W. (2008) *Beaches, Ruins, Resorts: The Politics of Tourism in the Arab World.* University of Minnesota Press, Minneapolis, Minnesota.

Heinz Housel, T. (2007) Australian nationalism and globalization: narratives of the nation in the 2000 Sydney Olympics' opening ceremony. *Critical Studies in Media Communication* 24(5), 446–461.

Hepple, L. (1986) The revival of geopolitics. *Political Geography Quarterly* 5(4, S1), S21–S36.

Herrera, L.M.G., Smith, N. and Vera, M.Á.M. (2007) Gentrification, displacement, and tourism in Santa Cruz de Tenerife. *Urban Geography* 28(3), 276–298.

Hillali, M. (2007) Du tourisme et de la géopolitique au Maghreb: le cas du Maroc. [Tourism and geopolitics in the Maghreb: the case of Morocco.] *Herodote* 127, 47–63, 201, 203–204 (in French).

Ho, E.L.-E. (2013) 'Refugee' or 'returnee'? The ethnic geopolitics of diasporic resettlement in China and intergenerational change. *Transactions of the Institute of British Geographers* 38(4), 599–611.

Hoerner, J.-M. (2007) Le tourisme et la géopolitique. [Tourism and geopolitics.] *Herodote* 127, 15–28, 199, 203 (in French).

Horejsova, T. and Paris, C.M. (2013) Tourism and the challenge of Arctic governance. *International Journal of Tourism Policy* 5(1–2), 113–137.

Huijbens, E.H. and Alessio, D. (2015) Arctic 'concessions' and icebreaker diplomacy? Chinese tourism development in Iceland. *Current Issues in Tourism* 18(5), 433–449.

Hyndman, J. (2015) The securitisation of Sri Lankan tourism in the absence of peace. *Stability: International Journal of Security and Development* 4(1). Available at: http://doi.org/10.5334/sta.fa (accessed 14 July 2016).

Hyndman, J. and Amarasingam, A. (2014) Touring 'terrorism': landscapes of memory in post-war Sri Lanka. *Geography Compass* 8(8), 560–575.

Isaac, R., Hall, C.M. and Higgins-Desbiolles, F. (eds) (2016) *The Politics and Power of Tourism in Palestine*. Routledge, Abingdon, UK.

Jenkins, J.M., Hall, C.M. and Mkono, M. (2014) Tourism and public policy: contemporary debates and future directions. In: Lew, A., Hall, C.M. and Williams, A. (eds) *The Wiley Blackwell Companion to Tourism*. Wiley-Blackwell, Oxford, UK, pp. 542–555.

Johnson, C. (2011) *The Neoliberal Deluge: Hurricane Katrina, Late Capitalism, and the Remaking of New Orleans*. University of Minnesota Press, Minneapolis, Minnesota.

Jones, L. and Sage, D. (2010) New directions in critical geopolitics: an introduction. With contributions of: Gearoid Ó Tuathail, Jennifer Hyndman, Fraser MacDonald, Emily Gilbert and Virginie Mamadouh. *GeoJournal* 75, 315–325.

Jordan, P. (2011) Kroatien ante portas. Was kommt auf die EU zu? [Croatia before the gates. What's in store for the EU?] *Geographische Rundschau* 63(4), 14–19 (in German).

Kandler, H. (2000) Die anatolische 'Bruchlinie' – chance fur ein neues Fremdbewusstsein bei Turken und Griechen? [The Anatolian 'faultline' – chance for new mutual recognition by Turks and Greeks.] *Orient* 41(1), 65–82 (in German).

Kaplan, R.D. (2009) The revenge of geography. *Foreign Policy* 172(May/June), 96–105.

Kearns, G. (2009) *Geopolitics and Empire: The Legacy of Halford Mackinder*. Oxford University Press, Oxford, UK.

Klein, N. (2007) *The Shock Doctrine: The Rise of Disaster Capitalism*. Metropolitan Books, New York.

Kristoffersen, B. (2014) 'Securing' geography: framings, logics and strategies in the Norwegian high north. In: Powell, R. and Dodds, K. (eds) *Polar Geopolitics: Knowledges, Resources and Legal Regimes*. Edward Elgar, Cheltenham, UK, pp. 131–148.

Lichtenberger, E. (2002) Österreich in Europa zu Beginn des 21. Jahrhunderts. [Austria in Europe at the beginning of the 21st century.] *Mitteilungen der Osterreichischen Geographischen Gesellschaft* 144, 7–26 (in German).

Luo, Q., Boccia, L.V., Han, C., Liu, X., Yu, F. and Kennett, C. (2010) Representing the opening ceremony: comparative content analysis from USA, Brazil, UK and China. *The International Journal of the History of Sport* 27(9–10), 1591–1633.

Mamadouh, V. (1998) Geopolitics in the nineties: one flag, many meanings. *GeoJournal* 46(4), 237–253.

Mamadouh, V. (1999) Reclaiming geopolitics: geographers strike back. *Geopolitics* 4(1), 118–138.

Megoran, N. (2008) Militarism, realism, just war, or nonviolence? Critical geopolitics and the problem of normativity. *Geopolitics* 13(3), 473–497.

Molinaro, I. (2002) Quebec in Europe: constraints and opportunities. *American Review of Canadian Studies* 32(2), 239–258.

Müller, D. (2015) Issues in Arctic tourism. In: Evengård, B., Larsen, J.N. and Paasche, Ø. (eds) *The New Arctic*. Springer, Dordrecht, the Netherlands, pp. 147–158.

Murphy, A.M., Bassin, M., Newman, D., Reuber, P. and Agnew, J. (2004) Is there a politics to geopolitics? *Progress in Human Geography* 28, 619–640.

Ojeda, D. (2013) War and tourism: the banal geographies of security in Colombia's 'retaking'. *Geopolitics* 18(4), 759–778.

Olson, R. (2002) Turkey–Russia relations, 2000–2001: containment or congagement? *Orient* 43(1), 79–94.

Ormond, M. (2014) Resorting to plan J: popular perceptions of Singaporean retirement migration to Johor, Malaysia. *Asian and Pacific Migration Journal* 23(1), 1–26.

Østreng, W., Eger, K.M., Fløistad, B., Jørgensen-Dahl, A., Lothe, L., *et al*. T. (2013) *Shipping in Arctic Waters: A Comparison of the Northeast, Northwest and Trans Polar Passages*. Springer, Dordrecht, the Netherlands.

Ó Tuathail, G. (1994) The critical reading/writing of geopolitics: re-reading/writing Wittfogel, Bowman and Lacoste. *Progress in Human Geography* 18, 313–332.

Ó Tuathail, G. (2010) Opening remarks. In: Jones, L. and Sage, D. New directions in critical geopolitics: an introduction. With contributions of: Gearoid Ó Tuathail, Jennifer Hyndman, Fraser MacDonald, Emily Gilbert and Virginie Mamadouh. *GeoJournal* 75, 315–325.

Paasi, A. (2005) Globalisation, academic capitalism and the uneven geographies of international journal publishing spaces. *Environment and Planning A* 37, 769–789.

Paasi, A. (2006) Texts and contexts in the globalizing academic marketplace: comments on the debate on geopolitical remote sensing. *Eurasian Geography and Economics* 47(2), 216–220.

Pain, R. (2009) Globalized fear? Towards an emotional geopolitics. *Progress in Human Geography* 33(4), 466–486.

Panitch, L. and Gindin, S. (2012) *The Making of Global Capitalism: The Political Economy of American Empire*. Verso, London.

Porter, L. (2009) Whose urban renaissance? In: Porter, L. and Shaw, K. (eds) *Whose Urban Renaissance? An International Comparison of Urban Regeneration Strategies*. Routledge, New York, pp. 456–478.

Power, M. and Campbell, D. (2010) The state of critical geopolitics. *Political Geography* 29(5), 243–246.

Puijk, R. (1999) Producing Norwegian culture for domestic and foreign gazes: the Lillehammer Olympic opening ceremony. In: Klausen, A.M. (ed.) *Olympic Games as Performance and Public Event: The Case of the XVII Winter Olympic Games in Norway*. Berghahn, New York, pp. 97–117.

Raymond, N. (2004) Perú y Costa Rica. Geopolítica del desarrollo turístico en América Latina. [Peru and Costa Rica. Geopolitics of tourism development in Latin America.] *Cuadernos Geograficos* 36, 55–72 (in Spanish).

Robinson, J. (2003) Postcolonialising geography: tactics and pitfalls. *Singapore Journal of Tropical Geography* 24, 273–289.

Rocheleau, D.E. (2015) Networked, rooted and territorial: green grabbing and resistance in Chiapas. *Journal of Peasant Studies* 42(3–4), 695–723.

Rowen, I. (2016) The geopolitics of tourism: mobilities, territory, and protest in China, Taiwan, and Hong Kong. *Annals of the American Association of Geographers*, DOI: 10.1080/00045608.2015.1113115.

Saldanha, A. (2002) Identity, spatiality and post-colonial resistance: geographies of the tourism critique in Goa. *Current Issues in Tourism* 5(2), 92–111.

Saraçoğlu, C. and Demirtaş-Milz, N. (2014) Disasters as an ideological strategy for governing neoliberal urban transformation in Turkey: insights from Izmir/Kadifekale. *Disasters* 38, 178–201.

Sarrasin, B. (2007) Géopolitique du tourisme à Madagascar: de la protection de l'environnement au développement de l'économie. [Geopolitics of tourism in Madagascar: from protection of the environment to economic development.] *Herodote* 127, 124–150, 201, 204–205 (in French).

Shapiro, J. (2008) *Cinematic Geopolitics*. Routledge, London.

Sharp, J. (2000) Remasculinising geo(-)politics? Comments on Gearóid Ó Tuathail's critical geopolitics. *Political Geography* 19(3), 361–364.

Sheppard, E. (2002) The spaces and times of globalization: place, scale, networks, and positionality. *Economic Geography* 78, 307–330.

Shin, Y.-S. (2004) Tourism development in North Korea: economical and geopolitical perspective. *Anatolia* 15(2), 150–163.

Sidaway, J.D. (2008) The dissemination of banal geopolitics: webs of extremism and insecurity. *Antipode* 40(1), 2–8.

Sigler, T.J. (2014) Panama as palimpsest: the reformulation of the 'Transit Corridor' in a global economy. *International Journal of Urban and Regional Research* 38(3), 886–902.

Silk, M. (2002) 'Bangsa Malaysia': global sport, the city and the mediated refurbishment of local identities. *Media, Culture & Society* 24(6), 775–794.

Smiraglia, C. (1994) Perche una nuova geografia dell Antartide? [Why a new geography of Antarctica?] *Memorie – Societa Geografica Italiana* 51, 163–172 (in Italian).

Smyth, H. (2005) *Marketing the City: The Role of Flagship Developments in Urban Regeneration*. Taylor and Francis, London.

Sparke, M.B. (2006) A neoliberal nexus: economy, security and the biopolitics of citizenship on the border. *Political Geography* 25(2), 151–180.

Sparke, M., Sidaway, J.D., Bunnell, T. and Grundy-Warr, C. (2004) Triangulating the borderless world: geographies of power in the Indonesia–Malaysia–Singapore Growth Triangle. *Transactions of the Institute of British Geographers* 29(4), 485–498.

Su, X. (2013) From frontier to bridgehead: cross-border regions and the experience of Yunnan, China. *International Journal of Urban and Regional Research* 37(4), 1213–1232.

Tietze, S. and Dick, P. (2013) The victorious English language. Hegemonic practices in the management academy. *Journal of Management Inquiry* 22, 122–134.

Timothy, D.J. (2002) *Tourism and Political Boundaries*. Routledge, London.

Traganou, J. (2010) National narratives in the opening and closing ceremonies of the Athens 2004 Olympic Games. *Journal of Sport & Social Issues* 34(2), 236–251.

Weaver, D.B. (2010) Geopolitical dimensions of sustainable tourism. *Tourism Recreation Research* 35(1), 47–53.

Xue, L., Kerstetter, D. and Buzinde, C.N. (2015) Residents' experiences with tourism development and resettlement in Luoyang, China. *Tourism Management* 46, 444–453.

Zhang, J.J. (2013) Borders on the move: Cross-Strait tourists' material moments on 'the other side' in the midst of rapprochement between China and Taiwan. *Geoforum* 48, 94–101.

Zimmerbauer, K. (2013) Unusual regionalism in northern Europe: the Barents Region in the making. *Regional Studies* 47(1), 89–103.

3 Tourism in the Geopolitical Construction of Central and Eastern Europe (CEE)

Derek Hall*

Seabank Associates, Maidens, Ayrshire, UK

In a geopolitical sense, 'Eastern Europe' as a region died rather suddenly at the end of the Cold War.

(Zeigler, 2002: 685)

This chapter briefly sketches classical geopolitical (de)constructions of CEE (Fig. 3.1) and the role of tourism as a reflection of changing ideological environments.

3.1 Introduction

Although often misperceived in the West (if at all) during the Cold War as relatively homogeneous, the countries of Central and Eastern Europe (CEE) possess tourism resources that embrace a diverse range of complex cultures, inspiring landscapes and myriad activities, coupled to often tortured histories, contested heritage and conflicting imagery. Indeed, mass visitation has often been unwelcome: the territories and peoples of CEE have been subject to invasions, conquests, mass migrations, bitter cleavages, grotesque demagogy, overt manipulation and not a little misrepresentation. Often viewed as no more than a pawn in big power politics, manoeuvring and rivalry, CEE has been trampled on, divided and subdivided, wooed and threatened, marketed and marketed to, and subjected to the neoliberal hegemony that engulfs us all (e.g. Bridger and Pine, 1998; see Part III Introduction, this volume). Little wonder that the term 'geopolitics' retains strong negative associations, and that the term 'visitor' may be regarded with some ambivalence.

3.2 Cast Within a History of 'Big Men'

The newly independent states of CEE that emerged out of the settlements of World War I offered a regional linchpin that some of the earliest and most influential geopolitical writings recognised as part of the territorial power struggle for control of Europe. These writings anticipated that the Great Powers would continue to vie for dominance in the perceived borderlands between Germany and (Soviet) Russia (Mackinder, 1904, 1919; Kjellén, 1917, 1920; Haushofer, 1927).

The continued strategic importance of the region was echoed in the opinions of a later generation of geopolitical writers in the chaos and aftermath of World War II. Then, American strategists (e.g. Spykman, 1944; Kennan, 1947) focused attention on the 'denial principle': that CEE should not fall under the influence of a power that was inimical to American interests.

Despite their efforts, the Yalta Agreement of 1945 had established, however tentative the intention, areas of hegemonic dominance: much

*E-mail: derekhall@seabankscotland.co.uk

Fig. 3.1. The countries of Central and Eastern Europe. (Redrawn from various sources.)

of CEE was yielded to a Soviet zone of influence, while the ensuing Greek civil war acted as a dynamic fault line between ideologies. Despite the attention-grabbing crises noted in Table 3.1, Western interest in the region waned as the Cold War superpower contest moved to the more chaotic domains of Asia. And for many in the West, CEE became a *terra incognita*; certainly a no-go (to) area for tourism.

In 1989, the European geopolitical game was renewed as a result of the largely unanticipated collapse of the Communist regimes and the subsequent competitive rush to fill the vacuum left by the removal of Soviet-inspired central political and economic planning structures. The institutions of international capitalism jockeyed for influence and market dominance: banks, accountancy firms, management consultants, insurance companies, private security firms, supermarkets, fast-food chains, property developers and real estate agents, religions and sects, as well as tour companies and travel agencies. In the face of this onslaught, the post-communist (some in name only) regimes appeared to respond as one

in wishing to be embraced by the Euro-Atlantic alliances.

The Yugoslav genocides that accompanied the territorial aggression there heightened a renewed sense of geopolitics in CEE, although at times it appeared that the Western response seemed more concerned with saving the historic built fabric of such tourism honeypots as Dubrovnik and Mostar than with the slaughter of thousands of defenceless people.

The marked regional differences between bloody chaos and bloodless calm that characterised an apparent end of the Cold War in Europe required substantial reappraisals of a 'future Europe', its spatial differentiation and connectivity, as well as new sources of power and influence.

Since the end of the 19th century, several spatial models of world power had been constructed based on a mix of such factors as historical continuity, changing ideological structures and technological innovations in communications and weaponry (Jones, 1955). These models tended to be both ethnocentric and prescriptive,

Table 3.1. Cold War events impacting on CEE's 'visitability'.

1943–1948	Sovietisation of CEE
1947–1948	Soviet blockade of Berlin and Western airlift to sustain West Berlin
1948–1954	Trieste/Istria zones of occupation
1953	Stalin dies; uprising in East Berlin
1955	Soviet withdrawal from eastern Austria
1956	Khrushchev's 'secret' speech denouncing much of 'Stalinism'; uprisings in Poland and Hungary
	200,000 flee west from the crushing of the 'Hungarian revolution'
1950s–1960s	Reforms in Yugoslavia encouraging mass international coastal tourism (and permitting labour emigration)
1961	Construction of the Berlin Wall; Cuban missile crisis
1968	Warsaw Pact invasion of Czechoslovakia on the basis of the 'Brezhnev Doctrine'
1979	Return to Poland of Karol Wojtyła as Pope John Paul II
1980	Moscow Olympics
1980–1981	Rise of Solidarność in Poland and the subsequent imposition of martial law (which saw, for example, armed 'air marshalls' stationed at both ends of aircraft cabins during domestic flights)
1981	Extreme austerity measures introduced in Romania
1984	Sarajevo Winter Olympics
1985	Election of Mikhail Gorbachev as CPSU General Secretary; Helsinki agreements on human rights in Soviet-dominated 'Eastern Europe'
1986	Rise to power of Milošević in Yugoslavia; Chernobyl nuclear reactor disaster in Ukraine
1989	Removal of official communist party rule in much of CEE; end of Warsaw Pact and CMEA
1990	German reunification
1991	Disintegration of the Soviet Union; beginnings of Yugoslav wars of succession

Notes: CEE = Central and Eastern Europe; CMEA = Council for Mutual Economic Aid; CPSU = Communist Party of the Soviet Union.

the twin flaws of classical geopolitics. But above all, they were dangerously oversimplistic.

The term 'geopolitics' derives from the studies of a Swedish political scientist, Rudolf Kjellén (Holdar, 1992; Marklund, 2015), a follower of the 19th century German geographer, Friedrich Ratzel, who developed an organic theory of state evolution. This suggests that states grow and decay in the manner of any living organism. Just as an organism needs food, so the state, in order to retain its vigour and continue to thrive, requires space in increasing quantity. According to Ratzel, territory for the state is an essential, life-giving force and boundaries are obstructive to the state's organic growth.

Armed with his concept of living space (*Lebensraum*), Ratzel influenced many students of politics. Among them was Karl Haushofer, whose name has become inextricably connected with the 'science' of geopolitics. Haushofer (1927) promoted Ratzel's notion of 'moveable frontiers': borders were temporary 'battle lines' that moved depending on the relative strengths of competing neighbouring states (O'Loughlin, 1999). Employing Ratzel's concepts of state growth and reacting to a perceived encirclement of the German-dominated Old World by Anglo-Saxon maritime power, Haushofer helped forge German strategy in both theory and practice. He and his students produced a mass of literature on the theme of Germany's perceived need for space, to counter such 'encirclement'. This captured the close attention of the Austrian artist, Adolf Hitler (de Blij, 1967: 105). Geopolitics in Germany thus became both a prescription for expansive territorial ambition and a justification for it; and the term became firmly associated with Nazi aspirations, racial determinism and genocide. Central and Eastern Europe was a primary target of this perverted thinking.

Earlier, H.J. Mackinder (Semmell, 1958; Kearns, 2009), a Scottish historical geographer, promoted the global view as one in which land power would increase as a result of more effective communication systems. At a time when Britain was still the pre-eminent world power,

Mackinder's *Geographical Pivot of History* (1904) – 'a defining moment in the history of geopolitics' (Ó Tuathail, 1996: 25) – drew attention to the fact that the Eurasian core ('Pivot Area', later 'Heartland') was inaccessible to ships of sea powers and thus capable of sheltering a great land power which might come to control the world.

Mackinder described his Eurasian Pivot Area (essentially Russia/USSR) as the source of powerful forces that had affected Europe, South Asia and the Far East. And his famous, later debunked, simplistic hypothesis was:

> Who rules East Europe commands the Heartland [Eurasia]
>
> Who rules the Heartland commands the World-Island [Eurasia and Africa]
>
> Who rules the World-Island commands the World
>
> (Mackinder, 1919)

Such an imperial perspective saw the world as a stage setting for the 'major powers' to act out their muscle flexing. Other peoples and places, in such circumstances, were 'merely the backdrop for action by "white men"' (Sidaway *et al.*, 2014: 174). Thus, a voiceless 'Eastern Europe' was firmly positioned within, and the nexus of, the global geopolitical map, complementing and perhaps helping to focus attention on the region's perceived strategic importance for both later Nazi Germany and the Soviet Union. Somewhat naïvely, however, Mackinder felt that effective control of the Heartland for only one purpose (dominance of the world) could be achieved only by the alliance of two or more states.[1] How far these formulations influenced German geopoliticians, especially Haushofer, and fed into the subsequent formulation of the (albeit short-lived) Ribbentrop–Molotov pact of 1939, continues to be debated.

Although Haushofer's actual impress upon German policy may not have been as great as some have supposed, the Nazi decisions of 1933–1939 appeared to be in accord with his ideas. But several war moves, notably the attack on the Soviet Union in 1941, were clearly contrary to them. Nevertheless, 'Haushofer contributed to that climate of opinions which regarded aggression and conquest as a natural and proper role for a powerful state' (Pounds, 1963: 410).

The reproduction of Mackinder's 1919 book in 1942 inspired the American Nicholas Spykman (1944), who felt that the wartime Allies should base their future policy on preventing any consolidation of the global 'rimland'. In the Cold War era that was to follow, this prescription became part of US 'containment' policy aimed at preventing the Soviet Union, and later China, from spreading communist influence into new areas *anywhere*.

In the post-war period, critics continued to point to the oversimplification, determinism and ethnocentricity of earlier geopolitical formulations (East, 1950; Hall, 1955). And by its association with the Nazis, the term 'geopolitics' became, in today's parlance, 'toxic'. Indeed, more than 20 years after the end of World War II, it could still be said that: 'Probably some decades will pass before the term comes into general use again to mean global strategic views' (de Blij, 1967: 137).

In the meantime, the geographical shift of Cold War focus to Asia indicated, almost by default, the West's acquiescence that CEE was 'safely' secured behind the Iron Curtain, an attitude that Węcławowicz (1996: 181) later categorised as a 'menace from the West'. Western non-intervention in Hungary in 1956 emphasised this stance.

The 'falling dominoes' theory which increasingly was to mesmerise US strategists, although the subject of much critical evaluation (e.g. Cohen, 1964; Murphey, 1966), was relevant to CEE in as much as it appeared to be adopted by Moscow in 1968. The Warsaw Pact intervention in Czechoslovakia in that year was justified by the (rather hastily and crudely constructed) 'Brezhnev Doctrine', which argued that if the survival of socialism was threatened in one country, it was the duty of fellow socialist countries to come to its assistance.

The Cold War represented a balance of imperialisms, a mutual equilibrium of hegemony. Like much geopolitical formulation before it, the domino theory – both Washington and Moscow versions – was narrowly deterministic, ethnocentric and a gross oversimplification of reality. Thus, 'the real complexity of human geographies in the places ... deemed strategic [was]... sometimes obscured or erased' (Sidaway *et al.*, 2014: 181).[2]

And such oversimplification would 'inform' popular Western (negative) constructions of much of CEE for almost half a century.

3.3 Cold War Geopolitics, State Socialist Tourism

If 'containment' was a much-used Cold War term in the West, it possessed a very different meaning for the everyday lives of citizens in much of CEE. The official attitude towards travel and tourism was one significant component of this. Cold War geopolitics was reflected strongly in the policies applying to this area of socio-economic activity, but, of course, 'geopoliticians' paid scant regard to the everyday practices of such a mundane sociocultural activity as leisure travel.

Earlier, the upheaval of World War I and the subsequent emergence of new nation states and ideologies, followed by economic depression, instability and political extremism, militated against any expansion of a tourism market for much of the region. Apart from religious pilgrimages, wealthy elites had dominated travelling for pleasure and education for two centuries, and only from the later 19th century, with the expansion of spas and a development of new holiday resorts coupled to improved communications, were the less prosperous middle classes able to stay in modest boarding houses and country cottages, the latter often in upland areas. The social base of tourism and organised leisure activity further broadened during the 1930s, notably stimulated by hiking and mountaineering associations in Czechoslovakia and Poland (Hall, 1991; Böröcz, 1996). Pan-Slavism is credited to have stimulated intraregional travel and touristic encounters during the interwar period (Sobe, 2006). For Polish people, deprived of their statehood until 1918, '... tourism was one of the most important instruments of patriotic upbringing, and it retained this character after independence' (Rogalewski, 1980: 115).

As Horáková (2010) has suggested, some pre-war tourism trends began to emerge in the very early post-war years, only to be snuffed out by the imposition of Soviet communism. In the case of Czechoslovakia, the last European 'domino' to fall, this imposition took place, through a coup, in 1948.

Replicating policies experienced from the 1920s onwards in the Soviet Union, the early post-war 'Stalinist' period in CEE saw basic characteristics and dogmas emanating from the dictatorship in Moscow: rapid economic growth based on heavy industrialisation and the dogmatic pursuit of unrealistic growth targets. Heightened by Cold War antagonisms (over Berlin and the Korean War, for example), and the insecurity of relatively young regimes consolidating power, any foreigners who visited were regarded with suspicion as potential enemies of the state. Thus, incoming foreign tourism was minimal and restricted to friendship and solidarity groups.

For one particular country after 1948, Horáková (2010: 63) identifies 'a great schism' and a 'relative incommensurability' between Czechoslovak tourism and that of Western Europe. This was a time of 'separation and reclassification of existing economic mechanisms, customs and traditions'. But alongside a rapid decline in international tourism, there was experienced an 'intense development' of organised domestic recreation. The value of labour resided in its health and vitality, although such echoes of Nazi practice tended to be avoided in the official prose employed.

Thus, the social dimensions of state socialism made provision for the well-being of (mostly urban-industrial) working families, and to this end subsidised enterprise- and trade union-sponsored facilities were developed for domestic, group-oriented tourism and recreation, including a comprehensive network of pioneer and youth holiday camps for schoolchildren located on coasts, by lakes, in forests and upland areas. Opened in 1925, *Artek*, on the Crimean coast, was the model for such camps (Shaw, 1991: see also Part II Introduction, this volume).

Being strictly subordinated to political, economic and ideological considerations, such domestic tourism was employed to create correct attitudes through 'socialist education' (Allcock and Przecławski, 1990: 5). Large families with low incomes, the elderly and rural peasant households appear to have been least well served by this system (Hall, 1991).

Outbound international tourism was minimal: exit visas for private travel abroad were rarely granted, little money was available for it, and those groups who had enjoyed foreign travel since at least the 19th century – the aristocracy, bourgeoisie and intelligentsia – had been eliminated, structurally or otherwise. State and party elites – the *nomenklatura* – now dominated any foreign travel that was available. Most of the invitations to Moscow were short on recreational opportunities; and in some cases did not involve a return component.

From the mid-1950s, following the hiatus after Stalin's death in 1953, dogmas began to be relaxed, living standards gradually rose and the need to emphasise, if only for propaganda reasons, international socialism saw a growing development of international tourism within the socialist bloc. Paralleling the growth of economic aid and cooperation within the Council for Mutual Economic Aid (CMEA), this phase tended to be characterised by the more developed societies generating most tourist outflows. Although the statistics of the period are poorly documented, a number of geographical studies of tourism were undertaken in the less developed, tourist-receiving countries (e.g. Losanoff, 1968; Swizewski and Oancea, 1978).

Yugoslavia largely bypassed this stage since, having been expelled from the Soviet bloc in 1948, tourism exchanges with the bloc countries were initially embargoed. Jeopardised by this expulsion, the Yugoslav economy was swiftly reoriented westwards, and, from the early 1950s, developed a tourism industry geared to Western markets, notably along the Slovenian and Croatian Adriatic coast (Cicvarić, 1980; Allcock, 1983).

From the 1960s, in the more advanced CEE countries at least, priorities began to be shifted towards the production of some consumer goods, including motor cars, ownership levels of which, however, remained relatively low. In some societies, rules governing private property ownership also began to be relaxed, encouraging the growth of second- and leisure-home ownership (Gardavský, 1977). Pressure for longer holidays and a 5-day working week subsequently took place alongside increasing urbanisation and leisure goods availability.

Although the 1970s and 1980s saw an easing of administrative constraints on individual travel to other European socialist countries, exit visa requirements posed more severe limitations on movements than did entry visas (Böröcz, 1990). In this way, forced substitution played an important part in intra-bloc movement, and, after all, Cuba and Vietnam were theoretically available fraternal destinations. Further influencing this development were factors of ethnicity – neighbouring states having cross-border co-ethnic minorities – and the question of individual countries' degree of internal liberalisation. Hungary's liberal and Westernised image within the Soviet bloc offered an enticing destination for many of the region's citizens, an attraction that was enhanced significantly during the summer of 1989.

When the West European package-holiday business was gathering momentum in the 1960s, 'Eastern Europe' had been poorly prepared to participate as a host region (see Chapter 21, this volume). A decade or so later, most of the region's economies felt the necessity to place an emphasis on attracting Western tourists in order to acquire hard currency. First Spain, and later Turkey, acted as role models. Tourism receipts in Turkey grew by 620% between 1980 and 1988, underlining the substantial and rapid economic impact that could be attained from a relatively low starting point when a new tourism destination was 'discovered', packaged and marketed (Buckley and Witt, 1990: 10). However, the ideological framework within which international tourism could develop differed markedly between Turkey and the Soviet bloc countries.

While some CEE countries had been gradually developing a Western-oriented tourism component, the economic circumstances of the 1970s brought increasing hard-currency debt, with varying prospects of repayment to Western financial institutions. During that decade, the purchase of Western technology with Western loans and credits on the understanding that they could be paid back either in kind, or from the profits of selling goods produced by the technology back to Western markets, failed to live up to expectations.

As a consequence, programmes of attracting hard-currency tourists were stepped up from the later 1970s. This was despite often inadequate and inappropriate administrative and infrastructural capacities.

Individual countries' reinterpretations of state socialism, expressing a diversity of cultural and historical factors, and the strengthening of critical pathway trajectories, clearly impacted upon the nature of tourism and leisure development. Yugoslavia had needed to adopt a necessarily pragmatic attitude that had encouraged a rapid growth in tourism by Westerners during the 1950s and 1960s, further stimulated by Western investment in hotel building and road construction along the Adriatic coast (Allcock, 1986; Hall, 2003; Bracewell, 2006). The name 'Yugotours' became familiar among the package-tour brochures stocked by European travel agencies. This decentralised socialist state took a clear regional lead, both in tourist numbers and income generated, to levels comparable with a number of major Western tourist economies.

As international tourism evolved, tourist flows in the region expressed growing differentiation. They became notably more asymmetrical, both in terms of intra-bloc tourism and in the region's continuing to act as a host for, rather than as the source of, international (extra-bloc) tourism. But until the end of the 1980s, the regional economic impact of international tourism remained relatively small, certainly by comparison with Western Europe. The World Tourism Organization (WTO, 1990: 18) records that for 1988, tourism receipts represented just 0.94% of the exports of 'European socialist societies'. By contrast, the figure for 'developed market economies' was 6.99%, and the world average was 6.85%.

Mackinder did not say, 'Who travels to Eastern Europe ... can travel the world'. But the imperious attitudes and language employed in the early part of the 20th century by those from the 'Big Powers' in dismissing Central and Eastern Europe, now, into the last decade of that century, took on a more condescending tone, as reflected in a Western tour brochure:

> The whirlwind of change in the Eastern Block [sic] ... has taken everyone's breath away. We must welcome such profound turnabouts as it makes travel there more accessible and increases our understanding of and friendship with the local people ... we have for some time experienced the growing desire among travellers to visit the new emerging societies of the Eastern World, and see something of the historic changes for themselves ...
>
> (Explore 1990, *East Europe & Siberia*, p. 3, cited in Hall, 1991: 112–113)

3.4   A Geopolitics of Reorientation

As interpreted by Kuczabski and Michalski (2014), Mach (1998) suggested four types of CEE post-communist 'transformation'.

1. *Substitution.* Institutional changes based on modernisation: a substitution of centralised and rigidly managed economy and its political super-structure with the 'modern' West European capitalist model. This assumes a rapid abandonment of the communist model.

2. *Transplantation.* This can exist in two versions. One presumes that certain elements of the old order remain unchanged. The other allows the continuing existence of the old institutional structure in which only certain elements of the new system are implemented.

3. *Recombination.* This implies that neither institutions nor individuals are able to perform rapid radical changes. 'Transformation' thus means modification and reconfiguration of existing elements.

4. *Retrogression.* Presumes that transformation can actually mean a return to organisational and mental forms of the pre-transformation times and thus steer the transformation itself towards collectivism and authoritarianism, and generate a fear of the future.

This model and its terminology is employed by Pavlo Doan and Viktoriia Kiptenko in Chapter 6, this volume, to evaluate the tortuous context that tourism has faced in Ukraine in its post-Soviet years.

Shortly after Mach's formulation, Smith (2002) explored three interconnected aspects of CEE's geopolitical and geoeconomic repositioning – the elements of Mach's 'substitution' (see also Box 1.1, this volume).

1. Neoliberal marketisation. The financing of transition through the European Bank for Reconstruction and Development (EBRD) and through the EU PHARE (Poland and Hungary: Assistance for Restructuring their Economies) and TACIS (Technical Assistance to the Commonwealth of Independent States and Georgia) programmes, tied to a particular set of political criteria with the monitoring of transition impacts through economic performance criteria and transition indicators (for example, see Chapters 1 and 23, this volume).

2. EU enlargement processes. The 1993 Copenhagen criteria for accession included the development and sustaining of a functioning market economy, the capacity to accommodate competitive pressure and market forces within the Union, the development of democracy, the rule of law, human rights and the protection of minorities, and the ability of countries to accept the obligations of the Union (including the 20,000 laws and regulations of the *acquis*), thus tying

EU accession criteria to economic, political and civic progress (for a positive expression of this, see Chapter 19, this volume).

3. Balkan post-conflict reconstruction. The construction of a region in crisis requiring international intervention, with the nature of that intervention in the form of capitalist marketisation (and international modes of governance: see Chapters 17 and 18, this volume).

In order to redefine and relocate their role and position on the European stage after the Cold War, the political elites of Central and Eastern Europe were keen to indicate that a new set of geographical realities had taken hold of the region (Dingsdale, 1999; Zeigler, 2002: 671; Fortier, 2006). The use of maps for propaganda purposes has a long geopolitical history (Hall, 1981). If history is written by victors, the same would seem to apply to cartography. If maps change after every war, then the Cold War was no different, with the flowering of what Zeigler (2002) refers to as 'persuasive cartography'.

If Mackinder had regarded CEE imperiously as the gateway – land and people to be trampled over – to the Eurasian 'heartland', the pivot of world history, Cohen (1991) saw it as one of the world's great 'gateway regions' through which the maritime and continental realms of Eurasia would be 'forged' (an interesting euphemism) into an interdependent economic system.

By the end of the 20th century, the Cold War term and concept of 'Eastern Europe' had almost ceased to exist. Interpretations of 'Central Europe' had returned in a rapid and forceful way, both to the geopolitical vernacular and to the lexicon of tourism marketing (e.g. Jordan, 2006). This semantic reversal was employed to project the region itself not only as a gateway but also as a central, focal element of Europe: a psychological westward shift away from the pejorative (and grossly inaccurate) concept of being 'Eastern' and thus 'Other' (e.g. Krejči, 2005).

A 'region' defined by superpower politics that had often been perceived during the Cold War as 'closed to the outside world' (but open with the Soviet Union) (Cohen, 1964) now sought to be just the opposite: open to the world but closed to Russia, a Euro-Atlantic repositioning that would culminate for some in European Union (EU) (and NATO – North Atlantic Treaty Organization) accession and the (not always

convenient) guardianship of EU external eastern borders, the symbolic edges of 'Europe'. '... NATO has not yet solved the key question of where the edge of Europe lies ...' (O'Loughlin and Kolossov, 2002: 579).

Just as studies have tended to treat the EU in geopolitical terms as an empire engaged with enlargement (Aalto, 2002), one of the more significant aspects of the NATO enlargement debate was the relative lack of attention paid to alternative perspectives (O'Loughlin, 1999). Most notably, renewed and heightened Russian fears of encirclement (Kennan, 1947) were ignored, with the result of Crimean (re)annexation (see Chapter 5, this volume) and conflict in Ukraine (Chapter 6, this volume).

This badly advised Euro-Atlantic geopolitical erasure was well articulated in Zeigler's (2002) research. As a means of representing post-Cold War repositioning and reimaging, he sought new national maps from CEE embassies in Washington DC. He found that five former Soviet republics employed maps to reposition themselves in Europe, one employing a new set of popular images, but many were drawn from an idealised pre-Communist past.

All three Baltic States emphasised a reconnection to other ('Western') countries around the Baltic Sea, highlighting the centrality of this sea and its Hanseatic heritage for northern Europe.[3] In all cases, Russia was marginalised and the Russian language avoided (despite these countries' significant Russian minorities: see Dostál and Jelen, 2015). 'The maps produced by the Baltic States heralded to the world their petition to relocate in a new neighbourhood' (Zeigler, 2002: 676).

Indeed, this cartographically reinforced aspiration was articulated across the 'region', with all countries' maps expressing a desire to position themselves in the centre of the continent, consigning both concept and use of 'Eastern Europe' to the dustbin of Cold War semantic history. These expressions well reflected Dijkink's (1996) concept of 'geopolitical cultures' – the combination of attitudes, beliefs, perceptions and fears that characterise citizens' world views (O'Loughlin and Kolossov, 2002) – and complemented the expansionist intentions of the Euro-Atlantic alliances.

In this way, for example, new Polish maps reversed the Cold War 'satellite state' analogy by setting Warsaw as the hub of an (albeit asymmetrical) European wheel, with all European capitals orbiting the Polish capital. In this representation, Moscow was marginalised and unorbited.

In a similar about-face fashion, both Slovenia and Croatia emphasised their (historic) connections with, and within, Central Europe, turning diametrically away from the Serbian heart of the former Yugoslavia, 'to escape from the gravitational pull of Belgrade' (Zeigler, 2002: 683). Given that the research was undertaken only months after the end of the Yugoslav wars of succession, this was hardly surprising.

As part of a means of inspiring their own citizens and providing iconographic nation-building tools, the maps produced by these countries in the 1990s – when 'in transition' between the Communist and Euro-Atlantic worlds – provided opportunities for each 'newly freed' country to formulate its own 'conceptions of a new European order in which they would enjoy greater centrality and higher status' (Zeigler, 2002: 685).

Yet such 'persuasive cartography' is only one element of a range of iconographic elements – changed place and road names, coins, currency, stamps (see Part II Introduction) and corporate logos – that can symbolise identity and re-imaging for inspiring a domestic audience, in building a new sense of the future and signalling to the outside world that here is a reinvigorated, reoriented society now far more welcoming, in the case of tourism, for example, to the requirements of marketised consumption.

While for Cohen in 1964, the Iron Curtain and the post-war division of Europe meant that 'Central Europe' was no more, for Zeigler in 2002 (685): 'Communist Eastern Europe never was in geographical Eastern Europe, it was always central to the continent, just marginalized by political history'.

Endnotes

[1] A dynamic variant of this thesis was to be chillingly reproduced in George Orwell's *1984* (1948).
[2] History almost appeared to repeat itself in the early 1990s (see Chapter 9, this volume).
[3] Although the dynamism of the Baltic Sea region is not unproblematic (Koch, 2015).

References

Aalto, P. (2002) A European geopolitical subject in the making? EU, Russia and the Kaliningrad Question. *Geopolitics* 7(3), 142–174.

Allcock, J.B. (1983) Tourism and social change in Dalmatia. *Journal of Development Studies* 20(1), 35–55.

Allcock, J.B. (1986) Yugoslavia's tourist trade: pot of gold or pig in a poke? *Annals of Tourism Research* 13(4), 565–588.

Allcock, J.B. and Przecławski, K. (1990) Introduction. *Annals of Tourism Research* 17(1), 1–6.

Böröcz, J. (1990) Hungary as a destination 1960–1984. *Annals of Tourism Research* 17(1), 19–35.

Böröcz, J. (1996) *Leisure Migration: A Sociological Study on Tourism*. Pergamon, Oxford, UK.

Bracewell, W. (2006) Adventures in the marketplace: Yugoslav travel writing and tourism in the 1950s–1960s. In: Gorsuch, A.E. and Koenker, D.P. (eds) *Turizm: The Russian and East European Tourist under Capitalism and Socialism*. Cornell University Press, Ithaca, New York, pp. 248–265.

Bridger, S. and Pine, F. (eds) (1998) *Surviving Post-Socialism: Local Strategies and Regional Responses in Eastern Europe and the Former Soviet Union*. Routledge, London.

Buckley, P.J. and Witt, S.F. (1990) Tourism in the centrally-planned economies of Europe. *Annals of Tourism Research* 17(1), 7–18.

Cicvarić, A. (1980) *Turizam i privredni razvoj Jugoslavije.* [*Tourism and Economic Development of Yugoslavia.*] Informator, Zagreb, Yugoslavia (in Serbo-Croat).

Cohen, S.B. (1964) *Geography and Politics in a Divided World*. Methuen, London.

Cohen, S.B. (1991) Global geopolitical change in the post-Cold War era. *Annals of the Association of American Geographers* 81, 551–580.

de Blij, H.J. (1967) *Systematic Political Geography*. Wiley, New York.

Dijkink, G.-J. (1996) *National Identity and Geopolitical Visions: Maps of Pride and Pain*. Routledge, London.

Dingsdale, A. (1999) Eastern Europe: a new regional geography of post-socialist Europe? *Geography* 84, 204–221.

Dostál, P. and Jelen, L. (2015) De-Russianisation of the western post-soviet space: between the thick and thin nationalising processes. *Geopolitics* 20(4), 757–792.

East, W.G. (1950) How strong is the Heartland? *Foreign Affairs* 29(1), 78–93.

Fortier, A.-M. (2006) The politics of scaling, timing and embodying: rethinking the 'new Europe'. *Mobilities* 1(3), 313–331.

Gardavský, V. (1977) Second homes in Czechoslovakia. In: Coppock, J.T. (ed.) *Second Homes: Curse or Blessing?* Pergamon, Oxford, UK, pp. 63–74.

Hall, A.R. (1955) Mackinder and the course of events. *Annals of the Association of American Geographers* 45(2), 109–126.

Hall, D.R. (1981) A geographical approach to propaganda. In: Burnett, A.D. and Taylor, P.J. (eds) *Political Studies from Spatial Perspectives*. Wiley, Chichester, UK, pp. 313–339.

Hall, D.R. (1991) Evolutionary pattern of tourism development in Eastern Europe and the Soviet Union. In: Hall, D.R. (ed.) *Tourism and Economic Development in Eastern Europe and the Soviet Union*. Belhaven, London, pp. 79–115.

Hall, D. (2003) Rejuvenation, diversification and imagery: sustainability conflicts for tourism policy in the eastern Adriatic. *Journal of Sustainable Tourism* 11(2–3), 280–294.

Haushofer, K. (1927) *Grenzen in ihrer geographischen und politischen Bedeutung. [The Meaning of Geographical and Political Borders.]* Karl Vowinckel, Berlin (in German).

Holdar, S. (1992) The ideal state and the power of geography: the life-work of Rudolf Kjellén. *Political Geography* 11, 307–323.

Horáková, H. (2010) Post-communist transformation of tourism in Czech rural areas: new dilemmas. *Anthropological Notebooks* 16(1), 59–77.

Jones, S.B. (1955) Global strategic views. *Geographical Review* 45(4), 492–508.

Jordan, P. (2006) Tourism and EU enlargement: a Central European perspective. In: Hall, D., Smith, M. and Marciszewska, B. (eds) *Tourism in the New Europe: the Challenges and Opportunities of EU Enlargement*. CAB International, Wallingford, UK, pp. 65–80.

Kearns, G. (2009) *Geopolitics and Empire: The Legacy of Halford Mackinder*. Oxford University Press, Oxford, UK.

Kennan, G.F. (1947) The sources of Soviet conduct. *Foreign Affairs* 25, 566–582.

Kjellén, R. (1917) *Der Staat als Lebensform. [The State as a Living Organism.]* S. Hirzel, Leipzig, Germany (in German).

Kjellén, R. (1920) *Grundriß zu einem System der Politik. [The Basis of our Political System.]* S. Hirzel, Leipzig, Germany (in German).

Koch, K. (2015) Region-building and security: the multiple borders of the Baltic Sea Region after EU enlargement. *Geopolitics* 20(3), 535–558.

Krejči, O. (ed.) (2005) *Geopolitics of the Central European Region: The View from Prague and Bratislava*. VEDA, Slovak Academy of Sciences, Bratislava, Slovakia.

Kuczabski, A. and Michalski, T. (2014) Ukrainian post-communist transformation: causes, consequences and threats. *Quaestiones Geographicae* 33(2), 171–180. Available at: http://geoinfo.amu.edu.pl/qg/archives/2014/QG332_171-180.pdf (accessed 19 July 2016).

Losanoff, E. (1968) Geographische Aspekte der Auslandstouristik in der Volksrepublik Bulgarien. [Geographical dimensions of foreign tourism in the Bulgarian People's Republic.] *Geographische Berichte* 13(2), 125–136 (in German).

Mach B.W. (1998) *Transformacja Ustrojowa a Mentalne Dziedzictwo Socjalizmu. [Systemic Transformation and the Mental Legacy of Socialism.]* Instytut Studiów Politycznych, (Polish Academy of Sciences), Warsaw (in Polish).

Mackinder, H.J. (1904) The geographical pivot of history. *Geographical Journal* 23, 421–444.

Mackinder, H.J. (1919) *Democratic Ideals and Reality: A Study in the Politics of Reconstruction*. Constable, London.

Marklund, C. (2015) The return of geopolitics in the era of soft power: rereading Rudolf Kjellén on geopolitical imaginary and competitive identity. *Geopolitics* 20(2), 248–266.

Murphey, R. (1966) China and the dominoes. *Asian Survey* 6, 510–515.

Ó Tuathail, G. (1996) *Critical Geopolitics: The Politics of Writing Global Space*. Routledge, London.

O'Loughlin, J. (1999) Ordering the 'Crush Zone': geopolitical games in post-Cold War Eastern Europe. *Geopolitics* 4(1), 34–56.

O'Loughlin, J. and Kolossov, V. (2002) Still not worth the bones of a Pomeranian grenadier: the geopolitics of the Kosovo war 1999. *Political Geography* 21, 573–599.

Orwell, G. (1948) *1984*. Secker and Warburg, London.

Pounds, N.J.G. (1963) *Political Geography*. McGraw-Hill, London.

Rogalewski, O. (1980) International tourism originating from Poland. *International Social Science Journal* 32(1), 114–127.

Semmell, B. (1958) Sir Halford Mackinder: theorist of imperialism. *Canadian Journal of Economics and Political Science* 24(4), 554–561.

Shaw, D.J.B. (1991) The Soviet Union. In: Hall, D.R. (ed.) *Tourism and Economic Development in Eastern Europe and the Soviet Union*. Belhaven, London, pp. 119–141.

Sidaway, J.D., Mamadouh, V. and Power, M. (2014) Reappraising geopolitical traditions. In: Dodds, K., Kuus, M. and Sharp, J. (eds) *The Ashgate Research Companion to Critical Geopolitics*. Ashgate, Aldershot, UK, pp. 165–187.

Smith, A. (2002) Imagining geographies of the 'new Europe': geo-economic power and the new European architecture on integration. *Political Geography* 21, 647–670.

Sobe, N.W. (2006) Slavic emotion and vernacular cosmopolitanism: Yugoslav travels to Czechoslovakia in the 1920s and 1930s. In: Gorsuch, A.E. and Koenker, D.P. (eds) *Turizm: The Russian and East European Tourist under Capitalism and Socialism*. Cornell University Press, Ithaca, New York, pp. 82–96.

Spykman, N. (1944) *The Geography of the Peace*. Harcourt, Brace and Company, New York.

Swizewski, C. and Oancea, D.I. (1978) La carte des types de tourisme de Roumanie. [Map of types of tourism in Romania.] *Revue Roumaine de Géologie, Géophysique et Géographie, Série Géographie* 23(2), 291–294 (in French).

Węcławowicz, G. (1996) *Contemporary Poland: Space and Society*. UCL Press, London.

WTO (World Tourism Organization) (1990) *Yearbook of Tourism Statistics*. WTO, Madrid.

Zeigler, D.J. (2002) Post-communist Eastern Europe and the cartography of independence. *Political Geography* 21(5), 671–686.

Part II:

Reconfiguring Conceptions and Reality

For those born during the last stages of, or after, the 'Cold War', the terms 'post-socialism' and 'post-communism' may possess little meaning. For others of us, the experience of political, cultural and economic change brought about in Europe during our lifetimes has been profound. On either side of the former European divide, our perceptions and understanding of the European space, its values and significance have required a reordering, a reorienting and a rediscovering.

As Peter Jordan argues in Chapter 4, if we have the impression that the Adriatic space is emerging as a cultural region, it is because we are reacting to the impact of the Cold War period, when European division bifurcated the Adriatic Sea. The Adriatic space is, in fact, re-emerging as a cultural region, which it had been for centuries, being shaped by powers from the Roman Empire onwards. Thus, as a counterpoint to conceptions of Central/Central and Eastern/ East-Central/Eastern Europe, Jordan's chapter looks at the cultural, regional and geopolitical role of the Adriatic as an East–West 'bridge', not least in its significance for tourism.[1] For example, dominating the eastern Adriatic, post-war Yugoslavia, although initially pursuing a Stalinist agenda, was, by the 1950s, preparing itself to accommodate mass coastal tourism from western markets at least a decade ahead of its Soviet bloc neighbours.

Jordan suggests that for Italy, the only remaining larger country, the Adriatic space is again open and accessible as its 'natural' and traditional 'playground': but such playgrounds come at a price. And this conception leads to a consideration of those eastern Adriatic countries pejoratively signified as the 'Western Balkans': a post-conflict semi-periphery of contestation and competing hegemonies that is addressed in later chapters (7, 17, 18, 23).

Part II of the book therefore challenges conceptions of tourism space and addresses contemporary areas of geopolitical contestation within it. In Chapters 5–7, these are seen to arise from the neoclassical fault line between hegemonic superpowers Russia and the EU/NATO, and the tourism consequences of contestation for the societies involved. The role and implications of tourism development are therefore examined within these arenas of contestation at a number of scales and levels.

Within a contemporary context of instability and uncertainty, John Berryman in Chapter 5 addresses Russians' real and mythical perceptions and imagery of Crimea, and the long-held role tourism (alongside more strategically significant factors) has played in these.

The hasty and unilateral[2] reunification of Crimea with Russia rendered the peninsula *de facto* under Russian control, while *de jure* within Ukrainian territory. To reinforce such a *de facto* control, the use of imagery and symbolism can be an important part of the narrative in establishing an appearance of legitimacy. As part of this process, the Russian Federation authorities were swift to issue 'national' postage stamps embracing images of Crimea: monuments and locations of historic and touristic importance, as well as the image shown in Fig. II.1: a cartoon of the Soviet-era *Artek* children's holiday centre in Crimea that allegedly had been allowed to run down within independent Ukraine. The stamp illustrated depicts a chunk of Crimea, including *Artek*, within the broad embrace of a clearly happy (now Russian) protective Bear Mountain, a popular topographic feature (see also Fig. 5.3).

But as Berryman suggests, without a better economic performance, Russia will be unable to maintain the pace of its military modernisation and have available the necessary funds for the development of Crimea's vital tourist industry (see, for example, Ivanov *et al.*, 2016). The bear's demeanour may yet change. Meanwhile, Crimea is a long-term obstacle to the normalisation of Ukraine–Russian relations, at the least, throwing up such surrogates as the *Eurovision Song Contestation*.

Ukraine's 'narrative' is intertwined inextricably with both the history and the very conception of Europe. The continent's evolution has been likened to 'an endless series of overlaid maps' (Ascherson, 2007, 2015). This has demanded of the citizens of Ukraine – located on an East–West cultural divide – a means to coexist within an historic contact zone (Plokhy, 2015). Such coexistence has been tested severely

Fig. II.1. 2015 Russian Federation postage stamp depicting the International Children's Centre *Artek* and Bear Mountain in Crimea.

in recent years. In Chapter 6, Pavlo Doan and Viktoriia Kiptenko's attempt to disambiguate the implications for the everyday practices of the tourism development of Ukraine's 'cultural hybridity' – overlapping a now major geopolitical fault line – helps to reveal the infinite complexity of nationhood.

> That most Europeans are oblivious, incapable of finding Ukraine on any map and liable to consider the country just another piece of flotsam from the wreckage of the USSR, is ironic, of course.
>
> (Bell, 2015)

But it is considerably more than ironic, and Western popular geopolitical judgements such as this fail to articulate the trauma of everyday life for those in both eastern and western Ukraine.

Doan and Kiptenko perform a considerable feat in examining the inextricable intertwining of Ukraine's complicated geopolitical trajectory with its tourism development path.

The formulation of a geopolitics of organised crime would be a useful, if empirically hazardous, endeavour (see, for example, Pickering-Iazzi, 2015). In a somewhat polemical piece, Granovac (2012) has argued that organised crime and corruption are typical 'side-effects' of globalisation and are becoming critical geopolitical factors. He has claimed that the USA and EU have been 'geopolitically outwitted' by such activities in the Balkans. As a beneficiary and exploiter of conflict and instability, organised crime and corruption have become entrenched, according to Granovac. But, he contends, its presence is a major argument for the 'civilising' processes of the EU to embrace the 'Western Balkans' fully, some of the implications of which are discussed in Chapters 17 and 18.

As this volume was being completed, data on large-scale tax avoidance obtained from the Panamanian law firm and 'corporate service provider' Mossack Fonseca were being disseminated, with their implications beginning to be assessed. Within such a global perspective, the power of 'grey' international finance is exemplified by Antonio Violante in Chapter 7 with an examination of the Russian financing and ownership of tourism and related real estate development in Montenegro.

Violante extols the sustainable tourism potential of Montenegro, pointing out that article 1 of the country's constitution actually stipulates that it is an 'ecological state'. The difference between theory and reality, of course, may be significant. The author argues that the country allowed entry to Russian capital, welcoming and embracing it on a wave of immediate results, to the point where such a high proportion of ownership of national assets could no longer be isolated from Montenegro's foreign policy. And this came at a time when Montenegro was actively pursuing EU and NATO membership.

With hegemonic competition for this strategically located Adriatic country being devised in Washington, Brussels and Moscow, Violante concludes that Montenegro's tourism expansion could prove to be a critical issue in the country's future political-economic trajectory, with Russia looking to protect its considerable interests.

In Montenegro, tourism and related real estate development is one of the central elements of a contestation acting out larger geopolitical tensions within and about Europe.

Endnotes

[1] The bridging epithet is one that occurs throughout this volume.
[2] Albeit the Crimean electorate voted 93% in favour of coming under Russian rule in a March 2014 referendum: the Kyiv authorities did not recognise the result (Dunkley, 2015).

References

Ascherson, N. (2007) *Black Sea: The Birthplace of Civilization and Barbarism.* Vintage Books, London.
Ascherson, N. (2015) *Black Sea: Coasts and Conquests: From Pericles to Putin.* Vintage Books, London.
Bell, I. (2015) New nation, old story. *The Herald* [Glasgow, UK] *Arts*, 12 December, pp. 10–11.
Dunkley, J. (2015) Russian news agency furious as Barclays closes its account. *The Independent* [London], 15 July, p. 50.
Granovac, B. (2012) Geopolitics and organized crime and corruption in the early 21st century with reference to the Balkans. *European Perspectives: Journal on European Perspectives of the Western Balkans* 4(1)[6], 79–94.
Ivanov, S., Idzhylova, K. and Webster, C. (2016) Impacts of the entry of the Autonomous Republic of Crimea into the Russian Federation on its tourism industry: an exploratory study. *Tourism Management* 54, 162–169.
Pickering-Iazzi, R. (2015) *The Mafia in Italian Lives and Literature: Life Sentences and their Geographies.* University of Toronto Press, Toronto, Canada.
Plokhy, S. (2015) *The Gates of Europe: A History of Ukraine.* Allen Lane, London.

4 The Adriatic as a (Re-)Emerging Cultural Space

Peter Jordan*

*Austrian Academy of Sciences, Institute of Urban
and Regional Research, Vienna, Austria*

4.1 Introduction

The Adriatic space is here conceived as the coasts of the Adriatic Sea and their functional hinterlands, rather than as the hydrological catchment. Since at least Roman times, this space has been characterised by a dense network of cultural relations. For long periods in history, it found itself either under a common rule (Roman Empire, Kingdom of the Ostrogoths, Eastern Roman, later called Byzantine, Empire) or was dominated by a power centred on its coasts (Venice).

But even in periods of divergent political affiliation, these cultural networks persisted. The rather narrow sea failed to act as a barrier to economic exchange, migratory movements, the flow of ideas and styles, or exchange of, for example, artists. As a result, the cultural landscape around the Adriatic shares many similarities.

Moreover, the inhabitants of all coastal regions have a lot in common. Italian is a language frequently spoken, or at least understood, along the eastern Adriatic coast down to Albania. This is true up to the present day, even though national movements have sought national distinctiveness from the beginning of the 19th century and invested much effort into emphasising divergences among the coastal populations. But

even the only major period of a significant political divide between the western and the eastern coasts of the Adriatic, i.e. the Cold War, 1945–1989, a subsequent renaissance of nationalism and regionalism was not able to swallow these commonalities or cultural similarities.

The chapter proceeds from the foundations of these all-Adriatic commonalities over the character of common cultural features and the reasons for a later interruption to their revival after the fall of communism. In detail, it endeavours to answer the following questions:

1. Which powers were shaping a common Adriatic cultural space and what was their lasting impact?
2. Which cultural features became common to the Adriatic space?
3. What caused a divide later?
4. In which fields, among them perhaps tourism, is a revival of trans-Adriatic connections and networks after 1989 most obvious?

Major reference works to be consulted in this context and which were used as sources for this contribution are Bertić (1987), Klemenčić (1993, 1997), Rugg (1994), Budak *et al.* (1995), Biondi *et al.* (1996), Fridl *et al.* (1998), Magocsi (2002), Jordan *et al.* (2003), Regan (2003), Lichtenberger (2005) and Jordan (2011).

*E-mail: peter.jordan@oeaw.ac.at

4.2 Powers that Shaped a Common Adriatic Cultural Space

Table 4.1 summarises the political and cultural impacts of the major powers that have dominated the Adriatic space from the Romans to the 20th century.

Most of the historical 'eras' of power impacts on the Adriatic cultural space that are outlined in Table 4.1 are spatially represented on subsequent maps (Figs. 4.1a–4.1i) as indicated in the table.

Table 4.1. Powers that shaped a common Adriatic cultural space.

Power	Impact on the Adriatic cultural space
Roman Empire, until 395 (Fig. 4.1a)	The western and eastern coasts were colonised intensively by a Roman, Latin-speaking population: the foundation of a common culture in the Adriatic space. Urban and transport networks were also established along the eastern coast, much denser than inland. Wholly part of a centralised state performing an important bridge function, cultural and economic contacts across the Adriatic were intensive, but not a heartland of the Empire, its centres being located elsewhere.
West Roman Empire, 395–476 (Fig. 4.1b)	Most of the Adriatic space (except modern Montenegro and Albania) was still under one rule. Roman settlement and culture also continued along the east coast. The sea continued to function as a bridge. Again, not the core region of the Empire, rather a periphery, although the last capital of the Empire, Ravenna, was located here.
Kingdom of Ostrogoths under Theoderic, until 526/552 (Fig. 4.1c)	Again, most Adriatic space was under one rule (except modern Montenegro and Albania). Roman settlement and culture, also on the east coast, was not discontinued (King Theoderic admired Roman culture and was, in cultural terms, very assimilative). The bridge function continued. Ravenna was the capital of the Kingdom, the northern Adriatic coastlands its heartland: it was a truly Adriatic state.
East Rome under Emperor Justinian, 527–565 (Fig. 4.1d)	East Rome expanded its rule over large parts of the Mediterranean, including all of the Adriatic space, almost restoring the ancient Roman Empire. Justinian resided temporarily in Ravenna. Since East Rome had preserved several aspects of Roman culture better than the West (e.g. architecture, Latin as the official language), it continued to shape the Adriatic space very much in the Roman cultural sense.
Byzantine Empire, 8th–12th century (Fig. 4.1e)	Following the Arab invasions, East Rome withdrew as a political power from the largest part of the Adriatic space and returned to its Greek roots in the cultural sense (from then on called Byzantine Empire). But Byzantium (Constantinople/İstanbul) preserved its status as the metropolis of the whole Mediterranean, as well as its cultural influence over the Adriatic space well beyond the 10th century. Although augmented by some new elements, this was still ancient Roman culture. A Romance population, albeit from the 7th century with a Slavonic substratum in the north (Regan, 2003: 113) and an Albanian substratum in the south (Schramm, 1994), remained in the cities of the east Adriatic coast speaking Dalmatian, an East-Romance language derived from vulgar Latin.
Venice, c.1000/13th century –1797 (Fig. 4.1f)	Founded in 812, Venice became independent of Byzantium in 1000 and began to extend its influence along the eastern Adriatic coast. It had changed fronts from the Byzantine east to the Frankonian-Latin west and now promoted Western-Latin culture as well as *romanitas* on the east Adriatic coast – thereby preserving the cultural commonality of the Adriatic space against further Byzantine (gradually becoming more Greek in character) and later Ottoman influence. A Venetian feudal and urban elite preserved a Latin, Romance culture. A Slavonic rural population majority in the north and its Albanian counterpart in the south behaved in a rather assimilatory manner. This resulted in a Western, Latin culture similar to the west coast, with the additional feature of bilingualism – Dalmatian, gradually replaced by Venetian and Slavonic.

Continued

Table 4.1. Continued.

Power	Impact on the Adriatic cultural space
	By the 13th century, Venice had brought most of the east (but not west) Adriatic coast under its political control. The central and southern parts of the Apennine Peninsula were, from the 13th century, dominated by French and Spanish rule with a rigid feudalism. This resulted in social and economic backwardness to the present day (the *Mezzogiorno* problem).
	Venetian coastal cities such as Ragusa (Dubrovnik), Cattaro (Kotor) and Durazzo (Durrës) exerted strong cultural influence on their hinterlands through trade connections.
	Consequentially, the Adriatic space was not under a common rule, but still represented a cultural community. Intensive trans-Adriatic cultural and economic relations existed. Many architects and artists from the Apennine Peninsula worked in Venetian coastal cities and vice versa. Fishermen of Chioggia also had their fishing grounds along the east coast (Jordan, 1997). The east coast provided Venice and cities of the Apennines Peninsula with timber, wine and olives. Albanian and Slavonic Christian refugees from the Ottoman Empire crossed the sea and settled.
	Although the Republic of Venice (being a merchant and seafaring, not a territorial, power) did not expand its rule over the whole east coast, it had its operational base in this space and was thus essentially an Adriatic state. From the 15th century onward, it also had the historical role of preventing the Ottoman Empire from intruding substantially into the Adriatic space.
Austria, 1797–1805	Austria 'inherited' Venetian Adriatic possessions, but, apart from promoting its Trieste seaport, had no further ambitions here and did not act as an Adriatic power. But Austria preserved the dominance of the Venetian upper class along the east coast and a feudal system (the Colonate), as also the cultural commonality of the Adriatic space. Under Austria, southern parts of the east coast (Dalmatia) declined into a political and economic periphery (like the southern sections of the west coast).
Napoleonic France, 1805–1813/15 (Fig. 4.1g)	Napoleonic France expanded its rule for a very short period over almost the entire Adriatic space (except Montenegro and Albania), but left a substantial and sustained impact as a West European power by the transfer of enlightenment and by administrative, economic and social modernisation. It thus promoted the cultural commonality of the Adriatic space. In political and economic terms, however, the Adriatic space was only a periphery of the Napoleonic Empire.
Austrian Empire, Austro-Hungarian Monarchy, 1813/15–1867 (Fig. 4.1h), 1867–1918 (Fig. 4.1i)	Again, Austria invested little energy in its Adriatic provinces, except for Trieste. A unified Italy (by 1870), as a dangerous competitor in the region promoting *irredenta* aspirations among compatriots outside the state, set the monarchy in motion. Belatedly, it began developing its Adriatic coastlands, but with limited success: emigration reached huge dimensions, and Dalmatia especially remained an extreme periphery.
	In the sociocultural sphere, the Austrian Empire and (from 1867) the Austro-Hungarian Monarchy continued to preserve the domination of the Venetian elite, who were affected and infected by the Italian national idea, against an increasingly self-conscious, now also nationally conscious, Slavonic substratum. This preserved the cultural commonality of the Adriatic space, albeit against already fierce counterforces (see Section 4.5).

4.3 Common Cultural Features of the Adriatic Space

4.3.1 Roman legacy

Architectonic and structural remnants of Roman cities are still visible all around the Adriatic.

This is true for Aquileia, for example, the most important Roman trading port in the northern Adriatic, with trading links to the eastern Alps, the upper Danube and the Pannonian Basin. Preserved here are the Roman Forum, the structures of the Roman port (Fig. 4.2) and the mosaic floor of an early Christian church. Roman architectonic

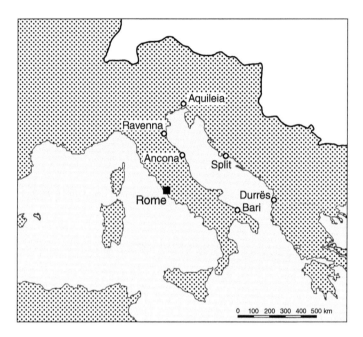

Fig. 4.1a. Late Roman Empire.

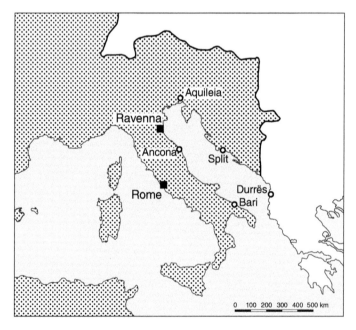

Fig. 4.1b. West Roman Empire (395–476).

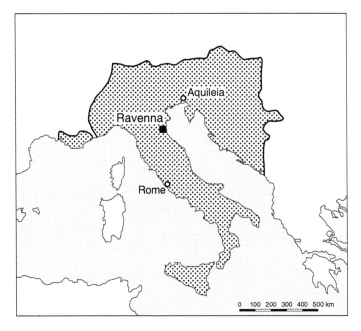

Fig. 4.1c. Kingdom of the Ostrogoths under Theoderic.

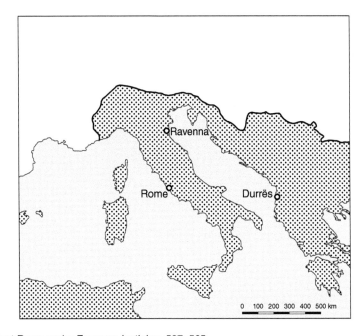

Fig. 4.1d. East Rome under Emperor Justinian, 527–565.

Fig. 4.1e. Byzantine Empire (9th century).

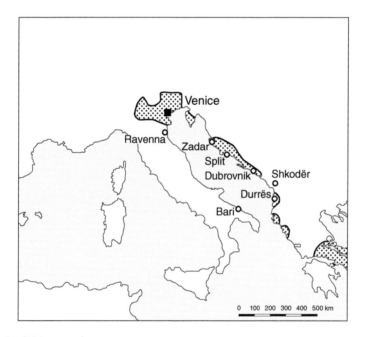

Fig. 4.1f. Venice (18th century).

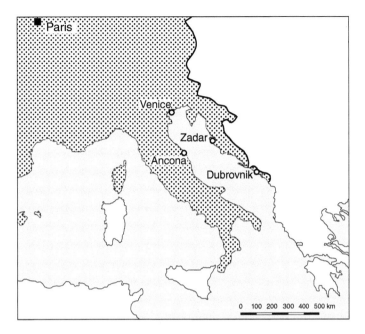

Fig. 4.1g. Napoleonic France, 1805–1813/15.

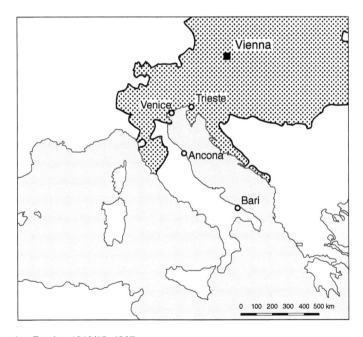

Fig. 4.1h. Austrian Empire, 1813/15–1867.

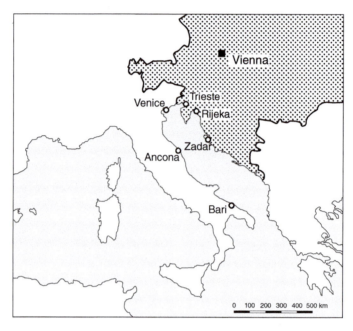

Fig. 4.1i. Austro-Hungarian Monarchy, 1867–1918. (From author's compilation from various sources.)

Fig. 4.2. The former Roman port of Aquileia, Italy. (Photograph courtesy of Peter Jordan.)

Fig. 4.3. Diocletian's Palace in Split, Croatia. (Photograph courtesy of Peter Jordan.)

highlights on the east coast of the Adriatic include the sixth-largest Roman arena, with seating for 23,000 spectators, and other Roman monuments in Pula, Diocletian's Palace in Split (Fig. 4.3), a Roman amphitheatre and Roman *thermae* in Durrës (western terminal of the *Via Egnatia*), as well as excavations of the Roman city Apollonia on the central Albanian coast.

In Ravenna, Roman-type monuments cannot be traced back to the times of the Roman Empire (before 395), but to its successor states: the Western Roman Empire and the Kingdom of Ostrogoths, which sustained Romanesque architecture and made Ravenna its capital. Examples along the west coast include Ancona's Arch of Trajan and the Roman column in Brindisi, eastern terminal of the *Via Appia* (after 109 AD, the *Via Traiana*).

Apart from visible and tangible cultural traces, the Roman Empire left a most important cultural legacy in at least four respects:

1. By tolerating Christianity (in 313 under Emperor Constantine) and by elevating it to the rank of the state church (in 391 under Emperor

Theodosius), this denomination became the common spiritual basis of the Adriatic space and of areas far beyond.

2. The Roman language, Latin, developed into: (i) modern Italian; (ii) Dalmatian – an East Roman language spoken in the cities of the east coast under the rule of Byzantium and, up to the early Modern Ages, on the island of Krk (Italian *Veglia*); and (iii) into Friulian and Venetian (the latter regarded as a dialect of Italian, but independently developed from vulgar Latin), which are still spoken. Italian is not only the official language of a large country but also has an excellent position as a trade and educational language with many speakers of other languages along the east Adriatic coast from Slovenia down to Albania.

3. Roman script finally penetrated the east coast, albeit against a long predominance of the Glagolitic script (*Glagolica*) among Croatian coastal dwellers (locally used as a sacred script until the late 19th century), and against Arabic script with Albanians and Bosniaks, who switched to Roman script only in 1908 and 1928, respectively. In Montenegro, and with Serbs in Bosnia-Herzegovina and Croatia, the

Cyrillic script is still in use. But especially in the Adriatic coastlands of Montenegro, the Roman alphabet has gained ground in most spheres of daily life.

4. Roman law has not only become fundamental for the Adriatic space but also for the Western European cultural and political system as a whole.

4.3.2 East Roman and Byzantine legacy

Architectonic traces of Byzantium, directly developed from ancient Roman art, can still be found around the Adriatic. A most impressive example is San Marco, the cathedral of Venice, which has been modelled after the lost Apostles Church in Byzantium. Ravenna exhibits significant East Roman and Byzantine influence, the Basilica di San Vitale, for example, completed in 547, is modelled on the Church of Hagia Sophia in Constantinople. Its mosaics depict East Rome's Empress Theodora and Emperor Justinian.

Many old churches along the east coast (Saint Euphrasius in Poreč/Parenzo, with its mosaics; the 8th century octagonal church of Sveti Donat in Zadar, Fig. 4.4) reflect East Roman and Byzantine cultural influence.

Another characteristic is the motive of Enthroned Christ (*Christus Pantocrator*) (closely related to the rather triumphant attitude of the Eastern Church), which can also be frequently found around the Adriatic.

4.3.3 Venetian legacy

Although Venice never acquired possessions along the west coast south of Cervia, and had no major cultural influence there, it contributed essentially to the cultural commonality of the Adriatic space by: (i) accepting as an expansive political and seafaring power the Papal, Western, Latin, later Catholic Church and by spreading it (together with Slovenes and Croats) to the east coast of the Adriatic; and (ii) enforcing the

Fig. 4.4. Sveti Donat in Zadar, Croatia. (Photograph courtesy of Peter Jordan.)

Romance cultural element with its language, societal model and architecture along the east coast.

Although founded by Byzantium, Venice later discontinued its relation with its founder and became a spearhead of the Western model of society, as well as of Western Christianity towards the East. This contributed to the spread of Catholicism to the cities on the eastern coast, which had been under Byzantine cultural domination, as well as among Albanians, elevating Roman Catholicism to a common cultural feature of the Adriatic space. Even along the coast of Montenegro, although otherwise a core area of the Serbian Orthodox Church, and in Albania, although the largest part of Albanians converted to Islam under Ottoman rule, Venetian Catholic mission has left traces to the present day. The 10% Roman Catholic minority in contemporary Albania plays a most active role in modern Albanian society, and the Catholic Albanian nun, Mother Theresa (although from the Albanian community of Skopje, Macedonia),

has become an 'icon' of Albanian identity (Fig. 4.5) (Jordan, 2015).

Venice preserved, by its possessions along the eastern Adriatic coast, a Romance population, architecture and language (Venetian, later Italian), into which individuals of other ethnic and linguistic groups were assimilated. Venice's impact was not terminated by its political end in 1797, but continued under Austrian rule up to World War I, as Austria did not question the societal dominance of Venetians. Although subject to substantial erosion later, at least in architecture and lifestyle, Venetian Romance cultural elements are clearly discernable today.

4.4 Dividing Factors

4.4.1 Migration of Slavs, 6th–7th century

In the 6th and 7th centuries, Slavonic tribes reached the east coast of the Adriatic (Regan,

Fig. 4.5. Monument of Mother Theresa at a major square in Shkodra, Albania. (Photograph courtesy of Peter Jordan.)

2003: 113) and populated most of it, except the cities, which remained Romance. They established the first Slavonic states under formal Byzantine supremacy, with heartlands on the coast, where infrastructure from Roman times was best developed. The first Croatian state was established on the northern Dalmatian coast; the Serbian principality Doclea, or Zeta, was founded in present-day Montenegro. While the Croatian state was influenced by Western, Latin culture, Doclea came under the influence of Byzantium, although zones of influence were fluid.

A very reasonable and well-documented theory of the linguist and toponymist, Gottfried Schramm (Schramm, 1994), maintains that Albanians are not autochthonous in what is Albania today, but were, after the year 800, evacuated from what is Bulgaria today by the Byzantine Empire and settled near Dyrrhachium (Durrës) to protect this important Adriatic bridgehead of the Empire against the Bulgarian Empire. Schramm's theory is based on Slavonic toponyms found and adopted by the Albanian settlers. This would mean that this section of the east Adriatic coast was settled by Slavonic people before the Albanians came in: a highly contested claim, but also supported by historians (see Schmitt, 2012).

The settlement of Slavs and Albanians on the eastern coast meant an ethnic division of the Adriatic space, but a cultural division to a minor extent only, since cities and elite culture remained Romance, and Croats as well as Slovenes came under the influence of the Latin Church and Western political powers. Also ethnic affiliation was not an important factor for personal and group identity before the 19th century.

4.4.2 Unification of Italy 1859–1870, rise of national ideas on the east coast

From the early 19th century, the national idea in the sense of Johann Gottfried Herder's cultural nation ('a nation is a group of people with common cultural characteristics'; Herder, 1774), as well as the nation state idea modelled after France, gained ground around the Adriatic and was first effected by the unification of Italy from 1859 to 1870. This did no harm to the cultural commonality of the Adriatic space,

but caused a political divide along the Adriatic between Italy and Austria–Hungary competing for supremacy here.

On the east coast, the rise of national ideas resulted at first in a foremost political, but increasingly also cultural, divide between the former Venetian, now Italian urban, and the Slavonic rural population. Later, Montenegro (1878) and Albania (1912) became small nation states at the expense of the Ottoman Empire. The first Yugoslavia, the Kingdom of the Serbs, Croats and Slovenes (1918–1941), conceived itself as a nation state composed of the three 'tribes'. As the strong power of the east coast, it resumed the previous Austro-Hungarian rivalry with Italy.

Italy's engagement on the east coast in the interwar period and during World War II, and its aspirations to dominate the Adriatic space (*mare nostro*), simulated full cultural harmony of the Adriatic space. But this was not real or sustainable. It deepened cultural divides and ended in expulsion and other human tragedies.

4.4.3 Europe's geopolitical divide, 1945–1989

This is the only significant period in history in which the Adriatic Sea lost its communicative function almost completely, and trans-Adriatic relations were reduced to a minimum. This resulted from: (i) Europe's division into two political and economic systems across Central Europe and the Adriatic Sea, although the Adriatic situation became less contentious as the two communist Adriatic states, Yugoslavia and Albania, fell foul of Moscow; (ii) the expulsion and flight of Italians from the east coast, which became Slavonic and Albanian, except for small remnants.

In this period of division, tourism was the main factor connecting the two coasts of the Adriatic. Due to communist Yugoslavia's policy of opening its borders for Western commercial tourism in the late 1950s and early 1960s and developing an adequate tourism infrastructure – much in contrast to all other communist countries in the first decades of the post-war period – Italian tourists also visited the Slovenian and Croatian coasts.

4.5 The Revival of an Adriatic Commonality after 1989

From the 1990s: (i) political and socio-economic systems on both coasts of the Adriatic were no longer antagonistic; (ii) a stronger power on the east coast (Yugoslavia) ceased to exist; and (iii) all countries now participated in the European integration process. This situation favoured a revival of the Adriatic cultural and economic commonality in several fields.

4.5.1 Minorities revived their networks

Just as Italian minorities along the Adriatic east coast intensified their connections with the motherland, so too did Slavonic and Albanian minorities on the opposite coast.

A Croatian group in the communes San Felice del Molise, Montemitro and Acquaviva Collecroce in the Campobasso Province (Molise region) is estimated (Italy conducts no ethnic census) at 2400–6000 persons. They go back to the second half of the 15th century, when Catholic Slavs from Dalmatia and Herzegovina fled from the Ottomans to the opposite Adriatic coast. Although many of them no longer speak Croatian, they have refreshed their contacts with Imotski, Ljubuški and Vrgorac, their supposed origins in the Dalmatian hinterland.

Albanians or Arbëresh are dispersed across wide areas of southern Italy and form the so-called *Arberia* in the sense of the totality of old-established Albanians on the Apennine Peninsula. Near to the Adriatic coast, they settled in the provinces of Campobasso (Molise region) and Taranto (Puglia region). Some of these groups were present on modern Italian territory by the end of the 13th century, but most came as refugees in the second half of the 15th century during (1460–1461) and after (1468) the final unsuccessful uprising against the Ottomans. Further groups arrived in the late 15th century and in the years 1534 and 1744. They originated from all areas inhabited by Albanians at the time, and mostly settled in thinly populated mountain regions. Today, they number an estimated 120,000. Their specific cultural identity is still evident in their language and adherence to a Greek-Catholic Church, united in 1536 with

Rome. This community has refreshed its contacts with the Albanian mother country since 1991. But there appears to have been little contact with post-communist Albanian migrants to Italy, since the majority of these settled in urban areas and were mostly of Muslim ancestry.

A definite rapprochement between the 2258 (population census 2002) Italians in Slovenia and the 17,807 (population census 2011) Italians in Croatia on the one hand and adjacent places and regions in Italy (mainly Trieste) occurred not only after the dissolution of Yugoslavia but also much earlier, due to relatively open borders. This group of Italians, concentrated on the west coast of Istria, but also in small numbers in the Kvarner region (Rijeka, Krk, Cres), can be regarded as successors of the Venetians, the former upper social stratum of the east coast. In Istria at least, they enjoy appropriate minority rights and preserve their language and culture well, not least due to the cultural prestige of Italy and Italian, as well as the economic attractiveness of adjacent northern Italy.

4.5.2 The Roman Catholic Church has recovered its position in society on the east coast

While religion in general, and Roman Catholicism in particular, had been banished to the private sphere during communist times, it subsequently recovered its former position in society. This is especially true for the Roman Catholic Church in Croatia, and also among Croatian minorities in Bosnia-Herzegovina and Montenegro. It is also significant for the Catholic minority and church in Albania, which play a more than proportionate role in society (Jordan, 2015). In this way, Catholicism as a former common Adriatic cultural feature has enjoyed a significant revival.

4.5.3 Revival of trans-Adriatic foreign direct investment and trade

Concerning foreign direct investment (FDI), Italy, with its traditional market economy and as a homeland of large enterprises, is a major investor in other Adriatic countries. According to

2014 data (WIIW, 2015), Italy is proportionately most active in Montenegro, where it has an FDI share of 12.4% and ranks second among foreign investors (after Russia: see Chapter 7, this volume). In Albania, Italy has a share of 11.6% and ranks third (after Greece and Canada: see Chapter 23, this volume) among foreign investors. Italy's engagement in Slovenia sees it with a share of 7.9% and fourth rank. Surprisingly small, however, is Italian FDI in Croatia, which had a huge tourism industry to privatise. With a share of just 2.8%, Italy ranks only ninth among foreign investors. This can perhaps be explained partly by the unfortunate experiences of Croatian tourism destinations in the interwar period, when Italian investors bought hotels just to close them down and remove competition. Italian investment in Bosnia-Herzegovina is also small (2.8%, eleventh rank).

In foreign trade, however, trans-Adriatic relations have become very close in all respects. Italy ranks first as Albania's trade partner in exports as well as in imports (2013: 31% and 46%, respectively) (Löchel, 2016); it ranks first also in Croatian exports and second (behind Germany) in Croatian imports (2014: 14% of both) (Državni zavod za statistiku, 2015). Italy also ranks second (behind Germany) as Slovenia's trading partner, with 15% exports and 11% imports (Statistični urad, 2015); and third in Bosnian imports (10%), second in exports (14%).

4.5.4 Trans-Adriatic tourism

It would be too much to say that trans-Adriatic tourism experienced a revival after the fall of communism, since Titoist Yugoslavia had opened itself early for Western commercial tourism and had long received large numbers of tourists from Italy. They usually ranked second or third among foreign tourists (Jordan, 1997). Indeed, it may even be said that tourism was the main factor connecting the two coasts of the Adriatic during the critical period of a bipolar Cold War Europe.

This relationship did not weaken, despite the dissolution of Yugoslavia. Even in the years of the Yugoslavian wars up to 1995, when tourism on the eastern Adriatic coast almost collapsed, Italians (besides Austrians and Czechs) were the most reliable guests and continued to come at least to the northern parts of the coast, where the situation was safe (Jordan, 1995). During the 2000s, communist Yugoslavia's generating market structure was almost re-established. In Slovenia in 2014, 15.8% of all foreign tourist nights were spent by Italians, Italy ranking first in terms of countries of origin (Statistični urad, 2015). In Croatia, Italy ranked fifth (behind Germany, Slovenia, Austria and the Czech Republic) in 2014 (7.3%) (Državni zavod za statistiku, 2015), and in Montenegro eighth (1.7%) (Zavod za statistiku, 2015). In Albania, with just 260,000 foreign tourist nights in 2014, an even larger share of Italians would not have had a significant economic impact (INSTAT, 2015).

Italians visit the eastern Adriatic coast mainly for its natural beauties and its opportunities to spend vacations near to nature, but appreciate also the fact that their language is understood almost everywhere and feel familiar in Venetian-type towns and cities. A dense network of touristic ferry lines connects the Italian with the Croatian coast (Direct Ferries, 2016): from Venice to Umag/Umago, Poreč/Parenzo, Rovinj/Rovigno and Pula/Pola on Istria; from Ancona to Zadar, Split and Stari Grad (on the island of Hvar); from Pescara to Hvar and Vela Luka (on the island of Korčula); and from Bari to Dubrovnik.

4.5.5 Montenegro's 'turn' to the Adriatic

Montenegro's Adriatic facade comprises by area the minor part of the country, but in economic terms has always been its most active part. It has been shaped by Venetian culture and still hosts a small Catholic Croatian minority exhibiting Western influence. What has changed in recent years is the country's general political orientation from a 'smaller Serbia' looking towards Belgrade and conceiving Montenegrins as Serbs in the national sense, to a multicultural society with a predominantly Adriatic orientation. This has been due to its political and economic dissociation from Serbia since 1998, starting with the first term of Milo Đukanović as president (1998–2002) and passing through the stages of union with Serbia (2003–2006) to full independence (since 2006).

4.5.6 Growing importance of Croatia's and Slovenia's Adriatic facades

Although Croatia has the longest coastline of all Adriatic countries (1778 km excluding islands: longer than that of Italy), it is predominantly a Central European country. Its capital and central region, as well as its demographic and economic cores, are located in the interior. But because the country's coast hosts about 90% of Croatia's tourism – the dominant branch of the economy – and attracts, not least for this reason, significant internal migration, it has certainly escaped its former role as an economic periphery.

This development started in communist times as a result of Tito's 'litoralisation' policy, but has continued after Yugoslavia's dissolution. In this context, it is also worth mentioning that the emotional relation of Croatians to the coast is very strong, due to its historical role (location of the first Croatian state) and the fact that Croatia's most prominent landmarks (Dubrovnik, Diocletian's palace in Split, Opatija, Roman arena in Pula) are located here. All this results in Croatia's Adriatic facade exerting more than proportional weight in the economic, political and cultural orientation of the country. Croatia shapes the Adriatic space to a considerable extent and is an important player in it.

To a much smaller but still significant extent, this applies also to Slovenia and its Adriatic facade. Again, tourism plays a role, but Slovenia's coast gained in importance because of the growth of Koper/Capodistria as a transit seaport for large parts of Central Europe. It has also developed such tertiary functions as the country's third university.

4.6 Conclusion

If we have the impression that the Adriatic space is emerging as a cultural region, it is because we are reacting to the impact of the Cold War period, when Europe was divided and this divide bifurcated the Adriatic Sea. The Adriatic space is, in fact, re-emerging as a cultural region, which it had been for centuries, being shaped by powers from the Roman Empire onwards.

It was the rise of national ideas from the second half of the 19th century and the bipolar nature of Europe after World War II that damaged cultural and other commonalities and let them almost fall into oblivion. But after 1989, they reappeared: in the fields of culture, economic and political relations, and not least in tourism. It is likely that this development will continue, even if European integration should not advance further. For the south-east European littoral countries, Albania and Montenegro, the Adriatic space is a convenient gateway to the European West. Increasingly, Croatia and Slovenia are presenting their Adriatic 'face', and for Italy, the only remaining larger country in the region, the Adriatic space is again open and accessible as its 'natural' and traditional 'playground'.

References

Bertić, I. (ed.) (1987) *Veliki Geografski Atlas Jugoslavije.* [*Great geographical atlas of Yugoslavia.*] SNL, Zagreb, Yugoslavia (in Serbo-Croat).

Biondi, N., De Menech, S. and Cecotti, F. (1996) *Il confine mobile. Atlante storico dell'Alto Adriatico 1866–1992.* [*The shifting border. Historical atlas of the Upper Adriatic 1866–1992.*] Istituto Regionale per la Storia del Movimento di Liberazione nel Friuli – Venezia Giulia, Edizioni della Laguna, Trieste, Italy (in Italian).

Budak, N., Jordan, P. and Lukan W. (eds) (1995) *Kroatien. Landeskunde – Geschichte – Kultur – Politik – Wirtschaft – Recht.* [*Croatia. Regional Geography – History – Culture – Politics – Economy – Law.*] Böhlau, Wien – Köln – Weimar, Austria/Germany (in German).

Direct Ferries (2016) Available at: http://www.directferries.co.uk/ferries_from_italy_to_croatia.htm (accessed 20 July 2016).

Državni zavod za statistiku – Republika Hrvatska (2015) *Statistički ljetopis 2015.* [*Statistical yearbook 2015.*] Državni zavod za statistiku, Zagreb, Croatia (in Croatian). Available at: http://www.dzs.hr (accessed 20 July 2016).

Fridl, J., Kladnik, D., Orožen Adamič, M. and Perko, D. (eds) (1998) *Geografski Atlas Slovenije.* [*Geographical Atlas of Slovenia.*] DZS, Inštitut za geografijo, Geografski inštitut Antona Melika, Ljubljana (in Slovenian).

Herder, J.G. v. (1774) Auch eine Philosophie der Geschichte zur Bildung der Menschheit. [Also a philosophy of history for the education of humankind.] Hartknoch, Riga (in German). Available at: http://www.deutschestextarchiv.de/book/show/herder_philosophie_1774 (accessed 20 July 2016).

INSTAT (Instituti i Statistikave) (2015) *Vjetari Statistikor 2014.* [*Statistical Yearbook 2014.*] INSTAT, Tirana (in Albanian). Available at: http://www.instat.gov.al/en/publications/books.aspx (accessed 20 July 2016).

Jordan, P. (1995) The Impact of the Wars in Croatia and Bosnia-Hercegovina on the Tourism of the Croatian Coast. In: Baraniecki, L. (ed.) *Conditions of the Foreign Tourism Development in the Central and Eastern Europe.* Institute of Geography, Wrocław University, Wrocław, Poland, pp. 71–86.

Jordan, P. (1997) *Beiträge zur Fremdenverkehrsgeographie der nördlichen Kroatischen Küste.* [*Contributions to tourism geography of the northern Croatian coast.*] Institut für Geographie und Regionalforschung, Klagenfurt, Austria (in German).

Jordan, P. (2011) Beyond national and regional ideas: the Adriatic space as a network and cultural region. In: Pagnini, M.P. (ed.) *Proceedings of the Second Conference of the Adriatic Forum, Construction and Deconstruction of Nationalism and Regionalism: A Long Journey to Europe.* Académie Européenne de Géopolitique, Montepellier, France, pp. 107–121.

Jordan, P. (2015) An exception in the Balkans: Albania's multiconfessional identity. In: Brunn, S. (ed.) *The Changing World Religion Map. Sacred Places, Identities, Practices and Politics, Vol. 3.* Springer, Dordrecht, the Netherlands, pp. 1577–1597.

Jordan, P., Kaser, K., Lukan, W., Schwandner-Sievers, S. and Sundhaussen, H. (eds) (2003) *Albanien. Geographie – Historische Anthropologie – Geschichte – Kultur – Postkommunistische Transformation.* [*Albania. Geography – historical anthropology – history – culture – post-communist transformation.*] Peter Lang, Vienna (in German).

Klemenčić, M. (ed.) (1993) *A Concise Atlas of the Republic of Croatia & the Republic of Bosnia and Hercegovina.* Leksikografski zavod Miroslav Krleža, Zagreb.

Klemenčić, M. (ed.) (1997) *Atlas Europe (Atlas of Europe).* Leksikografski zavod Miroslav Krleža, Zagreb.

Lichtenberger, E. (2005) *Europa. Geographie, Geschichte, Wirtschaft, Politik.* [*Europe. Geography, History, Economy, Politics.*] Wissenschaftliche Buchgesellschaft, Darmstadt, Germany (in German).

Löchel, C. (ed.) (2016) *Der Neue Fischer Weltalmanach 2016.* [*The New Fischer World Almanac.*] Fischer, Frankfurt am Main, Germany (in German).

Magocsi, P.R. (2002) *Historical Atlas of Central Europe.* University of Toronto Press, Toronto, Canada.

Regan, K. (ed.) (2003) *Hrvatski povijesni atlas.* [*Croatian historical atlas.*] Leksikografski zavod Miroslav Krleža, Zagreb (in Croatian).

Rugg, D.S. (1994) Communist legacies in the Albanian landscape. *Geographical Review* 84(1), 59–73.

Schmitt, O. (2012) *Die Albaner – eine Geschichte zwischen Orient und Okzident.* [*The Albanians – a History between Orient and Occident.*] Beck, Munich, Germany (in German).

Schramm, G. (1994) *Anfänge des albanischen Christentums. Die frühe Bekehrung der Bessen und ihre langen Folgen.* [*Outsets of Albanian Christianity. The early Conversion of the Bess and its lasting Impacts.*] Rombach, Freiburg im Breisgau, Germany (in German).

Statistični urad Republike Slovenije (2015) *Turizem (Tourism).* Statistični urad, Ljubljana (in Slovenian). Available at: http://www.stat.si/StatWeb/pregled-podrocja?idp=24&headerbar=21 (accessed 20 July 2016).

WIIW (Vienna Institute for International Economic Studies) (2015) *WIIW Database on Foreign Direct Investment in Central, East and Southeast Europe.* WIIW, Vienna. Available at: http://data.wiiw.ac.at/fdi-database.html (accessed 20 July 2016).

Zavod za statistiku Crne Gore (2015) *Statistički godišnjak 2015.* [*Statistical yearbook 2015.*] Zavod za statistiku, Podgorica, Montenegro (in Montenegrin). Available at: http://www.monstat.org/cg/index.php (accessed 20 July 2016).

5 Crimea: Geopolitics and Tourism

John Berryman*

Department of Politics, Birkbeck College, University of London, UK

5.1 Introduction

Crimea has long been an important focus for tourism and a source of Russian imagery. Its geopolitical history, however, has been both complicated and of no little significance, a significance that resonates strongly today.

What were the geopolitical and historical drivers of President Putin's startling March 2014 *coup de main* in the Crimea, and how has the accession of Crimea to the Russian Federation (RF) impacted on tourism in the peninsula? On the basis of an examination of the historical and geopolitical role of Crimea and Russia's position in the Black Sea region (Fig. 5.1), this chapter seeks to address these two questions.

5.2 The Historical and Geopolitical Role of Crimea

5.2.1 Russia's acquisition of Crimea

Seizure in 1696 of the Turkish fortress of Azov at the mouth of the Don River and the establishment of Taganrog on the Sea of Azov as a naval base for a southern fleet signalled Peter the Great's determination to challenge the Ottoman Empire's control of the Black Sea. Indeed, Peter seriously weighed the Black Sea against the Baltic Sea as Russia's prime gateway to Europe, and even considered making Taganrog Russia's outward-looking capital. However, at the end of another Russo-Turkish War, by the terms of the 1711 Peace of Pruth, Peter surrendered Azov, dismantled the fortress at Taganrog and destroyed the Azov fleet (Clarke, 1898: 7, 12; Anderson, 1995: 35–37, 72; King, 2005: 143–146; Trenin, 2008: 104).

After decades of confusion and drift succeeding Peter the Great, Catherine the Great annexed most of the right bank of Ukraine and pushed on down to the Black Sea. Controlled since the 15th century by the Crimean Khanate under the protection of the Ottoman Empire, the sparsely populated grasslands of the steppe now became the imperial province of 'New Russia' (*Novorossiya*) and Crimea was occupied.

The turning point in the struggle between the Russian and Ottoman Empires came at the conclusion of a 6-year war. By the 1774 Treaty of Kutchuk-Kainardji, Russia resecured the ports of Azov and Taganrog, plus the fortresses of Kerch and Kinburn at the mouth of the Dnepr River, and established a protectorate over an 'independent' Crimea. Access to the Black Sea coastline between the Dnepr and

*E-mail: johnberryman@blueyonder.co.uk

Fig. 5.1. Crimea and the Black Sea. (Redrawn from Mitchell, 1974: 406.)

Bug rivers was established, and Russia secured the right to send its merchant ships through the Turkish Straits and maintain warships in the Black Sea.

In 1779, shipyards for naval and merchant vessels opened at Kherson on the estuary of the Dnepr River, 3 years later a Russian Black Sea Fleet was established, and in 1783 Catherine seized the opportunity to annexe Crimea. Her favourite, Prince Grigorii Potemkin, was appointed governor of 'New Russia' and commander of the Black Sea Fleet, which moved to its main base at Sevastopol on the Crimean peninsula. Finally, new shipyards were established at Sevastopol and at Nikolaev, 40 miles up the Bug River (Anderson, 1966: xi–xii, 5–11; Daly, 1991: 106–107, 177; Sondhaus, 2001: 29; Kipp, 2002: 159–160).

The geopolitical significance of the Crimean peninsula therefore lay in its possession of Russia's first warm water port. Enjoying one of the finest natural harbours in the world, for more than two centuries Sevastopol has been the headquarters of the Russian Black Sea Fleet and the main base area for naval units that have operated in the Black Sea and the Mediterranean (Polmar, 1991: 18; Schwartz, 2014).

5.2.2 Sevastopol and the Russian Black Sea Fleet, 1783–1853

Enjoying limited access to the world's oceans, the Imperial Russian Navy could not hope to match the worldwide blue-water capability of the British Royal Navy. From its inception, therefore, the regional tasks of the Russian Black Sea Fleet were to match the Turkish Navy, provide wartime defence for Russia's new south-western flank, including the new Black Sea ports such as Odessa, Nikolaev and Mariupol, and serve as a 'secondary arm' to provide logistic and amphibious support for the efforts of the Russian army to deal with Muslim guerrillas down the Circassian coast of the Black Sea. In the course of these operations, Russia secured control of additional Black Sea ports such as Novorossisk, Tuapse, Ochamchira, Sukhumi and Poti (Maiorano, 1985: 56–57; Daly, 1991: ix–xii; Kipp, 2002: 152). As grain exports from these ports (and later oil exports from Batumi) became major sources of the Empire's revenues, defence of the Black Sea littoral and an ability to close the Black Sea to the fleets of Russia's enemies, while providing unimpeded access for Russian warships to project Russia's power into the vital export route of the Mediterranean, became the long-term goals of Russia's Black Sea policy (Gorshkov, 1979: 81–82; MccGwire, 1981: 211; Kagan, 2002: 250; King, 2005: 195–200).

The dilemma Imperial Russia confronted was that any attempt to seize control of the Turkish Straits – the Bosphorus, the Dardanelles and the enormous city of Constantinople – risked precipitating the collapse of the Ottoman Empire and opening the door to control being exercised by a stronger and possibly more hostile European power. Russia's Foreign Minister, Karl Nesselrode, therefore concluded that the wisest strategy was to maintain a weak Ottoman Empire, which could be persuaded not to side with Russia's enemies, and to work with the Great Powers to maintain the international regime for the Straits established by the Anglo-Turkish treaty of 1809 that specified that no non-Turkish warships could pass the Straits while Turkey was at peace (Tsygankov, 2012: 66, 75).

The 1841 Straits Convention embodied this international regime, which provided Russia with a measure of security against attacks from the Black Sea in wars in which Turkey was not a belligerent. However, the authorities in St Petersburg were aware that in the event of war between Turkey and Russia, British and other non-Turkish warships would be free to enter the Black Sea and attack Russia's ports (Anderson, 1966: 393; Sondhaus, 2001: 16–18, 29, 32–34). As a consequence, over the following decade, the imperial authorities pressed ahead with efforts to strengthen the defences of Sevastopol. Docks and forts were modernised and reinforced by British engineers, but lacking any rail or proper road links with Russia's vast hinterland, on the eve of the Crimean War, Sevastopol remained a second-class naval base providing facilities for a second-class Russian Black Sea Fleet (Clarke, 1898: 81; Sondhaus, 2001: 29).

5.2.3   The Crimean War and its aftermath, 1853–1871

Notwithstanding Russia's contribution to the defeat of Napoleon's *Grande Armee*, and her full post-1815 participation in the Congress System, as Russia's large military forces secured new gains in the Caucasus and suppressed the 1830

Polish and 1848 Hungarian revolts, western suspicions of Russian intentions rose. In March 1854, the liberal states of Britain and France intervened in another Russo-Turkish War and launched a preventive war to cut back and weaken Russia. Their primary objectives were to deny Russia control of Constantinople and the Turkish Straits, and thereby quash Russia's Mediterranean ambitions, to protect Britain's corridor to India and the Far East and French spheres of influence in the Near East, and to forestall possible further adverse shifts in the balance of power in Europe (Anderson, 1966: 391–392; Gough, 2014: 114–116; Berryman, 2015: 189).

Although sufficient to annihilate the Turkish fleet at Sinope in November 1853, the obsolete Russian Black Sea Fleet was no match for the large and modern Anglo-French fleets that were sent through the Turkish Straits into the Black Sea in the spring of 1854 (Clarke, 1898: 88–93). Enjoying complete command of the sea, the allies sought to seize Sevastopol and eliminate the Russian Black Sea Fleet. After an 11-month siege, Sevastopol was taken by British, French and Turkish forces in September 1855. For subsequent generations of Russians, the Crimean War underlined the vulnerability of Russia's Black Sea flank to seaborne attack through the Turkish Straits, while the bravery of the defenders of Sevastopol (vividly captured in Count Leo Tolstoy's *Sevastopol'skie rasskazy* ('Sevastopol Sketches')) came to symbolise the heroism of Russia's forces in resisting foreign invasions. The image was therefore firmly established in the Russian memory of Sevastopol as a city of 'Russian glory', rather than as a site of a Russian defeat (Plokhy, 2000: 374; Sasse, 2007: Chapter 3).

By the terms of the 1856 Treaty of Paris, the Black Sea was neutralised and Russia (together with the Ottoman Empire) was required to cease maintaining naval forces in the Black Sea and to remove all fortified naval installations and arsenals around its coast. Concluding that although a Black Sea Fleet was no longer available, naval suasion against the Ottoman Empire could once more be effected from the Mediterranean, in 1858 a small Russian Mediterranean Squadron was established, utilising a coaling station and naval depot at the Bay of Villafranca on the Sardinian coast (Kipp, 1972: 216, 221; Kipp, 1983: 157–158). In 1870, Russia finally seized the opportunity offered by the Franco-Prussian War to secure the abrogation of the Black Sea clauses of the treaty and open the way for the re-establishment of a Russian Black Sea Fleet.

5.2.4 Russia, Crimea and the Black Sea, 1877–1917

In 1877, Tsar Alexander II initiated another war with Turkey (despite reservations within his Ministries of War, Finance and Foreign Affairs). His move was in response to revolts against Ottoman rule in Bosnia-Herzegovina and Bulgaria between 1875 and 1876, and the failure of the Turkish authorities to implement the reforms demanded by the European powers (Fuller, 1992: 309–317). Since Russia's Black Sea Fleet was at this stage almost non-existent, there could be no thought of seizing Constantinople and the Turkish Straits by a swift naval *coup de main* (King, 2005: 194; McMeekin, 2011: 23). Turkish command of the Black Sea likewise ruled out the possibility of Russian forces receiving naval support during their southward advance on Constantinople. Hence, only at considerable cost was the great fortress of Plevna taken by Russian forces, and only with its forces almost at the gates of Constantinople was Russia able to secure Turkey's signature to an armistice and then a peace treaty at San Stefano, which established an enormous Bulgarian state enjoying access to the Aegean Sea.

As a Russian client, Bulgaria would serve as a springboard for an attack on Constantinople, and provide the Russian Navy with an eastern Mediterranean base. Confronting strong objections by the European powers, stiffened by London's despatch of a powerful Royal Navy squadron and landing force through the Dardanelles and the transport of 7000 native troops from India to Malta, Russia was unable to prevent the terms of the Treaty of San Stefano being superseded by the 'unfair' diplomatic arrangements of the 1878 Congress of Berlin, the centrepiece of which was a much reduced Bulgaria, stripped of its coastline on the Aegean Sea (Anderson, 1966: 197–219; Kipp, 1983: 165–168; Bartlett, 1996: 104–106; Sondhaus, 2001: 122–125, 227).

Chastened by its setbacks of 1856 and 1878, in 1882 Russia approved a 20-year naval building programme to produce a modern Black Sea Fleet. Since Russia could not import warships into the Black Sea through the Turkish Straits, the programme was undertaken in the shipbuilding yards of Nikolaev and Sevastopol (Clarke, 1898: 112–115, 156; Sondhaus, 2001: 147–148; Kipp, 2002: 162, 166). However, facilitated by the consolidation of a Franco-Russian alliance between 1892 and 1894, a small Russian Mediterranean Squadron was re-established. Utilising the facilities provided by what was now the French anchorage of Villafranca and the great French naval base at Toulon, the squadron consisted largely of Russian warships *en route* to the Far East, together with a few units temporarily detached from the Baltic Fleet (Clarke, 1898: 156; Marder, 1940: 175, 178–179, 182; Westwood, 1970: 8).

August 1914 saw the outbreak of war between the Central Powers of Imperial Germany and the Austro-Hungarian Empire and the *Entente* Powers of France, Russia and Britain. Having evaded a sea chase by the Royal Navy, on 10 August 1914 the German Navy's battle cruiser *Goeben* and light cruiser *Breslau* were allowed to enter the Dardanelles and were promptly incorporated into the Turkish Navy. Heavy German pressures in Constantinople, and Turkish dreams of reconquering Crimea, the Caucasus and even the Volga basin, led the Turkish government to reach the suicidal conclusion that its interests would be best served by an alignment with the Central Powers, rather than 'bandwagoning' with the *Entente* Powers. Hence, in late October 1914, the two powerful new German warships spearheaded surprise attacks by the Turkish Navy on Odessa, Novorossisk, Feodosia and Sevastopol (Halpern, 1994: 63, 224; Reynolds, 2011: Chapter 4; Sondhaus, 2014: 94–112; Rogan, 2015: 46–51). In response, in November 1914, Russia, Britain and France declared war on the Ottoman Empire, and by early the following year an Anglo-French attack on the Dardanelles was under way to enable British and French arms and equipment to be delivered to sustain Russia's war effort.

Against this backdrop of unprecedented *Entente* cooperation, in March 1915 London and Paris agreed that at the end of hostilities they would raise no objections to the annexation by Russia of Constantinople and the Straits (Anderson, 1966: 311–314, 322–326). And following the abdication of Tsar Nicholas II in March 1917, Britain and France reassured the new Russian Provisional Government that provided it maintained a commitment to the war, control of the Straits would be transferred to its authority. With the Bolshevik Revolution and Russia's withdrawal from the war, this secret agreement was rendered null and void. International supervision of the Straits would subsequently be established by the 1936 Montreux Convention. Although this Convention permits Russian warships to pass through the Straits in peacetime, Moscow remains unhappy with the considerable discretionary powers that the Turkish authorities can exercise (Global Security, 2015a).

5.2.5 The Soviet Union, Crimea and the Black Sea, 1918–1991

Unimpressed by Trotsky's delaying tactics at the Brest–Litovsk peace negotiations, a renewed advance of German forces on what was now Petrograd forced the Bolsheviks to sign a humiliating peace settlement on 3 March 1918 that ceded independence to 1 million square miles of Polish, Finnish, Baltic, Ukrainian and Transcaucasian provinces of the former Russian Empire. One million German and Austro-Hungarian troops now advanced into Baltic, Finnish and Ukrainian territory, and General Skoropadskyi was established as head of a German-backed puppet government in Kyiv. On the Black Sea coast, German forces occupied Odessa and Nikolaev, and by the end of April had entered Crimea and secured control of most of the Black Sea Fleet at Sevastopol. However, the suggestions of General Erich Ludendorff and General Max Hoffman in Berlin that the Crimean peninsula be developed as a resort facility or 'German Riviera' for German troops in the region were abandoned with the termination of the war in November 1918 (Kitchen, 1976: 241–244; Halpern, 1987: 542–555).

The withdrawal of German and Austrian troops from Ukraine and Crimea in turn only opened the way for armed intervention by the *Entente* powers to assist those White Armies in the Russian Civil War operating in the neighbourhood of the Black Sea. French forces despatched through the Turkish Straits landed at Odessa

and Sevastopol in December 1918, but were withdrawn by April 1919. Western support for the White forces of General Denikin was provided until March 1920, when the remainder of his Kuban troops were evacuated from Novorossisk. In November 1920, 130,000 troops and civilians of General Wrangel's White Army were evacuated by the Royal Navy from Crimea to Constantinople. Western intervention through the Black Sea in the Russian Civil War once more underlined the vulnerability of Russia's southwest flank (Acherson, 2015: 34–38; Berryman, 2015: 190–191).

With the victory of the Bolsheviks, in 1921 the Crimean Autonomous Soviet Socialist Republic (Crimean ASSR) was established as part of the Russian Socialist Federal Soviet Republic, and a few ships of the Russian Black Sea Fleet were salvaged. Only in the 1930s was a large-scale programme launched to reconstitute the Soviet Navy (Rohwer and Monakov, 2001). In exile in Munich after World War I, Skoropadskyi became co-founder of the *Volkischer Beobachter*,[1] and the goal of securing Ukraine was embraced by Hitler who, like Ludendorff and Hoffman, also saw Crimea as an ideal site for German colonisation. Although technically assigned to Ukraine in Nazi pre-war planning, by 1941 Hitler had determined that Crimea should be cleansed of its non-German population to provide for the resettlement of South Tyrol Germans, thereby resolving a festering dispute with his ally, Mussolini. Hitler rhapsodised that with the building of new motorways from Germany through the conquered territories, the beauty of Crimea would eventually become accessible to all Germans (Dallin, 1957: 253–257; Kershaw, 2000: 400–402, 434; Acherson, 2015: 26–28). In the event, such grandiose visions would not be realised. The 300-day German siege of Sevastopol in 1941–1942, followed by the bloody struggle of Soviet forces to resecure the base in 1944, cost the enormous total of 1.2 million lives and saw the complete destruction of the city (Lieven, 1999: Chapter 4).

While 2 million Ukrainians fought in the Red Army against German forces, two divisions of the Western Ukrainian-based Organization of Ukrainian Nationalists (OUN), plus the Western Ukrainian Galician 14th Waffen SS Division, fought alongside Nazi Germany against Soviet forces. These deep differences of identity within

Ukraine and Crimea were exacerbated by Stalin's deportation of the entire population of Crimean Tatars to Central Asia in 1944–1945 on the basis of a claim that they had cooperated with German forces (Sasse, 2007: 5, 75; Acherson, 2015: 30–32).

In June 1945, the Crimean ASSR became the Crimean *Oblast* of the Russian Soviet Federal Socialist Republic (RSFSR), and work commenced on the reconstruction of Sevastopol. Nine years later, in a clumsy gesture of recognition of the importance of the unity of Ukraine with Russia, Soviet leader Nikita Khrushchev transferred Crimea to Ukraine. No prior consultation was conducted with the largely Russian inhabitants of the peninsula, who were handed over to the jurisdiction of Ukraine like a sack of potatoes. However, the huge Soviet military presence at Sevastopol continued to be administered directly from Moscow, as had been the case since the 1948 decision of the Presidium of the RSFSR. Meanwhile, the publication in 1954 of the immensely popular study by Evgenii Tarle, *Gorod russkoi slavy: Sevastopol' v 1854–1855 gg* (*City of Russian Glory: Sevastopol in 1854–1855*) only further entrenched the strong identification of Russian people with their *gorod geroi* ('Hero City') (Plokhy, 2000: 37–38; Sasse, 2007: Chapter 5; Berryman, 2015: 191–192).

Through the Cold War, while strong Soviet naval forces ensured that the Black Sea remained a 'Soviet lake', the Mediterranean became an American and subsequently a 'NATO (North Atlantic Treaty Organization) lake', in which two carrier battle groups of the United States Navy (USN) Sixth Fleet were deployed, comprising around 40–50 warships and 150 aircraft. Initially, in 1958 a small number of Soviet diesel-powered submarines operated from a Soviet logistic support base at Vlora, on the coast of Albania, but following the Soviet split with Albania in 1961, they were expelled.

With the withdrawal of American *Jupiter*-class intermediate-range ballistic missiles from Italy and Turkey in 1963 in the aftermath of the Cuban missile crisis, USN nuclear-strike aircraft operating from attack carriers in the eastern Mediterranean were augmented by the deployment in the Mediterranean of nuclear-powered A-2 *Polaris* ballistic-missile submarines. In response, from 1964 a Soviet 5th Operational Squadron of around 20 ships became a feature of the Mediterranean naval balance, augmenting the forces of the Russian Black Sea Fleet based in Sevastopol. While the peacetime objective of the Soviet Mediterranean squadron to project power and influence mirrored that of the USN Sixth Fleet, its wartime objective was to neutralise the capacity of the American carriers and ballistic-missile submarines to launch strategic nuclear strikes against the Soviet Union. By the outbreak of the 1967 Arab–Israeli War, the Soviet Mediterranean squadron was a force of more than 40 ships and 12 submarines (MccGwire, 1973; Berryman, 1988: 205–208). As a reward for Soviet support for the Arab states, following the 1967 war an enlarged Soviet Mediterranean squadron of around 60 ships was able to use a range of facilities at the Egyptian ports of Alexandria, Port Said and Marsa Matrouh, and in 1972 facilities were made available at the Syrian ports of Latakia and Tartus. Following the Egyptian split with the Soviet Union in 1976, for the remainder of the Cold War and through the post-Cold War years, these Syrian facilities have provided the only stable support base for the Soviet/Russian Navy in the Mediterranean. Meanwhile, the deployment of Tu-22 *Blinder* anti-submarine warfare (ASW) aircraft and Tu-26 *Backfire* bombers from bases in the Crimea in the 1980s provided land-based air support for the Soviet Navy in the Black Sea and made life difficult for NATO naval forces in the Mediterranean. However, with cutbacks in military expenditure in the Gorbachev years, the Soviet Mediterranean squadron was reduced to an average of 30–40 ships (Maiorano, 1985: 61–64; Coutau-Begarie, 1989; Polmar, 1991: 19; Gorenburg, 2010; Global Security, 2015b).

5.2.6   The Russian Federation, Crimea and the Black Sea, 1991–2014

As a consequence of the implosion of the Soviet Union in 1991, the newly independent state of Ukraine assumed control of the north coast of the Black Sea and Crimea, while the coast between Sukhumi and Batumi became Georgian. Russia consequently lost access to 22 out of 26 harbours and naval bases around the Black Sea, out of which 19 (including Sevastopol) came under the control of Ukraine (Sanders, 2001: 102).

Anxious to resolve the issues of Ukraine's denuclearisation and the division of the Black

Sea Fleet between Ukraine and Russia, no attempt was made by the Kremlin to foment separatism among the large Russophile population in southeast Ukraine, nor was any support provided by President Yeltsin for Russian secessionists within Crimea nor for Russian nationalists within the *Duma* calling for Crimea's full independence or transfer to Russia's sovereignty. By 1997, Ukraine's denuclearisation had been settled, and in that year Ukraine signed an agreement to lease the bulk of Sevastopol's facilities to Russia for 20 years for the payment of almost US$100 million/year (Sasse, 2007: 232; Berryman, 2015: 193–194; Shapovalova, 2015: 232, 238–239). And in anticipation of the eventual expulsion of the fleet from Sevastopol, Russia began to develop alternative facilities at Novorossisk, pending the construction of a new base between Gelendzhik and Tuapse (Berryman, 2009: 177; Gorenburg, 2010).

With the complexities of Ukraine's denuclearisation and the Black Sea Fleet resolved, the central challenge confronting Moscow was the eastward enlargement of NATO. Despite its vehement protests, a weak Russia was unable to block the first phase of NATO enlargement in 1999, and, unprepared to pick a fight he could only lose, President Vladimir Putin's response to the second phase in 2004 was subdued. By this point, NATO had incorporated seven former Warsaw Pact states and three former Soviet republics. By contrast, although NATO Membership Application Plans (MAPs) for Albania and Croatia were approved at the 2008 NATO Bucharest Summit, MAPs for Georgia and Ukraine were not approved, due to European reservations. Having arrived in Bucharest for a NATO–Russia Council meeting, Putin made it clear to US President George W. Bush that the prospect of the emplacement of NATO military infrastructures on the territory of Ukraine (including Crimea) would pose an existential challenge to Russia's security and was a 'red-line issue'. Indeed, after Russia's war with Georgia in August 2008, there was an expectation that Kyiv would be next in Moscow's firing line (Berryman, 2015: 194–200; Hill and Gaddy, 2015: 360; Shapovalova, 2015: 248–249).

In the event, the unexpected 2010 electoral victory in Ukraine of President Viktor Yanukovich saw the signing of the Kharkov Accords, by which the lease of Sevastopol was extended for a further 25 years to 2042, and legislation was passed that indicated Ukraine would no longer pursue NATO membership but would revert to its earlier non-aligned status. Consequently, for the next 4 years, discussions of possible NATO membership for Ukraine disappeared from the international agenda, although by 2012–2013 there were signs that Russia was looking to expand its naval support facilities in the eastern Mediterranean to sustain a larger Russian Mediterranean Task Force (Nikolsky, 2014; Schwartz, 2014).

Against this background of a relative stabilisation of NATO–Russian relations, it was the efforts of the European Union (EU) to secure an Association Agreement with Ukraine in November 2013, which triggered the 'Euromaidan' demonstrations in Kiev. Spearheaded by far-right elements, the ousting of the elected government of Yanukovich in February 2014 was seen in Moscow as an 'extra-constitutional coup'. Fearing that the new authorities in Kyiv might seek to revoke the 2010 law specifying Ukraine's non-aligned status, apply for accelerated NATO membership and terminate the 2010 Sevastopol basing agreement, Moscow's decision to launch a special operation to secure Crimea represented the not unexpected determination of a Great Power to take swift pre-emptive action to deny potentially hostile military and naval forces the discretionary availability of the vital naval base of Sevastopol and the 189 other military bases on the peninsula (Sanders, 2014: 205; Berryman, 2015: 202; Marshall, 2015: 13–14).

Aware that the repercussions of this stunning fait accompli might be serious, as part of the special operation, K-300P *Bastion* mobile coastal defence anti-ship missiles were openly deployed on Crimean territory to demonstrate Russia's preparedness to protect the peninsula from military attack (*Russia Today*, 2015). The statement of Russia's Defence Minister, General Sergei Shoigu, that the Black Sea Fleet would receive more than US$2.3 billion in development funding underlined Moscow's determination to assert Russia's position in the Black Sea viz-à-viz its NATO neighbours of Turkey, Romania and Bulgaria (Daly, 2014; Sanders, 2014: 204–205; Schwartz, 2014; Marshall, 2015: 15). Apart from new ships, six new ultra-quiet diesel-electric *Kilo*-class submarines, fitted with *Kalibre* cruise missiles, would be deployed from improved facilities at Novorossisk (Bodner, 2014; Hoyle, 2015). In addition, the *Dnepr-M* missile attack early warning radar on Cape Khersones near Sevastopol would be upgraded or replaced with a new *Voronezh*-series radar. The Yevpatoria deep-space tracking and control station would be refurbished and reintegrated into the Russian space tracking network (Boltenkov and Shepovalenko, 2014; Bodner, 2015). Shoigu added that the modernised Black Sea Fleet would also be used to extend Russia's presence into 'long range sea zones', specifically the Eastern Mediterranean (*Moscow Times*, 2015c).

In his emotional address to Russia's Federal Assembly on 18 March 2014, seeking ratification of the treaty to admit Crimea and Sevastopol to the Russian Federation, President Putin underlined the special historical and symbolic significance of Crimea in the hearts and minds of the Russian people (Putin, 2014). In these changed geopolitical circumstances, how has Crimean tourism fared?

5.3   Crimean Tourism

From the time of Catherine the Great's spectacular tour of Crimea in 1787, the people of the Russian Empire were captivated by the climate and ravishing beauty of the peninsula. In the 19th century, Crimea became the summer retreat and 'luxurious playground' for the wealthy and the *literati* of tsarist imperial society, and the Crimean Riviera became the Russian equivalent of the *Cote d'Azur* (Sasse, 2007: 40–41) (Figs. 5.2 and 5.3). In Soviet times, although Sevastopol was off limits to foreign visitors, Crimea's coasts, beaches, palaces, sanatoria and private homes became an equally key destination for a more proletarian clientele, many coming from the heavy industrial cities of east Ukraine such as Donetsk, Zaporozhnye, and Kharkiv, and southern Russia. At its height, the more than 600 sanatoria and children's camps in Crimea attracted between 6 and 8 million annual visitors, and in the 1980s the Soviet Union sought to tap the hard currency European and international market with the construction of huge new Western-style hotels such as the Hotel Intourist Yalta, and the Cosmos in Moscow (Sasse, 2007: 166).

After the collapse of the Soviet Union, thanks to the deterioration of the Ukrainian economy, Crimea's development was starved of funds, and by 1994 the peninsula was attracting only 4 million visitors/year. However, Western cruise

Fig. 5.2. Livadia Palace – summer retreat of Tsar Nicholas II and site of the 1945 Yalta Conference. (From http://tirogek.taninhost.ir/crimea-yalta-conference.php.)

Fig. 5.3. Gurzuf beach and Bear Mountain. Chekhov's summer house is nearby. (From http://www. blacksea-crimea.com/WhereToStay/holapartments4.html#anchorGurzufapt.)

ships began paying visits to the Ukrainian ports of Odessa, Yalta and Sevastopol (which was now open to foreign visitors), and at their peak 130 cruise ship visits a year were being made, bringing with them more than 60,000 tourists (US–Ukraine Foundation, 2012; Hyde, 2014; Berman, 2015). Thanks in part to this international influx and an improvement in the Ukrainian and Russian economies, in 2012 Crimea received 6.13 million visitors and in 2013 5.9 million. Ukrainians made up approximately two-thirds of the tourists and Russians one-third (*Krimskii Konflikt*, 2014).

5.3.1 Tourism and annexation 2014

Following Russia's controversial annexation of Crimea in March 2014, Ukraine suspended all rail transportation and direct flights from Ukraine to Crimea. International flights to Crimea were suspended, leaving only Russian cities with direct connections to Simferopol's modern airport. With the exception of one visit to Yalta by a German vessel, all cruise ship visits to Crimea were terminated (*Moscow Times*, 2014). As a consequence of these measures, in 2014 the number of tourists visiting Crimea fell by a half, to 3 million. Seventy per cent of the visitors were now Russians, including some Russian refugees fleeing the insurgency in neighbouring south-east Ukraine; 28% were Ukrainians and 2% were from other countries. The availability of subsidised package tours and round-trip air tickets from Moscow and efforts by the Russian authorities to discourage officials in the security services from travelling abroad helped boost demand. However, given the absence of direct rail connections between Ukraine and Crimea and difficulties of road connections to Crimea through Ukraine, most of the Russians travelling to Crimea by road and rail used the Kerch ferry between Crimea and Russia. Having only limited capacity, the ferries struggled to cope with the vast increase in traffic (Yurchenko *et al.*, 2014).

Crimea's dependence on Ukraine for 80% of its water, 60–90% of its electricity and two-thirds of its natural gas unsurprisingly generated problems for the new authorities in Simferopol. In the past, Kyiv had exploited this dependence repeatedly to exert pressure for political compliance (Sasse, 2007: 167). In April 2014, Kyiv deliberately reduced the water supply to Crimea from the North Crimean Canal to a trickle, leading to widespread crop failures, while gas supplies were also disrupted. Moreover, in December 2014, Ukraine temporarily cut off electric power to Crimea in the midst of its own power shortages (*Moscow Times*, 2015b). In response, Moscow undertook to supply local power plants with additional generators, connect Crimea to the main Russian power grid and develop aquifers and a local desalination plant, and by the autumn of 2014 aquifers and pipelines were supplying fresh water to the North Crimean Canal and the largest cities in Crimea's eastern areas. In view of these hardships and difficulties, Crimea's Prime Minister, Sergei Aksyonov, conceded that the 2014 tourist season was a unique one, but expressed the hope that the following year Crimea would see 5 million visitors (Ash, 2014; Hanauer, 2014; IISS, 2014: viii; *Sputnik News*, 2015).

Recognising the need to modernise the legacy of the neglected and dilapidated infrastructure that Ukraine had bequeathed Crimea, Russia pledged to spend the huge sum of US$18 billion on development projects over the next 6 years. In March 2014, Russian Prime Minister, Dmitry Medvedev, announced the creation of a Russian Ministry for Crimean Affairs, and construction of a new road and rail bridge from mainland Russia to Crimea across the Kerch Straits was planned. However, the total projected cost of the bridge has grown seven-fold to 350 billion roubles (US$10.3 billion), and by the end of 2014 it was estimated that Russia's expenditure on Crimea was running at around US$4.5 billion/year, paying 75% of the Crimean government's budget, while subsidising pensions and other benefits for the 2.3 million local residents of Crimea (IISS, 2014: viii; Berman, 2015; Kenarov, 2015). Notwithstanding these transitional problems, including a local inflation rate of 42%, according to the Ukrainian division of the polling organisation, Growth from Knowledge (GfK), in association with the Kyiv-based Free Crimea Centre, after 1 year only 4% of Crimeans remained opposed to Russia's rule (*Moscow Times*, 2015a: Nechepurenko, 2015).

5.3.2   Resurgent tourism 2015

As a result of a sharp devaluation of the rouble in 2014 by almost 50%, triggered by a drop in world oil prices and the imposition of Western sanctions in retaliation for Russia's annexation of Crimea, the first quarter of 2015 saw a 31% and 38% reduction in the number of Russian visitors to Italy and Spain, respectively, as many Russians switched to cheaper destinations such as Turkey, Egypt, Greece, Cyprus and Montenegro (see Chapter 7, this volume) (Burgen *et al.*, 2015). However, thanks to renewed recommendations to Russian state employees in the security services not to travel abroad, many Russians chose domestic destinations for their vacations (*Moscow Times*, 2015e). Since childhood and family memories of Crimea are strong, many Russians chose to renew their acquaintance with the peninsula. Beautifully illustrated publications have helped to remind them of the attractions of Crimea and the special place it occupies in the historical imagery and identity of the Russian people (Sidyakin, 2015).

According to *Rosaviatsia* (Russia's Federal Air Transportation Agency), the tourist season for 2015 therefore opened with a 340% increase in visitors to Crimea in the first 4 months of the year, as compared to the same period in 2014. Almost 696,000 passengers flowed through Simferopol airport between January and April 2015, compared to just under 205,000 in 2014, and air arrivals in Crimea for Russia's Labour Day Holiday (1–4 May) 2015 numbered 44,233 passengers, compared to 16,511 in 2014 (*Moscow Times*, 2015d). Over the summer season, flights from Russian cities left for Crimea at frequent intervals throughout the day and night, and by the end of 2015 Crimea had received 4.6 million visitors (*Moscow Times*, 2016).[2]

5.4   Conclusion

Given the manner in which the hasty reunification of Crimea with Russia was effected, it is clear that,

> *De facto* under Russia's control, *de jure* Ukraine's territories, Crimea is deemed to become a long term obstacle to the normalization of Ukraine–Russian relations.
>
> (Shapovalova, 2015: 265)

In September 2015, an unofficial blockade of trucks delivering Ukrainian goods to Crimea was mounted by ultra-nationalist members of the Right Sector and Azov militia groups and disgruntled Crimean Tatars, critical of (Ukraine's) President Poroshenko for having failed to present a plan to return Crimea to Ukraine. Bowing to the pressures, Kyiv announced an official blockade. However, on 20 November (the second anniversary of the initiation of the Maidan demonstrations in Kyiv), these same groups blew up two electricity pylons carrying power from Ukraine to Crimea, and 2 days later blew up two more. For a time, attempts to repair the lines were blocked by these militants, and a state of emergency was declared in the peninsula. Additional generators were hastily supplied to Crimea from Tatarstan, and aware of the interconnections between the electricity grids of Ukraine and Russia, and Ukraine's dependence on Russian electricity supplies as well as on coal supplies from Russia and Donbas, the crisis was handled in a restrained manner by both Moscow and Kyiv (Jarabik, 2015). After an 11-day blackout, on 2 December power was restored to Crimea when the first of two new Russian undersea cables was switched on by Putin at a ceremony in Simferopol. Two more cables will be provided, restoring more than 90% of the peninsula's power needs (*Moscow Times*, 2015f).

With respect to the future of tourism in Crimea, since the shock of the Islamic State of Iraq and Syria (ISIS) downing of a Russian airliner over the Sinai desert in October 2015 and the Turkish shoot-down of a Su-24 jet fighter on the Syrian–Turkish border in November 2015, the Crimean authorities are hopeful that, notwithstanding the recent power blackouts and likely price increases in Crimean vacations by 15–30% in 2016, a proportion of the more than 6 million Russian tourists who have previously visited Egypt and Turkey each year will flock to Crimea (*Moscow Times*, 2016).

However, without a better economic performance, Russia will be unable to maintain the pace of its military modernisation and have available the necessary funds for the development of Crimea's vital tourist industry. Since the summer of 2015, angry exchanges between Simferopol and Moscow concerning the adequacy and delivery of funding and accusations of corruption have been reported (Bennetts, 2015; Matlack, 2015). The period ahead promises stormy weather in the Black Sea region and rough sailing for the Russian ship of state (Motyl, 2016).

Endnotes

[1] Newspaper of Germany's National Socialist Workers' (Nazi) Party from 1920.
[2] In August 2015, the author took return night flights from St Petersburg to Simferopol on packed 450-seat Boeing 777s.

References

Acherson, N. (2015) *Black Sea: Coasts and Conquests: From Pericles to Putin*. Vintage Books, London.
Anderson, M.S. (1966) *The Eastern Question 1774–1923: A Study in International Relations*. Macmillan, London.
Anderson, M.S. (1995) *Peter the Great*, 2nd edn. Longman, London.
Ash, L. (2014) Tourism takes a nosedive in Crimea. *BBC News*, 8 August. Available at: http://www.bbc.co.uk/news/magazine-28688478 (accessed 21 July 2016).
Bartlett, C.J. (1996) *Peace, War and the European Powers, 1814–1914*. Macmillan, Basingstoke, UK.
Bennetts, M. (2015) Where is Russian cash, asks Crimea's leader. *The Times* [London] 21 December, p. 38.
Berman, I. (2015) Paradise lost in Crimea: how Russia is paying for the annexation. *Foreign Affairs*, 8 September. Available at https://www.foreignaffairs.com/articles/ukraine/2015-09-08/paradise-lost-crimea (accessed 21 July 2016).
Berryman, J. (1988) The Soviet Union and Yugoslavia's defence and foreign policy. In: Milivojevic, M., Allcock, J.B. and Maurer P. (eds) *Yugoslavia's Security Dilemmas: Armed Forces, National Defence and Foreign Policy*. Berg, Oxford, UK, pp. 192–212.

Berryman, J. (2009) Russia, NATO enlargement and the new lands in between. In: Kanet, R.E. (ed.) *A Resurgent Russia and the West: The European Union, NATO and Beyond*. The Republics of Letters, Dordrecht, the Netherlands, pp. 161–186.

Berryman, J. (2015) Russian grand strategy and the Ukraine crisis: an historical cut. In: Sussex, M. and Kanet, R.E. (eds) *Power, Politics and Confrontation in Eurasia: Foreign Policy in a Contested Area*. Palgrave Macmillan, Basingstoke, UK, pp. 186–209.

Bodner, M. (2014) Russia sending new Stealth submarines to Crimea. *Moscow Times*, 17 September.

Bodner, M. (2015) Crimea annexation boosts Russia's deep space capabilities. *Moscow Times*, 5 March.

Boltenkov, D. and Shepovalenko, M. (2014) Russian defense arrangements in Crimea. *Moscow Defense Brief* May. Available at: http://mdb.cast.ru/mdb/5-2014/item4/article1/?form==print (accessed 21 July 2016).

Burgen, S., Kirchgaessner, S. and Luhn, A. (2015) Med's Russian lament: we wish you were here. *The Guardian*, 5 September, p. 25.

Clarke, Sir G.S. (1898) *Russia's Sea Power: Past and Present or The Rise of the Russian Navy*. John Murray, London.

Coutau-Begarie, H. (1989) The Soviet naval presence in the Mediterranean. In: Clark, S.L. (ed.) *Gorbachev's Agenda: Changes in Soviet Domestic and Foreign Policy*. Westview, Boulder, Colorado, pp. 271–286.

Dallin, A. (1957) *German Rule in Russia 1941–1945: A Study of Occupation Policies*. Macmillan, London.

Daly, J.C.K. (1991) *Russian Sea Power and 'The Eastern Question', 1827–41*. Macmillan, London.

Daly, J.C.K. (2014) Hot issue: after Crimea: the future of the Black Sea Fleet. *The Jamestown Foundation*, 22 May. Available at: http://www.jamestown.org/programs/hotissues/single-hot-issues/?tx_ttnews%5Btt_news%5D=42411&tx_ttnews%5BbackPid%5DBbackPid%5D=61&cHash=18fb1cd8a0f3 (accessed 21 July 2016).

Fuller, W.C. (1992) *Strategy and Power in Russia 1600–1914*. The Free Press, New York.

Global Security (2015a) *Montreux Convention 1936*. Available at: http://www.globalsecurity.org/military/world/naval-arms-control-1936.htm (accessed 21 July 2016).

Global Security (2015b) *Russian Naval Base at Tartus*. Available at: http://www.globalsecurity.org/military/world/syria/tartous.htm (accessed 21 July 2016).

Gorenburg, D. (2010) The future of the Sevastopol Russian naval base. *Russian Military Reform*, 22 March. Available at: http://russiamil.wordpress.com/2010/03/22/the-future-of-the-sevastopol-russian-navy-base?/?relat (accessed 21 July 2016).

Gorshkov, S.G. (1979) *The Sea Power of the State*. Pergamon Press, Oxford, UK.

Gough, B. (2014) *Pax Britannica: Ruling the Waves and Keeping the Peace before Armageddon*. Palgrave Macmillan, Basingstoke, UK.

Halpern, P.G. (1987) *The Naval War in the Mediterranean 1914–1918*. Allen & Unwin, London.

Halpern, P.G. (1994) *A Naval History of World War I*. UCL Press, London.

Hanauer, L. (2014) Crimea adventure will cost Russia dearly. *The Moscow Times*, 7 September.

Hill, F. and Gaddy, C. (2015) *Mr. Putin: Operative in the Kremlin*. Brookings Institute Press, Washington, DC.

Hoyle, F. (2015) Russia flexes muscles with new base in Black Sea. *The Times*, 24 September. Available at: http://www.thetimes.co.uk/tto/news/world/europe/article4215982.ece (accessed 21 July 2016).

Hyde, L. (2014) Crimean summer tourism disaster. *Kyiv Post*, 12 June. Available at: http://www.kyivpost.com/article/content/business/crimean-summer-tourism-distaster-3 (accessed 10 December 2015).

IISS (2014) *Strategic Survey 2014. The Annual Review of World Affairs*. The International Institute for Strategic Studies, London.

Jarabik, B. (2015) The Crimea blackout: electrifying Maidan. *Carnegie Moscow Center: Eurasia Outlook*, 25 November. Available at: http://carnegie.ru/commentary/?fa=62090&mkt_tok=3RkMMJWWfF9wsRouua7NZ (accessed 3 August 2016).

Kagan, F.W. (2002) Russia's geopolitical dilemma and the question of backwardness. In: Kagan, F.W. and Higham, R. (eds) *The Military History of Tsarist Russia*. Palgrave Macmillan, Basingstoke, UK, pp. 249–257.

Kenarov, D. (2015) Putin's peninsula is a lonely island. *Foreign Policy*, 6 February. Available at: http://foreign-policy.com/2015/02/06/putin-peninsula-lonely-island-crimea-annexation-russia-ukraine/?wp_login_redirect=0 (accessed 21 July 2016).

Kershaw, I. (2000) *Hitler 1936–45: Nemesis*. Allen Lane, The Penguin Press, London.

King, C. (2005) *The Black Sea: A History*. Oxford University Press, Oxford, UK.

Kipp, J.W. (1972) Consequences of defeat: modernizing the Russian navy, 1856–1863. *Jahrbücher für Geschichte Osteuropas* 20(2), 210–225.

Kipp, J.W. (1983) Tsarist politics and the naval ministry 1876–81: balanced fleet or cruiser navy. *Canadian-American Slavic Studies* 17(2), 151–179.

Kipp, J.W. (2002) The Imperial Russian Navy, 1696–1900: the ambiguous legacy of Peter's 'second arm'. In: Kagan, F.W. and Higham, R. (eds) *The Military History of Tsarist Russia.* Palgrave Macmillan, Basingstoke, UK, pp. 151–182.

Kitchen, M. (1976) *The Silent Dictatorship: The Politics of the German High Command under Hindenberg and Ludendorff, 1916–1918.* Croom Helm, London.

Krimskii Konflikt (News/Crimea/HTML) (2014) V 2014 godu kolichestvo turistov v Krymu umen'shilos v dva raza – do 3 mln. [In 2014 the number of tourists in Crimea reduced by twice – to 3 million.] 3 October (in Russian). Available at: http://gordonua.com/news/crimea/V-2014-godu-kolichestvo-turisto-v-Krymu-umenshilos-v-dva-raza-do-3-min-44376.html (accessed 21 July 2016).

Lieven, A. (1999) *Ukraine and Russia: A Fraternal Rivalry.* United States Institute of Peace Press, Washington, DC.

MccGwire, M. (1973) The Mediterranean and Soviet naval interests. In: MccGwire, M. (ed.) *Soviet Naval Developments: Capability and Context. (Papers Relating to Russia's Maritime Interests).* Praeger, New York, Chapter 25.

MccGwire, M. (1981) The rationale for the development of Soviet seapower. In: Baylis, J. and Segal, G. (eds) *Soviet Strategy.* Croom Helm, London, pp. 210–254.

McMeekin, S. (2011) *The Russian Origins of the First World War.* Belknap Press/Harvard University Press, Cambridge, Massachusetts.

Maiorano, A.G. (1985) Black Sea prophecy. *Proceedings of the US Naval Institute* III(1), 56–64.

Marder, A.J. (1940) *The Anatomy of British Sea Power. A History of British Naval Policy in the Pre-Dreadnought Era, 1880–1905.* Alfred A. Knopf, New York.

Marshall, T. (2015) *Prisoners of Geography. Ten Maps That Tell You Everything You Need To Know About Global Politics.* Elliott and Thompson, London.

Matlack, C. (2015) Crimea is now Putin's child: Russian security services are cracking down on alleged corruption in the newly annexed peninsula. *Bloomberg Business*, 24 July. Available at: http://www.bloomberg.com/news/articles/2015-07-24/crimea-is-now-putin-s-problem-child (accessed 3 August 2016).

Mitchell, D.W. (1974) *A History of Russian and Soviet Sea Power.* Andre Deutsch, London.

Moscow Times (2014) German cruise liner docks in Crimea despite Ukraine's opposition. *The Moscow Times*, 22 September.

Moscow Times (2015a) Inflation in Russia-annexed Crimea hits 42.5 percent in 2014. *The Moscow Times*, 15 January.

Moscow Times (2015b) Cash-strapped Russia to delay building highways in Crimea. *The Moscow Times*, 16 March.

Moscow Times (2015c) Russia says Crimean military buildup completed. *The Moscow Times*, 30 March.

Moscow Times (2015d) Simferopol airport sees passenger boom as Russians flock to Crimea. *The Moscow Times*, 6 May.

Moscow Times (2015e) Economic crisis forces Russians to spend vacations inside the country. *The Moscow Times*, 27 August.

Moscow Times (2105f) Russia restores Crimea power supplies. *The Moscow Times,* 3 December.

Moscow Times (2016) Crimea vacations will cost 30% more in 2016. *The Moscow Times*, 19 January.

Motyl, A. (2016) Lights out for the Putin regime: the coming Russian collapse. *Foreign Affairs*, 27 January. Available at: https://www.foreignaffairs.com/articles/russian-federation/2016-01-27/lights-out-putin-regime (accessed 3 August 2016).

Nechepurenko, I. (2015) One year after the annexation, Crimea still bracing for a brighter future. *The Moscow Times*, 5 March.

Nikolsky, A. (2014) Russian naval presence in the Eastern Mediterranean and the problems of projected naval basing. *Moscow Defense Brief*, February. Available at: http://mdb.cast.ru/mdb/2-2014/item1/article2/?form=print (accessed 21 July 2016).

Plokhy, S. (2000) The City of Glory: Sevastopol in Russian historical mythology. *Journal of Contemporary History* 35(3), 369–383.

Polmar, N. (1991) *The Naval Institute Guide to the Soviet Navy,* 5th edn. United States Naval Institute Press, Annapolis, Maryland.

Putin, V. (2014) Address by President of the Russian Federation 18 March. Available at: http://en.kremlin.ru/events/president/news/20603 (accessed 3 August 2016).

Reynolds, M.A. (2011) *Shattering Empires: the Clash and Collapse of the Ottoman and Russian Empires, 1908–1918.* Cambridge University Press, Cambridge, UK.

Rogan, E. (2015) *The Fall of the Ottomans: the Great War in the Middle East, 1914–1920*. Allen Lane, London.

Rohwer, J. and Monakov, M.S. (2001) *Stalin's Ocean-Going Fleet: Soviet Naval Strategy and Shipbuilding Programmes, 1935–1953*. Frank Cass, London.

Russia Today (2015) Putin in film on Crimea: US masterminds behind Ukraine coup helped train radicals. *Russia Today*, 15 March. Available at: http://rt.com/news/240921-us-masterminds-ukraine-putin/ (accessed 21 July 2016).

Sanders, D. (2001) *Security Co-operation between Russia and Ukraine in the Post-Soviet Era*. Palgrave Macmillan, Basingstoke, UK.

Sanders, D. (2014) *Maritime Power in the Black Sea*. Ashgate, Farnham, UK.

Sasse, G. (2007) *The Crimea Question: Identity, Transition, and Conflict*. Harvard University Press, Cambridge, Massachusetts.

Schwartz, P.N. (2014) Crimea's Strategic Value to Russia. *Centre for Strategic and International Studies*, 18 March. Available at: http://csis.org/print/48939 (accessed 14 November 2015).

Shapovalova, N. (2015) The role of Crimea in Ukraine–Russia relations. In: Bachmann, K. and Lyubashenko, I. (eds) *The Maidan Uprising, Separatism and Foreign Intervention: Ukraine's Complex Transition*. PIE-Peter Lang, Frankfurt, Germany, pp. 227–265.

Sidyakin, A.G. (2015) *Zolotaya ceredina Zemly: Krim.* [*Golden Centre of the World: Crimea.*] N. Orianda, Moscow (in Russian).

Sondhaus, L. (2001) *Naval Warfare 1815–1914*. Routledge, London.

Sondhaus, L. (2014) *The Great War at Sea: A Naval History of the First World War*. Cambridge University Press, Cambridge, UK.

Sputnik News (2015) New pipelines start supplying fresh water to Crimea. *Sputnik News*, 4 April. Available at: http://sputniknews.com/russia/20150404/1020474871.html (accessed 3 August 2016).

Trenin, D. (2008) Russia's perspective on the wider Black Sea region. In: Hamilton, D. and Mangott, G. (eds) *The Wider Black Sea Region in the 21st Century: Strategic, Economic and Energy Perspectives*. Centre for Transatlantic Relations, Washington, DC, pp. 103–117.

Tsygankov, A.P. (2012) *Russia and the West from Alexander to Putin: Honour in International Relations*. Cambridge University Press, Cambridge, UK.

US–Ukraine Foundation (2012) Crimea: Types of Tourism. Available at: http://www.traveltoukraine.org/crimea/types-of-tourism.php (accessed 21 July 2016).

Westwood, J.N. (1970) *Witnessses of Tsushima*. Sophia University, Tokyo.

Yurchenko, S., Dzhabbarov, U. and Bigg, C. (2014) Tourist season a washout in annexed Crimea. *Radio Free Europe/Radio Liberty*, 5 July. Available at: http://www.rferl.org/articleprintview/25446604.html (accessed 3 August 2016).

6 The Geopolitical Trial of Tourism in Modern Ukraine

Pavlo Doan* and Viktoriia Kiptenko
Taras Shevchenko National University, Kyiv, Ukraine

6.1 Introduction

Ukraine's geopolitical situation strongly determines the tourism role that this country can play since gaining independence in 1991, as tourism operates within the evolving international political and economic environment (Hall, 2008; Webster and Ivanov, 2014). The post-communist transformation of Ukraine has been acknowledged as being more complicated than its neighbours (Mach, 1998; Kuczabski and Michalski, 2014). How have the geopolitical challenges of the post-communist, post-independence transformation influenced tourism trends in the country?

In striving to answer this question, this chapter argues that contested fluctuations in Ukraine's geopolitical trajectory coupled to processes of decolonisation, denationalisation and decentralisation of governance have particularly affected the critical path of tourism development. Within this context, we examine the macro-parameters of tourism development and conduct an empirical enquiry into the current state of tourism in Ukraine.

Our analysis follows the chronology of official pronouncements and acts and evaluates their impact on tourism development processes, balanced with a consideration of the limitations imposed on the domestic environment.

The Cabinet of Ministers only established the rules on reporting travel statistics in 1995. The methodological approaches to tourism statistics have changed several times following the institutional transformations after 1991, but remain different to international practice, even after modifications to the reporting of border crossing statistics in 2006. These limitations complicate longitudinal analyses. Under these circumstances, we base our evaluations on: (i) reliable, in our opinion, assumptions of Ukrainian experts concerning official data before 2000 (notably Babarytska, 1997; Fedorchenko and D'orová, 2002; Grabovenska, 2013; Kyfiak, 2003; Lutak and Mikhalchuk, 2012); and (ii) consistent data produced by the Committee for Statistics of Ukraine (2015) since 2000. International sources, particularly those of the World Tourism and Travel Council (WTTC, 2015), ground our economic assessments.

Our study suggests that controversial geopolitical fluctuations have affected attempts to establish Ukraine's role in the international tourism arena negatively. It is our contention that the transformation of tourism governance and the evolution of its environment have mirrored the gradual decolonisation, denationalisation and decentralisation of governance within the country as a whole since 1991.

*Corresponding author. E-mail: doan.pavel@gmail.com

6.2 The Challenges of Geopolitical Choice: A Bed of Thorns

The very name of the country (which entered into use from the 12th century) suggests a duality, which is reflected in the perceptions of its international prospects both from outside and domestically. Recent linguistic claims (Pivtorak, 2001) on the etymology of the name *Ukraine* as 'homeland' or 'country, area' have failed to gain precedence over earlier interpretations of 'outskirts' or 'borderland'.

Ukraine's position in the state system of the Eurasian continent is often characterised as the 'geographic centre of Europe', or 'crossroads between West and East'. In addition, the river system and Black Sea access of the country sets it at a point of contact between north and south, from the Baltic to the Mediterranean.

This strategic situation, coupled with a valuable source of natural resources but with a lack of natural barriers, has seen Ukraine subjected to invasions, the territorial expansion of its neighbours and subsequent division. The country has experienced a succession of geopolitical orientations as a result of cultural impacts from ancient Greece, Byzantium and Normans, Western Europe and Moscow.

Dergachev (2006) points out the complex role of the geopolitical and social-cultural 'borderness' of the country. Despite its size and centrality, this marginality in relation to different 'civilizations' (Huntington, 1996) is reflected in the contrasting geopolitical orientations expressed within the western, central and south-eastern regions of Ukraine.

In addition, the post-communist transformation of Ukraine appears to be more complicated compared to its neighbours. Kuczabski and Michalski (2014) suggest that the country has endured three simultaneous processes of social transformation: decolonisation of governance, decentralisation of government and denationalisation of economy. Following Mach (1998), they argue that a non-linear process initially planned as 'transplantation' (essentially replacing communism with a market economy) turned to 'recombination' (with *nomenklatura* privatisation) and slipped to 'retrogression' (an establishment of the oligarchic model), which restrained real democratic and market transformation and stifled the country's revival.

Geographical and historical factors contextualise the diversity of geopolitical descriptions employed for Ukraine: Slavic-oriented, Black Sea–Balkans, Black–Baltic Seas, Black–Caspian Seas, Eastern or Western European (Dergachev, 2006; Mikhel', 2009; Usova, 2011; Koroma, 2013; Braychevskyy, 2014). Geopolitical and geoeconomic factors have strongly influenced the country's controversially meandering foreign policy path, with orientations towards Western Europe (European Union (EU) integration), Euro-Atlantics (EU and North Atlantic Treaty Organization (NATO) affiliation) and Russia-oriented policy (Commonwealth of Independent States (CIS) and Eurasian Economic Space (EES)), resulting in a compromise and attempted balance between the West and Russia.

6.2.1 The Declaration on the State Sovereignty of Ukraine (1990)

In 1990, the country stated its intention to establish a neutral state based on three nuclear-free principles: not to accept, not to manufacture and not to buy nuclear weapons. Further parliamentary Acts concerning state independence (*Decree*, 1991), nuclear-free status (*Statement*, 1991) and the referendum on independence (CSAHA, 1991) confirmed Ukraine's distinctive entry into international affairs.

6.2.2 The term of the first President of Ukraine, Leonid Kravchuk (1991–1994)

This period was characterised by the pursuit of a balance between seeking closer ties with Europe and continued cooperation with Russia. The parliamentary Act on domestic and foreign policy direction (*Decree*, 1993b) enshrined foreign policy cornerstones (Euro-Atlantic integration and good neighbour relations with Russia) and established the practice of balance between Europe and the USA and strong ties with Russia as a means of enhancing and sustaining long-term European security.

Thus, Ukraine joined the Euro-Atlantic Partnership Council (in 1992), signed the Agreement on partnership and cooperation between

Ukraine and the EU (in 1994, into force 1998) and joined the *Partnership for Peace* programme (in 1994).

At the same time, the need for continued dependence on eastern energy resources and markets for Ukrainian goods and services (tourism in particular) justified Ukraine's participation in the establishment of the CIS (former Soviet Union minus the Baltic States) in 1991 (*Agreement*, 1991), and saw the *Dagomys* treaty on the further development of relations between Ukraine and Russia in 1992 (*Agreement*, 1992).

Formally, the foreign policy course aimed towards EU and NATO membership would not be inaugurated until towards the end of the decade (see Table 6.1).

6.2.3 Leonid Kuchma's (1994–2005) term in office

The *Law on the Basis of the National Security of Ukraine* (2003) failed to clarify the country's geopolitical choice during this period.

In 2002, Ukraine received EU special neighbour status. In 2003, Kuchma formally inaugurated the European integration process and declared the aim of Ukraine was to sign a treaty on EU Association followed by adoption of the *Plan of Actions for Ukraine* by the European Commission (in 2004). And moves towards

NATO membership appeared to be taking shape up to 2004 (Table 6.1).

Along with permanent limitations in economic sovereignty, resource and other dependence on Russia, the latter's ambiguous claims for sovereignty over Crimea in 1994–1995 and conflict between Russia and Ukraine over the adjacent Tuzla island (2003) provided the context for the dramatic swings of foreign policy during this period. Treaties on the Black Sea Fleet (*Agreement*, 1997) and on Friendship between Russia and Ukraine (1997) contributed to a strategic partnership, and were coupled with Ukraine's adoption of an Agreement on the Eurasian Economic Space (2003). Further Russia-oriented endeavours of Premier Yanukovich's cabinet were seriously questioning the country's future, both domestically and on the international stage.

6.2.4 The Orange Revolution (November 2004–January 2005)

Protests against the falsification of presidential elections at the end of 2004 opened the most turbulent geopolitical period for Ukraine. It also acted to highlight the serious differences in outlook between the people of the western-central and eastern-southern regions of the country, the geopolitical consequences of which would be

Table 6.1. Steps on the path of reshaping Ukraine's non-aligned policy towards full membership of NATO. (From *Law*, 2003, 2004; *Decree*, 2004).

	Event	Year
1.	Adoption of Charter on special partnership	1997
2.	Establishment of the first NATO information and documentation centre in Eastern Europe	1997
3.	Programme of Ukraine–NATO cooperation	1998
4.	NATO mission in the country	1999
5.	The Declaration of the Council of National Security of Ukraine marked the course on reshaping the non-aligned policy towards full membership of NATO	2002
6.	Action Plan NATO–Ukraine	2002
7.	Ukraine–NATO Memorandum on support of NATO operations	2002
8.	Act of *Verkhovna Rada* (parliament) on free access of NATO forces to the territory of Ukraine	2004
	Ukraine's support to NATO actions in Balkans and Iraq	
	Kuchma's Act of the President stating that Ukraine needs 'significant deepening of relations with NATO and the EU as a guarantor of security and stability in Europe' rather than full membership (particularly of NATO)	July 2004

expressed a decade later to contextualise Russia's annexation of Crimea and its 'hybrid war' (Plokhy, 2015) in the Donbas region.

6.2.5 Viktor Yushchenko's presidency (2005–2010)

This period favoured European integration and the development of relations with NATO, and revived earlier goals in the military doctrine of Ukraine. From 2005 to mid-2006, Ukraine involved Western experts in developing the country's foreign policy, signed a 3-year Ukraine–EU plan (February 2005) and started a new phase of intensive dialogue with NATO (Vilnius meeting, April 2005). In 2005, the EU recognised the market economy status of Ukraine.

The first visit of a president of independent Ukraine to the USA (April 2005) boosted relations between the countries in trade, resource dialogue, military complex cooperation and political affairs (with regard to Georgia and Moldova, in particular). In February 2006, the USA granted Ukraine the status of a market economy state (which Russia and Kazakhstan had received in 2002) and eased mutual access to markets.

These developments were intertwined with a cooling of relations with post-Soviet countries, dissatisfaction with the role of the CIS and a questioning of the Russian Black Sea Fleet's future within the territory of Ukraine. Declarations of general support for the creation of a Eurasian Economic Space (EES) based on free-trade zone status without supranational bodies and a customs zone were combined with the endeavours of Ukraine to establish itself as a new regional leader. In practice, the Union of Democratic Choice (Baltic–Black–Caspian Seas region), initiated in December 2005, and GUAM (Georgia–Ukraine–Moldova), of February/March 2006, remained latent projects. None the less, they served to irritate the Kremlin and, coupled with a contested Russian gas price and conflicts in the Kerch area (Tuzla island), exacerbated differences between Russia and Ukraine.

Long-lasting parliamentary crises resulted in the Regions party gaining a majority and V. Yanukovich becoming prime minister (mid-2006 to 2007). During this and the Y. Tymoshenko cabinet period (2008–2009), a new 'strategic partnership' with Russia was forged

under political conditions put forward by Moscow (Sochi meeting, October 2006, and prolongation of the strategic treaty between the countries in 2008). It brought low gas prices and a rollback in relations with NATO and EU that was short-lived: 2008 saw the receipt of a NATO Action Plan letter and Ukraine's access to World Trade Organization membership; the EU's *Eastern Partnership for Ukraine* was declared the following year.

6.2.6 Viktor Yanukovich presidency (2010–2013)

The precarious balancing approach to foreign policy was now to collapse.

The *Law* (2010) *on the Foundations of Domestic and Foreign Policy* formalised the course to pursue European integration in parallel with pragmatic and friendly cooperation with Russia. The latter was marked by the broad framework of the Kharkov Agreement[1] and pressure to join the EES and the Eurasian Economic Union (EAEU, 2015). 'National pragmatism' in relations with NATO saw the termination of the Commission and National Centre on Preparations for the Euro-Atlantic Integration of Ukraine. However, the subsequent National Programme of Ukraine–NATO Cooperation for 2011 questioned Ukraine's 'non-aligned' status.

Several steps towards the EU were also under way: a protocol towards agreement on partnership and cooperation (November 2010), full membership of Ukraine in the European Energy Community (February 2011) and an initialled agreement on Association (March 2012). But these were brought to a halt when, on 21 November 2013, the Cabinet of Ministers suspended preparations for the Association Agreement (*Decree*, 2013).

6.2.7 Euromaidan protests (November 2013–February 2014)

The ousting of Yanukovich reopened the way for the EU Association Agreement (*Agreement*, 2014). Parliament abolished Ukraine's non-aligned status on 23 December 2014. Russia's unilateral annexation of Crimea and intervention in eastern

Ukraine finally clarified Russia's status as an enemy within the new military doctrine (*Decree*, 2015). By contrast, Ukraine was now pursuing full EU and NATO membership.

Thus, at the time this chapter was being written, Ukraine's geopolitical path had brought the country through thorns of establishment (1991–2004), years of turbulence (2005 to mid-2006/2008/2010–2013) to a firmly pro-Western orientation.

Initial signs of 'transplantation' (Mach, 1998; Kuczabski and Michalski, 2014) for the country's post-communist transformation had developed features of 'recombination' by 2005–2006. The controversial fluctuations of mid-2006 to 2013 raised hopes for a clear and distinct role for the country in the international arena, but then brought 'retrogression'. Now, the goal of a European future is raising major challenges for Ukraine as a state.

6.3 Tourism Resources

Ukraine possesses favourable resources for tourism (Lyubitsewa *et al.*, 2012). There is diversity and density of the natural and cultural base (Babarytska, 1997), with patterns of regional differentiation and specialisation (Doan, 2015), as exhibited in Fig. 6.1.

The comfortable period for summer travelling lasts from the end of spring to mid-autumn, varying from 105 days/year in the northern part of the country to 180 at the coastal areas of the Black and Azov seas. Unfortunately, the formerly prosperous coastal destinations of Crimea are currently suffering the consequences of Russian annexation.

Mountainous areas of the Carpathians, the north-west and south-west highlands, generate all-year activities, notably skiing, hiking, bicycling and kayaking. Bukovel resort is perhaps the best-known winter destination.

Mainly flat, lowland landscapes (75% of the country's surface), dense river systems and sparsely populated woodland areas (in the north) offer much potential for rural tourism. Biosphere reserves (Askania-Nova, Carpathian, Chornomorskyi and Dunayskyi), nature-protected reserves (e.g. Roztochchia, Medobory, Kaniv, Crimean Mountain and Forest, Kara-Dag and Martian

Cape), natural parks (over 40) and wildlife preserves (37% of the total area of protected territories of the country) offer prospects of green tourism and ecotourism. Notably, the Primeval Beech Forests of the Carpathians were listed as a UNESCO World Heritage Site in 2007 (UNESCO, 2015).

A wide range of rich mineral water springs have provided the basis for 46 international spa resorts, mostly situated in the L'viv, Khmelnitsky, Transcarpathian, Ternopil and Poltava regions. Noteworthy are the mud deposits of the lakes and salt lakes of the Crimea, Odessa, Kherson and Zaporizhzhiya regions. However, only one-third of the land area of Ukraine can be regarded as having a favourable ecological situation, although some areas of ecological disaster, notably Chornobyl (*Chernobyl'*), attract ('dark') tourists from around the world.

Ukraine possesses a rich cultural heritage (Lyubitsewa *et al.*, 2012). Attractions in the central and eastern parts of the country reflect the evolution and development of Ukrainian history and culture: Kiev (Kyiv) Rus, Kozaks [Cossacks]. Southern areas of the country contain numerous ancient monuments (e.g. Chersonese, Olvia, Kam'yani Mogyly). Folk culture and architecture are particularly rich in the west of the country. All of the country's UNESCO World Heritage Sites are shown on Fig. 6.1. A further 16 'candidate' attractions, together with those of the national project *7 Wonders of Ukraine*, form Ukraine's 'must-see' destinations (Seven Wonders of Ukraine, 2015; UNESCO, 2015). The nature of post-independence transformations in tourism governance now determines the potential of these valuable assets for tourism purposes.

6.4 '3D' Transformation of Tourism Governance and Business in Ukraine: Decolonisation, Denationalisation and Decentralisation

In the early 1990s, the newly independent country moved slowly and borrowed Soviet-era legislation during those first years of its development. Initially, the authorities responsible for tourism regulation and development in Ukraine differed little from former bodies.

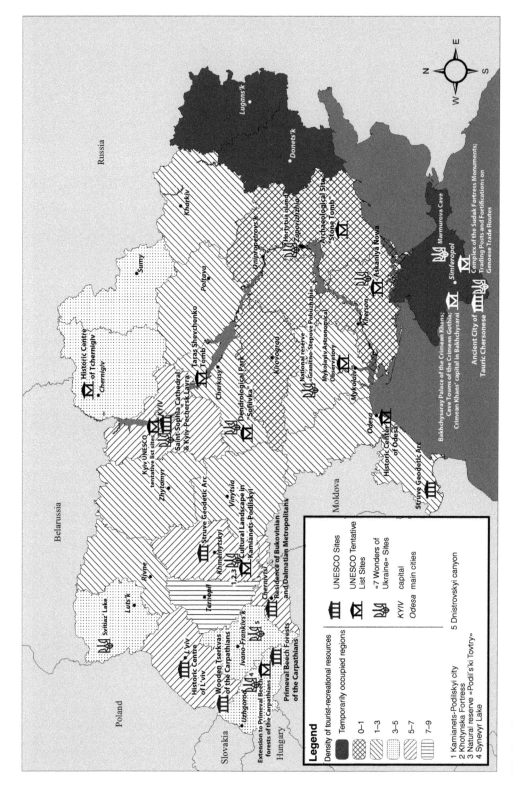

Fig. 6.1. Ukraine: location map of tourism resources. (From authors' compilation from Babarytska, 1997; Seven Wonders of Ukraine, 2015; UNESCO, 2015.)

The process of decolonisation, denationalisation and decentralisation as central elements of post-communist transformation were articulated in tourism in a number of ways: the establishment of governance institutions, the development of general and specific legislative regulation and gradual market reform of the business environment. The tourism focus evolved from inbound tourism and hospitality based on former Soviet norms to an internationalisation of activities, a transformation of the national health resort sector and a 'recombination' of institutions (1998, 2000, 2001), licensing and taxation rules by 2005. Elaboration of a wide-ranging tourism policy and promotion of the country's image abroad, aimed at European integration in 2005–2007, gradually gave way to attention being paid to infrastructure, business practice and, from 2011, taxation issues.

It is to be hoped that further moves will direct tourism along the path of sustainable development. Several national eco-labelling schemes have been introduced for hotels and other accommodation enterprises (Kiptenko and Doan, 2015). A legislative momentum has survived the serpentine path of tourism governance outlined in Table 6.2. Thus, the 1991 law *On environmental protection*, that of 1999 *On the ratification of the convention on access to information, public participation in decision making and access to justice in environmental matters*, the wide-ranging *On standardisation* (2001) and the 2010 legislation *On basic principles of the State environmental policy of Ukraine until 2020* have established a platform from which tourism sustainability policy and practice can develop and be enhanced.

6.5 Tourism Development in the Crucible of Geopolitical Trials

Patterns of travel have mirrored the country's geopolitical fluctuations (Fig. 6.2). During the period of establishing Ukraine's role in the international arena (1992–2004), the average ratio of outbound to inbound travellers was around 1.5:1, reaching a maximum of 2.1:1 in 2000. A drastic increase in inbound tourism overtook outbound travel during 2004–2008, reflecting new political-administrative measures.

For example, a 22% increase in inbound flows in 2007 largely reflected a simplification of the visa regime for 36 countries, including the EU, in 2006 (Lutak and Mikhalchuk, 2012; Grabovenska, 2013; Committee for Statistics of Ukraine, 2015).

After 2008, inbound travel slowly declined. The country's precarious geopolitical balancing act during 2010–2013 witnessed a 50% decrease in inbound and a 6% fall in outbound flows by 2014. Domestic travel slowly recovered from the declines of 1997–1998 and 2009, and had reached 1995 levels by 2011.

Investment levels crashed during the crisis of 1997–1998 and remained low, reflecting a further turn from 'recombination' (2005 to mid-2006) to 'retrogression' (mid-2006 and 2013) in state policy (Fig. 6.3). Nevertheless, in terms of tourism and travel's direct contribution to gross domestic product (GDP) and employment, from 2000 Ukraine exceeded the CIS and Russia by almost half until 2013, after which geopolitical tensions resulted in Russia's annexation of the Crimea (see Chapter 5, this volume) and the 'hybrid war' in eastern Ukraine (Plokhy, 2015). An inevitable decline in the role of tourism and travel in the national economy quickly followed (WTTC, 2015).

The uncertain pattern of outbound expenditures in Fig. 6.3 reflects well the geopolitical turbulence of 2005–2010, while earlier low levels rendered Ukraine particularly distinctive.

Tentative moves towards EU and NATO, paralleled with conciliation towards Russia during 2003–2004, could explain the growth in the share of visitor expenditure (2003–2007), while 'geopolitical controversies' influenced the fall of 2007–2011, and again from 2013.

An uncertain environment was significant for business tourism, which consistently represented 80–90% of inbound travel and 80–85% of outbound movement.

The acute geopolitical fluctuations between European and Eurasian leanings during 2005–2014 influenced regional patterns of travel flows both in and out of Ukraine. Figure 6.4 highlights the role of the 2008 financial crisis. Inbound flows from the CIS prevailed over the EU share and actually increased from 2008, until finally declining in 2013–2014 almost back to the 2008 level.

Table 6.2. Key elements in the transformation of tourism governance in Ukraine. (From *Decree*, 1992, 1993a, 2001, 2005, 2011a,b, 2014; Kyfiak, 2003; Kiptenko and Malynovska, 2009; Grabovenska, 2013; Uriadovyi Portal, 2015; WTM, 2015.)

Year	Action	Outcome
1992	Introduction of visa regulations	
1992	Establishment of the State Committee on Tourism	Set the decolonised platform for travel and tourism development. It functioned without regulations for almost a year.
1993	Cabinet of Ministers adopted Decree No 625 *On approval of the provisions about the State Committee of Tourism*	Determined the sphere of competence for state tourism policy and sector development: to promote inbound tourism and hospitality, improvement of infrastructure, training of qualified personnel, participation in international fairs and exhibitions, attraction of foreign investment and cooperation with international organisations.
1994	Law *On legal status of foreigners*	
1995	Law *On tourism*	Defined the legislative, organisational and socio-economic foundations of the state tourism policy, its goals and priorities. It aimed to safeguard constitutional rights (of recreation, freedom of movement, health care, safe environment and satisfaction of spiritual needs during tourist trips); and recognised the economic priority of the branch, declaring the need for the licensing of tour operators and travel agents. Provisions regarding types of tourism and their requirements, the concept of 'tourist recreational resources' and their sustainable use finally swept away Soviet practice.
1995	Law *On taxation of enterprises' income*	Marked the replacement of former centralised economic order by market-related steps in the taxation of enterprises and established appropriate tax rates. However, this law lacked regulations for tour operators and travel agents.
1996	Order of the State Committee of Tourism *On rules of usage and provision of hotel services*	Improved customer rights protection and encouraged further market transformation.
1997	Further Law *On added value tax*	Addressed tourism-related issues: the majority of tourism small and medium-size enterprises (SMEs) suffered heavily from a tax burden.
1998	Decree No 1400/98 *About the State Committee of Tourism* raised the responsibility of the State Committee to overall development of tourism and expanded the list of objectives of the body, including budgetary authority	Along with the promotion of national leisure and free-time usage by Ukrainians, their familiarisation with national heritage, this document pointed to the need for the sustainable use and preservation of tourism recreational resources. It enhanced the international role of the Committee – development of international tourism, expansion of cooperation with other countries and international tourism organisations, active participation in international projects – in line with the country's geopolitical trajectory. Market-oriented responsibilities included licensing tourism businesses, keeping appropriate registers, creating and supporting fair competition and coordinating tourism statistics.

Continued

Table 6.2. Continued.

Year	Action	Outcome
1998	Presidential Decree *On simple taxation system of subjects of small entrepreneurship*	Relief for business activities of travel agencies. SMEs could be registered as simple taxpayers and pay an annual fixed proportion of turnover or a monthly sum related to the national minimum wage.
1999	Membership of the United Nations World Tourism Organization (UNWTO)	
1999	Introduction of obligatory certification of hotel and restaurant services	Established international standard criteria: more competitive than Soviet-style services.
2000	State Committee for Youth Policy, Sports and Tourism assumed responsibility for the regulation of tourism	While the previous body lasted two years, this Committee existed for just one.
2000	Law *On licensing of certain types of economic activity*	Governance 'recombination' did not prevent further strengthening and tightening of legislation on tour operators' and travel agents' activities.
2001/2	Presidential Decree *On Reorganisation of the State Committee of Youth Policy of Ukraine*	Established the State Tourism Administration to replace the previous body.
2002	Provision No 331/2002: State Tourism Administration gained new responsibilities	Increased authority over: transformation of national health resort industry into a competitive and profitable sector; analysis and prognostication of tourism development; study of labour market; and training provision.
2002/3	Tourism policy *Development programme 2002–2010* included the creation and promotion of the positive image of the country abroad	*The state programme for the provision of a positive image of Ukraine for 2003–2006* initiated the process, but it lacked consistency. Less than half of planned tasks were completed because of inappropriate financing and lack of clear direction. Further image-building efforts were included in the state programme *On scientific-technological foundations of creation of software products of Ukraine for 2007–2010*, and in the programmes: for arts and culture support until 2012; for UEFA EURO-2012 Ukraine–Poland preparation; and *Investment image of Ukraine*.
2005	Introduction of visa-free entry to Ukraine by EU citizens (from 1 May)	
2005	Presidential Decree: *About the Ministry of Culture and Tourism* marks a 'recombination' in tourism governance with the creation of a Ministry for Culture and Tourism	The range of responsibilities widened: elaboration and implementation of state tourism, cultural and language policy, including determination of sectoral trends and prospects; approval of professional education content; coordination of tourism market activities; and attraction of inward investment. The State Office of Tourism and Resorts within the Ministry gained authority over European integration objectives within tourism and recreation.
2006	Introduction of visa-free entry extended to a total of 36 countries	

Continued

Table 6.2. Continued.

Year	Action	Outcome
2007	The *Licence requirements for tour operators' and travel agents' activity* imposed the obligation of bank guarantees, qualified staff and appropriate office practice and space	Provision for service quality improvements required a specialised element of tourism higher education (50% for tour operators, 30% for travel agents), or 3 years of experience. Business practice standards concerned norms of contracting and accountancy, dealing with documentation and statistical data, obligatory clients' insurance. Thus, in just over a decade (1996–2007) the regulation and quality of Ukrainian tourism services and business standards had been substantially strengthened.
2010	Presidential Decree: *On optimisation of central authority system* abolished the Ministry for Culture and Tourism	State tourism policy came under the authority of the Ministry for Infrastructure. This addressed the problem of poor tourism facilities, but diminished the role of the tourism sector in the national economy.
2010	Revocation of travel agents' licensing	Every SME now had the possibility to act as a travel agent regardless of its main activity. A rapid growth of tourism supply followed: 30% annual travel agency growth 2010–2012, with tour operators increasing 10–15% per year. A drop in demand and decrease in quality characterised strong market competition. Discounting instead of professional servicing became a key instrument of competition.
2011	Presidential Decree established the State Agency of Tourism and Resorts within the Ministry of Infrastructure	Gained authority over promotional material distribution, implementation of anti-corruption policy and budget efficiency.
2011	A New Tax Code of Ukraine	For tourism businesses, this left a number of issues unresolved. Imperfections over tour operators' VAT rebates remained, although the new Code retained a simple taxation system not unfavourable to travel agents.
2014	The Ministry of Economic Development and Trade gained tourism administration	This followed the critical political events of 2013–2014, but lasted little more than 6 months (September 2014–April 2015).
2015	The State Agency of Tourism and Resorts stopped accepting documents for tour operators' licences	Yet the Law *On licensing of certain types of economic activity* seemed to override this, representing a positive turn from 'retrogression'.
2015	A new Department of Tourism Development within the Ministry	First selection competition for officials appointed two ministerial advisors. The first Ukrainian delegation to represent the country at the London *World Travel Market*.

In 2012, the share of travellers to the EU exceeded the traditionally strong outbound flow to the CIS. In 2007–2008, inbound flows from the EU briefly surpassed the share of Russia. But in 2009, the situation reversed in favour of Russia until 2013, when, marked by a drastic geopolitical shift, the situation inverted again.

6.6   Case Study

The current situation (as at 2015/16) in Ukraine is the most serious trial during its independent history. The status of annexed Crimea and hostilities in eastern Ukraine have tested the power and authority of the state. These geopolitical

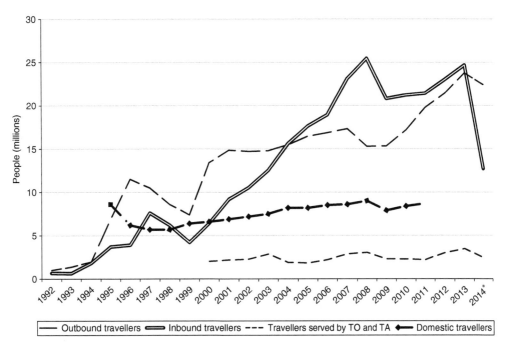

Fig. 6.2. Tourist flows of Ukraine, 1992–2014. (From Babarytska, 1997; Fedorchenko and D'orová, 2002; Kyfiak, 2003; Lutak and Mikhalchuk, 2012; Grabovenska, 2013; Committee for Statistics of Ukraine, 2015.) *Note:* TO = tour operator; TA = travel agent; 2014* = limited data due to occupation of part of Ukraine's territory.

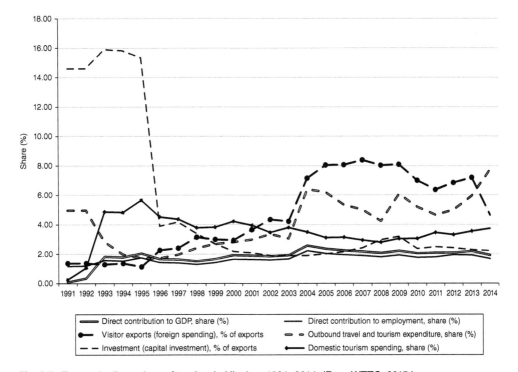

Fig. 6.3. Economic dimensions of tourism in Ukraine, 1991–2014. (From WTTC, 2015.)

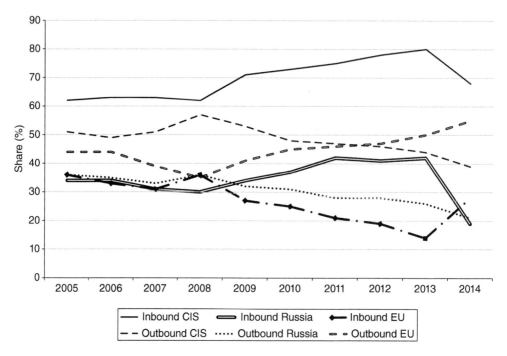

Fig. 6.4. Regional patterns of Ukraine's travel flows, 2005–2014. (From WTTC, 2015.)

circumstances have, of course, affected the general economic and business environment adversely, and tourism in particular.

This context provided the frame for our case study. We questioned 51 respondents out of approximately 5000 employees of tourism-related companies in Kyiv regarding the impact of geopolitical instability on their business. Owners of tourism-related companies (60%), senior managers or supervisors (30%) and other staff (10%) constituted the respondents' profile. The statistical sampling error of our analysis was 13.8%.

The results of the survey suggested that 73% of tourist companies acknowledged a negative impact on their business from the geopolitical and economic crises of 2013–2015. By contrast, around 6% of respondents stated that their business actually grew during that period.

Over half of all respondents (53%) confirmed that their companies had not changed the direction of their activity, while 45% reported changes to the destinations they specialised in. Thus, approaching half of the tourist companies in the country's capital employed

diversification as one of the instruments to resist the crisis and to strengthen their company's market share.

Tourism-related employment levels during 2013–2015 appear not to have changed much. Over a half of respondents (59%) answered that their staff base had remained at the same level. By contrast, 31% reported reduced numbers, while 8% affirmed that their company staff numbers had actually risen.

From spring 2015, the majority of Ukrainian tourism-related companies experienced a recovery, and 65% of respondents confirmed a rise in demand for their services from the beginning of the season. On the other hand, 31% did not.

Looking to the future, opinions were divided. Almost half (47%) of respondents perceived positive dynamics in demand, while 45% disagreed. Almost one-third of those interviewed (31%) noticed unusual activity of sales for packages to EU countries between March and the end of June 2015. In fact, the introduction of obligatory fingerprinting for every Ukrainian applicant for a Schengen visa from 23 July 2015

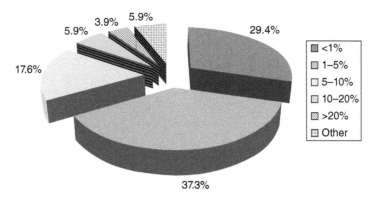

Fig. 6.5. Share of customers of tourist companies from temporarily occupied territories. (From authors' survey.)

is likely to have stimulated this minor revival of the market.

The heart of our survey constituted questions regarding demand for tourism products, visa difficulties and emigration problems among people from the temporarily occupied territories of eastern Ukraine (some districts of the Donetsk and Lugansk regions and Crimea). We discovered that people from these territories used services of tourism-related companies quite often (Fig. 6.5). In fact, the Donbas region used to be one of the richest in Ukraine and its citizens usually bought the most expensive packages. After the occupation, many people took the opportunity to move to different parts of Ukraine, but their official residence registration did not change. So, it would appear that wealthy people from the Donbas region have sustained a significant part of Ukraine's tourist flow.

At times of geopolitical instability, emigration tends to increase. Under such circumstances, foreign consulates might be expected to reject entry visa applications more often than usual. However, 78% of our respondents claimed that less than 1% of their clients had been rejected in seeking to obtain a visa.

We came across evidence that, since 2013, travellers had frequently applied for a Schengen country visa, and from that country had then entered another destination in the Schengen area. Such violations can lead to deportation. In fact, we discovered that 10% of respondents had experienced the problem of clients being deported for this reason. Twenty-six per cent of companies we interviewed confirmed that at

least one of their clients who bought a full package (tickets for transport, hotel, land transfers, insurance and visa) had not subsequently checked in to a booked hotel, had broken off all communication after departure and did not return to Ukraine after the planned end of the trip.

6.7 Conclusions

The limited history of Ukraine as a sovereign state has been typified by confused fluctuations in geopolitical orientation, reflecting the ambiguity of the country's strengths and weaknesses. The current pro-Western trajectory to integrate with the EU and NATO has emerged from 25 years of contentious post-communist transformations.

Tourism development in independent Ukraine has mirrored the simultaneous processes of decolonisation, denationalisation and decentralisation. The establishment of tourism governance institutions, the development of general and specific legislative regulation and the gradual market reform of the business environment have reflected the 'transplantation', 'recombination' and 'retrogression' modes of the state. The replacement of former Soviet norms by 1995 focused tourism development on inbound tourism and hospitality. This was followed by a further 'recombination' of institutions, the establishment of licensing and taxation rules, enhanced internationalisation of activities and a transformation of the health resort sector. Attempts to promote the country's image abroad from 2007 faced obstacles of business practice and taxation issues, especially from 2011. Patterns of inbound and outbound travel have reflected fluctuations in the country's geopolitical trajectory.

The unresolved and destabilising issues of annexed Crimea and hostilities in eastern Ukraine continue to affect the economic and business environment adversely, and particularly the tourism sector.

Our survey of tourism business representatives has indicated that survival is possible through a diversification of activities, despite the imperfect institutional context.

Endnote

[1] Signed on 21 April 2010, this document prolonged the stay of Russia's Black Sea Fleet in Sevastopol from 2017 until 2042.

References

Agreement (1991) *On the Establishment of the Commonwealth of Independent States.* State Archive of the Russian Federation, Moscow. Available at: http://www.rusarchives.ru/statehood/10-12-soglashenie-sng.shtml (accessed 25 July 2016).

Agreement (1992) *Between Russian Federation and Ukraine on Future Development of Interstate Relations.* Dagomys. Available at: https://www.referent.ru/1/24184 (accessed 25 July 2016).

Agreement (1997) *Between Ukraine and Russian Federation on the Status and Conditions of the Black Sea Fleet of Russian Federation in Ukraine.* Diplomaticheskiy vestnik, Moscow. Available at: http://zakon3.rada.gov.ua/laws/show/643_076 (accessed 25 July 2016).

Agreement (2014) *On Association between Ukraine, From One Side, and EU, European Society of Atomic Energy and their Member States, From the Other Side 2014.* Ofitsiynyi visnyk Ukrainy, Kyiv. Available at: http://zakon3.rada.gov.ua/laws/show/984_011/card6#Public (accessed 25 July 2016).

Babarytska, V. (1997) *Terytorialna organizatsiia kompleksu mizhnarodnogo turyzmu Ukrainy.* [*Territorial Organization of the Complex of International Tourism of Ukraine.*] Taras Shevchenko National University of Kyiv, Kyiv (in Ukrainian).

Braychevskyy, Y. (2014) Deciding on NATO: a necessary step or a premature move? *Geography and Tourism* 29, 87–100.

Committee for Statistics of Ukraine (2015) *Home page.* Available at: http://www.ukrstat.gov.ua/ (accessed 25 July 2016).

CSAHA (Central State Archives of Higher Authorities) (1991) *Details of the results of all-Ukrainian referendum* 1(28), 6. Available at: http://www.archives.gov.ua/Sections/15r-V_Ref/index.php?11 (accessed 25 July 2016).

Declaration (1990) *On the State Sovereignty of Ukraine* (1990) Vidomosti Verkhovnoi Rady, Kyiv. Available at: http://zakon3.rada.gov.ua/laws/show/55-12 (accessed 25 July 2016).

Decree (1991) *On Proclamation of Independence of Ukraine.* Vidomosti Verkhovnoi Rady, Kyiv. Available at: http://zakon5.rada.gov.ua/laws/show/1427-12 (accessed 25 July 2016).

Decree (1992) *Of the Cabinet of Ministers on Changes in the System of Executive Authorities Subordinate to the Cabinet of Ukraine.* Uriadovyi Kur'er, Kyiv. Available at: http://zakon1.rada.gov.ua/laws/show/616-92-%D0%BF/ed19921110 (accessed 25 July 2016).

Decree (1993a) *Of the Cabinet of Ministers on Approval of the State Committee of Ukraine for Tourism.* Uriadovyi Kur'er, Kyiv. Available at: http://zakon1.rada.gov.ua/laws/show/625-93-%D0%BF (accessed 25 July 2016).

Decree (1993b) *On the Main Directions of Foreign Policy of Ukraine.* Vidomosti Verkhovnoi Rady, Kyiv. Available at: http://zakon5.rada.gov.ua/laws/show/3360-12 (accessed 25 July 2016).

Decree (2001) *Of the President on Reorganization of the State Committee of Youth, Sports and Tourism of Ukraine.* Uriadovyi Kur'er, Kyiv. Available at: http://zakon2.rada.gov.ua/laws/show/1132/2001 (accessed 25 July 2016).

Decree (2004) *Of the President on the Military Doctrine of Ukraine.* Ofitsiynyi visnyk Ukrainy, Kyiv. Available at: http://zakon5.rada.gov.ua/laws/show/648/2004 (accessed 25 July 2016).

Decree (2005) *Of the President on the Ministry of Culture and Tourism of Ukraine.* Uriadovyi Kur'er, Kyiv. Available at: http://zakon4.rada.gov.ua/laws/show/680/2005 (accessed 25 July 2016).

Decree (2011a) *Of the President on Regulations on the State Agency for Tourism and Resorts.* Ofitsiynyi Visnyk Presydenta Ukrainy, Kyiv. Available at: http://zakon4.rada.gov.ua/laws/show/444/2011 (accessed 25 July 2016).

Decree (2011b) *Of the President 'Questions of Optimization of Central Executive Bodies'.* Uriadovyi Kur'er, Kyiv. Available at: http://zakon2.rada.gov.ua/laws/show/370/2011 (accessed 25 July 2016).

Decree (2013) *Of the Cabinet of Ministers on the Questions on Association Agreement Between Ukraine, From One Side, and EU, European Society of Atomic Energy and Their Member States, From the Other Side.* Ofitsiynyi visnyk Ukrainy, Kyiv. Available at: http://zakon3.rada.gov.ua/laws/show/905-2013-%D1%80 (accessed 25 July 2016).

Decree (2014) *Of the Cabinet of Ministers on Optimization of the System of Central Executive Authorities.* Uriadovyi Kur'er, Kyiv. Available at: http://zakon4.rada.gov.ua/laws/show/442-2014-%D0%BF (accessed 25 July 2016).

Decree (2015) *Of the President on the Decision of the National Security and Defense Council 'On the New Edition of the Military Doctrine of Ukraine'.* Ofitsiynyi visnyk Ukrainy, Kyiv. Available at: http://zakon3.rada.gov.ua/laws/show/555/2015 (accessed 25 July 2016).

Dergachev, V. (2006) Geopoliticheskaya transformatsia Ukrainy. [Geopolitical transformation of Ukraine.] *Vestnik analitiki,* 2 (in Ukrainian). Available at: http://dergachev.ru/analit/4.html (accessed 25 July 2016).

Doan, P. (2015) Lokal'ni systemy u terytorial'nomu upravlinni turyzmom v Ukraini. [Local systems in territorial administration of tourism in Ukraine.] Unpublished PhD thesis, Taras Shevchenko National University of Kyiv, Kyiv, Ukraine (in Ukrainian).

EAEU (Eurasian Economic Union) (2015) *Law Portal.* EAEU, Moscow. Available at: https://docs.eaeunion.org/en-us/ (accessed 25 July 2016).

Fedorchenko, B.K. and D'orová, T.A. (2002) Suchasny stan rozvytku turyzmu v Ukraini (1990-ti). [Current state of tourism development in Ukraine (1990s).] In: Fedorchenko, B.K. and D'orová, T.A. *Istoriia Turyzmu v Ukraini.* [*History of Tourism in Ukraine.*] Vyscha shkola, Kyiv (in Ukrainian). Available at: http://tourlib.net/books_history/fedorchenko62.htm (accessed 25 July 2016).

Grabovenska, S.P. (2013) *Suchasny stan i tendentsii rozvytku turystychnoi sfery Ukrainy.* [*The current state and trend of development of tourism in Ukraine.*] (In Ukrainian.) Available at: http://www.newbiznet.com.ua/index.php/ru/articles/80-market/335-2013-07-31-07-08-09 (accessed 25 July 2016).

Hall, C.M. (2008) *Tourism Planning: Policies, Processes and Relationships,* 2nd edn. Pearson Education, Harlow, UK.

Huntington, S.P. (1996) *The Clash of Civilizations and the Remaking of World Order.* Simon and Schuster, New York.

Kiptenko, V. and Doan, P. (2015) Destination Ukraine: tourism litmus of the transition to green economy. In: Reddy, M.V. and Wilkes, K. (eds) *Tourism in the Green Economy.* Routledge, Abingdon, UK, pp. 210–224.

Kiptenko, V. and Malynovska, O. (2009) Concept of program of creation and promotion of tourist image of Ukraine on target segments. *Geography and Tourism* 2, 30–40.

Koroma, N. (2013) Baltic-Black Sea geopolitical region: the national interests of Ukraine in this system of regional interactions. *Kyivskyy Geografichnyy Schorichnyk* 8, 229–233.

Kuczabski, A. and Michalski, T. (2014) Ukrainian post-communist transformation: causes, consequences and threats. *Quaestiones Geographicae* 33(2), 171–180. Available at: http://geoinfo.amu.edu.pl/qg/archives/2014/QG332_171-180.pdf (accessed 25 July 2016).

Kyfiak, V. (2003) Turyzm Ukrainy. [Tourism in Ukraine.] In: Kyfiak, V. *Organizatsiia tourystychnoy diialnosti v Ukraini.* [*Organization of tourism activities in Ukraine.*] Chernivtsi: Knyhy-XXI (in Ukrainian). Available at: http://tourlib.net/books_ukr/kyfjak_2.htm (accessed 25 July 2016).

Law (2003) *On the Basis of the National Security of Ukraine.* Vidomosti Verkhovnoi Rady, Kyiv. Available at: http://zakon5.rada.gov.ua/laws/show/964-15 (accessed 25 July 2016).

Law (2004) *On Ratification of the Memorandum of Understanding Between the Government of Ukraine and the Headquarters of United Armed Forces of NATO on Atlantic and the Headquarters of United Armed Forces of NATO in Europe Regarding Support to NATO Operations by Ukraine.* Vidomosti Verkhovnoi Rady, Kyiv. Available at: http://zakon3.rada.gov.ua/laws/show/1607-15 (accessed 25 July 2016).

Law (2010) *On the Foundations of Domestic and Foreign Policy of Ukraine.* Vidomosti Verkhovnoi Rady, Kyiv. Available at: http://zakon3.rada.gov.ua/laws/show/2411-17 (accessed 25 July 2016).

Lutak, O.M. and Mikhalchuk, L.V. (2012) Analiz ta otsiniuvannia informatsii pro osnovni turystychni potoky Ukrainy. [Analysis and evaluation of information about major travel flows in Ukraine.] *Actual Problems of Economics* 12(138), 217–225 (in Ukrainian). Available at: http://nbuv.gov.ua/j-pdf/ape_2012_12_29. pdf (accessed 25 July 2016).

Lyubitsewa, O., Kiptenko, V., Malska, M., Rutynskiy, M., Zanko, Y., *et al.* (2012) Geography of tourism of the Ukraine. In: Wyrzykowski, J. and Widawski, K. (eds) *Geography of Tourism of Central and Eastern Europe Countries*. University of Wrocław, Wrocław, Poland.

Mach, B.W. (1998) *Transformacja ustrojowa a mentalne dziedzinstwo socjalizmu. [Systemic transformation and the mental legacy of socialism.]* Instytut Studiow Politycznych Polskiej Akademii Nauk, Warsaw (in Polish).

Mikhel', D. (2009) Osnovni aspekty geopolitychnogo polozhennya Ukrainy ta ii zovnishn'opolitychny vymir. [Main aspects of geopolitical position of Ukraine and its foreign affairs dimension.] *Politologia* 110(9), 176–180 (in Ukrainian). Available at: http://goo.gl/d3kAZ6 (accessed 25 July 2016).

Pivtorak, G. (2001) *Pokhodzhennia ukraintsiv, rosian, bilorusiv ta yikhnikh mov. [Origin of Ukrainians, Russians, Belarussians and their languages.]* Academia, Kyiv. Available at: http://litopys.org.ua/pivtorak/pivt.htm (accessed 25 July 2016).

Plokhy, S. (2015) *The Gates of Europe: A History of Ukraine*. Allen Lane, London, UK.

Seven Wonders of Ukraine (2015) Nominations. Available at: http://7chudes.in.ua/nominaciyi/ (accessed 25 July 2016).

Statement on Non-nuclear Status of Ukraine (1991) Vidomosti Verkhovnoi Rady, Kyiv. Available at: http://zakon5.rada.gov.ua/laws/show/1697-12 (accessed 25 July 2016).

UNESCO (2015) *Ukraine: Properties Inscribed on the World Heritage List*. UNESCO, Paris. Available at: http://whc.unesco.org/en/statesparties/ua (accessed 25 July 2016).

Uriadovyi Portal (Government Portal) (2015) *Ministr Ekonomichnogo Rozvytku I Torgivli Pryznachyv Dvoh Radnykiv z Pytan' Turyzmu. [The Minister of Economic Development and Trade of Ukraine Appointed Two Advisers for Tourism.]* (In Ukrainian.) Available at: http://goo.gl/78lBWD (accessed 15 November 2015).

Usova, L.S. (2011) Foreign policy of Ukraine: between non-aligned and Euro-Atlantic integration. *Vlast'* (*Authority*) 7. Available at: http://goo.gl/QWOSpn (accessed 25 July 2016).

Webster, G. and Ivanov, S. (2014) Geopolitical drivers of future tourist flows. *Journal of Tourism Futures* 1(1), 58–68.

WTM (World Travel Market) (2015) *World Travel Market London.* WTM, London. Available at: http://www.wtmlondon.com/ (accessed 25 July 2016).

WTTC (World Travel and Tourism Council) (2015) *Data Gateway*. WTTC, London. Available at: http://www.wttc.org/datagateway/ (accessed 25 July 2016).

7 Under Pressure: The Impact of Russian Tourism Investment in Montenegro

Antonio Violante*

Department of Cultural Heritage and Environment, University of Milan, Italy

7.1 Introduction

Rarely can tourism be viewed in isolation. The (geo)political, economic, cultural and environmental context and implications of tourism development are well represented in this chapter. Within a context of contestation at both international and national levels, the chapter explores the intricate interweaving of tourism development, property investment and geopolitical influence. It examines how these interrelationships are played out in a recently independent Balkan country. While Montenegro (Fig. 7.1) is noted for the natural beauty of its Adriatic coastline and often majestic mountains, it is faced with a foreign policy balancing act between the geopolitical interests of East and West, within which tourism plays a prominent role. It is concluded that this balancing act will continue.

7.2 Montenegro: A Small Country with a Tourism Vocation

In 2006, Montenegro became an independent state for the second time, after a referendum that signalled the end of the federal union with Serbia. Prior to the official recognition of its first independence (by the Berlin Congress in 1878),

Montenegro had been under the nominal sovereignty of the Ottoman Empire for several centuries. The country lost its independence in 1918, when it was absorbed into the Kingdom of Serbs, Croats and Slovenes under the Serbian Karadjordjević dynasty (Sbutega, 2006: 364). In World War II, it was militarily occupied by Italy, and emerged from the war as a component of communist Yugoslavia.

During the political events of the past century, this small Balkan territory not only maintained but also reinforced two characteristics that in common perception may distinguish it from other European countries.

The first of these is that of a small, proud and secluded country with an indomitable population that, despite formal submission to other bigger powers (Ottomans, Serbian dynasty, Italy), has never been subjected to any other. Because of this fact, it has been considered an 'archaic natural park isolated from the world and history' in the words of Enzo Bettiza (Bettiza, 2000), who recalls a description of Montenegro attributed to the French linguist and Slavist Paul Garde:[1] 'Montenegro, le village d'Astérix'. This was later taken up by the geographer André-Louis Sanguin (2011a,b), who highlighted some of the characteristics of this 'rebel' territory, such as its minuscule dimensions and the fact that it was separated from its

*E-mail: antonio.violante1@unimi.it

Fig. 7.1. Montenegro: location map. (Redrawn from *Lonely Planet* and others.)

territorial context, very much like the famous French comic north-western Gallic village in Caesar's age, opposing the Roman invasion and led by their tiny Asterix.

The other Montenegrin trait lies in its self-identification as an 'ecological state', as confirmed both in its 1992 constitution during the Yugoslav Federal Republic years and in Article 1 of the independent Montenegro Constitution of 2007 (Comparative Constitutions Project, 2007: 2; Constitute, 2015: 7). Such designation has been motivated by the natural beauty of Montenegro's landscapes: pristine mountains, fauna and flora that are still partially primitive, five national parks (of 14,000 sq km) (Milutinović and Anđelić, 2004; Radojičić, 2005) and 292 km of coast, with priceless Venetian-built towns and monuments.

These characteristics, constitutionally promoted by the country's institutions, would appear to provide ideal conditions for the development of sustainable tourism (see UNDP, 2004; Ratkovic and Bulatović, 2013; Županović and

Kovačević, 2013). But Montenegro is also a land of myth.

The image of a touristically attractive place has been reinforced thanks to the 2006 movie *Casino Royale*, with Daniel Craig as James Bond, in which it is suggested that landscapes and the casino providing the film title are situated in Montenegro. Some tourism promotion websites have carried this further a little too imaginatively, with the idea of promoting 'extreme luxury and world famous casinos, that even induced a 007 franchise movie (Casino Royale) to be shot in a Montenegrin gambling spot' (New Montenegro, n.d.). But no movie scene – neither landscape nor interior – was ever shot in Montenegro. What was passed off as Montenegrin was actually shot in the Czech Republic, specifically in the town of Karlovy Vary (formerly Carlsbad). In this way, the small Balkan state is depicted inaccurately through Central European landscapes, of valleys surrounded by castles and late baroque towns. It would be natural to wonder why such mystification was necessary: yet it did contribute to the relaunch of Montenegrin's tourism image abroad.

After leaving behind fratricidal wars and NATO attacks at the end of the 1990s, former Yugoslavia was commonly perceived as covered with the stain of Balkan negativity, disambiguated so marvellously by Maria Todorova (1997) in her classic, *Imagining the Balkans*. This quality of the region retained its morbid attraction, representing a 'dark side' of the European conscience. The associations of such imagery may persist for Montenegro, alongside a memory of Lehar's operetta, *The Merry Widow*, whose scenario revolves around 'Pontevedro', an imaginary country purposely rhyming with Montenegro, which then was perceived exactly as an operetta state. The 'disturbing' Balkan world recalls Agatha Christie's, *Murder on the Orient Express*, a train that notoriously brings to mind spies, murders and international intrigue, so similar in fact to the *Casino Royale* train that carries James Bond through a fictional Montenegro.

Montenegro's tourism vocation and its contribution to the economy was an important component in federal Yugoslavia (Uskoković, 2004). Following the tumultuous period of transition in the last decade of the 20th century, the opportunity arose to relaunch the country from the very beginning of the new millennium. This was embodied in a conference supported by the Montenegrin ministry of tourism that took place in Cetinje (the country's once royal capital) in May 2002, where professors of the economic faculty of the University of Podgorica, and those of the hotel and tourism faculty situated in Kotor, examined the potential for further tourism development in various of the country's localities (e.g. Milutinović and Anđelić, 2004; Uskoković, 2004). In terms of employment, Montenegro's full-time labour market was calculated at 187,333 in 2005 (MTEP, 2007). The country's master plan for tourism for 2020 envisaged no less than 65,700 people employed in tourism by that time, 39,830 directly and 25,870 indirectly, although it was not clear if these figures were full-time equivalents (MTEP, 2008; Stranjančević and Kovačević, 2012).

In current terms, the importance of Montenegro's tourism sector is confirmed in data gathered by the World Travel and Tourism Council (WTTC, 2015): in 2014, travel and tourism contributed around 9.5% of the country's gross domestic product (GDP), compared to a European average of 3.4% and a world average of 3.1%. The unemployment rate in the sector for 2014 was high, too: 8.6%, compared to a traditional tourism country such as Italy at 4.8%. Significantly, however, Montenegro occupied the top spot in the world's ranking for the growth rate of investments in the tourism sector in 2015 (15.6%). By contrast, the European average was just 2.4%, and for neighbouring Croatia a mere 0.3%, while the Russian Federation saw a negative trend with –17.4% (WTTC, 2015). The reason for such investment was not hard to find.

7.3 Montenegro and Russia

Russia and Montenegro have a particularly friendly relationship that goes back to the 19th century when, by the 1878 Treaty of San Stefano, the tsar's empire guaranteed economic support for the small principality (Lampe, 1996: 57). Such a bond sprang from geopolitical motives: Russia's interest in having an outlet to the Mediterranean – even if it was indirect and through Montenegro – and common Slavic origins with a shared Orthodox Christianity. Good relations flourished with the matrimonial politics of the two reigning monarchies: on 7 August 1889, Saint Petersburg saw the wedding between Milica, the daughter of Nikola Petrović, Montenegro's prince, and grand duke Peter Nikolayevich Romanov, the first cousin of Tsar Alexander. On that occasion, the emperor defined Nikola as 'Russia's only sincere and loyal friend' (Sbutega, 2006: 309).

A military convention between the two countries signed in November 1910 established that Montenegro would make its military forces available to the tsar if he should ask; and that Montenegro could not enter into treaties with other countries without Russia's consent. In exchange, Russia would double its financial contributions to the Montenegrin army, aiding its modernisation. This was in addition to the financial support Russia provided to Montenegro in order to correct its commercial deficit, saving the country from bankruptcy (Sbutega, 2006: 319–320). With such agreements, the new kingdom of Montenegro (Prince Nikola became king in 1910) de facto became a protectorate of the world's biggest Slavic country.

7.4   A New Tourism?

A century later, the Russian interest in Montenegro has been mainly economic and touristic,
rather than political or strategic. Since 2008,
the two countries have shared a visa-free regime,
resulting in Montenegro becoming a favourite
destination for Russian tourists. In summer
2011, more than 20% of Montenegro's visitors
came from Russia, a number second only to
those coming from Serbia (27.9%) (Balkans.
com, 2011).

Serbian tourists visit because of a common
political past that lasted until 2006, a shared
language, geographic proximity with an attractive coastline (Serbia is landlocked) and prices
that are generally lower than in neighbouring
Croatia and Greece. However, despite having in
common the preference for seaside rather than
mountains, the requirements of Russian and
Serbian tourists in Montenegro are significantly
different. Serbian tourists are mostly families
with limited resources who choose Montenegro
because the beaches are free to use and there is
no obligation to rent sunbeds; take-away food is
available rather than having to eat in (more expensive) restaurants and there have been many
rooms to rent at low prices compared to the rest
of Europe (because supply has been greater than
demand).

On the other hand, Russian tourists see
Montenegro as a 'friendly window' overlooking
the Mediterranean. With its temperate climate,
it is an attractive alternative to the Black Sea,
with an exotic Balkan component that enhances
its allure. Since this is medium- to long-distance
tourism, it is affordable only for a particularly
wealthy clientele of medium- to high-income
groups and business magnates. Such 'tourists'
required apartments, resorts, hotels and luxury
villas, marinas for their yachts and quality infrastructures that Montenegro simply did not possess until the opening years of this century.

However, despite urban renewal, the imagined elite tourism did not produce the anticipated result. Since 2006, there has been much
building speculation to attract a wealthy clientele, especially Russians, that has resulted in a
'cementification' of the coastal area: next to
Venetian heritage palaces there are 'socialist'-
style buildings, hotels and public and private
modern constructions. Some complexes, such as

Dukley Gardens, just outside Budva, have been
built to high standards, with levels of internal
luxury that most Montenegrins can only dream
of. Yet they are built practically on the coastline,
occupying often prominent positions and de-
spoiling it, despite the 'ecological state' proclamation of Montenegro's constitution.

Investors' expectations had been to produce
a 'gentrification' not of residents but of tourists:
gone would be the 'poor' – mainly Serbs or Macedonians – while Western Europeans and wealthy
Russians would increase. The bubble of expectation regarding these new types of tourists continued to grow to 2013, stimulating an abnor-
mal growth of real estate prices and continued
building speculation. Banks and real estate
agencies proliferated.

Most of the new, gated communities being
built in Montenegro for 'tourists' have 24 h con-
cierge services and state-of-the-art security systems. It would appear that the new tourism
could be identified through wealthy people who
had the money and the will to invest in a 'Wild
West economy', but had no desire to mix with
the local population or to acknowledge Montenegrin reality. The selling point of these new
constructions was 'total security', yet criminality in the country is insufficient to justify the ob-
session with 24 h guards. Port infrastructures
increased in size and sophistication – especially
at Budva and Tivat – in part to accommodate the
new tourists' outsize yachts and motor launches.

7.5   Environmental Impacts of
Foreign Investments

Economically, by the end of the 1990s, Montenegro was already de facto the 'biggest' offshore
state of Europe (ironic, considering its actual
size): corruption and a significant grey economy
resulted from a lack of laws to eradicate corruption and illegality effectively, and from the arrival of numerous 'businessmen' of dubious legality from such countries as Russia and Italy.
Montenegro was hailed as a 'new Monte Carlo',
where it was possible to gamble, both in a casino
and in business (Masnata, 2006a,b). Immediately after the 2006 independence referendum,
the real estate boom began: it was easy to understand why. Due to a stunning natural environment, noticeable especially in the Bay of Kotor,

where mountains and sea are joined in an in-credible union, and prices are low compared to the rest of seaside Europe, Montenegro became a favourite target for foreign investors, especially Russian.

Yet according to Montenegro law, foreign-ers could not own real estate property without being part of a registered business company. As a consequence, there was a boom of newly cre-ated business associations, some of which were false and created ad hoc in order to purchase property.

A major public concern was how this boom was going to impact on the country's economy and environmental resources. In the latter case, the character of the coastal area has changed greatly because of new construction and mas-sive investments that have not always respected the style and the natural characteristic of the surrounding environment. The most obvious ex-ample is the previously mentioned *Dukley Gar-dens* complex in Budva: while it might appear luxurious, modern and pleasant to the eye from the coast it is built on, when observed from the opposite shore (from the old town), any eco-logical and architectural merits disappear (see light2tube, 2014). The development is also of dubious legality, as it restricts public access rights to the immediate shore.

The most obvious case of the change brought by this boom is that of the city of Budva: once a peaceful and charming small town, it became the epicentre of nightlife, and changed its appearance quite rapidly because of the *Environmental Plan of the Municipality of Budva* (Lajović, 2013).

Although presented to regulate new con-struction, the plan actually changed the purpose of various building sites, ruining natural green-ery in favour of high-end, exclusive buildings for a rich clientele (Lajović, 2012). Budva was pre-sented as the personification of the 'new Monte Carlo' (Plamenac, 2014), with plans for hotels and casinos, to exploit tourism potential and economic gain. If the aim was to have a modern city for a high-end, elite clientele, the realisation of such a goal was far from easy. Hitherto, tour-ism in the Budva area had been far from luxuri-ous, based on small-scale private accommoda-tion, considered as being family friendly, with budget prices and a 'homely' feel.

Now foreign investors were in, the lack of regulation and the high level of corruption saw

Budva gaining a reputation not only as the cap-ital of Montenegro tourism but also as the main focus for construction abuse and excessive ur-banisation. In the country's attempt to break free from the past and to open its doors to foreign investors, perceived as those who could save the failing economy and provide jobs for the local population, existing rules were interpreted liber-ally. The only positive side effect of the 'Russian wave' was the fact that when it came to money, any kind of ethnic and identity tensions among the locals disappeared.

7.6 Between East and West

There were many telltale signs that the Russian bubble had been created artificially, and that it would not last forever. Issues were raised about the legitimacy of money that was being brought into the country, often as cash in suit-cases (Montenegrin laws are much less restrict-ive in terms of cash limits, and there was much speculation involved due to lack of controls) (Bilefsky, 2008). Except for media accusations and several lawsuits brought (perhaps to ap-pease the population and to act as a distraction from other, more significant accusations), it ap-peared little could be done in the face of the Rus-sian 'invasion' of the country's economy. As state companies (producing aluminium, energy) were being wholly or partially sold to Russian in-vestors, it was clear that the controlling centre of power in the country was shifting. In the words of Blagoje Grahovac (senior adviser to the speaker of the parliament): '... whoever holds the upper hand economically will also do so pol-itically' (Bilefsky, 2008), implying that rules had been interpreted flexibly to accommodate a much-needed influx of money into a country that had slipped out of the EU's grasp.

Budva was the core of Russian interests, mostly because of its economic potential, and this was expressed on the ground through many bilingual billboards, menus in restaurants and business advertisements from local companies in a variety of employment sectors. The town was also home to the honorary Russian consul-ate, making business even easier. The local population lost sight of the long-term effects of such an 'invasion' and welcomed the Russians, with their Orthodox common roots, 'colourful' habits (relating to alcohol, food and a penchant for sad, 'soulful' music) and the wealth that was beginning to make its presence felt for those who were smart enough to grasp opportunities. The negative stigma usually attached to money of unclear provenience was perceived as a non-issue. Also, the older generation had studied Russian in school and many had worked in Russia in the past. On their side, Russians saw in Montenegro the calm oasis that their own country no longer seemed to offer (Hunin, 2012). The laid-back approach taken by Montenegrins (often caricatured as being lazy and slow) offered Russians the opportunity to concentrate and do business in a way that the frenzy of Moscow no longer allowed.

In 2012, the Russian press announced that Russian citizens owned at least 40% of Montenegro's real estate (ZM, 2012). And according to the Central Bank of Russia, of a total foreign investment in Montenegro in 2013 of around US$1.1 billion, 32% was traceable to Russian companies (Rapoza, 2015). Such a Montenegrin dependence on tourists and Russian investors had induced Croatian sources to describe the country as a 'Russian colony', accusing Prime Minister Milo Đukanović of 'manipulative strategies in post-independence privatizations for the benefit of non-Montenegrins' (Orešić, 2009).

However, in 2014 there was a decrease in the number of Russian tourists by around 15%, compared to the 300,000 Russian visitors of the previous year (Tomović, 2014a). The reasons for such an abrupt drop were both economic and political. On the one hand, the heavy devaluation of the rouble discouraged citizens from taking trips abroad, leading to a decrease of 30% in overall Russian outbound tourism (Vukićević, 2014).

Equally significantly, in 2013 a Russian presidential decree prohibited Russians from owning real estate outside their home country (Anon., 2013). This caused a huge problem for Russian officials who owned many properties along Montenegro's coasts.[2] Selling became the only option for them in order not to lose their official position back home. The Russian move was dictated by domestic interests. But it had clear international repercussions, not least for Montenegro's tourism and investment sectors.

On the other hand, the Ukraine crisis saw Russia and the EU on opposite sides, and Montenegro aligned with the latter to impose sanctions on Moscow, because of its own aims of joining NATO and the EU. By taking such a position, Podgorica certainly did not encourage a larger Russian presence in Montenegro. Russia stigmatised the Montenegrin ambitions of joining NATO and the EU as anti-Russian politics, and the number of charter flights from Russia to Montenegro was reduced (Anon., 2014b). Montenegrin officials claimed the reduction in Russian tourist numbers was purely the result of economic factors. However, according to Sergej Glazjev, economic advisor to Vladimir Putin, because of the Montenegrin prime minister's hostility, Russian companies and citizens were being deprived of their assets, although such claims were denied strongly by Obrad Mišo Stanišić from the Committee for the European Integration of the Montenegrin Democratic Party:

> Montenegro is not leading an anti-Russian or any other 'anti' policy toward any country in the world. Our national priorities and national goals are certainly Europe and Euro-Atlantic integration. These are our top priorities and we are conducting our policies according to them. If anyone believes that our national interests are directed against them, it is their right. But I repeat that this has nothing to do with anti-Russian or any other 'anti' policy.
>
> (Vukićević, 2014)

The somewhat colder relations between Russia and Montenegro left Podgorica with apparently conflicting goals: being forced to balance its desire to appear Western-oriented for NATO and EU accession aspirations, while having Russians own about 40% of the country, whether through real estate (Tomović, 2015a) or company shares. But the bubble had burst, and at the time of writing the Russian investment stronghold of Budva had many unsold units and inevitably prices had dropped.

The decrease in real estate demand was estimated at 20–30%, despite an increase in sales to Ukrainian citizens looking for a safer place in which to live and invest (Vukićević, 2015). Compared to the Russians, Ukrainians had much smaller budgets, limited to €20–30,000, and insufficient for the inflated price of Montenegrin seaside real estate.

Yet Russian tourism in Montenegro appeared to bounce back. From the first months of 2015, there was evidence, in contrast to most European tourism destinations, of an increase in reservations from Russia for destinations traditionally 'cheaper', such as Bulgaria and Montenegro (D'Amora, 2015):

> It's a paradoxical situation. On one hand the relations with Europe are bad, and on the other, European countries are urging Russian tourists to come because they are losing money.
>
> (Irina Tyurina, spokeswoman for the Russian Tourism Industry Union, quoted in D'Amora, 2015)

Montenegro benefited from such a paradox in the first half of 2015: according to the country's National Tourism Organization, tourists from Russia registered a 5% increase compared to the same period of the previous year, representing 22% of total arrivals, suggesting that Montenegro had managed to maintain its position in the Russian market. None the less, business fears were being voiced that Montenegro would never again be a 'hotspot' for Russians, as it had been from 2008 to 2013 (Tomović, 2015b).

According to Žarko Radulović, the head of the Montenegro Tourist Association, after the 2014 drop in numbers, the Russian tourists' return to the Montenegrin coast reflected reduced prices of air tickets and accommodation, and a rouble value adjustment. And although the European Travel Commission reported a 30% decrease in the numbers of Russian tourists visiting Europe during the first quarter of 2015, Montenegro and Romania were the exception to such a negative trend (Tomović, 2015b).

7.7 Conclusions: Moscow Does Not Like NATO's Courtship

Montenegro presents the example of how a country economically weakened by 20 years of wars, sanctions, poverty and an exponential growth of the grey economy can grasp an opportunity for short-term improvement while losing sight of the wider context. The country allowed entry to Russian capital, welcoming and embracing it on a wave of immediate results, to the point where such a high proportion of ownership of national assets could no longer be isolated from Montenegro's foreign policy.

The relationship with Russia bloomed until 2008, when the global financial crisis hit. Despite plummeting income and Putin's curb on property ownership abroad in 2013, the bond between the two countries remained strong in real estate, tourism and industry. Its impacts were felt in a number of different ways within the country. A small proportion of the population experienced wealth deriving from the influx of foreigners and their companies, selling land to them at exorbitant prices at the peak of the Russian 'invasion', or simply going into business as operating partners present on the ground. An even smaller section of the population, belonging to the ruling political class, enjoyed the benefits of state agreements that helped their own businesses significantly. However, the rest of the population grew unhappy, perceiving the Russian presence as a 'sell-out', and a form of modern servitude.

In November 2014, billboards appeared saying 'better a banana in the hand than a Russian boot on the neck'. These referred to an alleged comment made by Russia's Ambassador to Serbia, Alexander Čepurin, who supposedly compared Montenegro to a monkey lining up to join NATO in the hope of getting a banana (Anon., 2014a). Public expressions of protest clearly perceived the Russian influence as negative and threatening the prized history of Montenegrin liberty (Komnenić, 2014). Formal complaints were sent from Moscow, but the Montenegrin government denied any involvement in, or endorsement of, the protests (Tomović, 2014b).

Such tensions were expressed in a particular way when, at a Euro 2016 qualifying football match between Montenegro and Russia in Podgorica in March 2015, two Russian players were struck by missiles. As players began to brawl on the pitch, the game was abandoned and awarded to Russia (Langham, 2015; Veth, 2015).

The message was quite clear: Russia's influence was beginning to feel a burden, conditioning every foreign policy decision, including trying to persuade the government not to join sanctions against Moscow over Ukraine. And all the while Montenegro was actively pursuing EU and NATO membership.

It is the latter that made the situation escalate into full-blown diplomatic conflict: on 2

December 2015, NATO invited Montenegro to be its 29th member (Anon., 2015; Botelho, 2015; Santarpia, 2015). This was a strategic move for both NATO and the EU, aiming to extend their zone of influence over Montenegro, now perceived as being dangerously flooded with Russian money and political ties. Despite a lengthy accession process (12–18 months), Russia's voice was heard immediately, threatening repercussions and instilling fear in Montenegro's business class. Montenegrin officials saw NATO's invitation as a sign of improvement in terms of the democracy and reforms required by the Western world to bring the country out of its Balkan 'black hole'. More blatantly, it was clearly a strong message from NATO (and especially from the USA) that it would not countenance a Russian stronghold in the Balkans. Both superpowers aimed to gain a stronger strategic (and military) control over that part of the peninsula and the Adriatic, with Montenegro becoming an unwilling object of desire.

It is easy to conclude that Montenegro's tourism expansion could prove to be its most critical issue on the path to the 'civilised' Western world, with Russia wishing to protect its interests and transforming the soft power gained through investment into an intercession in the 'Euro-Atlantic' project.

Endnotes

[1] Professor emeritus at the University of Provence.
[2] These had included the nationalist mayor of Moscow, Yuri Luzhkov (Anon., 2007).

References

Anon. (2007) Oligarch finds a place in the sun in Moscow-on-Sea. *The Irish Times* [Dublin] 25 July. Available at: http://www.irishtimes.com/news/oligarch-finds-a-place-in-the-sun-in-moscow-on-sea-1.951241 (accessed 26 July 2016).

Anon. (2013) Russians put properties owned in Montenegro for sale. *Independent Balkan News Agency* [Belgrade, Serbia] 22 April. Available at: http://www.balkaneu.com/russians-put-properties-owned-montenegro-sale/ (accessed 9 September 2015).

Anon. (2014a) Ambasador čepurin o Crnoj Gori u NATO: 'I u politici postoje majmuni!' [Ambasador Chepurin on Montenegro in NATO: 'In politics there are monkeys!'] *Analitika* [Podgorica, Montenegro] 27 November (in Montenegrin). Available at: http://portalanalitika.me/clanak/124865/ambasador-cepurin-o-crnoj-gori-u-nato-j-u-politici-postoje-majmuni (accessed 15 September 2015).

Anon. (2014b) Ruski odgovor Crnoj Gori: Smanjićemo broj čarter letova ka Jadranu. [The Russian response to Montenegro: we will reduce the number of charter flights to the Adriatic.] *Vesti.rs* [Belgrade, Serbia] 6 December (in Serbian). Available at: http://www.vesti.rs/HiTech/Ruski-odgovor-Crnoj-Gori-Smanjicemo-broj-carter-letova-ka-Jadranu.html (accessed 10 December 2015).

Anon. (2015) Montenegro is formally invited to join NATO alliance. *Visit Montenegro* 3 December. Available at: http://www.visit-montenegro.com/montenegro-is-formally-invited-to-join-nato-alliance/ (accessed 10 December 2015).

Balkans.com (2011) Serbian and Russian tourists lead Montenegro's tourism in August. *Balkans.com Business News* [Belgrade, Serbia] 30 September. Available at: http://www.balkans.com/open-news.php?uniquenumber=121534 (accessed 26 July 2016).

Bettiza, E. (2000) Montenegro il villaggio di Asterix [Montenegro the village of Asterix]. *La Stampa* [Turin, Italy] 15 October (in Italian). Available at: http://web.sky.mi.it/forum/FAV2-00101D13/FOV2-00101D15/0005D4B7-70E903AC-0006B335?Templates=Bodies&FormID=96&Page=0 (accessed 12 December 2015).

Bilefsky, D. (2008) Despite crisis, wealthy Russians are buying coastal Montenegro. *New York Times* 1 November. Available at: http://www.nytimes.com/2008/11/01/world/europe/01balkans.html?pagewanted=all&_r=0 (accessed 12 November 2015).

Botelho, G. (2015) NATO formally invites Montenegro to join alliance, rankling Russia. *CNN* 2 December. Available at: http://edition.cnn.com/2015/12/02/europe/nato-montenegro-membership-invitation/ (accessed 10 December 2015).

Comparative Constitutions Project (2007) *The Constitution of Montenegro 19 October 2007*. Available at: http://www.comparativeconstitutionsproject.org/files/Montenegro_2007.pdf (accessed 12 December 2015).

Constitute (2015) Montenegro's Constitution of 2007. Available at: https://www.constituteproject.org/constitution/Montenegro_2007.pdf (accessed 26 July 2016).

D'Amora, D. (2015) Where Russian tourists will (and won't) go in 2015. *Moscow Times* 22 March. Available at: http://www.themoscowtimes.com (accessed 20 September 2015).

Hunin, J. (2012) Arrivano i russi. [The Russians have arrived.] *Voxeurop* [Roubaix, France] 16 November (in Italian). Available at: http://www.voxeurop.eu/it/content/article/3039501-arrivano-i-russi (accessed 23 August 2015).

Komnenić, P. (2014) Russia protests anti-Russian billboards in Montenegro. *Moscow Times* 28 November. Available at: http://www.themoscowtimes.com/article/512010.html (accessed 15 September 2015). Reprinted from *Reuters* 28 November 2014. Available at: http://www.reuters.com/article/us-montenegro-russia-billboards-idUSKCN0JC13F20141128#sBOewlTEAzgdSDQ8.97 (accessed 11 December 2015).

Lajović, V. (2012) U Budvi počinje izgradnja pet solitera. [In Budva the construction of five skyscrapers.] *Vijesti Online* [Podgorica, Montenegro] 1 October (in Montenegrin). Available at: http://www.vijesti.me/vijesti/u-budvi-pocinje-izgradnja-pet-solitera-94040 (accessed 10 December 2015).

Lajović, V. (2013) Građevinski lobi može da odahne. [Building lobby can feel relieved]. *Vijesti Online* [Podgorica, Montenegro] 8 February (in Montenegrin). Available at: http://www.vijesti.me/vijesti/gradjevinski-lobi-moze-da-odahne-112690 (accessed 10 December 2015).

Lampe, J.R. (1996) *Yugoslavia as History. Twice There Was a Country*. Cambridge University Press, Cambridge, UK.

Langham, R. (2015) Russia vs. Montenegro: a new Eastern European rivalry. *Futbolgrad* [New York] 4 October. Available at: http://futbolgrad.com/russia-vs-montenegro-a-new-eastern-european-rivalry/ (accessed 26 July 2016).

light2tube (2014) Dukley Gardens, Zavala, Budva, Montenegro. *YouTube* 15 March. Available at: https://www.youtube.com/watch?v=cfHuDAGvTFM (accessed 14 December 2015).

Masnata, R. (2006a) Montenegro, MonteCarlo? I. *Osservatoria Balcani i Caucaso* [Rovereto, Italy] 18 September (in Italian). Available at: http://www.balcanicaucaso.org/aree/Montenegro/Montenegro-Montecarlo-I-34507 (accessed 14 December 2015).

Masnata, R. (2006b) Montenegro, MonteCarlo? II. *Osservatoria Balcani i Caucaso* [Rovereto, Italy] 22 September (in Italian). Available at: http://www.balcanicaucaso.org/aree/Montenegro/Montenegro-Montecarlo-II-34543 (accessed 14 December 2015).

Milutinović, L. and Anđelić, M. (2004) Nacionalni parkovi u turizmu Crne Gore. [National parks in Montenegro's tourism.] In: *Turizam Crne Gora u Drugoj Potovini XX. Vijeka*. Report of Scientific Meeting Cetinje, 22–24 May 2002, Cetinje, Montenegro, pp. 263–276.

MTEP (Ministry of Tourism and Environmental Protection) (2007) *Bulletin No 59*. MTEP, Podgorica, Montenegro.

MTEP (2008) *Strategija razvoja turizma Crne Gore do 2020. Godine.* [*The Tourism Development Strategy of Montenegro by 2020.*] *The Master Plan – updated text*. The Government Printing Office, Podgorica, Montenegro.

New Montenegro (n.d.) Casinò in Montenegro. *New Montenegro* [Milan, Italy] undated (in Italian). Available at: www.newmontenegro.eu/turismo/casino-montenegro.aspx (accessed 16 September 2015).

Orešić, B. (2009) Ruska kolonija Crna Gora. [Montenegro a Russian colony.] *Globus* [Zagreb, Croatia] 4 September (in Croatian). Available at: http://globus.jutarnji.hr/svijet/ruska-kolonija-crna-gora?onepage=1 (accessed 20 September 2015).

Plamenac, B. (2014) Budva kandžama korupcije: afera aferu stiže. [Budva claws of corruption: scandal and scandals arrive.] *MONITOR online* [Podgorica, Montenegro] 11 April (in Montenegrin). Available at: http://www.monitor.co.me/index.php?option=com_content&view=article&id=5136:budva-u-kandama-korupcije-afera-aferu-stie-&catid=3538:broj-1225&Itemid=4803 (accessed 10 December 2015).

Radojičić, B. (2005) *Geografija Crne Gora: Prirodna Osnova.* [*Geography of Montenegro: Physical Basis.*] Unireks, Nikšić, Montenegro (in Montenegrin).

Rapoza, K. (2015) Despite Montenegro's 'Westward Ho', Russian investment unlikely to dissipate. *Forbes* [Jersey City, New Jersey] 30 November. Available at: http://www.forbes.com/sites/kenrapoza/2015/11/30/despite-montenegros-westward-ho-russian-investment-unlikely-to-dissipate/ (accessed 26 July 2016).

Ratkovic, R. and Bulatović, I. (2013) Impact of economic crisis on sustainable tourism (case: Montenegro). In: *Conference Proceedings, 2nd International Scientific Conference Tourism in Southern and Eastern Europe 2013, Volume 2*. University of Rijeka, Faculty of Tourism and Hospitality Management, Opatija, Croatia, pp. 355–370.

Sanguin, A.-L. (2011a) Montenegro in Rebecca West's *Black Lamb and Grey Falcon*. The literature of travellers as a source of political geography. *Geoadria* 16(2), 253–260.

Sanguin, A.-L. (2011b) Montenegro in Rebecca West's *Black Lamb and Grey Falcon*. The literature of travellers as a source of political geography. Paper presented at the IV Conference of the Adriatic Forum, *Geopolitical Issues of the Adriatic – Yesterday, Today, Tomorrow*. Department of Geography, University of Zadar, Zadar, Croatia, 16–18 September.

Santarpia, V. (2015) La Nato sfida la Russia e invita il Montenegro a entrare nell'alleanza. Mosca: 'Pronti a chiudere i rapporti'. [NATO challenges Russia and invites Montenegro to join the alliance: Moscow 'ready to end relations'.] *Corriere Della Sera* [Milan, Italy] 2 December (in Italian). Available at: http://www.corriere.it/esteri/15_dicembre_02/nato-sfida-russia-invita-montenegro-entrare-alleanza-mosca-pronti-chiudere-rapporti-ccbfb33e-98ef-11e5-85fc-901829b3a7ed.shtml (accessed 2 December 2015).

Sbutega, A. (2006) *Storia del Montenegro*. [*History of Montenegro*.] Rubbettino, Soveria Mannelli, Italy (in Italian).

Stranjančević, A. and Kovačević, B. (2012) Human resources in sports and recreational tourism in Montenegro coast: situation and perspectives. *Journal of the Geographical Institute 'Jovan Cvijic'* 62(1), 135–156.

Todorova, M. (1997) *Imagining the Balkans*. Oxford University Press, Oxford, UK.

Tomović, D. (2014a) Floods and Ukraine crisis threaten Montenegro tourism. *BalkanInsight* [Belgrade, Serbia] 16 June. Available at: http://www.balkaninsight.com/en/article/floods-and-ukraine-crisis-threaten-montenegro-tourism (accessed 20 September 2015).

Tomović, D. (2014b) Russia slams anti-Moscow billboards in Montenegro. *BalkanInsight* [Belgrade, Serbia] 28 November. Available at: http://www.balkaninsight.com/en/article/russia-protests-over-offensive-bilbords-in-montenegro-s-capital (accessed 18 December 2015).

Tomović, D. (2015a) Russian interest wanes in Montenegro real estate. *BalkanInsight* [Belgrade, Serbia] 19 February. Available at: http://www.balkaninsight.com/en/article/russian-interests-in-montenegro-s-real-estate-wanes (accessed 23 August 2015).

Tomović, D. (2015b) Russian tourists start returning to Montenegro. *BalkanInsight* [Belgrade, Serbia] 17 July. Available at: http://www.balkaninsight.com/eu/article/russian-tourism (accessed 20 September 2015).

UNDP (United Nations Development Programme) (2004) *Strategic Framework for Development of Sustainable Tourism in Northern and Central Montenegro: Roadmap for Development of 'Wild Beauty'*. UNDP, Podgorica.

Uskoković, B. (2004) Turizam u privrednom razvoju Crne Gore. [Tourism in the economic development of Montenegro.] In: *Turizam Crne Gora u Drugoj Potovini XX. Vijeka*. Report of Scientific Meeting Cetinje, 22–24 May 2002, Cetinje, Montenegro, pp. 9–18 (in Montenegrin).

Veth, M. (2015) Montenegro vs. Russia – the scandal of Podgorica. Futbolgrad [New York] 30 March. Available at: http://futbolgrad.com/montenegro-vs-russia-the-scandal-of-podgorica/ (accessed 26 July 2016).

Vukićević, J. (2014) New Russian threats to the Montenegrin economy. *Radio Slobodna Evropa* [RFE/RL, Prague, Czech Republic and Washington, DC] 16 December. Available at: http://www.slobodnaevropa.mobi/a/new-russian-threats-to-the-montenegrin-economy/26747113.html (accessed 20 September 2015).

Vukićević, J. (2015) Montenegro: spariti i russi, crolla l'immobiliare. [Montenegro: the Russians gone, real estate collapses.] *Osservatorio Balcani e Caucaso* [Rovereto, Italy] 16 March (in Italian). Available at: http://www.balcanicaucaso.org/aree/Montenegro/Montenegro-spariti-i-russi-crolla-l-immobiliare-159891 (accessed 20 September 2015).

WTTC (World Travel and Tourism Council) (2015) *Travel and Tourism. Economic Impact 2015 Montenegro*. WTTC, London. Available at: http://www.wttc.org/-/media/files/reports/economic%20impact%20research/countries%202015/montenegro2015.pdf (accessed 26 July 2016).

ZM (2012) Rusi vlasnici 40 odsto nekretnina u Crnoj Gori. [Russians own 40 per cent of real estate in Montenegro.] *Novi Magazin* [Belgrade, Serbia] 9 January (in Serbian). Available at: http://www.novimagazin.rs/svet/rusi-vlasnici-40-odsto-nekretnina-u-crnoj-gori (accessed 20 September 2015).

Županović, I. and Kovačević, J. (2013) Sustainable tourism development in Montenegro – actual situation and perspective. In: *Conference Proceedings, 2nd International Scientific Conference Tourism in Southern and Eastern Europe 2013, Volume 2*. University of Rijeka, Faculty of Tourism and Hospitality Management, Opatija, Croatia, pp. 447–461.

Part III:

Tourism and Transnationalism

A dimension that appeared to be beyond the foresight of neoclassical geopoliticians was the growth and significance of transnational economic power, but not through trade in the traditional sense. In seeking to upgrade technology and thus improve efficiency through gaining access to Western loans to purchase Western technology, the Soviet bloc in the 1970s and 1980s not only failed to take advantage of the potential 'efficiency gains' available but also did not appreciate that granting licenses for Western manufacturing giants – whatever their supposed political allegiances (e.g. Fiat) – to pursue their activities behind the 'Iron Curtain' was something of a Trojan horse.

By 1989, 'Western' multi/transnational corporations possessed the power to 'invade' Central and Eastern Europe (CEE) quietly, perhaps insidiously, in a way that even the war-mongering demagogues of the earlier 20th century would have admired.

This section of the book therefore examines, conceptualises and reflects on ways in which tourism- and leisure-related transnational corporations have (or have not) established their presence and exerted their influence in CEE countries.

Hana Horáková's Chapter 8 focuses firmly on tourism- and leisure-related developments as the source of contestation in her analysis of 'Dutch village' growth in rural areas of the Czech Republic. In such development, notable since the 1990s, she contends that there has been a 'striking complicity' between international tourism and neoliberal globalisation. The effects of the neoliberal forces of political and economic restructuring have encouraged local political elites to deploy tourism as a solution to rural socio-economic decline. But this process, in its turn, also became a *cause* of other severe problems, endangering social coherence and disrupting the physical landscape.

Highlighting social and cultural cleavages revolving around the contested narratives of modernity, Horáková points to tensions between values set under socialism (with the state as a key guarantor of development and well-being) and values derived from post-socialist modernity characterised by the key features of neoliberalism – a market economy, privatisation and decentralisation of political power.

She concludes that the incapability of both local power actors and marginalised subjects to resist the pressures of neoliberalisation open up issues about the nature of democracy and the form of representation in post-socialist Europe.

Piotr Niewiadomski's conceptualisation and analysis of the expansion of international hotel groups into CEE after 1989, in Chapter 9, is grounded in the very evident neglect of the cultural, economic and political diversity of the region by neoliberal orthodoxy in the earlier years of 'transition'. Employing the concepts of strategic coupling and path dependence, and undertaking an interview survey of decision makers in Poland, Niewiadomski highlights the

inability of local and regional institutions to facilitate the expansion of international hotel
groups adequately during the early 1990s.

Complementing this approach and offering
a conceptualisation of the role and power of
transnational hotel chains, Stanislav Ivanov
and Maya Ivanova, in Chapter 10, go on to
evaluate the limited extent of such chains' penetration in Bulgaria. Traditionally, Bulgarian
tourism has been associated with coastal resorts, and to a much lesser extent with spa and
ski centres (Bachvarov, 2006). More than a decade ago, Carter (2005) pointed to a number of
factors that determined the slow, early progress
of foreign direct investment (FDI) in the country.

Within this context, Ivanov and Ivanova
argue that apparent tokenism has operated in
the selection of Bulgaria as a host destination,
with major hotel corporations each being represented by only one or two affiliated properties in
the country. The authors raise the question as to
whether such corporations enter Bulgaria in
search of expansion opportunities and to offer a
greater choice of destinations for their customers, or because they are pursuing their own globalisation agenda for achieving wide geographic
presence regardless of the destinations entered.

While rounding off Part III of the book, Erika Nagy's Chapter 11 also provides a link with
the section that follows, *Borderlands* (and indeed
could also have been located in the subsequent
section, *Mobilities*).

In her chapter, Nagy focuses on consumption practices that have incorporated the crossing of national borders into the everyday lives of
local ('near-border') communities. Such practices have changed comprehensively in CEE
since the late 1980s. Employing examples from
Hungary, Nagy argues that the embedding of
CEE border regions in global flows and European
institutional space has induced multiple strategies and everyday practices that have played an
important part in relaxing deeply rooted ethnocultural conflicts and socio-spatial inequalities
'produced' by the spatial logic of capitalism.
However, the transformation of borders and related practices has been a contested process, as it
has challenged (re-)emerging nationhood, raised
new 'othering' processes, and has added new dimensions to polarisation processes active in CEE.

Nagy's chapter is therefore particularly useful, both in picking up themes established earlier
in the volume and in raising issues that are
addressed further in later chapters.

References

Bachvarov, M. (2006) Tourism in Bulgaria. In: Hall, D., Smith, M. and Marciszewska, B. (eds) *Tourism in the New Europe: The Challenges and Opportunities of EU Enlargement.* CAB International, Wallingford, UK, pp. 241–255.
Carter, F.W. (2005) Foreign direct investment in Bulgaria: the first ten years. In: Turnock, D. (ed.) *Foreign Direct Investment and Regional Development in East Central Europe and the Former Soviet Union.* Ashgate, Aldershot, UK, pp. 209–223.

8 Large-scale Tourism Development in a Czech Rural Area: Contestation over the Meaning of Modernity

Hana Horáková*

Metropolitan University Prague, Czech Republic

8.1 Introduction

Over the past 25 years, rural areas in the post-socialist countries have gone through wide-ranging processes of transformation that primarily affected the nature of rural economies. A rapidly changing rural environment has witnessed the emergence of new patterns of economic activity; among them tourism, which has been seen as a major agent for economic (re)development, and as a lifeline for rural communities.

The centrality of tourism in rural development has been recognised by many planners, managers and practitioners. There is a widespread perception that tourism offers salvation in local economic crises (Butler and Hall, 1998). The goals of tourism development in rural areas include the diversification of local economies, job creation, poverty alleviation, increased investment, population retention and community development, infrastructure and facility provision (Hall and Jenkins, 1998: 34; Giampiccoli and Saayman, 2014).

As many impact studies indicate, rural communities in general regard tourism favourably (Allen *et al.*, 1993). However, other tourism specialists advise local governments against considering tourism as a panacea for the long-standing problems of unemployment and economic problems. As the nature of rural tourism in general is to exploit rural environments for

recreational purposes, it brings with it the likelihood of new forms of impact, competition and conflict: since land has become redefined as a 'tourism resource' (Hughes, 1995: 53), there is a potential conflict between recreation and tourism uses, and other forms of land use; and other possible conflicts may emerge between non-tourist and tourist activities. As development always implies a power relation, potential conflicts lie in the contested nature of development and modernity; there are contradictory interpretations and claims about what development is, what the local interests are and how modernity is understood. Significant changes in the structure and identity of rural areas and communities may provoke ambivalent reactions on the part of local communities, including fears or resistance.

This chapter investigates the impact of development through tourism, as perceived by the residents of a Czech rural area (Lipno nad Vltavou) (Fig. 8.1) with regard to a large-scale tourism project that has been taking place in this area since the 1990s (Horáková, 2010). Lipno (in the following text the shortened name Lipno will be used) became one of the rural areas that fully adopted the concept of tourism as development (Higgins-Desbiolles, 2006; Davis and Morais, 2004). Tourism in Lipno has become the primary economic endeavour that dominates community life and upon which the local area is dependent.

*E-mail: hana.horakova@mup.cz

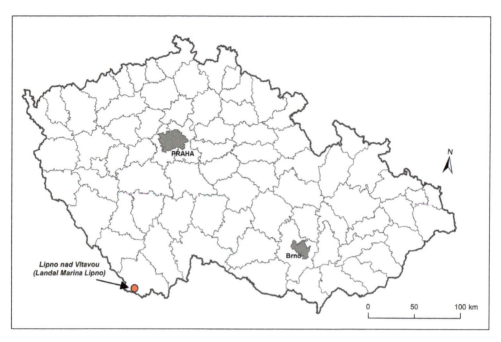

Fig. 8.1. Location of the research site in the Czech Republic. (Compiled by Hana Novotna.)

Although Lipno is one of the largest recreational resorts fuelled by rich foreign investment, built in a rural environment since the demise of state socialism, the concept of exogenous development through tourism is not entirely atypical in rural post-socialist Czech Republic. There are about 25 recreational resorts built for foreign, predominantly Dutch, clientele in various stages of implementation, situated in localities with a high touristic and recreational potential (Horáková and Fialová, 2014) (Fig. 8.2).

The Lipno area serves as a prime example of a large-scale, rapidly and extensively evolving, and largely exogenous (through foreign investment), tourism enterprise driven by the ideology and practice of neoliberalism. The study attempts to analyse a complex relation between neoliberalism (both in the form of discourse and practice) and transformation of the rural area under study. Specifically, it interrogates the appropriation of a post-socialist discourse of development to help justify the neoliberal goals of land privatisation and the intensification of tourism development of the region in the name of economic prosperity and modernity.

Rather than approaching neoliberalism as a top-down hegemonic political economic project,

the analysis will focus on the constitution of the processes of neoliberalisation and the ways in which different 'local neoliberalisms' are embedded within wider networks and structures of neoliberalism (Peck and Tickell, 2002). The goal is to identify neoliberal elements encountered in the local area and find out who promotes/opposes them, and how this neoliberalisation is, through the post-socialist discourse of development and modernity, negotiated and accepted by different actors and subjects.

I argue that the ways local actors perceive, reflect, or subvert and respond to the challenges of recent transformation through tourism are largely contingent on the way they have been able or willing to adapt to the social change brought about by the post-November 1989 political and economic restructuring. The ambiguous meanings of modernity, primarily the contested accounts of the socialist past and post-socialist present, are also instrumental in understanding the level of community engagement in tourism planning and decision making. The key research question is to what extent the socialist past affects ongoing processes and practices related to development through tourism, and how new developmental activities are affected by the legacy of socialism.

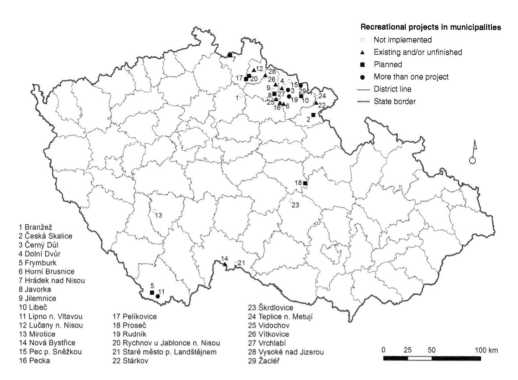

Fig. 8.2. Locations of recreational resorts built for foreign, predominantly Dutch, clientele in the Czech Republic. (Compiled by Dana Fialová.)

1 Branžež
2 Česká Skalice
3 Černý Důl
4 Dolní Dvůr
5 Frymburk
6 Horní Brusnice
7 Hrádek nad Nisou
8 Javorka
9 Jilemnice
10 Libeč
11 Lipno n. Vltavou
12 Lučany n. Nisou
13 Mirotice
14 Nová Bystřice
15 Pec p. Sněžkou
16 Pecka

17 Pelíkovice
18 Proseč
19 Rudník
20 Rychnov u Jablonce n. Nisou
21 Staré město p. Landštějnem
22 Stárkov

23 Škrdlovice
24 Teplice n. Metují
25 Vidochov
26 Vítkovice
27 Vrchlabí
28 Vysoké nad Jizerou
29 Žacléř

Given the divergence and diversity of the post-socialist condition, and the dilemma of continuity versus discontinuity, the chapter examines the contestation over the meaning of development and modernity in the rural area under study.

After presenting the conceptual and methodological framework derived from the post-socialist ethnography of change, the text introduces the case study of Lipno, focusing on the continuity and change in Lipno society and the predicament of its post-socialist development through tourism and examining the economic, physical and social impacts of tourism on the rural community. The last part discusses how the parallel and competing values revolving around the notion of modernity affect the residents' perceptions of the large-scale tourism project.

8.2 Conceptual and Methodological Framework

There are numerous models and theories that attempt to explain the nature, magnitude and type of social change induced by tourism, with respect to the relationship between community residents' perceptions of tourism and its impact. With regard to transition in general, and to post-socialist change in particular, this study adopts the concept of post-socialist rural change in which tourism plays an essential role, and one that accelerates the processes of modernisation and aspects of modernity in local perceptions and expressions. The impact of international tourism on the processes of transformation and strategies of development in the area under study is approached in two interrelated contexts: first, as one largely inseparable from the overall post-November 1989 transformation; and second, as a reflection of an ambiguous, complex process in which the post-socialist present blends with the socialist past.

As for the former, I argue that understanding the character and range of social change induced by tourism as one of the potential factors of endogenous development is a complicated task, since it is difficult to separate this change from the broader processes of post-socialist political and economic restructuring. Urbanisation and privatisation of rural resources, as well as their commodification and commercialisation, does not have to be caused only by tourism. Moreover, these modernisation factors are both a driver and a condition for constructing post-productivist rurality, typical of the shift from production to consumption (Horáková and Boscoboinik, 2012). Yet, though many rural municipalities can manage without tourism, its role in rural transformation is perceived as fundamental.

The predicament of clear separation between the changes induced by tourism and the broader transformation context is complicated by the nature of contemporary (post-)transition. This study is based on the assumption that the transformation to capitalism is not an unambiguous landmark from the socialist past, but is instead typified by an overlapping of the old system with the new one (Burawoy and Verdery, 1999). Unlike so-called 'transitology', the theory based on the assumption that the former socialist countries will follow the development path of Western capitalism (Verdery, 1996), I believe that a shift from socialist totalitarianism to (neo) liberal democracy has not been as swift, smooth and unilinear as predicted by transitologists. Conversely, I understand 'transition' as neither a complete break with the past nor a predictable historical process. The process of social change is one of continuity, hybridisation and rupture (Boyer, 2006).

Although post-socialist countries reject the preceding political orders, the long afterlife of the repercussions of the previous orders paradoxically keeps them alive (Hörschelmann and Stenning, 2008: 345). In sum, 25 years after the collapse of state socialism, post-socialist transformation processes (and their outcomes) are essentially ambiguous. Moreover, due to the non-linear and often contradictory nature of post-socialist change, transformations remain unfinished, uncertain and unpredictable (Burawoy and Verdery, 1999).

To avoid the epistemological flaws of the deterministic and neo-evolutionist paradigm of 'transition', the present study prefers an ethnographic approach and broader contextualising of the topic. By challenging the idea that only one 'road' leads to development, I want to show the various multi-linear responses to global challenges exercised by the rural society under study.

The task of studying the contradictions, paradoxes and ambiguities of post-socialism, as well as continuities and ruptures with socialist structures, institutions and ideologies is best approached by adopting the method of post-socialist ethnography that takes into account both historical continuity and human agency to act independently on various structural limitations. The focus is put on a pluralist interpretation of social, economic and political processes, structures and phenomena that take place (and are negotiated) in the local context. Post-socialist ethnography puts emphasis on the processes and meanings of post-socialist transformation as it is lived, experienced and negotiated at a grassroots everyday level (Burawoy and Verdery, 1999; Hann, 2002).

The paper is grounded methodologically in *iterative* social anthropological fieldwork (O'Reilly, 2005); a long-term research strategy based on systematic and focused revisits to the site over the course of 6 years (2008–2014), which helped to examine the complexity of rural space. I assume that the qualitative methods (participant and non-participant observation, semi-structured interviews and in-depth conversations) suit this research purpose much more effectively than quantitative research methods. They can reveal why certain people behave as they do. Participant observation was used at numerous social events organised by community members, whereas non-participant observation was aimed at the monitoring of certain interest groups – such as visitors and guests, the local community, etc. – with the aim of recording the movement of those studied in and around the tourism resorts and the village. Semi-structured interviews and in-depth conversations were designed to investigate community attitudes towards the tourism resorts. They were conducted with a wide range of people: local government officials, wage earners, owners of tourism enterprises, local intellectuals and ordinary village residents. Altogether, more than 50 people were interviewed in the course of the fieldwork, many of them several times. The collected data were then coded according to various research interests, such as 'attitudes towards tourism development' and 'involvement in tourism enterprise'.

Secondary data were drawn from various reports and analyses of the current state of tourism development in Lipno (Analýza, 2013; Kalabisová *et al.*, 2013), from the Czech Statistical

Office and Infocentrum Lipno nad Vltavou. To understand the nature of change in the community's life and to find out how the legacy of the socialist Lipno has affected contemporary social relationships, all issues of local newsletters dating back to 1989 were examined, and relevant data were drawn from the village chronicle.

8.3 Case Study

8.3.1 Continuity and change in the rural society of Lipno

Lipno nad Vltavou is a village in southern Bohemia lying near a lake of the same name on the left side of the Vltava river (Fig. 8.3). It is part of the touristic region of Šumava, which borders Germany and Austria. According to the 2014 census, the village has 654 inhabitants (Czech Statistical Office). The political, socio-economic and cultural history of the region was influenced heavily by twentieth century developments. Before World War II, the whole region was predominantly populated by German-speaking people. After 1945, many Germans were displaced due to post-war geopolitical arrangements. During the Cold War, Šumava became part of an inaccessible border belt where more than 80 small municipalities ceased to exist. A historical landmark in the development of the region was the decision of the former Czechoslovak communist government to construct a dam on the Vltava. As a result, several small villages were flooded, including Lipno.

During the 1950s, the Lipno area was gradually repopulated by ethnic Czechs and Slovaks, including Romanian Slovaks, who were recruited as temporary workers for the power station and dam construction. Originally, all the workers stayed in wooden lodgings, which, in the course of time, turned into the blocks of flats that formed the initial basis of the permanent settlement.

From 1958, when Lipno officially became a municipality, there was a steady demographic and socio-economic development. The main sources of livelihood for the residents under socialism were employment in the primary sector (power station and light industries such as timber rafting and woodworking, peat cutting and paper mills), agricultural activities and, to a certain extent, a tertiary sector. A relatively advanced local infrastructure was instrumental in developing vital local social life. Community associations, though organised compulsorily under an umbrella institution called the National Front, mushroomed.

Though Lipno is situated in a remote, peripheral area of the Czech borderland, it has a high touristic and recreational potential due to its highly valued landscape. Tourism development in the area started in the 1960s. The landscape became a magnet for second homes (weekend cottages and chalets), as well as for mass and individual recreation and tourism, both domestic and international. But before 1989, tourism was just a marginal source of income, as it could be developed in certain areas only, due to the close proximity of state borders that were closed by virtue of the Iron Curtain during the socialist era. Tourism activities (hiking, recreational fishing, yachting, skiing and collective summer sports) mostly related to the rural character of the setting. They could be characterised by the following terms: relaxing, low technological and non-competitive (Butler, 1998).

8.3.2 Post-socialist Lipno

The advent of economic restructuring oriented toward market economy brought about the economic decline in agriculture (the state farm's closure) and traditional light industries, followed by the closure of other local industries. The old, established patterns of development were abandoned and a new pattern of tourism was adopted by the local authorities, who thought they could capitalise on the area's 'under-development' caused by the proximity of the Iron Curtain. The acceptance of the concept of tourism as development was also possible because Lipno's land lay outside any nature conservation areas (Kalabisová *et al.*, 2013).

The role of local authorities in power redistribution and local development was paramount. Due to the vast change in public administration after 1989, even very small municipalities were endowed with democratically elected local governments, who became much more autonomous in deciding how local development should take place (Bernard *et al.*, 2011). This especially concerned the position of the Lipno mayor (who had been in office continuously since 1992),

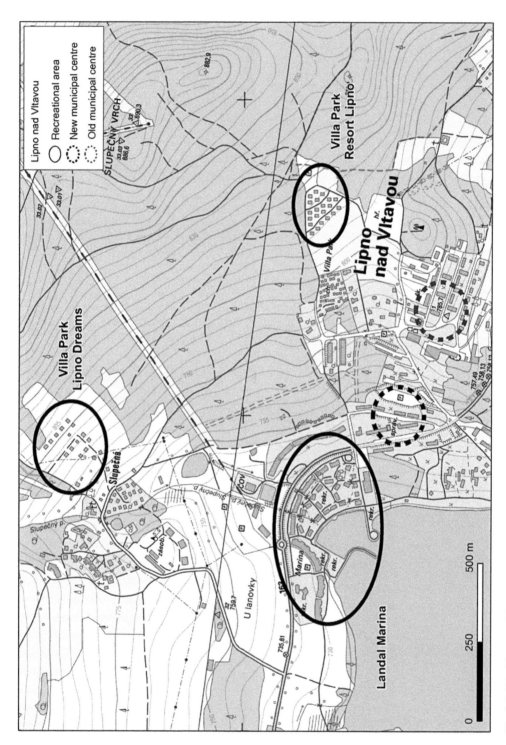

Fig. 8.3. The Lipno nad Vltavou village district. (Compiled by Dana Fialová.)

who was behind the agreement between rural political and business representatives and the Dutch company, Landal Green Parks, which bought land from both the municipality and local owners, and which between 1999 and 2005 built a tourist resort known as Landal Marina Lipno (Fig. 8.4). The resort is commonly referred to as a 'Dutch village'[1] because accommodation units are purchased by the Dutch, who either use them for their own recreation or they further rent them for profit – predominantly to other Dutch people. It stretches over an area of 13 ha (including a yacht marina), offering over 306 studios and apartments, with more than 1600 beds. So far, the resort remains the largest accommodation provider in Lipno.

The Dutch enterprise put a new marketing stamp on the destination and became a blueprint for further development plans that were typically externally oriented and large scale in nature. More land was sold and leased, both to foreign investors and Czech-based business corporations, for various tourism-related activities.

Similarly, local community properties were converted to tourist and other leisure-related purposes. New amenities were constructed, financed partly by public resources and partly by private enterprise.

Foreign investment was particularly focused on building accommodation facilities. The number of tourist nights has increased tenfold since 1997, reaching a level of 400,000/year (Analýza, 2013). There has been an increase in bed numbers by 840% in the past 20 years, and new beds are still being built. By 2012, more than 100 accommodation facilities provided 4978 beds (Infocentrum Lipno nad Vltavou).

One problem is that the number of beds has increased faster than tourist arrivals. As a result, there has been a steady decline in the occupancy rate since 2010. Another problem relates to the composition of the accommodation facilities. The major category is so-called apartment flats or houses registered as housing units, the construction of which is one of the most important types of investment in the village. Their foreign

Fig. 8.4. Landal Marina and Dutch houses, Lipno nad Vltavou. (Photograph courtesy of Hana Horáková.)

(largely Dutch) owners live outside the locality and use the flats themselves only occasionally, or they use them for short-term rentals to tourists. Thus, the prevalence of apartment flats pushes out classic accommodation facilities such as guesthouses, hotels or lodgings, which impacts negatively on the possibility of generating new jobs for local people (Kalabisová *et al.*, 2013).

Another substantial allocation of beds lies in the category of second homes, which serve a predominantly international clientele. They are vacant for most of the year, except for a couple of weeks during the winter and summer peak seasons. For the rest of the year, they resemble 'cold beds'.

Lipno has turned into a full destination resort situated in a rural host community, targeting both foreign and domestic clientele. The largest part of the foreign clientele is made up of Dutch (85%), followed by 10–12% comprising German tourists. According to recent statistics, the number of Czech visitors is increasing (Infocentrum Lipno nad Vltavou).

Outdoor recreational activities, facilities and attractions form the basis of the tourism industry and dominate this rural area; in fact, the location has become a stage for the activities themselves, rather than a key setting. Today's leisure activities are, however, different to and less complementary with the old patterns. They have been transformed from being passive and minor elements in the landscape to become active, competitive, highly technological and individualised (Butler, 1998; Hall *et al.*, 2003). The simple, traditional rural setting is no longer capable of meeting demands for the specialised contemporary forms of tourism and recreation (Horáková and Fialová, 2014: 192–206).

8.3.3 Economic, social and physical impacts

The growth and invasion of tourism to rural areas carries with it major consequences and impacts, both positive and negative (George *et al.*, 2009). From the economic point of view, Lipno sounds like a success story. Between 1994 and 2012, tourism contributed to the accumulation and capital appreciation of municipality property (its value rose 21 times: Analýza, 2013), and to the increase of the real estate tax revenue. The

positive economic situation has been reflected in a number of benefits for the local inhabitants (a reduced price of municipal waste collection; bargain rent in municipal flats; reduced entrance fees to some tourist attractions). The successful economic development has resulted in various awards for the area, such as Top Invest (2008) for the best investment (Lipno Ski resort) and Best of Realty (2012) for the 'best and most thoughtful urbanistic development, successfully combining public and private investment in tourism' (Infocentrum Lipno nad Vltavou).

Contrary to popular assumptions and arguments put forward by economic determinists who believe in the inevitability and desirability of tourism development, tourism is not a benign force of economic development. Many studies show that the promised benefits fail to materialise for the majority of people. In Lipno, a rise in the price of foodstuffs and public services, as well as the high rate of the real estate tax, affect the local population negatively. Despite the benefits, the new tourist infrastructure is unaffordable for the majority of the locals.

The complex nature of tourism requires impact assessments of the physical and sociocultural environments, as well as of the economic effects. Tourism development in Lipno, particularly its second phase (from 2005 onwards), corresponds to one of the most typical models of social carrying capacity, namely Butler's concept of resort cycle (Butler, 1980). It claims that as tourism development increases substantially, a number of negative effects on community life can occur. A trend toward the institutional ownership of land and a rapid growth in the number of second homes, recreational resorts and tourist attractions resulted in reduced access to what was originally public land. As the tourism enterprises engulf the rural community, the result is: (i) social disruption of the local community; and (ii) disruptive and irrevocable change of the physical environment (cf. Butler *et al.*, 1998). These two aspects are not mutually exclusive. The social effects can be exacerbated by the physical aspects, as is the case in Lipno, where unprecedented rapid construction of recreational units, second homes and tourist attractions impacts on social life.

First, the advent of large-scale tourism in Lipno has a severe impact on the physical environment. Its rapid growth has resulted in the transformation of the whole landscape and the village alike. The newly built tourist resorts and facilities, including the height, style and material of the buildings, have utterly changed the character of the local area, which has become a mere tourist 'sight' (cf. Cohen, 1978: 219). The impact of exogenous tourist projects on the physical environment is particularly harsh, owing to the sharp contrast between the tourist facilities built according to 'international standards' and the 'traditional' built environment. The environment is artificially transformed and adapted to the tastes and desires of tourists. Dewailly (1998: 123) used the term landscape 'under siege' to indicate the rapid transformation processes that no longer provide space for rurality, tranquillity and peace.

The interplay between the processes of post-November economic restructuring and large-scale tourism development affects the spatial structuring of the entire village. Tourism development resembles a centrifugal phenomenon: it starts around a core and then expands toward the periphery, while the core undergoes the most intensive ecological transformation. New buildings and shopping and entertainment facilities remind us of a 'resort landscape', even 'seaside resort', with an aesthetic value of its own (Cohen, 1978: 226). As the tourist enterprise tends constantly to expand, the same processes of commercialisation and defacement affect other parts of the village, which brings an intensification of transformational activities. The result is that the whole area – from the core to the periphery – is partly or completely transformed through tourism development. New tourist attractions and accommodation resorts are being built with the aim of supplementing or superseding those already existing. The rural place and space has become a stage for tourist activities.

The only place that has so far resisted this transformation is the original settlement of 'Old' Lipno, perceived as a periphery by the locals and tourists alike. Its physical separation was bolstered by the local authorities' decision to build a brand new village centre, commonly called the 'promenade', in the vicinity of the recreational resorts. This centre, with its restaurants, cafés, shops and other tourist-oriented services, makes a shop window of Lipno.

The construction of tourist infrastructure arouses ambivalent, often negative, reactions among the locals, including the owners of weekend cottages. Many consider it to be 'ugly', 'inappropriate for the rural environment', 'like *fata morgana*' or an 'architectural monstrosity'. Likewise, many experts as well as laypeople claim that it disrupts the character of the landscape and contributes to the loss of sense of place. On the other hand, the infrastructure is endorsed positively by many stakeholders, especially rural entrepreneurs who are economically reliant on tourism and the residents, who fully endorse the modernisation ethos promoted by the local power elite.

The impact of tourism on the sociocultural environment manifests itself less clearly and immediately, therefore it is difficult to monitor and measure. The most serious effects that were observed in the area include tourist pollution and the tourist trap nature of the destination, marginalisation of some layers of the local population and overall, 'touristification'. Tourist pollution indicates a set of undesirable effects of tourism on the local population; its environmental and social environment (Shaw and Williams, 2002). In Lipno, it manifests itself by overloading the public space, thus inducing high levels of stress in the locals because of the excessive number of tourists, particularly in the peak periods.

Marginalisation of the population indicates the (un)intentional pushing of residents out of the more 'prestigious' places in the destination. Concern to satisfy the residents' needs appears to be a low priority on the agenda of local politics. Those who do not participate in the tourism development are driven out to the peripheral zones of the destination and to the socioeconomic margins of local society. Marginalisation of the inhabitants and the feelings of not belonging are intensified by diverse restrictions in using the public space and infrastructure.

If the number of tourists and visitors in a destination is not regulated, it may contribute to the depreciation of the countryside capital (Garrod et al., 2006). The intensity of the depreciation is affected by: tourist numbers (in relation to the number of residents); seasonality; a level of economic dependency of the community on tourism; and the rate of regulation of tourism (Dewailly and Flament, 1993). Research results indicate that Lipno has succumbed to the tourist trap effect: tourist numbers are not regulated; instead, local political elites try to increase numbers through approving entrepreneurial projects focused on tourism in the village, or by supporting investment in constructing new accommodation facilities and tourist infrastructure, which in turn helps to increase the economic reliance of the community on tourism.

The overall process of the above-mentioned effects is 'touristification', characterised by the complex impact of tourism on local social life, contributing to a transformation of the village identity. The basic function of the place is being gradually pushed out while being transformed into a tourist destination. The needs of tourists and visitors are prioritised over the residents' needs and their lifestyles.

8.4 Neoliberalisation of Landscape and Community

The research topic of large-scale tourism development in Lipno is embedded in a wider context of post-socialist transformation that is taking place within the ideology and practice of neoliberalism. This section explores how the neoliberal forces affect social relations and how they impact on the account of the key concepts such as 'development', 'progress' and 'modernity'. It interrogates the process of forming the postsocialist discourse of development that legitimises neoliberal policies in the form of the privatisation, individualisation, marketisation, commercialisation and commodification of the Lipno landscape and community. This discourse, instrumental in the intensive touristification of the village in the name of economic prosperity and development, is compared with the discourse of socialist modernity.

Neoliberalism is a complex term that often means different things to different people (McCarthy, 2006). It is as much a political and ideological project as it is an economic, social and developmental project (Peck and Tickell, 2002). Current debates about neoliberalism distinguish at least two key conceptions. First, neoliberalism as a hegemonic, uniform, 'top-down' political-economic project bolstered by a singular ideology, and advanced by governments and international organisations, with similar effects worldwide (Bakker, 2005). A second conception presents neoliberalism as a 'process' and not a 'thing' (Bakker, 2005), as 'migrating technologies

of governance' that bring diverse outcomes depending on the interaction with local context. Rather than approaching neoliberalism as a hegemonic political-economic project and unitary ideology, Peck and Tickell argue that the analysis should focus on the '(re)constitution of the processes of neoliberalisation and the variable ways in which different "local neoliberalisms" are embedded within wider networks and structures of neoliberalism' (Peck and Tickell, 2002: 380).

In line with the second view, the present chapter conceptualises neoliberalism as a phenomenon that 'only manifests itself in hybrid formations' and 'cannot be reduced to any one of its constituent elements' (Peck, 2004: 403). The attempt is to identify neoliberal components that are successful in the researched area and to answer the question of who promotes them and why, and how is this neoliberalisation negotiated and accepted/declined by individual actors and subjects?

Neoliberalism is commonly conceptualised as being made up of three main pillars – resistance toward a Keynesian state, faith in civil society and its components, including NGOs and communities, and a focus on individuals as economic and social actors (McCarthy and Prudham, 2004). The key element of the neoliberal paradigm is the market economy. The programme of vast economic reforms to set up and develop the market economy was pursued immediately after the fall of communism in Czechoslovakia. The market was constructed as a symbol of 'civilisation' and 'modern society', as a part of *natural* social evolution, toward which Czech society was logically heading after the involuntary pause filled by an unsuccessful (because of being artificial) project of 'really existing socialism' defined by centrally planned economy (Holý, 2010: 149). As Holý (2010: 197) claims, the cultural construction of the 'natural' and 'artificial' does not only explain a problem-free acceptance of the discourse of market economy in the 1990s but also it can be understood as a key metaphor of Czech culture that is frequently used in a number of other discourses – political, ecological and gender.

Post-socialist Lipno has used market forces in the process of (re)creating and evaluating landscape and community. Local authorities formulated developmental goals in accord with free competition among private entrepreneurs, both foreign and local, and presented them (inward and outward of the community) as instruments for improving economic performance.

The second element that is in line with the classic definition of neoliberalism is the emphasis on private property. Privatisation became the fundamental factor of economic restructuring in post-November 1989 Czechoslovakia. Similarly to the market economy, private property was construed as 'natural', as opposed to the 'artificiality' of centralised economy (Holý, 2010: 158). As has already been stated, the process of the privatisation of rural resources in Lipno was launched when the local authorities decided to purchase land with the aim of consolidating it and offering it to prospective private investors. The development of the municipality through such a large-scale tourism project proved to have ambivalent effects – entirely positive for the investors and developers, and devastating for the community, especially its social coherence.

The third basic element is a strong impetus toward the devolution of governance functions and empowering non-state actors, including communities led by the belief that communities could manage their resources better than the state. The assumption of self-governing community is one of the defining features of neoliberal rule (McCarthy, 2006). The imperative of deregulation and decentralisation was justified, in a similar way to the above-mentioned neoliberal components, by the failure of the former socialist state in managing the country, particularly in economic terms (the so-called economy of shortage). Contrary to the commonly anticipated outcome of the 'retreat of government' under neoliberalism, in Lipno, neoliberal reforms have instead expanded certain aspects of state power, executed by means of local political actors while silencing the former local actors (community associations). The engine of strategic change has been the village mayor, who made his own vision of development that he promoted both in cooperation with much of the local business elite, and with international financial actors. He legitimised developmental goals of land privatisation and consolidated an economic narrative of the efficiency of large-scale tourism enterprise that will ensure the economic and demographic survival and prosperity of the local community.

8.4.1 Contestation over the meaning of modernity

The rhetoric and practice of neoliberalism as a part of modernisation policy, with its inherent free-market environmentalism, has been embraced enthusiastically by the Lipno political and economic elite. The model of post-socialist modernity shaped by the Western-oriented emphasis on a self-regulated market economy is accentuated, in contrast to the project of socialist modernity, which is presented as being to blame for the overall moral and economic devastation of the country, the local landscape and the community. The aim is to replace socialist modernity, which is viewed as being outdated and obsolete. These two large-scale modernisation projects, socialist and capitalist, while sharing a common goal, namely to construct an entirely new social, political and economic order, and to reorient society toward a future ideal by dislodging its past as a 'negative other' (Brandstädter, 2007: 134), define themselves in direct opposition to each other. As Holý (2010: 13) points out, the emerging post-November discourses either develop the socialist narratives or they are constructed in opposition to the official discourses under socialism. Both implicit and explicit framing of the dominant discourse into the narrative of the unsuccessful socialist project, promulgated by the local political and business elite, has facilitated a smooth, trouble-free privatisation process of public resources. This is what Harvey (2003) calls accumulation by dispossession, that is 'the enclosure of public assets by private interests for profit, resulting in greater social inequity' (Bakker, 2005: 543).

Post-socialism thus creates space for cultural struggles between two modernisation projects backed by two opposing ideologies – socialism and capitalism. These struggles are over the meaning and ownership of modernity (Brandstädter, 2007: 134–135). The 'Western' concept of modernity is presented as 'natural', as an ideal to be pursued, as was clear from the interviews with the local power elite (especially the mayor), from the specially designed analyses (Kalabisová *et al.*, 2013; Analýza, 2013) and from media representation. In the logic of the dichotomised discourses on modernity, the following quotes chosen from diverse sources (an outside expert on architecture; a blogger; a regional politician) show the tendency of negating the former (socialist) period while presenting Lipno as a historical 'non-entity', as if there were no people, no history, no development (Horáková and Fialová, 2014: 328–329):

> In 1989 Lipno had some 240 inhabitants who still lived in dilapidated lodging houses in the middle of the woods, higgledy-piggledy, with asbestos cement roofing.
>
> (Vítková, 2006)

> The marina has grown on a greenfield site, filled with bush. There was just mud and havoc. Today there is a tastefully built small town.
>
> (An Internet user)

> Surely enough there is no other village in Southern Bohemia that could boast of similar development that serves to the satisfaction of local people. It is unbelievable, as Lipno was not a historical municipality but in fact a dam construction site.
>
> (Former senator and mayor of the nearby town, cited in Analýza, 2013)

The attempt to represent the village as a place without history is in stark contrast to a historical memory captured by the village chronicle, which contains a newspaper article of September 1969:

> What emerged over the dam is a very modern village with 200 flats. ... Lipno amazes with its tidiness and taste, vast greenery and flowerbeds all around the settlement. Though the village welcomes around 5,000 domestic and international visitors a day in summer, it remains clean and tidy. Sidewalks are paved, banisters are shining with newness, rose flowerbeds are tidy, street lightning is everywhere.
>
> (The Cronicle of Lipno)

The representation of current Lipno deprived of any meaningful past prevails among the residents with close contacts to the local entrepreneurial elite. As one of the informants claimed,

> Lipno used to be like the bush but now it is being civilised. If we go 'to town', one has to get dressed, not like in a village. Lipno links village with town. Our children won't be country bumpkins anymore.

The newly built-up landscape is associated with 'civilisation' and 'modernisation'. The new village centre confers prestige; now, the urbanites will no longer look down on the villagers.

The master narrative of post-socialist modernity is rooted in the teleology of 'transition', which assumes that the former socialist countries must follow the development path of Western capitalism (Verdery, 1996). As such, it does not take into account any continuity with the former regime; neoliberalism is viewed as the *sole* source of social change and development (Kalb, 2002). Thus, the dominant narrative is modelled by, and reinforced with, the equally powerful discourse of anti-communism based on the widespread societal rejection of socialism and socialist categories. Those labelled as 'communists', irrespective of their real affiliation to the Party in the past or current political preferences, are depicted as the antithesis of progress and modernity. The stereotypical image of a communist indicates a person dependent on paternalist state; as naturally lazy, as a result of a poor socialist work morale; somebody who is envious of the economic success of others. In the language of Lipno's political and business elite, those who do not support the tourism project are 'lazy and spoilt by socialism'. They argue that such locals do not work properly; some of them even do not want to work at all because 'living on the dole suits their human nature better'. This argument was used to account for the above-average rate of unemployment in Lipno in 2013, 13.40%[2] (Czech Statistical Office).

Kalabisová *et al.* (2013: 121) put it unequivocally: the main reason is a 'long-term unwillingness of a narrow group of local inhabitants to work'. Such reasoning, however, fails to explain why the unemployment rate before 2012 was much lower: it even dropped from 11.27% in 2006 to 7.39% in 2008. After that there was a steep rise, to reach the level of 2013. It is obvious that 'cultural' factors obscured the real reasons embedded in the recent economic crisis.

The dominant narrative of progressiveness silences other 'alternative' discourses as obsolete. Any calls for a slower pace of 'modernisation' sound backward and obscurantist. Yet, though the post-socialist discourse of development and modernity is hegemonic and omnipresent, the research outcomes point to certain layers of the local population that do not identify with it. These are not only socio-economically marginalised individuals who share largely positive memories of socialist modernisation and/or those who are severely afflicted by post-socialist modernisation but also the middle-class residents who are against the current large-scale transformation through tourism that results in a radical change of the village structure and identity. They do not like the uncontrollable tourism development that engulfs the landscape. As one informant claims, development in Lipno 'has been running riot' and 'things got out of hand'. Such disagreement, however, remains largely in the form of private grumbling and is not translated into any public action. Hence, the tourism development project is accompanied by an extremely low level of community participation. The attitude of the majority of locals toward tourism development is overwhelmingly characterised by passivity and indifference.

The inability to influence tourism-related development is caused by a number of mutually intertwined factors. First, the prevailing feelings of powerlessness echoed in a common saying, 'one cannot do anything about that', are conditioned by an apparent uselessness of the residents' residual, 'unproductive' social capital composed of horizontal bonding (kin, neighbour or vocational) based on the 'particularised trust' (Kovács, 2012: 115) inherited from the socialist era. As Lampland (2002: 41) argues, 'neither qualifications nor friendships from the socialist period are sufficient to ensure success' in the post-socialist environment. Social capital must be renewed and enhanced in order to be used as an asset in the new milieu. By lacking the 'effective', vertical social capital, these residents cannot comply with the requirements of post-socialist progress and modernity.

Second, this inability is exacerbated by a lack of communication and cooperation opportunities in the community. There is no 'local' pub or club in the village where residents could discuss matters freely.

Third, non-interference in the development plans and decisions of the local power elite can be equally explained by the nature of rural public life under socialism. As Mandel (2002: 282) points out, all formal organisational activity was linked to the state ideology of socialism with the aim of directing and controlling cultural expressions for political purposes. Forty years of socialism, when people were prevented from interrogating the decisions made by the power elite, have resulted in a high degree of apathy and unwillingness to engage in public affairs, strengthened by

the current frustration and disillusionment with the post-socialist development. As one informant said,

> there is no point in going to the polls, you never change anything. There will be the same people on the ballot as before, there is nobody to vote for.

Fourth, another factor that can contribute to explaining the overall lack of agency is the absence of, or limited information about, the privatisation and development processes. Very few local people were informed of any plans or invited to participate in discussions concerning the launching of the tourism projects. As some bitterly admit, they even feel discouraged from attending regular meetings of the local government to discuss the policies and plans for tourism, though, legally, access should be free to everybody interested.

8.5 Conclusion

Among many similar tourism development projects that have emerged in a Czech rural environment in the past 15 years, Lipno is unique in a number of aspects. The scale, pace and nature of transformation through tourism is unprecedented. It touches upon all dimensions of rural social organisation – the patterns of economic livelihood, settlement patterns and spatial arrangements and choices of leisure activities. It necessarily arouses extensive media coverage, which is, however, not paralleled with any active local response. The lack of community participation in planning and implementing such tourism projects is reflected in the serious negative effects, namely a disruption of the landscape and community life.

This chapter has attempted to point out a striking complicity between international tourism and neoliberal globalisation (Salazar, 2013; Duffy, 2014). The effects of the neoliberal forces of political and economic restructuring encouraged the local political elite to adopt tourism as a 'rural response to globalisation' and as a 'mechanism' for development (George *et al.*, 2009: 12). While this strategy was deployed as the solution to the socio-economic decline of the village, it turned out to be rather a *cause* of other severe problems, endangering social coherence and disrupting the physical landscape. The findings suggest that though tourism-related development does confer economic benefits on some people, most residents feel that these gains seem too small in comparison to what is lost.

Lipno society has changed significantly, shifting from an egalitarian to a 'competitive' type of society, which brings about new power and social relations, competing social and cultural practices and tensions in rural place making.

The outcomes reveal pluralistic accounts of the post-socialist rural development through tourism. They show that the rivalry in the community is caused predominantly by the ambivalent meanings of development and modernity. Hence, the major point of difference, highlighting social and cultural cleavages, emerges on a discursive level and revolves around the contested narratives of modernity. The major conflict among the residents relating to the tourism development is caused by tensions between values set under socialism (with the state as a key guarantor of development and well-being) and values derived from post-socialist modernity enhanced by the key features of neoliberalism – market economy, privatisation and decentralisation of political power. The process of neoliberalisation accompanied by the lack of community participation has been instrumental in creating new parameters of progress and backwardness. Privatisation, commodification and commercialisation have noticeably deepened social difference in Lipno society. A new hierarchy between central and marginal worlds emerges; these worlds intersect both physical and symbolic zones, and are accompanied by distinct, often incompatible, practices and lifestyles. The former is composed of those who identify fully with the post-socialist discourse of modernity as the only possible way of development. The latter involves those who failed to join the tourism projects and comprises the category of culturally, partly socio-economically marginalised citizens.

In the situation where the post-socialist development project in rural Lipno is dominated by the local political elite and foreign capital interests, practically unopposed by the local community, it would be too naïve to expect that in the near future power will be disseminated to grassroots initiatives and institutions, and community interests will be inserted into the tourism planning processes. The incapability of both local power actors and marginalised subjects to resist the pressures of neoliberalisation open up issues about the nature of democracy and the form of representation in post-socialist Europe.

Endnotes

[1] The term 'Dutch village' is a vernacular name for standardised recreational houses owned by the Dutch in Czech villages. It is used in public discourse, predominantly by Internet users, to assert strong criticism of this new form of tourism. Recently, the usage of the term has increasingly appeared in official reports and documents, and also in academia.

[2] The rate of unemployment in the region in 2013 was 7.12% (Czech Statistical Office).

References

Allen, L.R., Long, P.T., Perdue, R.R. and Kieselbach, S. (1993) Impact of tourism development on residents' perceptions of community life. *Journal of Travel Research* 27(1), 16–21.

Analýza (2013) *Rozvoj obce Lipno nad Vltavou od počátku 90. let.* [*Development of Lipno nad Vltavou since the Early 1990s.*] Incoma GfK, Prague (in Czech).

Bakker, K. (2005) Neoliberalizing nature? Market environmentalism in water supply in England and Wales. *Annals of the Association of American Geographers* 95(3), 542–565.

Bernard, J., Kostelecký, T., Ilner, M. and Vobecká, J. (eds) (2011) *Samospráva venkovských obcí a místní rozvoj.* [*Local Government in Rural Municipalities and Local Development.*] SLON, Prague (in Czech).

Boyer, R. (2006). How do institutions cohere and change? In: James, P. and Wood, G. (eds) *Institutions and Working Life.* Oxford University Press, Oxford, UK.

Brandstädter, S. (2007) Transitional spaces: postsocialism as a cultural process. *Critique of Anthropology* 27(2), 131–145.

Burawoy, M. and Verdery, K. (1999) *Uncertain Transition. Ethnographies of Change in the Postsocialist World.* Rowman and Littlefield, Lanham, Maryland.

Butler, R.W. (1980) The concept of the tourist area life-cycle of evolution: implications for management of resources. *Canadian Geographer* 24(1), 5–12.

Butler, R.W. (1998) Rural recreation and tourism. In: Ilbery, B. (ed.) *The Geography of Rural Change.* Addison Wesley Longman, Harlow, UK, pp. 211–232.

Butler, R.W. and Hall, C.M. (1998) Image and reimaging of rural areas. In: Butler, R.W., Hall, C.M. and Jenkins, J. (eds) *Tourism and Recreation in Rural Areas.* John Wiley, Chichester, UK, pp. 115–122.

Butler, R.W., Hall, C.M. and Jenkins, J. (eds) (1998) *Tourism and Recreation in Rural Areas.* John Wiley, Chichester, UK.

Cohen, E. (1978) The impact of tourism on the physical environment. *Annals of Tourism Research* 5(2), 215–237.

Cronicle of Lipno, The. Kept and stored by Vicki Neubauerová, Lipno nad Vltavou, Czech Republic.

Czech Statistical Office (2015) Available at: https://www.czso.cz/csu/czso/home (accessed 15 May 2015).

Davis, J.S. and Morais, D.B. (2004) Factions and enclaves: small towns and socially unsustainable tourism development. *Journal of Travel Research* 43, 3–10.

Dewailly, J.M. (1998) Images of heritage in rural regions. In: Butler, R.W., Hall, C.M. and Jenkins, J. (eds) *Tourism and Recreation in Rural Areas.* John Wiley, Chichester, UK, pp. 123–137.

Dewailly, J.M. and Flament, E. (1993) *Géographie du turisme et de loisirs.* SEDES, coll. DIEM, Paris.

Duffy, R. (2014) Interactive elephants: nature, tourism and neoliberalism. *Annals of Tourism Research* 44, 88–101.

Garrod, B., Wornell, R. and Youell, R. (2006) Re-conceptualizing rural resources as countryside capital: the case of rural tourism. *Journal of Rural Studies* 22, 117–128.

George, W.E., Mair, H. and Reid, D.G. (2009) *Rural Tourism Development. Localism and Cultural Change.* Channel View Publications, Bristol, UK.

Giampiccoli, A. and Saayman, M. (2014) A conceptualisation of alternative forms of tourism in relation to community development. *Mediterranean Journal of Social Sciences* 5(27), 1667–1677.

Hall, C.M. and Jenkins, J.M. (1998) The policy dimensions of rural tourism and recreation. In: Butler, R.W., Hall, C.M. and Jenkins, J. (eds) *Tourism and Recreation in Rural Areas.* John Wiley, Chichester, UK, pp. 19–42.

Hall, D., Roberts, L. and Mitchell, M. (eds) (2003) *New Directions in Rural Tourism.* Ashgate, Farnham, UK.

Hann, C.M. (2002) *Postsocialism. Ideals, Ideologies and Practices in Eurasia.* Routledge, London.

Harvey, D. (2003) The 'new' imperialism: accumulation by dispossession. *The Socialist Register 2004*, 63–87.

Higgins-Desbiolles, F. (2006) More than an 'industry': the forgotten power of tourism as a social force. *Tourism Management* 27(6), 1192–1208.

Holý, L. (2010) *Malý český člověk a skvělý český národ.* [*The Little Czech and the Great Czech Nation.*] SLON, Prague (in Czech).

Horáková, H. (2010) Post-communist transformation of tourism in Czech rural areas: new dilemmas. *Anthropological Notebooks* 16(1), 59–77.

Horáková, H. and Boscoboinik, A. (eds) (2012) *From Production to Consumption: Transformation of Rural Communities.* LIT Verlag, Berlin.

Horáková, H. and Fialová, D. (2014) *Transformace venkova. Turismus jako forma rozvoje.* [*Transformation of Rurality. Tourism as a Form of Development.*] Aleš čeněk, Prague (in Czech).

Hörschelmann, K. and Stenning, A. (2008) Ethnographies of postsocialist change. *Progress in Human Geography* 32(3), 339–361.

Hughes, G. (1995) The cultural construction of sustainable tourism. *Tourism Management* 16(1), 49–59.

Infocentrum Lipno nad Vltavou. Available at: www.lipno.info/infoservis/ (accessed 27 July 2016).

Kalabisová, J., Plzáková, L., Studnička, P. and Tinková, V. (2013) *Měření efektů cestovního ruchu v obci Lipno nad Vltavou.* [*Measuring the Effects of Tourism in the Village of Lipno nad Vltavou.*] Vysoká škola hotelová, Prague (in Czech).

Kalb, D. (2002) Afterword: globalism and postsocialist practices. In: Hann, C.M. (ed.) *Postsocialism. Ideals, Ideologies and Practices in Eurasia.* Routledge, London, pp. 317–334.

Kovács, K. (2012) Rescuing a small village school in the context of rural change in Hungary. *Journal of Rural Studies* 28, 108–117.

Lampland, M. (2002) The advantages of being collectivized: cooperative farm managers in the postsocialist economy. In: Hann, C.M. (ed.) *Postsocialism. Ideals, Ideologies and Practices in Eurasia.* Routledge, London, pp. 31–56.

McCarthy, J. (2006) Neoliberalism and the politics of alternatives. *Annals of the Association of American Geographers* 96(1), 84–104.

McCarthy, J. and Prudham, S. (2004) Neoliberal nature and the nature of neoliberalism. *Geoforum* 35(3), 275–283.

Mandel, R. (2002) Seeding civil society. In: Hann, C.M. (ed.) *Postsocialism. Ideals, Ideologies and Practices in Eurasia.* Routledge, London, pp. 279–296.

O'Reilly, K. (2005) *Ethnographic Methods*. Routledge, Oxford, UK.

Peck, J. (2004) Geography and public policy: constructions of neoliberalism. *Progress in Human Geography* 28(3), 392–405.

Peck, J. and Tickell, A. (2002) Neoliberalizing space. *Antipode* 34, 380–404.

Salazar, N. (2013) *Envisioning Eden: Mobilising Imaginaries in Tourism and Beyond*. Berghahn, Oxford, UK.

Shaw, G. and Williams, A.M. (2002) *Critical Issues in Tourism: A Geographical Perspective*. Blackwell, Oxford, UK.

Verdery, K. (1996) *What Was Socialism, and What Comes Next?* Princeton University Press, Princeton, New Jersey.

Vítková, L. (2006) Marina Lipno – Přístav uprostřed lesů. [Marina Lipno – in the midst of the woods.] *Umělec* 3 (in Czech). Available at: http://divus.cc/praha/cs/article/marina-lipno-a-port-in-the-middle-of-the-woods (accessed 3 August 2016).

9 The Expansion of International Hotel Groups into Central and Eastern Europe after 1989 – Strategic Couplings and Local Responses

Piotr Niewiadomski*

School of Geosciences, University of Aberdeen, UK

9.1 Introduction

The collapse of communism in Central and Eastern Europe (CEE) in 1989 and the subsequent re-orientation of the formerly communist states to capitalism and liberal democracy signified one of the most dramatic geopolitical shifts in the world's history. It redrew the map of Europe and brought about a completely new structure of political and economic relations, both on the European continent and in the rest of the world (Hudson, 2000). The former communist states' triumphant and (almost) unanimous decision to embark on the path of transition to democracy and a form of market economy (Amsden *et al.*, 1994; Gowan, 1995; Kołodko, 2000; Sokol, 2001) hallmarked the onset of a political and economic experiment of an unprecedented scale – the construction of capitalism and liberal democracy from the ruins of communism (Smith, 1997; see also Grabher and Stark, 1998).

The mode of transition that the CEE countries adopted at the recommendation of the array of Western multilateral organisations was deeply rooted in the ideology of neoliberalism (Smith and Pickles, 1998; Bradshaw and Stenning, 2004). Defined in terms of the structural adjustments necessary to replace the old system with a new

one, the transition was to be based on the rapid implementation of a stock set of appropriate policies and reforms to facilitate the emergence of a market economy and democratic relations. The main objective was to dismantle the former socialist institutional structures and develop new, democratic and free market-orientated arrangements (Smith, 1997). The whole neoliberal project revolved around the golden formula of two interrelated transitions – political and economic – both of which were seen as a precondition for the desired reintegration with the Western world. While the political transition included political liberalisation, democratisation and free elections, the economic transition was to bring economic liberalisation, internationalisation, marketisation, deregulation and privatisation (Smith and Pickles, 1998; Sokol, 2001; Bradshaw and Stenning, 2004).

Meanwhile, rather than fostering political stability and economic convergence with the West, the transition assumed different forms in different places, simultaneously becoming a source of multiple unexpected social, political and economic problems (Sokol, 2001; Dunford and Smith, 2004). Although the rightness of the ongoing geopolitical shift and the overall direction of the economic and political changes was hardly questioned, the reality of transition on the ground,

*E-mail: p.niewiadomski@abdn.ac.uk

which contrasted starkly with what the neo-liberal project had promised, laid serious doubts on the appropriateness of the ongoing reforms. The striking disjuncture between the expect-ations which the geopolitical reorientation of the CEE region generated and the measureable effects of the transition that could be observed on the ground at various spatial scales derived from the universal nature of the neoliberal orthodoxy and its inherent neglect of the economic, social and political diversity of CEE (Bradshaw and Stenning, 2004). As a result, the geopolitical and economic changes at the national and supra-national level brought about a range of unex-pected local responses that were determined by different historical experiences, earlier paths of growth, different pre-existing institutional con-texts and varying local capacities to accommo-date the proposed changes (Smith and Pickles, 1998). Importantly, these responses differed not only between regions, localities and communi-ties but also between sectors of the economy. The hotel sector – one of the key subsectors of the tourism production system and the main focus of this chapter – can serve here as a good example.

Because of the communist governments' ideological preoccupation with the development of heavy industries, tourism – like other service industries – was of very low significance among the priorities of communist administrations (Scott and Renaghan, 1991; Hall, 1992; Williams and Balaž, 2002; Johnson and Vanetti, 2004). As a result, the CEE hotel sector, which between 1945 and 1989 remained almost entirely in the hands of the state, was largely underinvested and underdeveloped (Jaakson, 1996; Johnson, 1997; Błądek and Tulibacki, 2003; Witkowski, 2003; Johnson and Vanetti, 2004). Moreover, because of the political divide between the East and the West, the CEE market was cordoned off from the global economy and the investment and expert-ise that international hotel corporations would have brought had they been allowed to expand into CEE. Although the situation started to change as early as in the 1970s, and some limited pene-tration of international hotel brands was al-lowed in some states (notably Hungary and Poland), it was still too little to foster any sig-nificant upgrading. For all these reasons, when communism collapsed, the CEE hotel industry found itself lagging far behind its Western coun-terpart in terms of the number and condition of hotels, the range of extra facilities and the skills and knowledge possessed by hotel staff (Jaakson, 1996; Johnson, 1997; Błądek and Tulibacki, 2003; Witkowski, 2003).

As crucial elements of a successful transi-tion to capitalism, the ongoing internationalisa-tion of the CEE economies and the increasing openness of the CEE region to foreign firms were anticipated to offer a solution to the problems that the tourism industry and its subsectors were facing. This was similar to numerous other CEE industries, where, due to the lack of local capital, a key role in bringing much desired up-grading was accorded to foreign direct invest-ment (FDI) (Hardy, 1998; Pavlinek, 2004). Also in the hotel sector, great hopes were pinned on the expected influx of foreign corporations. It was assumed that international hotel groups would import the newest knowledge and tech-nology, implement modern marketing and man-agement practices and help improve the neglected hotel infrastructure (Franck, 1990; Healey, 1994). The simultaneous re-evaluation of tour-ism in the CEE economies as a hard currency earner (Franck, 1990; Johnson and Vanetti, 2004), as well as the growing recognition of the fact that 'the lack of modern hotels and com-mercial facilities is constraining the develop-ment of the private sector' (EBRD, 1994: 27), were additional important reasons why inter-national hotel groups were to be welcomed in CEE. It was believed that the prospects of strong economic development and the general tourist attractiveness of CEE, both of which were ex-pected to translate into high levels of demand for hotel services, would prove sufficient to attract foreign hotel investors and operators (Lock-wood, 1993; Healey, 1994; Johnson and Iunius, 1999;). Unfortunately, even though the interest was indeed mutual, the expansion of inter-national hotel groups into CEE in the 1990s was hampered by a vast array of unexpected factors. Local responses to the expansion, which were rarely in line with the pro-transition enthusiasm of the CEE national governments, proved to play a significant role in determining the expansion's pace and scope. It is these responses that lie at the heart of this chapter.

The chapter draws from the research pro-ject carried out in 2008 and 2009. The main aim of the project was to enquire into the com-plex interrelations between expanding hotel groups and the emerging post-communist institutional contexts across CEE. Although the project focused on three different states, due to limited space the following analysis concentrates on the case of Poland – one of the biggest hotel markets in CEE. The data presented in Section 9.3 derive from 58 semi-structured interviews. Twenty-four of them were carried out with development executives from all 23 international hotel groups from the world's top 50 (according to the ranking found in Gale, 2008) that were active in the CEE market when the project started. The following 30 interviews were conducted in Poland with general managers of international hotels, hotel developers, representatives of the local hotel industry, representatives of local governments and trade unions and hotel consultants from international consultant firms based in Poland. The remaining four interviews were carried out with hotel analysts based outside CEE.

The remainder of this chapter consists of two sections and conclusions. Section 9.2 reviews the literature in which the following analysis is grounded. Further to a brief discussion of mutual relationships between geopolitics and tourism, it discusses the concepts of strategic coupling and path dependence that frame the whole analysis. An explanation of how these two notions can be combined in tourism research with the lens of geopolitics is also provided. Section 9.3 offers an empirical analysis. Various capabilities and attitudes of regional institutions in CEE (and in Poland in particular) further to the fall of communism are discussed, and the different ways in which they influenced the pace and scope of the expansion of hotel groups are also analysed. The last section offers conclusions.

9.2 Geopolitics, Strategic Coupling and Different Spatial Scales

As Weaver (2010: 48) noted, 'contemporary geopolitical discourses rarely mention tourism, and the tourism literature is rarely, if ever, framed within an explicitly geopolitical context'. Given that the term 'geopolitics' refers to the interrelationships between space, territoriality, territory and power (Cohen, 2003) (see Chapters 1 and 2, this volume), this reciprocal neglect of the relations between geopolitics and tourism is somewhat surprising.

Because international tourism is only made possible by the sovereign powers that the origin and the destination state possess and exercise, it is essential to recognise that tourism – particularly in its international form – is an inherently geopolitical phenomenon (Weaver, 2010). Importantly, this argument applies fully to both the constantly growing cross-border tourist flows (the number of international tourist trips reached the level of 1.087 billion in 2013 and is anticipated to increase almost twofold by 2030; UNWTO, 2014) and the complex multi-actor international tourism industry that facilitates and serves these flows. Indeed, just like tourism as a human activity involves a mass movement of people across national borders, the international expansion of the tourism production system – arguably the world's largest industrial complex (Lundberg et al., 1995) – inevitably relies on cross-border flows of capital, commodities, labour and expertise (Reiser, 2003; Hazburn, 2004; Hannam, 2013), none of which would be possible if adequate geopolitical relations between given states (or blocs of states) were not established.

By the same token, geopolitical relations at the national and supranational level can largely determine the fate of various tourist destinations at the subnational level. While, on the one hand, individual destinations may fall victim to the geopolitical imperatives of their respective national authorities (e.g. when the national government puts the tourism-dependent prosperity of local communities at risk by means of getting involved in a political conflict; Bianchi, 2007; Hannam, 2013), on the other, any relaxation of political tensions at the international level may generate new developmental opportunities for individual tourist destinations. Moreover, given that tourism has the potential to facilitate regional peace, foster friendly relationships between historical enemies and reduce economic inequities between different countries and regions, it may also often help improve geopolitical relations (Weaver, 2010). Thus, following Weaver (2010), who explored the relationships between geopolitics and sustainable tourism at various spatial scales, this chapter recognises that as much as geopolitical changes at the national and supranational level may have varying implications on tourism and the tourism industry at the sub-national level, local tourism-related responses to these changes will always be place and context dependent, and will therefore always differ. It is mainly on this premise that the analysis presented later in this chapter is based.

In this context, the chapter employs the concepts of strategic coupling and path dependence to explain why, in the CEE hotel industry, the promptness of geopolitical changes at the national and supranational level could hardly be reflected at lower geographical scales, and why the responses of the regional and local institutions to the expansion of international hotel groups – a much desired effect of the CEE hotel sector's economic and political reorientation to the West – did not match the standards set by the triumphant enthusiasm of the national administrations.

Although the concept of strategic coupling derives from economic geography, rather than any discipline where geopolitical relations are a core subject, its sensitiveness to different spatial scales and relations between them makes it particularly helpful in addressing the focus of this chapter. Associated with the much wider global production networks framework (Henderson *et al.*, 2002; see also Hess and Yeung, 2006; Coe *et al.*, 2008; Coe and Hess, 2011), the concept of 'strategic coupling of global production networks and regional assets, an interface mediated by a range of institutional activities across different geographical and organizational scales' (Coe *et al.*, 2004: 469) offers a middle ground perspective on how regional development can be fostered (see also Yeung, 2009; Coe and Hess, 2011). While, on the one hand, it pays attention to regional assets and endogenous growth factors within the region (such as technological and human resources) that are an essential precondition for development to take place, on the other, it emphasises the role of extra-regional processes in how regions develop, i.e. how regional assets fit the needs of translocal actors and how regions can slot into their global production networks (Coe *et al.*, 2004).

Regional development is thus a context-dependent outcome of the complementarity of regional assets and strategic needs of foreign firms. Moreover, the idea of strategic coupling also recognises that a key role in this set of processes is always played by regional institutional

formations and their capacity to unleash regional potential (to mould and promote regional assets) in order to fit the strategic needs of external firms, and thus 'hold down' translocal actors and their global production networks (Coe *et al.*, 2004; Coe, 2009; Coe and Hess, 2011; MacKinnon, 2012). Thus, strategic coupling processes derive from the intentional actions of two groups of actors (both of which decide to pursue a common objective) and result in time- and space-contingent coalitions between them (MacKinnon, 2012).

Particularly important here is also the fact that, as MacKinnon observed,

> the process of strategic coupling can be viewed in evolutionary terms, suggesting that regional institutions' capacities to bargain with TNCs [transnational corporations] will reflect the legacy of previous strategies and forms of investment.
>
> (MacKinnon, 2012: 231–232)

It is mainly for this reason why the concept of path dependence – a key notion of evolutionary economic geography (EEG) – is of enormous significance in framing the following analysis in combination with the concept of strategic coupling. Assuming that the economic landscape does not tend towards a unique equilibrium but rather it evolves in ways shaped by its history and past trajectories of growth (Martin and Sunley, 2006; Boschma and Martin, 2007, 2010), the concept of path dependence recognises that the evolution and historical transformations of regional institutions (and regional assets) should be fully acknowledged as an important set of factors shaping the relations between extra-local actors and their production networks on the one hand and the regions into which they expand on the other (MacKinnon, 2012).

In this respect, it is hardly surprising that the idea of path dependence gained much prominence in research on the variety of forms that the neoliberal transition unexpectedly assumed across CEE. In stark contrast to the neoliberal orthodoxy that was based on the idea of capitalism as a single ideal type that could be uniformly and universally implemented overnight, the idea of path dependence points towards the multiplicity of political and economic systems emerging in CEE, simultaneously emphasising their evolutionary nature (Smith and Pickles, 1998; Sokol,

2001; Bradshaw and Stenning, 2004). By means of recognising that the political and economic landscape is constituted out of the past social relations that are not replaced but reworked in a complex way (Smith, 1997), it stresses the complexity of post-communist transformations in CEE – 'the variety of strategies, techniques and effects that constitute transition-in-process – actually existing transition' (Smith and Pickles, 1998: 5). The research by Williams and Balaž (2000, 2002), who analysed the path-dependent nature of the Czech and Slovak tourism sector's post-communist development, clearly demonstrates that the concept of path dependence is also fully applicable to the tourism industry and its subsectors. The remainder of this chapter adopts the ideas of strategic coupling and path dependence to enquire into the disjuncture between the opportunities that the geopolitical changes in CEE created for both international hotel groups and the regions of CEE and the capacities of the CEE regional institutions to take advantage of these opportunities to the initially expected standards. Figure 9.1 illustrates in graphic form the applicability of these two concepts to the focus of this chapter.

9.3   Local Responses to the Expansion of International Hotel Groups: Capabilities and Attitudes

The unprecedented growth opportunities for international hotel groups that the geopolitical reorientation of CEE seemed to have created encouraged massive excitement in the hotel industry. The plethora of various regional assets in which CEE was abundant (Lockwood, 1993; Healey, 1994; Johnson and Iunius, 1999) seemed to be a 'perfect match' with the enthusiasm about the opportunities to expand into the formerly closed CEE market that international hotel groups shared (especially given that their domestic markets, as well as numerous other markets in the world, were already saturated). Unfortunately, the expansion into what was expected to be a land of opportunity brought disappointment and disillusionment, as a result of which the enthusiasm evaporated and the ambitious plans of smooth expansion had to be replaced by scepticism and cautiousness (Johnson and Iunius, 1999; Rotter, 2002). Although the persistently low degree of political stability and the high level of economic uncertainty (e.g. unstable exchange

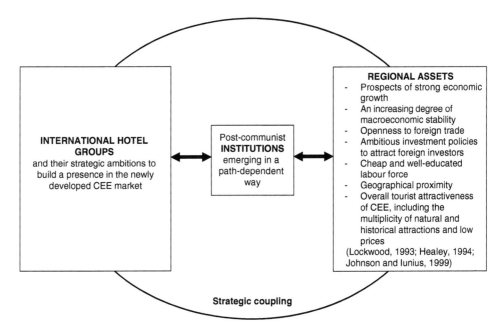

Fig. 9.1. Strategic couplings between international hotel groups and regional assets in CEE following the fall of communism in 1989. (From author's compilation, inspired by Coe et al., 2004: 470, Figure 1.)

rates, high inflation) were still hampering the expansion the most (Scott and Renaghan, 1991; Healey, 1994), the factors that unexpectedly affected the expansion in as strong a way derived from the unclear and emerging status of post-communist institutions across CEE. Rather than shaping and promoting regional assets to attract foreign hotel groups, due to the persisting influence of the communist legacies, the regional institutions of CEE proved to be not entirely capable of mediating strategic couplings between the assets of the CEE regions and the extra-local hotel industry actors that were looking to tap the previously closed CEE market. As a development executive from an international hotel group active in CEE confirmed:

> Initially there was a high level of excitement about Eastern and Central Europe following the change in 1989 and the 1990s. And then suddenly the realisation came that institutions are not there and property rights are not properly established.
>
> (Interviewee, November 2008)

A development executive from a different hotel group active in CEE also observed:

> A lot of these countries are very young democracies and it's not only the bad economic system but also the political system that is in transformation ... And not all of these countries are successful... And there are issues of corruption and there are a lot of sorts of problems that are probably logical or at least sort of natural for countries that are transforming. And that makes it more difficult to do business there.
>
> (Interviewee, April 2009)

First and foremost, the incapabilities of regional institutions originated from unregulated legal systems at the national level. As the decision to embark on the transition to capitalism and liberal democracy did not automatically replace the former communist legal systems with new, transparent and progressive ones, transforming the laws inherited from the communist period and passing all necessary legislations proved to be a complicated and time-consuming process. As one of the quotes above suggests, the most serious source of legal obstacles for investors and expanding hotel groups that the regional institutions were not able to cope with on their own was the issue of reprivatisation and land ownership.

While countries such as Estonia and the former Czechoslovakia completed the restitution process in a more or less smooth and clear-cut way, and all the land that had been nationalised previously by the communist authorities was passed back to its original owners, a proper reprivatisation reform was never passed in Poland. As a result, in the early 1990s, it was hardly possible in Poland to obtain a clear title on land, not to mention that purchasing land for investments was associated with the risk of a lawsuit with pre-communist owners which foreign hotel developers were not willing to take (Niewiadomski, 2016). Although the problem of unregulated land ownership was not caused by the regional authorities, their day-to-day activities were affected the most. For instance, the unregulated ownership of a considerable proportion of plots in various cities effectively prevented the respective regional institutions from elaborating comprehensive city development plans – a necessary precondition for a building permit (Niewiadomski, 2016). As a senior official from the regional government in one of the biggest Polish cities confirmed:

> In 1989 pretty much everything was in the hands of the state. And since then Poland has failed to pass a proper re-privatisation reform. Every case has to be considered individually and every individual has to claim their rights in a lawsuit. Many of them have already succeeded but not all ... And it is not something that differs between regions, it is a national-level problem. And this is the main reason why so many Polish cities do not have comprehensive city development plans and why issuing building permits is sometimes so difficult. If there is no development plan, no permit can be issued. And this makes the procedures much, much longer.
>
> (Interviewee, June 2009)

The institution of a public ground lease (the so-called perpetual usufruct, i.e. leasehold of public land for 99 years instead of passing full ownership), which was often used by the regional governments and which was hard for foreign investors to understand, was another discouraging factor from the perspective of foreign hotel developers (Niewiadomski, 2016). Importantly, the incapabilities of the regional institutions in Poland also derived from the unclear and not very transparent division of responsibilities between the different levels of administration. It was only in 1999 that the two-level system (regions and municipalities), which had been implemented during the communist era and in which regions were hugely dependent on the central administration, was replaced by a three-level system (regions, counties, municipalities) where a notable proportion of decision-making responsibilities was devolved to the local and regional authorities. Thus, not only was it initially risky to make any investments but also it was not always clear where different permits should be sought (Niewiadomski, 2016). Finally, the political attitudes of the regional authorities to foreign ownership of Polish land often made the whole process even more complex. The fear of being sold out and exploited, which in the Polish case was rooted not only in the communist past but also (or even mostly) in the memory of World War II, and which was often cultivated by extreme political parties for their own populist purposes, was often the source of widespread suspicion and open hostility towards foreign investors (Franck, 1990; Healey, 1994). Indeed, the enthusiasm about the geopolitical changes that was evident at the national level was not always fully reflected at lower geographical scales. As a development executive from an international hotel group active in CEE commented:

> It's an emotional thing and in any city where a hotel is developed, even though the land belongs to a private person, it's a very much politically sensitive thing ... Sometimes there are mayors who are progressive, young and fit, like in Wrocław for example. They understand the business rationale behind it. And then there are other mayors who are not so open and not so flexible.
>
> (Interviewee, February 2009)

Unregulated land ownership and the problems with getting a clear title on land, the lack of comprehensive city development plans, the unclear division of responsibilities between various levels of administrations and the varying political and cultural attitudes of regional and local authorities, all of which made the administrative procedures in the 1990s unnecessarily complex and long, were the very source of what was usually considered to be the most typical heritage of communism – corruption and bureaucracy (Niewiadomski, 2016). A development executive from an international hotel group active in CEE confirmed:

> Yes, we have found corruption in some areas and we have also found a lot of bureaucracy.

> And again, that's why we don't feel comfortable in making any investments at this point. We think it has to be done by somebody who knows this bureaucracy and of course when we talk about corruption we're not going to go to any deals when we can see that things are not done properly.
>
> (Interviewee, February 2009)

Although the problem of corruption (particularly with regard to the restitution process and the privatisation of the state-owned hotel enterprises) was initially a decisive factor hampering the expansion of international hotel investors and operators into CEE in the 1990s (Scott and Renaghan, 1991; Lockwood, 1993; Healey, 1994; Johnson and Vanetti, 2004), a significant number of CEE countries managed to tackle (or at least considerably reduce) this problem relatively quickly. By contrast, various forms of bureaucracy proved to be a serious issue for many years to come. As a development executive from one of the international hotel groups active in Poland that not only operate or franchise hotels but also invest directly in real estate, confirmed:

> In Poland – and I think it's the same thing in the other CEE countries – the main thing we face is the long and quite complicated administrative procedures. And it can take quite long to get everything right with the land register, planning and building permit and all of that. That's quite a long process ... Just a very simple thing can take a very long time because you need signatures, and you need a lot of official documents and the paperwork. The paperwork is just massive. So, yes, we take that as one of the factors that slow down the development.
>
> (Interviewee, December 2008)

As a hotel industry expert from an international consulting company based in Poland further explained:

> The problem is that there is still this past syndrome coming from the communist times and that has a lot to do with this inefficiency that is all in the administrative capacities, inside of each one of the sidelines – federal, municipal, regional or local offices. You know, the mayor can make a decision for the city, but by the time it gets approved by the general assembly, by the time it gets stamped, by the time the clerks get all these stamps, we're talking months and years.
>
> (Interviewee, June 2009)

A senior official from the regional government in one of the biggest Polish cities also critically confirmed:

> Some procedures are truly unnecessary ... Because we do different projects with Germans or French we can see how much easier the procedures in their projects are and how complex they are in ours. These procedures, this amount of documentation which we need to file are all a serious hurdle, a serious barrier ... We of course can see every day that many of those procedures could be simpler, but 20 years is too little to complete such a thorough transformation of the whole system and the old way of thinking.
>
> (Interviewee, July 2009)

However, this inefficiency of administrative capacities across CEE did not derive solely from the fact that the CEE legal systems were 'in the making' and that for some years after the collapse of communism many laws remained unclear. As the hotel industry expert quoted above further commented, the problem of bureaucracy was also deeply rooted in the personal (political and cultural) attitudes of CEE officials. Referred to by the interviewee as a 'lack of will power to make things actually happen' (Niewiadomski, 2016: 279) or, more generally, as a 'mentality issue', such attitudes originated from the lack of business culture under the communist regime and the fact that the need for enhanced collaboration between the private sector and public administration – so obvious for developed societies – was too new in the 1990s to be understood completely by the CEE states (Johnson and Vanetti, 2004). As the interviewee continued:

> There's certain reasons why this is very difficult to break. We need to remember that an administrator sitting behind the desk and making 1500 PLN [approximately €400] a month has absolutely no incentive, especially if you cannot corrupt him. Because in the old days it moved faster because you could put envelopes under the table and now I would say that's 98 per cent gone. So there are absolutely no incentives for them to do anything rapidly, to make any decisions or sign anything that they could be fired for. So they sit at these desks unless somebody presses them and says 'hey, Mr Kowalski, where is this whatever file that has been with us for three years?' Otherwise it's just hung.
>
> (Interviewee, June 2009)

Another important factor that determined the nature of local responses to the expansion of hotel groups into CEE in the early 1990s, and which therefore largely affected its scope and pace, was the local and regional authorities' shortage of knowledge of the hotel business. Not only were the authorities usually not able to provide hotel investors and operators with credible information on the market (e.g. in terms of identifying appropriate plots of land for hotel investments or indicating where the demand for hotel services might emerge in the future) but also they were not experienced enough to tailor their expectations towards hotel investors to the needs of the local community. As a result, the regional and local governments' ambitious preferences for luxury hotels with large conference and spa facilities and under the most famous brands could hardly be matched by the strictly demand-orientated international investors and operators. Such discrepancies between what the regional governments expected and what hotel groups were willing to offer were often a source of misunderstandings, leading to many project failures. As a development executive from an international hotel group active in CEE confirmed:

> When you ask a mayor what type of hotel they would like, they would invariably always say 'oh, I want a 5-star hotel with big conference facilities and big spa facilities'. But it may not make economic sense... It is then our job to say 'well, hang on, you know, we've got to make this work financially, so let's try to bring the two interests together and we recommend, for example, 150 rooms and not 250 rooms, the largest conference room should be for 200 people and not for 400 people, and it should be a 4-star hotel, not a 5-star hotel'. It's our job then, to kind of explain to these people what the right hotel concept for the region is.
>
> (Interviewee, February 2009)

While all the obstacles hampering the expansion of international hotel investors and operators into CEE described above pertained to the stage of property development, the problems that the few existing internationally branded hotels experienced in CEE at the stage of operations (i.e. once the hotel opened its doors), and which were therefore relatively easy to anticipate, also initially proved to be discouraging factors for potential new players. Given that the interests of the city in a multiplicity of local business, cultural and political events, which all translate into higher levels of tourism traffic, are convergent with those of hotels, hotels have no choice but to rely on an institutional infrastructure responsible for city marketing. In the early 1990s, such infrastructure in CEE was either non-existent or, at best, not developed and experienced enough to help local and regional governments promote their assets properly, create appropriate investment conditions and thus attract international companies. The tourism-related institutional infrastructure inherited from the communist system was not fully able in such a short time to adjust to the requirements of the new system and assume the responsibilities that it had never had to fulfil before. As a senior official from the regional government in one of the most famous tourist cities in Poland confirmed:

> Let me put it this way... One of the weaknesses of all Polish cities is the very poor marketing, the lack of professional marketing, the lack of a strong city brand and the lack of marketing of that brand.
>
> (Interviewee, June 2009)

Given that Poland was one of the largest and most quickly developing markets in CEE, and that the potential of numerous cities as attractive tourist and business destinations was recognised relatively quickly, it offers in this respect a particularly interesting case. Rather than helping address the problem, the plethora of institutions that started emerging in the 1990s to market their cities initially fostered the chaos. While some of these institutions were established as departments of local government, some of them were founded as NGOs, as a result of which their sources of funding and their actual responsibilities varied widely (they could range from carrying out marketing activities and elaborating educational programmes in the area of tourism to analysing the market, providing information for expanding firms and even proposing new legislation). Not only was it difficult, therefore, to coordinate their activities at the national level but also the whole structure was very unclear, and thus of very little use to expanding hotel groups. For this reason, in places where such institutions were in their infancy or where there was simply too much chaos, various initiatives designed to imitate the missing infrastructure were organised directly by representatives of the industry. The Warsaw Destination Alliance (WDA), established by a few upscale hotels in Warsaw in order to promote the Polish capital as a business and tourist destination, can serve here as the best example of this (Niewiadomski, 2016).

As demonstrated by the case of the hotel industry presented above, in the 1990s the regional and local institutions of CEE were hardly able to catch up with the prompt geopolitical shift that the majority of national governments in the CEE region embarked on enthusiastically. Indeed, rather than fostering the economic and political openness that was declared at the national level, they were, in fact, largely hindering (although mostly unintentionally) the expansion of foreign hotel investors and operators into CEE. Rooted in the communist legal, political, economic and sociocultural past, the local responses to the expansion inevitably proved to be path dependent in nature. However, it is also necessary to recognise that the overall situation has not remained as bad as it might have been seen to be in the early 1990s.

Although the quotes above suggest that at least some of the problems had not entirely receded into insignificance before 2008 and 2009, when the interviews were carried out, some important improvements started taking place as early as the late 1990s. Twenty years after the fall of communism, it was easy to see that large-scale corruption was no longer a problem, that hotel projects were very seldom at risk because of bureaucratic hurdles, that the legal systems across CEE were developed much more in line with what could be observed in Western Europe (mostly because of the influence of the European Union) and that the capabilities and attitudes of regional and local institutions were at least sufficient to promote regional assets, create adequate investment conditions for foreign firms and thus make strategic couplings with international hotel investors and operators fully possible and successful for both sides.

9.4 Conclusions

This chapter has combined the lens of geopolitics with the concepts of strategic coupling and path dependence to explain the inability of regional and local institutions in CEE to facilitate adequately the expansion of international hotel groups into the CEE region in the early 1990s. It has been demonstrated that although it was hoped that international hotel investors and operators would bring upgrading to the CEE hotel industry, which, further to the fall of the communist regime, found itself in a much neglected condition, and thus in striking need of help from foreign firms, the various responses to the expansion observed at the subnational levels initially hampered, not fostered, the whole process.

Various legal problems inherited from the communist past, such as unregulated land ownership, the unclear division of responsibilities between different levels of administration and the unnecessarily complex and lengthy administrative procedures, all of which accounted for massive bureaucracy (often augmented by serious threats of corruption), largely constrained the potential of regional institutions to mediate strategic couplings between extra-local actors and regional assets. In addition, legal problems were often accompanied by the lack of professional knowledge of hotel development, together with an array of different political and cultural attitudes, which from the perspective of foreign firms were less than adequate and which in various institutional environments often made foreign hotel groups feel unwelcomed, or at least unsupported. Thus, the communist legacies and the largely path-dependent nature of the regional institutions' post-communist development proved to be the decisive source of the disjuncture between the opportunities created by the changes in the geopolitical situation at the national and supranational level and the degree to which these opportunities could be taken advantage of at subnational scales. Indeed, regional and local

institutions were either unable, or in some cases most unwilling, to meet the expectations generated by the enthusiasm associated with the onset of large-scale geopolitical changes.

The above analysis of the expansion of international hotel groups into CEE after 1989 leads to two sets of conclusions. First, apart from emphasising that the international development of the tourism production system hinges on the geopolitical relations between different countries (and blocs of countries), it demonstrates that the geopolitics of tourism and the tourism industry is inherently multi-scalar in nature, and therefore it will never be accounted for comprehensively without due attention to the specific economic, political and sociocultural features of the places that the international flows of tourists and tourism-related capital interconnect. Second, more generally and beyond the case of the tourism industry, the analysis presented above shows that even the most favourable changes in the geopolitical situation at the supranational level are not automatically supported by the processes occurring at lower scales if appropriate conditions are not met. This, in turn, attests to the fact that political, economic and sociocultural processes taking place at various scales and in varying institutional contexts may be largely asynchronous – something that in the case of post-communist changes in CEE has been well captured by the notion of systemic transformation – 'a plurality of transitions in a dual sense ... a multiplicity of distinctive strategies ... not one transition but many occurring in different domains' (Stark, 1992: 301). Because of its highly place-specific nature, tourism as a human activity, as well as the whole tourism industry, offers an interesting case through which these relationships can be explored in more depth.

References

Amsden, A., Kochanowicz, J. and Taylor, L. (1994) *The Market Meets its Match: Restructuring the Economics of Eastern Europe.* Harvard University Press, Cambridge, Massachusetts.

Bianchi, R. (2007) Tourism and the globalisation of fear: analysing the politics of risk and (in)security in global travel. *Tourism and Hospitality Research* 7, 64–74.

Błądek, Z. and Tulibacki, T. (2003) *Dzieje Krajowego Hotelarstwa – od Zajazdu do Współczesności: Fakty, Obiekty, Ludzie.* [*The History of the Polish Hotel Industry – from an Old Inn to Contemporary Times: Facts, Establishments, People.*] Palladium Architekci – Błądek, Mańkowski, Poznań, Poland (in Polish).

Boschma, R. and Martin, R. (2007) Editorial: constructing an evolutionary economic geography. *Journal of Economic Geography* 7, 537–548.

Boschma, R. and Martin, M. (2010) The aims and scope of evolutionary economic geography. In: Boschma, R. and Martin, R. (eds) *The Handbook of Evolutionary Economic Geography*. Edward Elgar, Cheltenham, UK, pp. 3–39.

Bradshaw, M. and Stenning, A. (2004) Introduction: transformation and development. In: Bradshaw, M. and Stenning, A. (eds) *East Central Europe and the Former Soviet Union*. Pearson, Harlow, UK, pp. 1–32.

Coe, N. (2009) Global production networks. In: Kitchin, R. and Thrift, N. (eds) *The International Encyclopedia of Human Geography*. Elsevier, Oxford, UK, pp. 556–562.

Coe, N. and Hess, M. (2011) Local and regional development: a global production networks approach. In: Pike, A., Rodriguez-Pose, A. and Tomaney, J. (eds) *The Handbook of Local and Regional Development*. Routledge, London, pp. 128–138.

Coe, N., Hess, M., Yeung, H., Dicken, P. and Henderson, J. (2004) 'Globalizing' regional development: a global production networks perspective. *Transactions of the Institute of British Geographers* 29, 468–484.

Coe, N., Dicken, P. and Hess, M. (2008) Global production networks: realizing the potential. *Journal of Economic Geography* 8, 271–295.

Cohen, S. (2003) *Geopolitics of the World System*. Rowman and Littlefield, Oxford, UK.

Dunford, M. and Smith, A. (2004) Economic restructuring and employment change. In: Bradshaw, M. and Stenning, A. (eds) *East Central Europe and the Former Soviet Union*. Pearson, Harlow, UK, pp. 33–58.

EBRD (European Bank for Reconstruction and Development) (1994) *Annual Report 1994*. EBRD, London.

Franck, C. (1990) Tourism investment in Central and Eastern Europe. *Tourism Management* 11, 333–338.

Gale, D. (2008) Hotels' 325. *Hotels* 7, 38–52.

Gowan, P. (1995) Neo-liberal theory and practice for Eastern Europe. *New Left Review* 213, 3–60.

Grabher, G. and Stark, D. (1998) Organising diversity: evolutionary theory, network analysis and post-socialism. In: Pickles, J. and Smith, A. (eds) *Theorising Transition: The Political Economy of Post-Communist Transformation*. Routledge, London, pp. 54–75.

Hall, D. (1992) The challenges of international tourism in Eastern Europe. *Tourism Management* 13, 41–44.

Hannam, K. (2013) 'Shangri-La' and the new 'Great Game': exploring tourism geopolitics between China and India. *Tourism Planning and Development* 10(2), 178–186.

Hardy, J. (1998) Cathedrals in the desert? Transnationals, corporate strategy and locality in Wrocław. *Regional Studies* 32, 639–652.

Hazburn, W. (2004) Globalisation, reterritorialisation and the political economy of tourism development in the Middle East. *Geopolitics* 9(2), 310–341.

Healey, N. (1994) The transition economies of Central and Eastern Europe: a political, economic, social and technological analysis. *Columbia Journal of World Business* 29, 61–70.

Henderson, J., Dicken, P., Hess, M., Coe, N. and Yeung, H. (2002) Global production networks and the analysis of economic development. *Review of International Political Economy* 9, 436–464.

Hess, M. and Yeung, H. (2006) Guest editorial. *Environment and Planning A* 38, 1193–1204.

Hudson, R. (2000) One Europe or many? Reflections on becoming European. *Transactions of the Institute of British Geographers* 25, 409–426.

Jaakson, R. (1996) Tourism in transition in post-Soviet Estonia. *Annals of Tourism Research* 23, 617–634.

Johnson, C. and Iunius, R. (1999) Competing in Central Eastern Europe: perspectives and developments. *International Journal of Hospitality Management* 18, 245–260.

Johnson, C. and Vanetti, M. (2004) Market developments in the hotel sector in Eastern Central Europe. *Advances in Hospitality and Leisure* 1, 153–175.

Johnson, M. (1997) Hungary's hotel industry in transition 1960–1996. *Tourism Management* 18, 441–452.

Kołodko, G. (2000) *From Shock to Therapy: The Political Economy of Post-Socialist Transformation*. Oxford University Press, Oxford, UK.

Lockwood, A. (1993) Eastern Europe and the former Soviet states. In: Jones, P. and Pizam, A. (eds) *The International Hospitality Industry: Organizational and Operational Issues*. Pitman/Wiley, New York, pp. 25–37.

Lundberg, D., Krishnamoorthy, M. and Starvey, M. (1995) *Tourism Economics*. Wiley, New York.

MacKinnon, D. (2012) Beyond strategic coupling: reassessing the firm–region nexus in global production networks. *Journal of Economic Geography* 12, 227–245.

Martin, R. and Sunley, P. (2006) Path dependence and regional economic evolution. *Journal of Economic Geography* 6, 395–437.

Niewiadomski, P. (2016) The globalisation of the hotel industry and the variety of emerging capitalisms in Central and Eastern Europe. *European Urban and Regional Studies* 23(3), 267–288.

Pavlinek, P. (2004) Regional development implications of foreign direct investment in Central Europe. *European Urban and Regional Studies* 11, 47–70.

Reiser, D. (2003) Globalisation: an old phenomenon that needs to be rediscovered for tourism? *Tourism and Hospitality Research* 4, 306–320.

Rotter, K. (2002) Łańcuchy i systemy hotelowe w Polsce. [Hotel groups and chains in Poland.] *Turystyka i Hotelarstwo* 2, 9–22 (in Polish).

Scott, J. and Renaghan, L. (1991) Hotel development in Eastern Germany: opportunities and obstacles. *Cornell Hotel and Restaurant Administration Quarterly* 32, 44–51.

Smith, A. (1997) Breaking the old and constructing the new? Geographies of uneven development in Central and Eastern Europe. In: Lee, R. and Wills, J. (eds) *Geographies of Economies*. Edward Arnold, London, pp. 331–344.

Smith, A. and Pickles, J. (1998) Theorising transition and the political economy of transformation. In: Pickles, J. and Smith, A. (eds) *Theorising Transition: The Political Economy of Post-communist Transformations*. Routledge, London, pp. 1–22.

Sokol, M. (2001) Central and Eastern Europe a decade after the fall of state-socialism: regional dimensions of transition processes. *Regional Studies* 35, 645–655.

Stark, D. (1992) The great transformation? Social change in Eastern Europe. *Contemporary Sociology* 21, 299–304.

UNWTO (United Nations World Tourism Organization) (2014) *Tourism Highlights*, 2014. UNWTO, Madrid.

Weaver, D. (2010) Geopolitical dimensions of sustainable tourism. *Tourism Recreation Research* 35(1), 47–53.

Williams, A. and Balaž, V. (2000) Privatisation and the development of tourism in the Czech Republic and Slovakia: property rights, firm performance and recombinant property. *Environment and Planning A* 32, 715–734.

Williams, A. and Balaž, V. (2002) The Czech and Slovak republics: conceptual issues in the economic analysis of tourism in transition. *Tourism Management* 23, 37–45.

Witkowski, C. (2003) *Hotelarstwo – cz. II: Międzynarodowe Systemy Hotelowe w Polsce.* [*The Hotel Industry – Part Two: International Hotel Groups in Poland.*] Wyższa Szkoła Ekonomiczna w Warszawie, Warsaw (in Polish).

Yeung, H., (2009) Regional development and the competitive dynamics of global production networks: an East Asian perspective. *Regional Studies* 43, 325–351.

10 Conceptualising Transnational Hotel Chain Penetration in Bulgaria

Stanislav Ivanov* and Maya Ivanova

Varna University of Management, Varna, Bulgaria, and Zangador, Varna, Bulgaria

10.1 Introduction

If international tourism is an underestimated agent of globalisation, then the transnational corporations (TNCs) that inhabit the tourism and hospitality sectors are a significant driving force of that process, not least in terms of their requirement for consistency of product quality and complementarity of operational standards. Transnational hotel chains are no exception, and the geopolitical power they wield in many tourism destination economies (in terms of employment provision and standards, skill requirements, infrastructural stimulation, foreign direct investment (FDI) encouragement and revenue generation) may be substantial. Within the countries of Central and Eastern Europe (CEE), the penetration and role of TNCs is often nuanced, and in this chapter the options open to TNC hotel chains in their expansion process are reviewed and examined in relation to the Bulgarian market.

In the field of international business and marketing, hotel chains have a special place due to their specific characteristics: they are multi-unit enterprises that operate in a highly capital-intensive service industry and in countries with a diverse business environment (Ivanova and Ivanov, 2015a). Although there is a significant research literature dealing with the internationalisation of hotel chains (Littlejohn, 1997; Littlejohn *et al.*,

2007; Johnson and Vanetti, 2008), researchers have only recently focused on hotel chains' development in CEE in general (Wu *et al.*, 1998; Oana and Milla, 2009; Niewiadomski, 2015, 2016; Cosma *et al.*, 2014) and in Bulgaria in particular (Ivanova, 2013; Ivanova and Ivanov, 2014, 2015b,c).

The expansion process of a hotel chain includes four stages, connected with four strategic decisions, elaborated in Table 10.1: whether to start the expansion process and to internationalise; which destinations to enter; the choice of entry mode (equity or non-equity); and the selection of a local partner if a non-equity entry mode or joint venture is adopted.

As this chapter discusses the entry of international hotel chains in Bulgaria (Fig. 10.1), it focuses on the last three stages of this process. Specifically, the chapter elaborates the strategic decisions that the hotel chain's management team needs to make during the chain's expansion and evaluates how these decisions are reflected in the actual entry of hotel chains in the context of Bulgaria.

10.2 Theoretical Background

10.2.1 Analytical frameworks

There is no uniform theory of hotel chain expansion. The discussion of the strategic decisions

*Corresponding author. E-mail: stanislav.ivanov@vumk.eu

Table 10.1. Theoretical framework of the managerial decisions in a hotel chain's expansion process. (From authors' compilation.)

	Decisions in the expansion process of a hotel chain			
	Whether?	Where?	How?	With whom?
Definition	The decision to start the process of a chain's expansion and internationalisation	Choice of a destination to enter	Choice of an entry mode	Selection of a local partner
Analytical frameworks	• Eclectic theory (Dunning and McQueen, 1981; Hill et al., 1990; Dunning, 2000) • Transaction costs approach (Williamson, 1981; Teece, 1986; Erramilli and Rao, 1993) • Resource-based view (Barney, 1991; Barney and Arikan, 2001)	• Eclectic theory • Transaction costs approach	• Agency theory (Eisenhardt, 1989) • Eclectic theory • Transaction costs approach • Resource-based view • Syncretic theory (Contractor and Kundu, 1998)	• Agency theory • Partner selection approach (Geringer, 1991)
Factors influencing the hotel chain's decision	• Firm specific factors • Home country specific factors	• Host country general specific factors • Host country tourist industry and hotel industry specific factors	• Product specific factors • Firm specific factors • Host country specific factors • Home country specific factors • Entry mode characteristics	• Task-related criteria • Product-related criteria • Partner-related criteria
Sample publications dealing with the hotel chain's decision	Rodtook and Altinay (2013); Brida et al. (2015)	Dunning and McQueen (1981); Dunning (2000); Johnson and Vanetti (2005); Pranić et al. (2012); Zhang et al. (2012); Assaf et al. (2015)	Contractor and Kundu (1998, 2000); Rodriguez (2002); Chen and Dimou (2005); Quer et al. (2007); Oana and Milla (2009); Leon-Darder et al. (2011); Alon et al. (2012); Choi and Parsa (2012); Martorell et al. (2013); Niewiadomski (2016); Baena and Cerviño (2015); García de Soto-Camacho and Vargas-Sánchez (2015)	Altinay (2006); Holverson and Revaz (2006); Li et al. (2006); Xiao et al. (2008); Brookes and Altinay (2011); Ivanova and Ivanov (2015b)

Fig. 10.1. Bulgaria: location map. (Redrawn from *CIA Factbook* and *Magellan Geografix.*)

that the hotel chain management team needs to take during the expansion process is usually within the context of several analytical frameworks, briefly sketched in Box 10.1.

10.2.2 Choice of destination

The choice of a destination is usually the first decision to be made after the hotel chain management team has decided to initiate the expansion/internationalisation process. The company has the choice of simultaneous and/or consecutive entry into several destinations (Cuervo-Cazurra, 2011), depending on its resources (resource-based view) after careful evaluation of the locational advantages of countries (eclectic theory). Not all destinations are made equal.

Two groups of factors influence the choice of a destination by the hotel chain's management team (Dunning and McQueen, 1981; Dunning, 2000; Johnson and Vanetti, 2005; Assaf *et al.*, 2015). These are: (i) host country general specific factors, such as global location, political stability, economy, social and cultural resources, including labour availability, transport and communications infrastructure, legal/tax regimes and destination image; and (ii) host country tourism and hotel industry specific factors that include the hotel sector's characteristics and performance levels, government tourism policy and quality of tourist infrastructure.

Hotel chains enter destinations that create a favourable business environment for foreign investors as a result of legislation, taxation, market potential for chains' growth and other factors listed above that lead to low potential transaction costs, especially contract enforcement costs (transaction costs approach). However, a hotel chain may enter a destination that is not so attractive but it does so in order to: (i) achieve a broader geographic coverage of countries in its portfolio; (ii) have presence in a particular region; or (iii) gain a competitive advantage over other chains by entering a destination not offered by them (see also Moghaddam *et al.* (2014) for a critique of the internationalisation motives as stipulated by the eclectic theory). Therefore, the internal strategic objectives and motives of the hotel chain may play a role in the selection of a destination to enter beyond the host country's general and tourism/hotel industry specific factors.

Box 10.1. Analytical frameworks for hotel chain expansion policy

Resource-based view (From Barney, 1991; Barney and Arikan, 2001)

This perceives the firm as a bundle of resources that form the basis of its competitive advantage. The company achieves superior performance through the effective and efficient use of its internal valuable, rare, inimitable and non-substitutable resources for creating and applying unique capabilities and learning (Foss, 1996). The company continuously expands in order to deploy the maximum of its resources. The resource-based view is adopted as an analytical framework with regard to the international expansion and modal choice (Contractor and Kundu, 1998; Choi and Parsa, 2012).

Agency theory (From Eisenhardt, 1989)

This is used to analyse the 'principal–agent' relationships between the hotel chain and member hotels. In franchise and marketing consortia, the individual hotel acts as an agent of the hotel chain that is its principal, while in management contracts and leaseholds, the principal is the hotel owner(s) and the role of the agent is played by the hotel chain. The 'principal–agent' relationship generates sources of potential conflict for three main reasons: (i) both sides in the relationship have different and sometimes contradictory interests. For example, the chain is interested in the high quality of the product, which, however, requires additional costs for the hotels and decreases their financial results; (ii) there is an asymmetry of information flow: the principal has less information about the operational issues taking place in the hotel than the agent itself; (iii) the asymmetry of information leads to a moral hazard faced by the principal, who is never sure that the agent is acting properly. This requires additional costs for contractual and operational control incurred by the principal. Within the context of hotel chains, the agency theory is used in the analysis of the entry modes and the partner selection process (Panvisavas and Taylor, 2008; Ivanova and Ivanov, 2015a).

Transaction costs approach (From Williamson, 1981; Teece, 1986; Erramilli and Rao, 1993)

This approach evaluates the 'make or buy' decision faced by the firm – whether to produce something by itself or to buy it from the market – and therefore sets the efficient economic boundaries of the firm. The decision is based on the comparison of the transaction costs associated with the production and the purchase of the item. The transaction costs include: search and information costs (related with obtaining information about the market availablity of the product, suppliers, prices); negotiation costs (connected with the drafting and signing of a mutually agreeable contract); and contract enforcement costs (associated with the monitoring and control to assure that each party will fulfil its contract obligations and will not be involved in opportunistic behaviour) (see also Hollensen, 2014). The transaction costs approach may serve as the framework for analysis of the decision to internationalise, the choice of a destination and the choice of an entry mode.

Eclectic theory (From Dunning and McQueen, 1981; Dunning, 2000)

The eclectic theory uses an 'ownership–location–internalisation' (*OLI*) framework in order to analyse the internationalisation process of multinational corporations and hotel chains in particular. According to the eclectic theory, a hotel chain located in one country will affiliate with hotels in other countries (i.e. it will initiate the expansion/internationalisation process) if it has some competitive or ownership (*O*) advantage over hotel chains and/or independent hotels in other countries and it is economically efficient to combine its assets with the factor endowments located (*L*) in those foreign countries (Dunning and McQueen, 1981: 202). The chain would choose to utilise its ownership advantages only if it boasts internalisation (*I*) advantages, i.e. it is more efficient for the chain to deliver the service by itself through a high level of control types of entry modes like equity modes, management contract or lease. The OLI framework is adopted to analyse the initiation of the internationalisation process (if the chain has ownership advantages), choice of a destination (if the destination has locational advantages) and the choice of an entry mode (the internalisation advantages for the chain). Comparing the resource-based view and the eclectic theory, we can firmly say that the eclectic theory is more encompassing than the resource-based view, because the ownership advantages in the OLI frameworks are linked with the resources, competences, capabilities and learning within the organisation from the resource-based view. Furthermore, the transaction cost approach is reflected in the internalisation advantage in the OLI framework. Therefore, the eclectic theory incorporates both the resource-based view and the transaction cost approach.

Continued

Box 10.1. Continued.

Syncretic theory (From Contractor and Kundu, 1998)

Developed in regard to modal choice, this tries to combine the agency theory, transaction cost approach and the resource-based view (with an accent on intangible organisational capabilities and corporate knowledge). According to the theory, the choice of entry mode depends on three groups of factors: country specific and firm structural and firm strategy and control factors. Comparing the eclectic and the syncretic theories, we see that both have similar coverage. For example, the locational advantages in the eclectic theory are transposed as country-specific factors in the syncretic theory; the ownership and the internalisation advantages of the eclectic theory are mostly reflected in the firm-specific structural factors and strategic and control factors in the syncretic theory. Therefore, the two theories overlap to a great extent. None the less, to the best of our knowledge, the syncretic theory has not been applied outside the modal choice.

10.2.3 Choice of entry mode

A hotel chain may choose between two groups of entry modes – equity or hierarchical modes (full ownership and partial ownership, or joint venture), and non-equity or contractual modes (management contract, franchise, marketing consortium and lease), depending on the capital involvement of the hotel chain (Ivanova, 2013). Equity modes require financial involvement of the chain in the capital of the hotel's owner, while this is not the case when non-equity modes are used. The characteristics, advantages and disadvantages of the different entry modes have been widely discussed in the research literature from the viewpoints of the chain and of the member hotel (Cunill, 2006; Ivanov and Zhechev, 2011; Ivanova, 2013; Niewiadomski, 2014; Ivanova and Ivanov, 2015c). Research results are mixed regarding whether the choice of the entry mode by the chain actually affects its performance (Barbel-Pineda and Ramirez-Hurtado, 2011; Kosova et al., 2013).

Which type of affiliation a chain would use when entering a destination depends on various factors summarised below (Contractor and Kundu, 1998; Chen and Dimou, 2005; Alon et al., 2012; Martorell et al., 2013). Usually, the literature groups the factors into firm and host country specific. However, we consider this grouping to be too limiting and to overlook the role of the hotel chain's product, the inherent characteristics of the entry modes per se and the specific legislation of the chain's home country. We therefore divide the factors influencing choice of entry mode into five groups (Box 10.2).

10.2.4 Choice of a partner

The last decision in the expansion process refers to partner selection. It is a decision that the chain's management team has to take when they have decided to use non-equity mode or joint venture as an entry mode in the destination. If full ownership was chosen as an entry mode, then the chain does not need to decide on who its local partner would be. The partner selection is a bilateral process – the chain selects a local partner hotel, while the owners/managers of the local hotel select a hotel chain. Despite its importance, the partner selection from the viewpoint of the chain and/or the local hotel has received less attention compared to entry mode choice (Holverson and Revaz, 2006; Li et al., 2006; Brookes and Altinay, 2011; Ivanova and Ivanov, 2015b).

From an agency theory perspective, selecting the proper partner is vital for the chain because: first, in the case of franchise or marketing consortium, the local partner is responsible for the hotel service delivery and quality management process; and second, if an inappropriate local partner is selected regardless of the type of entry mode, the hotel chain will incur high transaction costs for monitoring and control of the fulfilment of the contract obligations, thus decreasing its financial performance.

The literature identifies various partner selection criteria used by hotel chains (Altinay, 2006; Bierly and Gallagher, 2007; Holmberg and Cummings, 2009; Brookes and Altinay, 2011), which Geringer (1991) divides into task- and partner-related criteria. According to Geringer,

---

Box 10.2. Factors influencing hotel chains' choice of entry mode

---

Product specific factors

These deal with the characteristics of the hotel chain's product: the complexity of services offered and the level of standardisation. Higher complexity of the services offered by the chain would force it to use entry modes with greater control. A higher level of standardisation allows the chain to multiply the product concept via franchising because its control is eased.

Firm specific factors

These are the characteristics of the hotel chain itself:

- size, growth and profitability;
- strategy and control factors: perceived strategic importance of the need for size in global operations, reservation system and brand, investment in training, economies of scale, chain's ability to exercise management control and maintain quality, centralisation of operation;
- international expertise and experience; degree of internationalisation of the hotel chain (share of hotels located abroad; geographical dispersion of affiliated properties);
- market segment of operation;
- country of origin (home country);
- number of years of operation.

From the perspectives of agency theory and the transaction costs approach, when companies increase in size, the costs for implementing control increase, and thus chains would tend to use non-equity modes (Martorell *et al.*, 2013). On the other hand, a chain's greater international experience (resource-based view) would favour the equity mode, because the chain may not need a local partner for its entry into a destination. Further, within the syncretic theory framework, the greater the perceived importance of the firm's strategic and control variables, the higher an emphasis the chain would put on control, and would tend to favour the equity modes.

Host country specific factors

These include:

- economic: level of economic development; unemployment; openness/degree of penetration of foreign investment (FDI to GDP ratio);
- country risk: political, economic, legal;
- market potential;
- cultural distance between home and host countries;
- host country legislation;
- availability of funding and local partners.

Usually, chains would prefer non-equity modes when the country risk is high or the cultural distance between the home and host countries is high (Contractor and Kundu, 1998; Rodrigez, 2002; Martorell *et al.*, 2013), in order to decrease their financial exposure to risk. The host country's legislation may predetermine the choice – for example, a local partner is a compulsory requirement for foreign investors in the United Arab Emirates (UAE).

Entry mode specific factors

These are characteristics that hotel chain managers consider when evaluating their choice options (Ivanova, 2013):

- principal–agent relationship;
- operational and outcome-based control provision;
- resource requirements of the specific entry mode (human resources, finances);
- degree of (de)centralisation of the decision-making process.

Continued

Box 10.2. Continued.

In a franchise and marketing consortium, the chain is the principal and the local partner is the agent, while in management contract and lease, the roles are reversed. According to agency theory, the agent has more information about operations and financial results than does the principal. Therefore, if the chain prefers a higher level of control over the operations of the hotel, but still opts for the non-equity modes, it would need to choose management contract or lease. A franchise and marketing consortium would further decentralise the operational decision-making process from the chain to the member hotels and require less resources than management contract, lease and equity modes, because the chain is not involved in the daily operations of the properties.

The **home country's legal and tax treatment** of the entry modes may also play a role in the selection of entry mode if the chain's different types of revenue (royalty fee, franchise fee, marketing fee) receive different tax treatment.

---

task-related criteria refer to those variables which are intimately related to the viability of a proposed venture's operations regardless of whether the chosen investment mode involves multiple partners. The variables could be tangible or intangible, human or nonhuman, in nature.

(Geringer, 1991: 45)

Within the context of hotel chain expansion, the task-related criteria are directly linked to the local partner's capabilities to deliver the hotel service to the customers in proper quality and quantity, and include: competent employees; qualified managers; local market knowledge; and strategic fit of/synergy benefits from the integration of the two partners' resources (e.g. the hotel chain's brand positioning matches the product of the local hotel).

The partner-related criteria include those that are not direcly linked to the hotel service delivery process but may have a significant impact on the relationship between the chain and its local partner, such as: the partner's organisational size (e.g. number of owned/operated properties); image in the local community; financial results and performance; strategy/ reasons for entering in the partnership with the chain; and their propensity to trust. A compatibility of corporate cultures is also vital.

Considering that the hotel industry is location bound and that the service delivery process takes place in a specific physical setting (Ivanov and Zhechev, 2011), we differentiate a third group of criteria, in addition to Geringer's (1991) task- and partner-related criteria: 'product-related criteria' (Ivanova, 2013). Within this group are included all the tangible characteristics of the property that determine and facilitate the service delivery process: location and accessibility of the property; the hotel's official categorisation; characteristics and condition of the property; and potential to adapt the property to the chain's standard.

Usually, the hotel chains include questions in the application forms which potential franchisees/ consortium members complete that cover most of the above criteria. They are used for initial screening and subsequent selection of potential partners, but may also be used for periodic evaluation of the partnership itself.

10.3 Market Penetration of Global Hotel Chains in Bulgaria

In 2015, Bulgaria had 3163 accommodation establishments (with ten or more rooms), which were highly concentrated geographically, such that around two-thirds of all beds in the country were concentrated within the three regions on the Black Sea coast (Fig. 10.1): Burgas, Varna and Dobrich. Currently, the main tourist products include mass summer 5S (sea, sun, sand, spirits and sex) tourism on the coast and winter ski tourism in the mountains. The heritage of Thracian civilisation, cultural, golf, eco-, spa/ wellness, wine, rural and city-break tourism are also promoted.

10.3.1 Choice of a destination

Table 10.2 shows the presence of international hotel corporations in Bulgaria ordered by the number of affiliated hotels in the country. In total, 63 hotels are affiliated with the brands of 33 international hotel chains belonging to 25 hotel corporations. Data in Table 10.2 reveal no major patterns in the factors influencing chains' presence in the country. Bulgaria is the host destination for:

- global corporations with a wide geographic presence in around 100 or more countries (e.g. Best Western, Hilton Worldwide, Accor) with thousands of affiliated hotels, but also companies with a regional presence (Alkoçlar, REWE Group, Easy hotels) that have only several tens of affiliated properties;
- corporations with well-developed multi-branding strategies (Accor, Wyndham, Inter-Continental, Starwood), and chains with only one brand (Iberostar, Kempinski, Sentido);
- corporations headquartered in countries with geographical proximity to Bulgaria (European Union member state or Turkey), and companies registered in the USA, China, UAE;
- corporations from countries with high cultural proximity to Bulgaria (Turkey, Spain), and companies from countries with low cultural proximity (USA, Switzerland, Germany).

Our correlation analysis between the number of hotels in Bulgaria affiliated with international chains on the one hand, and the country- and company-specific factors on the other, did not reveal any statistically significant correlation. Our regression analysis (not shown in the tables) further confirmed the lack of any statistically significant relationship. On the other hand, the fact that most of the corporations have only one or two affiliated hotels in Bulgaria might suggest potential tokenism – that the international hotel corporations do not intend to expand in Bulgaria, but choose the country in order to establish a minimal presence and a profile. Probably, their managers do not consider the hotel market in Bulgaria to be large and profitable enough to sustain the presence of more properties under their brands, especially in the case of luxury brands. The low cost image of the destination and its relatively low ranking on Transparency International's Corruption Perception Index (2015)[1] could be factors that further justify the strategy of international hotel corporations of maintaining a minimal presence in the country.

10.3.2 Choice of an entry mode

Table 10.3 presents the chain affiliation of accommodation establishments in the country in 2012 and 2015. The data show that the market penetration of hotel chains in Bulgaria is very low – less than 5% of the accommodation establishments are affiliated with a hotel chain (domestic or international). Although in recent years the share of affiliated hotels has risen, it none the less remains very low. Table 10.3 also reveals that international chains show a preference for the non-equity types of entry mode: a marketing consortium is the most popular, followed by management contract and franchise. By contrast, the domestic chains predominantly use ownership as a way to expand domestically.

International chains affiliate mostly with high-category hotels (4 and 5 stars) and only two of their properties have been categorised as 1 or 2 stars. International chains also prefer hotels with a large number of rooms – half of the hotels affiliated with them have in excess of 150 (one has more than 700 rooms). Regarding location, international chains almost exclusively have a presence within urban (Sofia, Plovdiv, Varna, Ruse, Pleven) and seaside destinations (the Black Sea coast), while domestic chains are well represented in mountain resorts (Bansko, Borovets, Pamporovo, Chepelare) as well. This geographic concentration of international hotel brands could be attributed to the specific market segments of these destinations. Sofia, as the capital, and Plovdiv and Varna, as the second and third largest cities, respectively, have well-developed, all-year business and events tourism sectors that make these cities attractive for brands targeted at business travellers (Novotel, Radisson Blu, Sheraton, Hilton, Holiday Inn, Ramada, Park Inn, Golden Tulip). Of course, being a large city that is visited for city breaks as well, Sofia hosts such mid- and low-priced brands as Easyhotel, Ibis, Best Western. The international chains that have affiliated hotels located in seaside resorts are mostly oriented towards the mass leisure market: Melia, Sol hotels, Iberostar, LTI hotels, RIU, Prima Sol hotels.[2]

Table 10.4 shows the cross-tabulation of the entry modes used by the international chains, and the characteristics of the member hotel. The data reveal that management contract and franchise are usually used for high-category hotels

Table 10.2. International hotel chains' presence in Bulgaria. (From authors' compilation.)

Hotel corporation	Headquarters location	Number of hotel brands	Number of hotels	Number of rooms	Number of countries present	Number of brands in Bulgaria	Number of hotels in Bulgaria	Number of rooms in Bulgaria	Cultural proximity between chain's home country and Bulgaria[a]
HotelREZ Hotels and Resorts	UK	1	656	37,784	27	1	10	627	n.a.
Best Western	USA	7	4,000	303,522	113	3	9	405	3.738038
REWE Group/ DER Touristik	Germany	3	39	15,316	9	3	8	1,930	1.519870
Melia Hotels International	Spain	8	316	83,709	35	2	6	2,254	0.632499
RIU Hotels and Resorts	Spain	1	105	45,390	19	1	6	2,002	0.632499
Accor	France	17	3,792	495,072	92	2	3	592	0.909239
Carlson Rezidor Group	USA	7	1,092	172,234	87	2	2	219	3.738038
Hilton Worldwide	USA	12	4,440	731,851	97	2	2	441	3.738038
Hotusa	Spain	7	2,595	233,550	53	1	2	88	0.632499
Sentido Hotels	Germany	1	67	n.a.	13	1	2	428	1.519870
Wyndham Hotels Group	USA	15	7,700	668,500	71	1	2	759	3.738038
Alkoçlar Hotels	Turkey	1	10	n.a.	2	1	1	94	0.621433
Barcelo Hotels and Resorts	Spain	1	95	29,375	16	1	1	294	0.632499
Design Hotels	Germany	1	288	22,262	55	1	1	71	1.519870
Easy Hotels	UK	1	21	1,900	9	1	1	57	n.a.
Global Hotel Alliance	UAE	33	495	108,400	76	1	1	159	n.a.
Iberostar Hotels and Resorts	Spain	1	79	26,806	13	1	1	636	0.632499
Intercontinental Hotel Group	UK	12	4,963	726,876	96	1	1	130	n.a.

Continued

Table 10.2. Continued.

Hotel corporation	Headquarters location	Number of hotel brands	Number of hotels	Number of rooms	Number of countries present	Number of brands in Bulgaria	Number of hotels in Bulgaria	Number of rooms in Bulgaria	Cultural proximity between chain's home country and Bulgaria[a]
Kempinski	Switzerland	1	75	20,101	32	1	1	159	2.394011
Leading hotels of the world	USA	1	416	60,095	80	1	1	159	3.738038
Preferred hotels	USA	5	687	136,228	80	1	1	151	3.738038
Shanghai Jin Jiang International Hotels Ltd/Louvre Hotels Group	China/France	6	1,136	93,475	47	1	1	90	0.909239[b]
Small luxury hotels of the world	UK	1	525	24,984	80	1	1	125	n.a.
Starwood Hotels	USA	10	1,271	362,623	86	1	1	184	3.738038
Youth Hostel Association/ Hostelling International	UK	1	4,000	n.a.	90	1	1	12	n.a.

Notes: [a]Based on the six cultural dimensions of the Hofstede–Minkov framework (power distance, individualism, masculinity, uncertainty avoidance, long-term orientation, indulgence); formula for calculation as in Contractor and Kundu (1998); source of data for the calculations: The Hofstede Centre (2015). [b]Difference with France, where the Louvre Hotels Group was registered when it entered the Bulgarian market.

Table 10.3. Chain affiliation of accommodation establishments in Bulgaria. (From authors' compilation.)

	2012[a]		2015[b]	
	Foreign chains	Domestic chains	Foreign chains	Domestic chains
Total number of accommodation establishments affiliated with hotel chains	108		139[c]	
Total number of accommodation establishments	2758		3163	
Hotel chains' market penetration	3.91%		4.39%	
Number of chains operating in the country	28	12	33	18
Number of affiliated accommodation establishments	47	61	63	80
Full ownership or joint venture	2	56	1	75
Management contract	15	10[d]	21	10[d]
Franchise	14	–	17	–
Marketing consortium	22	–	27	–
Number of accommodation establishments affiliated with hotel chains by category				
1 star	–	–	1	–
2 stars	1	4	1	9
3 stars	5	15	12	18
4 stars	30	33	38	43
5 stars	11	9	11	10
Number of accommodation establishments affiliated with hotel chains by size				
Up to 50 rooms	9	12	15	21
51–100 rooms	8	22	11	23
101–150 rooms	6	6	6	9
Over 150 rooms	24	22	31	27
Number of accommodation establishments affiliated with hotel chains by location				
Urban	21	10	33	16
Seaside	21	27	25	40
Mountain	4	23	3	23
Other	1	1	2	1

Notes: Several hotels belong to two foreign hotel chains simultaneously (to one chain through franchise/management contract and to another through a marketing consortium). [a]As at 1 December 2012. [b]As at 1 November 2015. [c]Four of the hotels are fully owned by a domestic hotel chain and have simultaneously joined an international marketing consortium. [d]Some of the management companies and the hotel owner companies belong to the same holding, have the same or connected physical persons as owners. Numbers reflect the officially stated type of affiliation on the websites of the hotel and the hotel chain, although the authors suspect that all or most hotels affiliated with domestic chains are owned by the chains or connected companies (Ivanova and Ivanov, 2014).

(4 and 5 stars), while 3-star hotels are affiliated mostly with marketing consortia, and these differences are statistically significant (χ^2 = 23.310, p <0.05). The same pattern is observed regarding the size of the hotel – management contract and franchise are used for large properties (over 100 rooms), while for smaller hotels (up to 100 rooms), the chains use a marketing consortium (χ^2 = 36.714, p <0.01). For the smallest properties (up to 50 rooms), the marketing consortium is even the exclusive type of affiliation. Finally, urban properties are usually affiliated via a marketing consortium, while for seaside hotels, chains prefer management contract and franchise (χ^2 = 26.201, p <0.01).

The results in Table 10.4 are not surprising. Management contract is a suitable entry mode for large and high-category properties that can generate sufficient revenues to cover the management costs of the chain (Ivanov and Zhechev, 2011). In Bulgaria, these hotels are predominantly located on the Black Sea coast; hence, most of the hotels affiliated via management contract are seaside hotels. On the other hand, the Bulgarian hotel market has very low prices – for 2013, the average price per one overnight was 24.47 BGN (€12.5) for 1- to 2-star hotels, 35.68 BGN (€18.2) for 3-star hotels and only 53.50 BGN (€27.3) for 4- to 5-star hotels (Ivanov, 2014). These low prices, and the predominant

Table 10.4. International hotel chains' type of entry mode in Bulgaria (as at 1 November 2015). (From authors' compilation.)

		Entry mode			Chi-squared (degrees of freedom)
	Ownership	Management contract	Franchise	Marketing consortium	
Number of properties	1	21	17	27	
Category					
1 star	0	0	0	1	23.310**
2 stars	0	0	1	0	(12)
3 stars	0	0	2	10	
4 stars	0	15	13	11	
5 stars	1	6	1	5	
Hotel size					
Up to 50 rooms	0	0	0	16	36.714***
51–100 rooms	0	2	4	5	(9)
101–150 rooms	0	2	2	2	
More than 150 rooms	1	17	11	4	
Location					
Urban	0	7	5	22	26.201***
Seaside	1	11	12	1	(9)
Mountain	0	2	0	3	
Other	0	1	0	1	

Note: **Significant at 5% level; ***significant at 1% level.

price competition of the hotels, do not allow them to pay a franchise fee from their current revenues or to increase their prices to cover it. Chains' strict franchise service operation manuals may frighten the potential local partners as well, while the marketing consortium is much more flexible as an entry mode, sets fewer requirements (product- and task-related criteria) for the chains' local partners and some of them may find it more attractive than the franchise, especially the owners of the smallest properties (of up to 50 rooms).

10.3.3 Choice of a local partner

In recent research on the selection criteria hotel chains use to choose their local partners in Bulgaria, Ivanova and Ivanov (2015b) found that the international hotel chains considered product-related criteria (property-related characteristics) as the most important. Task-related criteria (competent employees, qualified managers, local market knowledge) and partner-related factors (the hotel's image in the local community and its financial results

and performance) were evaluated as much less significant in the partner selection process. These findings probably reflect the fact that international chains have their own service standards that are imposed on the affiliated hotels, they send managers to run the hotels (in the case of management contracts) and provide training for hotel employees and managers. Because of these practices, the physical and locational attributes of the building are more important to the chains than the task- and partner-related criteria such as the quality of available labour.

10.4 Conclusion

This chapter has addressed the decision-making processes that international hotel corporations engage in during their expansion procedures, and has focused on the entry and presence of these corporations in Bulgaria. Our findings have shown that country- and firm-specific factors play little role in the presence of these organisations in the country. On the contrary, it appears that potential tokenism exists in the selection of Bulgaria as a host destination, with major hotel corporations each being represented by only one or two affiliated properties in the country. This raises the question as to whether these corporations enter Bulgaria in search of expansion opportunities and to offer a greater choice of destinations for their customers, or because they are pursuing their own globalisation agenda for achieving wide geographic presence regardless of the destinations entered.

This chapter has also shown that the chains and their partners have a strong preference for non-equity entry modes (franchise, marketing consortium and management contract). Most affiliated properties have a large number of rooms and are located in urban or seaside areas.

Most importantly, the market penetration of hotel chains in the country is extremely low (less than 5%), indicating that a huge market potential exists in the country. A potential that has yet to be realised. While international hotel chains have focused on the capital, Sofia, and the ever-expanding seaside resorts (as well as major cities), they have paid little attention to the country's mountain resorts.

Multinational corporations in general, and international hotel chains in particular, have been subject to significant criticism regarding the outflow of money from host countries' economies for payment of affiliation fees, repatriation of profits, use of foreign employees and managers, tax avoidance and the destruction of smaller and weaker local enterprises (Kulsuvan and Karamustafa, 2001; Otusanya, 2011; Dwyer, 2014). Yet international hotel chains may offer tangible and significant benefits for their local partners. They have strict quality control procedures, substantial marketing knowledge and expertise, elaborate training programmes and work with numerous online travel agencies and other distributors (Ivanov and Zhechev, 2011). Their relatively small but growing presence in Bulgaria may help improve the competitiveness of the local hotel industry and its visibility on the global tourist marketplace.

Endnotes

[1] Joint 69th place, out of 175 countries, in 2014.
[2] Nationally, there would seem to be a degree of seasonal complementarity between the summer Black Sea resorts, winter mountain resorts and all-year urban attractions. But, as accommodation is not only separated geographically but also is mostly under different ownership patterns, the majority of hotels along the coast and most in the mountains operate seasonally. In the few hotels on the coast and in the mountains that fall under common ownership, staff are rotated, with 6 months on the coast, 5 in the mountains and 1 month's annual leave.

References

Alon, I., Ni, L. and Wang, Y. (2012) Examining the determinants of hotel chain expansion through international franchising. *International Journal of Hospitality Management* 31, 379–386.

Altinay, L. (2006) Selecting partners in an international franchise organisation. *International Journal of Hospitality Management* 25(1), 108–128.

Assaf, A.G., Josiassen, A. and Agbola, F.W. (2015) Attracting international hotels: locational factors that matter most. *Tourism Management* 47, 329–340.

Baena, V. and Cerviño, J. (2015) New criteria to select foreign entry mode choice of global franchise chains into emerging markets. *Procedia – Social and Behavioral Sciences* 175, 260–267.

Barbel-Pineda, J.M. and Ramirez-Hurtado, J.M. (2011) Does the foreign market entry mode choice affect export performance? The case of the Spanish hotel industry. *Journal of Business Economics and Management* 12(2), 301–316.

Barney, J. (1991) Firm resources and sustained competitive advantage. *Journal of Management* 17(1), 99–120.

Barney, J. and Arikan, A. (2001) The resource-based view: origins and implications. In: Hitt, M.A., Freeman, R.E. and Harrison, J.S. (eds) *The Blackwell Handbook of Strategic Management*. Blackwell, Oxford, UK, pp. 124–188.

Bierly, P.E. and Gallagher, S. (2007) Explaining alliance partner selection: fit, trust and strategic expediency. *Long Range Planning* 40(2), 134–153.

Brida, J.G., Driha, O.M., Ramón-Rodríguez, A.B. and Scuderi, R. (2015) Dynamics of internationalisation of the hotel industry: the case of Spain. *International Journal of Contemporary Hospitality Management* 27(5), 1024–1047.

Brookes, M. and Altinay, L. (2011) Franchise partner selection: perspectives of franchisors and franchisees. *Journal of Services Marketing* 25(5), 336–348.

Chen, J.J. and Dimou, I. (2005) Expansion strategy of international hotel firms. *Journal of Business Research* 58(12), 1730–1740.

Choi, G. and Parsa, H.G. (2012) Role of intangible assets in foreign-market entry-mode decisions: a longitudinal study of American lodging firms. *International Journal of Hospitality and Tourism Administration* 13(4), 281–312.

Contractor, F.J. and Kundu, S.K. (1998) Modal choice in a world of alliances: analyzing organizational forms in the international hotel sector. *Journal of International Business Studies* 29(2), 325–357.

Contractor, F. and Kundu, S. (2000) Globalization of hotel services: an examination of ownership and alliance patterns in a maturing service sector. In: Aharoni, Y. and Nachum, L. (eds) *Globalization of Services. Some Implications of Theory and Practice*. Routledge, Abingdon, UK, pp. 296–319.

Cosma, S., Fleșeriu, C. and Bota, M. (2014) Hotel chain's strategic options to penetrate the Romanian market. *Amfiteatru Economic* 16(8), 1352–1365.

Cuervo-Cazurra, A. (2011) Selecting the country in which to start internationalization: the non-sequential internationalization model. *Journal of World Business* 46, 426–437.

Cunill, O.M. (2006) *Growth Strategies of Hotel Chains: Best Business Practices by Leading Companies*. The Haworth Press, New York.

Dunning, J. (2000) The eclectic paradigm as an envelope for economic and business theories of MNE activity. *International Business Review* 9(2), 163–190.

Dunning, J. and McQueen, M. (1981) The eclectic theory of international production: a case study of the international hotel industry. *Managerial and Decision Economics* 2(4), 197–210.

Dwyer, L. (2014) Transnational corporations and the globalization of tourism. In: Lew, A.A., Hall, C.M. and Williams, A.M. (eds) *The Wiley Blackwell Companion to Tourism*. John Wiley and Sons, Chichester, UK, pp. 197–209.

Eisenhardt, K. (1989) Agency theory: an assessment and review. *The Academy of Management Review* 14(1), 57–74.

Erramilli, M.K. and Rao, C.P. (1993) Service firms' international entry-mode choice: a modified transaction cost approach. *Journal of Marketing* 57(3), 19–38.

Foss, N. (1996) Capabilities and the theory of the firm. *Revue d'Économie Industrielle* 77(3), 7–28.

García de Soto-Camacho, E. and Vargas-Sánchez, A. (2015) Choice of entry mode, strategic flexibility and performance of international strategy in hotel chains: an approach based on real options. *European Journal of Tourism Research* 9, 92–114.

Geringer, J.M. (1991) Strategic determinations of partner selection criteria in international joint venture. *Journal of International Business Studies* 22(1), 41–61.

Hill, C.W.L., Hwang, P. and Kim, W.C. (1990) An eclectic theory of the choice of international entry mode. *Strategic Management Journal* 11(2), 117–128.

Hofstede Centre, The (2015) *National Culture*. The Hofstede Centre, Helsinki, Finland. Available at: http://geert-hofstede.com/national-culture.html (accessed 28 July 2016).

Hollensen, S. (2014) *Global Marketing*, 6th edn. Pearson Education, Harlow, UK.

Holmberg, S. and Cummings, J. (2009) Building successful strategic alliances. Strategic process and analytical tool for selecting partner industries and firms. *Long Range Planning* 42(2), 164–193.

Holverson, S. and Revaz, F. (2006) Perceptions of European independent hoteliers: hard and soft branding choices. *International Journal of Contemporary Hospitality Management* 18(5), 398–413.

Ivanov, S. (2014) *Hotel Revenue Management: From Theory to Practice*. Zangador, Varna, Bulgaria.

Ivanov, S. and Zhechev, V. (2011) *Marketing v hotelerstvoto*. [*Hotel Marketing*.] Zangador, Varna, Bulgaria (in Bulgarian).

Ivanova, M. (2013) Affiliation to hotel chains as a development opportunity for Bulgarian hotels. Doctoral dissertation, University of Economics-Varna, Bulgaria. Available at: http://ssrn.com/abstract=2346377 (accessed 28 July 2016).

Ivanova, M. and Ivanov, S. (2014) Hotel chains' entry mode in Bulgaria. *Anatolia* 25(1), 131–135.

Ivanova, M. and Ivanov, S. (2015a) The nature of hotel chains: an integrative framework. *International Journal of Hospitality and Tourism Administration* 16(2), 122–142.

Ivanova, M. and Ivanov, S. (2015b) Affiliation to hotel chains: requirements towards hotels in Bulgaria. *Journal of Hospitality Marketing and Management* 24(6), 601–608.

Ivanova, M. and Ivanov, S. (2015c) Affiliation to hotel chains: hotels' perspective. *Tourism Management Perspectives* 16, 148–162.

Johnson, C. and Vanetti, M. (2005) Locational strategies of international hotel chains. *Annals of Tourism Research* 32(4), 1077–1099.

Johnson, C. and Vanetti, M. (2008) Internationalization and the hotel industry. In: Woodside, A. and Martin, D. (eds) *Tourism Management: Analysis, Behaviour and Strategy.* CAB International, Wallingford, UK, pp. 285–301.

Kosova, R., Lafontaine, F. and Perrigot, R. (2013) Organizational form and performance: evidence from the hotel industry. *The Review of Economics and Statistics* 95(4), 1303–1323.

Kulsuvan, S. and Karamustafa, K. (2001) Multinational hotel development in developing countries: an exploratory analysis of critical policy issues. *International Journal of Tourism Research* 3(3), 179–197.

Leon-Darder, F., Villar-Garcia, C. and Pla-Barber, J. (2011) Entry mode choice in the internationalisation of the hotel industry: a holistic approach. *The Service Industries Journal* 31(1), 107–122.

Li, S.C.Y., Wong, M.C.S. and Luk, S.T.K. (2006) The importance and performance of key success factors of international joint venture hotels in China. *Chinese Economy* 39(6), 83–94.

Littlejohn, D. (1997) Internationalization in hotels: current aspects and developments. *International Journal of Contemporary Hospitality Management* 9(5/6), 187–192.

Littlejohn, D., Roper, A. and Altinay, L. (2007) Territories still to find – the business of hotel internationalisation. *International Journal of Service Industry Management* 18(2), 167–183.

Martorell, O., Mulet, C. and Otero, L. (2013) Choice of market entry mode by Balearic hotel chains in the Caribbean and Gulf of Mexico. *International Journal of Hospitality Management* 32(1), 217–227.

Moghaddam, K., Sethi, D., Weber, T. and Wu, J. (2014) The smirk of emerging market firms: a modification of the Dunning's typology of internationalization motivations. *Journal of International Management* 20, 359–374.

Niewiadomski, P. (2014) Towards an economic-geographical approach to the globalisation of the hotel industry. *Tourism Geographies* 16(1), 48–67.

Niewiadomski, P. (2015) International hotel groups and regional development in Central and Eastern Europe. *Tourism Geographies* 17(2), 173–191.

Niewiadomski, P. (2016) The globalisation of the hotel industry and the variety of emerging capitalisms in Central and Eastern Europe. *European Urban and Regional Studies* 23(3), 267–288.

Oana, D. and Milla, J.L. (2009) Spanish hotel international expansion: evolution and tendency. The role of Eastern Europe. *Annals of the University of Oradea: Economic Science* 1(1), 181–187.

Otusanya, O.J. (2011) The role of multinational companies in tax evasion and tax avoidance: the case of Nigeria. *Critical Perspectives on Accounting* 22, 316–332.

Panvisavas, V. and Taylor, J.S. (2008) Restraining opportunism in hotel management contracts. *Tourism and Hospitality Research* 8(4), 324–336.

Pranić, L., Ketkar, S. and Roehl, W.S. (2012) The impact of macroeconomic country specific factors on international expansion of US hotel chains. *Tourismos* 7(1), 155–173.

Quer, D., Claver, E. and Andreu, R. (2007) Foreign market entry mode in the hotel industry: the impact of country- and firm-specific factors. *International Business Review* 16(3), 362–376.

Rodriguez, A.R. (2002) Determining factors in entry choice for international expansion. The case of the Spanish hotel industry. *Tourism Management* 23(6), 597–607.

Rodtook, P. and Altinay, L. (2013) Reasons for internationalization of domestic hotel chains in Thailand. *Journal of Hospitality Marketing and Management* 22(1), 92–115.

Teece, D. (1986) Transaction cost economics and the multinational enterprise. An assessment. *Journal of Economic Behavior and Organization* 7(1), 21–45.

Transparency International (2015) *Corruption Perceptions Index, 2014.* Transparency International, Berlin, Germany. Available at: http://www.transparency.org/cpi2014/results (accessed 28 July 2016).

Williamson, O. (1981) The economics of organization: the transaction cost approach. *The American Journal of Sociology* 87(3), 548–577.

Wu, A., Costa, J. and Teare, R. (1998) Using environmental scanning for business expansion into China and Eastern Europe: the case of transnational hotel companies. *International Journal of Contemporary Hospitality Management* 10(7), 257–263.

Xiao, Q., O'Neill, J. and Wang, H. (2008) International hotel development: a study of potential franchisees in China. *International Journal of Hospitality Management* 27(3), 325–336.

Zhang, H.Q., Guillet, B.D. and Gao, W. (2012) What determines multinational hotel groups' locational investment choice in China? *International Journal of Hospitality Management* 31(2), 350–359.

11 New Consumption Spaces and Cross-border Mobilities

Erika Nagy*

Centre for Economic and Regional Studies, Hungarian Academy of Sciences, Békéscsaba, Hungary

11.1 Introduction

The recent migration crisis that European countries face and the unfolding re-regulation of cross-border flows introduced by national governments raised memories that had been forgotten quickly by those who live in the former 'eastern bloc' – such as being stopped, searched and asked nasty questions by customs officers and frontier guards at border-crossing stations.

Even in the communist era, when the territorialised power of the (nation) state was performed clearly and forcefully, diverse social practices emerged that challenged state control, such as shopping trips, petty trading and smuggling – addressing basic needs, as well as demand for goods of particular symbolic value in the shortage economies (Kornai, 1980; Vörös, 1997; Chelcea, 2002; Hetesi et al., 2007). National boundaries were reinterpreted and challenged further in the transition period by international political discourses and the related changes in institutional practices that transformed the meanings and identities attached to borders (Johnson et al., 2011; Kuus, 2011; Scott, 2014). Both the multiplicity of strategies and interactions crossing national borders, and an embedding of the everyday lives of 'borderlanders' in the material reality of the European common market, question the relevance of recent policies

that rely on renaturalising national borders. Such (geo)political action calls for further open discussion that should rest on a deeper understanding of social practices embedded in changing border regimes.

In this chapter, I focus on consumption practices that incorporated the crossing of national borders into the everyday lives of local ('near-border') communities. Such practices have changed thoroughly in Central and Eastern Europe (CEE) since the late 1980s, as a consequence of the transformation of the state–market–society nexus in the post-Cold War political context:

1. Changing consumption practices were embedded in the contradictory processes of the political transition that embraced the redefinition of nationhood (Young and Light, 2001) – exploited by national political elites to bring forward and make accepted the reforms that fundamentally transformed social relations (Harvey, 2005; Szalai, 2006). As a consequence, the newly established national border regimes of CEE were embedded in the highly uneven landscapes of economic development and political power (Popescu, 2008; Ehrlich et al., 2012) produced by the spatial logic of emerging capitalisms.
2. Consumption patterns were particularly shaped by the entry of retail transnational corporations (TNCs) that orchestrated economic

*E-mail: nagye@rkk.hu

restructuring across CEE by enhancing competitive pressure in distributive services, building their transnational supply networks and (along with commercial property developers) by introducing new forms and spaces of consumption and raising new, consumption-related identities (Coe, 2011; Nagy, 2012). Although major retailers' strategies were anchored strongly in national regulatory frameworks, as well as in local spaces (Wrigley *et al.*, 2005), they challenged territorialised state power in various ways.

3. While consumers of border regions were subjected to the space-producing logic of retail capital, and also to the spatial organisation of state power, the embedding of CEE economies and political systems into European institutional structures enhanced the scope for cross-border mobility and cooperation. Such processes questioned the state-centred doctrine of border control and raised political conflicts and new 'othering' discourses related to various boundaries (and underlying power relations) of and within Europe (Popescu, 2008; Kuus, 2011; Balogh, 2014; Scott, 2014).

To reveal the multiplicity of cross-border consumption practices and the underlying social relations, I rely on the critical reinterpretations of geopolitics that placed the complex spatialities of power in focus and considered borders as manifestations of state power employed to exclude 'others' and control domestic space (Ó Tuathail, 1994). Moreover, I put critical geographical arguments for embracing also the socio-spatial practices of various non-state agents at the very centre of this chapter to reveal the multiplicity of social relations that are constantly making and remaking the borders (Johnson *et al.*, 2011; Dodds *et al.*, 2013). This approach allows me to focus on border-related strategies and practices and also to anchor my analysis in the political economic concept of consumption.

In this chapter, I argue for understanding institutional and corporate strategies related to border regions as the responses of local agents to their perceived marginalities in capital flows, shrinking systems of collective consumption and in national political spaces – by (re)valorising their fixed assets through extending and exploiting their networked relations across scales and by mobilising various border-related identities.

I argue also for understanding the consumption-related strategies of powerful local agents – having clear class and urban bias – as the engines of growing socio-spatial inequalities within border regions, marginalising low-income groups and transferring social problems to less powerful localities. Finally, I link these arguments to earlier critiques on the neoliberalisation of national and European policies (Brenner, 2009; Hudson and Hadjmichalis, 2014).

The following analysis deals with Central and East European cross-border consumption practices, with a particular focus on three Hungarian–Romanian border regions – referring also to other case studies (Fig. 11.1) and wider CEE processes – that were reshaped unevenly by the above structural changes. I shall discuss the relevant theories, linking the critical geopolitical approach focused on everyday practices to the political economic interpretation of consumption (Section 11.2). In Section 11.3, I give a brief overview of retail restructuring and the changing social role of consumption in the East Central European context (11.3.1), and analyse cross-border consumption practices and the related strategies along the Hungarian–Romanian border (11.3.2–11.3.4.). Finally, I summarise how socio-spatial inequalities are reproduced in/through cross-border consumption (Section 11.4).

11.2 Global Flows, National Borders, Local Practices – Conceptualising Cross-border Consumption

Academic debates revolving around the changing consumption practices in CEE embraced political economic explanations as well as 'culturalist' approaches focused on the consumption-led (re)construction of identities under post-socialism. Although both streams were concerned with profound consumption-related social changes, it was the former that provided a framework for a systematic critical analysis of changing consumption landscapes as manifestations of uneven development[1] in the context of CEE emerging capitalisms explicitly. This approach – anchored in Marx's widely discussed and contested concept of commodity fetishism – focuses not just on the act of consumption but also on the underlying systems of exchange, in which the social

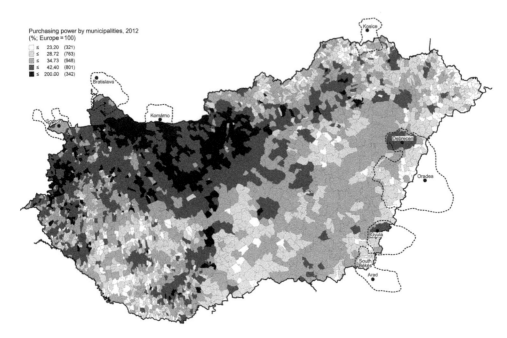

Fig. 11.1. Purchasing power inequalities in Hungary at the municipal (LAU2) scale (2014) and the target areas of the fieldwork. (From Gfk Hungary, 2015.)

(class, gender, ethnic, power) relations of capitalism are manifested (Lowe and Wrigley, 1996; Goss, 2006). Accordingly, consumption should be understood as an integral part of the production processes – of the circulation of capital – that is controlled increasingly by powerful agents (e.g. by major retailers) capitalising on their intermediary role by linking producers and customers across scales and creating new aesthetics and institutional contexts for 'reproducing desire' in the era of global capitalism (Harvey, 1995; Zukin and Maguire, 2004).

This conceptualisation leads us to understand consumption as a socially and spatially uneven process shaped primarily by the strategies of major retailers through the organisation of consumption spaces, centralised logistic systems and global sourcing (Lowe and Wrigley, 1996; Dicken, 2007). However, as retailing became transnational, the agents of the sector grew increasingly dependent on host markets in terms of regulations, supply networks, consumption culture and property market processes (Wrigley *et al.*, 2005; Faulconbridge, 2010). For this, relying on the arguments for linking political economic and 'culturalist' approaches,[2]

I analyse cross-border practices in the context of the interlinked and competing strategies of retailers as well as of various local agents – political elites, public institutions, entrepreneurs and consumers – to understand consumption as a culturally and politically embedded process.

Cross-border practices are particular social acts, in which various geopolitical strategies manifest and reproduce socio-spatial inequalities. This means:

1. For major retailers, a national border raises not just the problems of adaptation to various host market contexts but also challenges them through intra-firm (inter-store) competition within their territorialised organisational structures. However, at the same time, the near-border situation allows them to exploit the price differentials in neighbouring countries stemming not only from national regulations (e.g. VAT rates) but also from uneven development (e.g. labour prices and various levels of penetration of 'modern' retail formats) (Gereffi, 1999; Kovács, 2008).

2. National borders are sources of power for state bureaucracy in controlling and filtering transnational flows to stimulate (uneven) economic development and to protect sovereignty (Popescu, 2008; Balogh, 2014). However, the refashioning of the state–market–society nexus in a neoliberal manner across Europe that stimulated socio-spatial polarisation in the access to 'public goods' (Harvey, 2005; Brenner *et al.*, 2010; Nagy *et al.*, 2015) made local agents of border regions exploit their near-border situation in response to a 'meltdown' of the welfare state.

To understand consumption practices in the context of the space-producing logic of capital, as well as of spatial practices of state power (i.e. the construction of national borders and various spatial hierarchies), I discuss *cross-border* consumption as a set of geopolitical practices by mobilising the extended concept of critical geopolitics. I consider national borders as the manifestations of spatialised power constantly reshaped by national and international discourses (Ó Tuathail and Agnew, 1992; Agnew, 2011), and also by the daily practices of various (state and non-state) agents challenging and/or reproducing the established institutional structures (Johnson *et al.*, 2011). This approach allows me also to reveal how territorialised and non-territorial (networked, place-based) agencies interact and conflict in border regions.

My analysis rests on a two-tiered methodology.

1. To reveal cross-border consumption practices, I discuss here the results of two series of case studies (2010; 2013–2015) focused on three regions along the Romanian–Hungarian border (Fig. 11.1). The case study areas exhibited different trajectories in the era of rapidly changing border regimes and market restructuring from the early 1990s on, such as the *Debrecen–Oradea metropolitan region* (Hungary/Romania), *Gyula* (Hungary), a small urban centre for a declining rural space and the *South-Békés region* (Hungary) marginalised by shrinking public services and also by corporate strategies over two decades. The strategies of local agents – including entrepreneurs, municipal officials, NGOs, locally embedded TNCs and governmental bodies – were revealed through semi-structured interviews.

2. The results of the qualitative research were analysed in the context of local, regional and national statistics and documents, relying also

on earlier scholarly work on changing border regimes and retail restructuring in CEE, as well as on market reports. I refer to fieldwork results from Slovak–Hungarian and the Austrian–Hungarian border regions[3] in my analysis (Fig. 11.1).

11.3 Changing Cross-border Consumption Practices and the Related Strategies along the Romanian–Hungarian border

11.3.1 The context: retail restructuring and changing consumption patterns in Central and Eastern Europe

The liberalisation of post-socialist markets, the privatisation processes and the entry of transnational agents transformed consumption practices across CEE from the early 1990s. Yet these changes were shaped by national and local histories of socialism, when consumption grew as a source of identity through variegated practices – by having/not having access to goods and also by getting scarce items through horizontal informal relations and recontextualising/recycling them (Verdery, 1999; Stenning *et al.*, 2011). Consumption was dependent also on cross-border trading that stimulated the rise of petty traders (from Yugoslavia, and later from Poland) and various illegal/semi-legal activities that were undermining state control. Cross-border exchange was stimulated by the variegated landscape of 'socialist' economies, such as by the rise of the 'second economy' in Hungary in the 1980s (the introduction of enterprising and improved access to goods) in contrast to the strict state control over resources in Romania (Kolosi, 2000; Chelcea, 2002).

The introduction of market institutions in CEE stimulated the entry and rapid expansion of retail TNCs seeking higher returns in risky, uncertain markets (Hess, 2004). The process was embedded in the globalisation of retail capital – driven by the declining return of capital within the sector and also in the property markets of the core economies. The resulting thorough restructuring of the CEE retail sector had three stages:

1. Early transformation characterised by privatisation, liberalisation and decentralisation (spatially equalising) processes.

2. The period of intensive internationalisation (from the late 1990s).

3. The era of saturation and rapid centralisation after the EU accessions. The emerging consumption landscape was highly uneven and shaped primarily by corporate strategies exploiting surplus capacities (in building a CEE-wide supply network), as well as the 'post-shortage' condition of consumption (Coe, 2011; Nagy, 2012). The latter manifested itself in uncertainty and loss of trust amid the rapid changes of the 1990s (Shevchenko, 2002), and later in building new identities as consumers, related to class, modernity, traditions and nationality (Patico and Caldwell, 2002; Klumbyte, 2009; Eglitis, 2011). Recent reviews suggest that consumption motives have grown highly diverse, including the use of digital technologies to rationalise choices and save time, the rise of ethical consumption and the spread of re-cycling as a way of saving money and of reinterpreting consumption as a social act (Gulyás, 2008; Cetelem, 2015).

Unevenness was also shaped by various structures and regulation contexts of national markets. In Hungary, privatisation and the enterprising

rush of the early 1990s was followed by rapid centralisation of the sector in terms of capital, organisation and consumption spaces, stimulated primarily by transnational retailers from the late 1990s (Fig. 11.2). The entry of such agents accelerated the introduction and spread of innovations in distribution and retailing, making the national market highly contested and centralised from the early 2000s. Retail restructuring – encouraged by a belated and inconsistent regulatory framework until 2006 – stimulated the polarisation of consumption practices along incomes, education skills and residential location (AC Nielsen, 2005; TÁRKI, 2008).

Retail restructuring in Romania entered the second stage after the EU accession in 2007. However, transformation of the sector, and also of consumption practices, was spectacular and resulted in a rapid centralisation, driven primarily by the growth of the supermarket segment. The development of discount stores, hypermarkets, as well as specialist shops in shopping malls and the introduction of e-retailing facilities stimulated a further decline of the traditional scenes of consumption (independent small shops and markets). The changes were

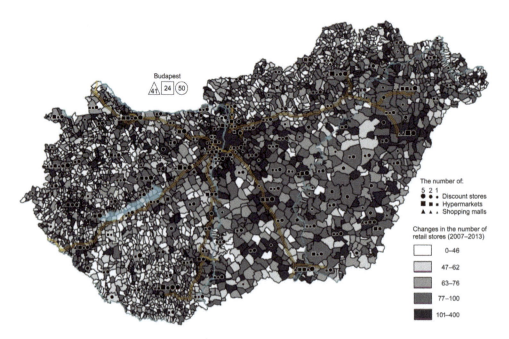

Fig. 11.2. Changes in the retail store stock (2007–2013) and the spread of new retail formats in Hungary (2014) at the municipal (LAU2) scale. (From author's calculations based on TEIR (Regional Information System), Hungary, and on corporate websites.)

driven mostly by retail TNCs expanding quickly in the emerging market[4] that recovered quickly after the financial crisis (from 2011) (AC Nielsen, 2005; Buzilá, 2011; Planet Retail, 2014).

Retail restructuring contributed to ongoing socio-spatial polarisation across CEE (Nagy, 2005); nevertheless, at the same time, it enhanced the opportunities for local elites to build local strategies on consumption. In near-border centres, such strategies were encouraged by major retailers' localisation strategies that relied on cross-border flows in enhancing capital return and revalorising local investments in the contested market contexts (Michalkó, 2004; Kovács, 2008). Meanwhile, rural spaces – particularly, low-income, immobile households – were marginalised by major retailers' localisation strategies that stimulated the rise of differentiated, multi-tiered consumption strategies (Michalkó, 2004; Nagy et al., 2015). Accordingly, a wide spectrum of cross-border consumption patterns emerged across CEE border regions. However, such practices were shaped also by the processes of state restructuring that differentiated citizens as consumers of public goods. Thus, in the following sections, cross-border consumption is discussed in the context of both powerful agents' (state and retail capital) space-making logic.

11.3.2 Strategies for growth and tackling peripherality in the Oradea–Debrecen urban region

The socio-spatial transformation of the Debrecen–Oradea[5] region was embedded in the unfolding political economy of the CEE transition – the systemic crisis (industrial decline, social polarisation), the selective recovery of local industries stimulated by transnational flows and the reorganisation of state space that enhanced the autonomy and the responsibilities of local communities (Pickles and Smith, 2007; Smith and Swain, 2010). Recovery came earlier (in the late 1990s) in Debrecen and rested on the growth and restructuring of manufacturing, health industries, knowledge-based services and retail. Oradea entered the take-off period in the early 2000s, as a European node of distributive services.

The restructuring of the local economies stimulated by the influx of capital, the enhanced competition on local and regional retail markets and the recontextualisation of the border region within Europe – free flows, enhanced networking, EU funding – incited local political and economic elites in both cities to develop multi-tiered strategies in which various forms of consumption had a central role. These strategies were the manifestations of neoliberal urban policies emerging across Europe (discussed by Jessop, 2002; Swyngedouwe et al., 2002; Amin and Thrift, 2007) and rested on the commodification of local culture and urban space, delegating various tasks related to 'public good' to NGOs and market agents and on employing exceptionality ('flexible') measures in development policies.

Although, both cities faced similar structural problems, their scope within the national administrative political systems was different. The act on municipalities provided fairly wide autonomy in strategy making and fund-raising for local agents in Debrecen. The city had no rival as a regional centre, which made it one of the prime targets for retail investment outside Budapest. Local leaders positioned the city as the primary cultural centre for east Hungary and also for north-west Romania (inhabited by a substantial Hungarian minority), employing an ethnocultural definition for the 'nation'. By contrast, in Oradea, the scope of local agents was limited by strong state control over development resources and public financing exercised by county-level public administrative bodies, through which party politics – often having ethnocultural connotations – infiltrated into regional and local development policies. Moreover, as a local politician suggested, Oradea '...has always been lagging behind one of our competitors' (i.e. Bucharest as the primary national centre and Cluj Napoca in the north-west region). Thus, local leaders have relied on Europe-wide networking and cross-border relations as the engine for development.

The growth and the increasing diversity of cross-border relations was embedded in the major shifts and turns in the discourses and institutional practices related to national borders in Hungary and Romania, such as:

- The dissolution of the communist regimes (1989/1990), followed by the redefinition of bilateral political relations based on mutual acceptance of the geopolitical status

quo and of international law as a framework for settling problems related to ethnic
minorities and national borders (1996)[6] –
embedded in international and national
discourses on building European identities
in the applicant countries (Moisio, 2002).

• The unfolding of cross-border relations
(2000–2004/2007): the re-regulation of
cross-border flows from 2001 on, including
abolishing the visa system (EU/Romania),
introducing a new cross-border control
system (providing 7-day permits for those
who live within 35 km distance from the
border, 2003), and building local institutional capacities to exploit pre-accession
and cross-border cooperation (CBC) funds.

• After the EU accessions (2004, 2007): intensified multiple networking and enhanced
flows within settled national regulation
frameworks.

The key agents (our interviewees) of the increasingly complex and multi-scalar net of social relations were local political leaders supported by the emerging 'project class' (Kovách
and Kucerová, 2006), public institutions, risk-
taking enterprises (TNCs and local small and
medium-size enterprises (SMEs)) and NGOs. In
the following, I introduce briefly three processes
in which their strategies were entangled.

1. Consumption restructuring in the region
was driven by the spatial logic of retail capital: in
the early 1990s, small capitals were mobilised to
exploit unaddressed demand in the transition
markets, predominantly through traditional
channels (convenience stores, open markets).
The entry of TNCs and the introduction of new
formats on Debrecen's market changed the scene
thoroughly by the late 1990s,[7] resulting in an
increasingly centralised consumption landscape
at the regional and local scale. The process was
supported by the local municipality through a
fairly liberal regulation regime, as retail restructuring fitted the concept of a regional/transborder
service centre, and also the ideology of the
consumer citizen of the post-shortage society
(Klumbyte, 2009; Eglitis, 2011).

In Oradea, a single new mall was opened,
and local retail was dominated by traditional
shopping spaces until 2008 (Colliers International, 2011). The uneven transformation of
national and local markets stimulated the

growth of cross-border shopping, which was enhanced further by Romania's EU accession.
Shoppers coming from Romania – dominantly
(60%) from County Bihor – targeted primarily
the hypermarkets in Debrecen (accounting for
75% of contributors of this format in 2008)
(Tömöri, 2012); the well-off also frequented the
branded shops of the shopping malls (4–5% of
the visitors/7–8% of the turnover annually). As
the executives of the new formats in Debrecen
indicated, their cross-border contributors were
attracted primarily by the 'reliable quality of
goods and services they cannot get at home'.
Thus, the key agents of Debrecen's retail sector
exploited the 'modernisation gap' of the two
markets by attracting the higher-income, mobile
groups of the border region – introducing a new
dimension of socio-spatial inequalities by the
early 2010s.[8]

In parallel, a group of mediators emerged in
the 'grey' segment of cross-border retailing that
provided basic goods for traditional convenience
stores and open market sellers in Romania frequented by lower-income consumers. They
sourced their supply in the major stores of Debrecen (Metro, Tesco) and/or on the local open
market. Although such businesses carried considerable risks – the mediators combined formal
and informal relations to exploit price differences and the relaxed border control – they were
also sources of learning and trust ('ties that
bind': Granovetter, 1985). This experience assisted their move into the 'formal' zone of retailing as national regulations grew tighter and
market prices grew more balanced.

2. The above changes were embedded in extensive urban revitalisation programmes introduced by local political leaders and bureaucrats
to regenerate declining inner spaces in both cities in the 2000s. Such projects were financed
dominantly by EU ERDF (European Regional Development Fund) and were linked with developing the commercial function of the urban
centres. The rise of new branded spaces in the
cities rested on the coalition of retail capital and
neoliberal local state – such as in the case of the
Forum shopping mall (2008) in the centre of
Debrecen, near a new cultural complex (theatre,
Museum of Modern Arts, Kölcsey Cultural
Centre) (Fig. 11.3). The latter was a tier of the
local political elite's growth strategy, funded by
central governmental and EU programmes, and

Fig. 11.3. The Forum shopping mall (right) and the cultural centre (left) in Debrecen. (Photograph courtesy of Erika Nagy.)

devoted to making Debrecen the primary centre for 'high' culture for the well-off visitors from eastern Hungary and north-west Romania (Nagy, 2012). In response to the enhanced cross-border competition (retail investments in Oradea), the executives of local shopping centres exhibited the malls as public spaces and entered partnerships with local cultural institutions to refocus their markets.

The municipality of Oradea also mobilised major human and institutional capacities to raise EU funding for revitalising and 'selling' local built heritage and cultural services as tourism products. Here, local programmes were linked even more clearly to the social transformation of urban space, by promoting gentrification and reorganising the hinterland to channel suburbanisation (Timár and Nagy, 2012). The latter was framed by the Oradea Metropolitan Area (OMA)[9] and exploited by local leaders to ease housing shortages and respond to the social tensions raised by economic restructuring. This element of local policy had a cross-border dimension, as suburbanisation processes had reached the villages on the Hungarian side by 2010. For rural communities, the arrival of new residents from Romania was key for their local 'revitalisation' strategy, and they entered various bilateral agreements with Oradea municipality on institutional cooperation (education, transportation development, cultural exchange, raising EU funding) to improve local services and access of the villagers to the urban labour market and consumption facilities.[10] This systematic organisation of the cross-border hinterland rested on a political turn – the entry of Hungary's minority party into local and county bodies – and on the EU integration process. However, the spread of the OMA stimulated political conflicts with ethnocultural connotations in Oradea that had to be managed very skilfully by Hungarian minority politicians.

3. The health 'industry' was also an emerging segment of cross-border consumption. Public health care had been underfinanced, poorly organised and lacked proper technical and academic background in Romania since the 1990s. Hungarian medical services were also poorly financed, but rested on high-quality training (University of Debrecen, Faculty of Medicine) and R&D background. Two major coalitions emerged to exploit institutional and market potentials.

- The one formulated by public institutions and NGOs (e.g. the Catholic Church in Oradea and various organisations of professionals in both cities) targeted the improvement of the quality and accessibility of services in Romania through joint training programmes and the setting up of new facilities (an eye clinic, orthopaedic and gynaecological ambulances) in Oradea involving specialists from Hungary, and through developing information and diagnostic systems (a joint EU-funded project of

city hospitals of Debrecen and Oradea). However, the new services were not fully integrated into the Romanian public health system; thus, their introduction marginalised the poor and immobile rural dwellers.

- A 'marketed' model of health services also emerged mobilising professional knowledge, institutional capacities and social relations in Debrecen. The city had developed as a regional medical service centre in the past 15 years, based on the capacities of local public hospitals and on private surgeries and clinics. The latter provided high-quality services for well-off patients (30–50% from Romania, mostly from Oradea), and an 'extra' income for the staff working as entrepreneurs (while having a low-paid, full-time job in public institutions). The development of a medical 'industry' stimulated investments in sports facilities and leisure services involving private (e.g. Aquaticum Spa resort) and public funding (Főnix Sports Hall), which were ranked by major retailers as key factors of their competitiveness and were considered as pillars of the urban development strategy by local leaders.

The emerging cross-border urban region was the scene of emerging coalitions and development strategies that were enacted by cross-border networks of institutions, firms, NGOs and individuals. However, the case study suggested that cross-border relations were dominated by powerful urban agents and inter-urban linkages that channelled private and public investments dominantly into urban spaces. In this way, new dimensions of inequalities emerged in urban–hinterland relations in terms of access to goods and services, as well as to knowledge and information (e.g. on raising EU funding), supported by the spatial logic of capital, the centralising national policies and also by normative, output-oriented EU policies. Nevertheless, equalisation processes were also occurring in the region due to permanent learning, institutional capacity building and networking, through which the Oradea region 'caught up' with Debrecen (e.g. in mobilising EU funding) and rural municipalities had access to EU funding and information to ease the deficits in local public services.

11.3.3 A prosperous spa town in a peripheral border region – Gyula

The history of Gyula – a small border town of 30,365 inhabitants (2014) – reflects clearly how the entangled processes of modernisation and geopolitical changes produced socio-spatial inequalities on the European semi-periphery (Wallerstein, 2010). The city was marginalised in major railway constructions, which eroded its regional market centre roles and limited capital accumulation to local resources (1860s–1914). It has lost its economic hinterland because of the border changes in 1920 and, finally, it ceased to be a county seat within the highly centralised spatial administrative structure of the communist regime (1950) (Nagy *et al.*, 2012). As a response, strategies for tackling peripherality under various regimes were developed by local actors who relied on Gyula's resources – focusing on quality food production, exploiting cultural heritage and the natural conditions for spa services, introducing local brands that survived regime changes, and a political platform for local development in the long term. Gyula, as a small town and a near-border community, exhibits a relevant context for analysing the social (consumption) relations shaped by 'othering' discourses dominated by party politics and supranational institutions, and the translation of such discourses into the daily practices of 'borderlanders' (van Houtum and Pijpers, 2007; Kuus, 2011; Balogh, 2014).

In the 1990s, the town faced a transition-led economic decline, particularly in local textile and food industries. The latter resulted directly from the entry of transnational retail capital: TNCs enhanced their market control through buyer-driven commodity chains, pushing local suppliers toward contested market segments and unequal bargaining on the terms of exchange. Due to its size and the lack of businesses attractive to foreign investors, local leaders developed a strategy focused on the development of the urban economy by combining 'marketed' services (tourism, retail) and the capacities of the public institutions (administration, health, culture). An important element of this was the exploitation of local brands – traditional food, the spa and the historical town image, and the multicultural character of Gyula[11] – to stimulate growth.

The engine of change was a small group of local leaders, headed by the mayor and her team leading the local coalition for tourism development and accessing EU funding for urban revitalisation and spa development,[12] taking off in the late 1990s. The strategy was backed also by the expertise of the regional centre of the national tourism development agency (Tourinform) and by an NGO (DARIB), involving the key agents of the sector in the local coalition and also helping their networking activities in Hungary and beyond. The cooperation facilitated concerted and systematic fund-raising and marketing activities, and provided a 'critical mass' of investments for mobilising private capital – the entry of retail TNCs (Interspar, Tesco, Schwarz/Lidl, from 2008), Hunguest (a Central European hotel chain) and smaller-scale developments in the catering and hotel business sector. As a result, tourism-related services were enhanced in terms of quality and quantity, the local property market was revived and employment in services increased by 14% (2001–2014). The process was supported by the involvement of the county hospital in the spa development (rehabilitation services). In turn, growing tourism contributed to the rise of a wide range of 'marketed' health services provided by the hospital's specialists. Paradoxically, the growth of this segment was stimulated by cutbacks in the public health-care system, which produced underutilised capacities in the hospital (in diagnostic, operative and also in the rehabilitation phases) – opening a way for income generation for public institutions.

This model rested largely on the changing border regime in terms of funding, Europe-wide networking (knowledge flows, marketing) and of cross-border relations. The latter was limited to the vigorously growing shopping tourism from Romania in the 1990s. Although Romanian consumers contributed largely to local retail businesses, they were considered as immediate 'others' associated with 'improper' behaviour and 'backwardness' in this early period.

As political relations were settled and the Romanian economy was taking off, cross-border flows intensified and the borderland status was redefined after 2000. The proportion of Romanian contributors in local leisure and health services was increasing, outnumbering all other groups of foreign visitors by 2010. Their combined trips, ranging from 1-day spa-and-shopping visits to 2-week family vacations, were growing in quantity and also in the size of the catchment area. Local businesses refocused their services to meet new customers' needs (e.g. by improving language skills) and made use of cross-border cooperation in exporting services, constructing regional supply chains (catering), externalising services (e.g. laundry for hotels) and hiring Romanian-speaking staff. As visitors from Romania were growing in number, they were perceived by locals as 'ones like us' and as 'guests who appreciate quality'. Old 'othering' was fading – assisted by the growing number of Gyula-Arad joint EU projects – and was soon replaced by new 'others' from outside of the EU (mostly from Serbia), who had all the labels that previously were associated with Romanians.

While the above changes generated growth and involved more and more households in the service industries,[13] economic restructuring produced new jobs in the worst-paid sectors, reinforced the seasonality of local labour demand and increased the gap between the urban and rural labour markets in terms of accessibility, incomes and stability (availability of full-time jobs). Inequalities were also enhanced by the Gyula-centred restructuring of retail spaces and the rise of health-care 'business', marginalising the poor, who were confined to the shrinking public pool of services and who had no access to social support – unlike the Debrecen–Oradea region, where NGOs took this role. Thus, while Gyula's economy was increasingly networked and opened to cross-border flows, the town's immediate rural hinterland was increasingly peripheralised – perceived as a new 'othering' process by the village dwellers.

11.3.4   Being a consumer in a rural ghetto – border-related practices in South Békés

Traditionally, South Békés is associated with the richness of natural assets needed for specialised food production, which provided a basis for prosperity and stability until the late 1980s. However, since then the region has been hit by economic decline, loss of control over local resources, emigration and the disintegration of local communities. As a consequence, retail investments and new retail forms are scarce, even in small towns, and local consumers are dependent on local retailers and service providers, who exploit their oligopolistic market position (relatively high prices, limited range of goods). Meanwhile, traditional forms of self-supply and solidarity are fading due to increasing poverty (Fig. 11.1).

The consumption practices of local communities are interwoven with various informal/ semi-formal activities. They range from cross-border petty trade satisfying basic needs – pursued openly in public market places and silently agreed by local leaders, even though this is a source of tax abuse – to illegal businesses adapting flexibly to various border regimes, such as fuel trading (1990s), tobacco smuggling (early 2000), human trafficking and prostitution (recently). However, for the majority of villagers, the border has no direct impact on their lives. As an interviewed local intellectual suggested

> ...Here we live in the middle of nowhere. We are not good customers, as we do not have good incomes. Instead, we have an emerging small kingdom of one or two great men [major landowners and local leaders] and only the local state helping local people, just to survive. We are back into the 19th century.

As the interview suggests, the region is captured in a modernisation trap in which local communities lack all forms of capital to exploit the new border regime and individuals become increasingly dependent on a few key agents in terms of income raising and consumption. Low-income households' dependence is reinforced also by the social subsidy system, which is shrinking, controlled by the local state and in which in-kind support (food and fuel) has a major share. Such social relations indicate the emergence of a rural ghetto, where consumption is limited to basic needs and exploited to control the community.

11.4   Conclusions

The embedding of CEE border regions in global flows and European institutional space has induced multiple strategies and diverse everyday practices that seem to have a decisive role in relaxing deeply rooted ethnocultural conflicts and socio-spatial inequalities 'produced' by the spatial logic of capitalism. However, the transformation of borders and related practices was a contested process, as it challenged (re)emerging nationhood (Young and Light, 2001; Popescu, 2008; Scott, 2014), raised new 'othering' processes (Kuus, 2011; Balogh, 2014) and added new dimensions to the polarisation processes in CEE.

The strategies employed to exploit the border context ranged from enhancing the profitability of TNCs investing in Hungarian border regions – by relying on labour assets, price and market structure differentials – to daily survival by getting involved in various forms of illegal trade (e.g. Horváth and Kovách, 1999; Kovács, 2008; Tömöri, 2011). Cross-border consumption became a key aspect of the daily lives of 'borderlanders'. A new set of related practices emerged that were shaped by the spatial logic of retail capital, as well as by the strategies of local agents responding to their peripheral position produced by capital flows and to state restructuring. Changes in such practices were urban-centred processes, driven by international investors in coalition with powerful local agents seeking new sources of growth and to tackle social conflicts through exploiting local assets (including the near-border status) – all embraced by neoliberal local policies focused on consumption (Szalai, 2006; Brenner, 2009). Although small towns (e.g. Gyula, Komárom/Komarno, Sopron) were also targeted by major retailers (Fig. 11.2), and local institutional and private capital was mobilised for enhancing local services, such places became highly vulnerable to global crises (e.g. Fig. 11.4), and relations with their hinterland have been weakened considerably. However, the most striking dimension of socio-spatial inequalities was (is) the urban–rural nexus in the context of cross-border consumption. The case studies suggest that the majority of rural communities lack institutional capacities, expertise and networked relations to exploit their cross-border situation, while they are marginalised by capital flows and by shrinking public services. Thus, 'rural ghettoisation' – ongoing across CEE since the transition (Virág, 2010) – is exacerbated by the rise of new centralities and marginalities along the border.

Fig. 11.4. Smach supermarket (run by the Delhaize Group) closed down in Mezőkovácsháza, a small market centre in the 'Dél-Békés' region. (Photograph courtesy of Erika Nagy.)

Endnotes

[1] As defined by Smith, 1991.

[2] I refer here to the debate on the relevance of the political economic approach towards understanding the role of consumption in the context of global capitalism, in particular to the arguments of Granovetter (1985), Hudson (2004), Miller (2005) and Goss (2006) for considering agency and sociocultural embedding of economic actions, including consumption.

[3] I rely here on the results of the 'Innotárs' project (210 interviews conducted in cross-border urban regions (Fig. 11.1)) and on the project results supported by the National Research, Development and Innovation Office – OTKA/NKFIH grants 114468 (Change and Continuity in Hungarian Spatial Imaginaries: Nationality, Territoriality, Development and the Politics of Borders) and 109296 (Institutional and Individual Responses to State Restructuring in Different Geographical Contexts).

[4] The Schwarz Group (Kaufland, Lidl); Carrefour; Rewe Group; Metro Group; Auchan; Delhaize Group (including the Mega Image supermarket chain since 2000).

[5] Debrecen (203,506 inhabitants in 2015) is a medium-size town, regional centre and county seat in Hungary, 60 km from the border; Oradea (196,367 inhabitants in 2012, 73.1% Romanian, 24.9% Hungarian, 1.2% Roma, 0.8% others) is a medium-size town, county seat with metropolitan status in Romania, 11 km from the border. These two towns are founders of the Bihar-Bihor Euroregion (2002) with County Bihor (Romania) and County Hajdú-Bihar (Hungary).

[6] Known as the 'Treaty between the Republic of Hungary and Romania on Understanding, Cooperation and Good Neighbourhood'.

[7] Two malls, a hypermarket and a Metro store had been opened by 1998; by 2014, two further malls (on- and off-centre), one hypermarket, a number of supermarkets and discount stores had also been added to the local stock (see also Fig. 11.2) by the 'Top 10' retailers. In parallel, the number of stores was declining – primarily hitting peripheral urban and rural spaces (Tömöri, 2011).

[8] Recently, major transnational and domestic retailers have challenged the Debrecen-centred cross-border shopping model by introducing new retail forms, such as shopping malls (7), DIY stores and hypermarkets (4) and mushrooming supermarkets and discounters targeting the Bihor county market (600,000 inhabitants), where, in 2012, the GDP/capita was 50% higher than the Romanian average (Colliers International, 2011; Planet Retail, 2014).

[9] Metropolitan zones (12 in all) were proposed by the Act on Regional Development of Romania (2006). Major urban centres were permitted to organise services and set up development plans covering their hinterland (also defined by the Act).

[10] Similar strategies were employed by rural communities in the Bratislava region (Hardi et al., 2009), and in north-east Hungary (providing second homes for the well-off from Kosice).

[11] Gyula has a Romanian, a German and a Roma minority; it is the primary cultural and education centre of the Romanian diaspora in Hungary.

[12] The municipality has had a majority ownership (93%) in the local spa complex since the transition.

[13] As employees and also as seasonal accommodation service providers – annually, 500–700 households.

References

AC Nielsen (2005) *Emerging Markets. Retail and Shopper Trends. Report.* The Nielsen Company, Vienna.

Agnew, J. (2011) The origins of critical geopolitics. In: Dodds, K., Kuus, M. and Sharp, J. (eds) *Ashgate Research Companion to Critical Geopolitics.* Ashgate, Farnham, UK, pp. 19–32.

Amin, A. and Thrift, N. (2007) Cultural-economy and cities. *Progress in Human Geography* 31(2), 143–161.

Balogh, P. (2014) *Perpetual Borders. German–Polish Cross-border Contacts in the Szczecin Area.* Stockholm University, Stockholm.

Brenner, N. (2009) Open questions on state rescaling. *Cambridge Journal of Regions, Economy and Society* 2, 123–139.

Brenner, N., Peck, J. and Theodore, N. (2010) Variegated neoliberalization: geographies, modalities, pathways. *Global Networks* 10(2), 182–222.

Buzilá, N. (2011) *The Romanian Retail Market – Present and Perspectives.* Faculty of Economic Science, Tibiscus University, Timişoara, Romania.

Cetelem (2015) Cetelem körkép 2015. A fogyasztás Európában – 2009–2014, az évek, amelyek mindent megváltoztattak. [Cetelem Panorama 2015. Consumption in Europe – from 2009 to 2014 , the years that changed everything.] Available at: https://www.cetelem.hu/sites/default/files/korkep/cetelem-korkep-2015.pdf (accessed 29 July 2016).

Chelcea, L. (2002) The culture of shortage during state socialism: consumption practices in a Romanian village in the 1980s. *Cultural Studies* 16(1), 16–43.

Coe, N. (2011) Geographies of production II. A global production network A–Z. *Progress in Human Geography* 36(3), 389–402.

Colliers International (2011) *Valuation Report. ERA Park, Oradea*. Colliers, Bucharest. Available at: http://www.abcapproperty.com/cms/images/File/OtherMatters/draft%20valuation%20report%20Era%20Oradea%20041511%20Final.pdf (accessed 29 July 2016).

Dicken, P. (2007) *The Global Shift. Mapping the Changing Contours of the World Economy*. Sage, London.

Dodds, K., Kuus, M. and Sharp, J. (2013) Introduction: geopolitics and its critics. In: Dodds, K., Kuus, M. and Sharp, J. (eds) *Ashgate Research Companion to Critical Geopolitics*. Ashgate, Farnham, UK, pp. 1–18.

Eglitis, D. (2011) Class, culture, and consumption: representations of stratification in post-communist Latvia. *Cultural Sociology* 5(3), 423–446.

Ehrlich, K., Kriszan, A. and Lang, T. (2012) Urban development in Central and Eastern Europe – between peripheralization and centralization? *disP – The Planning Review,* 48(2), 77–92.

Faulconbridge, J.R. (2010) TNCs as embedded social communities: transdisciplinary perspectives. *Critical Perspectives on International Business* 6(4), 273–290.

Gereffi, G. (1999) International trade and industrial upgrading in the apparel commodity chain. *Journal of International Economics* 48, 37–70.

GfK (2015) *Purchasing Power Hungary*. GfK Geomarketing, Bruchsal, Germany.

Goss, J. (2006) Geographies of consumption: the work of consumption. *Progress in Human Geography* 30(2), 237–249.

Granovetter, M. (1985) Economic action and social structure: the problem of embeddedness. *American Journal of Sociology* 91, 481–510.

Gulyás, E. (2008) Interpretations of ethical consumption. *Review of Sociology* 14(1), 25–44.

Hardi, T., Hajdú, Z. and Mezei, I. (2009) *Határok és városok a Kárpát-medencében. [Borders and towns in the Carpathian Basin.]* MTA RKK, Pécs-Győr, Hungary.

Harvey, D. (1995) *The Condition of Postmodernity. An Enquiry into Origins of Cultural Change*. Blackwell, Oxford, UK.

Harvey, D. (2005) *A Brief History of Neoliberalism*. Oxford University Press, Oxford, UK.

Hess, M. (2004) Global production networks. Dealing with diversity. In: Haak, R. and Tachiki, D.S. (eds) *Regional Strategies in a Global Economy*. IUDICIUM Verlag, Munich, Germany, pp. 31–52.

Hetesi, E., Andics, J. and Veres, Z. (2007) Az életstílus-kutatás eredményeinek fogyasztásszociológiai interpretációs dilemma. [The sociology of lifestyle research results: consumption interpretation dilemmas.] *Szociológiai Szemle [Sociology Review]* 3–4, 117–135.

Horváth G.K. and Kovách, I. (1999) A feketegazdaság (olajgazdaság és KGST-piac) és a vállalkozói Kelet-Magyarország. [The black economy (oil-market economy and Comecon) and entrepreneurship in Eastern Hungary.] *Szociológiai Szemle [Sociology Review]* 3, 28–53.

Hudson, R. (2004) Conceptualizing economies and their geographies: spaces, flows and circuits. *Progress in Human Geography* 28(4), 447–471.

Hudson, R. and Hadjimichalis, C. (2014) Contemporary crisis across Europe and the crisis of regional development theories. *Regional Studies* 48(1), 208–218.

Jessop, B. (2002) Liberalism, neoliberalism and urban governance: a state-theoretic perspective. In: Brenner, N. and Theodore, N. (eds) *Spaces of Neoliberalism: Urban Restructuring in North America and Western Europe*. Blackwell, Oxford, UK, pp. 105–125.

Johnson, C., Jones, R., Paasi, A., Amoore, L., Mountz, A., Salter, M., *et al.* (2011) Interventions on rethinking the border in border studies. *Political Geography* 30(2), 61–69.

Klumbyte, N. (2009) Post-socialist sensations: nostalgia, the self and alterity in Lithuania. *Lietuvos Etnologija* 9(18), 93–116.

Kolosi, T. (2000) *A terhes babapiskóta. A rendszerváltás társadalomszerkezete. [The pregnant sponge finger. Social restructuring and transition.]* Osiris, Budapest.

Kornai, J. (1980) *Economics of Shortage*. North-Holland, Amsterdam.

Kovách, I. and Kucerová, E. (2006) The project class in Central Europe: the Czech and Hungarian cases. *Sociologia Ruralis* 46(1), 3–21.

Kovács, A. (2008) A kiskereskedelem területi jellegzetességei a szlovák-magyar határtérségben. [Spatial characteristics of the retail trade in the Slovak–Hungarian border region.] *Tér és Társadalom* [*Space and Society*] 3, 97–107.

Kuus, M. (2011) Europe's eastern expansion and the re-inscription of otherness in East-central Europe. *Progress in Human Geography* 28(4), 472–481.

Lang, T. (2015) Socio-economic and political responses to regional polarisation and socio-spatial peripheralisation in Central and Eastern Europe: a research agenda. *Hungarian Geographical Bulletin* 64(3), 171–185.

Lowe, M. and Wrigley, N. (1996) Towards the new retail geography. In: Wrigley, N. and Lowe, M. (eds) *Retailing, Consumption and Capital*. Longman, Harlow, UK, pp. 3–30.

Michalkó, G. (2004) *A bevásárlóturizmus. A turizmus termékei I.* [Shopping tourism. Tourism items I.] Kodolányi János Főiskola, Székesfehérvár, Hungary.

Miller, D. (2005) Consumption as a vanguard of history. In: Miller, D. (ed.) *Acknowledging Consumption*. Routledge, London, pp. 1–53.

Moisio, S. (2002) EU eligibility, Central Europe, and the invention of applicant state narrative. *Geopolitics* 7(3), 89–116.

Nagy, E. (2005) Strategies of international investors in Hungary's emerging retail market. In: Turnock, D. (ed.) *Foreign Direct Investment and Regional Development in East Central Europe and the Former Soviet Union*. Ashgate, Aldershot, UK, pp. 267–290.

Nagy, E. (2012) Bargaining, learning and control: production of consumption spaces in post-socialist context. *Europa Regional* 20(1), 42–54.

Nagy, E., Timár, J., Nagy, G. and Velkey, G. (2015) The everyday practices of the reproduction of peripherality and marginality in Hungary. In: Lang, T., Ehrilch, K., Sgibnev, W. and Henn, S. (eds) *Understanding Geographies of Polarization and Peripheralization.* Palgrave-MacMillan, Basingstoke, UK, pp. 135–156.

Nagy, G., Nagy, E. and Timár, J. (2012) The changing meaning of core–periphery relations of a nonmetropolitan 'urban region' at the Hungarian–Romanian border. *disP – The Planning Review* 48(2), 93–105.

Ó Tuathail, G. (1994) The critical reading/writing of geopolitics: re-reading/writing Wittfogel, Bowman and Lacoste. *Progress in Human Geography* 18, 313–332.

Ó Tuathail, G. and Agnew, J. (1992) Geopolitics and discourse: practical geopolitical reasoning and American foreign policy. *Political Geography* 11, 190–204.

Patico, J. and Caldwell, M.L. (2002) Consumers exiting socialism: ethnographic perspectives on daily life in postcommunist Europe. *Ethnos* 67(3), 285–294.

Pickles, J. and Smith, A. (2007) Post-socialist economic geographies and the politics of knowledge production. In: Tickell, A., Sheppard, E. and Peck, J. (eds) *Politics and Practice in Economic Geography.* Sage, London, pp. 151–162.

Planet Retail (2014) *European Grocery Retailing*. Planet Retail Ltd, London. Available at: http://www.planetretail.net/presentations/ApexBrasilPresentation.pdf (accessed 29 July 2016).

Popescu, G. (2008) The conflicting logics of cross-border reterritorialization: geopolitics of Euroregions in Eastern Europe. *Political Geography* 27(4), 418–438.

Scott, J.W. (2014) *Bordering, Border Politics and Cross-border Cooperation in Europe*. EU Borderscapes Working Papers, 7. Karelian Institute, University of Eastern Finland, Joensuu, Finland. Available at: http://www.euborderscapes.eu/fileadmin/user_upload/Working_Papers/EUBORDERSCAPES_Working_Paper_7_Scott.pdf (accessed 24 August 2016).

Shevchenko, O. (2002) 'Between the holes': emerging identities and hybrid patterns of consumption in post-socialist Russia. *Europe–Asia Studies* 54(6), 841–866.

Smith, A. and Swain, A. (2010) The global economic crisis, Eastern Europe, and the former Soviet Union: models of development and the contradictions of internationalization. *Eurasian Geography and Economics* 51(1), 1–34.

Smith, N. (1991) *Uneven Development. Nature, Capital and the Production of Space,* 2nd edn. Blackwell, Oxford, UK.

Stenning, A., Smith, A., Rochovska, A. and Swiatek, D. (2011) *Domesticating Neoliberalism. Spaces of Economic Practice and Social Reproduction in Post-socialist Cities.* Wiley-Blackwell, Oxford, UK.

Swyngedouw, E., Moulaert, F. and Rodriguez, A. (2002) Neoliberal urbanization in Europe: large-scale urban development projects and the new urban policy. *Antipode* 34(3), 542–577.

Szalai, E. (2006) *Az újkapitalizmus és ami utána jöhet.* [*The new capitalism, and what may come after it.*] Új Mandátum Kiadó, Budapest.

TÁRKI (2008) Fogyasztói szegmentáció.. [Customer segmentation.] TÁRKI, Budapest, p. 44. Available at: http://www.tarki.hu/hu/research/gazdkult/fogyasztoi_szegmentacio.pdf (accessed 29 July 2016).

Timár, J. and Nagy, E. (2012) Urban restructuring in the grip of capital and politics: gentrification in East-Central Europe. In: Csapó, T. and Balogh, A. (eds) *Development of the Settlement Network in the Central European Countries: Past, Present, and Future.* Springer Verlag, Berlin-Heidelberg, Germany, pp. 121–135.

Tömöri, M. (2011) A határon átívelő kiskereskedelem tereinek társadalomföldrajzi vizsgálata Debrecenben és Nagyváradon. [Socio-geographical study of cross-border retail spaces of Debrecen and Oradea.] Unpublished PhD thesis, University of Debrecen, Debrecen, Hungary.

Tömöri, M. (2012) Retail without borders: the example of Debrecen (Hungary) and Oradea (Romania). *Central European Regional Policy and Human Geography* 3(1), 53–62.

van Houtum, H. and Pijpers, R. (2007) The European Union as a gated community: the two-faced border and immigration regime of the EU. *Antipode* 39(2), 291–309.

Verdery, K. (1999) Fuzzy property rights power and identity in Transylvania's decollectivization. In: Burawoy, M. and Verdery, K. (eds) *Uncertain Transitions: Ethnographies of Change in the Postsocialist World.* Rowman and Littlefield, Oxford, UK, pp. 53–82.

Virág, T. (2010) *Kirekesztve. Falusi gettók az ország peremén.* [Excluded . Rural ghettoes at the edge of the country]. Akadémiai Kiadó, Budapest.

Vörös, M. (1997) Életmód, ideológia, háztartás. A fogyasztáskutatás politikuma az államszocializmus korszakában. [Lifestyle, ideology, household. Consumption research politics of the Communist era.] *Replika* 26, 17–30.

Wallerstein, I. (2010) Bevezetés a világrendszer-elméletbe. [Introduction to world-systems theory.] Harmattán, Budapest.

Wrigley, N., Coe, N.M. and Currah, A. (2005) Globalizing retail: conceptualizing the distribution-based transnational corporation (TNC). *Progress in Urban Geography* 29(4), 437–457.

Young, C. and Light, D. (2001) Place, national identity and post-socialist transformations? An introduction. *Political Geography* 20(8), 941–955.

Zukin, S. and Maguire, J.S. (2004) Consumers and consumption. *Annual Review of Sociology* 30, 173–197.

Part IV:

Borderlands

I'm not crazy about borders; I can't honestly say
I hate them either. It's just that they scare me,
that's all, and I always get uncomfortable when
I get too close to one.

(Kapllani, 2010: 1)

CEE's national boundaries have long been a
subject of contention and debate, as well as of
historical, geographical and political study (e.g.
Thuen, 1999). The changing nature of the EU's
internal and external borders is a significant factor in European spatial reconfiguring, mobility
and tourism dynamics, and for local development. Border conceptualisation underwent a
'processual shift' during the 1990s, from 'border'
to 'bordering', and, more recently, critical attention has turned to the potential of 'borderscapes'
as a focus of analysis in helping to understand
new forms of belonging and 'becoming' (Brambilla, 2015).

Borders and border regions have attained a
particular role in the European discourse as
active spaces where links and contacts for deeper
integration are being established, not least in
order to receive funds from the European Commission. As a consequence, political elites have
appreciated the importance of cross-border
collaborative projects. These notably embrace
regions marginalised in former times. However,
the imposition of exogenous and elite-driven
models for border region development have not
been consistent in taking account of the interests and customs of local people, including patterns of local ownership and knowledge. This is

critical for promoting cross-border cooperation
as a form of governance (Tamminem, 2012).

Different levels of governance can meet at
borders, and diverse identities, self-definitions and
perceptions of 'otherness' interact. Such continuities and discontinuities can simultaneously unite
and divide. European processes have created new
types of neighbourly political spaces to adminis-
ter, while devising instruments to strengthen border controls at the Union's external limits. Such
controls, the lack of them, or their improvisation
in the face of large-scale migrant/refugee mobility, have called into question the very nature of
cooperation and policy consistency within the
Union (see also Part VI of this volume).

Building on Poland's strong tradition of
border studies, in the first chapter (12) of Part
IV, Sylwia Dołzbłasz focuses on the changing
roles of a state border conditioned by dynamic
geopolitical factors, and its significance for tourism and related mobilities, employing detailed
empirical enquiry and participant observation
in the mountainous section of the Polish–Czech
borderland. This is a border that, within a century, has been transformed from separating empires to becoming a barrier between communist
states and finally to evolving into an internal
border of the EU, enjoying unhindered passage
within the Schengen area.

Dołzbłasz's chapter analyses the influence
of the border's changing character on the transformation of transborder connections and local
development. The author discusses the issue of

transborder tourism development and addresses issues relating to border perception among tourists. In shaping the transborder region, the presence of an integrating factor is crucial to complement jointly held, coherent developmental goals. Transborder tourism based on the region's attractive natural conditions can be a significant element enhancing that process.

High geopolitics can exert profound local impacts on such mobilities as tourism in sensitive borderland areas. Jussi Laine's Chapter 13 draws on experience from the border between Finland and the Russian Federation, where interaction and cross-border mobility have reflected political, ideological and sociocultural change. The border here is seen to act as an illuminating laboratory in which the relationship between tourism and the symbolic, psychological and physical nature of international borders, and the geopolitical climate that maintains them, may be studied.[1]

In the wake of the Soviet Union's collapse, Finnish–Russian tourism began to develop rapidly, and its nature changed remarkably. A more open border, and the stark contrasts it revealed, projected great opportunities for tourism. This potential was not fully grasped, as the historical barrier effect of the border remained deeply etched in people's minds on the Finnish side and tourism to Russia remained susceptible to the impacts of high geopolitics. By contrast, tourism from Russia became a regular commercial activity.

In response to NATO and EU enlargement, however, Russia's policies towards its Western neighbours changed the perceived role of the border from a bridge back to a barrier. Laine argues that both Finland and the EU seem to have lost faith in sociocultural communication and in the transformation process in Russia. This has resulted in the privileging of formal relations at the expense of more locally oriented initiatives, with profound impacts for the practice of tourism between the countries.

At the same time, further north, Syrian and Afghani refugees apparently have been directed across the border from Russia into Kirkenes, Norway (on bicycles, as it is forbidden to cross the border there on foot). Russia's apprehension concerning refugee/migrant mobility has been poorly appreciated in the West (see, for example, Vinogradova *et al.*, 2015). While just seven refugees crossed into Kirkenes in 2014, by late 2015,

while EU attention was focused on refugees/migrants approaching from south-eastern Europe and north Africa, 200 were crossing this northern border per day (see Fig. 25.1), while the number of cross-border Russian shoppers fell some 20–25%, from a 2014 figure of 320,000 (Higgins, 2015; Kingsley, 2015).

The next two chapters highlight a theme and a location rarely addressed in the English language literature (although see Aalto, 2002; Kropinova and Bruce, 2009): the exclave role of Kaliningrad in tourism development and cross-border relations. The question of the issue's neglect is reason enough to include two chapters on the phenomenon. But this volume is privileged to be able to feature complementary chapters written by Russian experts in the field who are able to approach the issue from different perspectives: from the Russian centre/outside (a Moscow view) and from the periphery/within Kaliningrad itself.

The geographical situation of the Kaliningrad *Oblast'* (region), some 1100 km to the west of Moscow and an exclave of the Russian Federation surrounded by EU member states, is unique in Europe. Alexander Sebentsov and Maria Zotova, in Chapter 14, relate that debate over the economic development of the region, as an exclave has taken place since the collapse of the USSR. Such debate has also proceeded over the choice of a development model for the region: either to remain a Russian military outpost – a role that rendered the *Oblast'* closed to foreign tourists for decades – or to become a laboratory for cooperation with the EU. Sebentsov and Zotova affirm that any resolution of Kaliningrad's exclave issues (including tourism) is only possible if the interests of Russia as a whole, as well as those of regional and international stakeholders, are given equal consideration.

In her evaluation of tourism development from within Kaliningrad, Elena Kropinova in Chapter 15 points to the fact that the Kaliningrad *Oblast'* is now characterised by a relatively high level of international tourism compared to other regions of the Russian Federation, and that tourism is now one of the region's economic priorities. This is likely to be boosted in 2018, particularly in terms of infrastructure development, as Kaliningrad acts as one of the Russian cities hosting the FIFA World Cup tournament:

increasing numbers of both Russian and foreign tourist arrivals are expected. The influx of Russian visitors will be accelerated by a depreciation of the rouble, encouraging Russian tourists to stay 'within' their own country.

Kropinova herself has been in the forefront of strengthening collaboration and cooperation with EU neighbours through cross-border programmes and initiatives. The roles and implications of these are examined.

Endnote

[1] This borderland has also been the subject of a classic early post-war study (Mead, 1952).

References

Aalto, P. (2002) A European geopolitical subject in the making? EU, Russia and the Kaliningrad question. *Geopolitics* 7(3), 142–174.

Brambilla, C. (2015) Exploring the critical potential of the borderscapes concept. *Geopolitics* 20(1), 14–24.

Higgins, A. (2015) Avoiding risky seas, migrants reach Europe with an Arctic bike ride. *New York Times* (New York) 9 October. Available at: http://www.nytimes.com/2015/10/10/world/europe/bypassing-the-risky-sea-refugees-reach-europe-through-the-arctic.html?_r=0 (accessed 3 August 2016).

Kapllani, G. (2010) *A Short Border Handbook*. Portobello, Edinburgh, UK.

Kingsley, P. (2015) Syrians fleeing war find new route to Europe – via the Arctic Circle. *The Guardian* (London) 29 August. Available at: http://www.theguardian.com/world/2015/aug/29/syrian-refugees-europe-arctic-circle-russia-norway (accessed 3 August 2016).

Kropinova, E. and Bruce, D. (2009) A new Russian window to the West: the province of Kaliningrad. In: Holloway, J.C. (ed.) *The Business of Tourism*, 8th edn. Pearson Education, Harlow, UK, pp. 717–731.

Mead, W.R. (1952) Finnish Karelia: an international borderland. *Geographical Journal* 118(1), 40–57.

Tamminem, T. (2012) Re-establishing cross-border cooperation between Montenegro, Kosovo and Albania: the Balkans Peace Park and local ownership. *Slavica Helsingiensia* 41, 125–151.

Thuen, T. (1999) The significance of borders in the East European transition. *International Journal of Urban and Regional Research* 23(4), 738–750.

Vinogradova, M.V., Kulyamina, O.S., Koroleva, V.A. and Larinova, A.A. (2015) The impact of migration processes on the national security system of Russia. *Mediterranean Journal of Social Sciences* 6(3)(S5), 161–168.

12 From Divided to Shared Spaces: Transborder Tourism in the Polish–Czech Borderlands

Sylwia Dołzbłasz*

Department of Spatial Management, Institute of Geography and Regional Development, University of Wrocław, Poland

12.1 Introduction

By their very nature, mountain borders tend to form a strong barrier between neighbouring countries. Moreover, the spatial barrier is often reinforced by functional constraints resulting from, for example, the scarcity of infrastructural connections (Rudaz, 2009). The existence of strong political and administrative barriers between adjacent countries deepens the marginal position of the mountain border area, resulting in a lack of cooperation and connections between the actors from the regions divided by a state border.

Another scenario is also possible: the common mountainous area develops a network of connections between various types of stakeholders to generate collective action and movement (see Rudaz, 2009), which may result in the emergence of a transborder region in the literal sense. Under these circumstances, the mountainous character of such areas does not create barriers, but it becomes an integrating element conditioning the development of connections and cooperation between actors of the border region. A *sine qua non* for the development of such an optimistic scenario is a significant reduction in the role of the state border as a barrier, as well as favourable geopolitical conditions and joint/coherent development goals. The development of transborder tourism based on attractive natural conditions could be the significant element that enhances the shaping of a transborder region.

This chapter focuses on the changing roles of a state border conditioned by geopolitical factors, using the example of the mountainous parts of the Polish–Czech borderland. This is a border that, within a century, has been transformed from separating European empires to becoming a barrier between communist states, and finally to evolving into an internal border of the European Union (EU), permitting unhindered passage within the Schengen area (see Fig. 12.1).

The chapter analyses the influence of the border's changing character on the transformation of transborder connections and local development. For this purpose, the chapter discusses the issue of transborder tourism development and addresses issues relating to border perception among tourists.

In order to study the influence of the border on shaping cross-border tourism, survey research was carried out among tourists visiting the Jizera Mountains, one of the ranges situated in the Polish–Czech border region, and, additionally, in-depth interviews were conducted with local leaders. The research was also based on data concerning changes in the line of the national

---

*E-mail: sylwia.dolzblasz@uwr.edu.pl

Fig. 12.1. The changing geopolitics of the study area. (a) Until WW1; (b) interwar period; (c) since 1993. (From author's reworking of historical maps of Europe.)

border and spatial planning (construction, transport network) in the studied area. Selected data on cross-border projects co-financed with EU funds and realised in the area under investigation were also used in the research.

12.2 Borders and Their Changing Role

The issues examined in this chapter fall under the scope of 'border studies', an interdisciplinary research area (Newman and Paasi, 1998; Brunet-Jailly, 2005) within which the subject of transborder relations and the development of a borderland is complex (Paasi, 2011). Originally, borders were perceived mainly in terms of lines (Jones, 2009). In recent years, however, as a result of intensified integration processes in Europe, the transformations of the post-Cold War period and globalisation, the perception of borders has been modified considerably. The role of research into processes and relationships within borderlands is increasing, because

> state borders are at the same time social, political and discursive concepts, and not just statistical categories situated between countries.
> (Newman and Paasi, 1998: 197)

Today, the border is understood no longer as merely a physical barrier separating one country from another, but as a socio-spatial construction, exhibiting and voicing the existing diversities of human practices and as a site at and through which socio-spatial differences are communicated (van Houtum, 2005).

During the past decade, borders have commonly been said to be losing their 'barrier' function but, at the same time, boundary enforcement has been observed in a wide variety of circumstances (Amilhat-Szary, 2007). The idea of a 'borderless world' turned out to be utopian rather than real (Paasi, 2012). Even in Europe, despite processes of EU integration, results have not been as significant as the vision of 'a borderless Europe' might imply (Strüver, 2004).[1] This stems from the fact that the existence of national borders presents not only formal legal barriers, but also mental, cultural, spatial and economical ones (Palmeiro Pinheiro, 2009; Rippl *et al.*, 2010; Brunet-Jailly, 2011). Moreover, as Anderson and O'Dowd (1999) have pointed out, every state border and border region is unique. Thus, it seems that the effects of vanishing political barriers will occur with varying intensity, not only at different national borders but also within particular borderlands (Dołzbłasz and Raczyk, 2012).

With the appropriate conditions resulting from the progress of globalisation and integration, the role of the border as a barrier can be reduced, but its negative effects may not disappear completely (Ackleson, 2005). While the border can be a barrier and bring problems, it can also provide certain opportunities and bring benefits (Agnew, 2008; van der Velde and Spierings, 2010; Sohn and Lara-Valencia, 2013). For example, disparities in the socio-economic development level observed in adjacent areas on either side of the border are often followed by differences in prices; but this in turn enhances transborder shopping tourism, which can be a significant factor for the local economy. What is important, then, is that both the negative and positive effects of the border can be felt at the same time (Dołzbłasz, 2015).

It is necessary to emphasise the mobile nature of political borders, where mobility is not understood in a physical sense but in the context of shifting borders, mainly as the consequence of their variable level of closure/openness, change of function and changes in perception of them among inhabitants and tourists. The starting point for the idea of a mobile space (Walther, 2009; Retaillé and Walther, 2011; Więckowski, 2013) assumes that in changing historical circumstances, one element of the spatial structure dominates the system, thereby reorienting relations between places. In West Africa, for example, the creation of state borders has given birth to a new generation of markets. In the area under investigation, by contrast, liberalisation of the regime associated with the national border has led to a new feature: the development of transborder tourism. The changes observed are a result of processes of integration, but most of all, transborder cooperation and the mobilisation of local actors. As Paasi (2012) notes, borders are no longer lines in the ground, but they still influence boundary-producing practices.

Political boundaries affect the flow of tourists, their choice of destination, planning, infrastructure development and the marketing of tourism (Timothy, 2001). Cultural and linguistic similarity is also important, because many tourists are more inclined to cross the border if the language on the other side is the same as, or similar to, their own. However, there are also many tourists who are looking for differences while travelling. When considering the impact of borders on tourism, three main types of connection can be distinguished: borders as a barrier (real and perceived); borders as a destination; and borders as a modifier of the tourism landscape (Timothy, 2001). Indeed, borders influence tourism in many respects and in different ways and, at the same time, tourism has an influence on the border landscape (Więckowski, 2010).

12.3   Determinants of Development of the Polish–Czech Borderland

When analysing borderland transformation processes, one should take into consideration the area's complex character. Transborder relations are determined not only by political, institutional and financial factors but also by factors specific to particular regions (van Houtum, 1999), such as natural topographic features. Types of landforms and other physical geographical features shape the character of the borderland that affects the current processes of integration. Also important is how these local features have been influencing socio-economic development of border areas over time, as regards, for example, a settlement network, transport networks, economic structures. The presence of valuable natural landscapes and protected areas, or, on the contrary, highly industrialised urban areas, affects a borderland's functioning, transborder practices and potential fields of cooperation.

In the functioning of the Polish–Czech borderland, an important role has been played by, among other things, the change in the course of history of state borders over the years, the transformation of the political system in Poland and the Czech Republic in the 1990s, and favourable Polish–Czech relationships. The pace of the transformation process in the Polish–Czech border region in recent years has been affected mostly by the two countries' accession to the EU in 2004, which intensified transborder cooperation. The other key factor has been the removal of EU internal borders with entry to the Schengen Zone (since 2007).

Mutual contacts on a larger scale, including transborder tourism, were brought about following the political and socio-economic transformation of 1989. From 1945 until the 1990s, the possibility to create cooperative relationships (between the institution and/or between people) was very limited and practically non-existent. This was due mainly to the minimal permeability of the border (and in some periods, even the lack of it), the centrally planned economic systems and stringently reinforced security apparatus of the countries[2] on either side of it. The inhabitants of the borderland were not able to socialise with people on the other side of the border or, for example, to experience transborder tourism and shopping trips (at least by legal means; illegal border trade activities were, however, obvious and commonplace) (Dołzbłasz, 2015).

The crucial determinant shaping transborder interconnections in the Polish–Czech border area is the similarity in socio-economic development on both sides of the border (see Topaloglou *et al.*, 2005; European Union, 2010; Knippschild, 2011). A striking similarity can also be observed in relation to regional issues encountered (e.g. joint mountain region, reorganisation of traditional branches of industry) and development objectives (e.g. economic development, EU integration processes, tourism development) (Pokluda, 2005; Vaishar *et al.*, 2013). Further, the cultural barrier is slight, with few negative national stereotypes (Dębicki, 2010), a positive attitude towards neighbouring nations, shared historical experience of post-socialism and language similarity.

The current Polish–Czech border was established in 1993 (after the dissolution of Czechoslovakia)[3] and runs mainly across a mountainous region but, paradoxically, it proved to be less of a barrier than, for example, the Polish–German river border. Although mountains restrict the freedom of movement, the relatively high number of border crossings[4] has facilitated local traffic greatly. The character of relations in the Polish–Czech border region is influenced to a great extent by environmental factors. As a touristically attractive area with mountain tourism, winter sports and a great number of historic buildings, the borderland is enhanced by the recognition of its great natural value through the designation of numerous national and landscape parks. Touristic attractiveness not only facilitates but also 'determines' the potential directions of cooperation through the unique character of the area.[5] This contributes to a strong, clear objective of cooperation. There is considerable potential for integration, with favourable conditions for the creation of a truly transborder region (Dołzbłasz and Raczyk, 2010). At the same time, however, it is desirable to avoid the creation and consolidation of a 'cooperation monoculture' dominated by tourist-oriented activities.

12.3.1 Transborder cooperation

On the Polish–Czech border, cooperation within formal EU regional development programmes was initiated in 1995 within the framework of PHARE Cross-border Cooperation (CBC).[6] Euroregions, established through a bottom-up process, played the most important role in the shaping of cross-border cooperation in the pre-accession period (Furmankiewicz, 2007). After accession

to the EU, as in other member countries, this main role was played by Interreg IIIA (Church and Reid, 1996; Perkmann, 1999), and subsequently by Interreg IVA programmes in the framework of European Territorial Cooperation (ETC; 2007–2013).[7]

An analysis of transborder projects realised within the framework of the Czech Republic–Republic of Poland Interreg IIIA CBC Programme (2004–2006) found that cross-border cooperation in the Polish–Czech border region was shaped mainly by the area's mountainous character. Tourism-related projects (about 37%), involved mainly non-physical investment, with a significant proportion of undertakings involved in providing joint services for the tourism sector (about 20%). These included, for example, a joint tourist information system, joint promotion and marketing activities and tourist events. An important role was also played by property investment and basic infrastructure projects. Such a project structure reflects the influence of the environmental factors that directed the programme towards transborder tourism (Dołzbłasz and Raczyk, 2015). Subsequent transborder projects implemented under the Czech–Poland CBC Programme (2007–2013) within ETC also concerned tourism (over 20% of projects), with a share of physical investment projects (12%). These, for example, helped establish transborder tourist trails. The spatial distribution of projects (Fig. 12.2) shows a clear prevalence in close proximity to the border. An important role was played by the tourist attractiveness of particular regions and the existence of spa and tourism resorts. The high level of permeability of the Polish–Czech border influenced the spatial aspect of cooperation significantly, and its positive role in shaping the transborder region.

12.4 Perceptions of the Border in the Transborder Tourist Area

In order to answer the question about the character of the changes in the Polish–Czech borderland on the way 'from divided to shared spaces', the rest of this chapter focuses on perceptions of the border among tourists. To this end, a more in-depth analysis of the role of the border in local tourism was conducted, based on a questionnaire

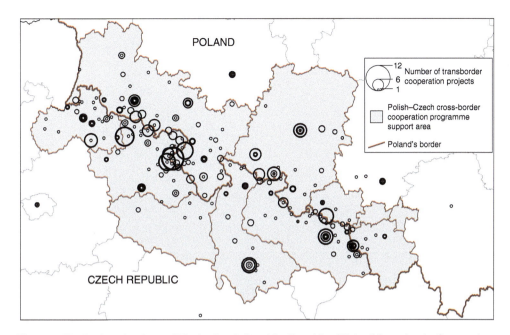

Fig. 12.2. Distribution of projects within the Czech Republic–Republic of Poland Cross-border Cooperation Operational Programme, 2007–2013. (From author's elaboration based on data from the Joint Technical Secretariat of the Czech Republic–Republic of Poland Cross-border Cooperation Operational Programme 2007–2013.)

survey in Orle, a tourist centre in the Jizera Mountains (Fig. 12.3).[8] The study included 200 respondents of Polish and Czech nationality (purposive sampling, proportional quota sampling). It was carried out on weekends and workdays in the period May–July 2011. An analysis of frequency and cross tabulation (contingency) was undertaken.

The area under investigation is located in south-western Poland (Lower Silesian Voivodship), in the Western Sudetens of the Jizera Mountains (Fig. 12.4). These territories have, historically, been a dynamic border region and their nationalities have changed over the ages. Given the latitudinal course of the mountain ranges, which constitute a natural barrier, the border has most often run along the highest peaks, dividing the two national units into the southern and northern side of the mountains. These lands were under the control of the medieval Kingdom of Poland and then the Kingdom of Bohemia. In the 16th century, along with Bohemia, the region fell into the hands of the Austrian Hapsburgs, and in the 18th century it passed to Prussia. The border between the

Prussians and Austria ran through the Jizera Mountains and basically corresponded (with later small modifications) to the Czech–German border of 1918–1939 and the Polish–Czech border of 1945–1993. Since 1993, it has been the border between Poland and the Czech Republic (see Fig. 12.1). The incorporation of Lower Silesia into Poland after the World War II was accompanied by a comprehensive change of population. Previous changes of national affiliation of these terrains were generally not followed by such far-reaching changes.

Changes in local land use of the Jizera Mountains have been connected with geopolitical changes. Until World War II, two settlements existed on the main ridge of the mountains: Gross-Iser and Karlsthal (now Orle). The former was established in the 17th century. Following World War II, Gross-Iser started to disappear as a result of resettlement. Of the over 50 buildings (including three tourist lodges and two inns) existing in the 1930s (and still existing after World War II, albeit disused), only one remains; the rest were destroyed in the 1950s. The history of the only building left standing from former

Fig. 12.3. Orle, on the Polish side of the border. (Photograph courtesy of Sylwia Dołzbłasz.)

Gross-Iser is characteristic of the borderland; it was originally a schoolhouse, but after 1945, under the conditions of the closed, impassable Polish–Czech border and stringent constraints imposed on movement in the border region, it became a watchtower for the frontier guards (and that is the reason why it was the only building from the whole settlement to survive). Since 1989 and the lifting of restrictions in the border area, the building has become a tourist lodge called *Chatka Górzystów* (Hikers' Cabin).

The settlement of Karlsthal has a similar history of a rise and fall that is closely connected with the presence of the border. A glassworks was established here in the 18th century, around which the settlement developed. After the factory was closed in 1890, it was used as a foresters' lodge. In the 1930s, a watchtower of the German border guard and customs service was put up, and after World War II, it was occupied by Polish border guards. Only four buildings from the whole settlement have survived, in which the Orle tourist station has been located since the 1990s.

The history of tourism development in the Sudetens dates back to the 16/17th century, when tourists first started to explore this area (mainly attending spas). The most significant development factors for the emergence of mass tourism at the end of the 19th century were, apart from an attractive environment, very good railway connections (built due to intensive industrial use of the Sudetens and proximity to important urban centres such as Breslau (Wrocław), Dresden and Berlin). The Sudetens, and especially the Giant and the Jizera mountains, comprised a cross-border region before World War I. This was expressed by the socio-economic links between entities operating on both the Austrian and German sides, which subsequently contributed to improvements such as extensive expansion of the cross-border transport infrastructure. Tourism was a central element of the region's cross-border character (Staffa, 2005; Potocki, 2009).

These cross-border links were somewhat loosened in the interwar period (after the establishment of Czechoslovakia), and the contacts were radically limited and politicised by the

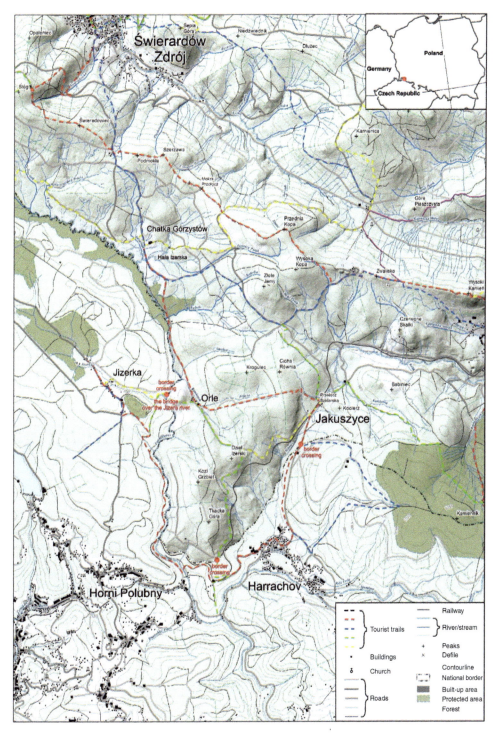

Fig. 12.4. The southern part of the Jizera Mountains. (From author's elaboration based on selected elements of topographic maps.)

Communist regime after 1945. In the sphere of tourism, one could speak about almost complete isolation of the Polish and Czech Sudetens after World War II (Staffa, 2005; Potocki, 2009).

The borderland nature of the Jizera Mountains had a major influence on the development of post-war tourism in this region. A large part of it was inaccessible to tourists for many years. Geopolitical changes, particularly the reduction in the role of the border as a barrier since the 1990s, led to the redevelopment of transborder tourism and influenced the dynamic processes of shaping the transborder region. Now Orle and a non-government organisation associated with it play a significant role in Polish–Czech cross-border cooperation at the local level. Good relationships with Polish and Czech local government authorities and their involvement in transborder collaboration also enhance transborder region creation. A genuine will for joint actions and awareness of the need to shape such a tourism region is tangible among local NGOs and self-governments. As many authors emphasise, personal relationships (such as the informal meetings of mayors from neighbouring communities) and positive attitudes towards counterparts on the other side of the border can be key elements in the effectiveness of cross-border cooperation (e.g. Fall, 2009).

Different events are organised by Polish and Czech actors during both the winter and summer seasons, such as skiing competitions (e.g. 'Izerski Tour' and 'Retro Tour'), photographic competitions, astronomical observations, music concerts, bike retro tours, art exhibitions and glass workshops. The majority of these activities draw on the multicultural traditions of this area and relate to the region's past. Most of these cultural, touristic and sports events are organised jointly by Polish and Czech actors, and among the participants one can find Polish, Czech and German tourists, as well as residents of the region (author's interviews with local leaders).

In the author's survey, 80% of respondents considered that the possibility of crossing the national border outside of border crossing points was a major convenience, made available since 2007. Almost all tourists visiting Orle were aware of being in direct proximity to the national border, and 73% perceived this as an attraction. For just 8% of tourists interviewed, the border was (still) a barrier.

The border constituted a barrier slightly more often for bicycle tourists than for those on foot.[9] Presumably, this is the result of cyclists having fewer possibilities than walkers to cross the border because of the physical limitations on bike trails in mountains. The border was perceived as a barrier most often by tourists who came from outside of the region, a view not shared by the majority of residents, suggesting that the more often residents of border regions have to deal with the border and the inhabitants of neighbouring countries, the less often do they exhibit negative stereotypes about nationalities or the feeling that the national border is a significant barrier.

Among tourists visiting the Jizera Mountains, the majority planned to visit the neighbouring country. None of the respondents indicated a feeling of any kind of impediment in crossing the Polish–Czech border; this applied equally to Czechs crossing to the Polish side and Poles crossing to the Czech side. The respondents of both groups expressed intentions to cross the border often, indicating that the Jizera Mountains function effectively as an area of transborder tourism.

The national border was taken into consideration in planning the route of trips by only 25% of tourists. This might suggest that the Polish–Czech Jizera Mountains are perceived as one, coherent touristic region and the fact that it has a national border running through it does not constitute a hindrance; it could also mean that the border is not regarded as an attraction in itself.

The tourist respondents did not express any negative associations with the border (Fig. 12.5), and for some it held positive associations (over 17%). A significant percentage of tourists associated the Polish–Czech border with freedom of travel. Male respondents in particular equally often cited towns and villages of the border area (Poles provided Czech ones, while Czechs provided Polish ones), which on the one hand reflected their knowledge of the area's geography and, on the other, was undoubtedly an expression of perceived tourist destinations in the Polish–Czech border area. Associations referring to gastronomy are characteristic here, more frequent among men than among women (for example, Polish men visiting their neighbouring country motivated by the longstanding Czech beer tradition).

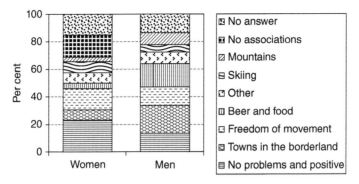

Fig. 12.5. Associations with the Polish–Czech border in its local dimension among tourists (by sex) in the Jizera Mountains in 2011. (From author's field survey.)

Associating the border with skiing and mountains was relatively rare (around 10%). This appeared to result from the fact that respondents crossing the border were looking for activities and experiences different from those on their own side: skiing and mountain activities are available on both sides of the border. Among older age groups, freedom of travel was often emphasised, perhaps reflecting the fact that such people remember from their own experiences the time when the border was closed. As such, they appreciate the current state of affairs more than those with no such experiences. On the other hand, the older respondents less often cited specific border towns and villages (over 20% of respondents below the age of 40 and only 5% among tourists aged over 50). This demonstration of younger tourists having a better knowledge of the area on the other side of the border probably results from the fact that they travel more often, taking for granted the freedoms of Schengenicity.

12.4.1 The microgeopolitics of border mobilities

In the context of geopolitical changes, the reconstruction of the bridge on the Jizera River in 2005 constituted an important event, in both practical and symbolical terms (Fig. 12.6). The bridge joining the village of Orle (Karlsthal at the time) with Jizerka (Fig. 12.7) and Horni Polubny (see Fig. 12.4) had functioned for many years and was used by both local inhabitants and tourists. After 1945, as a result of the delineation of the Polish–Czechoslovak border along the Jizera riverbed,

the bridge (and the entire borderline area) was inaccessible and lost its touristic importance; it was finally demolished around 1982. Attempts to reconstruct it were undertaken in the 1990s. Neighbouring Polish and Czech communities promoted this idea, together with local activists, in particular the Izera Society. In 2004, with both countries' accession to the EU, Poland and the Czech Republic agreed to rebuild the bridge as a border crossing point, and it was newly inaugurated the following year (Towarzystwo Izerskie, 2015).

It was emphasised by respondents on numerous occasions that the liberalisation of regulations connected with the border traffic significantly influenced the shaping of the movement of tourists. It enabled, among other things, the connection of tourist routes and the organisation of cross-border touristic and sports events. EU membership, the possibility of obtaining funding from the Polish and Czech cross-border cooperation programmes, and the involvement of local governments and NGOs in the field resulted in numerous local development projects, both material investments and non-financial ones. They made it possible, on the one hand, to bring local communities of the Polish–Czech border area closer together, and on the other, to develop the tourist industry in this area.

Among the motives for crossing the border, the most frequently cited by respondents was hiking/mountain biking (almost 40%) and wanting to see tourist attractions on the other side (approximately 25%) (Fig. 12.8). In terms of weight, the next motive for Poles was gastronomy/beer (more often among men than among

Fig. 12.6. Border bridge over the Jizera river. (Photograph courtesy of Sylwia Dołzbłasz.)

Fig. 12.7. Jizerka on the Czech side of the border. (Photograph courtesy of Sylwia Dołzbłasz.)

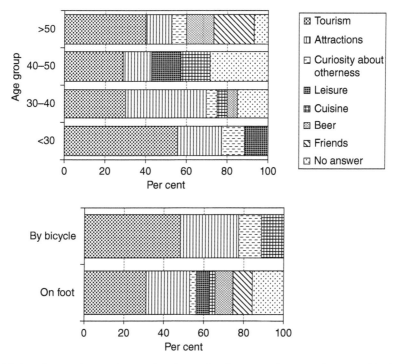

Fig. 12.8. Motives for crossing the border given by tourists (by age and means of transport) in the Jizera Mountains in 2011. (From author's survey.)

women); Czech beer and *knedle* (a speciality of Czech cuisine) enjoy great popularity among Poles. For Czechs, the next motive is curiosity about 'the other side', as well as meeting friends. 'Friendship' motives were given more often by women than by men, and by the oldest age group. Other motives (such as prices, trade) were very rarely mentioned. There was a clear relation between the motive of visiting attractions and the higher education of respondents, as well as the 30–40 age group. Among bicycle tourists, touristic motives were significantly dominant; other motives were mentioned much more rarely among them than among walking tourists. Motives of relaxation were important for respondents in the older age groups (over 40 years).

Although objectively there is a great need for improvement in the infrastructure of the transborder mountain areas, the tourists' assessment in relation to this local area was relatively favourable (Fig. 12.9). Over 25% expressed the view that nothing needed to be done to facilitate movement in the Polish–Czech border area, considering that removal of the border function had been sufficient. However, for tourists moving about

by foot or bicycle, the most important aspect for improvement was the need to connect Polish and Czech trails better and to create a coherent network of bilingually marked trails. The next most important desired action was the production of maps and guidebooks for the whole Polish–Czech border region in both languages. The proportion of respondents suggesting the need for improvements to cross-border transport, which is not at a particularly satisfactory level,[10] was lower than might have been expected (Fig. 12.9).

Despite the removal of the official border crossings in 2007, after 4 years around 70% of tourists in the Jizera Mountains still made use of these specific locations to cross the national border. Of the others, only 14% of tourists were crossing the border outside of tourist trails. This reflects the limits placed by the course of the Jizera River along the border, as well as the occurrence of cross-border protected areas, rendering random border crossings hindered or forbidden.

On an average weekend trip, according to the survey respondents, tourists travel to the area of the neighbouring country twice, but approximately 10% go three or four times. Respondents said that their visits to other ranges of the Sudeten Mountains were much less frequent. The frequency of crossing borders was clearly higher among tourists with a higher education and a younger age. In addition, tourists from regions far from the border showed greater cross-border mobility, which might reflect the fact that they generally visited the Polish–Czech mountains less frequently, and thus their curiosity about 'the other side' was greater than that of tourists who lived closer and those who came to the Jizera Mountains more frequently.

Opinions regarding the need for a clear demarcation of the Polish–Czech border in the area saw an equal split (45% of respondents in both cases) between those who believed that the border should be visible (with border posts, rocks, plinths and the like) and those who did not. This desire for visibility was more often expressed by men (56%) than by women (35%), and by bicycle tourists (52%). Older age groups tended to feel that there was no need to mark the border: only 28% from the 40–50 age group believed there was a need, in comparison with approximately 50% of younger groups (Fig. 12.10). It seemed that many years of living with the closed or difficult-to-cross border resulted in a greater acceptance of its current openness and lack of demarcation. Overall, a lower proportion of Czechs than Poles felt the need for demarcation.

It is characteristic that, while benefitting from the positive effects of the elimination of borders, a significant number of tourists nevertheless want to know when they are still in their own country and when they are in their neighbours' country. A similar situation has arisen elsewhere. For example, in the divided city of Tornio-Haparanda, on the Finland–Sweden border at the top of the Gulf of Bothnia, a common urban centre is being constructed, but the inhabitants have voted to mark the border, symbolically yet distinctly, within the urban area (http://www.haparandatornio.com/).

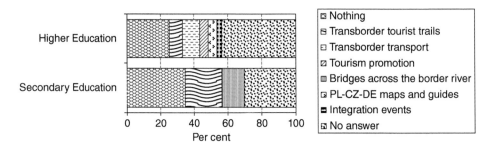

Fig. 12.9. Opinions regarding what should be done to facilitate movement in the Polish–Czech border area among tourists (by education) in the Jizera Mountains in 2011. (From author's survey.)

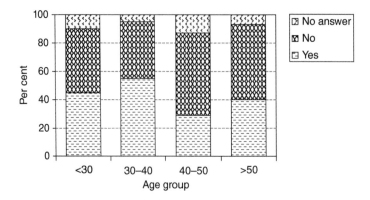

Fig. 12.10. Opinions regarding the need for clear marking of the Polish–Czech border in the area among tourists (by age) in the Jizera Mountains in 2011. (From author's survey.)

On the basis of the study carried out, we can state that the Jizera Mountains constitute an area of transborder tourism where the border has, to a considerable extent, lost its divisive character and is not perceived as a barrier. Tourists who are aware of being in a border region consider access to the 'other side' to be an additional value for fulfilling their touristic goals.

12.5 Conclusion

Within a century, the Polish–Czech border has been transformed from separating European empires to becoming a barrier between communist states and finally to evolving into an internal border of the EU, allowing unhindered passage within the Schengen Zone. It is a good example of a border that, without significant changes of its course, has had its character modified many times and, as a consequence, has exerted a significant impact on the development of adjacent border areas.

This chapter has shown how geopolitical change at a number of levels has exerted a local impact on the function of settlements in the Jizera Mountains Polish–Czech border area. Economic activity in this area evolved from a glassworks, forestry services offices, customs office premises and a borderland protection army station to become, eventually, a significant transborder tourism centre closely related to the traditions of the Jizera Mountains. Prior to post-war communism, these mountains had played an important role as a developing transborder tourist region, particularly before World War I. It is characteristic of such areas, which were once inaccessible because of their proximity to the national border, that through political change and a consequent functional change in the nature of the border, they have become tourist areas where the border itself has become part of the tourist attraction.

Geopolitical impress can be observed even in such peripheral areas as the Jizera Mountains. Current favourable geopolitical conditions have reduced the role of the state border as a barrier. In shaping the transborder region, a key issue seems to be the presence of an integrating factor, as well as joint, coherent developmental goals. Transborder tourism based on the region's attractive natural conditions can be the significant element enhancing that process.

In the Polish–Czech borderland, tourists now move about freely across and on both sides of the border, and take part in many shared touristic and cultural events. Strong cross-border connections, in the field of tourism, are now clearly visible. The border is no longer a barrier; its permeability possesses an intrinsic value and assists the process of transformation from a divided to a shared space.

Acknowledgements

I would like to thank the *Towarzystwo Izerskie* (Jizera Society), and in particular Stanisław Kornafel, for all their help in conducting the surveys presented in this chapter. I would also like to thank Monika Roszczewska for her extensive help in the cartographic work.

Endnotes

[1] During the writing of this chapter, European border cooperation strategy appeared to be in some disarray in the face of continued flows of refugees from the Middle East.

[2] Some permeability of the Polish–Czechoslovakia border did, however, exist for a few years in the 1960s and 1970s.

[3] The line of the border was the same as between Poland and Czechoslovakia during the period 1945–1992.

[4] The total number before joining the Schengen Zone was about 113, including 23 for small border traffic only and 42 on tourist trails.

[5] This reinforces Stefanick's (2009) observation that protected areas, which are numerous in mountainous border regions, can constitute an environmental barrier but at the same time can act as the basis for the development of transborder environmental conservation.

[6] The PHARE Programme aimed to assist applicant countries in preparation for EU accession. The PHARE Cross-Border Cooperation programme's objective was to support changes in the border regions of these countries by implementing cross-border projects.

[7] European Territorial Cooperation (ETC), better known as Interreg, is one of the three goals of the European Union cohesion policy. The overarching objective of ETC is to promote a harmonious economic, social and territorial development of the Union as a whole. Interreg is built around three strands of cooperation: cross-border (Interreg A), transnational (Interreg B) and interregional (Interreg C). Five programming periods have succeeded each other: Interreg I (1990–1993), II (1994–1999), III (2000–2006), IV (2007–2013) and V (2014–2020).

[8] This chapter comprises part of a wider study with the aim of analysing the integration process in the Polish–Czech borderland, which also features a spatial analysis carried out of the road and rail connections and tourist trails.

[9] As for the method of reaching the area under examination, walking tourism (51%) was a little more popular than bicycle tourism (43%).

[10] Although in 2010, after many years of effort, cross-border rail connections were reactivated on the old route that had operated before World War II.

References

Ackleson, J. (2005) Constructing security on the U.S.-Mexico border. *Political Geography* 24, 165–184.

Agnew, J. (2008) Borders on the mind: reframing border thinking. *Ethics and Global Politics* 1(4), 175–191.

Amilhat-Szary, A.-L. (2007) Are borders more easily crossed today? The paradox of contemporary trans-border mobility in the Andes. *Geopolitics* 12, 1–18.

Anderson, J. and O'Dowd, L. (1999) Borders, border regions and territoriality: contradictory meanings, changing significance. *Regional Studies* 33(7), 593–604.

Brunet-Jailly, E. (2005) Theorizing borders: an interdisciplinary perspective. *Geopolitics* 10, 633–649.

Brunet-Jailly, E. (2011) Special section: Borders, borderlands and theory: an introduction. *Geopolitics* 16, 1–6.

Church, A. and Reid, P. (1996) Power, international networks and competition: the example of cross-border cooperation. *Urban Studies* 33(8), 1297–1318.

Dębicki, M. (2010) *Stereotypy Czechów wobec Polaków na Pograniczu – Regionalne Zróżnicowanie oraz Determinanty stanu Rzeczy.* [Czech stereotypes of Poles in the borderland – regional diversity and factors determining the state of affairs.] Wydawnictwo Uniwersytetu Wrocławskiego, Wrocław, Poland (in Polish).

Dołzbłasz, S. (2015) Symmetry or asymmetry? Cross-border openness of service providers in Polish–Czech and Polish–German border towns. *Moravian Geographical Reports* 23(1), 2–12.

Dołzbłasz, S. and Raczyk, A. (2010) The role of the integrating factor in the shaping of transborder co-operation: the case of Poland. *Quaestiones Geographicae* 29(4), 65–73.

Dołzbłasz, S. and Raczyk, A. (2012) Transborder openness of companies in a divided city: Zgorzelec/Görlitz case study. *Tijdschrift voor Economische en Sociale Geografie* 103(3), 347–361.

Dołzbłasz, S. and Raczyk, A. (2015) Different borders – different co-operation? Transborder co-operation in Poland. *Geographical Review* 105(3), 360–376.

European Union (2010) *First Espon Synthesis Report, 2013, New Evidence on Smart, Sustainable and Inclusive Territories.* European Union, Brussels.

Fall, J.J. (2009) Beyond handshakes: rethinking cooperation in transboundary protected areas as a process of individual and collective identity construction. *Revue de Géographie Alpine* 97(2), 73–84.

Furmankiewicz, M. (2007) International co-operation of Polish municipalities: directions and effects. *Tijdschrift voor Economische en Sociale Geografie* 98(3), 349–359.

Jones, R. (2009) Categories, borders and boundaries. *Progress in Human Geography* 33(2), 174–189.

Knippschild, R. (2011) Cross-border spatial planning: understanding, designing and managing cooperation processes in the German–Polish–Czech borderland. *European Planning Studies* 19(4), 629–645.

Newman, D. and Paasi, A. (1998) Fences and neighbours in the postmodern world: boundary narratives in political geography. *Progress in Human Geography* 22(2), 186–207.

Paasi, A. (2011) A border theory: unattainable dream or a realistic aim for border scholars? In: Wastl-Walter, D. (ed.) *The Ashgate Companion to Border Studies.* Ashgate, Farnham, UK, pp. 11–32.

Paasi, A. (2012) Mobile and not-so-mobile borders. Abstract, 2012 Annual Meeting of Association of American Geographers, New York.

Palmeiro Pinheiro, J.L. (2009) Transborder cooperation and identities in Galicia and northern Portugal. *Geopolitics* 14, 79–107.

Perkmann, M. (1999) Building governance institutions across European borders. *Regional Studies* 33(7), 657–667.

Pokluda, F. (2005) Orlicko: a rural microregion on the Czech-Polish state border. *EUROPA XXI* 13, 173–184.

Potocki, J. (2009) *Funkcje Turystyki w Kształtowaniu Transgranicznego Regionu Górskiego Sudetów.* [*Functions of Tourism in Forming the Cross-Border Mountain Region of the Sudetes.*] Wydawnictwo WTN, Wrocław, Poland (in Polish).

Retaillé, D. and Walther, O. (2011) Spaces of uncertainty: a model of mobile space in the Sahel. *Singapore Journal of Tropical Geography* 32, 85–101.

Rippl, S., Bücker, N., Petrat, A. and Boehnke, K. (2010) Crossing the frontier: transnational social integration in the EU's border regions. *International Journal of Comparative Sociology* 51(1–2), 5–31.

Rudaz, G. (2009) Territorial redefinition and the governance of mountain regions. *Revue de Géographie Alpine* 97(2), 27–37.

Sohn, C. and Lara-Valencia, F. (2013) Borders and cities: perspectives from North America and Europe. *Journal of Borderlands Studies* 28(2), 181–190.

Staffa, M. (2005) Historia poznania Karkonoszy i rozwój osadnictwa. [History of the Giant Mountains' explorations and development of settlement.] In: Mierzejewski, M.P. (ed.) *Karkonosze. Przyroda Nieożywiona i Człowiek.* Wydawnictwo Uniwersytetu Wrocławskiego, Wrocław, Poland, pp. 23–50 (in Polish).

Stefanick, L. (2009) Transboundary conservation: security, civil society and cross-border collaboration. *Journal of Borderlands Studies* 24(2), 15–37.

Strüver, A. (2004) Everyone creates one's own borders: the Dutch–German borderland as representation. *Geopolitics* 9(3), 627–648.

Timothy, D.J. (2001) *Tourism and Political Boundaries.* Routledge, London.

Topaloglou, L., Kallioras, D., Manetos, P. and Petrakos, G. (2005) A border regions typology in the enlarged European Union. *Journal of Borderlands Studies* 20(2), 67–89.

Towarzystwo Izerskie (2015) *Towarzystwo Izerskie.* [Jizera Society.] Orle, Poland (in Polish). Available at: http://www.towarzystwoizerskie.org/ (accessed 3 August 2016).

Vaishar, A., Dvořák, P., Hubačíková, V. and Zapletalová, J. (2013) Contemporary development of peripheral parts of the Czech–Polish borderland: case study of the Javorník area. *Geographia Polonica* 86(3), 237–253.

van der Velde, M. and Spierings, B. (2010) Consumer mobility and the communication of difference: reflecting on cross-border shopping practices and experience in the Dutch–German borderland. *Journal of Borderlands Studies* 25, 191–205.

van Houtum, H. (1999) Internationalisation and mental borders. *Tijdschrift voor Economische en Sociale Geografie* 90, 329–335.

van Houtum, H. (2005) The geopolitics of borders and boundaries. *Geopolitics* 10(4), 672–679.

Walther, O. (2009) A mobile idea of space. Traders, patrons and the cross-border economy in Sahelian Africa. *Journal of Borderlands Studies* 24(1), 34–46.

Więckowski, M. (2010) Tourism development in the borderlands of Poland. *Geographia Polonica* 83(2), 67–81.

Więckowski, M. (2013) Eco-frontier in the mountainous borderlands of Central Europe. The case of Polish border parks. *Journal of Alpine Research* 101(2), DOI: 10.4000/rga.2107.

13 Finnish–Russian Border Mobility and Tourism: Localism Overruled by Geopolitics

Jussi Laine*

Karelian Institute, University of Eastern Finland, Joensuu, Finland

13.1 Introduction

High geopolitics can exert profound local cross-border impacts on mobilities such as tourism in sensitive borderland areas. Global travel and tourism not only are determined by an individual's choices and preferences but also are increasingly influenced by geopolitical events and their resulting economic conditions and uncertainty. This study draws on the experience from the border between Finland and the Russian Federation[1] (Fig. 13.1), where interaction and cross-border mobility have reflected political, ideological and sociocultural change. It is suggested that the border provides an illuminating laboratory in which the relationship between tourism and the symbolic, psychological and physical nature of international borders, and the geopolitical climate that maintains them, may be studied.

In the past two decades, Russia has become a key contributor to tourism growth in Europe. This growth has been especially visible in Finland, where the rapid increase in Russian tourists has seen them become the largest group of foreign tourists visiting the country. This chapter focuses on cross-border tourism in particular, and shows that tourist flows in both directions have been clearly defined by the development of the tourism industry and its related facilities, but even more importantly by the broader geopolitical

changes affecting the border and broader relations across it. Geopolitical stand-offs like the recent Ukraine crisis (see Chapters 5 and 6, this volume) have generated severe impediments to travel and tourism by thwarting the movement of people, as has been apparent in travel both to and from Russia (see also Chapters 14 and 15, this volume). In addition to their impact on tourist flows, external shocks caused by geopolitical events also influence related jobs and economies.

If the situation today is to be better understood, a brief examination of the historical context within which Finnish–Russian tourism has evolved is necessary. Finland's post-World War II relationship with the Soviet Union, and more recently with Russia, has been shaped by a common history, Cold War realities and the lessons learned from devastating armed conflicts, but also by pragmatism, interdependencies and the simple equations between supply and demand. Dictated by the 1948 Agreement of Friendship, Cooperation and Mutual Assistance, post-World War II Finnish foreign policy towards the Soviet Union was based on the principle of 'official friendship'. Although the border was heavily guarded by two armies, a sound and trusting relationship with the Soviet Union was sustained to avoid future conflicts with the ideologically alien superpower on Finland's doorstep. While such friendship was orchestrated at the state level, it was

*E-mail: jussi.laine@uef.fi

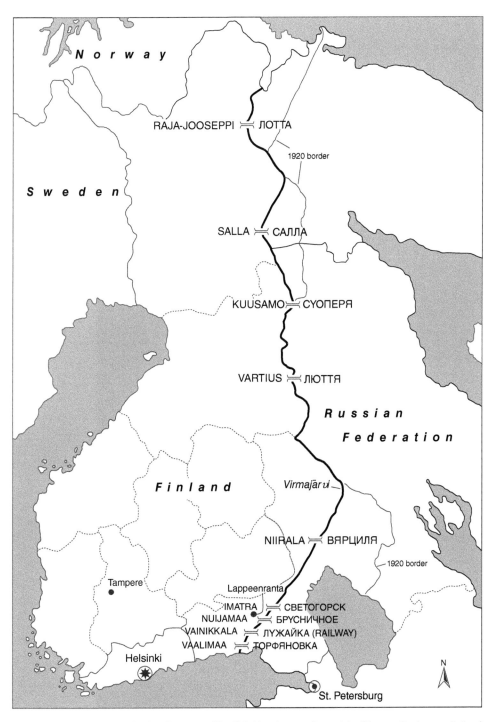

Fig. 13.1. The Finnish–Russian border area, with official border crossing points. (From author's compilation.)

effected through para-diplomatic links, within which tourism played an important role.

As the geopolitical situation improved in the wake of the Soviet Union's collapse, Finnish–Russian tourism began to develop rapidly, and its nature changed remarkably. A more open border, and the stark contrasts it revealed, projected great opportunities for tourism. This potential has not, however, been fully grasped. The border remains deeply etched in people's minds, in spite of the fact that the institutional border has subsided. In contrast to the past, tourism has become a regular commercial activity based on pull and push factors, yet Finnish tourism to Russia still seems especially susceptible to the impact of high geopolitics.

To appreciate the big picture and find explanations for both cross-border mobility and its lack, we must look beyond mere geographical proximity and distance decay. Tourism is far from being apolitical: it is affected by high politics, and it also provides the means to conduct politics. The crisis in Ukraine can be seen as a tipping point that brought an end to the post-Cold War status quo in Europe and signalled a resumption of the Great Power competition. In Finland, it fostered a general sense of unpredictability surrounding Russia and cast it, once again, as a threat, impelling Finland to adopt a completely new foreign and security political position, but also changing the image of Russia as a tourist destination, and more generally in the eyes of many. Russia's increasingly assertive domestic policies and its policies towards its various neighbours have altered the perceived role of the border from a bridge back to a barrier. This has also been apparent at European Union (EU) level, where the securitisation emphasis alongside the prevailing new 'realism' in EU foreign policy have increasingly changed the 'ring of friends' rhetoric to one of a 'secure neighbourhood'.

Both Finland and the EU more broadly seem to have lost their faith in sociocultural communication and in the transformation process in Russia. This has resulted in the privileging of formal relations at the expense of more locally oriented initiatives, with a profound impact on tourism between the countries.

13.2 Theoretical Premise

Many studies of tourism have traditionally focused on the tourist him or herself and have revolved around the pull and push factors influencing tourist behaviour and decision making (e.g. Crompton, 1979; Hirschman and Holbrook, 1986). Those who consider the future of the tourism industry tend to focus on economic and geographic perspectives, or on the impact of demographic and technological change and development on the industry (e.g. Yeoman, 2012). However, the impact of major (geo)political upheavals on tourism and related mobility has received relatively little attention. In attempting to fill this gap, this chapter illustrates how the development of tourism not only reflects the existing world but also modifies it through the formation of new and different kinds of behaviour and consumption. Tourism is not apolitical. The development of the field has diverse, complex and contradictory economic, political, social, cultural and environmental impacts (Dehoorne et al., 2014). There is also a close connection between political stability and economic security and increased levels of travel and tourism (Madankan and Ezzati, 2015).

Studies of cross-border tourism have generally approached borders as barriers that limit travel and the growth of tourism (Wachowiak, 2006). Tourism as an activity is fundamentally a combination of consumption and recreation. This is especially noticeable in border areas, as ease of access allows these more than other regions to be destinations for shopping (Timothy, 2005). Residents of border areas thus have more direct relations with people from adjacent countries (Honkanen et al., 2015). The impact of tourism is often particularly important for border areas, which are peripheral – in many senses of the word. Tourism must therefore also be considered in terms of regional development. Opportunities of cross-border tourism have increased as a result of national and regional policies promoting good neighbourly relations and contacts (Prokkola, 2008.)

The role of the border per se naturally plays a key role in cross-border tourism. Tourism – no less than other forms of economic and sociocultural activity – is affected by the existence of political borders (Timothy, 2001). Borders do not only demarcate jurisdictions and pose physical barriers to mobility, but they also continue to influence socio-spatial behaviours and attitudes, how we perceive different places and how we perceive and interpret our own actions (Hallikainen, 2003; Laine, 2013). Borders help us to create and perceive the differences indispensable for the construction of contexts and meanings (Hall, 1999), and to make sense of the otherwise complex society we inhabit (Paasi, 1999). The geopolitical knowledge an individual accumulates through perception, but also through ignorance, stereotypes and prejudices, shapes their feelings, opinions and ideas towards their own country, its neighbours and their place in the world (Laine, 2013). It is thus important to study the extent to which people are willing to adopt official geo-visions, as well as the extent to which actions and decisions at state level are affected by the perceptions and preferences at lower levels (Kolossov, 2003).

Borders, whether real or imagined, can pose barriers to international travel because of the specific functions and methods of demarcation, as well as the experiences and expectations of individual travellers concerning the border itself or what lies on the opposite side (Timothy, 2001; Laine, 2013). On the other hand, borders themselves can be a curiosity for tourists who seek to experience something out of the ordinary (Timothy and Butler, 1995). Borders may act as tourist attractions when they offer a unique spectacle in the cultural landscape, or when their influence on the borderlands is so strong that the economic, legal and cultural differences they create become significant attractions in themselves (Timothy, 2001).

Both these tendencies are apparent on the Finnish–Russian border, at times even in a somewhat contradictory manner. During the Soviet era, the border was perpetually exploited as a border that divided. Despite the disappearance of its role as an ideological dividing line between East and West following the collapse of the Soviet Union, for many Finns the border still has deep symbolic meanings. The border still functions as a cultural, political and economic dividing line that exists deep in the national memory (Paasi, 2011).

However, these differences are pushed aside when the border is crossed for shopping or recreational tourism purposes (Izotov and Laine, 2012). On the other hand, the border itself has become a tourist destination. The easternmost point of Finland and continental EU at Virmajärvi has now been made accessible to tourists, and is the only place where the border zone may be entered without a special permit. The tenser

geopolitical climate seems only to have increased the popularity of such visits, as they allow a 'mystical' Russia to be seen without actually having to cross the border.

Although the role of a tourist's individual decision making cannot be ignored, the aim here is to underline that tourism does not occur in a vacuum, but various factors form the context within which individual decisions are made. Tourism is a major international industry that functions within an evolving political and economic environment (Webster and Ivanov, 2015). It is thus essential to study how historical, cultural, economic, infrastructural and especially geopolitical circumstances affect cross-border tourist flows. It has been suggested that they form a complex and dynamic interplay, a 'bandwidth of unfamiliarity', between rational and emotional differences that have either positive or negative impacts on cross-border mobility (Spierings and van der Velde, 2008).

While certain differences maintained by a border – in price levels, tax and currency exchange rates, product selection or quality – tend to fuel cross-border mobility, differences in language, administrative structures, political arrangements, border-related policies, or general societal stability may reduce it. In many cases, borders are still quite tangible constructions. Crossing can still take time, effort and money.

Tourism is also a form of consumption (Timothy, 2005). Shopping is the main reason for travelling for millions of tourists each year, and it plays a key role in Finnish–Russian cross-border tourism. Shopping denotes more than the activity of buying products and commodities: it must also be understood as a leisure activity. Borders are often crossed in search of activities or services unavailable on the other side. These include the enjoyment of unique landscapes and visiting heritage sites, and various outdoor activities, but also gambling and sex tourism. Border regions are prime locations for such activities, because visitors from neighbouring regions do not have to go far into foreign territory to find their 'dens of iniquity' (Timothy, 2000). Motivations to shop on the other side depend not only on border crossing procedures, but also on contrast, awareness and willingness to travel (Bar-Kołelis and Wiskulski, 2012).

If there are many formalities associated with crossing a border, it may serve to discourage people, however much they may wish to travel. A destination's attraction may be diminished if it becomes too similar to the point of departure (Timothy, 1999). This is particularly the case if tourism is analysed in terms of consumer mobility; like shopping practices, cross-border tourism is often stimulated by differences between countries. Awareness is needed of what the other side of the border has to offer, whereas willingness to travel depends on both rational and emotional factors.

Destinations are chosen because of the perceived pleasures or benefits they provide. People are encouraged to visit a destination because of the images they have developed through various media (Urry, 1995). Geopolitical discourses or 'scripts' as presented by the media are powerful and, because they divide up the world, may lead to wars and conflicts over territory and resources (O'Tuathail, 2002). These discourses make their way into everyday practice through the media and, indeed, tourism (see Chapters 20 and 25, this volume). The media are effective in creating and enforcing images and imaginaries that harm the reputation of particular places as tourist destinations. Reported risks to security or health, for example, are especially effective in this respect.

13.3 Historical Positioning and Peculiarities

Finnish–Russian relations are a broader phenomenon than the usual bilateral relations between two states, and tourism between the two is no exception. The border has played a key role in the development of tourism, which itself has reflected broader geopolitical changes. The inception of Finnish–Russian cross-border tourism can be dated to the era when Finland was still, as an Autonomous Grand Duchy, part of the Russian Empire. When the Swedish Empire relinquished the territory of modern Finland to the Russian Empire in 1809, border formalities were simplified, and travel from Russia to Finland increased. During this period of autonomy, Finland maintained a national economy and a customs border with Russia. However, the border was otherwise open, and crossing it was very much a formality. Finland was in some ways a 'foreign country' to Russians, whose opportunities

to travel to other parts of Europe were limited for political reasons (Kostiainen *et al.*, 2004), and it became a popular holiday destination for the upper class of St Petersburg in particular.

The Russian Revolution of 1917 changed everything, not least where cross-border mobility and tourism were concerned. Finland took advantage of the turmoil to explore the possibility of independence. Following the Bolshevik seizure of power in Russia later that year, Finland seized the opportunity and declared its independence on 6 December 1917. The heavily guarded military border that was erected following the peace treaty between the independent Republic of Finland and Soviet Russia in 1920 halted all forms of interaction, and the border remained practically closed until the end of World War II. This is clearly illustrated in Fig. 13.2, which shows both the share of the Soviet Union/Russia in Finnish imports and exports, and the permeability of the border for tourism. Although cross-border tourism is not directly included in trade figures, its role as an economic activity is still significant.

In 1948, Finland and the Soviet Union signed the Agreement of Friendship, Cooperation and Mutual Assistance, which determined all forms of interaction between the two states and their respective citizens based on the principle of 'official friendship'. Friendship was not limited to intergovernmental relations, but was also effected through para-diplomatic links across the border. Various, more or less official, delegations consisting of politicians, but also of artists, teachers, athletes, various experts, trade union representatives and friendship groups, were sent by Finnish state agencies, particularly the Ministry of Education, and they received special treatment in the Soviet Union (Kostiainen, 1998). These trips, Kostiainen (1999) points out, have to be understood in the context of the Finnish–Soviet special relationship. Whereas the relationship between the two countries had been very tense before World War II, in the post-war world many saw a closer relationship and increased cross-border interaction as necessary. Tourism played an important role here, even if all cross-border trips remained highly regulated and had to be carefully prepared in advance.

After the war, tourism activities were actively developed in both countries, as they were seen as making a significant contribution to exports. Given the statist model of the Soviet economy,

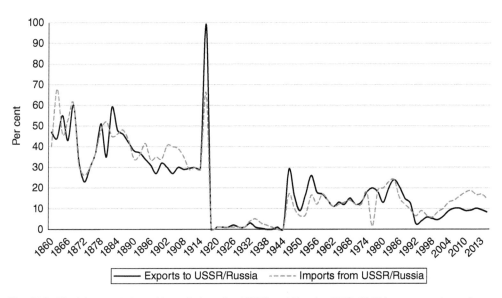

Fig. 13.2. Finnish exports to and imports from the USSR and Russia, 1858–2015 (as a percentage of total exports/imports). (From The Finnish Customs (http://uljas.tulli.fi/).)

tourism was highly politicised. Cultural exchange and tourism were, however, greatly influenced by ideological bias on the Finnish side. Most trips to the Soviet Union were organised by friendship societies and closely connected travel agents who viewed the Soviet Union very positively. The most important player was the Finland–Soviet Union Society (now the Finland–Russia Society), which had been established on 15 October 1944 – less than a month after the armistice ending the Continuation War (between Finland and the Soviet Union) had been signed. The Institute for Cultural Relations between Finland and the Soviet Union was established in 1947 for the purpose of coordinating and undertaking research related to the Soviet Union, and advancing Finno-Soviet scientific and educational cooperation in the spirit of good-neighbourly relations. Joint seminars were organised with Soviet academics, but such scientific tourism provided few academic results.

An important moment in the history of Finnish, and broader Western, tourism was witnessed on 1 July 1958, when the first road border crossing point to the Soviet Union was opened at Vaalimaa.[2] Prior to this, the border could only be crossed by rail. The 1973 energy crisis marked another turning point in tourism between Finland and the Soviet Union. As increased fuel prices

made flying significantly more expensive, many chose the Soviet Union as their holiday destination because of its geographical proximity. Cross-border tourism was further encouraged by the 1974 Finnish–Soviet treaty on travel affairs, which aimed to develop various forms of tourism between the two countries, as well as making obtaining a visa easier. Within 10 years, the number of tourists doubled in both directions. The number of Finnish tourists continued to grow: in 1956, only some 300 Finns had visited Leningrad (St Petersburg), but by the early 1980s the figure was about 100,000/year. The number of border crossings in general rose from approximately 2000/year to more than half a million. Official agreements concerning the number of tourists annually in both directions were concluded between the states, as were tourist itineraries. Whereas in 1970 Soviet tourists could travel in Finland via only two predefined routes, by 1980 this had grown to 13 (Abrasimov, 1984).

However, as the tourism sector in the Soviet Union remained underdeveloped, the number of inbound tourists had to be limited. Despite this, the tourism flow remained rather one-sided. But the number of Soviet tourists to Finland grew steadily during the 1970s and, of the capitalist countries, Finland was clearly the most popular destination for Soviet tourists. Yet, even by 1983, for example, while approximately 330,000 Finns visited the Soviet Union, only 30,000 Soviet tourists visited Finland. They did, in fact, form the third largest group of foreign visitors to Finland, but this was still less than 10% of the number of Finnish tourists to the USSR. Soviet tourist numbers remained low principally because of the restrictions ('exit visas') placed on travel abroad. To be allowed to leave the Soviet Union, one had to be trustworthy, which usually meant being a member of the Communist Party.

Finnish delegations to the Soviet Union included a number of what Kostiainen (1998) has called 'Soviet sympathisers', but the share of people crossing the border out of simple curiosity increased steadily throughout the 1970s and 1980s. Increased efforts to boost cross-border interaction reflected President Kekkonen's proclamation of an 'active' relationship with the Soviet Union, and encouraged reciprocal travel from the USSR to Finland. It has to be understood that all forms of cross-border interaction at the time, from trade to tourism, were organised as 'exchanges' based on bilateral, centralised reciprocal agreements (Kostiainen, 1998). Although tourism was presented as a means to build peace and friendship between Finland and the Soviet Union in official rhetoric, the reality was more calculated and controlled. From the Soviet perspective, foreign travel was considerably more complicated than domestic travel, because it involved the possibility that Soviet citizens would have to interact with people with a contrasting world view (Kostiainen et al., 2004). Alongside the fear of foreign influence, travel was hindered by the Cold War era attitudes on both sides of the border, as well as by various bureaucratic barriers, ranging from difficulties in obtaining visas, the lack of an exchangeable currency and artificially high travel costs. When abroad, Soviet citizens had to follow preapproved travel routes and stay overnight only in officially designated accommodation facilities.

Conscious efforts were also made to use tourism as a form of Cold War propaganda (Juvonen, 2013). The competition between the different economic systems was not limited to the development of space research and military equipment; it was also politically important to show that the Soviet citizen lived in good conditions. Foreign travel was not necessarily a matter of wealth for a Soviet citizen: the right to travel had to be earned by being loyal and trustworthy in the eyes of the Communist Party. It was considered of great importance that foreigners gained the best possible image of the Soviet Union – both when they visited the country and when they met Soviet citizens in their own countries. Soviet tourists were monitored closely to protect them from exposure to too many foreign influences. Those allowed to travel also had to be capable of acting as torchbearers for the Soviet Union's superior social system. The Soviet state-run travel agency, Intourist, aimed to exert a strong influence on the content of Soviet tourist trips abroad. Itineraries and travel programmes of tourist groups travelling to Finland had to be checked and preapproved by Intourist, whose agents ordered changes to any aspects with which they were dissatisfied. Intourist also planned trips to the Soviet Union from abroad, again with the aim of showcasing the superior Soviet system.

The freer conditions brought about by *glasnost* and *perestroika* in the late 1980s also had an impact on tourism, but mainly from an economic perspective. The application process Soviet citizens had to go through changed, but it did not get any easier. It was no longer required to apply for a travel permit from the CPSU (Communist Party of the Soviet Union) Central Committee: this could now be bought directly from Intourist, although the quality control of tourist groups was still done by the party administration (Juvonen, 2013). As a result, tourism actually decreased. In the midst of the reforms, travel agencies and other tourism-related companies also became self-sustaining and commercially oriented businesses. The tourism industry was developed, but on a small scale. Foreign tourists were allowed to visit only certain cities and regions, although their number grew in tandem with the increase in the general openness of the Soviet system.

13.4   Post-Soviet Trends

After the collapse of the Soviet Union, the border began gradually to open, as is shown by the numbers crossing the border (Fig. 13.3). Easier passage across the border encouraged Finns who had been resident in areas ceded to the Soviet Union after the war, along with their descendants, to satisfy their curiosity and visit places that

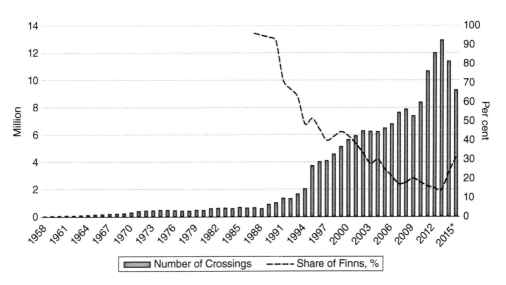

Fig. 13.3. Total number of border crossings and the share of Finns at the Finnish–Russian border, 1958–2015. (From The Finnish Border Guard (http://www.raja.fi/facts/the_border_guard_in_figures).) *Estimate

had been largely inaccessible to them hitherto. Elderly Finns visited their former home towns and territories, looking for traces of Finnishness, their own roots and what was left of the houses in which they had spent their childhood (Izotov and Laine, 2012). The boom in tourism this created was largely unexpected, and local tourist businesses struggled to adjust after years of total state control. 'Nostalgia tourism' stimulated cross-border cooperation and, despite the slow start, also supported the local economy on the Russian side. Many Finns also crossed the border for cheap alcohol, cigarettes and other consumer goods; some were lured across the border by the availability of prostitution. Finland also benefited from the increased transit tourism flow between East and West. The Finnish tourism infrastructure was utilised effectively and Finland functioned as an intermediate stopping point, especially for travel from Western Europe and the USA to Russia, and vice versa.

Crossing the border also became easier from the other direction. Finland was the closest destination for Russians, travel to which required little in the way of planning. Although Finns still made most of the border crossings at the beginning of the 1990s, the share of Russians crossing grew rapidly with the freer conditions of the post-Soviet era (Fig. 13.3). Much of this is explained by the huge increase in Russian visitors to Finland, rather than any marked decrease in Finns

travelling to Russia. It is apparent that the development of cross-border traffic volumes is linked with general economic development, which in turn is often linked with the geopolitical climate. When Finland joined the EU in 1995, many Russians now saw Finland as a convenient gateway to the rest of the Union. As Fig. 13.3 shows, the number of border crossings declined temporarily with the beginning of the financial crisis in 2008, but increased sharply as the Russian economy recovered and the Russian population became more affluent (see also Chapters 14 and 15, this volume). Records were broken in 2013, when the Finnish–Russian border was crossed close to 13 million times, with the great majority of crossings now being made by Russians. Since then, the tenser geopolitical climate caused by the Ukraine crisis and its ripple effects has resulted in the number of border crossings dipping considerably.

Most of the incoming border traffic from Russia is related to tourism or shopping tourism, both of which bring wealth and jobs to Finland. Not only do Russians form the largest share of incoming visitors to Finland, but the average Russian spends more on both products and services than other visitors during their stay in Finland. Shopping is also an important motive for Finns, even if what they buy is remarkably different. Whereas Russians come to Finland to spend their savings, Finns often cross the border to buy products that are significantly cheaper than they are in Finland (Kononenko and Laine, 2008).

As shopping plays such an important part in Finnish–Russian cross-border tourism, so does the exchange rate. Between 1990 and 1998, the number of Russian tourists with registered overnight stays in Finland increased steadily by 20–30%/year. The Russian financial crisis of August 1998 resulted in a marked devaluation of the rouble, and Russian tourism to Finland plummeted as travel, goods and services suddenly became considerably more expensive (Figs 13.4 and 13.5). As one might expect, Finnish tourism to Russia intensified, as the weak rouble strengthened Finns' relative purchasing power. The incoming Russian tourist flow rebounded in 2000, after which it grew quite steadily for several years. In early 2010, tourism was increasingly developed with a specific focus on Russian tourists by many Finnish cities.

The rapid growth in overnight stays by Russians since 2006 was largely supported by the financial upswing and an increasingly affluent middle class. The accommodation statistics do not correlate directly with the border crossing statistics, because geographical proximity means that many Russians make day trips to Finland. A significant percentage of incoming Russian tourists stay overnight with relatives or friends,

or in cottages/houses they own, which are not recorded in the accommodation statistics: in 2014, Russians made more than 3.8 million trips to Finland, yet only 615,116 registered in official accommodation establishments. The mismatch is also partly explained by transit tourism, as many Russians use Finland as a gateway to other European destinations; for example, by taking advantage of low-cost air carriers that operate from Finland.[3] The impact of the reduced tourist flow from Russia on the Finnish accommodation sector has been significant; for example, the number of nights spent by Russian tourists in March 2015 was down by almost 50% compared to March 2014; the December 2014 statistics were down by 52% from December 2013. The reduced tourist flow from Russia has hurt the border area most: South Karelia has seen a decline in the number of overnight stays of almost 60%.

While the duration of the trips made by Russians has shortened – overnight trips have become day trips to save on accommodation costs – in terms of the actual number of trips, Finland remains the number one destination for Russian tourists.[4] The figures can, however, be misleading, as statistics hide the fact that many of the crossings are made by the same people, often for the purpose of informal trade. Most

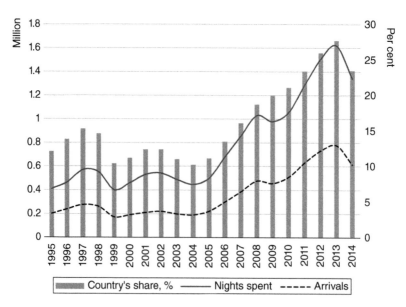

Fig. 13.4. Arrivals and nights spent in all official accommodation establishments in Finland by Russians, as well as the share of Russians of all incoming tourists. (From Official Statistics of Finland, 2015.)

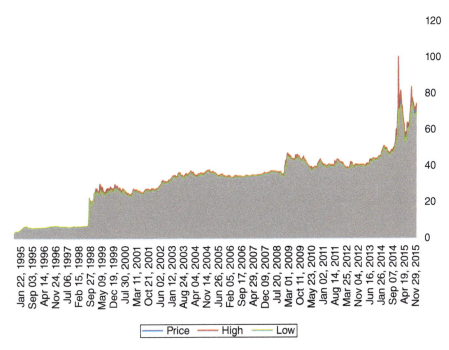

Fig. 13.5. Development of the foreign exchange rates between the Euro and the Russian rouble, 1995–2015. (From European Central Bank, 2015.)

trips are, in fact, for shopping purposes and not actual holiday visits: the most popular holiday destination for Russian tourists in the past has been Turkey. Many Russian day-trippers purchase fish and meat, the import of which Russia has banned as a countermeasure to EU sanctions. However, the amount spent by Russian tourists in Finland has shrunk, resulting in a reduction in revenue of hundreds of millions.[5]

Exchange rate fluctuations also explain much of the changes in cross-border traffic in the past 2 years. The deteriorating trade relationship resulting from anti-Russian sanctions and the related counter-embargo has seen the value of the rouble collapse, and inflationary pressure has eroded incomes and Russian travellers' spending power. This has significantly hindered Russians' ability to travel abroad, as many destinations have become less affordable. The European Travel Commission (ETC) confirms that travel from Russia has fallen as a direct consequence of geopolitical tensions (ETC, 2014a). In its more detailed report on the Crimea Crisis's impact on tourism, the ETC (2014b) explains that its escalation has resulted in an abrupt change in travel trends, and Finland has been among the most

affected because of its proximity to north-west Russia and the dominance of cross-border traffic. The current climate of economic uncertainty, fear of hostile attitudes towards Russians and slower visa processing, amplified by media coverage, have all contributed to diverting travel from Russia to non-European destinations (ETC, 2014b).

The number of Finnish tourists travelling to Russia has, in turn, increased because of the depreciation of the rouble against the euro, suggesting that economics trump pure politics as a determining factor for Finns. Given that most of the tourism facilities and many shops on the Finnish side of the border have been designed with Russian tourists in mind, the reduction of the incoming tourist flow has had severe consequences. Many companies have had to lay off employees, some have had to cease operations and in certain shops, established especially for Russian customers, net sales have fallen by up to 75% since the beginning of 2015 (TAK, 2015). The reduced tourist flow has also resulted in a number of flight routes being cancelled.[6] Interestingly, the tenser geopolitical climate resulted in travel from Finland to Russia being quite stable or even decreasing for several years, but it spiked at the end of 2014, when the rouble weakened significantly. In 2015 (January–October), Finns' share of border crossings increased to 31%, the highest figure in more than 10 years.

Outbound tourism from Russia has been further reduced by the general economic crisis that has prompted the Russian government to encourage its citizens to spend their vacations and money at home. The patriotic wave that has swept the country following the annexation of Crimea in March 2014 has led many Russians to spend their holidays on the Black Sea peninsula. As an indication of this, the Consulate General of Finland in Russia was expected to grant about half a million visas in 2015, compared with almost one million for the previous year – the first dip in the number of issued visas since the collapse of the Soviet Union. In general, times are tough for many Russians, and this is also reflected in tourism. For example, in St Petersburg, real wages have fallen by more than 10% and pensions by almost 7% as a result of inflation. Although fewer Russian tourists are crossing the border, Finland has maintained its position as an important destination for Russian tourists, who have abandoned their plans for more exotic holidays in long-haul destinations and instead visited Finland, which is easy and relatively cheap to get to.

Russians have been directly advised to travel domestically, and recent statistics suggest that many have followed this advice. In some cases, the advice has been reinforced by exaggerated statements published widely in the Russian media. A good example of this is the recent, widely publicised, claim by Anna Popova, the head of the Russian Federal Service for Surveillance on Consumer Rights Protection and Human Wellbeing (*Rospotrebnadzor*), that Russians should not travel out of the country because of an array of health risks. In her comments, carried by *Interfax* (6 December 2015), Ms Popova urged Russians to spend their holidays at home because of the risk of diphtheria in Finland. No case of the disease has been reported for years, but, according to Popova, the risk of infection has increased because Finland has recently accepted a large number of refugees, most notably from Syria and Iraq. In Russia, she claimed, the epidemiological situation is stable and there is no risk of catching life-threatening infections.

Ms Popova went on to advise Russians not to travel to the USA because of the risk of bubonic plague; and to avoid Poland because of increased cases of hepatitis, tuberculosis and HIV, while other favourite Russian holiday destinations, such as Egypt and Turkey, should be avoided because of security risks. The statement clearly echoed the stand taken by both President Putin and Foreign Minister Lavrov, who strongly recommended Russian citizens not to travel to Turkey following the November 2015 shooting down of a Russian fighter jet after it had allegedly entered Turkish airspace. Ms Popova added that the threat of terrorism in Turkey was no less than in Egypt, where a Russian passenger jet in flight was destroyed by a bomb the previous month. As both countries have been visited by millions of Russian tourists annually in the past, the decision to halt flights and practically ban travel is a major blow to the tourism industry and the sizeable revenue both Turkey and Egypt have gained from Russian visitors. It also reduces the options for Russian tourists in search of sunnier climes. (Geo)politics can thus exert profound impacts on various forms of mobility such as tourism.

13.5   Conclusions

Geopolitics and the economic trends and uncertainties generated by it are closely associated with tourism both in terms of its quality and quantity. The Finnish–Russian case exemplifies how politics have been involved in the long history of the development of tourism between the countries. Tourism between Finland and the Soviet Union differed in many ways from today's tourism between Finland and Russia. Crossing the Iron Curtain was a complex political, economic and social undertaking. During the Cold War especially, tourism – like any other activity – was inextricably linked with the constant political and ideological competition between the socialist and capitalist world views, and involved much mutual suspicion and fear. In the contemporary climate's security-oriented new realism, formal relations have again been privileged at the expense of local initiatives, and the bridging role of borderlands has reverted to the role of a filter, if not a barrier.

Geopolitical events and the actions of key players all have an impact on the perceived role of borders and on mobility across them. At the same time, the ways in which state borders are framed politically and exploited pragmatically, and above all the ways they are perceived in cultural-geographical terms, all influence tourist experiences and expectations. An individual tourist's motivation may depend on various factors. As the Finnish–Russian case demonstrates, tourism is more than an ephemeral phenomenon of social life, but functions within the wider processes of economic and political development.

Endnotes

[1] The Russian Federation is hereafter referred to as Russia.

[2] At first, the border crossing point was open in certain months only. By 1966, traffic had increased to the extent that it was decided to keep the crossing point open year-round, but only during daylight hours. It was not until 1993 that the border crossing point was opened to traffic 24 h/day.

[3] In recent years, Russians have formed a significant share of the passengers using the Tampere airport and a majority of the passengers of the Lappeenranta airport. Furthermore, thanks to the high-speed rail connection between St Petersburg and Helsinki, Helsinki airport has even been marketed as the second airport for congested St Petersburg.

[4] The neighbouring countries belonging to the Commonwealth of Independent States (CIS) are not included in the comparison.

[5] In 2013, Russian tourists spent more than €1.3 billion in Finland, while the figure was €966 million in 2014. The 2015 figures have yet to be published (Visit Finland, 2015).

[6] Ryanair stopped flying from Lappeenranta Airport in south-east Finland as the stream of Russians crossing the border for cheap flights to Europe diminished. Finnair announced that it would suspend flights between Helsinki and Nizhny Novgorod, Kazan and Samara.

References

Abrasimov, P.A. (1984) Matkailu – tärkeä osa maidemme välistä yhteistyötä. [Tourism – an important part of cooperation between our countries.] *Matkailusilmä [Tourist Eye]* 1, 4–5 (in Finnish).

Bar-Kołelis, D. and Wiskulski, T. (2012) Cross-border shopping at Polish borders. Tri-City and the Russian tourists. *Geojournal of Tourism and Geosites* 1(9), 43–51.

Crompton, J.L. (1979) Motivation for pleasure vacation. *Annals of Tourism Research* 6, 408–424.

Dehoorne, O., Depault, K., Ma, S. and Cao, H. (2014) International tourism: geopolitical dimensions of a global phenomenon. In: Cao, B., Ma, S. and Cao, H. (eds) *Ecosystem Assessment and Fuzzy Systems Management*. Springer, New York, pp. 389–396.

ETC (European Travel Commission) (2014a) *European Tourism 2014 – Trends & Prospects*. Quarterly Report Q3/2014. Brussels.

ETC (2014b) *European Tourism amid the Crimea Crisis*. A report produced by the European Travel Commission and Tourism, Economic (an Oxford Economic Company), Brussels.

European Central Bank (2015) Eurosystem. European Central Bank, Frankfurt, Germany. Available at: https://www.ecb.europa.eu/stats/exchange/ (accessed 4 August 2016).

Hall, S. (1999) *Identiteetti*. *[Identity.]* Vastapaino, Tampere, Finland (in Finnish).

Hallikainen, A. (2003) *Venäjän Kahdet Kasvot. Maakunnallisten ohjelma-asiakirjojen ja vertailuaineiston välittämä Venäjä-kuva. [The two faces of Russia: the images of Russia presented in the programme documents of regional councils and in the comparison material.]* Tampere University Press, Tampere, Finland (in Finnish).

Hirschman, E.C. and Holbrook, M.B. (1986) Expanding the ontology and methodology of research on the consumption experience. In: Brinberg, D. and Lutz, R.J. (eds) *Perspectives on Methodology in Consumer Research*. Springer, New York, pp. 213–251.

Honkanen, A., Pitkänen, K. and Hall, C.M. (2015) A local perspective on cross-border tourism. Russian second home ownership in Eastern Finland. *International Journal of Tourism Research*, DOI: 10.1002/jtr.2041.

Izotov, A. and Laine, J. (2012) Constructing (un)familiarity: role of tourism in identity and region building at the Finnish–Russian border. *European Planning Studies* 21(1), 93–111.

Juvonen, E. (2013) Rappiota rajan takaa: turismi Neuvostoliiton ja Suomen välillä 1956–1991. [Decline behind the border: tourism between the Soviet Union and Finland, 1956–1991.] University of Jyväskylä, Jyväskylä, Finland (in Finnish).

Kolossov, V. (2003) 'High' and 'low' geopolitics: images of the foreign countries in the eyes of Russian citizens. *Geopolitics* 8(1), 121–148.

Kononenko, V. and Laine, J. (2008) *Assessment of the Finnish–Russian Border: The Case of Vaalimaa Border Crossing Point*. The Finnish Institute of International Affairs Working Papers 57, Helsinki.

Kostiainen, A. (1998) Mass tourists, groups and delegates. Travel from Finland to the Soviet Union from 1950 to 1980. In: Peltonen, A. and Heikkinen-Rummukainen, M. (eds) *Trends in Russian Research on Tourism*. The Finnish University Network for Tourism Studies, Savonlinna, Finland, pp. 46–50.

Kostiainen, A. (1999) The vodka trail: Finnish travellers' motivation to visit the former Soviet Union. In: Toivonen, T. and Ahtola, J. (eds) *Travel Patterns: Past and Present*. The Finnish University Network for Tourism Studies, Savonlinna, Finland, pp. 33–48.

Kostiainen, A., Ahtola, J., Koivunen, L., Korpela, K. and Syrjämaa, T. (2004). *Matkailijan Ihmeellinen Maailma. Matkailun Historia Vanhalta Ajalta Omaan Aikaamme*. [Traveller's Wondrous World. History of tourism from the old times to our own time.] Suomalaisen kirjallisuuden seura, Helsinki (in Finnish).

Laine, J. (2013) *New Civic Neighborhood: Cross-border Cooperation and Civil Society Engagement at the Finnish–Russian Border*. University of Eastern Finland, Joensuu, Finland.

Madankan, A. and Ezzati, E. (2015) The impact of geopolitical factors on tourism in the Middle East. *Journal of Applied Environmental and Biological Sciences* 5(S4), 128–133.

Ó'Tuathail, G. (2002) Post-cold war geopolitics: contrasting superpowers in a world of global dangers. In: Johnson, R.J., Taylor, P. and Watts, M. (eds) *Geographies of Global Change*, 2nd edn. Blackwell, Oxford, UK, pp. 174–189.

Official Statistics of Finland (OSF) (2015) Accommodation statistics. Statistics Finland, Helsinki. Available at: http://www.stat.fi/til/matk/index_en.html (accessed 4 August 2016).

Paasi, A. (1999) The political geography of boundaries at the end of the millennium: challenges of the de-territorializing world. In: Eskelinen, H., Liikanen, I. and Oksa, J. (eds) *Curtains of Iron and Gold. Reconstructuring Borders and Scales of Interaction*. Ashgate, Aldershot, UK, pp. 9–24.

Paasi, A. (2011) A border theory: an unattainable dream or a realistic aim for border scholars? In: Wastl-Walter, D. (ed.) *The Ashgate Research Companion to Border Studies*. Ashgate, Aldershot, UK, pp. 11–31.

Prokkola, E.-K. (2008) Resources and barriers in tourism development: cross-border cooperation, regionalization and destination building at the Finnish–Swedish border. *Fennia* 186(1), 31–46.

Spierings, B. and van der Velde, M. (2008) Shopping, borders and unfamiliarity: consumer mobility in Europe. *Tijdschrift voor Economische en Sociale Geografie* 99(4), 497–505.

TAK (2015) News. TAK, Lappeenranta, Finland. Available at: http://en.tak.fi/news/ (accessed 4 August 2016).

Timothy, D.J. (1999) Cross-border partnership in tourism resource management: international parks along the US–Canada border. *Journal of Sustainable Tourism* 7(3–4), 182–205.

Timothy, D.J. (2000) Borderlands: an unlikely tourist destination? *IBRU Boundary and Security Bulletin* 8(1), 57–65.

Timothy, D.J. (2001) *Tourism and Political Boundaries*. Routledge, London.

Timothy, D.J. (2005) *Shopping Tourism, Retailing and Leisure*. Channel View, Clevedon, UK.

Timothy D.J. and Butler R.W. (1995) Cross-border shopping: a North American perspective. *Annals of Tourism Research* 22(1), 16–34.

Urry, J. (1995) *Consuming Places*. Routledge, London.

Visit Finland (2015) *Statistic Service Rudolf. Visit Finland Visitor Survey, Travel Accounts*. Visit Finland, Helsinki. Available at: http://visitfinland.stat.fi/PXWeb/pxweb/en/VisitFinland/?rxid=b09ee2ee-0031-40d5-85a9-7ef77797450b (accessed 4 August 2016).

Wachowiak, H. (2006) Introduction. In: Wachowiak, H. (ed.) *Tourism and Borders. Contemporary Issues, Policies and International Research*. Ashgate, Aldershot, UK, pp. 1–6.

Webster, C. and Ivanov, S. (2015) Geopolitical drivers of future tourist flows. *Journal of Tourism Futures* 1, 58–68.

Yeoman, I. (2012) *2050 – Tomorrow's Tourism*. Channel View, Bristol, UK.

14 Kaliningrad as a Tourism Enclave/Exclave?

Alexander Sebentsov* and Maria Zotova
Laboratory for Geopolitical Studies, Russian Academy of Sciences, Moscow, Russia

14.1 Introduction

Until 1991, the Kaliningrad *Oblast'* (region) was a contiguous part of the Soviet Union. It was closed to foreigners (largely because of the stationing here of the country's Baltic naval fleet) and therefore featured on no international tourism maps.

Incorporated into the Russian Soviet Federative Socialist Republic (RSFSR) as part of the westward expansion of the USSR into former eastern Prussia at the end of World War II, Kaliningrad's lack of contiguity with the rest of Russia was then less of a concern. Indeed, it was part of the western bastion of the Soviet Union protecting the 'hero city' of Leningrad.

With the (re-)establishment of the Baltic States' (Estonia, Latvia, Lithuania) independence (and that of Belarus) in 1991, the Kaliningrad region became physically detached from the rest of Russia; and since 2004, Kaliningrad has been surrounded on its landward sides by member states of the European Union (EU) (Poland and Lithuania) (Fig. 14.1).

Such 'exclavity' clearly poses problems for economic development, social integration and political relations. The role and nature of (international) tourism can be seen as a barometer for a number of these geopolitically related issues.

Debates over the economic development of the Kaliningrad region as an exclave have taken place since the collapse of the USSR in 1991. Numerous papers have analysed different aspects of the impact of 'exclavity' on the socio-economic development of the region (Vinokurov, 2007; Klemeshev, 2009; Fedorov *et al.*, 2013; Rozhkov-Yurevskiy, 2013; Sebentsov and Zotova, 2013; Gareev and Eliseeva, 2014; Gimbitsky *et al.*, 2014). Such debate has also taken place over the choice of a development model for the region: either to stay a Russian military outpost, as the 'unsinkable aircraft carrier' in Eastern Europe, or to become a laboratory for cooperation with the EU (Klemeshev and Mau, 2011).

According to most researchers, any resolution of Kaliningrad's exclave problems (including tourism) is only possible if the interests of Russia as a whole, as well as those of regional and international stakeholders, are given equal consideration. The Kaliningrad region must be regarded as the centre of an EU–Russian partnership. The development of tourism, which is considered a potential growth sector for the region, may also become one of the results of this partnership, including cross-border cooperation (Dragileva, 2006; Korneevets and Kropinova, 2010; Kropinova, 2010; Richard *et al.*, 2015). For this current research,[1] the authors undertook two study visits to the Kaliningrad region (in 2012

*Corresponding author. E-mail: asebentsov@gmail.com

Legend:

● Main cities

▢ Vehicle checkpoints:

1. Nida–Rybachiy; 2. Sovetsk–Panemune; 3. Pogranichiy–Ramonishkay;
4. Chernyshevskiy–Kibartay; 5. Gusev–Goldap; 6. Bagrationovsk–Bezledy
7. Mamonovo II–Gjehotki, 8. Mamonovo I–Gronovo

▨ Territory of local border traffic

KD = Kaliningrad Oblast'; TG = Taurage; MP = Marijampole

Fig. 14.1. The Kaliningrad neighbourhood. (From authors' compilation.)

and 2014) and interviewed representatives of the tourism business sector, scientists, the regional authority and non-profit organisations.

14.2 'Exclavity'

'Exclavity' influences all aspects of life in the Kaliningrad region, including the development of tourism. For a visit here, both Russian and foreign tourists have to cross the state border. Kaliningraders also need to cross borders if they want to walk through Red Square in Moscow or to visit the Hermitage in St Petersburg.

'Exclavisation' has been a gradual process, allowing the regional economy and local citizens

time to adapt to it. In the 1990s, the negative influence of the borders on the development of tourism was minimal, as the freedom of movement for citizens did not change much. Nation building in Lithuania and in Belarus had not yet become a serious obstacle for Russian citizens wishing to visit the region. For foreign citizens, the region was open for visiting, and for Poles a visa-free regime was even introduced.

In the 2000s, 'exclavisation' started to affect both the movements of Russian and foreign citizens. Thus, whereas previously residents of the Kaliningrad region could visit Poland and Lithuania without a visa and only with their national passports, from 2003 such travel required a special visa (at that point, however, people were issued multi-entry visas for free). Special transit documents for railway and other land transport were issued for transit to Russia and back.

From 2005, transit to Russia required a foreign passport (except for direct air and ferry travel). In 2007, a Schengen visa – with Lithuania and Poland now within that EU free movement area – was needed for Kaliningraders wishing to visit a neighbouring country. Taking into account that Russia followed the principle of reciprocity in its visa policy, Moscow's response regarding the citizens of Lithuania and Poland was swift. On the other hand, the Agreement between the Russian Federation and the Republic of Poland on the rules of local border traffic (LBT) facilitated, from July 2012, mutual visits for the citizens of the Kaliningrad region and neighbouring Polish voivodships (*wojewodztwa*, or provinces).

Travel conditions in the region changed significantly in comparison with the Soviet period, when the development of tourism in the Kaliningrad region was limited by the prohibition on visiting a range of territories due to a high level of militarisation.

Unsurprisingly, the number of tourists visiting Kaliningrad increased dramatically. In comparison with the end of the 1980s, when around 400,000 Russian tourists visited the region, in 2014 the total number of tourists reached 0.6 million. About a half of the 562,400 Russian tourists in that year came from Moscow (27.9%) and St Petersburg (22.7%). As in Soviet times, Russian tourists consider visiting the Kaliningrad region mostly for cure and health reasons (48%), in combination with cultural tourism (28%) (MTKR, 2015).

After Kaliningrad region's opening up to foreigners from 1991, German tourists were among the first to come to the region, seeking 'nostalgic tourism'. In the early 1990s, these were mainly Germans who had been born and brought up in the territory of former East Prussia. In the late 1990s/early 2000s, they were joined by their children and grandchildren and by curious Germans interested in their own history. This type of tourism is a common phenomenon for the Russian–Polish and several parts of the Russian–Lithuanian cross-border territories, where the citizens of Germany comprise a significant part of the tourist flow. In Poland, their proportion ranges from 17% to 25% in Sopot and Gdansk to 59% in Olsztyn (GUS, 2015). In Lithuania,

besides visiting the capital (74,400 people in 2014), German tourists often visit former Prussian territories (county of Klaipeda – 52,900, county of Alytus – 8000 people) (LS, 2015).

In general, cultural (46%) and business (35%) tourism prevails in the structure of foreign tourism in the Kaliningrad region (UFMS, 2014). According to official statistics, the highest number of foreign tourists was received in 2006, when 81,700 foreign citizens crossed the border with tourism visas. By contrast, the number was down to 37,600 in 2014.

Besides the Germans, whose proportion has remained around 60–70% during the post-Soviet period, the highest number of foreign tourists arrive from Lithuania and Poland (on average 3–5% for each country). The contribution of other countries is insignificant. In general, the main increase in the total number of tourists has been provided by Russian citizens, whose numbers have increased to comprise 68.3% in 1997 but 93.7% of total inbound tourists in 2014 (Fig. 14.2) (MTKR, 2015).

14.3 Local Border Traffic as the Basis for Developing Incoming Tourism

In 2014, 2.205 million citizens were recorded arriving in the territory of the Kaliningrad region through border checkpoints, an increase of 6.8% compared to 2013 (Fig. 14.3). A significant part of this increase is conditioned by the LBT agreement between Russia and Poland, which has substantially facilitated mutual visits for the inhabitants of Kaliningrad *Oblast'* and the neighbouring Polish territories using special LBT cards (UFMS, 2014, 2015).

Thus, 1.738 million foreign citizens arrived in the Kaliningrad region through checkpoints along the border with Poland in 2014, representing three-quarters of the total number of foreign arrivals. By comparison, 413,652 foreign citizens arrived from Lithuania and 53,841 through Khrabrovo airport (UFMS, 2015).

In 2013, 88% of Russian–Polish border crossings were made by Polish citizens (GUS, 2015), about 50% of these having used LBT cards.[2] Around 90% of the Poles who visited the Kaliningrad region in 2013 lived within 100 km

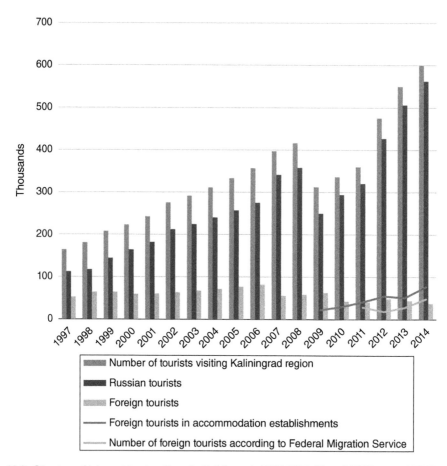

Fig. 14.2. Structure of inbound tourism flows in Kaliningrad, 1997–2014. (From MTKR, 2014; UFMS, 2014, 2015.)

of the state border, mostly in the neighbouring Warmian–Mazurian and Pomeranian voivodships. The main purposes of visit declared by the Polish citizens can be classified as: 92.1% crossed the border for shopping; 5.5% for 'tourism'; 1.2% for 'private purposes'; and 0.6% for business affairs. Analysis of the migration flows in the Federal Migration Service of the Kaliningrad region reports highlights the nature of the region as a border territory, with multiple border crossings undertaken by both Polish and Lithuanian citizens. This is predominantly on a short-term basis, as day trips form 97% of the total volume of mobility flows.

On the one hand, formal criteria would not allow defining this category of foreigners as tourists, as they do not stay overnight. On the other hand, most of them can be classified as 'visitors'[3] making a tourism trip, even a short one (Alexandrova and Stupina, 2013: 50–57). On average,

such a visitor spent 260 zloty/trip in 2013 (around €60), 88% of which was on the purchase of fuel, 6% on alcoholic beverages, 2.2% on tobacco and around 2% on tea, sweets and other food items.

Almost 90% of the Polish visitors going shopping do not travel more than 30 km from the border. This means that they do not reach Kaliningrad city itself, limiting themselves to visiting their nearest petrol station. In 2013, 58% of Poles who crossed the border visited the Kaliningrad region several times a month, and 38% did so several times a week. According to the data of the Federal Customs Service, a Polish visitor on average spends between 40 and 90 min in the Kaliningrad region. This is just the time needed for replenishing fuel, buying food and getting back to Poland.

Thus, not only the ordinary citizens of the neighbouring voivodships of Poland but also even those who regularly visit the Kaliningrad

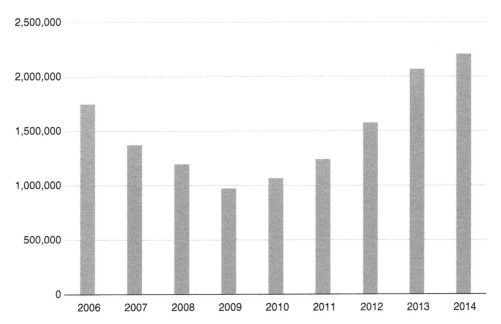

Fig. 14.3. The number of people arriving in the Kaliningrad region through border checkpoints, 2006–2014. (From MTKR, 2014; UFMS, 2015.)

region are not sufficiently interested in it as a destination for excursions or vacation. According to T. Omansky, head of the Polish Cultural Centre in Kaliningrad, the principal reason for this limited interest is the lack of information about interesting and attractive events, together with the holding of negative stereotypes. For example, a survey of 675 students of the Baltic Federal University (Kaliningrad) and the universities of Gdansk (Poland) and Klaipeda (Lithuania) undertaken by the authors showed that, despite the introduction of the LBT regime, 88% of Lithuanian and 68% of Polish students had never been to Russia, while the vast majority of their Russian coevals had visited neighbouring countries at least once. Some 28% of Polish students associated Kaliningrad with such negative stereotypical factors as 'poverty', 'low living standard', 'grey economy', 'smuggling', 'war', 'vodka', 'alcoholism', 'AIDS', 'Stalin', 'cold', 'absence of freedom', 'USSR', 'mafia', 'labour camps'. Only 5% of the respondents offered positive associations, while 68% gave neutral ones.

Thus, in order to help attract tourists from the neighbouring Polish voivodships, it is necessary to set up an efficient information system about upcoming events (concerts, festivals, retail sales)

taking place in the region. The Polish experience in attracting tourists from Kaliningrad could provide useful knowledge for regional government and local business. Nowadays, every citizen of Kaliningrad may find information about actual commercial offers for shopping and vacation in the neighbouring voivodships of Poland arranged in one brochure. Such a brochure often has an insert card that offers discounts in all the restaurants, shops and hotels that publish advertisements in this magazine. These brochures are often distributed by post, in malls, filling stations and tourist information centres, as well as at checkpoints. They could be used to promote regional tourism products within the framework of a tourism brand theme (e.g. 'Kaliningrad – the Amber Land').

A special certification scheme for shops, restaurants, hotels and information centres to indicate their 'visitor friendliness' (for example, speaking Polish) could also become a part of the information system. Such an approach has proven itself in Poland's Pomeranian and Warmian–Mazurian voivodships, where places in possession of a Russian menu and Russian-speaking staff have a sticker 'Russian friendly, *Zdravstvuyte!*' ('Hello!') on their doors.

14.4 Tourism as a Priority for Regional Development and Cross-border Cooperation

During the period 1991–1999, tourism was being proposed as a priority for regional development and international cooperation (Kropinova, 2009, 2010). Cross-border cooperation in tourism at this time was extremely limited and realised mostly within the framework of the Russian–Polish (1992) and the Russian–Lithuanian (1999) councils for cross-border cooperation. There were a number of important questions to discuss, such as establishing new checkpoints, delimitation and demarcation of the border (in the case of Lithuania) and environmental protection.

In the late 1990s/early 2000s, with the participation of the Kaliningrad region, five Euroregions were formed. They provided the framework for the development and discussion of numerous projects, including those in the field of tourism. For some of the Euroregions ('Lyna-Lava' and 'Sesupe'), tourism became the sole sphere of activity, with no more than modest results (some local initiatives such as annual rafting on the border river) due to lack of funds.

From the beginning of the 2000s, when regional strategies were developed, tourism acquired the role of a priority sector within the regional economy. The influence of tourism also characterised the programmes of cross-border cooperation, which became the main institutional instrument of cooperation between the Kaliningrad region and border regions of the neighbouring countries (see Fig. 14.4). The work on Cross-border Cooperation (CBC) Programmes, regional strategies and regional programmes for tourism development was launched at the same time, and highlighted simultaneous stages of cooperation in the tourism field during the first decade of this century.

14.4.1 The first stage, 2003–2006

This period was connected with the preparation of the first CBC Programme for Lithuania, Poland and Russia (2004–2006) and the elaboration of new regional strategic documents (AKO, 2003, 2005) directly linked with the development of tourism.

The CBC Programme for Lithuania, Poland and Russia was launched just after the enlargement of the EU, and was realised within INTERREG IIIA/TACIS (Technical Assistance to the Commonwealth of Independent States and Georgia). One of the sections of the programme was devoted to tourism (measure 1.4, 14 projects), with the purpose of the

> development of cross-border tourism and recreation industry, modernization of infrastructure, preservation of cultural objects with cross-border importance.
>
> (European Commission, 2006: 82)

According to our analysis of the programme, 42 out of 162 realised projects were directly connected with tourism development.

Despite the fact that EU enlargement led to a strengthening of the barrier functions of the Kaliningrad regional border with neighbouring EU member countries, both the CBC Programme and the regional strategies were permeated with the idea of creating a common tourism and recreational space. Thus, many projects of the programme appealed to the common historical past of the cross-border territories (e.g. 'On the trail of the castles in the Baltic Sea region – revitalisation and promotion of the objects') and to the common cultural space (e.g. 'Development of the common cultural space in the Euroregion of Neman', 'Conservation of cultural heritage of Eastern Prussia and strengthening of the regional identity'). Other CBC Programmes emphasised the possibilities of the common use of cross-border ecosystems – Vistula and Curonian lagoons, numerous rivers and lakes (e.g. 'Opening the water tourism route in the Curonian Lagoon: Klaipeda–Kaliningrad') (European Commission, 2006).

The Kaliningrad regional development programme for tourism sought that the 'formation of a common tourism and recreational space' should take place within the framework of CBC. It emphasised the great potential of a common Prussian heritage to attract a large number of tourists. However, this demanded significant funds for the restoration of appropriate monuments. Thus, it could not be realised within the framework of the CBC Programmes because of the limited financial resources available through TACIS, and a lack of experience. These factors limited the participation of the Kaliningrad

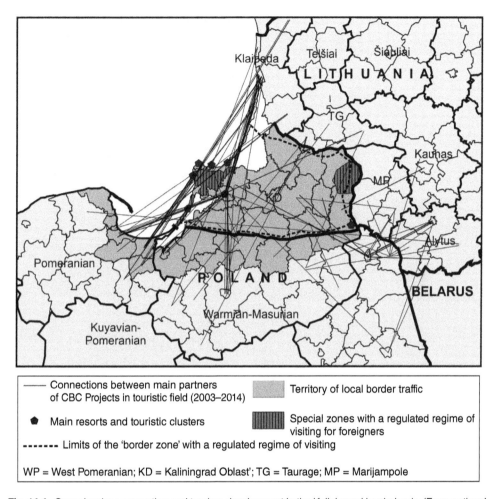

Fig. 14.4. Cross-border cooperation and tourism development in the Kaliningrad borderlands. (From authors' compilation.)

region in the programme: there was too high a threshold for national co-financing (10%). Thus, the main beneficiaries of the projects were mostly the Polish and Lithuanian partners.

Far more attention was paid in the Kaliningrad tourism development programme to the idea of promoting the region as 'The Amber Land'. In this draft concept, the traditions of extraction, refinement and historical ways of amber transportation were seen as 'the specific element of the historical and cultural heritage of the region'. In the framework of the programme, a range of projects was to be launched, such as the creation of a trade-artisan Amber Street in Kaliningrad city, together with international routes (Large, Middle and Small Amber Rings) through parts

of the so-called Great Amber Way. These routes, besides the Kaliningrad region, would need to include mostly border territories of the neighbouring states. Such plans remained on paper only.

14.4.2 The second stage, 2007–2013

This period was characterised by a gradual change in priorities in the development of tourism. The new regional strategy and programme for the development of the tourist industry adopted in 2007 did not elaborate a specific Kaliningrad brand (AKO, 2007). There was no mention of 'The Amber Land' in the documents. By contrast, 'flagship projects' such as a special economic zone for tourism development ('Curonian Spit') and a gambling zone ('Amber') were considered as the main attractions for tourists. The creation of a common tourism and recreational space was now seen only as a longer-term aim, possibly the result of the border complications arising from EU enlargement and extension of the Schengen area.

In 2007, the Kaliningrad region participated in the development of a new CBC Programme 'Lithuania–Poland–Russia' (2007–2013) that took previous experiences into account. Thus, instead of a complicated financing arrangement from different funds and European programmes (INTERREG, TACIS, PHARE (Poland and Hungary: Assistance for Restructuring their Economies)), a common financial system was created with equal rules and procedures – the European Neighbourhood and Partnership Instrument (ENPI). The co-finance threshold for applicants was lowered, and there were more possibilities for adapting the priorities proposed by the European Commission to comply better with the actual requirements of the programme territories. With the Russian Federation making its financial contribution to the programme, the participation of the Kaliningrad region became more equal. Tourism became one of the key priorities of cooperation: 16 out of 60 projects.

A special emphasis in the programme was placed on the joint creation, preparation and development of the technical and economic basis for cross-border tourism products, joint activity on their promotion, classification and certification, and for the training of guides. Such an approach was consonant with the aims of the existing development strategy (European Commission, 2008). An important step towards the creation of a joint tourism product was the development of a chain of tourist information centres in the borderland for exchanging news, information, materials and commercial offers for tourists, including, for example, in Sovetsk and Kaliningrad city.

These projects generally continued ideas developed in the preceding project period, and almost all were realised in the field of cultural and historical tourism. With the development of joint tourism routes, the restoration or creation of en route attractions took place. For example, the Russian–Lithuanian project 'From the Tilsit peace treaty of 1807 towards the Taurage convention of 1812'[4] was launched to preserve, restore and develop for tourism, common historical cultural heritage such as the Queen Louise bridge (on the border between the countries), the monument of Queen Louise in Sovetsk and tourist infrastructure in the centres of Sovetsk and Tourage.

Most of the cross-border projects were a kind of mirror in that the partners used each other's experience to increase their own tourism potential and to modernise tourism infrastructure. Such projects saw (Kaliningrad partner named first) the reconstruction of parks in Svetlyi and Malbork (Poland), Kaliningrad city and Jurbakas (Lithuania), Chernyakhovsk and Suwałki (Poland), the creation of adventure parks in Ozersk and Elk (Poland), the foundation of an archaeological museum in Elbląg (Poland) and the reconstruction of the Friedland Gate museum, within one of Kaliningrad's original 13 city gates.

14.4.3 The third stage, from 2014

Despite the unfavourable external conditions, the Kaliningrad region and the neighbouring areas of Lithuania and Poland actively participated in the development of new CBC Programmes for 2014–2020. It was decided to develop cooperation bilaterally – Russia–Poland and Russia–Lithuania – during this period. As in previous years, the participants of the programmes could choose and adapt to their mutual interests the priorities proposed by the European Commission. To date, the draft documents available demonstrate that tourism is still a priority in the field of cross-border cooperation. In the Polish–Russian Programme, the main emphasis is to be made on the development of cross-border tourism, the creation of a network for cooperation between travel agencies and the joint development and promotion of existing tourism centres (Kozak et al., 2013). In the Lithuanian–Russian Programme, efforts are to be concentrated on the joint promotion of local culture and the conservation of common historical and natural heritage (*Lithuania – Russia Cross-Border Cooperation Programme*, 2014). Thus, the idea of the cross-border tourism and recreation space is accommodated in these programmes.

In the strategic documents of the Kaliningrad region concerning the development of tourism (AKO, 2012), on the contrary, there is no mention of creating a common tourism product with neighbouring Poland and Lithuania. The obvious brand 'Königsberg – the capital of East Prussia' dropped out of sight from the State Programme of Kaliningrad *Oblast'* 'Tourism' (AKO, 2013), despite the attention paid to the restoration of the cultural heritage objects within this programme.

In the strategy of development of the Kaliningrad region, it is stated that the main factor for restraining the growth of competitiveness of the region on the Russian and international level is the absence of a 'landmark' attraction. This type of project is considered as a likely major source for generating tourism flows and creating the potential for the development of a full-scale tourism cluster. Such 'landmark' projects are represented by the Kaliningrad Aquarium Complex being constructed in conjunction with the Museum of the World Ocean (ships and maritime artefacts located along the Pregolya River), theme parks and gambling zones.

These 'landmark' projects are, in their turn, closely connected with the Kaliningrad region tourism brands to be promoted. Thus, the concept of 'Russia in Europe' is aimed to promote the Kaliningrad tourism product in Russia, while the concept of 'European Russia' with the strapline of a 'theme park of international importance' is directed toward foreign tourists. The strategy again has the concept 'The Amber Land', which implies the aim to realise three landmark projects – 'Amber Heart of Russia' (Kaliningrad), 'Amber Ring of Russia' (tourism clusters in the inner areas of the region) and 'From Spit to Spit' (bicycle route with camping sites along all the Baltic coast). The latter in many aspects develops ideas of previous CBC programmes.

One of the few 'landmark' projects that draws on Prussian heritage and creates a cross-border tourism and recreational space is the project 'The Old Town', which looks to the restoration of historical buildings in the centre of Kaliningrad city.

Thus, despite the fact that tourism is a priority for both regional development and cross-border cooperation, the CBC programmes naturally promote the common theme of the tourism potential of the regions – the cultural heritage of Eastern Prussia. For Kaliningrad region's concept of tourism development, on the contrary, the positioning of the tourism product acts to differentiate it from neighbouring territories. On the one hand, this approach seems strange, as the brand 'Eastern Prussia' may be considered as already formed. On the other hand, the absence of this brand in the official strategy is possibly connected with the permanent phobias of the federal centre towards probable separatist tendencies in the 'western outpost' of the country. Some local experts who actively participate in cross-border cooperation share these fears. Nowadays, Kaliningrad society is comprised of many newcomers and their descendants, and is relatively isolated from the rest of the Russian territory because of its 'exclavity'. From their very childhood, the people living here are being brought up in an 'other' cultural landscape, surrounded by cultural monuments that are barely connected with the history of their country.

> In the framework of the cross-border cooperation programmes and the other international projects, the European Union has overwhelmed the Kaliningrad region with its monuments. A Kaliningrad pupil, who is given Lermontov or Pushkin poems to learn at class, anyhow is taken on tour to the tomb of Kant. And they erected new monuments to Chopin, Kant, Danilatis, Queen Louise and other personalities of the European culture. They create the surrounding where there is a lack of Russian culture. This landscape changes rapidly, the German toponymy is restored... Without their own roots the youth begin to accept the German past as their own...
>
> (Interviewee, local expert, former coordinator of foreign projects)

Kaliningrad's relative isolation and being surrounded by other countries may lead, in time, to a transfer of identity for the local inhabitants. If this possibility is taken into consideration, the branding concept of 'Russia in Europe' sounds far safer than the concepts of 'Russian West' or 'European Russia', which could emphasise the specificity and difference of the region compared to the rest of Russia.

14.5 Cross-border Cooperation in the Field of Tourism: The Main Obstacles and Opportunities

The basic natural advantages providing the competitiveness of the Kaliningrad region as a tourism destination are its variety of favourable landscapes, seaside location, resort centres and a large number of cultural and historical heritage objects. These provide the potential for almost all types of tourism, including recreational (beach), cultural, business, health care and ecological. Significant possibilities for the development of cruise (sea and river) and rural tourism are also notable.

In both CBC and state programmes for tourism development, a number of barriers impede the realisation of this potential. These include transport accessibility, visa issues, a language barrier, poor level of small enterprise development and administrative constraints. Most of these obstacles, although features of the Russian Federation, acquire peculiarities in the Kaliningrad region because of its 'exclavity'. However, cross-border cooperation might become a tool that would allow at least some of them to be overcome.

The nature of state borders remains one of the main barriers to cooperation. When questioned, 80% of direct participants in the CBC Programmes INTERREG IIIA/TACIS 2004–2006 and ENPI 2007–2014 stated that the border regime was a substantial factor limiting the opportunities for a joint solution of problems in economic, sociocultural and institutional spheres (Kozak *et al.*, 2013). Border barriers also constitute the main obstacle for the formation of a common tourism and recreation space, which is the main priority of CBC programmes in the field of tourism.

In order to provide additional opportunities for tourists wishing to visit the Kaliningrad region, the Office of the Russian Ministry of Foreign Affairs (MFA) in Kaliningrad, as an experiment starting from 1 February 2002, began to issue short-term visas for a 72-h visit to the region. The citizens of Schengen countries, together with those of Great Britain and Japan, have been able to obtain a visa in one of the three consular offices situated by the Polish border, in Mamonovo (checkpoint Mamonovo 1 – Gronovo) and Bagrationovsk, and also in Khrabrovo (international airport). Such a visa can only be obtained if buying a tourism product from one of six certified travel agencies. In reality, the travel agencies sell travel insurance cover, which costs US$65 together with the visa. The travel agency accepts a tourist's documents, transfers them to the regional Kaliningrad office of the MFA and the latter pastes the Russian visa into a tourist's passport at the point of crossing the border. According to the MFA Office's data, the citizens of Germany, France, Great Britain, the Scandinavian countries and Poland have used this service most.

Interviews with staff of the MFA Office in Kaliningrad have suggested that only 500–1500 foreign tourists have actually used this facility annually. Because of this low demand, coupled with the negative atmosphere created by new rules concerning the issuing of a Schengen visa for Russians, this 'experiment' will be curtailed from the end of 2016.

According to representatives of the certified travel agencies interviewed, one of the reasons for low take-up of the 'border visa' service was the short period of its validity, and the fact that a visa could be issued on working days only, strictly from 09:00 h until 18:00 h. The travel agencies highlighted that in the case of cancellation or delay of a flight a tourist risks being delayed in the transit zone of the airport for a long time. The tourism information centre and the department for international and interregional tourism activity of the Ministry for Tourism of the Kaliningrad region agree that it is necessary to expand the practice of issuing border visas in order to increase the popularity of the service. According to several surveys undertaken for the Ministry for Tourism, foreign citizens prefer to stay in the Kaliningrad region for up to 10 days (MTKR, 2014, 2015).

In our opinion, efficient visa facilities with a 'soft' visa regime for foreign tourists are vitally necessary. The projected image of the Kaliningrad region as 'Russia in Europe' is not very interesting because of the lack of objects capable of attracting tourists. The Prussian heritage is much more attractive for foreign tourists, and it would be more effective to promote this in cooperation with Lithuania and Poland within the framework of the common brand 'Former Eastern Prussia'. Visa formalities are currently the main obstacle in the way of promoting such a product.

On average, citizens of the EU are able to visit 160–170 countries without a visa, or with a visa issued at the border. Thus, for instance, the citizens of Germany may freely visit 173 countries, Latvians 160, Lithuanians 159 and Poles 158 (Henley & Partners, 2015). EU citizens are, therefore, not accustomed to obtaining visas in order to visit other countries. In the case of the Kaliningrad region, some special conditions (compared to the rest of Russia) for foreign visitors should apply.

In this case, 'exclavity' may be of positive effect, as tourists could arrive with a special visa that excluded any opportunity to enter the main Russian territories without a border control.[5] Other opportunities for free entry to the Kaliningrad region already exist. Since 2009, open entry (for no more than 72 h) to the region has been available for foreigners in tourist groups arriving by cruise vessels. However, there are infrastructural limitations on the development of cruise tourism: notably the lack of specialised harbours (although preparation for the construction of a special terminal in Pionerskiy is in progress). Thus, according to the Kaliningrad River and Sea Fleet Agency, from 2011 until 2013 the seaport of Kaliningrad took only 15 cruise ships. By contrast, in 2012 the neighbouring port of Klaipeda (Lithuania) took 44 cruise ships, and that of Gdynia (Poland) 70 (Vylejagina and Strigin, 2013).

The regime of the border zone from the Russian side together with the small number of border checkpoints also impose substantial limitations to the development of cross-border tourism. The amendments to the law on the state border adopted by the State *Duma* (parliament) in 2005 restored Soviet-era limitations on mobility and economic activity in border areas. Initially, 35% of all the Kaliningrad region's towns, including Sovietsk, Bagrationovsk and the most tourist-attractive resort towns (Svetlogorsk, Yantarnyi and Zelenogradsk), were included in the border zone. In 2013, this area was reduced by 60%. However, many places considered as potential tourism attractions remain inside the designated border area. These include Rominta Forest, with bicycle routes on the border with Poland, and Vistytis Lake, on the border with Lithuania, where it was planned to create a large recreation zone. According to the latest regional tourism development programme (AKO, 2013), Vistytis Lake is a designated potential tourism cluster: 'European Baikal'.

There is also an insufficient development of the cross-border infrastructure. Although 21 checkpoints are set up in the Kaliningrad region, only 15 of them are de facto working (eight road, five rail, one each for sea and air). Despite the construction of new checkpoints (in 2010,

the large Mamonovo–Gzehotky checkpoint was constructed), most are overloaded on both the Russian–Polish and the Russian–Lithuanian borders. In the framework of CBC programmes and according to the plans of the Russian Border Service, some of these checkpoints are being modernised (e.g. Chernyakhovsk–Kibartay), and new roads and bridges are being constructed (e.g. in the area of the Sovietsk–Panemune checkpoint).

The border regime hampers the development of water tourism, which is one of the important aspects of both the CBC programmes and the strategic planning documents. The fact that rivers such as the Neman and Sesupe cross the state border severely complicates their use for tourism purposes. Occasional exhibition sailings are only possible as part of events supported by the regional authorities of the cross-border regions and connected with cross-border cooperation projects. For the same reason, EU plans for an international water route 'E-70' are difficult to realise, although within the framework of the CBC Programme 'Lithuania–Russia' (2014–2020) there are infrastructure projects concerning several Russian elements of this route (e.g. the creation of vessel berths on the spit of the Pregol and Deym rivers in Gvardeysk).

State borders cross the Curonian and Vistula lagoons, again considerably limiting the development of water tourism. The connection between river stations at Baltiysk (Kaliningrad) and Elbląg (Poland) is difficult; the checkpoints necessary for the development of navigation and yachting are absent; there are no special rules for crossing the sea border for vessels of such type; and the entry of vessels from third countries into the Curonian and Vistula lagoons is complicated.

Thus, only in 2013, within the framework of a state–private partnership, was it possible to open a seasonal checkpoint 'Rybachiy–Nida', which will potentially help develop Russian and international yachting. The checkpoint operates on request and has an extremely small number of entries per season (no more than 20).

The possible solution to these problems is to expand the LBT regime to the water checkpoints. However, the bureaucracy and necessity for numerous consultations with the Russian, Lithuanian and Polish legislations, together with the European regulations, remain obstacles. The other possible way of overcoming the fluvial border constraints is an expansion of the 72-h visa-free entry regime to the owners and passengers of sporting, sailing and pleasure boats.

Other problems impeding the development of incoming tourism include the existence of special zones with a regulated regime (i.e. restrictions) for foreigners. Such zones, whose borders have appeared on tourism brochures only quite recently, include significant territories of the region in the Nesterovskiy and Krasnoznamenskiy districts, and even the resorts of Zelenogradsk and Gurievsk. Taking into account that it is impossible to reach many of the resorts without entering these zones, non-stop transit is allowed. In the Baltiyskiy town district, such a closed zone, covering most of its territory, is an obstacle to the development of cross-border tourism cooperation along the Baltic spit. One of the 'landmark' projects of the region, the construction of a bicycle route 'From Spit to Spit' (from Poland through Kaliningrad to Lithuania, or vice versa) passes through a border area closed to foreigners for military reasons. Construction is to be finished by 2018, but if current conditions remain, the route's use by foreigners will evidently be difficult.

14.6   Conclusion

The successful development of the Kaliningrad region in most aspects is ultimately derived from positive international, including cross-border, cooperation. Tourism is one of the few spheres of cooperation where the 'negative' aspects of Kaliningrad's geographical position could become a powerful driver of development. The exclave character offers conditions for on-the-spot direct provision of entry visas, which could have a positive effect on attracting foreign tourists. Of course, negotiations with the EU on the facilitation of the visa regime must take into account regional and federal interests.

Cross-border tourist routes promoted in the framework of CBC programmes may also play an important role in attracting foreign tourists. The historical and cultural heritage of Eastern Prussia, being common for the Kaliningrad region and for the neighbouring parts of Poland and Lithuania, is one of the main factors attracting foreign tourists. An easing of the visa regime and development of cross-border cooperation in the field of tourism would aid the formation of a common space for the three countries' tourism product connected to Eastern Prussia and its capital, Königsberg. An additional cross-border brand could be 'The World Amber Way', whose potential tourist routes expand into the territories of neighbouring countries. A more active promotion of this brand in the CBC programmes with Poland and Lithuania may be useful for the region. Other regional brands (such as 'Russia in Europe') may also contribute to attracting foreign tourists, although they have less chance to become the focus of cross-border cooperation and are likely to attract mostly Russian tourists.

Cross-border cooperation is not able to remove all of the obstacles to tourism development. However, it allows for the solving of a complex of problems connected with the border regime and its infrastructure, joint use of cross-border ecosystems and the regulation of economic activity in the cross-border tourism sphere. There is a remarkable potential for attracting tourists to Kaliningrad from the neighbouring regions of Lithuania and particularly of Poland, especially taking into account the LBT agreements.

For many Poles, regular visits to the Kaliningrad region are part of their everyday life. But the main purpose of their visit is to purchase the cheaper Kaliningrad petrol and a few other goods. In order to change this situation, Polish and Lithuanian experience in the field of promoting regional tourism products should be drawn on. The study and the application of such experience should be incorporated into the framework of the CBC Programmes 2014–2020 'Poland–Russia' and 'Russia–Lithuania'.[6]

Endnotes

[1] The study is supported by a grant from the Russian Science Foundation (Project No 14-18-03621).
[2] In October 2014, more than 80,000 cards were issued to Polish citizens.

[3] According to the United Nations World Tourism Organization (UNWTO, 2016) methodology, a visitor is a traveller making a trip to any destination beyond their habitual residence with any principal purpose other than being employed at the premises registered in the country or in the place of visit.

[4] Meetings of two emperors were held in a pavilion set up on a raft in the middle of the Neman River close to Tilsit (Sovetsk). The first treaty, signed on 7 July 1807, ended the war between Imperial Russia and the French Empire and began an alliance between the two. The second treaty, signed on 9 July 1807, concerned Prussia's terms of surrender. Queen Louise, as the wife of King Friedrich Wilhelm III, met with the Emperor Napoleon I to plead unsuccessfully for favourable terms after Prussia's disastrous losses in the war. Ironically, the Tauroggen convention signed on 30 December 1812 at Taurage (now a small city in Lithuania), close to Sovetsk, opened the door for the Russian army to invade against Napoleon.

[5] Such approaches have been tried in other countries. Thus, on arrival at the Chinese island of Hainan, a tourist, being a part of an at least two-person group, may obtain a 21-day entry visa for US$30: such facilities are available 24 h, 7 days a week. Similar opportunities are given to the tourists visiting a range of insular territories of the UK.

[6] In July 2016 the local border traffic regime was 'temporarily' suspended by the Polish and Russian Governments after Poland announced its intention to suspend the regime for local movement across the border with Russia and Ukraine. (A note to this effect was received by the Russian Embassy in Warsaw on June 30.) This was done in line with stepping up security measures ahead of the NATO summit in Warsaw on July 8–9 and International Youth Days in Kraków on July 26–31. Local people and local governments in the Kaliningrad region and adjacent Polish regions want the border traffic regime reinstated. With its continued suspension they remain hostages to higher level (geo)politics (see also Chapter 13, this volume).

References

AKO (Administration of Kaliningrad Oblast') (2003) *Strategies of Socioeconomic Development of the Kaliningrad Region as the Cooperation Area for the Period until 2010.* Administration of Kaliningrad Oblast', Kaliningrad, Russia (in Russian).

AKO (2005) *State Program for Development of Tourism and Recreation in the Kaliningrad Region for the Period of 2002–2006.* Administration of Kaliningrad Oblast', Kaliningrad, Russia (in Russian).

AKO (2007) *Target-Oriented Program of Kaliningrad Oblast': 'Development of Kaliningrad Oblast' as Touristic Centre During 2007–2014 years'.* Administration of Kaliningrad Oblast', Kaliningrad, Russia (in Russian).

AKO (2012) *Strategy of Social and Economic Development of Kaliningrad Oblast' for Long-range Outlook.* Administration of Kaliningrad Oblast', Kaliningrad, Russia (in Russian).

AKO (2013) *State Program of Kaliningrad Oblast' 'Tourism'.* Administration of Kaliningrad Oblast', Kaliningrad, Russia (in Russian).

Alexandrova, A.Y. and Stupina, O.G. (2013) *Touristic Regional Studies. Influence of Regional Integration on Global Tourism Market.* KNORUS, Moscow (in Russian).

Dragileva, I.I. (2006) Transborder cooperation in south-east Baltic tourism development. Unpublished PhD dissertation, St Petersburg State University, St Petersburg, Russia (in Russian).

European Commission (2006) *Triple Jump. Projects of Lithuania, Poland and Kaliningrad Region of Russian Federation Neighbourhood Program (2006).* European Commission, Brussels. Available at: http://ec.europa.eu/regional_policy/archive/country/commu/docoutils/interregiiia_triplejump.pdf (accessed 4 August 2016).

European Commission (2008) *Cross-Border Cooperation Programme 'Lithuania–Poland–Russia' on 2007–2013.* Final Project of Programme. European Commission, Brussels.

Fedorov, G.M., Zverev, Yu.M. and Korneevets, V.S. (2013) *Russia on Baltic: 1990–2012 Years.* Immanuel Kant Baltic Federal University, Kaliningrad, Russia (in Russian).

Gareev, T.R. and Eliseeva, N.A. (2014) Commodity flow model for an exclave region: rent-seeking in the 'transitional period' of the special economic zone. *Baltic Region* 1, 72–90 [Immanuel Kant Baltic Federal University, Kaliningrad, Russia.]

Gimbitsky, K.K., Kuznetsova, A.L. and Fedorov, G.M. (2014) The development of Kaliningrad regional economy: a new stage of restructuring. *Baltic Region* 1, 56–71.

GUS (Central Statistical Office) (2015) *Tourism in 2014.* GUS, Warsaw.

Henley & Partners (2015) *The Henley & Partners Visa Restrictions Index 2015. Global Travel Freedom at a Glance.* Available at: https://www.henleyglobal.com/files/download/HP/hvri/HP%20Visa%20Restrictions%20Index%2020151001.pdf (accessed 4 August 2016).

Klemeshev, A. (2009) Russian exclave on the Baltic Sea: evolution of exclavity and ways to overcome it. *Baltic Region* 2, 86–97.

Klemeshev, A.P. and Mau, G.M. (eds) (2011) *Strategies for Development of Kaliningrad Region*. Immanuel Kant Baltic Federal University, Kaliningrad, Russia (in Russian).

Korneevets, V. and Kropinova, Ye. (2010) The 'Lithuania–Poland–Russia' neighbourhood program in the framework of the formation of the cross-border tourism region in the South-eastern Baltic and the promotion of the sustainable development of the territory. *Vestnik* 7, 152–156 [Immanuel Kant Baltic Federal University, Kaliningrad, Russia] (in Russian).

Kozak, M., Płoszaj, A., Rok, J. and Smętkowski, M. (2013) *Experts' report on European Neighbourhood Instrument Programme"Poland–Russia"in period 2014–2020*. Centre for European and Local Studies 'EUROREG', Warsaw University, Warsaw.

Kropinova, E.G. (2009) Tourism as a priority of regional development. *Vestnik* 3, 92–100 (in Russian).

Kropinova, Ye. (2010) International cooperation in the field of tourism and formation of cross-border tourist regions in the Baltic Sea area. *Vestnik* 1, 113–119 (in Russian).

Lithuania–Russia Cross-Border Cooperation Programme 2014–2020 4th Draft (2014) Vilnius.

LS (Statistics Lithuania) (2015) *Tourism in Lithuania 2014*. Statistical Department of Lithuania, Vilnius.

MTKR (Ministry of Tourism of Kaliningrad Region) (2014) *Analytical Report about Sample Survey of Kaliningrad's Population to Monitor the State of the Tourism Industry (II Quarter 2014)*. Scientific-Technical Centre 'Perspektiva', MTKR, Kaliningrad, Russia (in Russian).

MTKR (2015) *Statistical Database of Ministry of Tourism of Kaliningrad Region*. MTKR, Kaliningrad, Russia (in Russian).

Richard, Y., Sebentsov, A. and Zotova, M. (2015) The Russian exclave of Kaliningrad. Challenges and limits of its integration in the Baltic region. *Cybergeo: European Journal of Geography* article 402. Available at: http://cybergeo.revues.org/26945 (accessed 4 August 2016).

Rozhkov-Yurevskiy, Yu. D. (2013) Political and Geographical Features of Development of Kaliningrad Region as Exclave Region. Unpublished PhD dissertation, Immanuel Kant Baltic Federal University, Kaliningrad, Russia (in Russian).

Sebentsov A. and Zotova M. (2013) Geography and economy of the Kaliningrad region: limitations and prospects of development. *Baltic Region* 4, 81–94 Available at: http://journals.kantiana.ru/w.php?link=/upload/iblock/1eb/Sebentsov%20A.,%20Zotova%20M._81-94.pdf (accessed 4 August 2016).

UFMS (Administration of the Federal Migration Service in Kaliningrad Region) (2014) *Analytical Report about Migration Situation and Activity of UFMS of Russia in Kaliningrad Oblast' for Realization of State Migration Policy in Region in 2013*. UFMS, Kaliningrad, Russia (in Russian).

UFMS (2015) *Analytical Report about Migration Situation and Activity of UFMS of Russia in Kaliningrad Oblast' for Realization of State Migration Policy in Region in 2014*. UFMS, Kaliningrad, Russia (in Russian).

UNWTO (United Nations World Tourism Organization) (2016) *International Recommendations for Tourism Statistics 2008*. Department of Economic and Social Affairs. Statistics Division, UNWTO. Available at: http://unstats.un.org/UNSD/trade/IRTS/IRTS%202008%20unedited.pdf (accessed 9 August 2016).

Vinokurov, E.Y. (2007) *Theory of Exclaves*. Terra-Baltic, Kaliningrad, Russia (in Russian).

Vylejagina, U. and Strigin, A. (2013) An empty harbor. *Russian Gazette* 3 September. Available at: http://www.rg.ru/2013/09/03/reg-szfo/kruizy.html (accessed 1 February 2016).

15 An Evaluation of Tourism Development in Kaliningrad

Elena Kropinova*

Institute of Recreation, Tourism and Physical Education, Immanuel Kant Baltic Federal University, Kaliningrad, Russia

15.1 Introduction

This chapter briefly sets out the development of and influences on tourism in Kaliningrad. The factors and peculiarities of tourism and recreation in this exclave region of the Russian Federation (RF) (Fig. 15.1) are considered and evaluated. The tourism potential is assessed and possible development directions are outlined.

The Kaliningrad *Oblast'*,[1] due to its natural, cultural and historical potential, is characterised by a relatively high level of tourism development, especially international tourism, compared to other regions of the Russian Federation. Tourism is now one of the economic priorities of the *Oblast'*, whose population is approaching 1 million. In 2018, Kaliningrad will be one of a total of 11 Russian cities hosting the FIFA World Cup tournament. The global attraction of such a mega-event will stimulate considerably the further development of tourism infrastructure here.

Until 1945, the territory of the modern Kaliningrad *Oblast'* was a part of East Prussia. Climatic conditions favoured the development of maritime resorts here from the late 19th century. Such resort towns as Rauschen (now Svetlogorsk), Kranz (Zelenogradsk) and Pillau (Baltiysk) were particularly popular with Europeans (Kropinova and Bruce, 2009). As Königsberg – the capital of the East Prussian province – the city was known as one of the most beautiful (because of its Hanseatic architecture) and comfortable (owing to the implementation of garden city principles) in Europe.

After World War II, by the decision of the Potsdam peace conference, approximately one-third of the territory ($15,100 \text{ km}^2$) of the former East Prussia was transferred to the Soviet Union, and two-thirds to Poland. The part attached to the Soviet Union became the Königsberg *Oblast'*, but from 1946 became Kaliningrad *Oblast'*.

15.2 Factors of Tourism Development: SWOT Analysis

Both positive and negative factors are combined in the development of tourism in the region, as characterised in Table 15.1.

15.3 Tourism Statistics for the Kaliningrad *Oblast'*

In terms of absolute numbers of international tourist arrivals, only St Petersburg, Moscow and the Vladimir region exceed Kaliningrad within European Russia. In relative terms, per 1000 population, the *Oblast'* is ranked first.

*E-mail: ekropinova@kantiana.ru

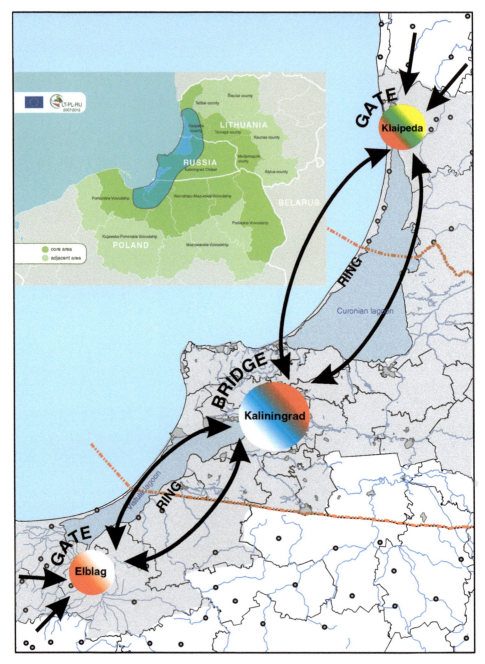

Fig. 15.1. Kaliningrad: within the framework of project strategy: lagoons as a crossroads for tourism and interactions of peoples of the south-east Baltic. (From Crossroads 2.0 Project, 2007–2013.)

However, Fig. 15.2 suggests that other indicators are more modest.

The performance indicators of tourism development in the *Oblast'* for 2002–2014, with the exception of the number of beds in spa and cure hotels and resort hostels, are also more favourable in comparison with average Russian rates (Fig. 15.3).

These data testify to tourism specialisation within the Kaliningrad *Oblast'* and its enhancement

Table 15.1. SWOT analysis for tourism development in Kaliningrad *Oblast'*. (From Fedorov, 2014; Kropinova, 2014; Kropinova and Anokhin, 2014; MTK, 2015.)

Quality	Details
Strengths	– Temperate climate, transitional from maritime to continental
	– Rich in hydrotherapeutic resources: mineral waters and therapeutic muds
	– Infrastructure for medical tourism: 19 spas with 4000 beds
	– Resorts of federal importance at: Svetlogorsk-Otradnoe and Zelenogradsk (Fig. 15.4)
	– Further potential for medical tourism with the Federal Centre for Cardiovascular Surgery of the Ministry of Healthcare (opened in 2013), and plans for a Federal Centre for Oncology
	– Rich historical and cultural heritage: medieval castles (19 sites), churches, fortifications (63 monuments): 1660 sites protected as objects of historical and cultural heritage of federal, regional and local significance, with more than 100 museums
	– Cultural events of national and international significance: in 2015, the 2000-capacity music theatre, Yantar Hall (Amber Hall), was built (Fig. 15.5)
Weaknesses	– Transport accessibility: high air fares and dependence on subsidies
	– The necessity for Russian citizens to have an international passport to travel by rail to and from the *Oblast'*
	– Time-consuming and costly visa regimes with foreign countries
	– Strong competition from neighbouring Baltic resorts in Poland and Lithuania and from Russian Black Sea resorts
Opportunities	– Unique in Russia: The Museum of the World Ocean (www.world-ocean.ru/en/)
	– Increased competition between tourism enterprises and quality upgrading
	– Growing demand for high-quality medical services and medical tourism, for nature-oriented and rural tourism
	– Reorientation of Russian citizens towards holidays in domestic resorts
	– Further and higher education establishments training tourism-related specialists
	– Image of the *Oblast'* as a centre for health and wellness tourism with recreation, rehabilitation and relaxation available
	– Participation in local and international cross-border routes: Great Amber Route, Baltic Fort Route, Great Silk Road, E70 and EuroVelo
	– Development of event tourism: FIFA World Cup 2018, International Humour and Music Festival of KVN: *Wailing KiViN*[2]
	– Waterborne cross-border tourism, in the Curonian and Vistula lagoons, on rivers and lakes
Threats	– Higher prices for tourism services compared to neighbouring countries
	– Lower quality of service compared to neighbouring countries
	– Deterioration of the ecological situation
	– Uncertain geopolitical situation concerning the border regions of the exclave

during the 2000s. By contrast, the spa sector has lagged behind: by 2014, the number of places in cure hotels and resort hostels per 1000 inhabitants was only 18% higher than the national average, and for 2002–2014, the number of places in such accommodation actually declined, while the figure for Russia increased slightly.

15.4 Stages of Kaliningrad's Development as a Russian Tourism Destination

The tourism industry in the Kaliningrad *Oblast'* has undergone significant changes since the USSR's demise in 1991, as summarised in Table 15.2. The resulting pattern of inbound tourism (1997–2014) can be seen in Fig. 15.6.

15.5 Changing Geopolitical Contexts

From 2003, there was a tightening of cross-border movement as a result of the introduction of national visas prior to Lithuania and Poland joining the EU's Schengen Zone. However, a Facilitated Transit Document (FTD), which is issued for travelling by road with a foreign passport, simplified transit traffic through the territory of Lithuania, and has remained to the present day.

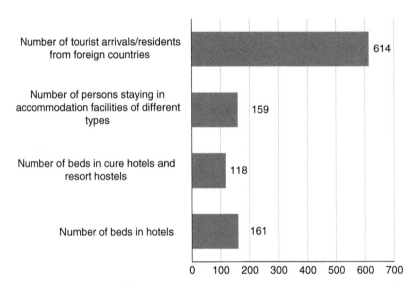

Fig. 15.2. Selected relative (per 1000 inhabitants) indicators of tourism development in the Kaliningrad *Oblast'* as a percentage against RF rates, 2014. (From Federal State Statistics Service.)

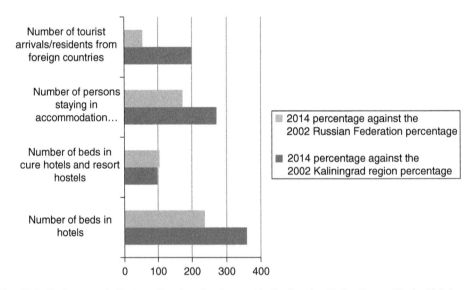

Fig. 15.3. Performance indicators of tourism development in the Russian Federation and in the Kaliningrad *Oblast'* in 2014 as a percentage against 2002. (From Federal State Statistics Service.)

The global financial crisis of 2008 brought a significant decline in tourist arrivals from 2009. It also coincided with the bankruptcy of the regional airline, KD Avia. These events resulted in a reduction of Russian tourist arrival numbers by more than 100,000, and almost halved foreign arrivals (see Fig. 15.3). From 2013, Russian tourism companies were forced to look for new markets following a sharp decline in demand for outbound trips that resulted from three inter-related factors:

- a tense geopolitical situation following Ukraine's 'revolution' and Russia's reincorporation of Crimea
- weakness of the rouble against foreign currencies, exacerbated by weakening global oil and gas prices

Fig. 15.4. The promenade in the resort town of Zelenogradsk (former Kranz), 2015. (Photograph courtesy of Elena Kropinova.)

Fig. 15.5. The music theatre, Yantar Hall (Amber Hall). (Photograph courtesy of Elena Kropinova.)

Table 15.2. Relationship between stages of tourism development, socio-economic and geopolitical conditions. (From Golunov and Vardomsky, 2002; Roberts, 2004; Ginsburg, 2009; Skyscanner, 2010; Fedorov, 2014; Rosstat, 2014, 2015; Kropinova *et al.*, 2015; RATA, 2015.)

Period	Stage of tourism development	Development characteristics
Before 1939	German, pre-Soviet	*Socio-economic:* East Prussia is a developed province of Germany *Tourism:* the resorts of East Prussia are tourism destinations
1950–1991	'Autarkic period of regional tourism', the Soviet period	*Socio-economic:* command–administrative system of management and economic planning *Tourism:* – system of special permits for visiting spa and cure resorts – dominated by Soviet domestic tourism with a steady inflow of tourists – accommodation facilities focused on year-round health and cure tourism: health spas, health and recreation resorts, *pensions* involving treatment – Kaliningrad's national strategic role precluded foreign tourism – five hotels: 90% of tourism enterprises were concentrated along the coast, where an extensive resort complex was established
1992–1995	'Start-up for international tourism'	*Socio-economic:* Free Economic Zone (FEZ *Yantar*) (1991–1996) covers the whole *Oblast'* *Tourism:* – opening for international arrivals: first groups primarily business and scientific – visa-free regime with Lithuania, voucher system with Poland – privatisation process begun – health and cure facilities transformed into tourist accommodation – development of cultural, historical and educational tourism – stakeholders in tourism considerably expanded
1996–2002	'Push-up for international tourism'	*Socio-economic:* Federal law 'On the Special Economic Zone in the Kaliningrad *Oblast'* (1996–2016)' encouraged citizens to travel abroad regularly *Tourism:* – infrastructure for international tourist arrivals developed – first foreign transport companies: trains to Berlin and Gdynia, SAS (Scandinavian Airline Sysem) to Copenhagen (1998–2003) – visa-free entry to Poland and Lithuania – Lithuanian, Polish, Swedish and German consulates opened to save residents having to travel to Moscow for a visa – foreign language guidebooks on Kaliningrad published – sharp rise in foreign tourist arrivals – nostalgia tourism: 59% of foreign tourists are German
2003–2009	'Kaliningrad – the centre of European tourism'	*Socio-economic:* Special Economic Zone (SEZ) status continues *Tourism:* – 72-h visas for tourists from the Schengen states, UK and Japan issued at three entry points (valid until January 2017) – *Oblast'* becomes a platform of interaction for Russia–EU joint programmes – regional airline, KD Avia, 2007/8: Kaliningrad becomes a transit hub – Russian tourist arrivals growth: 212,000 in 2002 to 430,000 in 2008 – foreign arrivals growth: 60,000 in 2002 to 92,000 in 2008 – arrivals peak in 2008, then the global financial crisis hits – old hotels refurbished, new accommodation built to a higher quality – domestic air routes to 13 Russian cities – direct air links to 18 foreign cities – operation of LOT Polish Airlines 2002–2008 – hospitality industry learning from European best practice

Continued

Table 15.2. Continued.

Period	Stage of tourism development	Development characteristics
2010–2013	The period of tourism's recovery after the global economic crisis of 2008	*Socio-economic:* cross-border cooperation projects in 'Lithuania–Poland–Russia' programme of ENPI (European Neighbourhood and Partnership Instrument), including tourism – agreement between Polish and Russian governments on local border traffic regulation – economic recovery – cross-border cooperation *Tourism:* – initiation of 'anchor sites' projects – federal subsidies for air travel to and from Moscow and St Petersburg (2012+) help to stabilise the inflow of Russian tourists – growth of cross-border tourism and recreation – steady growth in arrivals numbers from 2010: by 2013 back to 2008 levels – SAS air operations 2011–2013 – Air Berlin flights to/from the German capital from 2011 contribute to stabilisation of foreign tourism numbers (about half of are whom German) – entry of hotel transnational corporations (TNCs): Radisson Blue (2010) and Ibis (by Accor) (2013) – water border checkpoint on the Curonian Lagoon opened for foreign yachts and other small boats (2012)
2014 to present	Consolidation of 'anchor sites' and stimulation of domestic tourism	*Socio-economic:* EU economic sanctions against Russia over Crimea – a weakening of the Russian rouble *Tourism:* – Russian citizens' rejection of travelling abroad, searching for new holiday destinations inside Russia – Kaliningrad *Oblast'* resurgence as a domestic centre for spa and health, cultural and historical tourism – development of new destinations within the *Oblast'*: implementation of 'anchor sites' projects funded by federal and regional sources: Viking open-air museum 'Ancient Sambia' in the Curonian Spit national park; adventure park in Ozersk district (a near-border municipality with Poland); extensive promenade in Yantarny (eastern Baltic Sea coast); holographic exhibition on cultural traditions of Kaliningrad and Elbląg (Poland), in the Friedland Gate museum – decline of foreign tourist arrivals: by 5% for first quarter of 2015, notably 20% decline for German arrival numbers, 31% for Polish visitors and 19% for Lithuanians – compensation through projected growth of up to 20% in Russian tourist arrivals

- a growth of nationalist sentiment among Russians preferring Russian (including Crimean) resorts.

Further, the wider international situation saw a decline in foreign tourist arrivals in Russia as a whole: 2% in the first quarter of 2015, with a 9% decline in business arrivals (Rosstat, 2014, 2015). Within the Kaliningrad *Oblast'*, preliminary results of surveys conducted in 2015 suggested that a decline in foreign tourism would possibly reach up to 30–40% by the end of the year.

From in-depth interviews conducted with the owners of a number of travel agencies in

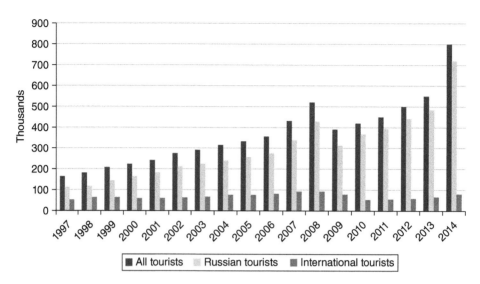

Fig. 15.6. The trend of inbound tourism in the Kaliningrad *Oblast'* (in thousands), 1997–2014. (From author's compilation from the Federal State Statistics Service in the Kaliningrad *Oblast'*, 1997–2015.)

summer 2015, the author concluded that tourism operators specialising in both inbound and outbound tourism were in a better position to recover. They were able to compensate for the loss of foreign tourists by receiving increased numbers of Russian visitors. In numerical terms, the increase was likely to be about 20% against the previous year. However, this growth was more significant in receipt terms because Russian tourists stayed longer than foreign tourists, resulting in higher expenditures per arrival. There are also significant spatial consequences: notably, Russian-oriented tourism contributes to the development of inner areas and peripheries where foreigners may not wish, or may not be permitted, to travel. Russian visitors more actively take tours into the hinterland areas, and also are more likely to stay overnight at cottages and farmhouses, creating added value in the rural municipalities of the *Oblast'*.

15.6 Prospects for Tourism Development

Local experts (Kropinova and Zaitseva, 2015) have elaborated both a baseline and a target scenario for tourism development within the Kaliningrad *Oblast'* to 2030 (Fig. 15.7). The baseline scenario assumes a retention of 2015's (domestic) positive

dynamics (+20%) for 2–3 years, followed by a deceleration of 5–6% per year. This growth notwithstanding, internal development opportunities will not be realised in full, partly reflecting a reduction in federal funding for a number of infrastructure projects aimed at developing tourism directly or indirectly. But key projects will be maintained, such as airport modernisation, the facilities for the FIFA World Cup 2018, responses to increasing demand for domestic travel and to a growing popularity of the recently created new 'anchor' projects such as the Yantar Hall music theatre and a yacht marina on the river Trostyanka in the Zelenogradsk municipality.

Implementation of the baseline scenario will be enhanced by the projects in Table 15.3.

15.7 Summary and Conclusion

The development of tourism in the Kaliningrad *Oblast'* of the Russian Federation has been going on concurrently with strengthening collaboration and cooperation between Russia and EU countries in general and the Baltic region in particular.

Table 15.4 summarises the factors that can be identified as having affected tourism development in the Kaliningrad *Oblast'*.

In the current geopolitical and geoeconomic conditions, and taking into account the rapid

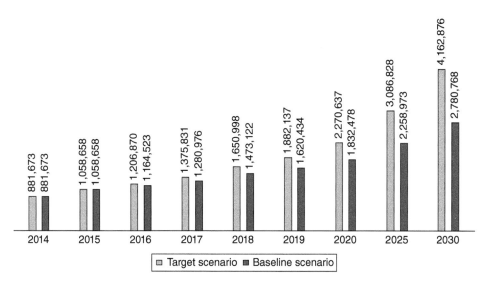

Fig. 15.7. Forecast of tourist arrivals in the Kaliningrad *Oblast'*, 2015–2030 (in absolute numbers). (From Zaitseva and Kropinova, 2015.)

Table 15.3. Key tourism development projects. (From Kropinova, 2013; Kropinova and Anokhin, 2014; Kropinova and Zaitseva, 2015; Kropinova *et al.*, 2015; New Kaliningrad, 2015.)

Project	Details
FIFA World Cup 2018	Kaliningrad is among 11 Russian host cities for the last rounds of the tournament, chosen because of its convenient geographical location for both Russian and foreign fans
Modernisation of Khrabrovo Airport	*Oblast'* accessibility will be improved. There will be an expected increase in passenger traffic up to (total *Oblast'* arrivals of) 5 million/year, compared to the current 2 million
	Near the boundary of the Kaliningrad *Oblast'* in Warmia-Mazury district (Poland), a new airport was opened in 2016
Lithuania–Poland–Russia CBC Programme	Launching of new centres of tourist attraction, created as a result of the programme's projects
Project of CBC Programme *Crossroads 2.0: Lagoons as crossroads for tourism and interactions of peoples of south-east Baltic: from history to the present*	Construction of the Viking open-air museum and Ancient Sambia. The Common Strategy and Action Plan on conservation and sustainable use of the natural, cultural and historical heritage of the cross-border area of Lithuania, Poland and Kaliningrad *Oblast'* adjacent to the Curonian and Vistula lagoons (see Fig. 15.1)
VILA 'Opportunities and Benefits of Joint Use of the Vistula Lagoon' project	Joint use of the Vistula Lagoon Russian–Polish land and water area for tourism
Czech Airlines Prague service	Regular flights to be launched in summer 2016, planned in cooperation with the Russian low-cost airline, S-7, providing links with other Russian regions
	This can be viewed as a further attempt to establish Kaliningrad as a transit hub, particularly for Russian travellers
Federal programme 'Development of the Transport System of Russia (2010–2020)'	Includes the ambitious project to construct a deep-water port in Pionerskii, a resort town on the Baltic Sea coast
	This will contribute to the development of cruise and ferry services between Kaliningrad, St Petersburg and other Baltic ports

Continued

Table 15.3. Continued.

Project	Details
Redevelopment/rejuvenation of Kaliningrad's historic centre	Project 'Heart of the City' is based on the results of an international urban planning competition that attracted more than 40 international participants. The best projects are to be implemented in the 40 ha central area
Establishment of a gambling zone	Kaliningrad is one of just four approved sites where gambling is legally permitted in the Russian Federation. The Yantarnaya (Amber) casino will be part of the Amberland gambling zone being developed along the Baltic Sea coast since 2014

Table 15.4. Factors influencing tourism development. (From Kropinova, 2013.)

Generic factor	Details
Institutional	Establishment of: – the Free Economic Zone (FEZ) – the Special Economic Zone (SEZ) – the Amberland gambling zone The creation of state institutions dealing with tourism development: – the Agency for Tourism – the Ministry of Tourism – the Tourism Development Corporation of Kaliningrad *Oblast'* – the Development Corporation of Kaliningrad *Oblast'*
Geopolitical	– Transformation from a military outpost of the Soviet era to a platform of Russia–EU cooperation – Establishment of transborder and cross-border tourism regions with Lithuania and Poland – Introduction of local border traffic with Poland and of 72-h tourist visas to visit the *Oblast'* – Well-known tensions in relations between Russia and the EU in recent years have made it difficult to implement the concept of EU–Russia cooperation, negatively affecting the above developments
Socio-economic	– Strengthening the social and economic impacts of an increased flow of Russian tourists – Implementation of federal and state programmes to create new tourism sites in the region – Increasing the contribution of tourism in the creation of added value
Resources	– Estimated above-average resource potential for tourism and recreation development in comparison with other Russian regions – The *Oblast'* is relatively similar to its nearest competitors, including the neighbouring regions of the south-eastern coast of the Baltic Sea – the Polish tri-cities (Gdańsk, Gdynia, Sopot), Lithuanian Neringa and Palanga – Both the volume and quality of tourist services have failed to realise potential – New and better-quality consumer-oriented tourism products are required: for example, the sea and lagoons have almost never been used. It is essential to integrate this potential and to create opportunities for Kaliningrad to enter the cruise tourism market in the Baltic Sea
Innovation	Cross-border cooperation is of special significance in the creation of innovative forms of tourism within: – the European Neighbourhood and Partnership Instrument (ENPI) – Neighbourhood Programme 'Lithuania–Poland–Kaliningrad *Oblast'* of the Russian Federation' (2004–2006) – Cross-border Cooperation Programme 'Lithuania–Poland–Russia' (2007–2013) – establishment of joint transborder and cross-border tourist routes, such as the Baltic Amber Necklace, Baltic Sea Fort Route, EuroVelo and E70 Special attention should be given to the development of a unified marketing policy for joint promotion of the transborder region – 'Polish Tri-Cities – Kaliningrad (Russia) – Klaipeda (Lithuania)', as well as to participation in Euro–Asian transborder tourist routes such as the Silk Road and the Great Amber Road

development of tourist potential of the Kaliningrad *Oblast'*, an increase of both Russian and foreign tourist arrivals is expected. An influx of Russian tourists will be accelerated by a depreciation of the rouble, encouraging Russian tourists to stay in their own country and support the national tourism market. The Kaliningrad region is among the top ten Russian destinations where special attention is paid to tourism infrastructure development and to the pursuit of event tourism. In its turn, an influx of foreign tourists is likely to be stimulated by the favourably low exchange rate and by the preservation of privileges for foreign tourists, such as retaining local border traffic rules and 72-h visas, as well as by the further development of cross-border cooperation.

Endnotes

[1] There are 46 *oblast'* and 39 *kraya*, units of local administration, in the Russian Federation.

[2] KVN is the Russian abbreviation for 'Cheerful and Resourceful Club' and KiViN is the youth version. It is called 'Wailing' as the teams must not just make jokes, but have to sing. From 1996 until 2014, this festival had taken place at Jurmala, near Riga (Latvia), but EU sanctions imposed against Russia resulted in venues being changed to Sochi for the KVN and to Svetlogorsk for the KiViN (see also RIA Novosti, 2015).

References

Crossroads 2.0 Project (2007–2013) Lagoons as crossroads for tourism and interactions of peoples of South-East Baltic: from the history to present. Project of CBC Programme, Kaliningrad, Russia.

Federal State Statistics Service. Available at: http://www.gks.ru/ (accessed 8 August 2016) (in Russian).

Fedorov, G. (2014) Border position as a factor of strategic and territorial planning in Russian regions in the Baltic. *Baltic Region* 3(21), 58–67.

Ginsburg, E.S. (2009) Improving spatial organization of air transport in Russia. Extended abstract of PhD dissertation. Scientific Library of abstracts and theses. Available at disserCat: http://www.dissercat.com/content/sovershenstvovanie-prostranstvennoi-organizatsii-aviatsionnogo-transporta-rossii#ixzz3ta2gLfpy (accessed 8 August 2016) (in Russian).

Golunov, S.V. and Vardomsky, L.B. (eds) (2002) *Security and Trans-border Cooperation in Russia's New Borderlands.* AEFIR, Moscow. Available at: http://www.obraforum.ru/book/chapter4.htm (accessed 8 August 2016) (in Russian).

Kropinova, E.G. (2013) Cooperation between the EU and Russia in the sphere of innovative development of tourism: case for the Cross-Border Cooperation Programme 'Lithuania–Poland–Russia'. *Baltic Region* 4, 48–57.

Kropinova, E.G. and Anokhin, A.Yu. (2014) The development of new trans-border water routes in the south east Baltic: technique and practice. *Baltic Region* 3, 121–136.

Kropinova, E. and Bruce, D. (2009) A new Russian window to the West: the Province of Kaliningrad. In: Holloway, J.C. (ed.) *The Business of Tourism*, 8th edn. Pearson Education, Harlow, UK, pp. 717–731.

Kropinova, E.G. and Zaitseva, N.A. (2015) Development scenarios for the development of tourism in the Kaliningrad region until 2030. *Regional Research* 4(50), 126–132. Available at: http://regis.shu.ru/eng/ (accessed 8 August 2016) (in Russian).

Kropinova, E.G., Zaitseva, N.A. and Moroz, M. (2015) Approaches to the assessment of the contribution of tourism into the regional surplus product: case of the Kaliningrad Region. *Mediterranean Journal of Social Sciences* 6(3) Special issue 5, 275–282.

Kropinova, K.A. (2014) The Great Amber Route – a myth or fact? In: Spirina, M.J. and Toropyginaja, A.A. (eds) *Tourism in EuroAsian Space: Reality and New Tendencies. Part I.* Conference on the EuroAsia Scientific Cooperation Forum, 4–5 December, SPB: MIEP pri MPA EvrAeES, pp. 165–175 (in Russian).

MTK (Ministry of Tourism of the Kaliningrad Region) (2015) *Report by the Minister on Tourism.* MTK, Kaliningrad, Russia. Available at: www.gov39.ru/docs/drond_2015.docx (accessed 30 October 2015) (in Russian).

New Kaliningrad (2015) Czech Airlines plans to launch airline 'Kaliningrad-Prag'. Available at: https://www.newkaliningrad.ru/news/briefs/community/7267649-czech-airlines-sobiraetsya-zapustit-reysy-kaliningrad-praga.html (accessed 8 August 2016) (in Russian).

RATA (2015) 72-hour visas remain. *RATA*: daily electronic newspaper of the Russian Association of Tourism Agencies. Available at: http://www.ratanews.ru/news/news_12112010_1.stm (accessed 1 November 2015).

RIA Novosti (2015) 'Wailing Kivinen' will move from Jurmala to Svetlogorsk. *LNR Media* [Palm Harbor, FL] 26 February. Available at: http://latestnewsresource.com/en/news/golosjaschij-kivin-pereedet-iz-jurmaly-v-svetlogorsk (accessed 23 December 2015).

Roberts, L. (2004) Capital accumulation – tourism and development processes in Central and Eastern Europe. In: Hall, D.R. (ed.) *Tourism and Transition: Governance, Transformation, and Development*. CAB International, Wallingford, UK, pp. 53–63.

Rosstat (2014/2015) Data of Rosstat, Russian Federal Statistics Bureau. Available at: webpage of Federal Tourism Agency: http://www.russiatourism.ru/contents/statistika/statisticheskie-pokazateli-vzaimnykh-poezdok-grazhdan-rossiyskoy-federatsii-i-grazhdan-inostrannykh-gosudarstv/kolichestvo-pribyvshikh-grazhdan-inostrannykh-gosudarstv-na-territoriyu-rossiyskoy-federatsii/ (accessed 1 November 2015) (in Russian).

Skyscanner (2010) LOT returned to Kaliningrad. *Skyscanner* [Edinburgh] 28 April. Available at: http://www.skyscanner.ru/news/lot-vozvrashchaetsya-v-kaliningrad (accessed 1 November 2015) (in Russian).

Zaitseva, N.A. and Kropinova, E.G. (2015) Tourism. In: *Scientific Research Works on the Development of Individual Sections of the Socio-economic Development of the Kaliningrad Region for the Long Term until 2030*. Immanuel Kant Baltic Federal University and HSE- St Petersburg No 06/10-2015, Kaliningrad and St Petersburg, Russia (in Russian).

Part V:

Identity and Image

As a mediator between ethnic minorities, host residents and tourists, ethnic gastronomy holds a potentially important role in the geopolitics of urban and ethnic tourism. Marta Derek's Chapter 16 exemplifies the Polish case. Derek highlights a number of insightful ironies. Eating out was not a popular pastime in communist-era Poland, and this aspect of urban living only took on significance in the late 1980s. Yet the seed for one of the capital's major ethnic cuisines – Vietnamese – was sown under the communist regime, when large numbers of Vietnamese students came to study in Warsaw and later stayed on in the city.

In this otherwise 'mono-ethnic' capital of Poland, Derek argues that ethnic gastronomy represents an important factor in contributing to the 'globalising' of local populations. Significantly, however, there is little evidence in Warsaw's restaurants of cuisine from other CEE countries being available.

In geopolitical terms, ethnic restaurants have also become a 'frontline' area for ideological conflict, given the ISIS attacks on both French and 'ethnic' restaurants in Paris in November 2015.[1] If one of the aims of this group was, as one media commentator put it, to explore and exploit the fault lines between different nationalities and ethnic groups, then the geopolitical role of cosmopolitan bars and restaurants in European cities will have been magnified. And in this way, the geopolitics of terrorism transfers its spatial significance from contested territory and boundaries to shared city centres and collective fear: exploiting the psychology of a threatened quotidian.

The everyday becomes a focus of uncertainty in Europe, as it has been in the Middle East for so long. And the faces of young Europeans killed in terrorist attacks while enjoying themselves, out on a Friday night, become familiar through television, newspapers and social media in a way that has never been granted to the thousands more Iraqis, Syrians and Afghanis killed as 'collateral damage' in wars within those faraway places of which we prefer to know so little.

A central aspect of Balkan post-conflict reconstruction has been for international interventionist agencies to socially (re)construct south-eastern Europe as different from other parts of CEE: as 'Other', or even 'anOther Other'. But then 'Balkan'/'the Balkans', as more than just a geographical designation for south-eastern Europe, has long held pejorative connotations (Todorova, 1997).

Smith (2002: 664) has argued that, as particularly employed by the EBRD, south-eastern Europe became a classifiable category defined on the basis of a lack of progress towards a market-based economy. He determined that post-conflict economic reconstruction, in the aftermath of the Yugoslav wars of succession in the 1990s, was here given the role not only of 'securing the hegemony of capitalist transition' but also of being the mechanism by which the 'goals of peace, stability and prosperity' (World Bank, 2000: 2) could be achieved.

The agenda of economic reform revolved around the key tenets of the structural adjustment programmes implemented earlier in 'East Central Europe' (by spatial implication, no longer 'Other'). According to Smith (2002: 665), these reforms were 'pushed through forcibly' by the EU through the signing of the Stability Pact for South-eastern Europe in 1999, which aimed to secure lasting peace, prosperity and stability, foster effective regional cooperation, create vibrant market economies and integrate the countries of the region into European and Atlantic structures (Friis and Murphy, 2000), thus echoing the World Bank's position for overseeing neoliberal hegemony in the region.

While a significant academic tourism literature has grown around post-conflict themes (e.g. Novelli *et al.*, 2012), the changing conceptualisation of peace and stability, intervention and international governance has likewise stimulated a considerable literature that has only occasionally been engaged with by tourism scholars. These literatures are drawn on in the following two chapters, focusing on the former Yugoslav territories of Bosnia and Herzegovina and Kosovo, respectively.

Chapter 17 by Rahman Nurković and Derek Hall examines the geopolitical context for the development of tourism in rural areas of Bosnia and Herzegovina. It draws on concepts of inverse peripherality and centrifugal governance, and is set within a context of institutionalised territorial division, resulting from the genocidal conflict of the first half of the 1990s. If tourism is now considered to be one of the country's leading sectors, a promoter of positive images and a symbol of intercommunal cooperation, the authors pose the question of how can it promote the country effectively when that country is so fundamentally divided and fragmented, with significant elements of its population expressing orientations towards neighbouring (and in tourism terms, competing) countries?

Nurković and Hall are not the first to conclude (e.g. Čaušević and Lynch, 2013) that tourism's socio-political and economic roles in Bosnia and Herzegovina would be far more effective if tourism was regulated centrally; that enhancing the country's image can only be brought about if

promoted with a unity of purpose. The widespread protests across the country in 2014 'undermined the rarely questioned ethno-nationalist ideological hegemony' (Mujkić, 2015: 623), and a subsequent economic and social 'compact' offered prospects for longer-term political reform (Kurtović, 2015; Maistorović *et al.*, 2015).

Starkly similar issues apply in Kosovo, albeit within a different context. In Chapter 18, Derek Hall and Frances Brown evaluate the role and relevance of tourism in contemporary Kosovo, drawing on concepts of double peripherality, contested heritage and the commoditisation of nature.

The Kosovo conflict exerted a profound impact on the philosophy and practice of international governance in Europe (see, for example, Tamminem, 2011). While conceptions of post-conflict tourism development are well rehearsed, the spatialised nature of Kosovo's contested and dissonant heritage, the complications of an array of international interventionist institutions and the commoditisation of nature all act to blur the role of tourism as an integrating agency.

In both chapters, Čaušević and Lynch's (2013: 148) contention that '. . . the natural environment . . . does not lend itself to ethnic labelling' is implicitly challenged.

In recognising three distinct periods for the role of tourism in Romania – development, stagnation and decline – Gheorghe and Alexandru (2001) argued that these were shaped by geopolitical factors. Yet geopolitical critiques of sociocultural development have been slow to emerge from the country. This volume, however, presents two contrasting studies *pour encourager les autres.*

Daniela Dumbrăveanu, Anca Tudoricu and Ana Crăciun, in Chapter 19, trace the political evolution of 'big events' in Romania, from the geopolitical manoeuvrings of the first decade of the 20th century up to the present day. They highlight the demonstration effects of how the mayor of Sibiu, during that town's year of being a European City of Culture in 2007, was able to move on to become the country's president. This was seen as an early 'reward' from the country's EU accession. Within this context, the chapter draws out paradoxes and divisions in attitudes towards, and interpretations of, heritage and identity: between western and eastern Europe, between generations in their appreciation of (high) culture and between 'cultural guardians' in their attempts to render culture more accessible.

The impress of neoliberalism is never far away, even if it does encourage museums and other cultural institutions to reach out and engage with a wider cross-section of society on the basis of trying to generate necessary funding in an era of meagre governmental support. The thread running through such issues in this chapter is the geopolitical nature of commemorating contested histories through the evolving nature of Romania's participation in the European Night of Museums event. Given the violent nature of Romania's anti-communist 'revolution' in 1989 and the nastiness of the regime that preceded it, recollection and representation of communist times is still a sensitive area rife with tension and potential hostility, even at a personal level. This is emphasised by the fact that only recently have the archives of the period begun to be opened up.

Although advances have been made in the field of memory studies (e.g. Marschall, 2015), the subject of presenting and interpreting an unwanted past, its contested memories and histories is still poorly researched in Romania. The authors claim that little multidisciplinary joint research has been undertaken, and there is minimal teaching of communism at university level. While there may be justifiable reasons for this, such a geopolitics of erasure is not healthy for a large contemporary European country. Extending the teaching, researching and interpretation of an unwanted past could help provide a focus for future coherent strategies encompassing culture, civil society and social reconciliation. Thus, for example, employing a former political prison to present an exhibition 'offers a rarefied field of knowledge for discourse production' (Wight, 2016: 60).

As Neil Taylor points out in Chapter 21, during the communist period, if tourism authorities decided to change itineraries, accommodation or transport provision at short notice, there was little that Western travel companies could do, apart from terminate relations, which was often not in their interests. Pity then the hapless individual traveller who had scant opportunity for redress if anything went wrong, which it often did, during their sojourn 'on the other side'. *Lonely Planet*'s unfortunately timed (April 1989) *Eastern Europe on a Shoestring* (Stanley,

1989) articulated such travellers' vulnerabilities in its chapter on Romania:

> Here independent travellers share the everyday problems of the people as nowhere else. Tourist facilities exist everywhere, but they're geared to the big spender. For shoestring travellers Romania can be the adventure of a lifetime, but only in summer when it's possible to camp.
> (Stanley, 1989: 369)

And if you wanted on-the-spot information from a reliable source, the main national tourist office (ONT) in Bucharest city centre:

> ... answers questions. The service here varies from friendly to unbelievably rude ...
> (Stanley, 1989: 383)

Likewise, accommodation for the less-well positioned traveller in Bulgaria was far from welcoming:

> Bulgaria would be a fairly inexpensive country if it weren't for the price of the hotels. While condemning discrimination abroad Bulgaria has created a mini-apartheid system at home, based on national origin. Western tourists are required to stay at the better Balkantourist hotels. Cheaper local hotels, guesthouses and dormitories are often reserved for Bulgarians only. In Sofia they compromise and let you stay at the 2nd class hotels while paying 1st class prices.
> (Stanley, 1989: 446)

It is in the long shadow of such a travellers' disenfranchised and relatively powerless past[2] that Alexandru Gavriş and Ioan Ianoş explore, in Chapter 20, the recently found power – and useful research resource – of travellers' blogs (Bosangit *et al.*, 2015). Is the 'freedom' to transmit globally positive and negative impressions of places a significant democratisation of the tourism (consumption) process? Does the collective nature of blogging about a particular destination promote images that can influence planning and development processes within those destinations? The examples of the 'marginal' capital cities of Bucharest and Sofia suggest that it can.

And then there are tourism photographs. Millions of them. The online platform *Instagram*, established in 2010, claimed to have 400 million users in 2015, with 58 million posts tagged *#travel* and 21 million with *#holidays*. In June 2015 alone, it was calculated that in excess of 3.8 million travel-related photographs were posted to the app (Coldwell, 2015/16). As with blogs, the impact of digital photography applications on how tourists document their travels is immense. Sharing in real time, 'trending' and the 'viral' consumption and reproduction of images has produced cycles of creation and recreation, highlighting, distorting, even manufacturing destination images and experiences, both as fragments and as totalities. But social media are also to blame for the cult of the 'selfie' (Dinhopl and Gretzel, 2016; Lyu, 2016). This ultimate indulgence of egocentrism – the foreframing of the itinerant self – recruits other places and cultures, as tourism has always done, but to new heights of narcissistic exclusion.

For many, particularly older, travellers, this would seem

> ... arrogant, and a distraction from travel in the purest sense, which is about developing a connection with the place you're in, rather than relentlessly celebrating your being there.
>
> (Coldwell, 2015/16: 73)

If economics has been viewed traditionally as being comprised of millions of small decisions combining to produce large outcomes, then the geopolitical power of the Web, of social media platforms and apps, in harnessing millions of verbal and visual perspectives, is of global significance. And not, of course, merely in relation to destination image.

Thus, the new hegemony of platform providers has facilitated bloggers and others to employ the geopolitics of cyberspace. This shift of power in the definition and promotion of destination images is articulated well in Gavriş and Ianoş's chapter. A liberating force for tourists it may be, but for destination hosts and residents? And what of the apparently divisive and inflationary intervention of such 'facilitators' as *Airbnb*, *Wimdu* and *9Flats* in encouraging the pervasive presence of tourists in residential areas (Arias Sans and Quaglieri Dominguez, 2016; Cole, 2016; Oskam and Boswijk, 2016)? The asymmetry of virtual space geopolitics is a clearly underexplored and evolving area.

Chapter 20 therefore provides empirical support to the growing base of academic tourism research focused on blogs, and contextualises it for an area that is less explored – capital city tourism in less-visited urban spaces.

Endnotes

[1] A facet of what Fregonese (2009) refers to as 'urbicide'.
[2] All of the situations and practices quoted above are, of course, not unknown across Europe to this day.

References

Arias Sans, A. and Quaglieri Dominguez, A. (2016) Unravelling Airbnb. Urban perspectives from Barcelona. In: Paolo Russo, A. and Richards, G. (eds) *Reinventing the Local in Tourism*. Channel View, Bristol, UK, pp. 209–228.

Bosangit, C., Hibbert, S. and McCabe, S. (2015) 'If I was going to die I should at least be having fun': travel blogs, meaning and tourist experience. *Annals of Tourism Research* 55, 1–14.

Čaušević, S. and Lynch, P. (2013) Political (in)stability and its influence on tourism development. *Tourism Management* 34, 145–157.

Coldwell, W. (2015/16) Something to declare. *Compass* [Cox & Kings, London, UK] 23, 72–73.

Cole, L. (2016) How Airbnb is reshaping our cities. *Geographical* 88(5), 34–39.

Dinhopl, A. and Gretzel, U. (2016) Selfie-taking as touristic looking. *Annals of Tourism Research* 57, 126–139.

Fregonese, S. (2009) The urbicide of Beirut? Geopolitics and the built environment in the Lebanese civil war (1975–1976). *Political Geography* 28, 309–318.

Friis, L. and Murphy, A. (2000) 'Turbo-charged negotiations': the EU and the Stability Pact for South Eastern Europe. *Journal of European Public Policy* 7(5), 767–786.

Gheorghe, M. and Alexandru, I. (2001) Géopolitique regionale et évolution du tourisme international en Roumanie. [Regional geopolitics and the evolution of international tourism in Romania.] *Geographica Slovenica* 34(1), 177–188 (in French).

Kurtović, L. (2015) 'Who sows hunger, reaps rage': on protest, indignation and redistributive justice in post-Dayton Bosnia–Herzegovina. *Southeast European and Black Sea Studies* 15(4), 639–659.

Lyu, S.O. (2016) Travel selfies on social media as objectified self-presentation. *Tourism Management* 54, 185–195.

Maistorović, D., Vučkovac, Z. and Pepić, A. (2015) From Dayton to Brussels via Tuzla: post-2014 economic restructuring as europeanization discourse/practice in Bosnia and Herzegovina. *Southeast European and Black Sea Studies* 15(4), 661–682.

Marschall, S. (2015) Tourism memories of the erased city: memory, tourism and notions of 'home'. *Tourism Geographies* 17(3), 332–349.

Mujkić, A. (2015) In search of democratic counter-power in Bosnia–Herzegovina. *Southeast European and Black Sea Studies* 15(4), 623–638.

Novelli, M., Morgan, N. and Nibigira, C. (2012) Tourism in a post-conflict situation of fragility. *Annals of Tourism Research* 39(3), 1446–1469.

Oskam, J. and Boswijk, A. (2016) Airbnb: the future of networked hospitality businesses. *Journal of Tourism Futures* 2(1), 22–42.

Smith, A. (2002) Imagining geographies of the 'new Europe': geo-economic power and the new European architecture on integration. *Political Geography* 21, 647–670.

Stanley, D. (1989) *Eastern Europe on a Shoestring*. Lonely Planet, Hawthorn, Victoria, Australia.

Tamminem, T. (2011) *Des Frontières Convoitées aux Marches de l'Union Européenne: la Gouvernance Européenne de l'Espace Politique dans les Balkans du Sud après la Guerre du Kosovo (1999–2008).* [*The Coveted Frontiers of EU Borderlands: European Governance of Political Space in the South Balkans after the Kosovo Conflict (1999–2008).*] Tampere University Press, Tampere, Finland (in French).

Todorova, M. (1997) *Imagining the Balkans*. Oxford University Press, Oxford, UK.

Wight, A.C. (2016) Lithuanian genocide heritage as discursive formation. *Annals of Tourism Research* 59, 60–78.

World Bank (2000) *The Road to Stability and Prosperity in South East Europe: A Regional Strategy*. World Bank, Washington, DC.

16 Multi-ethnic Food in the Mono-ethnic City: Tourism, Gastronomy and Identity in Central Warsaw

Marta Derek*

Faculty of Geography and Regional Studies, University of Warsaw, Poland

16.1 Introduction

Exotic restaurants featuring cuisine from other lands are an integral part of the urban landscape. Although they have existed for many centuries, historically their patrons belonged to the same ethnic group as the restaurant owners. Beginning in the second half of the 20th century, the trend has gradually changed – ethnic bars and restaurants have become popular with both the local population and tourists who are eager to discover ethnic diversity. Moreover, ethnic food outlets are operated by both members of the respective community and others.

World War II and subsequent geopolitical changes turned Poland into a mono-ethnic country. During the communist era, eating out was not part of Polish culture. Families and friends tended to look to themselves within their homes to provide entertainment and eat together, rather than going out formally – a trend that is still common nowadays. For around 40 years, catering services were state controlled and monocultural. Before the transition to a market economy in 1990, the sector was of very little importance. Despite this history, however, ethnic gastronomy reached Poland, notably in its principal cities. The multi-ethnic cuisines that sprang up reflect an attractive world that Poland was cut off from for many years.

This chapter explores how global trends in multi-ethnic food are articulated in the mono-ethnic city of Warsaw. Taking the city's central borough, *Śródmieście*, as a case study, we discuss the importance of ethnic gastronomy in 'globalising' the local population. Up to 31% of central Warsaw's eating establishments offer ethnic cuisine. However, their principal market is not tourists but local residents and workers, who have become 'taste tourists'. This 'eating to travel' trend is driven by globalisation, which has exerted a strong influence on Polish eating habits generally.

16.2 Current Catering Facilities in Cities

Catering facilities are among the most frequently used tourism services (Ashworth and Tunbridge, 1990). Tourism studies have considered them either as secondary elements or as important tourism facilities (Jansen-Verbeke, 1986; Law, 1993; Page, 1995; Page and Hall, 2003). However, many such facilities are used primarily by local residents: food is a necessity, but it is also an important cultural element. People eat out both because there is no alternative available at home and for pleasure. For example, Warde and

**E-mail: m.derek@uw.edu.pl

Martens (2000) note that in the UK, eating out for pleasure has become increasingly widespread over the past 100 years. In cities, where it is difficult to distinguish between residents and tourists, many establishments reflect the needs of the local community and tourism only complements the existing usage pattern (Page, 1995).

In large cities, restaurants, bars and cafes have manifold roles, and food consumption is only one angle of approach. These establishments can play an important role in creating the urban product; they broaden the appeal of a city and attract new workers and residents. As Clark (2003) suggests, people who are considering where to live and work have more than food on their plate:

> The presence of distinct restaurants redefines the local context, even for persons who do not eat in them. They are part of the local market baskets of amenities that vary from place to place.
>
> (Clark, 2003: 104)

Restaurants and bars can be considered as services associated with gentrification (e.g. Cook and Crang, 1996; Terhorst *et al.*, 2003; Maitland and Newman, 2008). Together with studios and offices, antique shops and art galleries, their impact on the urban space cannot be neglected.

One notable phenomenon in the expansion of eating establishments over the past few decades is the increase in the number of restaurants and bars serving ethnic cuisines. They are particularly visible in large cities, which van den Berghe calls 'the most fertile ground for the blossoming of ethnic cuisines'. He goes on to note that in the urban context,

> ethnic cuisines flourish not only within the confines of the urban ethnic community; it jumps across ethnic boundaries and gets marketed as a form of internal tourism.
>
> (van den Berghe, 1984: 393)

Driver (1983, cited in Warde, 1998), in his study of the UK, attributes the expansion of ethnic restaurants and bars to immigration, entrepreneurial ambition among migrant communities and the ability to adapt exotic cuisines to British tastes. While 30 or 40 years ago the growing number of ethnic eateries was not the result of consumer demand, it clearly is the case now. Cities foster the expansion of ethnic restaurants

and bars as a way to demonstrate their cosmopolitan outlook. As Molz suggests, cities

> seek to attract a greater variety of foreign food outlets to demonstrate their urban worldliness and appeal to a growing taste for diversity.
>
> (Molz, 2007: 80)

16.3 The Development of Ethnic Gastronomy in Cities

History shows that ethnic restaurants have been popular in cities through the ages. In medieval times, Jewish restaurants were found in Warsaw, Kraków and Prague, while Armenian eateries were popular in Lviv. However, their patrons belonged to the same ethnic group as the restaurant owners (Kowalczyk and Derek, 2010). In North America, Gabaccia (1998) noted that in the 1900s, consumers lacked cosmopolitan palates and bought much of their food from entrepreneurs 'of their own kind'. The phenomenon of ethnic cuisine as an attraction for customers from other ethnic groups was not seen until the second half of the 20th century. In the UK, for example, the rapid expansion of Chinese, Indian and Middle Eastern restaurants took place between the mid-1950s and the mid-1970s (Driver, 1983, cited in Warde and Martens, 2000). In the USA, the appearance of restaurants offering ethnic cuisine accelerated during the 1970s and 1980s (Turgeon and Pastinelli, 2002).

The popularity of ethnic cuisines has been influenced by geopolitical processes. A number of studies suggest that globalisation processes are responsible for changes in food consumption in the tourism sector (e.g. Warde, 1998; Hall and Mitchell, 2002; Richards, 2002; Mak *et al.*, 2012). These ongoing processes have increased both the supply and the demand for ethnic food. Supply is not only reflected in the increased mobility of people (labour and migrants) but also in the ideas, products, technologies and services that have influenced the food that is available. Changes in transport and technology mean that the industrial world has better access to a greater range of foods and produce than ever before (Hall and Mitchell, 2002), while global distribution has made it possible to prepare and supply diverse menus. As Cook and Crang put it, we can 'give our tongues a holiday' because a world of 'foreigners' and 'foreign flavours' has come to cosmopolitan London.

(Cook and Crang, 1996: 137)

On the demand side, mobile tourists have become more adventurous in what they eat. Travelling creates another source of demand – on returning home, tourists seek to extend their holiday by visiting a restaurant that serves the cuisine of the country or region they have just visited. Their consumption patterns change; what was once foreign is now local (Hall *et al.*, 2003). As Richards points out,

> tourists themselves are contributing to gastronomic mobility, by creating a demand in their own countries for foods they have encountered abroad.

(Richards, 2002: 3)

This influence can also work in the opposite direction. Cohen and Avieli (2004) argue that tourists' familiarity with ethnic cuisines mitigates their reluctance to patronise local eateries (see also Turgeon and Pastinelli, 2002), although this effect is more limited, for a number of reasons.

The media is another factor that influences demand for ethnic gastronomy. Culinary programmes shown on television, in food magazines and by 'celebrity chefs' all create new patterns of cooking and eating. As Bell and Valentine note

> recent years have seen the proliferation of food professionals, mediatisers and celebrities ... food writers, critics and broadcasters ... show us not only how to cook, but tell us what, when, where, how – and even why – to eat and drink. ... the food media make stars of the foodstuffs themselves.

(Bell and Valentine, 1997: 5–6)

Ethnic foods have become another star. Evidence for the trend is seen in supermarkets, which have introduced dedicated oriental food aisles (e.g. Carrefours in Warsaw), or 'ethnic weeks', where products from a particular country or region are promoted (e.g. Lidl in Poland runs Italian, Spanish, French and Asian weeks).

16.4 Ethnic Gastronomy for Local Residents and Tourists

As mentioned earlier, for many years eating establishments were understood as either secondary elements of tourism or as important tourism facilities. Recently, however, eating out on holiday has become not only a necessity but also an attraction. It reflects the 'consumption' of local heritage, comparable to visits to historical sites and museums (Hjalager and Richards, 2002). Tourists not only visit a destination, they also 'taste' it. Restaurants, bars and cafes have become attractions in their own right as places where tourists can enjoy the local food and experience the country's ethnic diversity and culinary traditions. Ethnic food can therefore become part of a multicultural, cosmopolitan urban tourism product. As Molz argues,

> in the case of round-the-world travellers ... culinary tourism is not necessarily about knowing or experiencing another culture through food but rather about using food to perform a sense of adventure, curiosity, adaptability, and openness to any other culture.

(Molz, 2007: 79)

She states that

> culinary tourists are eating the Other (as something distinct from their own culture), but they are also eating the differences between various Others.

(Molz, 2007: 79)

In today's cities, these 'various Others' can be seen in their clusters of ethnic restaurants.

Ethnic gastronomy is very popular among local residents; for them it represents a substitute for travelling, as they can taste the exotic without going to exotic places. Bell and Valentine (1997) talk about 'kitchen table tourism', which refers to the ability to travel without leaving home, town or the city. In a similar vein, Molz (2007) notes that urban consumers in the West can travel vicariously, simply by visiting the ethnic restaurants in their own neighbourhood. This remark is confirmed by Turgeon and Pastinelli (2002) in their study of ethnic restaurants in Quebec, Canada. Furthermore, Zelinsky points out,

> The diners at ethnic restaurants don't go just for the food. They also hunger for an exotic dining experience. Ethnic restaurants offer an effortless journey to a distant land where the waiter recites a menu of alien delights in charmingly accented English.

(Zelinsky, 1987; cited in Mitchell and Hall, 2003: 76)

Some authors have argued that eating in such places represents culinary tourism, which occurs when people 'travel to eat' local delicacies abroad, and when they 'eat to travel' by consuming foreign foods at home (Molz, 2007).

16.5 Eating Out: A Recent Phenomenon in Post-communist Warsaw

Warsaw is Poland's biggest city and number one tourist destination (2.9 million tourists in 2014, 37% of whom were foreigners).[1] Large parts of the city were destroyed during World War II. It was initially rebuilt under the communist regime, and since 1989 it has been redeveloped in a totally different geopolitical context. Eating out is a post-1989 phenomenon. Traditionally, Poles ate at home. Before World War II, this reflected the organisation of work (between 1918 and 1939, farmers constituted 60% of the population) and the meaningful social role of the shared meal at home (Domański et al., 2015). At that time, food provided outside of the home was also considered of poor quality, suspicious and unhealthy (Brzostek, 2010).

This trend was reinforced during the communist period, when the vast majority of Poles ate at home. An opinion poll carried out in Warsaw in the 1960s showed that although almost 34% of the city's residents ate outside the home, the overwhelming majority of these patronised factory canteens, while very few visited restaurants and bars (Peratlatkowicz, 1963). Respondents gave several reasons for this: long waiting times in restaurants, dirty and untidy premises, impolite service, an unpleasant ambience and a lack of menu choice (Peratlatkowicz, 1963). Cost was not necessarily a factor. An average meal in a bar was something that many people could have afforded; the problem was its usually poor quality. In many memories from that time, the food is described as basically inedible (Brzostek, 2010). A better meal was, in turn, expensive, and therefore only more affluent consumers could have afforded it.

Another reason for not eating out was simply a lack of establishments: in the mid-1960s, there were around 350 eating establishments in Warsaw, compared to more than 1500 in Budapest and a similar number in Prague (Brzostek, 2010). The culinary symbol of the period was the so-called 'milk bar' (bar mleczny), a cheap, state-subsidised, self-service canteen that offered a few dairy-based dishes. It should be underscored, however, that the situation of the catering sector evolved in parallel with regard to the political change occurring through the various stages of communism between 1945 and 1989.

The proliferation of eating establishments began in the 1980s and early 1990s. In big cities, it was manifested in two contradictory trends: cheap Vietnamese (called Chinese) street food on the one hand and expensive, luxury restaurants catering for an expanding number of affluent groups within post-communist society on the other (Sarzyński, 2009). Over the next few years, an increasingly wealthy society and lifestyle changes led to further expansion of both the number and range of opportunities, although the situation remained far from that found in Western Europe. According to statistics from the Polish magazine Polityka, a typical Pole spent €140 in restaurants, cafes and bars per year, compared to €901 in France, €806 in Spain, €775 in Germany and €739 in the UK (Sarzyński, 2009). Research conducted by Domański et al. (2015) suggests that 55% of Poles eat out in a restaurant at least once a year. Research has shown that the young are the most active: 83.6% of 15- to 25-year-olds declare they go to a restaurant, while the proportion decreases with age, falling to 41% for those over 65 years of age. Other important factors are level of education (84.2% with university degrees eat out compared to 13.1% of those who finished only basic compulsory school), work and social status. These findings reinforce the understanding that restaurants in Poland are patronised mostly by the middle class, and, unsurprisingly, that this can be explained primarily in financial terms (Domański et al., 2015). However, if we look at more day-to-day practices, only 2% of Poles eat out in a restaurant a few times a week, 2.8% do so once a week, 20% once a month and 27.8% a few times per year (Domański et al., 2015). This study is consistent with other research reporting statistics for eating out not only in restaurants but also in other catering facilities (Felisiak, 2014), and suggests that most people eat out only for special social occasions. This means that, in Poland, eating out remains a niche phenomenon, despite its recent expansion. Cost is an important factor. Consequently, gastronomy is not big business in Poland, and this is reflected in the ethnic characteristics of the establishment owners.

16.6   The Mono-ethnic City of Warsaw…

Unlike many other European metropolises, contemporary Warsaw lacks ethnic diversity and ethnic districts. Since 1945, Poland has been an overwhelmingly mono-ethnic and monocultural country: according to the national census of 2011, up to 97% of Poland's inhabitants declared themselves as Poles. With respect to migrants, official statistics show that there were only 175,066 foreigners (0.45% of the population) in the country at the end of 2014. The largest groups were (in thousands): Ukrainians (41), Germans (20.2), Russians (10.7), Belarusians (9.9), Vietnamese (9), Italians (5.6), French (4.8), Chinese (4.8), Bulgarians (4.5) and British (4.5). Regarding Warsaw in particular, estimates of the number of migrants fluctuate between 10,700 and 45,000 (Winiarska, 2014) (the number varies depending on the source and data collection method). This is equivalent to a mere 0.6–2.5% of the resident population. Even assuming that these numbers are underestimates (illegal immigration is not taken into account in official statistics), foreigners are still very much a 'niche phenomenon' in both Warsaw and Poland. Given these low numbers of migrants, Warsaw can be termed a mono-ethnic city. It is difficult to identify any ethnic districts or enclaves, although migrants tend to congregate in certain parts of the city. Therefore, the question arises: how can ethnic cuisine exist in a mono-ethnic city such as Warsaw?

16.7   … and Its Multi-ethnic Food

In the communist period, outlets offering ethnic food were extremely rare. There was, however, a 'recommendation' for opening restaurants featuring cuisines from other socialist countries (one restaurant per one country) in big cities. These actions were supported by interstate agreements, as this was the only way to ensure the supply to these restaurants of products normally unavailable on the market (Brzostek, 2010). As a result, between the 1950s and 1970s, restaurants serving Russian ('Trojka'), Chinese ('Szanghaj') and Bulgarian ('Sofia') cuisines were opened in Warsaw. It should be noted that this trend was common in many CEE capitals, where restaurants called 'Warschau', 'Bukareszt', 'Budapest' or 'Habana' were being opened at that time (Brzostek, 2010).

Even though these establishments were successful, they could not have changed the generally non-existent ethnic catering sector in Warsaw during communist times. Ethnic gastronomy began to spring up from the beginning of the 1990s. Cetnarska and Kowalczyk (1995) showed that in 1994 there were 45 establishments serving ethnic cuisines. Most (40; 88.8%) were concentrated in the city centre. Seven years later, research by Kaczorek (2002) indicated that their number had increased to 422; a more than tenfold increase. These ethnic eateries offered 29 different cuisines and constituted 20% of all catering establishments. Under half (130; 36.5%) were located in Warsaw's central borough, Śródmieście, where services such as public administration, trade, education, science, culture, health and transport were concentrated. It is also the city's most important tourist district, with more than half of hotel beds and many tourist attractions. The comparison of these two studies suggests that between 1994 and 2001, not only the number of establishments but also their location changed. Restaurants and bars moved out of the city centre to residential areas (Kaczorek, 2002; Kaczorek and Kowalczyk, 2003).

More than 10 years later, research conducted by the current author (Derek, 2013) in Śródmieście showed that between 2001 and 2013, the number of ethnic eateries had continued to grow.[2] This study focused on bars and restaurants that provided meals on the premises, while other catering facilities (such as takeaway food establishments) were not taken into account. The results are shown in Table 16.1 and Fig. 16.1. A total of 191 establishments (131 restaurants and 60 bars) were identified, reflecting a growth rate of 45% compared to 2001. They served 30 different cuisines and constituted

Table 16.1. Restaurants and bars serving ethnic food compared to other culinary establishments in Warsaw's borough of *Śródmieście*, 2013. (From Derek, 2013.)

Type of cuisine	Restaurants	Bars	Total
Establishments serving ethnic food, by cuisine:	131	60	191
Italian	37	1	38
Japanese	25	5	30
Turkish and Middle Eastern	0	20	20
Asian	6	12	18
Vietnamese	5	12	17
French	8	1	9
Indian	7	0	7
Mexican	7	0	7
Thai	3	3	6
American	3	3	6
Chinese	3	2	5
Spanish	4	0	4
Other ethnic cuisines[a]	23	1	24
Polish cuisine	58	6	64
Other eating establishments	157	200	357
Total	**346**	**266**	**612**

Note: [a]Cuisines served in just one or two establishments: Balkan, Bulgarian, Georgian, Lebanese, Russian, German, Argentine, Brazilian, Czech, Flemish, Galician, Greek, Japanese–Korean, Yemeni, Nepalese, Nigerian, Ukrainian and Hungarian.

31% of all culinary establishments, indicating that facilities had grown in popularity.

The study showed that the most popular cuisines in Warsaw reflected global trends: Italian, Japanese, Turkish and Middle Eastern, Asian or Vietnamese. With one exception, none were established as a result of in-migration.

Italian cuisine was the most popular (38 establishments, 20% of all ethnic restaurants and bars; Fig. 16.1), but it was neither specific to Warsaw nor to Poland. Italian cuisine has enjoyed a worldwide reputation since the 1970s. Its success is connected to two developments: the large-scale emigration of Italians to North America, and its compatibility with modern eating habits and cooking styles (Hjalager and Antonioli Corigliano, 2000). It is currently one of the most popular cuisines in Europe and the USA. For example, the survey conducted by Warde and Martens (2000) of 576 people in the UK showed that Italian was the most popular ethnic cuisine. Similarly, Brożek (2007) found that it was also the most popular ethnic cuisine in the centre of Warsaw in 2003. However, Derek (2013) showed that only 13 out of 38 restaurants or bars were owned or managed by an Italian. Which raises the question of how ethnic is ethnic food?

Another example of a global cuisine that is popular in central Warsaw is Japanese (30 establishments, 16% of all ethnic restaurants and bars; Fig. 16.1). Unlike Italian cuisine, this is a very recent phenomenon in the capital city. The first Japanese restaurant (called 'Tokyo') was established in 1992, and by 2003 there were still only four such restaurants in the central borough (Brożek, 2007). However, the owner of one Japanese restaurant, interviewed for a culinary magazine 5 years later, suggested that between 2003 and 2008 more than 120 'sushi establishments' had been opened in Warsaw and its surroundings (Ignacionek, 2008). This phenomenon is more the result of global trends, termed by Scarpato and Daniele (2002: 301) as 'global sushization', than the presence of a significant Japanese diaspora. Bestor points out,

> from an exotic, almost unpalatable ethnic specialty, then to haute cuisine of the most rarefied sort, sushi has become not just cool, but popular,

> (Bestor, 2000: 56–57)

and argues that the process took off in the 1970s in North America.

Derek (2013) showed that out of the 30 Japanese establishments in the city centre, only

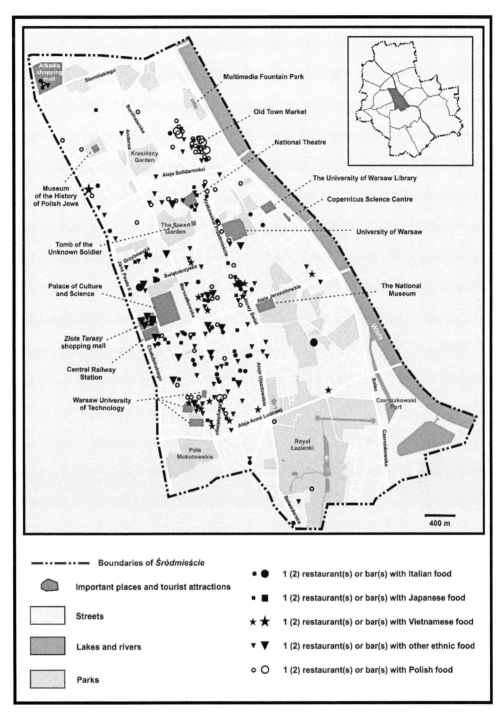

Fig. 16.1. Spatial distribution of restaurants and bars serving ethnic food in Warsaw's borough of *Śródmieście*, 2013. (From author's own fieldwork.)

6 had a Japanese owner or chef, while 3 had a Korean chef. In 13 establishments, neither the owner nor the staff were Japanese or Korean. Once again, this raises questions about the authenticity of this 'ethnic' cuisine. Yet, as Bestor suggests, the phenomenon is consistent with global trends,

> throughout the world, sushi restaurants operated by Koreans, Chinese, or Vietnamese maintain Japanese identities. In sushi bars from Boston to Valencia, a customer's simple greeting in Japanese can throw chefs into a panic.
>
> (Bestor, 2000: 61)

The only cuisine that is both popular and based on a long history of immigration into Warsaw is Vietnamese (17 establishments, 9% of all ethnic restaurants and bars; Fig. 16.1). Although Asian cuisine has a longstanding international reputation, in this case the reasons for the phenomenon are different. Vietnamese migrants make up the biggest ethnic group (from outside Europe) in Poland, and the population is estimated to be up to 30–35,000 (although official statistics suggest a much lower figure, as mentioned above). The first arrivals were students, who were the subject of international agreements between Poland and the then Democratic Republic of Vietnam designed to strengthen cooperation between the two countries during the communist period (Halik, 2008). At that time, Poland actively supported the development of solidarity between countries from the Soviet Bloc and the developing world. Approximately 4000 students arrived in the 1960s and 1970s. In the 1970s, they constituted the biggest group of foreign students (about 30% of the total).

These pioneers laid the groundwork for the subsequent, more numerous, waves of economic migrants in the 1990s and after Poland's 2004 EU accession. Research shows that the Vietnamese work mostly in trade and catering. The majority are self-employed or work for other Vietnamese, notably in microenterprises (Wysieńska, 2012). Consequently, the results of the research reported in Derek (2013) are unsurprising: in 15 of the 17 'Vietnamese' bars or restaurants, either the chef or the owner (or very often both) was Vietnamese, and in many cases the staff also. Furthermore, Vietnamese owned or cooked in many other establishments serving Asian cuisine (13 out of 18 Asian eateries).

It would be reasonable to expect, therefore, that the food served in these establishments is authentically ethnic.

However, this is not always the case. An interesting study of the evolution of the authenticity of Vietnamese food in Warsaw is given by Szymańska-Matusiewicz (2012). She argued that in the 1990s and at the beginning of the 2000s, Vietnamese cuisine was adapted to Polish tastes and became far from 'authentic'. In the second half of the 2010s, however, the trend changed and 'real' ethnic food (re)appeared. Customers, especially younger ones, began to patronise bars that served food to native Vietnamese in their workplaces (notably in the *Stadion Dziesięciolecia*, a huge former outdoor market famous for its multi-ethnic traders). This can be seen as a part of a global phenomenon, described in the following terms by Bell and Valentine:

> a true cosmopolitan would, of course, pour scorn on corporate chains peddling 'inauthentic' cuisines, and search for out-of-the-way places where the genuine article is still available, untouched by homogenising forces.
>
> (Bell and Valentine, 1997: 117)

Vietnamese eating establishments quickly responded to demand by changing their menus. As a result, *pho*, a traditional noodle soup, is now on the menu of most Vietnamese bars or restaurants (Szymańska-Matusiewicz, 2012). Nonetheless, one of the most popular dishes is still 'breaded chicken' (*kurczak w cieście*), a dish that is far-removed from authentic ethnic food.

16.8   Discussion

Warsaw has a relatively small non-Polish resident population, but, paradoxically, a high proportion of ethnic restaurants and bars. However, these food outlets do not reflect migration and mobility trends. Official statistics show that the largest groups of migrants are Ukrainians, Germans and Russians – but none has developed a culinary presence. The only notable ethnic group operating in the catering business is Vietnamese. Other dominant cuisines are those found elsewhere in the West: Italian and Japanese. The relatively large Italian, French and British communities in Warsaw work in transnational corporations rather than run their own restaurants (a relatively poor business opportunity). This suggests that migration, considered to be one of the most important influences on eating habits, is being replaced by global trends. This leads to disparities between the ethnic nature of the food that is served and the ethnicity of the people involved in its management and production. It is doubtful how much of the food prepared by non-ethnic staff is authentic, assuming that there is such a thing as 'authentic' cuisine.

This trend is, of course, not limited to Poland. Harbottle (1997; cited in Warde, 1998) shows that most chefs in French restaurants in Britain are not French, and that Greek and Turkish outlets are managed primarily by Iranians. Moreover, as Kalcik points out, one does not have to be authentic to be ethnic,

> The authenticity of recipes and other foodways is not as important as the fact of making what is a recognizably ethnic dish. Practitioners of ethnic cookery have developed substitutes, or significant modifications, which are acceptable because the use of the food so presented is symbolic.
>
> (Kalcik, 1984: 56)

Ethnic food outlets in Warsaw cater for locals rather than tourists. Unlike many Western European cities, there are no distinct ethnic districts that could become tourist attractions. Ethnic food is not a well-established element of the 'urban product', its authenticity is questionable and it does not seem to be an important tourist attraction.

Most outlets are located in the south-eastern part of the Śródmieście (Fig. 16.1), an area with a high concentration of offices, ministries and higher education. Apart from local residents, the business community is the main target for establishments in the area. Their location suggests that short-term business travellers and convention attendees have a significant (but not crucial) role, but there is no published research to confirm this hypothesis.

Tourists congregate in the Old Town, where most eating establishments serve Polish cuisine (Fig. 16.1). The area is more popular with foreign tourists than with national tourists, and it is reasonable to expect that non-Polish visitors are the main target group. A 2014 survey of domestic and international visitors shows that out of all of the foreign tourists who visit Warsaw,

60% visit this area. On the other hand, it is on the itinerary of only 37% of domestic tourists who visit the city (Ipsos, 2014). For their part, foreign tourists appear to be more interested in Polish than in other ethnic cuisines.

Ethnic restaurants remain an important attraction for local residents, in the form of 'kitchen-table tourism' (Bell and Valentine, 1997). Ethnic food acts as a substitute for travelling – people 'eat to travel'. This raises the question of the consequences of such behaviours. As mentioned earlier, exotic cuisines encourage people to travel to other countries, a phenomenon that Mitchell and Hall (2003) call the pre-travel phase of the food tourism experience. Conversely, travelling encourages people to taste different food back at home. However, a further insight into these relations is provided by Gwiazdowska and Kowalczyk (2015), who asked 330 students of the University of Warsaw about their eating and travelling habits. They found a weak relationship between travelling abroad and tasting other cuisines, and concluded that the current context of globalisation, the Internet and migration meant that travelling was only one reason for wanting to taste other cuisines.

Another interesting aspect of the Polish context relates to outbound tourism statistics. The 'top ten' countries visited by Polish tourists are Germany, the UK, Italy, the Czech Republic, France, Spain, Croatia, Greece, Austria and Slovakia (Janczak and Patelak, 2014). With the exception of Italy, none of these countries are well represented by eating establishments in Warsaw. On the other hand, neither Vietnam nor Japan appears in the top ten. In fact, these two countries do not appear in official statistics at all, as they only include countries receiving annually more than 100,000 Polish tourists. We can therefore conclude that ethnic food does not encourage Polish people to travel (at least not to the countries associated with many of Warsaw's ethnic food restaurants), and that eating in ethnic restaurants and bars seems to be a substitute, rather than an incentive, for travel. Further research could explore this phenomenon in more detail.

Poles rarely ate out during the communist period, due mainly to poor-quality food and a lack of eating establishments. It is ironic that this period saw the arrival of the 'core' of the now dominant ethnic cuisine entrepreneurs (the Vietnamese). Although at that time they were students, rather than restaurant owners, their presence in Warsaw laid the ground for later waves of immigrants who arrived from the 1990s. Finally, it should be noted that although the communist period witnessed the arrival of immigrants from many other developing countries, none have had such a significant influence on the development of cuisine.

16.9   Conclusions

Beginning in 1989, Poland has experienced a tremendous change in its political, economic, social and cultural environment. The collapse of communism and the transition to a market economy was a huge geopolitical change that influenced all areas of life. Poland opened up to the world and began to follow many new, notably Western, trends. One example is eating out – a new practice for Poles. Food outlets began to spring up from 1989, along with greater prosperity and lifestyle changes. Catering services, based on private ownership of the property, were an early development. The proliferation of ethnic restaurants and bars was a significant feature of this process. Nowadays, although ethnic minorities have never had a significant presence in Warsaw, either in terms of numbers or influence, ethnic cuisine is a very visible phenomenon in the city's landscape. Every third restaurant in the central borough of Śródmieście serves ethnic food.

Food is a reflection of global unification trends in cities, urban spaces and tourist destinations. It is also an important element of globalisation. Consequently, the large number of Italian or Japanese restaurants in Warsaw, despite an absence of appropriate ethnic minority residents, should not be surprising. Globalisation has made many national, local or regional dishes international. The growth in ethnic restaurants reflects global trends far more than migration patterns. As Scarpato and Daniele note,

the sense of place has completely been reshaped in a global village that is no longer only a geographic dimension but, instead, the result of a new cartography drawn according to the characteristics of different lifestyles.

(Scarpato and Daniele, 2002: 302)

Drawing on Derek (2013), we observe that ethnic gastronomy is an important factor in 'globalising' local populations. The range of ethnic foods available in other European metropolises such as Berlin, Paris or London far outstrips the Polish provision. In these cities, ethnic food is usually prepared and served by members of the appropriate ethnic community. Their cosmopolitan and multicultural character has become an important attraction, especially for international tourists. However, in Poland, ethnic gastronomy is an important attraction for local residents seeking to experience other cultures. In their study conducted in Quebec, Canada, Turgeon and Pastinelli (2002) suggest that eating in ethnic restaurants expresses a desire to explore the world and consume it; similarly, Warsaw residents 'eat to travel'.

More than 150 years ago, Brillat-Savarin (1862) wrote: '*Dis-moi ce que tu manges, je te dirai ce que tu es*' ('Tell me what you eat and I will tell you what you are'). If we apply this aphorism, paraphrased in the saying 'We are what we eat', to the proliferation of ethnic cuisines in Warsaw, it seems that the city's inhabitants are well adapted to the multi-ethnic, globalised world. Furthermore, if the popularity of ethnic cuisines in Warsaw is seen as a reflection of society's geopolitical context, then Poles place themselves firmly in a globalised world, rather than just the Central and Eastern European region. This is seen in the fact that in central Warsaw. the most popular cuisines are those found in many other cities around the world. In contrast, no country within the region has influenced Polish eating habits, despite relatively high levels of immigration from Ukraine, Russia and Belarus. There appears to be no such a thing as a Central European or post-Soviet influence on urban ethnic food outlets. In central Warsaw, there are more Mexican restaurants than Russian, Czech, Hungarian and Ukrainian put together. Poles seem to prefer to travel to the 'global village' rather than to Central and Eastern Europe.

The findings of this chapter are, however, limited to Poland's biggest city. Its cosmopolitan character, as well as its privileged position on the tourist and business map of Poland, renders Warsaw receptive to the development of ethnic gastronomy. Further research is required to find out how the sector's situation looks in other Polish cities and towns. Another interesting direction of future research could be a comparative analysis of Warsaw with other Central and Eastern European capital cities, like Prague, Budapest, Vilnius or Riga. More work is still needed in this area.

Endnotes

[1] Number of tourists who stayed overnight in tourist accommodation establishments with 10 or more beds. Data derived from the Central Statistical Office of Poland (GUS) (http://stat.gov.pl/en/).
[2] The fieldwork took place during October 2013 with the help of students from the Faculty of Geography and Regional Studies, University of Warsaw, studying Tourism Planning and Management.

References

Ashworth, G.J. and Tunbridge, J.E. (1990) *The Tourist-Historic City*. Belhaven, London.
Bell, D. and Valentine, G. (1997) *Consuming Geographies: We Are Where We Eat*. Routledge, Oxford, UK.
Bestor, T.C. (2000) How sushi went global. *Foreign Policy* 121, November–December, 54–63.
Brillat-Savarin, J.A. (1862) *Physiologie du goût or méditations de gastronomie transcendante*. [*Physiology of Taste or Meditations on Transcendental Gastronomy*.] Charpentier, Libraire-Éditeur, Paris (in French).
Brożek, M. (2007) Zmiany w przestrzennym zróżnicowaniu bazy gastronomicznej w dzielnicy Warszawa-Śródmieście na przestrzeni lat 1994–2003. [Changes in spatial differentiation of culinary establishments in Warsaw's borough of Śródmieście between 1994 and 2003]. MSc thesis. University of Warsaw, Faculty of Geography and Regional Studies, Warsaw (in Polish).
Brzostek, B. (2010) *PRL na widelcu*. [*The Polish People's Republic on a Fork*.] Baobab, Warsaw (in Polish).
Cetnarska, H. and Kowalczyk, A. (1995) Infrastruktura turystyczna i paraturystyczna. [Tourist services.] In: Żakowski, W. (ed.) *Warszawa jako centrum turystyczne: raport o stanie turystyki*. [*Warsaw as the tourist centre: a report on tourism*.] University of Warsaw, Faculty of Geography and Regional Studies, and Warsaw City Hall, Department of Sport and Tourism, Warsaw, pp. 23–46 (in Polish).
Clark, T.N. (2003) Urban amenities: lakes, opera, and juice bar: do they drive development? In: Clark, T.N. (ed.) *The City as an Entertainment Machine*. Research in Urban Policy 9. Elsevier, Oxford, UK, pp. 101–140.
Cohen, E. and Avieli, N. (2004) Food in tourism. Attraction and impediment. *Annals of Tourism Research* 31(4), 755–778.
Cook, I. and Crang, P. (1996) The world on a plate: culinary culture, displacement and geographical knowledges. *Journal of Material Culture* 1(2), 131–153.
Derek, M. (2013) Kierunki rozwoju usług gastronomicznych w warszawskiej dzielnicy Śródmieście. [Trends and developments in eating establishments in Warsaw's borough of Śródmieście.] *Prace i Studia Geograficzne* 52, 85–100 (in Polish).
Domański, H., Karpiński, Z., Przybysz, D. and Straczuk, J. (2015) *Wzory jedzenia a struktura społeczna*. [Eating patterns and social structure.] Scholar, Warsaw (in Polish).
Driver, C. (1983) *The British at Table, 1940–80*. Chatto and Windus, London.
Feliksiak, M. (2014) Zachowania żywieniowe Polaków. [Poles' culinary behaviours.] *Komunikat z badań CBOS* 115, CBOS, Warsaw (in Polish).
Gabaccia, D.R. (1998) *We Are What We Eat. Ethnic Food and the Making of Americans*. Harvard University Press, Cambridge, Massachusetts.
Gwiazdowska, K. and Kowalczyk, A. (2015) Zmiany upodobań żywieniowych i zainteresowanie kuchniami etnicznymi – przyczynek do turystyki (kulinarnej?) [Changes in culinary customs and attention to ethnic cuisines – contribution to (culinary?) tourism.] *Turystyka kulturowa* 9, 6–24 (in Polish). Available at: http://turystykakulturowa.org/ojs/index.php/tk/article/view/639/593 (accessed 9 August 2016).
Halik, T. (2008) Relacje polsko-wietnamskie. [Polish–Vietnamese relations.] In: Kulesza, M. and Smagowicz, M. (eds) *Wietnamczycy w Polsce. Perspektywy adaptacji społeczno-zawodowej*. [*The Vietnamese in Poland. Perspectives of socio-professional adaptation*.] Instytut Profilaktyki Społecznej i Resocjalizacji, Uniwersytet Warszawski, Warsaw, pp. 8–22 (in Polish).
Hall, C.M., Sharples, L. and Smith, A. (2003) The experience of consumption or the consumption of experiences? Challenges and issues in food tourism. In: Hall, C.M., Sharples. L., Mitchell, R., Macionis, N. and Cambourne, B. (eds) *Food Tourism Around the World. Development, Management and Markets*. Butterworth-Heinemann, Oxford, UK, pp. 314–335.
Hall, M. and Mitchell, R. (2002) Tourism as a force for gastronomic globalization and localization. In: Hjalager, A.M. and Richards, G. (eds) *Tourism and Gastronomy*. Routledge, London, pp. 71–87.
Harbottle, L. (1997) Fast food/spoiled identity: Iranian migrants in the British catering trade. In: Caplan, P. (ed.) *Food, Identity and Health*. Routledge, London, pp. 87–110.

Hjalager, A.M. and Antonioli Corigliano, M. (2000) Food for tourists – determinants of an image. *International Journal of Tourism Research* 2, 281–293.

Hjalager, A.M. and Richards, G. (2002) *Tourism and Gastronomy.* Routledge, London.

Ignacionek, E. (2008) Sushi – pomysł na biznes. [Sushi – a good idea for business.] *Poradnik Restauratora* 10 (in Polish), Available at: http://www.poradnikrestauratora.com.pl/archiwum/pazdziernik-10-2008, Kultura---Sushi---pomysl-na-biznes,Rok-2008,17,72.html (accessed 9 August 2016).

Ipsos (2014) *Raport z badania opinii turystów odwiedzających Warszawę w 2014 roku. [A Report of the Research on Tourist Flow in Warsaw in 2014.]* Ipsos Sp. z o.o. A report prepared for Warsaw City Hall, Warsaw, (in Polish).

Janczak, K. and Patelak, K. (2014) *Uczestnictwo Polaków w wyjazdach turystycznych w 2013 roku. [Poles' Participation in Tourists' Flow in 2013.]* Łódź, Poland (in Polish). Available at: https://d1dmfej9n5lgmh. cloudfront.net/msport/article_attachments/attachments/74006/original/Aktywno%C5%9B%C4%87_turystyczna_mieszka%C5%84c%C3%B3w_Polski_2013_FINAL_-_14_07_2014.pdf?1435825204 (accessed 17 August 2016).

Jansen-Verbeke, M. (1986) Inner-city tourism: resources, tourists and promoters. *Annals of Tourism Research* 13(1), 79–100.

Kaczorek, A. (2002) Gastronomia etniczna w Warszawie. [Ethnic Gastronomy in Warsaw.] MSc thesis. University of Warsaw, Faculty of Geography and Regional Studies, Warsaw (in Polish).

Kaczorek, A. and Kowalczyk, A. (2003) Modele lokalizacji usług gastronomicznych na obszarach miejskich. [Location models of eating establishments in urban areas.] *Prace i Studia Geograficzne* 32, 191–203 (in Polish).

Kalcik, S. (1984) Ethnic foodways in America: symbol and the performance of identity. In: Keller Brown, L. and Mussell, K. (eds) *Ethnic and Regional Foodways in the United States. The Performance of Group Identity.* University of Tennessee Press, Knoxville, Tennessee, pp. 37–65.

Kowalczyk, A. and Derek, M. (2010) *Zagospodarowanie turystyczne. [Tourism Planning and Management.]* PWN, Warsaw (in Polish).

Law, C.M. (1993) *Urban Tourism. Attracting Visitors to Large Cities*, Mansell, London.

Maitland, R. and Newman, P. (2008) Visitor–host relationships: conviviality between visitors and host communities. In: Hayllar, B., Griffin, T. and Edwards, D. (eds) *City Spaces – Tourist Places: Urban Tourism Precincts.* Butterworth-Heinemann, Oxford, UK, pp. 223–242.

Mak, A.H.N., Lumbers, M. and Eves, A. (2012) Globalisation and food consumption in tourism. *Annals of Tourism Research* 39(1), 171–196.

Mitchell, R. and Hall, C.M. (2003) Consuming tourists: food tourism consumer behavior. In: Hall, C.M., Sharples, L., Mitchell, R., Macionis, N. and Cambourne, B. (eds) *Food Tourism Around the World. Development, Management and Markets.* Butterworth-Heinemann, Oxford, UK, pp. 60–80.

Molz, J.G. (2007) Eating difference. The cosmopolitan mobilities of culinary tourism. *Space and Culture* 1(10), 77–93.

Page, S. (1995) *Urban Tourism.* Routledge, London.

Page, S. and Hall, C.M. (2003) *Managing Urban Tourism.* Pearson Education, Harlow, UK.

Peratlatkowicz, R. (1963) *Gastronomia warszawska w opinii mieszkańców miasta. [Warsaw gastronomy in the opinion of the city's residents.]* OBOP, Warsaw (in Polish). Available at: http://www.tnsglobal.pl/archiwumraportow/1961/11/30/gastronomia-warszawska-w-opinii-mieszkancow-miasta/#more-2171 (accessed 9 August 2016).

Richards, G. (2002) Gastronomy: an essential ingredient in tourism production and consumption? In: Hjalager, A.M. and Richards, G. (eds) *Tourism and Gastronomy.* Routledge, London, pp. 3–20.

Sarzyński, P. (2009) Nowe upodobania kulinarne Polaków. Sushi z kaszą. [The new culinary tastes of Poles. Sushi with groats.] *Polityka*, 26 August (in Polish). Available at: www.polityka.pl/tygodnikpolityka/spoleczenstwo/299628,1,nowe-upodobania-kulinarne-polakow.read (accessed 9 August 2016).

Scarpato, R. and Daniele, R. (2002) New global cuisine: tourism, authenticity and sense of place in postmodern gastronomy. In: Hjalager, A.M. and Richards, G. (eds) *Tourism and Gastronomy.* Routledge, London, pp. 296–313.

Szymańska-Matusiewicz, G. (2012) *Dlaczego Wietnamczycy wyjeżdżają z Polski? [Why Do Vietnamese Leave Poland?]* Komentarz Instytutu Sobieskiego nr 118 (in Polish). Available at: http://www.sobieski.org.pl/komentarz-is-118/ (accessed 9 August 2016).

Terhorst, P., van de Ven, J. and Deben, L. (2003) Amsterdam: it's all in the mix. In: Hoffman, L.M., Fainstein, S.S. and Judd, D.R. (eds) *Cities and Visitors. Regulating People, Markets, and City Space.* Blackwell, Oxford, UK, pp. 75–90.

Turgeon, L. and Pastinelli, M. (2002) 'Eat the world': postcolonial encounters in Quebec City's ethnic restaurants. *Journal of American Folklore* 115(456), 247–268.

van den Berghe, P.L. (1984) Ethnic cuisine: culture in nature. *Ethnic and Racial Studies* 7(3), 387–397.

Warde, A. (1998) Eating globally: cultural flows and the spread of ethnic restaurants. In: Kalb, D., van der Land, M., Staring, R., van Steenbergen, B. and Wilterdink, N. (eds) *The Ends of Globalization. Bringing Society Back In.* Rowman and Littlefield, Lanham, Maryland, pp. 299–316.

Warde, A. and Martens, L. (2000) *Eating Out: Social Differentiation, Consumption and Pleasure.* Cambridge University Press, Cambridge, UK.

Winiarska, A. (2014) *Mapowanie migrantów w Warszawie. [Mapping migrants in Warsaw.]* A draft document prepared for the project: 'Wzmocnienie trafności i skuteczności działań na rzecz cudzoziemców w Warszawie' [Strengthening the relevance and effectiveness of foreigners' actions in Warsaw] conducted by Fundacja Obserwatorium, Urząd Miasta Warszawy, Ośrodek Ewaluacji i Stowarzyszenie Vox Humana for the program Obywatele dla Demokracji [Citizens for Democracy], financed by EOG (in Polish). Available at: http://docplayer.pl/2655375-Mapowanie-migrantow-w-warszawie-opracowanie-wstepne.html (accessed 12 August 2016).

Wysieńska, K. (2012) Społeczność wietnamska w Polsce oraz w wybranych krajach regionu i świata. [The Vietnamese community in Poland and in selected countries of the region and the world.] In: Wysieńska, K. (ed.) *Sprzedawać, gotować, budować? Plany i strategie Chińczyków i Wietnamczyków w Polsce. [To sell, to Cook, to Build? Plans and Strategies of the Chinese and the Vietnamese in Poland.]* Instytut Spraw Publicznych, Warsaw (in Polish).

Zelinsky, W. (1987) You are where you eat. *American Demographics* 9(7), 31–33, 56–61.

17 Rural Tourism as a Meeting Ground in Bosnia and Herzegovina?

Rahman Nurković[1]* and Derek Hall[2]

[1]*Department of Geography, University of Sarajevo, Bosnia and Herzegovina;*
[2]*Seabank Associates, Maidens, Ayrshire, UK*

17.1 Introduction

This chapter raises more questions than it answers. It examines the geopolitical context for the development of tourism in rural areas of Bosnia and Herzegovina (BiH). In so doing, the chapter draws on concepts of inverse peripherality and centrifugal governance, and is set within a context of institutionalised territorial division, derived from the outcomes of previous genocidal conflict. The point of departure for the chapter is informed by two conventional notions:

1. That regional inequalities were intensified by the conflict of the first half of the 1990s and its outcomes. These heightened core–periphery effects at both national and regional levels, with a strong concentration of employment activity reinforced in the four regional centres of Sarajevo, Mostar, Banja Luka and Tuzla (Fig. 17.1) (Nurković, 2012b);
2. That tourism can be perceived as a non-threatening activity (Čaušević, 2010: 48), and that this can apply particularly to tourism in rural areas, which can be

> ...based on promotion of the natural environment and which does not lend itself to ethnic labelling.
> (Čaušević and Lynch, 2013: 148)

17.2 In the Shadow of Dayton

In the aftermath of the Yugoslav wars of accession, the 1995 Dayton Agreement (Box 17.1) reinforced nationalist divisions and left the newly independent state of Bosnia and Herzegovina divided and fragmented.

Underlying such territorial complications is the fact that:

> In Bosnia–Hercegovina there have been three potential 'nations' associated with long-term ethnic cleavages between Croats, Serbs and Muslims. The Bosnian Croats and Bosnian Serbs have been able to link themselves to a greater Croatia and a greater Serbia respectively whilst the Muslims have had an identity defined by their religious affiliation and a territorial dimension related to the former Yugoslav republic of Bosnia–Hercegovina that includes large areas dominated by Croats and Serbs. Hence, in the past, there has been a less clearly stated link between the Muslims and a well-defined territorial claim ... ethnic divisions, etched so profoundly in the recent conflict, were often regarded as relatively insignificant by the Muslims at many times in the past.
> (Robinson *et al.*, 2001: 964)

Designed to assist post-conflict consolidation, but not intended specifically to normalise social relations across the state (Dahlman and

---

*Corresponding author. E-mail: rahmannurkovic@hotmail.com

© CAB International 2017. *Tourism and Geopolitics* (ed D. Hall)

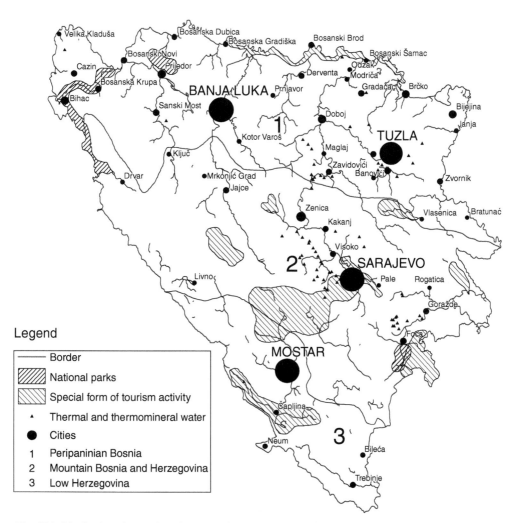

Fig. 17.1. Distribution of natural tourism attractions in Bosnia and Herzegovina. (From first author's compilation.)

ÓTuathail, 2005), Dayton established a fragmented, ethnically based, administrative spatial structure that

> legitimised exclusivist projects ... [through] ... the apartheid-like logic of international diplomacy's political anthropology.
> (Campbell, 1999: 395)

According to Chandler (2000), the Agreement relied on 1991 census maps of ethnicity that then helped determine the nature of partition, despite the highly politicised conditions in which that census was carried out. Dayton conflated 'ethnic' with 'national', producing a partition on ethnic lines to create separate 'national' spaces.

> ...the complex constitution of the country, the enormous numbers of ministries, deputies, canton governments, entities and municipal governments confuse and create problems when it comes to establishing consensus in respect of development agreements ... [such that there is a] reluctance of the officials to commit themselves to a planning process which involves responsibilities and sacrifices.
> (Alipour and Dizdarević, 2007: 217, 211)

Parallel, multiple state-building trajectories persist, confounding international neoliberal development processes (Keranen, 2013). Despite, or perhaps because of, the lack of an overarching body to coordinate tourism, rural and regional development, the country has been

Box 17.1   Key terms of the Dayton Peace Agreement

November 1995 in Dayton, Ohio (USA), the presidents of Bosnia–Herzegovina, Croatia and Yugoslavia (Serbia–Montenegro) signed the peace accord to end 4 years of fighting, to formally establish the Republic of Bosnia and Herzegovina, and to despatch a 60,000-strong NATO-led implementation force to preserve peace.

An international body, the Office of the High Representative (OHR), was established to ensure the implementation of the Agreement.

The State 'government', the Council of Ministers, is responsible for policies and decisions in the fields of diplomacy, economy, inter-entity relations and other matters as agreed by the entities, which are:

• the Federation of Bosnia and Herzegovina (FBiH: 51% territory), partly contiguous with Croatia, was established with ten regional cantons, each of which has its own government; mostly Bosniak (Muslim)-Croat.
• the Republika Srpska (RS: 49% territory), partly contiguous with Serbia, embraced municipal governance; mostly Serb.
• Brčko District, not an 'entity' but located on the border between BiH, Croatia and Serbia, and strategically important for all three ethnic groups, functions as a multi-ethnic district under the provision of the OHR.

Governmental bodies are divided between these three and the State.

These bodies' spatial fragmentation exacerbates the complexity of the country's administrative division (Fig. 17.2).

(From Robinson *et al.*, 2001; Alipour and Dizdarević, 2007; Čaušević and Lynch, 2011.)

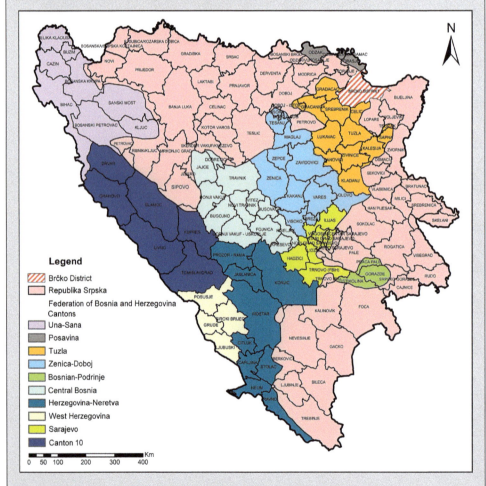

Fig. 17.2. Territorial administrative divisions of Bosnia–Herzegovina. (From first author's compilation.)

awash with exogenously derived plans and strategies; for example, *EU Multi-annual Indicative Planning Document* (European Commission, 2011), *Country Strategy 2011–2013* (Austrian Development Corporation, 2011), *Action Plan for 2015–2017* (Council of Europe, 2015). And according to the European Commission 2015 progress report on BiH,

> Cooperation between the State-level, Entity-level and Brčko District parliaments has yet to be improved.
>
> (European Commission, 2015: 6)

For more than two decades, the potential for tourism development has been constrained by such administrative, political and ethnic division and inconsistent levels of authority and responsibility. For tourism, as in other development sectors, these obstacles have impeded positive image building, brand development, planning and coherent overall policy strategy. Hence, the great irony facing tourism development is the potential for cultural diversity and multi-ethnicity to become one of the most important tourism attractions and branding attributes (Box 17.2), while currently representing one of the greatest obstacles to a comprehensive and systematic branding of Bosnia and Herzegovina as a single tourism destination.

Tourist boards are organised at local level (cantons and municipalities), including two organisations at entity level. A tourism association at the state level has existed, but lacks both a legal basis and financial viability.

Confused and conflicting images are generated by bodies that may be pursuing individual, perhaps even mutually exclusive, competing agendas. Through an analysis of some 12 of the country's various tourist boards' websites, Čutura *et al.* (2008) found an overall disconnection and low level of interactivity, as well as a lack of multilingual pages.

> It is almost absurd that ... most of these web sites cannot be connected with the country of B&H in any way. ... There is no strategy for [the] promotion [of] the image of B&H through the official web sites of tourist boards [and, for example] a visitor of [the] web site of [the] Tourist Organization of Republika Srpska could easily think that this region is situated in [the] Republic of Serbia because of the domain name used (.sr).
>
> (Čutura *et al.*, 2008: 801)

Čutura *et al.* (2008) concluded that the only communication constant they found in the image of Bosnia and Herzegovina on the tourist boards' websites was 'Diversity without unity'.

17.3　Tourism, Rural Development and Division

Several researchers from within the country have pointed to the 'important differences which exist between rural areas'. And while this '[d]iversity of rural areas is [a] significant element of the rural development policy, as well as [the] development of agro-tourism' (Ćejvanović *et al.*, 2009: 8), this argument is almost promoted as a rural development justification, or at least explanation, for the

---

Box 17.2　Critical imagery of Bosnia and Herzegovina (BiH)

Lonely Planet guidebook

> Bosnia and Hercegovina (BiH) describes itself as the 'heart-shaped land', which is surprisingly accurate anatomically. Emotionally too, the deep yet unimposing human warmth of this craggily beautiful country fits the bill ... rekindling that intriguing East-meets-West atmosphere born of Bosnia's fascinatingly blended Ottoman and Austro-Hungarian histories.
>
> (Elliott, 2009: 101)

UK Foreign Office Advisory

> Unexploded landmines remain a real danger, particularly in isolated areas in the mountains and countryside.... Flooding and landslides, in part due to heavy rainfall in May and August 2014 have also moved minefields and destroyed minefield markings. ... Protests, often at short notice, can be expected across major cities in Bosnia and Herzegovina. ... Most visits to Bosnia and Herzegovina are trouble-free.
>
> (FCO, 2016)

continued spatial administrative separation and fragmentation within the country.

BiH does not have a common policy for rural development, and basic principles of regional policy to sustain rural and regional development are poorly represented or absent (Mirjanić and Rokvić, 2013). Yet, of course, the sustainability of rural areas requires the implementation of a strong development policy.[1]

Rural areas in Bosnia and Herzegovina represent a significant share of its territory and society. They cover more than 90% of the territory and are inhabited by 57.2% of the population (BHAS, 2014). The most economically active demographic group – the 25- to 49-year-olds – is least well represented in agrarian areas. But the last official census data available covering the whole country are from 1991,[2] since when the spatial and structural nature of the country's population has changed dramatically (Nurković, 2013). Estimates suggest that while the country's population increased by 5% between 1991 and 2010, the rural population decreased by that proportion (Nurković, 2012b), and rural depopulation continues. Hidden rural unemployment is substantial.

Given the importance of Serbia and Croatia for their co-ethnics in BiH, there is much cross-border participation in different forms of mobility. In 2015, about 15,500 BiH residents were recorded as travelling on a daily basis for work to Croatia, Serbia or Montenegro (Nurković, 2012a; BHAS, 2016).

Tourism is now regarded as one of the leading branches of the BiH (rural) economy (Mlinarević *et al.*, 2008), but a wide range of constraints persist to inhibit a unified and coordinated approach to tourism planning and development (Box 17.3).

Box 17.3 Constraints on tourism planning and development

Structural

- symbolic structural violence is embedded within the post-Dayton social territorial structures
- dominance of elites with vested interests
- large, duplicated bureaucracies
- dependency on foreign economic aid, yet insufficient foreign capital investment
- significant grey economy, including tourism tax fraud
- unreliable statistical data partly resulting from such fraud
- overall fragmentation of tourism organisation, with tourism clusters operating independently from each other with a duplication of tasks and focus on short-term aims
- consequent unclear framework structures for tourism development initiatives
- poor infrastructure development, especially obsolete and war-damaged transport and communication
- inconsistent quality of accommodation
- lack of overarching support and information for cross-cultural cooperation

Operational

- lack of strategic indicators of destination planning
- absence of environmental analysis
- lack of overall destination community vision
- inability to implement key principles of sustainable development
- planning limited to superficial overviews
- little interest in pursuing a comprehensive or holistic approach
- lack of interpretive materials in potential source market languages
- poor marketing
- persistence of minefields and isolated explosives in a number of rural areas

Exogenous

- absence of low-cost airlines
- continuing external perceptions of political instability and conflict
- strong re-emergence of Croatia and Slovenia, and to some extent Montenegro, as competing destinations

(From Alipour and Dizdarević, 2007; Nastav and Bojnec, 2007; Vitic and Ringer, 2007; Nurković, 2009, 2013; Čaušević and Lynch, 2013; Morić, 2013b.)

Until recently, the tourism sector had not been important within the country. But in terms of overall visitor numbers and overnight stays, the volume of tourism is gradually returning to pre-conflict levels (Figs 17.3 and 17.4). Most foreign tourists continue to be from other countries of the former Yugoslavia (Fig. 17.5, Table 17.1).

In the face of a tradition of heavy industry and powerful energy and forestry interests, the tourism lobby remained weak. Within the former Yugoslav federation, tourism tended to be associated with the seaside (Kobasić, 1981), although the long importance of winter sports centres (reinforced by the 1984 winter Olympics) and spa resorts, and the pilgrimage role of Medūgorje after the 1981 'apparition' there, represented important inland attractions within BiH. Rural tourism was poorly developed (Table 17.2), but the United Nations World Tourism Organization (UNWTO) has shown that demand for services on family-owned farms has been constantly growing globally since around 1995, and that the highest growth rates have been recorded in some countries of southern and eastern Europe

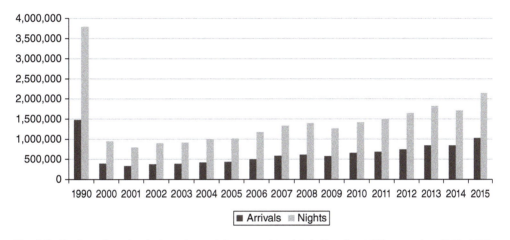

Fig. 17.3. Total number of arrivals and overnight stays of tourists in Bosnia and Herzegovina, 1990–2015. (From BHAS, 1990–2015.)

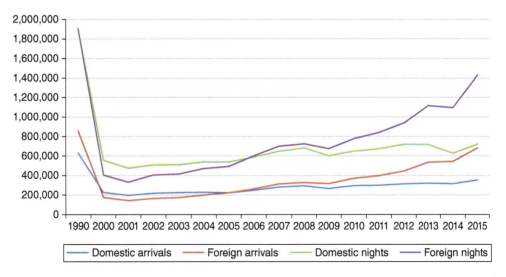

Fig. 17.4. Arrivals and nights of domestic and foreign tourists in Bosnia and Herzegovina, 1990–2015. (From BHAS, 1990–2015.)

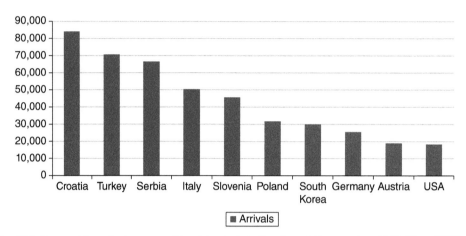

Fig. 17.5. Ten most important sources of tourist arrivals in Bosnia and Herzegovina, 2015. (From BHAS, 1990–2015.)

Table 17.1. Most important sources of foreign tourists and overnight stays in Bosnia and Herzegovina, 2007–2015. (From BHAS, 2007–2015.)

Countries	Arrivals/*Overnight stays* (thousands)				
	2007	2009	2011	2013	2015
Croatia	50.2	50.8	64.0	82.2	84.1
	108.1	*93.6*	*130.3*	*169.9*	*187.8*
Turkey	11.3	13.7	25.9	55.7	70.7
	29.1	*31.9*	*50.4*	*105.4*	*121.6*
Serbia	56.9	56.2	54.2	62.7	66.5
	131.5	*120.9*	*114.4*	*131.6*	*138.0*
Italy	17.6	15.4	26.4	29.3	50.3
	33.1	*32.7*	*54.5*	*62.7*	*122.3*
Slovenia	36.4	34.6	41.3	42.0	45.6
	68.3	*60.8*	*70.0*	*75.8*	*85.8*
Poland	–	12.6	22.6	33.8	31.7
	–	*33.5*	*65.9*	*80.8*	*71.7*
South Korea	–	–	–	11.6	30.0
	–	–	–	*12.8*	*34.1*
Germany	17.8	17.2	17.2	21.2	25.5
	39.6	*40.9*	*37.6*	*44.7*	*53.1*
Austria	11.7	13.0	14.8	17.3	17.9
	22.5	*22.7*	*27.9*	*30.9*	*35.0*
USA	8.5	6.7	8.5	10.3	17.4
	21.9	*19.5*	*20.5*	*22.9*	*38.4*
France	9.3	9.3	9.6	11.4	15.7
	19.5	*24.8*	*24.9*	*26.9*	*49.1*
Kuwait	–	–	–	8.1	11.1
	–	–	–	*34.1*	*37.0*
Montenegro	6.6	7.8	7.7	9.5	10.4
	7.5	*9.5*	*19.2*	*22.3*	*24.0*
Total (whole	**306,452**	**310,942**	**391,945**	**528,579**	**678,271**
figures)	*694,507*	*671,128*	*836,005*	*1,108,905*	*1,425,761*

Table 17.2. Typologies of rural areas' tourism in Bosnia and Herzegovina. (From Roberts and Hall, 2001; Ćejvanović et al., 2009; Nurković, 2009; Kajtaz, 2010a,b; Pećanac, 2010; Alibabić et al., 2012; Kuhar.ba, 2015.)

Rural tourism		Tourism in rural areas	
Wildlife/ ecotourism	Diverse landscapes: spectacular mountains, forests, rivers, lakes, national parks and beaches, birdwatching, nature photographing. The numbers and structure of nature visitors are unknown.	Health spa tourism	Strong growth in the past two decades: spa resorts offer a series of modern and high-quality treatments, at competitive prices. There are 15 thermal centres, and 8 offer high-quality thermal/mineral water. Most need upgrading and modernising.
'Eco-rural tourism'	Almost a dozen 'eco-villages' have been established in partnership with companies promoting renewable energy and 'healthy foods' to raise ecological awareness and promote healthy lifestyles.	Winter sports	Adjacent to Mount Igman, next to the Sarajevo plain, infrastructure was developed for the 1984 Winter Olympics: trails for biathlon with a shooting range (one of the most modern of its kind in the world), cross-country skiing trails and fully equipped 60 km training; two ski jumps of 70 and 90 m, with spectator stands that can accommodate 25,000.
Gastronomy	Home-made brandy, juices, meat products, home-made dairy products, bread, grain products, fruit. Bosnian cuisine is distinguished from other south Slav gastronomy by not using hot spices; meals are prepared by slow simmering in their own juices with a lot of vegetables. This is claimed to render it closer to French cuisine. Good quality wine is produced. Lacking a unified approach within the country, overall marketing is poor.	Cultural tourism/ religious pilgrimage	A crossroads for cultures and civilisations: three world religions meet, each with its shrines. Međugorje: a globally popular pilgrimage site for Roman Catholics, with more than 1 million annual visitors (hopelessly skewing already insufficient BiH tourist statistics). Here, the largest number of visitors arrive by bus and frequently stay in private homes, without being registered. Capacity has risen to perhaps more than 15,000 beds in this parish, which comprises five villages of 5000 residents and more than 200 souvenir shops.
Education related	Agricultural visits and participation: activities on farms, outdoor schools, youth education programmes.	Sports- related	Horse-riding, paragliding, rafting, canoeing, biking, hiking, running, hunting, fishing, mountaineering.

(Ćejvanović et al., 2009: 9). It has long been recognised that tourism in rural areas is one of the factors that can have an important role in the reconstruction and sustainable development of villages (Lukić, 2000). The demonstration effects of such development in neighbouring countries have been significant.

But considerable investments have been needed to modernise BiH's existing, and to create new, accommodation capacities and to improve transport and other rural infrastructures. Use of private housing capacities has been important in raising available tourism accommodation stock and increasing rural incomes. But in BiH, a number of tourist arrivals and overnight stays in family agricultural holdings is not recorded separately in cantonal tourism data and thus is not entered into the official statistical publications.

BiH's diverse landscapes and range of natural attributes offer substantial potential for a wide range of tourism-related activities in rural areas, both active and passive, 'new' and 'traditional' (Butler, 1998; Roberts and Hall, 2001) (Table 17.2, Fig. 17.1).

Although the spatial plan of BiH for the period 1981–2000 envisaged an integrated approach to nature protection that would have encompassed some 15% of the country's territory, at the turn of the century a mere 0.55% of BiH was protected (NEAP BiH Directorate, 2003). After the war, fragmentation and disturbance of habitats, together with over-exploitation of natural resources and the introduction of alien species, have resulted in dramatically increased environmental degradation. Although now 2.6% of the state territory is designated as protected areas (Table 17.3), even these are claimed to be under threat (Đug and Dresković, 2012).

In accordance with the Dayton Peace Agreement, all environmental legislation was retained from the former Yugoslavia until superseded by the adoption of new laws. In 2003, such new legislation was intended to harmonise with EU law. However, separate and incompletely adjusted frameworks persist in the two entities, and there is no defined single strategy or overarching coordinating agency for protected area designation at state level. The primary objectives of establishing a protected area network (PAN) and strengthening the capacity and capability of governmental institutions are urgently required.

17.4 Rural Tourism as a Meeting Ground?

Although conflict ended more than 20 years ago, and BiH should be regarded less as a post-conflict environment and more in terms of a *post*-post-conflict context,

> ...it may appear naïve to suggest that a sector such as tourism could play a positive role in a conflict-affected or post-conflict situation of fragility, especially given concerns over its ability to deliver sustainable and equitable growth ... However ... tourism could provide opportunities to advance the reconciliation process and contribute to the prevention of structural conflicts.
>
> (Novelli *et al.*, 2012: 1449)

As a consequence, the role of tourism development in post-conflict contexts has become a popular academic discourse, not least in relation to BiH. Čaušević and Lynch (2011), for example, have drawn on Bloch's (1982) concept of double burial – focusing on symbols of rebirth in funeral rituals – to produce the notion of 'phoenix tourism' that can assist post-conflict recovery and reconciliation.

Indeed, this role is the premise on which the work of Čaušević (2010) and Čaušević and Lynch (2009, 2013) is based. The latter argue that tourism appears to have been ahead of other sectors in BiH in encouraging partnership between those previously in conflict. By definition a social activity, they view tourism as a fertile ground for a more collaborative approach within the country. In its encouragement of joint projects between different stakeholders and communities, tourism, it is argued, can aid reconciliation:

> ... tourism is the one of a few economic sectors which has initiated intra-group, cross-entity and

Table 17.3. Major protected areas.

National Parks	Designated	Area (sq km)	
Sutjeska	1965	173	RS
Kozara	1967	34	RS
Una	2008		NW Bosnia (FBiH)
Nature parks			
Hutovo Blato (a Ramsar[3] bird migration site)	1995	74	Herzegovina (FBiH)
Blidinje	1995	6	Herzegovina (FBiH)

cross-border cooperation projects, despite the difficult socio-political context.

(Čaušević and Lynch, 2013: 154)

As noted earlier, somewhat pejoratively, it is often emphasised 'that every rural area in Bosnia and Herzegovina represents a particular individuality and distinctiveness' (Nurković and Drešković, 2013: 738). This heterogeneity may act to reinforce political separation, or it can be employed to encourage cooperation through complementarity.

In pursuing a 'phoenix' role in BiH, the concept of clustering of rural tourism services and activities would seem an appropriate spatial approach (Morić, 2013a). Clusters – spatial concentrations of complementary organisations and institutions involved in value-added activities – can stimulate cooperation and partnership from a modest base that can expand and develop (Briedenham and Wickens, 2004; Augustyn and Thomas, 2007), thereby generating a number of potential benefits (Box 17.4).

Such potential roles and benefits of clustering can be exemplified through the concept of theme trails. These are:

> networks of regional attractions that are marketed under a mutual theme in order to bring potential visitors into a region. At the same time they are networks of actors – municipalities, associations, and institutions with either economic or cultural backgrounds – trying to cooperate effectively.
>
> (Meyer-Cech, 2005: 137)

As a model, neighbouring Montenegro has eight theme trails, with participating members ranging in number from 5 to 60. Most of the trails are based on food, three are cross-border initiatives, and all have been generated by organisations exogenous to the areas in question: NGOs or foreign development agencies. Given the increasing emphasis on traditional cuisine and heritage as attractions in BiH, such trails might seem ideally suited to the country's conditions.

But such development of tourism in BiH raises two major issues:

1. As has been widely found, a major challenge to cross-cultural tourism development is the management of post-conflict emotions and issues surrounding contested heritage. Heritage can be related to identity creation (Bandyopadhyay *et al.*, 2008), which, in a post-conflict context, can be employed positively or negatively. Rather than acting as a vehicle for reconciliation, dissonant, contested 'heritagisation' can become the catalyst for recreating differences and reigniting intercommunity hostility (Miller, 2006; Poria and Ashworth, 2009);

2. In the absence of an overarching national body to plan and coordinate tourism development, rural tourism development in particular appears to be taking place in isolated clusters, both within the country but, perhaps more importantly, in a number of cross-border projects funded by the EU's IPA (Instrument for Pre-Accession Assistance) programme, various NGOs and neighbouring countries.

To what extent is the encouragement of such cross-border collaboration projects actually fostering centrifugal rather than centripetal forces, and

---

Box 17.4 Potential benefits of clustering tourism activities in rural areas

- acting as an element in a strategic shift towards sustainable development
- overcoming fragmentation in disadvantaged areas
- providing a framework for SMEs (small and medium-sized enterprises) to pursue cooperation and collaboration
- helping to alleviate poverty and promoting entrepreneurship in local areas
- reducing economic leakages with locally or regionally sourced inputs, thus enhancing the 'authenticity' of experience
- fostering a positive image and brand creation through the integration of stakeholders into a coherent and attractive service provision

(From Morić, 2013a: 98)

thus assisting the persistence of division and fragmentation within BiH? The metaphorical elephant in Dayton's living room is surely the corollary to BiH's internal division and fractionism: that contiguous neighbouring countries with co-ethnics in BiH (i.e. Serbia and Croatia) will continue to exert a disproportionate influence on the areas and activities inhabited by those co-ethnics, not least in terms of tourism development and the source of tourists, as a form of clientelism. Clearly, priority should be given to cross-internal border cooperation and development within BiH.

Otherwise, within the country's own relative marginality, an emphasis on rural tourism collaboration and development between the borderlands of Herzegovina and western Bosnia with Croatia (e.g. Center for Civil Initiatives, 2013) and between the borderlands of Republika Srpska and Serbia (e.g. Kokor, 2011) could act as forces of inverse peripherality whereby the borderlands sympathetic to adjacent countries become more important than the heartland (especially Bosniak-inhabited) areas of the interior. In the absence of an overarching national body to plan and coordinate such development, a form of centrifugal governance[4] is likely to persist, and perhaps accelerate.

This may be reinforced by a degree of mutual exclusivity expressed in the interests and destinations of foreign tourists from different source areas: a variation of the 'cultural proximity' (Kastenholz, 2010), 'self-congruity' (Beerli et al., 2007) and self-selecting segmentation recognised in the research literature. Thus,

large numbers of Roman Catholics (including significant numbers of Croatians, the largest foreign tourist group) naturally converge on Medūgorje in Herzegovina, while tourists from Serbia (until recently, the second largest foreign group) visit Orthodox monasteries, nature sites and other attractions within Republika Srpska. Perhaps with these issues in mind, Özlen and Tulić (2013) recommend that BiH removes visa requirements for tourists from the Middle East as an important target group.[5]

17.5 Conclusion

If tourism is now considered to be one of the country's leading sectors, a promoter of positive images and a symbol of intercommunal cooperation, how can it effectively promote the country when that country is so fundamentally divided and fragmented, with significant elements of its population expressing orientations towards neighbouring (and in tourism terms, competing) countries?

From a series of stakeholder interviews, Čaušević and Lynch (2013) found much evidence to suggest that tourism's sociopolitical and economic roles in Bosnia and Herzegovina would be far more effective if tourism was regulated centrally; that enhancing the country's image could only come about if promoted with a unity of purpose. And if this requirement is necessary for tourism development, how far is it also appropriate for other aspects of an integrated civil society?

Endnotes

[1] The Federation Agriculture Ministry's 2012 project, *Model for Rural Development*, was tainted by several arrests – including the then Minister – on charges of abuse of office in relation to the strategy (Anon., 2015).
[2] Data from the 2013 census were still being processed at the time of writing.
[3] International Convention on Wetlands.
[4] This is a loose obverse of the concept of centripetal governance put forward by Gerring et al. (2005).
[5] During the writing of this chapter, it was announced that a Dubai developer was to build 'thousands of housing units, hotels and the largest shopping center in Bosnia' (Reuters, 2015), which would create 'at least 10,000 local jobs'. This would be located close to the site of the 1984 Winter Olympics, below the Bjelasnica and Igman mountains. The aim was stated as 'to turn Bosnia and Herzegovina into a tourism leader of southeast Europe and to put its rich natural resources at the disposal of local and international clients' and thereby help change the country's image, presumably for the better.

References

Alibabić, V., Mujić, I., Rudić, D., Bajramović, M., Jokić, S. and Šertović, E. (2012) Traditional diets of Bosnia and the representation of the traditional food in the cuisine field. *Procedia – Social and Behavioral Sciences* 46, 1673–1678.

Alipour, H. and Dizdarević, L. (2007) A conceptual sustainability approach to tourism planning and development in post-war Bosnia and Herzegovina (BiH). *Tourism and Hospitality Planning & Development* 4(3), 211–230.

Anon. (2015) Bosnia and Herzegovina: former Agriculture Minister among five arrested for 'Farm incentives fraud'. *Organized Crime and Corruption Reporting Project* [Washington, DC] 29 September. Available at: https://www.occrp.org/en/daily/4439-bosnia-and-herzegovina-former-agriculture-minister-among-five-arrested-for-farm-incentives-fraud (accessed 9 August 2016).

Augustyn, M. and Thomas, R. (2007) Small firms in the new Europe: key issues, conclusions and recommendations. In: Thomas, R. and Augustyn, M. (eds) *Tourism in the New Europe: Perspectives on SME Policies and Practices*. Elsevier, Oxford, UK, pp. 227–236.

Austrian Development Corporation (2011) *Bosnia and Herzegovina Country Strategy 2011–2013*. Austrian Development Corporation, Vienna.

Bandyopadhyay, R., Morais, D.B. and Chick, G. (2008) Religion and identity in India's heritage tourism. *Annals of Tourism Research* 35(3), 790–808.

Beerli, A., Díaz Meneses, G. and Moreno Gil, S. (2007) Self-congruity and destination choice. *Annals of Tourism Research* 34(3), 571–587.

BHAS (Bosna i Hercegovina Agencija za Statistiku) (1990–2016) *Statistics of BiH*. Available at: http://www.bhas.ba/?lang=en (accessed 9 August 2016).

Bloch, M. (1982) Death, women and power. In: Bloch, M. and Parry, J. (eds) *Death and Regeneration of Life*. Cambridge University Press, Cambridge, UK, pp. 211–231.

Briedenham, J. and Wickens, E. (2004) Tourism routes as a tool for the economic development of rural areas: vibrant hope or impossible dream? *Tourism Management* 25(1), 71–79.

Butler, R. (1998) Rural recreation and tourism. In: Ilbery, B. (ed.) *The Geography of Rural Change*. Addison Wesley Longman, Harlow, UK, pp. 211–232.

Campbell, D. (1999) Apartheid cartography: the political anthropology and spatial effects of international diplomacy in Bosnia. *Political Geography* 18, 395–436.

Čaušević, S. (2010) Tourism which erases borders: an introspection into Bosnia and Herzegovina. In: Moufakkir, O. and Kelly, I. (eds) *Tourism, Peace and Progress*. CAB International, Wallingford, UK, pp. 48–64.

Čaušević, S. and Lynch, P. (2009) Hospitality as a human phenomenon: host–guest relationships in a post-conflict Bosnia and Herzegovina. *Tourism and Hospitality: Planning and Development* 6(2), 121–132.

Čaušević, S. and Lynch, P. (2011) Phoenix tourism: post-conflict tourism role. *Annals of Tourism Research* 38(3), 780–800.

Čaušević, S. and Lynch, P. (2013) Political (in)stability and its influence on tourism development. *Tourism Management* 34, 145–157.

Ćejvanović, F., Đurić, A. and Vujić, T. (2009) The competitiveness of tourism and rural tourism offer in Bosnia and Herzegovina through application of the marketing approach. Paper presented at 113th EAAE Seminar, *The Role of Knowledge, Innovation and Human Capital in Multifunctional, Agriculture and Territorial Rural Development*, Belgrade, Serbia, 9–11 December. Available at: https://core.ac.uk/download/files/153/6689999.pdf (accessed 9 August 2016).

Center for Civil Initiatives (2013) Rural development. *Center for Civil Initiatives* [Zagreb, Croatia] 19 January. Available at: http://www.cci.hr/en/?s=revival+of+cross-border+partnership&lang=en (accessed 21 February 2016).

Chandler, D. (2000) *Bosnia: Faking Democracy after Dayton*. Pluto Press, London.

Council of Europe (2015) *Action Plan for Bosnia and Herzegovina 2015–2017*. Council of Europe, Strasbourg, France.

Čutura, M., Mabić, M. and Brkić, J. (2008) Communicating country's image through the official web sites of tourist boards in Bosnia and Herzegovina. Proceedings of 4th International Conference: *An Enterprise Odyssey: Tourism-Governance and Entrepreneurship*. University of Zagreb, Cavtat, Croatia, pp. 792–802. Available at: https://www.researchgate.net/profile/Marija_Cutura2/publication/228269806_Comunicating_

Country's_Image_Through_the_Oficial_Web_Sites_of_Tourist_Boards_in_Bosnia_and_Herzegovina/ links/0c960522853cd8bb76000000.pdf (accessed 4 February 2016).

Dahlman, C.T. and Ó Tuathail, G. (2005) The legacy of ethnic cleansing: the international community and the returns process in post-Dayton Bosnia–Herzegovina. *Political Geography* 24(5), 783–800.

Đug, S. and Drešković, N. (2012) Nature protection in Bosnia and Herzegovina: state and perspectives. *Journal for Geography* 7(1), 69–80.

Elliott, M. (2009) Bosnia and Hercegovina. In: McAdam, M., D'Arcy, J., Deliso, C., Dragičević, P., Elliott, M., Marić, V., *et al*. (eds) *Western Balkans*, 2nd edn. Lonely Planet, Footscray, Victoria, Australia, pp. 101–168.

European Commission (2011) *Instrument for Pre-Accession Assistance (IPA) Multi-annual Indicative Planning Document (MIPD) 2011–2013 Bosnia and Herzegovina*. European Commission, Brussels.

European Commission (2015) *Bosnia and Herzegovina 2015 Report*. European Commission, Brussels.

FCO (UK Foreign and Commonwealth Office) (2016) *Foreign Travel Advice: Bosnia and Herzegovina*. Foreign and Commonwealth Office, London. Available at: https://www.gov.uk/foreign-travel-advice/bosnia-and-herzegovina (accessed 1 January 2016).

Gerring, J., Thacker, S.C. and Moreno, C. (2005) Centripetal democratic governance: a theory and global enquiry. *American Political Science Review* 99(4), 567–581.

Kajtaz, A. (2010a) Magic of Međugorje. *Turist* [Sarajevo] 25, 22–23.

Kajtaz, A. (2010b) New BiH brand. *Turist* [Sarajevo] 26, 52–53.

Kastenholz, E. (2010) 'Cultural proximity' as a determinant of destination image. *Journal of Vacation Marketing* 16(4), 313–322.

Keranen, O. (2013) International state building as contentious politics: the case of post conflict Bosnia and Herzegovina. *Nationalities Papers: The Journal of Nationalism and Ethnicity* 41(3), 354–370.

Kobasić, A. (1981) Lessons from planning in Yugoslavia's tourist industry. *International Journal for Tourism Management* 2(4), 223–239.

Kokor, E. (2011) Bosnia and Serbia: EU support for developing rural tourism. *eKapija* [Belgrade, Serbia] 27 May. Available at: http://www.ekapija.com/website/bih/page/434541_en/disclaimer.php (accessed 21 February 2016).

Kuhar.ba (2015) Arhive kategorije: Bosanska kuhinja. [Archive category: Bosnian cuisine.] (In Bosnian). Available at: www.kuhar.ba/recepti/bosanska-kuhinja (accessed 9 August 2016).

Lukić, A. (2000) Ruralni turizam – Čimbenik integralnog razvitka ruralnih prostora Hrvatske. [Rural tourism – a factor of integrated development of rural areas in Croatia.] *Geografski Horizont* 1(2), 7–31 (in Croatian).

Meyer-Cech, K. (2005) Regional cooperation in rural tourism trails. In: Hall, D., Kirkpatrick, I. and Mitchell, M. (eds) *Rural Tourism and Sustainable Business*. Channel View, Clevedon, UK, pp. 137–148.

Miller, P.B. (2006) Contested memories. The Bosnian genocide in Serb and Muslim minds. *Journal of Genocide Research* 8(3), 311–324.

Mirjanić, S. and Rokvić, G. (2013) Evolution of rural development policy in Bosnia and Herzegovina. In: Cvijanović, D., Subić, J. and Vasile, A.J. (eds) *Sustainable Agriculture and Rural Development in terms of the Republic of Serbia*. Institute of Agricultural Economics, Belgrade, pp. 889–906.

Mlinarević, M., Perić, J., Bačić, K., Smolćić-Jurdana, D., Stipanović, C., Cerović, Z., *et al*. (2008) *Strategija Razvoja Turizma Federacije Bosne i Hercegovine za period 2008–2018. [Tourism development strategy of the Federation of Bosnia and Herzegovina, 2008–2018.]* Federalno Ministartsvo Okoliša i Turizma, Sarajevo, Bosnia and Herzegovina (in Bosnian).

Morić, I. (2013a) Clusters as a factor of rural tourism competitiveness: Montenegro experiences. *Business Systems Research* 4(2), 94–107.

Morić, I. (2013b) The role and challenges of rural tourism development in transition countries: Montenegro experiences. *Turizam* 17(2), 84–95.

Nastav, B. and Bojnec, Š. (2007) The shadow economy in Bosnia and Herzegovina, Croatia and Slovenia: the labor approach. *Eastern European Economics* 45(1), 29–58.

NEAP BiH Directorate (2003) *National Environmental Action Plan for Bosnia and Herzegovina*. NEAP Directorate, Sarajevo, Bosnia and Herzegovina.

Novelli, M., Morgan, N. and Nibigira, C. (2012) Tourism in a post-conflict situation of fragility. *Annals of Tourism Research* 39(3), 1446–1469.

Nurković, R. (2009) Influence of tourism on the regional development of Bosnia and Herzegovina. *International Journal of Euro-Mediterranean Studies* 2(2), 201–214.

Nurković, R. (2012a) Geographic views on regional planning and development of Bosnia and Herzegovina. In: Schrenk, M., Popovich, V.V., Zeile, P. and Elisei, P. (eds) *Proceedings REAL CORP 2012: Re-mixing the City – Towards Sustainability and Resilience?* Schwechat, Austria, pp. 315–319.

Nurković, R. (2012b) Socio-economic transformation of Bosnia and Herzegovina. In: Bański, J. (ed.) *Local and Regional Development – Challenges and Policy Issues*. Polish Geographical Society, Warsaw, pp. 149–161.

Nurković, R. (2013) Influence of tertiary activities on local and rural development in Bosnia and Herzegovina. In: Osmanković, J. and Pejanović, M. (eds) *Local Economic and Infrastructure Development of SEE in the Context of EU Accession*. Academy of Sciences and Arts of Bosnia and Herzegovina, Sarajevo, Bosnia and Herzegovina, pp. 245–257.

Nurković, R. and Drešković, N. (2013) Regional development problems of the rural settlements in Bosnia and Herzegovina. *Chinese Business Review* 12(11), 736–746.

Özlen, M.K. and Tulić, M. (2013) Situation of tourism in B&H (agencies perspective and new solutions). *International Journal of Academic Research in Accounting, Finance and Management Sciences* 3(3), 162–170

Pećanac, A. (2010) Vacation for true nature lovers. *Turist* [Sarajevo] 25, 44–45.

Poria, Y. and Ashworth, G.J. (2009) Heritage tourism – current resource for conflict. *Annals of Tourism Research* 36(3), 522–525.

Reuters (2015) Dubai developer to build $4.8bln tourist resort in Bosnia. *Al Arabiya* [Dubai, UAE] 10 October. Available at: http://english.alarabiya.net/en/business/property/2015/10/10/Dubai-developer-to-build-4-8-bln-tourist-resort-in-Bosnia.html (accessed 9 August 2016).

Roberts, L. and Hall, D. (2001) *Rural Tourism: Principles to Practice*. CAB International, Wallingford, UK.

Robinson, G.M., Engelstoft, S. and Pobric, A. (2001) Remaking Sarajevo: Bosnian nationalism after the Dayton Accord. *Political Geography* 20, 957–980.

Vitic, A. and Ringer, G. (2007) Branding post-conflict destinations: recreating Montenegro after the disintegration of Yugoslavia. *Journal of Travel and Tourism Marketing* 23, 127–137.

18 Interrogating Tourism's Relevance: Mediating Between Polarities in Kosovo

Derek Hall* and Frances Brown
Seabank Associates, Maidens, Scotland, UK

18.1 Introduction

While a significant academic tourism literature has grown around post-conflict themes (Novelli *et al.*, 2012; see Chapter 17, this volume), the changing conceptualisation of peace and stability, intervention and international governance has likewise stimulated a considerable literature (Chandler, 2015; Randazzo, 2016). Much of this has resulted from the nature and outcomes of processes pursued in South-eastern Europe in the aftermath of the Yugoslav wars of succession in the 1990s.

The focus of this chapter, landlocked Kosovo, nestles among the Dinaric Alps, which rise to over 2600 m, within an upland basin of between 400 m and 700 m elevation, and shares borders with Albania, Montenegro, Serbia and the Former Yugoslav Republic of Macedonia (FYROM) (Fig. 18.1) (see also Wilkinson, 1955).

Kosovo was the poorest region in former Yugoslavia, with a per capita social product just a quarter of the Yugoslav average in 1989 (Bevc, 1993). Gross domestic product halved between 1990 and 1995, and although recovering since the end of conflict, it remains the lowest in south-eastern Europe (WIIW, 2013).

When considered in terms of superficial tourist numbers (a mere 50,074 in 2013), income derived (from just 83,883 tourist nights) (Table 18.1),

image generated[1] and (lack of) priority accorded to it, international tourism in Kosovo would appear to be of limited significance. Conversely, large numbers of Kosovars now travel to the Albanian and Montenegrin coasts for their holidays (1.38 million to Albania in 2014: see Chapter 23, this volume), a factor which does little for Kosovo's balance of payments.

Any evaluation of tourism in Kosovo must acknowledge the reality of double peripherality. The pejoratively ascribed 'Western Balkans' is viewed from the West – not least by potential tourism markets – as both troublesome and marginal, with Kosovo doubly so. And within Kosovo, the place of tourism has been at best marginal in the priorities of institutions of governance.[2]

Such double peripherality is exacerbated by the paradox that for centuries Kosovo has represented the heart of the Serbian Orthodox Church and the emotive core of a Serbian state. Kosovo no longer resides in Serbia, and Serbia refuses to recognise Kosovo as a separate, sovereign state. The region of Kosovo has also been long inhabited by ethnic Albanians, and was central to the rise of 19th century Albanian nationalism and the subsequent establishment of an Albanian state. Kosovo has remained outside of that state.

This paradox has sustained a sense of insecurity as a central component of group psychology – some parallels with Northern Ireland

*Corresponding author. E-mail: derekhall@seabankscotland.co.uk

Fig. 18.1. Kosovo: regional location. (Redrawn from various sources.)

Table 18.1. Kosovo: main sources of international visitors, 2008 and 2013. (From KAS, 2014.)

Country	2008		2013	
	Visitors	Nights	Visitors	Nights
Albania	3,213	3,311	7,778	10,515
USA	2,450	5,593	5,302	9,315
Turkey	1,694	2,099	4,949	8,237
Germany	734	4,517	4,259	6,497
Italy	1,089	2,427	3,704	5,280
Switzerland	1,452	2,325	2,591	5,038
UK	1,487	3,919	1,916	3,623
Croatia	931	1,060	1,771	3,795
Slovenia	1,289	1,823	1,467	4,627
FYR Macedonia	1,195	1,374	1,034	1,432
France	288	488	989	1,537
Serbia	250	233	725	1,418
Totals	**24,616**	**46,910**	**50,074**	**83,883**[3]

may be discerned here (e.g. Dowler, 2013; Mac Ginty, 2015) – one result being the polarised and mutually exclusive nature of some of the most important tourist destinations in the country.

Indeed, any focus on heritage within Kosovo's tourism development processes risks helping to perpetuate rather than alleviate cultural divisions. This suggests the need for substantial diversification of the Kosovo tourism product away from contested heritage, both to attract a potentially wider market base and to provide a non-(contested) cultural meeting ground for tourism stakeholders from different communities.

The chapter also addresses questions concerning the extent to which the appropriation and re-territorialisation of nature – through 'peace parks', 'peace ecology' and transboundary recreational areas – offers a means whereby tourism can escape the exclusiveness of cultural heritage and contribute to local and regional cooperation.

The purpose of this chapter, therefore, is to explore some of the concepts offered for, and the reality of, tourism development processes within a context of double peripherality, contested heritage and the commoditisation of nature in this new country whose 'independence' is both divisive and protected by external agencies, witnessing outcomes of polarisation and paradox.

18.2 Tourism, Intervention, Localism

Even in the early 1980s, before the explicit resurgence of Serbian nationalism, Yugoslavia's autonomous province of Kosovo was by far the least developed region of the country. It resided at the bottom of most socio-economic indicators (Hall, 1994) and, by 1989, no Kosovo destination featured in the list of Yugoslavia's top 30 tourist resorts (Allcock, 1991: 253–254).

Yet Kosovo was recognised to possess considerable tourist potential: a range of environmental, cultural and historical attractions for 'sedentary and recreational tourism' in spas and mountains, with towns possessing the foundations for business/conference tourism, notably the capital Prishtina. Hunting was then recognised as a lucrative use of natural resources. But the region was relatively neglected, with no marketing strategy or programmes to attract visitors, no evaluation of potential demand, nor coordination of a travel and tourism sector (Vukadinović, 1983).

Serbia's further suppression of Albanian culture and economic life from the later 1980s, and ultimate armed conflict, with the massacre of civilians and flight of 300,000 ethnic Albanians to neighbouring countries, removed any short-term prospects for conventional international tourism.

NATO (North Atlantic Treaty Organization) air strikes against Belgrade in 1999, and the subsequent removal of Yugoslav (Serbia–Montenegro) troops from Kosovo, were followed by an influx of international military and civilian interventionist institutions. This contrasted with the outflow of large numbers of ethnic Serbs, such that by 2011, Kosovo's population, enumerated at just under 1.8 million, exhibited a transformed composition (Table 18.2).

In 1999, the UN mission in Kosovo (UNMIK) and the Organization for Security and Cooperation in Europe (OSCE) became the leading civilian international institutions following NATO's deployment of a Kosovo protection force (KFOR).[4] The Kosovo National Assembly's 2008 independence declaration (Box 18.1) specifically welcomed the European Union's (EU) Rule of Law Mission (EULEX) and an International Civilian Office (ICO). These further contributed to the country's institutional complexity, policy overlap and top-down governance.

> While international armies of monitors, peacekeepers and administrators appear to be ever more necessary for Balkan stability, there is less and less of a role for the people of the region in deciding their own futures.
>
> (Chandler, 1999: 124)

Or, as Judah simply put it:

> All of this was confusing. It was unclear as to who was actually going to be in control.
>
> (Judah, 2008: 145)

In Europe until the 1980s, 'international intervention' as a category of statecraft was considered a violation of international law and of its founding concept of sovereignty. But the meaning of 'intervention' has become increasingly ambiguous and wide-ranging. Reframed through the

Table 18.2. Kosovo: population by ethnicity (%), 1948–2011. (From KAS, 2014.)

Ethnicity	1948	1953	1961	1971	1981	2011
Albanian	68.0	64.3	67.1	73.7	77.4	91.0
Serb	24.1	24.1	23.5	18.4	13.2	3.4
Other (Bosniaks, Turks, Roma, Ashkali, Gorani)	7.9	11.6	9.4	8.0	9.4	5.6

Box 18.1   Kosovo: international and national governance

United Nations Security Council (UNSC) resolution 1244 set up an interim UN Administration to run the country until Kosovo developed its own state institutions, while remaining legally part of 'Yugoslavia'. In November 2005, the 'Contact Group' (USA, Russia, UK, Germany, France and Italy) agreed guiding principles for negotiations between Belgrade and Prishtina, with UN Envoy Marti Ahtisaari moderating, devising a plan for 'supervised independence', which Russia and China openly opposed. In July 2007, negotiations failed. Kosovo, with the backing of the US and key EU member states, declared its independence in February 2008 as a democratic, secular and multi-ethnic republic. It was assumed that 'independence' would require the role of UNMIK to be phased out.

Serbia condemned the declaration as violating UNSC Resolution 1244. The UN General Assembly called on the International Court of Justice (ICJ) to give an advisory opinion on the legality of Kosovo's declaration. The ICJ's opinion – legally non-binding but anticipated to hold 'moral' influence – delivered in July 2010, stated that the declaration of independence was not in violation of international law. In September 2010, the UN General Assembly called for a new round of negotiations.

These have included the Brussels Agreement – the *First Agreement on Principles Governing the Normalization of Relations* (or '15-points') – negotiated and concluded in April 2013 (although not actually signed by either party) under EU auspices. Its purpose is to integrate Serb-majority municipalities in northern Kosovo into the Kosovo legal system, while providing certain guarantees.

Under the Principles, neither Kosovo nor Serbia may block the other party's progress towards EU accession, but Serbia's uncompromising non-recognition of Kosovo has constrained its EU candidacy aspirations. Belgrade has accepted, however, that progress in implementing the Brussels agreement is a prerequisite for EU accession talks.

(From Chandler, 2006; Brosig, 2011; Obradović-Wochnik and Wochnik, 2012; Radeljić, 2014; Rossi, 2014; Beha, 2015.)

Responsibility to Protect (R2P) principle (Olsson, 2015), notions of intervention and humanitarian action have become intertwined, leading to the neoliberal assumption of intervention becoming the norm and non-intervention the exception to be justified or denied (Malmvig, 2006).

Several observers have argued that the imposition of decisions, which the international bureaucracy expresses in capacity-building terms as being in the public interest, has tended to strengthen external mechanisms of governance while undermining domestic institutions of government, weakening political institutions and discouraging public participation in the political sphere (Chandler, 2006; Kostovicova and Bojičić-Dželilović, 2006).

Such impositions have been viewed as ethnocentric, hierarchical and acting to marginalise alternatives, displaying little concern for pre-existing forms of governance, civil society or cultural sensitivities (Devic, 2006; Mac Ginty and Richmond, 2013).

Partly in response to such perceived insensitivities, critical approaches to peace building and interventionism have tried to place local agents at the centre of the debate (Randazzo, 2016).

The resulting 'local turn' has laid emphasis on bottom-up, identifiably location-specific agency, to contribute to a 'trickle-up' development process. This is the context in which tourism can establish a role in contributing to small-scale business- and project-based collaboration and cooperation.

However, unlike the Republika Srpska in Bosnia and Herzegovina (Chapter 17, this volume), Kosovo Serbs have no formally recognised form of governance other than four municipalities centring on the area of north Mitrovica in northern Kosovo.[5] These have become, informally, almost an exclave of contiguous Serbia[6] and have been hostile to visitors, particularly since the 2008 independence declaration. These municipalities require a continuing KFOR presence, and they represent a major challenge for national integration (Clark, 2014).

Enhanced autonomy for all the country's municipalities would appear necessary, somewhat paradoxically, to assist such integration (Beha, 2015), harnessing consociational power-sharing arrangements similar to those established in Bosnia and Herzegovina (Rossi, 2014). While this would further weaken central authority, it could reduce the potential for ethnic conflict, encourage local self-government and preserve the overall territorial integrity of the country. But is Bosnia an exemplary model for Kosovo?

Reassurance of destination safety is a critical consideration for tourism development, and although the signing of the Dayton Peace Agreement for Bosnia and Herzegovina in 1995 might have been effective in restoring tourists' confidence in that country, such a process – despite the 2013 Brussels Agreement (see Box 18.1) – continues to evolve in Kosovo, sustaining uncertainty and insecurity.

18.3 Conceptual Approaches to Recreational Space: (i) The Contestation of Cultural Heritage

Kosovo has been the meeting ground of competing cultures and national ideals, and, in consequence, of contested heritage. The country's visitor attractions mostly, though not in equal measure, comprise Serbian Orthodox, Turkish Ottoman and Albanian Islamic and national (istic) sites and activities (Fig. 18.2, Table 18.3). Some of the most sacred sanctuaries of the Serbian Orthodox Church continue to need KFOR protection (Fig. 18.3), and the apparently mutually exclusive recognition of Serbian and Albanian culture is mundanely expressed in the obliteration of the other's language in official bi/trilingual signs and notices (Fig. 18.4).

While, for some tourists, conflict sites may become cultural markers, elements of 'dark tourism', for many communities they will continue to evoke painful memories (Novelli *et al.*, 2012). Participation in the identification and interpretation of such dissonant or contested heritage becomes part of the transitional justice process. Failure to reach such accommodation can create new divisions; rather than becoming a vehicle for reconciliation, tourism merely reinvigorates long-held resentment and animosity.

But harnessing tourism as a pathway to socioeconomic recovery and development eventually requires former victims and perpetrators of conflict to cooperate in a setting where reconciliation

Fig. 18.2. Kosovo: location of main visitor attractions. (Redrawn from *maps.com* and others.)

Table 18.3. Kosovo: major visitor attractions (the following categories are not necessarily well defined). (From Regent Holidays, 2013; authors' fieldwork.)

'National' Kosovar	
Prishtina	National Library/University
	Museum of Kosovo
	Emin Gjiku Ethnographic Museum
Peja/Peć	Haxhi Zeka kulla (traditional fortified house)
	Regional ethnographic museum (Tahir Beg Inn)
	Rugova Spring Water bottling factory
Dranoc village	Kulla restoration
Novobrdo/Novobërdë	Fortress and adjacent mines

Ethnic/nationalist Albanian (Islamic)	
Prizren	League of Prizren monument and museum (Albanian national awakening, 1878)
Prishtina	Skanderbeg monument (15th century Albanian national hero)
Prekaz	Adem Jashari memorial (UÇK: Ushtria Çlirimitare e Kosovës; or KLA: Kosovo Liberation Army)
	Martyrs' cemetery (UÇK)

Serbian secular	
Brezovica	Resort village
Istok/Istog	Trofta trout farm complex
Velika Hoča	Petrović Winery

Serbian/Orthodox	
Prizren	Church of the Virgin of Leviša/Lady Ljevis
	Holy Archangels Monastery
Gračanica	Orthodox Church and Monastery complex
Kosovo Polje	1389 Battle site monuments (Serbian defeat by Ottomans)
Peja/Peć	Peć Patriarchate ('spiritual seat of the Serbian nation')
Dečani/Deçan	Visoki Dečani Monastery (UNESCO World Heritage Site)
Velika Hoča	Winery of Visoki Dečani Monastery

Roman Catholic	
Letnica	Black Madonna church
Prishtina	Mother Theresa statue (contemporary Albanian nationalist iconography: see also Chapter 4, this volume)

Ottoman/Turkish (Islamic)	
Prizren	Emin Pasha, Sinan Pasha mosques
	Gazi Mehmed Pasha baths
	Kalaja fortress ruins
	Ottoman bridge
	Helveti tekke
Prishtina	Çarshi/Bazaar mosque
Gazimestan	Sultan Murat mausoleum
Vushtrri	Nine-arch stone bridge
Peja/Peć	Old bazaar
	Bajrakli mosque
Gjakova/	Old market
Đakovica	Hadum Aga mosque
	Bektashi tekke
	Taylor's Bridge: 190 m 11-arched stone bridge

Continued

Table 18.3. Continued.

Environmental	
Sharr Mountains	National park
Ulpiana	Classical (Roman and Byzantine) archaeological site
Drelaj	Rugova valley family farm (a working B&B on the 'Green Path' hiking trail)

Fig. 18.3. Visoki Dečani Monastery World Heritage Site: a tourist guide negotiates the paperwork with KFOR site protectors prior to visitors' admission. (Photograph courtesy of Derek Hall.)

Fig. 18.4. Serbian language obliterated from a trilingual notice outside the National Museum, Prishtina. (Photograph courtesy of Derek Hall.)

and societal healing may be a long and complex process: the 'management of post-conflict emotions' (Brewer and Hayes, 2011: 7).

As noted in Chapter 17, this volume, Čaušević and Lynch (2013) view tourism as a fertile ground for a more collaborative approach within south-eastern Europe, and the same authors have explored the role of tour guides in the transition of conflict issues into new heritage (Čaušević and Lynch, 2011). Certainly, tourism business and project development activities have the potential to contribute to a strengthening of reconciliation and socio-economic underpinnings through collaboration between communities.

Although small scale, the facilitating role of tourism guides, agencies and tour companies may assist different stakeholders and communities in embracing cooperation, collaboration and networking in business-driven activities. On a standard tour of Kosovo marketed by Regent Holidays (Bristol, UK) and managed locally by Intours & Travel (Prishtina), more than 40 major attractions/sites are included in the guided itinerary (see Table 18.3). As ethnic Albanian father and daughter, the tour managers are clearly well experienced in negotiating visits to and managing interaction within and between communities; for example, forewarning the tour group of a particularly difficult Serbian Orthodox functionary, or expressing strong personal friendships with a number of Serbian entrepreneurs.

The itinerary itself is strongly and deliberately balanced between the sites and attractions – sacred and secular – of different cultural groups, geographical areas and commercial stakeholders, avoiding only the Mitrovica area of northern Kosovo because of its continuing hostility to outsiders. Yet within the circumstances of each attraction, there is only limited evidence of intercommunal interaction.

As becomes evident on such a tour, Ankara has been investing significant resources in the restoration and protection of sites of Turkish Ottoman heritage in Kosovo. These include the renovation of revered Sultan Murat I's tomb,[7] on the site of the critical Gazimistan/Kosovo Polje battlefield of 1389 (Recepoğlu, 2007),[8] along with a number of mosques and other Ottoman-period buildings and institutions. Significantly, Turkish visitor numbers to Kosovo trebled between 2008 and 2013, and their visitor nights quadrupled during this period (see Table 18.1).

Turkey has also intensified cooperation in education and culture (e.g. Aktuna, 2014), with the Middle East Technical University said to have been considering opening a campus in Kosovo. These developments complement Turkey's support for Kosovo's independence,[9] in the belief that, to achieve lasting peace in the region, the final status of Kosovo needs to be resolved (Bulut, 2006; Eralp, 2010).

In exerting such 'soft power', Turkey's role may be seen as ambivalent: assisting physical reconstruction while potentially exacerbating cultural mutual exclusion and perpetuating Serbian hostility.

18.4   Conceptual Approaches to Recreational Space: (ii) Peace Ecology, Ecotourism and the Commoditisation of Nature

Johan Galtung (1969) posited two conditions of peace: negative, where there is merely an absence of direct violence; and positive peace, requiring additionally the absence of other forms of violence such as cultural and structural violence, and the emergence of social justice. The former still prevails in Kosovo.

Just as Milošović was beginning to impose Serbian ultranationalism on Kosovo (see Endnote 6), elsewhere much rhetoric was being employed to promote the notion that tourism could act as a serious contributor to global understanding, trust and world peace (D'Amore, 1988). Through cultural exchange, it was argued, benefits derived for both hosts and guests could promote mutual understanding on a global scale. More measured arguments (e.g. Brown, 1998; Litvin, 1998) recognised that while a peaceful environment was usually essential to enable tourism to flourish, tourism could not of itself create peace. Indeed, it is clear that tourism can act as both a source and an object of far from peaceful acts.

More recently, the concept of peace ecology has promoted the notion that:

> Conservation efforts can serve to promote mutuality and social justice, and ... Cooperative and collaborative projects can likewise work to restore and maintain the environment.
>
> (Amster, 2016: 175/6)

'Peace parks' and related transboundary protected areas (TBPAs) are promoted in part as broadly contributing to a culture of peace and co-operation alongside more mundane ecological objectives (Hammill and Besançon, 2007). Taking a lateral step away from Galtung's (1969) conceptions, Ali (2007) distinguishes between 'soft peace', where two or more contiguous countries involved in a transboundary park development are on good terms, and 'hard peace', where such bordering countries need to overcome animosity.

In contrast to Ali's distinction, Hargreaves embraces the ideals of peace parks enthusiastically:

> Peace Parks are truly trans-national, cross-border regions of special environmental significance. They are designated as protected areas, not only to preserve their ecology and in some cases their inhabitants' employment and way of life, but also as symbols of a better world, where wildlife and human beings can move freely over terrain which may belong to different countries but is unencumbered by the bellicose trappings of statehood: borders, flags, fences, soldiers, police, even minefields.
> (Hargreaves, 2004: 151)

Thus, a major role of peace parks can be identified as transforming the meanings and significance of borders without changing their physical position, implicitly requiring a redefinition of the role of the state in such borderlands (see also Chapter 12, this volume), and the engagement of external actors. As such,

> ... peace parks are highly political interventions that are far from the neutral conservation strategies ... [they] are ideologically related to neo-liberal forms of management that are promoted through appeals to global governance, which is in itself a political choice.
> (Duffy, 2007: 66)

In contributing to a 'pluralisation of political spaces', such interventions draw in

> a myriad of different actors, both state and non-state, as well as public and private. These newly created webs of cross-border contacts raise the question of what 'national' means ...
> (Basic, 2006: 217)

Large areas of upland Kosovo bordering Montenegro, Albania and FYROM are embraced by a range of local, national and international projects and programmes variously aiming to achieve environmental, peace and security, ecotourism and other socio-economic objectives (Box 18.2). In this commodification of nature,

the presence of a bewildering roll-call of NGOs, international interventionist organisations and professional consultancy businesses appears to mirror the nature of governance within the country as a whole.

NGOs have emerged as primary partners in development initiatives as neoliberal development strategies have shifted from structural adjustment programmes (SAPs) towards more political objectives of institutional engineering, notably 'good governance'. Professionalised, with close links to governments and transnational institutions, their ambiguous position arises from the difficulty of defining 'non-governmental action', and disambiguating the nature of 'NGO' as a signifier (Jeffrey, 2013).

This is exemplified in Box 18.2 in the contrast between the activities of large, professional, well-funded international organisations such as WWF and IUCN, and the focused and modest achievements of B3P. There is clear evidence of progress in supporting local populations to benefit financially from small-scale outdoor tourism deploying limited infrastructure (e.g. Lietti, n.d.).

But critiques of such international commoditisation of nature have demonstrated the way in which inappropriate semantics and rhetoric may constrain practical collaboration. For example, the 'Balkans Peace Park' is not a peace park in the sense of reconciling those involved in past conflict, because most (although not all) local people in the area covered by the 'park' in all three countries are ethnic Albanians, and local cross-border relations have not been problematic here (but see Tamminem, 2012). Thus, in Ali's (2007) terms, this is a 'soft peace' context. Further, unsurprisingly, the term *Balkan* is not well accepted in the region. Local people consider it an imposed name that has nothing to do with their culture but is a synonym of 'primitive' and 'barbarian', an ascription of 'otherness' (see, for example, Todorova, 1997). More widely, environmentalist discourse can be perceived as threatening property rights with the fear of possible privatisation of the environment (Hara, 2009; Gabioud, 2012).

The Balkans Peace Park concept is not alone in revealing confused objectives of 'peace', tourism and conservation. Yet Kosovo needs peace parks, both physical and metaphorical: less to straddle external borders than to act as internal meeting grounds across physical, cultural and psychological barriers.

Box 18.2   Environmental interventionist hierarchy?

1. European Ecological Green Belt

Mikhail Gorbachev was one of the more notable proponents for the creation of this post-Cold War symbol of reunification that would link up a number of pre-existing protected areas along the former Iron Curtain's forbidden zones in which wildlife had flourished. Formally initiated in 2003, the belt consists of three routes: the Fennoscandian and Baltic, from the Barents Sea down to the Gulf of Finland; a Central European belt, from the Baltic down to the Adriatic; and a more complicated south-eastern European route. Its vision includes symbolic joint cross-border activities in nature conservation and sustainable development.

The European Green Belt Association embraces 23 governmental and non-governmental organisations from 14 countries, including Kosovo. Project partners are EuroNatur, part of BUND (Friends of the Earth, Germany), and the German Federal Agency for Nature Conservation (BfN).

In 'Green Belt Balkan' EuroNatur's partners are: BfN, BUND, IUCN (International Union for Conservation of Nature, Gland, Switzerland), and local partner organisations including PPNEA (Preservation of Natural Environment in Albania) and MES (Macedonian Ecological Society). Sponsors include: MAVA Foundation (Gland), BfN, German Lufthansa, DBU (German Federal Environment Foundation), GIZ (German Society for International Cooperation).

2. Dinaric Arc Parks

Begun as a 3-year project in 2012 by WWF (World Wide Fund for Nature) to create an association of nature and national parks in Albania and all the Yugoslav successor states within the Dinaric alpine range, this project is funded by the Norwegian Ministry of Foreign Affairs and the MAVA Foundation.

As part of this programme, the Environment for People in the Dinaric Arc project is being implemented by IUCN and SNV (the Netherlands) as well as WWF. Six cross-border areas are embraced by the project in five countries. Objectives: establishing public–private partnerships; increasing awareness of the value of local biodiversity; identifying transborder actions in the fields of tourism, agriculture and forestry; evaluating the potential for establishing transboundary protected areas; creating platforms for coordinated actions of decision makers.

Overall, the Dinaric Arc Initiative aims to secure the preservation of the region's 'wealth and integrity' through the establishment of a network of protected areas, the promotion of cultural diversity, an empowering of local organisations supporting sustainable development and an integration of environmental standards in policies and practices.

It represents 'collaboration between WWF, IUCN, UNESCO-BRESCE, UNDP, UNEP, FAO, EuroNatur, SNV, REC, ECNC, and CIC backed up by the "Big Win" commitment made by the governments of the Dinaric Arc countries at the 9th Conference of the Parties to the Convention on Biological Diversity (CBD COP 9)' of 2008.

3. Transboundary protected areas

Some 11% of Kosovo territory is protected by law, and Kosovo's *State of Nature Report* (MESP and AMMK, 2015) claims the state is participating in cross-border nature protection initiatives with all its contiguous neighbours.

In particular, moves towards establishing two transborder protected areas were kick-started by UNEP, with feasibility studies published in 2010: (i) Sharr–Korab–Dešat across Kosovo's south and south-east borders with Albania and FYROM. Declared a national park in Kosovo in 1986, these mountains are home to brown bear and lynx. (ii) Prokletije/Bjeshkët e Nemuna, in the west and north-west extends across borders with Albania, Montenegro and Serbia; this is still at the proposal stage.

4. Small initiatives

A well-publicised (UK-led) and long-evolving project is B3P, the Balkans Peace Park project, which was registered as a charity in the UK in 2004. Its objective is 'to establish a protected area including territory from Montenegro, Albania, and Kosovo … to encourage exchange between the three countries and establish ties in a region long subject to war and strife'. Embracing local education, training and small-scale ecotourism development, the project remains an officially unrecognised entity.

Continued

Box 18.2   Continued.

Focused on the Rugova Valley in the west of the country, and led by Associazione Trentino con i Balconi, the project Vertical Action 2C *Valorization of Environmental Tourism* within the framework of EU Programme Seenet II *A translocal network for the cooperation between Italy and South-east Europe* has helped to establish a well-marked paths network within the valley (Fig. 18.5), as well as 'a network of ideas, passions, knowledge, people, associations and institutions'. Locally available materials produced include a *Green Path* handbook (Lietti, n.d.) and a series of ecotourism-related leaflets (e.g. Anon., n.d. a,b) produced under the auspices of Peja/Peć municipality.

(From Terry *et al.*, 2006; UNEP, 2010a,b; Hallik, 2013; MESP and AMMK, 2015; http://www.euronatur.org/project-areas/project-areas-a-z/; https://www.dbu.de/2535.html; http://en.mava-foundation.org/what-we-fund/list-of-projects/; http://www.dinaricarc.net/; https://www.cbd.int/cop9/; http://grassrootsvolunteering.org/volunteer_opportunities/balkan-peace-park-project.)

Fig. 18.5. A Green Path hiking and bike trails information board, Drelaj, Rugova Valley. (Photograph courtesy of Derek Hall.)

18.5   Conclusions

This commentary on tourism's role in contemporary Kosovo has been placed within a framework of the changing conceptions and reality of peace and stability, intervention and international governance. We have suggested that, currently, those seeking to promote tourism find themselves in a situation of double peripherality. While conceptions of post-conflict tourism development are well rehearsed (see Chapter 17, this volume), the

spatialised nature of Kosovo's contested and dissonant heritage, the complications of an array of international interventionist institutions and the commoditisation of nature all act to blur the role of tourism as an integrating agency.

Clearly, Kosovo needs micro-peace initiatives – perhaps micro-peace parks – as part of a reconciliation effort slowly building from the bottom up. The role that tourism may or may not play in this much-needed process is perhaps low on the list of priorities for decision makers. This is not the case, however, for those dynamic individuals and groups working within and across communities to establish a solid foundation for a functioning tourism sector in Kosovo.

Tourism in Kosovo may not offer a source of peace and security, but in the longer term it can be one element employed in overcoming prejudice and mutual exclusion through its requirement for business and project collaboration. Unfortunately, mutually exclusive ethno-territorial informal institutions, currently sustaining grey economies, have vested interests in maintaining polarised division, and stand as one practical obstacle in the way of this objective.

Can EU accession processes yet overcome the Gordian knot left over from atrocities spanning three decades? How far can external aspirations and demand, as expressed through international tourism, be translated into intercommunal collaboration? And who are the real beneficiaries of so much international interventionist activity?

Endnotes

[1] Reka (2011) found that UK residents interviewed still had a dominant image of Kosovo as a 'war torn country' and potentially unsafe, an image, he argued, that was reinforced by superficial media reporting.

[2] An official document acknowledged that ecotourism development had been 'prohibited' by 'lack of infrastructure, investment, plans and concrete projects', and called for the preparation of a national strategy (MESP and AMMK, 2015: 100).

[3] Of the total recorded domestic and international visitor nights (138,750) for 2013, 63% were spent in the Prishtina municipality. The second most popular area, Prizren, hosted just 6.3% (KAS, 2014).

[4] But this was seen from further to the east, long before the Crimea/Ukraine crises, as part of NATO's setting up a series of military protectorates (Albania, Bosnia, Macedonia and Kosovo) edging into Russia's historic zone of influence (Stepanova, 1999; Wallender, 1999; O'Loughlin and Kolossov, 2002).

[5] There is a relatively scattered distribution of Serbs across the rest of the country.

[6] Through which an alleged flourishing grey economy exists (Grahovac, 2012).

[7] Although just his internal organs were buried here, this is the only tomb of an Ottoman sultan located outside of Turkey (Şenyurt, 2012).

[8] A place treated as a neo-sacred Pyrrhic victory site by Serbs, and the rallying point where Milošević launched his ultranationalistic anti-Albanian campaign at the 600th anniversary gathering.

[9] This recognition by the Turkish government was controversial in view of the country's own Kurdish self-determination demands.

References

Aktuna, M.E. (2014) Structural analysis of current condition of Kosovo Yashar Pasha Mosque and strengthening proposals. Unpublished MSc thesis, Middle East Technical University, Ankara, Turkey. Available at: http://etd.lib.metu.edu.tr/upload/12617478/index.pdf (accessed 10 August 2016).

Ali, S.H. (2007) Introduction: a natural connection between ecology and peace? In: Ali, S.H. (ed.) *Peace Parks: Conservation and Conflict Resolution.* MIT Press, Cambridge, Massachusetts, pp. 1–18.

Allcock, J.B. (1991) Yugoslavia. In: Hall, D.R. (ed.) *Tourism and Economic Development in Eastern Europe and the Soviet Union.* Belhaven, London, pp. 236–258.

Amster, R. (2016) Transborder peace ecology. In: Amster, R. *Peace Ecology.* Routledge, Abingdon, UK, pp. 152–176.

Anon. (n.d. a) *Rugova: Destination of Rock Climbing.* Peja Municipality, Directorate for Economic Development, Peja (Peć), Kosovo.

Anon. (n.d. b) *Rugova: The Secret of Untouched Nature.* Peja Municipality, Directorate for Economic Development, Peja (Peć), Kosovo.

Basic, N. (2006) Transnationalism in the Balkans: an introduction. *Ethnopolitics* 5(3), 217–221.

Beha, A. (2015) Disputes over the 15-point agreement on normalization of relations between Kosovo and Serbia. *Nationalities Papers: The Journal of Nationalism and Ethnicity* 43(1), 102–121.

Bevc, M. (1993) Rates of return to investment in education in former Yugoslavia in the 1970s and 1980s by region. *Economics of Education Review* 12(4), 325–343.

Brewer, J. and Hayes, B.C. (2011) Post-conflict societies and the social sciences: a review. *Contemporary Social Sciences* 8(1), 5–18.

Brosig, M. (2011) The interplay of international institutions in Kosovo between convergence, confusion and niche capabilities. *European Security* 20(2), 185–204.

Brown, F. (1998) *Tourism Reassessed: Blight or Blessing?* Butterworth Heinemann, Oxford, UK.

Bulut, E. (2006) 'Friends, Balkans, statesmen, lend us your ears': the trans-state and state in links between Turkey and the Balkans. *Ethnopolitics* 5(3), 309–326.

Čaušević, S. and Lynch, P. (2011) Phoenix tourism: post-conflict tourism role. *Annals of Tourism Research* 38(3), 780–800.

Čaušević, S. and Lynch, P. (2013) Political (in)stability and its influence on tourism development. *Tourism Management* 34, 145–157.

Chandler, D. (1999) The Bosnian Protectorate and the implications for Kosovo. *New Left Review* 235, 124–134.

Chandler, D. (2006) *Empire in Denial: The Politics of State-building.* Pluto Press, London.

Chandler, D. (2015) Reconceptualizing international intervention: statebuilding, 'organic processes' and the limits of causal knowledge. *Journal of Intervention and Statebuilding* 9(1), 70–88.

Clark, J.N. (2014) Kosovo's Gordian knot: the contested north and the search for a solution. *Nationalities Papers: The Journal of Nationalism and Ethnicity* 42(3), 526–547.

D'Amore, L. (1988) Tourism – the world's peace industry. *Journal of Travel Research* 27(1), 35–40.

Devic, A. (2006) Transnationalization of civil society in Kosovo: international and local limits of peace and multiculturalism. *Ethnopolitics* 5(3), 257–273.

Dowler, L. (2013) Waging hospitality: feminist geopolitics and tourism in West Belfast, Northern Ireland. *Geopolitics* 18(4), 779–799.

Duffy, R. (2007) Peace parks and global politics: the paradoxes and challenges of global governance. In: Ali, S.H. (ed.) *Peace Parks: Conservation and Conflict Resolution.* MIT Press, Cambridge, Massachusetts, pp. 55–68.

Eralp, D.U. (2010) *Kosovo and Turkey: What Lies Ahead?* SETA Policy Brief, Ankara.

Gabioud, V. (2012) Improving inter-state relations through transboundary peace parks. Unpublished MA Thesis. University of Bradford, Bradford, UK. Available at: https://bradscholars.brad.ac.uk/bitstream/handle/10454/5865/Gabioud,%20Maria%20Victoria.pdf?sequence=3&isAllowed=y (accessed 10 August 2016).

Galtung, J. (1969) Violence, peace, and peace research. *Journal of Peace Research* 6(3), 167–191.

Grahovac, B. (2012) Geopolitics and organized crime and corruption in the early 21st century with reference to the Balkans. *European Perspectives – Journal on European Perspectives of the Western Balkans* 4(1)[6], 79–94.

Hall, D. (1994) *Albania and the Albanians.* Pinter, London.

Hallik, M. (2013) Report: The Balkans Peace Park (B3P) Project: Development and Peace Building from Ground Up. School of Social and International Studies, University of Bradford, Bradford, UK. Available at: http://www.brad.ac.uk/social-sciences/media/socialsciences/ceer/2013/Maarja.pdf (accessed 10 August 2016).

Hammill, A. and Besançon, C. (2007) Measuring peace park performance: definitions and experiences. In: Saleem, A.H. (ed.) *Peace Parks: Conservation and Conflict Resolution.* MIT Press, Cambridge, Massachusetts, pp. 23–39.

Hara, S. (2009) Peace Through Tourism: A Case-study of the Balkans Peace Park Project. Unpublished MA Thesis. University of Bradford, Bradford, UK. Available at: https://bradscholars.brad.ac.uk/bitstream/handle/10454/5873/Dissertation.pdf?sequence=1&isAllowed=y (accessed 1 January 2016).

Hargreaves, R. (2004) Mountains for peace in the Balkans. *The Alpine Journal* 151–160. Available at: http://www.alpinejournal.org.uk/Contents/Contents_2004_files/AJ%202004%20149-160%20Hargreaves%20Balkans.pdf (accessed 31 December 2015).

Jeffrey, A. (2013) Non-governmental organisations. In: Dodds, K., Kuus, M. and Sharp, J. (eds) *The Ashgate Research Companion to Critical Geopolitics.* Ashgate, Farnham, UK, pp. 387–403.

Judah, T. (2008) *Kosovo.* Oxford University Press, New York.

KAS (Kosovo Agency of Statistics) (2014) *Statistical Yearbook of the Republic of Kosovo 2014.* KAS, Prishtina.

Kostovicova, D. and Bojičić-Dželilović, V. (2006) Europeanizing the Balkans: rethinking the post-communist and post-conflict transition. *Ethnopolitics* 5(3), 223–241.

Lietti, L. (n.d.) *Green Path: Rugova Valley – Kosova.* SEENET, Brussels.

Litvin, S.W. (1998) Tourism: the world's peace industry? *Journal of Travel Research* 37(1), 63–66.

Mac Ginty, R. (2015) Where is the local? Critical localism and peace building. *Third World Quarterly* 36(5), 840–856.

Mac Ginty, R. and Richmond, O.P. (2013) The local turn in peace building: a critical agenda for peace. *Third World Quarterly* 34(5), 763–783.

Malmvig, H. (2006) *State Sovereignty and Intervention. A Discourse Analysis of Interventionary and Non-interventionary Practices in Kosovo and Algeria*. Routledge, London.

MESP (Ministry of Environment and Spatial Planning) and AMMK (Kosovo Environmental Protection Agency) (2015) *State of Nature Report 2010–2014*. MESP/AMMK, Prishtina.

Novelli, M., Morgan, N. and Nibigira, C. (2012) Tourism in a post-conflict situation of fragility. *Annals of Tourism Research* 39(3), 1446–1469.

O'Loughlin, J. and Kolossov, V. (2002) Still not worth the bones of a single Pomeranian grenadier: the geopolitics of the Kosovo war 1999. *Political Geography* 21, 573–599.

Obradović-Wochnik, J. and Wochnik, A. (2012) Europeanising the 'Kosovo Question': Serbia's policies in the context of EU integration. *West European Politics* 35(5), 1158–1181.

Olsson, C. (2015) Interventionism as practice: on 'ordinary transgressions' and their routinization. *Journal of Intervention and Statebuilding* 9(4), 425–441.

Radeljić, B. (2014) Official discrepancies: Kosovo independence and Western European rhetoric. *Perspectives on European Politics and Society* 15(4), 431–444.

Randazzo, E. (2016) The paradoxes of the 'everyday': scrutinising the local turn in peace building. *Third World Quarterly* 37(8), 1351–1370.

Recepoğlu, A.S. (2007) *Sultan Murat Tomb and Kosovo*. 'Siprint' Basimevi, Prizren, Kosovo.

Regent Holidays (2013) *Kosovo in Depth/Kosovo Guide*. Regent Holidays, Bristol, UK.

Reka, S. (2011) An investigation into the image of Kosovo as a tourism destination. Paper presented at Regional Science Conference *Stable Local Development Challenges and Opportunities*, Peja, Kosovo, 3–4 June. Available at: http://www.dukagjinicollege.eu/shqiperim_reka.pdf (accessed 17 January 2016).

Rossi, M. (2014) Ending the impasse in Kosovo: partition, decentralization, or consociationalism? *Nationalities Papers: The Journal of Nationalism and Ethnicity* 42(5), 867–889.

Şenyurt, O. (2012) Kosova'da Murad Hüdavendıgâr Türbesı v eek yapilari. [Murat Hüdavendıgâr tomb and outbuildings in Kosovo.] *METU JFA* [Ankara] 29(2), 285–311 (in Turkish).

Stepanova, E.A. (1999) *Explaining Russia's Dissention on Kosovo*. Policy Memo Series No 57, Program on New Approaches to Russian Security, Harvard University, Cambridge, Massachusetts.

Tamminem, T. (2012) Re-establishing cross-border cooperation between Montenegro, Kosovo and Albania: the Balkan Peace Park and local ownership. *Slavica Helsingiensa* 41, 125–151.

Terry, A., Ullrich, K. and Riecken, U. (eds) (2006) *The Green Belt of Europe: From Vision to Reality*. IUCN, Gland, Swizerland.

Todorova, M. (1997) *Imagining the Balkans*. Oxford University Press, Oxford, UK.

UNEP (United Nations Environment Programme) (2010a) *Feasibility Study on Establishing a Transboundary Protected Area Prokletije/Bjeshkët e Nemuna Mountains*. UNEP Interim Secretariat of the Carpathian Convention (ISCC), Vienna.

UNEP (2010b) *Feasibility Study on Establishing a Transboundary Protected Area Sharr/Šar Planina – Korab – Dešat*. UNEP Interim Secretariat of the Carpathian Convention (ISCC), Vienna.

Vukadinović, G. (1983) Organizacija turističke privrede Autonomne Pokrajine Kosovo. [Organization of the tourist economy of the Autonomous Province of Kosovo.] *Economia* [Belgrade] 6, 447–455 (in Serbo-Croat).

Wallender, C. (1999) *Russian Views on Kosovo*. Policy Memo Series No 62, Program on New Approaches to Russian Security, Harvard University, Cambridge, Massachusetts. 1999).

WIIW (2013) *WIIW Handbook of Statistics 2013: Central, East and Southeast Europe*. Vienna Institute for International Economic Studies, Vienna.

Wilkinson, H.R. (1955) Yugoslav Kosmet: the evolution of a frontier province and its landscape. *Institute of British Geographers, Transactions and Papers* 21, 171–193.

19 European Night of Museums and the Geopolitics of Events in Romania

Daniela Dumbrăveanu,* Anca Tudoricu and Ana Crăciun
Faculty of Geography, University of Bucharest, Romania

19.1 Introduction

This chapter focuses on the changing nature of events in Romania and the geopolitical dimensions of this change. The chapter has one major aim, within which are two key objectives. Our aim is to examine the geopolitical role of events in past and contemporary Romania. The first objective considers the European Capital of Culture – Sibiu 2007, its impacts and the implications of hosting such a prestigious, year-long event for city residents, local authorities and politicians. Second, through the role of the European Night of Museums event, the chapter evaluates the geopolitics of a country coming to terms with its sometimes brutal communist past.

Culture, history, art, places and spaces can be made accessible to society in two major ways: through the collections and exhibits of institutions such as museums, and through planned events. Both events and museums have a long history of interacting with their public in a variety of ways: of influencing the micropolitics of how citizens view their society and their own identity. These roles have become increasingly complex: from conserving, preserving and promoting values, to enhancing views, educating, stimulating and reawakening an appreciation of non-economic materialities.

Events can be considered as catalysts for enhancing places and spaces by impacting on social, cultural and economic life and the environment, and the identities associated with them. Events can offer contexts to provide meaning and purpose for particular actions.

Museums are usually well-established institutions known for their important role in preserving and exhibiting a variety of shared values (expressed through their collections). They also have a crucial role in passing on these shared values as heritage through presenting and interpreting contributions both to human progress and to local or national identity. To this end, for several decades, museums have embraced the hosting of events, often in cooperation with other bodies.

19.2 Events as Catalysts for Development

Events have developed into an 'industry' in their own right (Getz, 2007) because of the variety and complexity of the roles they can play in society. The purpose of each event will depend on the organiser's vision and needs. For example, entrepreneurs will view the role of events as income generators (Saayman and Saayman, 2004), and are more likely to focus their attention on managing participation fees, sponsorship, media and the services that are being offered to participants (Araujo and Bramwell, 1999; Moscardo, 2007). But there are also media events that do not directly generate income, perhaps being part of an organisation's marketing strategy, image promotion, brand, or even ideology. Such meetings, conventions, workshops, openings and exhibitions as components of the marketing strategies of corporations, associations and different stakeholders can be highly cost-effective marketing tools (Jiwa *et al.*, 2009; Pinto, 2013). By contrast, community-oriented events are used for fundraising, propaganda or active participation (Webber, 2004), raising the awareness of the group and self-identity.

Events can stimulate development, reappraisal and change (Richards and Wilson, 2004; Herrero *et al.*, 2006; Paiola, 2008; Žižek, 2014). They possess the potential to enrich the culture of particular places and the experience of the public, residents, visitors and tourists. Cultural events are especially significant in this respect, in that they can symbolise and exhibit the shared values of a group, promoting, consuming, appraising and debating these values on a public stage.

19.3 Cities as Stages for Events

Events can be regarded, metaphorically, as fulfilling for urban life the same role as blood does for the human body: of nurturing, refreshing and reinvigorating. Events provide diversity, interaction and awareness, generating enthusiasm, involvement and active participation. At a time when every town or city appears to be pursuing strategic place marketing, to focus on qualities of 'livability, investibility and visitability' (Kotler *et al.*, 1993: 18), events have become a 'critical component of urban development strategy across the globe' (Richards and Palmer, 2010: 2).

Hosting events has become almost obligatory for cities that attempt to enter the arena of competing identities in order to boost their economic and social development attractiveness: to express a distinctive identity in a world ever dominated by the blandness of globalisation. Events have become an important part of distinctiveness strategies because they can stimulate collaboration among stakeholders and can be utilised for a wide range of urban objectives, while remaining low cost, dynamic and flexible (Richards and Rotariu, 2015). Events also reflect

the need for self-image, a focus with which to identify at both a personal and a group level.

Much cultural funding is directed today towards the institutions whose projects, products and outputs can be measured by performance indicators (Richards and Palmer, 2010). This is why many social, economic and infrastructural development strategies underline the benefits of events. These can include: quality of life enhancements, creative activity, growth in visitor and tourist numbers, creation of partnerships, opportunities for education and entertainment, investment from external sources, intensified local engagement with citizens, firms and institutions, a chance to celebrate human skills and endeavour, intense media exposure and the discipline of immovable deadlines (Graham Devlin Associates, 2001; City of Cape Town, 2015). In this respect, cities' events calendars seek to include a wide variety of festivals that contribute to their development.

Tourist markets are an important consideration in the development, timing and location of events (Anholt, 2006), and tourism promotional literature often places events and 'eventfulness' at its core. Examples include: 'Celebrate your stay in Minneapolis with some of these fabulous, unique events!' (Meet Minneapolis, 2015); 'Berlin's ... classical to traditional, lifestyle to avant-garde, there is always something going on...the programme for theatre stages... of daily events...' (Visit Berlin, 2015).

In a metaphorical sense, the city can become the stage where communities perform their past and present experiences. Events can be the setting for their performance. The place, the community and the events shape the performance by creating a web of relationships. This web links the stage with the performers and the performances (Hayllar *et al.*, 2008), creating a 'playscape' that generates a particular sense of place and belonging, and which contributes to fundamental place identity. On the other hand, tourists and visitors, by accepting the invitation to be part of the performance, become leading actors who may challenge the 'performance' of the residents. Since they arrive with an external viewpoint and an earnest curiosity, they can bring lateral perspectives to the experience. For example, exhibiting an interest in such sensitive topics as contested memories of shared histories, cultural awareness can be mutually enriched.

19.4 Cultural Events and the Sense of Place

Events are known for their power to add and give meaning to places. They celebrate, entertain, incite and stimulate the senses, offering the participant an experience out of the ordinary. According to Tuan:

> an object or place achieves concrete reality when our experience of it is total, that is, through all the senses as well as with the active and reflective mind.
>
> (Tuan, 2001: 18)

Events are consumed and experienced collectively, creating

> linkages between people and groups within communities, and between the community and the rest of the world.
>
> (Saayman and Saayman, 2004: 630)

Events can generate a celebratory atmosphere to stimulate a more diverse cultural dimension of place and of life. Through this celebratory dimension, the eventscape becomes a vivid culturescape, often subject to debate and reinterpretation of what is being celebrated. Celebrating the past, memories of places and people can become increasingly engaging when performed in a context of art and culture: even memories of dark times. Since one of the roles of events is to invite and encourage 'negotiations' on a broad range of values and elements of identity, events such as the Night of the Museums (examined below) can be an effective tool in 'negotiating' a wide variety of themes, including contested memories and histories.

19.5 Events as a Manifestation of Past Political Power

Events can be employed to direct, redirect and focus public opinion. They can also be used as a means of introducing new ideas, particularly regarding sensitive, contested or controversial aspects of important issues for the community or wider public. Whether media events (Dayan and Katz, 1994; Bennett *et al.*, 2008) or mega-events such as the Olympic Games (Burbank *et al.*, 2001; Broudehoux, 2007), events can create 'empowering landscapes', the geopolitics of which may operate at a number of levels

(see Chapters 1 and 2, this volume). Politicians, event industry managers, commercial sponsors, equipment manufacturers, local authorities, professional associations and NGOs can take advantage of such eventscapes to introduce novelty, cater for curiosity, reinforce self-validation, raise awareness among participants and influence the beliefs and behaviour of host communities.

In the past century, in Romania, events were employed as instruments to serve political strategies. Regimes used them as promotional tools on the international stage, to position the country in a global context in order to promote its political views and interests.

At the beginning of the 20th century, Romania was facing the need to express its identity as a newly born European monarchy and to strengthen its position as a Latin country surrounded by Slavic nations. For this purpose, in 1906, King Carol I opened the Romanian National General Exhibition. This celebrated three important anniversaries for the country: 25 years since the proclamation of Romania as a unified monarchy, 40 years of successfully ruling Romania and 1800 years since Trajan's campaign of conquering Dacia to become a Roman province. The exhibition's landscape designer, the French-born Eduard Redont, was commissioned to produce a design to express Romania's vision of itself. Within the exhibition area, avenues were given symbolic names reinforcing Romanian history; squares and junctions were named after great historical figures who were admired by the royal family.

The exhibition was significant in portraying an accurate image of the geopolitical context of the era, not least in terms of the countries participating. Austria–Hungary's participation was a geopolitical necessity since 'the empire was physically and economically one of the largest neighbors of the Kingdom of Romania' (Albert, 2015: 125). France, Italy and Switzerland were all Roman countries, and their participation contributed to a celebration of Latinity and the roots of Romanian culture. By contrast, the presence of the German Empire at the exhibition had a double meaning: on the one hand, 'it was a counter-weight to Austria–Hungary in vying for cultural superiority in Central Europe' (Albert, 2015: 125), and on the other, it held strong cultural significance since the King of Romania was of German origin.

Thus, the exhibition acted as a stage for the major players of Middle Europe to act out a proxy geopolitical chess game in a diplomatic environment that would soon be swept away by World War I, ignited by events further south.

During the communist period, cultural events had a double role. Most aimed to promote communism and express its self-claimed liberalism, while also acting as an expression of, and instrument for, reinforcing the power of its ideology within an international context. An example of this was the *Golden Stag* international music festival, which emerged during Romania's period of 'de-Sovietization', the beginning of its nationalist turn. The *Golden Stag* festival was, purposefully, held in Braşov (between September 1950 and December 1960, the city was called 'Lenin'). Geographically located in the centre of the country, Braşov represented the heart of a united and independent Romania[1] eager to reposition and promote itself on the new map of Europe and of the communist bloc. When Ceauşescu became leader of the Communist Party in 1965, he intended to gain the support of the people in his effort to transform Romania from a poor European country to an industrialised economic power. The *Golden Stag* festival, organised for 4 successive years (1968–1971),

> represented a step forward for renewing Romania's cultural relations with the West, which had suffered since the proclamation of the Popular Republic at the end of 1947. It also represented an effort to integrate Romanian television within the European broadcasting scene, showcasing it as adhering to the same standards of quality.
>
> (Matei, 2013: 20)

The most controversial cultural event in Romania's recent history was *Cenaclul Flacăra*, a cultural and artistic festival held between 1973 and 1985. It generated 1615 music and poetry shows all over Romania, creating a vivid movement among the communist youth (TVR.RO, 2015). It was, and still is, considered a paradox. On the one hand, it was the only regular event that promoted folk culture enjoying less draconian censorship during the most restrictive period of Romanian communism. On the other hand, it was organised around the personality cult of its founder, poet Adrian Păunescu (1943–2010) (a highly controversial former communist poet and post-communist, left-wing politician). Criticised

by some people, appreciated by others, *Cenaclul Flacăra* produced widely appreciated music and literature; but it was also used as propaganda, being considered 'the megaphone of the Romanian communism' (Cărtărescu, 2010). Part of the paradox was the positive impact it had on the participants who joined and created a community, a movement, a lifestyle:

> Cenaclul Flacăra was a laboratory which produced good songs at all times. They were interweaving with that generation, they were emblems of the soul of that generation, they were picturing the drama of the days we lived.
>
> (Victor Socaciu, quoted in Ologeanu and Suciu, 2005)

At an individual level, by being the only way of celebrating youth and youthfulness, *Cenaclul Flacăra* became an element of personal heritage for people of that generation. Although the music produced and performed would not normally be associated with partying, since it was mostly of a patriotic and militant folk genre, many young people would, none the less, adopt it as birthday party music. The patriotic nature of *Cenaclul Flacăra* performance, music and poetry was particularly related to themes of unity, 'territorial integrity', equal opportunities, 'brotherhood among ethnic groups' and international peace. The capitalist world was portrayed as a permanent threat to the communist countries.

This rather radically direct celebration of patriotism was a very 'thick' safety curtain that was employed successfully to keep heavy censorship away, allowing the leading figure of Adrian Păunescu to develop into a sort of social hero for the young spirit. This personality with its own cult was thereby afforded a platform to address a limited number of non-ideological and non-communist themes during spontaneous poetry performances.

19.6   Events as a Vehicle for Contemporary Political Power: European Capital of Culture

The post-communist era has brought a dramatic change in all fields and has had an enormous impact on the Romanian cultural scene by opening borders (literally and metaphorically), encouraging diversity and embracing globalisation, especially after accession to the European Union in 2007. Cultural mega-events, such as Sibiu being declared European Capital of Culture (ECoC) in 2007, have been used to promote European values, to stimulate civic pride (essential for a community facing an identity crisis) and to help create cultural strategies and cities' identities (Santos *et al.*, 2015).

The ECoC staged in Sibiu was the first to be hosted in one of the post-2004–2007 EU accession countries, and it challenged the city's and the country's capacity to organise it effectively and manage it efficiently (Richards and Rotariu, 2010a). The event brought many positive impacts: helping to overcome the identity crisis of being both a Transylvanian and a Romanian city during a period of deep political instability; re-establishing local pride; raising the international profile of the city; stimulating long-term cultural development; attracting international visitors; improving social cohesion; and upgrading infrastructure. But one of its most significant contributions was to generate a country-wide positive attitude towards European events, fostering a climate of European cooperation, creativity and innovation (Richards and Rotariu, 2010b).

As a consequence, the event managed to stimulate competitiveness for subsequent ECoCs. Fourteen Romanian cities applied (Capitală Europeană a Culturii, 2015b)[2] and four (Baia Mare, Bucharest, Cluj-Napoca and Timişoara) reached the final shortlist in December 2015 (Capitală Europeană a Culturii, 2015a). In September 2016 Timişoara was declared the winner.

Whether the aim is for urban regeneration (Balsas, 2004) or branding and positioning (Nobili, 2005), entering the competition has become almost obligatory in Romania. Sibiu's success as an ECoC generated great interest in the country, not least from politicians. This is because it projected on to the national political stage a new dynamic type of political leader who appeared to stand in stark contrast to a national political scene crippled by corruption and ignorance. This was Sibiu's ECoC mayor, Klaus Iohannis, an ethnic German and local politician from the German Democratic Forum, who was subsequently propelled into the leadership of the National Liberal Party (NLP) and then into Romania's presidency.

This nationally successful political career could explain the interest shown by the 14 Romanian cities in ECoC 2021. Half of the mayors of these cities are NLP members and the other half cover a wide variety of political affiliations, including independents and a Hungarian minority representative. Aspirants clearly hope that the status of ECoC city mayor would help shape (in some cases even reshape) a further successful political career.

The democratic process of a city mayor winning popular support to become the country's president is not new in Romania. The precedent was set by Traian Băsescu, former mayor of Bucharest (2000–2004) and subsequent national president (2004–2014), so that in 2014 Romanians voted to replace one national president, a former capital city mayor, with another, the former mayor of a European Capital of Culture.

Three of the country's four post-communist presidents are associated with radically distinctive types of events: Ion Iliescu (December 1989–1992; 1992–1996; 2000–2004) presided over street riots resulting in a loss of life; Traian Băsescu, paradoxically associated with recurrent protests against corruption rather than being associated with the big event celebrating Romania 'becoming a European country' in 2007; and Klaus Iohannis who (at the time of writing) is only associated with events during his mayoral days, dominated by the ECoC.

19.7 The European Night of Museums – From Bridging Towards Bonding

The European Night of Museums (ENoM) is an event that challenges the way people think about culture. It is a night-time celebration of cultural diversity and shared identity that annually offers museums and other cultural institutions the opportunity to present and promote themselves and their activities for the benefit of residents and tourists, within a wider European context.

The first such event, *Lange Nacht der Museen* (Long Night of Museums), took place in Berlin in 1997 (Kultur Projekte Berlin, 2016). Its unexpected success became a source of inspiration for other cities. Local authorities recognised the wide range of opportunities it offered, particularly in terms of placing culture and tourism at the core of development strategies (Dumbrăveanu *et al.*, 2014). As a result, in 1999, the Minister of Culture and Communication in France launched

Le Printemps des Musées (The Spring of Museums), which was adopted by all countries that signed the Council of Europe cultural convention.

The event's primary aim was soon modified from being a tourist attraction to becoming dedicated to the rediscovery of museums' collections and of shared cultural identities. The initiative was followed by *Nuit Blanche* (White Night), an important event that focused on using cities as cultural stages and making art accessible to visitors as well as to residents. In 2005, this became the European Night of Museums, organised for the Saturday closest to International Museum Day, 18 May (ICOM, 2015). It is currently held in 33 countries, the institutions involved using their capital cities as hubs for networking types of events (Dumbrăveanu *et al.*, 2014).

ENoM has two main aims (ICOM, 2015), accessibility and collaboration: to make museums more accessible to the general public (particularly the young), and to encourage collaboration between museums at a European level while generating a festive atmosphere in which museums can promote themselves. From dusk to dawn, a variety of presentations takes place organised by museums in partnership with NGOs, cultural institutions and local authorities, most of them engaging youth participation through volunteering.

As an international event, the European Night of Museums can generate meaning and sense of place. It is a mixture of cities' identities, contributing to a broader image of European heritage. Since 2013, ENoM's fifth year, the event has been held under the patronage of the United Nations Educational, Scientific and Cultural Organization (UNESCO). In 2015, 4000 museums and 1270 cultural institutions participated in the event (Paulet, 2015). Participation grows annually, influenced by an appreciation of the levels of museology (Box 19.1) achieved.

Thus, in recent years, the term 'museum' has gained new attributes that render it a more interactive and socially oriented institution: the 'participatory museum' (Simon, 2010). But such changes have not been adopted universally, for political, philosophical and financial reasons. As a consequence, in Europe, western and eastern museums attained different levels of engagement with the public. Western museums that mastered the new museology shifted their emphasis from rigorous academic research and conservation work to a more educational- and entertainment-oriented strategy, collaborating in partnerships to develop attractive projects and ventures, while opening up and encouraging the public and local communities to participate.

By contrast, museums in Central and Eastern Europe (CEE) had remained largely reluctant to take this step and continued to display in a static, conservative, non-engaging way. Crucially, in their efforts to become competitive, accessible and dynamic, CEE museums have needed to confront one of their most challenging tasks: representing their communist past.

As a result, there remain significant differences across the continent in participants' expectations and motivations towards ENoM. In Western Europe, the event tends to be more focused, with participating cultural institutions pursuing a common purpose. The event appears as a pre-planned itinerary of activities, predominantly taking place indoors. By contrast, in CEE, ENoM is more a celebration of institutions, in a festive outdoor atmosphere.

The different approaches indicate an advanced level of museology in Western Europe, where cultural managers possess the advantage of knowing their participants' and visitors' profile, helping to anticipate expectations more precisely. Museums' capacity to educate and entertain the public is expressed through interactive and

---

Box 19.1   Museology

Derived from the original French conception of *muséologie*, it was adopted internationally in 1950 to define the philosophy behind museums (Deloche, 2001). As an applied science, it represents an archive of studies regarding museums' history, physical conservation and other forms of research. Since 1984, *la nouvelle muséologie* has stressed 'the social role of museums and its interdisciplinary character, along with its new styles of expression and communication' (Desvallées *et al.*, 2010: 55). This shift of focus from the object to the story contrasts with the 19th century notion that 'a museum is a well-arranged collection of labels, illustrated by specimens' (Brown Goode in Tilden, 1957: 13).

diverse programmes and the communication skills of the curators. Thus, in France, two million visitors have attended ENoM events in 3 successive years (2013–2015), twice the number of participants in 2005 (Paulet, 2015). In most Western European countries, there has been an almost constant number of participants in recent years, reflecting a sharing of common needs, interests and expectations. Audiences now know what to expect since the Night of Museums is part of a larger cultural events calendar.

On the other hand, countries of CEE experience a different approach. In Russia, museum studies show that a significantly high percentage of the population is not interested in museums. Nevertheless, research has indicated that events such as European Night of Museums have brought more visitors to museums and have played a major role in improving their image in visitor perceptions (Grinkevitch, 2014; Abakina et al., 2015). ENoM is now hosted by more than 20 Russian cities (Gordin and Dedova, 2014), and is focused mainly on attracting 20- to 40-year-olds. This is both the largest demographic group and the one least attracted to museums. Other ex-communist countries, including Bulgaria and Romania, exhibit the same trend.

In Romania, as revealed by the authors' surveys, the main stated reason for the adult population not visiting museums is a lack of time. This reflects a fundamental problem of museology: the failure to capture attention and involve the public. In 2014, there were 739 museums in Romania (a declining number), of which 37 were in Bucharest. The European Night of Museums in Romania (ENoMiR) is coordinated by the National Network of Romanian Museums (RNMR), a non-governmental organisation that also plays an important role in organising the event. It is a network that has increased its membership from 33 in 2006 to 66 in 2014 (Bujdei, 2014), and it currently works at both national and international levels through affiliation to the Network of European Museum Organisations (NEMO) (Rețeaua Națională a Muzeelor, 2008). By organising ENoMiR since 2005, RNMR has encouraged the participation and cooperation of all cultural institutions in order to assist in nurturing a better integrated development of creative industries in Romania. However, not all museums in Romania are members of RNMR. Most of them are trying to take a step forward by

participating in ENoMiR even if their resources are limited, since participation almost guarantees an improved museum image.

In a context in which museums lack the experience of assuming their roles other than being the preservers of national/local values, the ENoM tends to be both a paradox and an excellent opportunity for 'showing off'. ENoMiR is a colourful celebration, a stage for everyone, where visibility is the most important element. Here, the public sets the rules: the event attempts to meet the needs of a democratic society still learning how to deal with the freedom of expression and to come to terms with its past. This is the most important reason for increasing numbers of participants. ENoM finds itself at the heart of two types of bridge-building act: institutional and intergenerational. The latter is subtle, yet significant. Older generations are mostly drawn to ENoM by simple actions denied by their communist past, such as access to setting the rules, participating in the show or being able to act outdoors at night within a social group. The young, without experience of the communist past, are mostly attracted by curiosity and a desire to learn through entertainment.

In earlier ENoMs, most participating Romanian organisations were museums. Since 2014, other types of institutions such as the National Bank, Romanian Orthodox Churches (notoriously conservative) and, most notably, Jilava prison (an infamously oppressive place during the communist years) have taken part to open their doors to visitors. The best-attended attraction for 2 successive years was Bellu Cemetery.[3]

Visitors' enthusiasm for less frequented places springs from the curiosity of exploring them in different circumstances (Bellu Cemetery) or by gaining access to otherwise inaccessible institutions (Jilava prison). Indeed, former communist prisons, whether still in use, abandoned or opened to the public, have increasingly attracted Romanians' attention. But despite a willingness to visit former communist torture places, the communist past as a whole is still far from being accepted and laid to rest in Romania. As well as the political complexity of the issue, simply discussing people's lives under communism can create tension and conflicts generated by personal experiences of those times. Most people who retain nostalgia for the communist past are either those who enjoyed its privileges and/or are now failing to cope with the post-communist instability and pace of life. By contrast, there are those who have not yet come to terms with the communist past and blame their current unhappy situation on it. Hence, the experience of communism in Romania remains a contested history for many.

19.8 Exhibiting Communism – A Recurrent Challenge in Romania

Romania has made faltering steps towards coming to terms with its communist past. And, of course, for most former communist countries' residents the feelings generated from living under communism were hugely different from those of the curiosity held by foreigners during their brief visits. Since the fall of communism, all former communist countries have faced difficulties in dealing constructively with foreigners' eagerness, even enthusiasm, to (vicariously) experience the past symbols of communist realities. Thus, in Germany, although the Berlin Wall had long been an attraction in the West, after (re)unification, the authorities wanted to remove it quickly, and were reluctant to address the story behind it (Light, 2000). In Romania, following the events of December 1989, Bucharest's residents wanted The House of The People (currently the Parliament House) destroyed, because it held a variety of negative feelings for them. Yet, paradoxically, now the building is perceived as the most significant symbol of the capital city, especially by foreign visitors (see Chapter 20, this volume) and increasingly by Romanians themselves, even if the nation has still not come to terms with its communist past and with the Ceauşescus, both of which the Palace represents so monumentally.

Elsewhere in CEE, despite the fact that in the 1990s almost all public monuments related to the communist regime were destroyed or removed (to storage), the communist past began to be debated and represented as objective history. Examples of this include Prague's Museum of Communism, the Czar PRL-Life under Communism Museum in Warsaw, the Museum of Soviet Occupation in Kyiv and the Museum of Occupations in Tallinn.[4] By contrast, Romania has been slow in dealing with this past (as part of emotional

heritage), and this remains one of the biggest challenges for museums and museology in the country.

A vast majority of history museums, memorial houses or other types of Romanian public institutions still exclude communism and communist-era artefacts from their collections. They do not acknowledge, present, explain, perform or raise awareness of the communist past, let alone preserve or value it. Only a few rather insubstantial attempts to present and interpret this past in museums or through other types of art have been made.[5] In contrast to other former communist countries, Romania still does not possess any museum dedicated to communism, the dictator, other significant institutions or political figures from that era.

However, recently large numbers of top-secret communist files were declassified and, at a stroke, the victims of the former regime and their stories were brought under the spotlight. Defining the concept of 'victim of communism' is work still in progress by IICCMER (Institute for the Investigation of Communist Crimes and the Memory of the Romanian Exile).[6] It is widely known that among the large numbers of people incarcerated and murdered in notorious communist prisons, many intellectuals, poets, philosophers, priests, students and political figures opposing the regime died being physically and mentally tortured. Political and social torture was extended to their families and deeply affected their lives. The most notoriously brutal communist prisons were located at Sighetu Marmaţiei, Jilava–Bucharest, Piteşti, Râmnicu Sărat, Aiud and Gherla (Fig. 19.1). Sighetu Marmaţiei is now a museum, while the others are still functioning as prisons, although they have begun opening their doors to present some form of *their* communist past. According to our survey, this 'opening up' has gained momentum as the result of IICCMER's activities and the growing concern of Romanians to learn more about victims of communism.

One of the most visited museums – by far the best developed and managed in Romania – is the Memorial of the Victims of Communism and of the Resistance located in the former prison at Sighetu Marmaţiei, Maramureş county (Fig. 19.2). It is adjacent to the International Centre for Studies into Communism; both were opened in 1993. Despite its location near the border with

Fig. 19.1. Location of former communist detention centres and prisons in Romania. (From authors' own compilation.)

Fig. 19.2. Inside former Sighetu Marmaţiei prison, now The Memorial of the Victims of Communism and of the Resistance. (Photograph courtesy of Ana Crăciun.)

Ukraine, the former prison is a vivid annual participant in the Night of Museums event. It invites the audience to face a powerful emotional experience by taking it through an impressive amount of information based on complex research studies and work undertaken by IICCMER.

In 2015, Jilava prison (still operating as a penitentiary) in Bucharest, opened its gates to the public for the first time, as part of ENoMiR. A major attraction was the viewing of *Bless you, prison*, an emotional documentary film about its former prisoners, the victims of communism. Since 2014, the recounting of victims' stories has become a powerful driver for celebrating their memories. As this trend has grown across the country, a second stage has been reached whereby surviving victims of communism imprisoned and tortured inside the walls of those prisons are themselves invited to take part in events organised and developed by museums. The double aim of these programmes is, first, for museums to understand better how to value, interpret and present the communist past while retaining respect for the people involved; and, second, to respond to surviving victims' therapeutic need to be understood within the context of their suffering. Participation within, and exposure provided by, ENoMiR has proved to be an effective way to release powerful memories as part of a shared identity and contested past. This is particularly significant as the museum events become part of a city or national stage. Being able to move the story of the victims of communism from *inside* the walls of their prisons to *outside*, on to the streets of the city, takes the cathartic step of having their pain expressed and performed on a stage.

19.9   European Night of Museums in Bucharest

Night of Museum events need to be representative of the community in order to bring benefits. ENoMiR is seen to have been a success in Bucharest, particularly because of the ways in which the community has shared and embraced it, where each participant has become a performer on the city stage. To some extent, the city becomes a live museum. ENoMiR gives back public space to the public, to whom it belongs (Fig. 19.3). In a country where, during the most oppressive years of

Fig. 19.3.   European Night of Museums in Bucharest. (Photograph courtesy of Codrin Prisecaru.)

communism, even small groups strolling in public were banned, or today when touching museum exhibits may still be forbidden, ENoMiR overturns unpopular rules. It is a symbol of a cultural revolution, reinforced by the 24-h-city concept, radically different from communist times. ENoMiR is a symbol of freedom, extending cultural programmes aimed at regenerating parts of the city by improving its nightlife and night-time economy (Lovatt and O'Connor, 1995; Heath, 1997).

Most of the empirical evidence in this chapter is based on the authors' extended in-depth surveys, debates, questionnaires and interviews undertaken in 2013, 2014 and 2015 with ENoMiR participants, visitors, decision-making personnel, authorities and managers. Most respondents were approached in Bucharest or were residents of the city.

The first Romanian ENoM was organised by Antipa Natural History Museum in May 2005, when it inaugurated a series of cultural performances inside its premises, supported, with lower profile activities, by the National Art Museum, National Museum of Contemporary Art and National Museum of History. This was a success and grew in importance, with participant museum numbers increasing annually (Table 19.1).

In addition to further museums, a diversity of institutions and organisations have also sought to participate, including for 2015, churches (Zlătari Church, The Russian Church) and former communist prisons, some still functioning as prisons. Numbers of participant visitors have increased, and ENoM Bucharest seems to be

Table 19.1. The European Night of Museums in Romania – facts and figures. (From INS, 2015; Reţeaua Naţională a Muzeelor, 2008; authors' 2013–2015 field survey data.)

ENoMiR	2005	2015
Number of participant museums	4	21
Number of other participant institutions	0	11
Number of participant visitors – total	n/a	645,321
ENoM Bucharest 2014 Number of participant visitors	**Per cent of 2014 national** museum visitors	**Per cent of 2014 ENoMiR** national total
191,956	5.96	29.7
ENoM in Europe	2014 Number of participant visitors	
Rome	210,000	
Vienna	208,000	
Bucharest	191,956	
Barcelona	160,000	
ENoM European top event sites	2014 Number of participant visitors	
Centre Pompidou (Paris, France)	25,825	
Bellu Cemetery (Bucharest, Romania)	25,000	
National Museum Zadar (Zadar, Croatia)	18,127	
Natural History Museum (Vienna, Austria)	16,790	
Berlin Cathedral (Berlin, Germany)	8,700	
Colosseum (Rome, Italy)	3,000	
Bucharest as museum site and attraction	2014	
Total number of museums	37	
Share of national total (%)	5	
Number of visitors: per cent of national total	13.51	
Number of inhabitants per museum	26,993	
Total number of museum visitors	5,998	
Romania as a museum site attraction	2014	
Average daily museum attendance	40	
Average weekly museum attendance	281.66	

responsible for shaping the ENoMiR: almost 6% of the nation's annual museum visits take place here at this time, and approaching one-third of all ENoMiR participants attend in the capital (Table 19.1).

In a European context, the success of ENoM Bucharest is comparable to such cities as Rome, Vienna and Barcelona, and its most visited site (Bellu Cemetery) enjoys attendance comparable with the Pompidou Centre in Paris (Table 19.1). And while 3% of the French total population attended ENoM, in Romania the figure was 3.2% (Noapteamuzeelor.ro, 2015; Paulet, 2015). Overall, Romania and its capital appear to enjoy comparable levels of participation with major European countries and cities.

From the authors' surveys, a profile of the ENoM Bucharest participant visitor is gradually emerging (Table 19.2). Most participants make multiple visits, the stated reasons for which include 'the rare opportunity to consume a pleasant night atmosphere of the city streets' and finding the event 'attractive, engaging and educational'. Motivational factors across the survey

years suggest a growing appreciation of the value and significance of museum collections and exhibits. Educational programmes are attracting an increasing share of visitors.

While ENoM is clearly a success for visiting participants, the question of how museums develop their relationship with the public is still being addressed. In particular, people's 'heritage' relationship with the country's painful recent past, the way it is addressed and depicted, is still evolving.

19.10   Summary and Conclusions

The Romanian eventscape has changed significantly, particularly since communism collapsed and notably since EU accession. This change has been stimulated through two vehicles. The European Cultural Capital title was successful for Sibiu in 2007. Its demonstration effect, expressed in a variety of social, economic and political aspects, has stimulated intense competition for ECoC 2021. Three of the four shortlisted Romanian

Table 19.2. European Night of Museums Bucharest – participants' profile. (From authors' 2013–2015 field survey data.)

Predominant age groups	Share of total sample (%) ($n = 486$)
18–30	34.6
31–50	38.1
Gender: F	60
M	40
Education level:	
Higher education degree	72.5
Participation: ENoM visit occurrence	
Single time	39.2
Multiple visits	60.8
ENoM participants' museum attendance	
1–3 times/year	67.9
6–9 times/year	13.7
ENoM participation	
Family visits	44.4
Social group visits	41.9
Participants' main attractions	(Multiple attractions offered = >100%)
Performances included in the event	39.7
Night activity	36.7
Socialising	34.8
Participants' motivation	(Multiple attractions offered = >100%)
Understanding museum collections' value	69.8
Joining workshops and seminars of the event	29.1
Joining the educational programmes	15.6

cities – Bucharest, Cluj Napoca and Timişoara – are literally and metaphorically already a capital of some kind. Bucharest is the current administrative capital of the country, Cluj Napoca has always been and seen itself the capital of Transylvania, while Timişoara is the capital of the Banat region of western Romania. Both Transylvania and Banat are historic cultural regions. Also, the former and current Mayor of Cluj Napoca, Emil Boc, is a former prime minister. As a European geopolitical intervention, ECoC 2021 has stimulated regional competition and identity, as well as a broader awareness of European values.

Clearly, the biggest success in cultural events belongs to ENoMiR and ENoM Bucharest. Its success resides in the new approaches taken to tackle the museum–visitor–community relationship. It also reflects the way museums have become increasingly involved in education and responding to peoples' desire for understanding their history, particularly the communist past.

Despite its apparent success, it would be premature to conclude that ENoMiR has managed to influence policies addressing the recent past, its unwanted memories and contested histories. It is a challenging task to interpret and present communism for both foreign visitors and the Romanian public in a country whose citizens have lived through severe oppression, many of whom continue to be unable to come to terms with it. But the process has, at least, begun, and the future is encouraging. The leading figure of RNMR, Dragoş Neamu, also an active member of the NEMO Board, was very recently appointed councillor of Ministry of Culture, as this chapter was being completed.[7]

Currently, ENoM member museums in Bucharest and across the country are attracting significant and increasing numbers of a public eager to be active and to learn. Observations and survey evidence between 2013 and 2015 has shown that ENoM's success has its roots in the outcomes derived from core museums being joined by other institutions such as performing arts associations, churches and prisons. Through such collaboration, they assist access to the unknown, dark or even brutal communist past. The task of tackling this past more effectively lies in ENoMiR member institutions moving from a 'bridging' to a 'bonding' role, following the example of Western museums and institutions in further considering public needs and expectations through actions that can extend beyond the one-night event.

Since the Romanian public is split into at least two main groups in terms of how they relate to recent history, particular attention needs to be paid to the communal interests of this past. The subject of presenting and interpreting an unwanted past, its contested memories and histories, is still poorly researched. Little multidisciplinary, joint research has been undertaken, and there is minimal teaching of communism at university level. While there may be justifiable reasons for this, such geopolitics of erasure is not healthy for a large contemporary European country. Extending the teaching, researching and interpretation of an unwanted past could help provide a focus for future coherent strategies encompassing culture, civil society and social reconciliation.

Endnotes

[1] Current Romanian territory is the result of a historical unification act involving its three principalities (Walachia, Moldova and Transylvania), which was completed in December 1918.

[2] Alba Iulia, Arad, Bacău, Baia Mare, Brăila, Braşov, Bucharest, Cluj-Napoca, Craiova, Iaşi, Sfântu Gheorghe, Suceava, Târgu Mureş and Timişoara.

[3] Bellu Cemetery, also known as Bellu's Garden of Souls, is the most representative monumental cemetery in Romania, hosting almost 20% of the historical monuments of the capital city. It is also important due to its memorial function, since it shelters the bodies of the most significant Romanian personalities. It was visited by around 25,000 people in 2015.

[4] Arguably, these are aimed equally at foreign tourists and domestic residents.

[5] An exception is the role of films such as *Red Rats* (1990); *Memorial of Suffering* (1991); *The Death of Mr Lăzărescu* (2005); *12:08 East of Bucharest* (2006); *The Paper Will Be Blue* (2006); *4 Months, 3 Weeks, 2 days* (2007); *Tales from a Golden Age* (2009); and *The Autobiography of Nicolae Ceauşescu* (2010).

[6] IICCMER – *Institutul de Investigare a Crimelor Comunismului şi Memoria Exilului Românesc* (Institute for the Investigation of Communist Crimes and the Memory of the Romanian Exile) is a governmental institution that studies, documents and encourages public awareness of communist history in Romania through research, educational, editorial and museum projects.

[7] Not only was the new 2015 government claiming to be less political and more technocrat, but (with an ethnic German President), to appoint the leader of an NGO as counsellor for the Ministry of Culture really was an achievement.

References

Abakina, T.V, Derkachev, P.V., Filatova, L.M. and Scherbakova, I.V. (2015) *Aspects of Increasing Accessibility of Russian Museums and Evaluation of Attendance*. National Research University Higher School of Economics, Working Paper WP BRP/43/MAN/2015, Moscow. Available at: http://www.hse.ru/pubs/share/direct/document/167444828 (accessed 11 August 2016).

Albert, S. (2015) The nation for itself: the 1896 Hungarian Millenium and the 1906 Romanian National General Exhibition. In: Filipova, M. (ed.) *Cultures of International Exhibitions 1840–1940: Great Exhibitions in the Margins*. Ashgate, Farnham, UK, pp. 113–136.

Anholt, S. (2006) *Competitive Identity: The New Brand Management for Nations, Cities and Regions*. Palgrave Macmillan, London.

Araujo, L.M.D. and Bramwell, B. (1999) Stakeholder assessment and collaborative tourism planning: the case of Brazil's Costa Dourada Project. *Journal of Sustainable Tourism* 7, 356–378.

Balsas, C.J.L. (2004) City centre regeneration in the context of the 2001 European capital of culture in Porto, Portugal. *Local Economy* 19, 396–410.

Bennett, W.L., Lawrence, R.G. and Livingston, S. (2008) *When the Press Fails: Political Power and the News Media from Iraq to Katrina*. University of Chicago Press, Chicago, Illinois.

Broudehoux, A.-M. (2007) Spectacular Beijing: the conspicuous construction of an Olympic metropolis. *Journal of Urban Affairs* 29, 383–399.

Bujdei, L. (2014) Directorul MŢR, Virgil Niţulescu, a fost ales preşedinte al Reţelei Naţionale a Muzeelor din România. [The director of the Romanian Peasant Museum, Virgil Niţulescu, was elected president of the Romanian National Museum Network.] *Mediafax* [Suceava, Romania] 12 June (in Romanian). Available at: http://www.mediafax.ro/cultura-media/directorul-mtr-virgil-nitulescu-a-fost-ales-presedinte-al-retelei-nationale-a-muzeelor-din-romania-12745551 (accessed 10 September 2015).

Burbank, M., Andranovich, G. and Heying, C. H. (2001) *Olympic Dreams: The Impact of Mega-events on Local Politics*. Lynne Rienner, Boulder, Colorado.

Capitală Europeană a Culturii (2015a) *Baia Mare, Bucureşti, Cluj-Napoca şi Timişoara, pe lista scurtă a oraşelor preselectate. [Baia Mare, Bucharest, Cluj-Napoca and Timişoara, on the short list of the preselected cities.]* Capitală Europeană a Culturii/MiCapitală Europeană a Culturii (2015a) *Baia Mare, Bucureşti, Cluj-Napoca şi Timişoara, pe lista scurtă a oraşelor preselectate. [Baia Mare, Bucharest, Cluj-Napoca and Timişoara, on the short list of the preselected cities.]* Capitală Europeană a Culturii/Ministerul Culturii, Bucharest, Romania (in Romanian). Available at: http://www.capitalaculturala2021.ro/noutati_doc_24_baia-mare-bucuresti-cluj-napoca-si-timisoara-pe-lista-scurta-a-oraselor-preselectate_pg_0.htm (accessed 11 December 2015).

Capitală Europeană a Culturii (2015b) *Dosarele oraşelor ale căror candidaturi au fost acceptate. [The application forms of the cities which were nominated.]* Capitală Europeană a Culturii/Ministerul Culturii, Bucharest, Romania (in Romanian). Available at: http://www.caCapitală Europeană a Culturii (2015b) *Dosarele oraşelor ale căror candidaturi au fost acceptate. [The application forms of the cities which were nominated.]* Capitală Europeană a Culturii/Ministerul Culturii, Bucharest, Romania (in Romanian). Available at: http://www.capitalaculturala2021.ro/noutati_doc_22_dosarele-oraselor-ale-caror-candidaturi-au-fost-acceptate_pg_0.htm (accessed 13 November 2015).

Cărtărescu, M. (2010) Senatul EVZ: de partea întunecată a forţei. Bucureşti. [The EVZ senate: taking the dark side of force.] *evz.ro* [Bucharest, Romania] 18 November (in Romanian). Available at: http://www.evz.ro/senatul-evz-de-partea-intunecata-a-fortei-912899.html (accessed 16 April 2015).

City of Cape Town (2015) *Events Strategy 2015–2017*. City of Cape Town, Cape Town, South Africa. Available at: https://www.capetown.gov.za/en/visitcapetown/Documents/Events_Strategy_2015_2017.pdf (accessed 11 August 2016).

Dayan, D. and Katz, E. (1994) *Media Events.* Harvard University Press, Cambridge, Massachusetts.

Deloche, B. (2001) *Le Musée Virtuel: vers une Éthique des Nouvelles Images.* [*The Virtual Museum: Through an Ethic of New Images.*] Presses Universitaires de France, Paris (in French).

Desvallées, A., Mairesse, F. and de Mariemont, M.R. (2010) *Key Concepts of Museology.* Armand Colin, Paris.

Dumbrăveanu, D., Tudoricu, A. and Crăciun, A. M. (2014) The Night of Museums – a boost factor for the cultural dimension of tourism in Bucharest. *Human Geographies* 8, 55–63.

Getz, D. (2007) *Event Studies: Theory, Research and Policy for Planned Events.* Elsevier Butterworth-Heinemann, Oxford, UK.

Gordin, V. and Dedova, M. (2014) Cultural innovations and consumer behaviour: the case of Museum Night. *International Journal of Management Cases* 16, 32–40.

Graham Devlin Associates (2001) *Festivals and the City: the Edinburgh Festivals Strategy.* Unpublished report for City of Edinburgh Council, Edinburgh, UK.

Grinkevitch, V. (2014) Seventy percent of Russians not interested in museums. *Open Economy* [Moscow] 14 August. Available at: http://opec.ru/en/1735130.html (accessed 10 September 2015).

Hayllar, B., Griffin, T. and Edwards, D. (2008) *City Spaces – Tourist Places: Urban Tourism Precincts.* Butterworth-Heinemann/Elsevier, Oxford, UK.

Heath, T. (1997) The twenty-four hour city concept – a review of initiatives in British cities. *Journal of Urban Design* 2, 193–204.

Herrero, L.C., Sanz, J.Á., Devesa, M., Bedate, A. and Barrio, M.J.D. (2006) The economic impact of cultural events: a case-study of Salamanca 2002, European Capital of Culture. *European Urban and Regional Studies* 13, 41–57.

ICOM (International Council of Museums) (2015) *International Museum Day.* ICOM, Paris. Available at: http://network.icom.museum/international-museum-day (accessed 11 August 2016).

INS (Institutul Naţional de Statistică) (2015) *Baza de date Tempo – Turism.* [*National Statistics Institute, Tempo-Tourism Database.*] INS, Bucharest (in Romanian). Available at: http://statistici.insse.ro/shop/?lang=ro (accessed 10 June 2015).

Jiwa, S., Coca-Stefaniak, J.A., Blackwell, M. and Rahman, T. (2009) Light night: an 'enlightening' place marketing experience. *Journal of Place Management and Development* 2, 154–166.

Kotler, P., Haider, D.H. and Rein, I.J. (1993) *Marketing Places: Attracting Investment, Industry, and Tourism to Cities, States, and Nations.* Free Press, New York.

Kultur Projekte Berlin (2016) *36th Long Night of Museums.* Kultur Projekte Berlin, Berlin. Available at: http://www.visitberlin.de/en/event/08-27-2016/36th-long-night-of-museums-2016 (accessed 24 August 2016).

Light, D. (2000) An unwanted past: contemporary tourism and the heritage of communism in Romania. *International Journal of Heritage Studies* 6, 145–160.

Lovatt, A. and O'Connor, J. (1995) Cities and the night-time economy. *Planning Practice & Research* 10, 127–134.

Matei, A. (2013) The Golden Stag Festival in Ceausescu's Romania (1968–1971). *View Journal Of European Television History And Culture*, North America, 1. Available at: http://rdbg.tuxic.nl/euscreen-ojs/index.php/view/article/view/jethc015/38 (accessed 6 February 2015).

Meet Minneapolis (2015) Events Calendar. Meet Minneapolis, Minneapolis, Minnesota. Available at: http://www.minneapolis.org/visitor/calendar/ (accessed 20 September 2015).

Moscardo, G. (2007) Analyzing the role of festivals and events in regional development. *Event Management* 11, 23–32.

Noapteamuzeelor.ro (2015) Noaptea Muzeelor I Sărbătoarea europeană a muzeelor. [The Night of Museums I The European celebration of museums.] (In Romanian.) Available at: http://www.noapteamuzeelor.ro/ (accessed 10 August 2015).

Nobili, V. (2005) The role of European Capital of Culture events within Genoa's and Liverpool's branding and positioning efforts. *Place Branding* 1, 316–328.

Ologeanu, C. and Suciu, M. (2005) Cenaclul Flacăra – Două generaţii în blugi. [Cenaclul Flacăra – Two generations in blue jeans.] *Jurnalul.ro* [Bucharest] 5 November (in Romanian). Available at: http://jurnalul.ro/special-jurnalul/cenaclul-flacara-doua-generatii-in-blugi-33936.html (accessed 7 September 2015).

Paiola, M. (2008) Cultural events as potential drivers of urban regeneration: an empirical illustration. *Industry and Innovation* 15, 513–529.

Paulet, A. (2015) La Nuit des Musées a attiré 2 millions de visiteurs. [The Night of Museums has attracted 2 million visitors.] *Le Figaro* [Paris] 18 May (in French). Available at: http://www.lefigaro.fr/arts-expositions/2015/05/18/03015-20150518ARTFIG00060-la-nuit-des-musees-a-attire-2-millions-de-visiteurs.php (accessed 11 August 2016).

Pinto, L. (2013) Using events as a marketing technique. In: Reimer, L. (ed.) Inside Blackberry BUSINESS BLOG. Available at: http://bizblog.blackberry.com/2013/09/how-to-use-events-as-a-business-marketing-tool/ (accessed 19 August 2015).

Reţeaua Naţională a Muzeelor (2008) About the network. Available at: http://www.muzee.org/romania/index. php?option=com_content&task=blogcategory&id=2&Itemid=10 (accessed 15 September 2015).

Richards, G. and Palmer, R. (2010) *Eventful Cities: Cultural Management and Urban Revitalisation.* Butterworth-Heinemann, Oxford, UK.

Richards, G. and Rotariu, I. (2010a) 2007 European Cultural Capital in Sibiu – preliminary findings concerning the impact on major stakeholders. *Studies in Business and Economics* 5, 146–155.

Richards, G. and Rotariu, I. (2010b) The impact of the 2007 European Cultural Capital in Sibiu: a long term perspective. Unpublished paper, Munich Personal RePEc Archive, Munich, Germany. Available at: https://mpra.ub.uni-muenchen.de/22532/ (accessed 30 January 2016).

Richards, G. and Rotariu, I. (2015) Developing the eventful city in Sibiu, Romania. *International Journal of Tourism Cities* 1, 89–102.

Richards, G. and Wilson, J. (2004) The impact of cultural events on city image: Rotterdam, cultural capital of Europe 2001. *Urban Studies* 41, 1931–1951.

Saayman, M. and Saayman, A. (2004) Economic impact of cultural events. *South African Journal of Economic and Management Sciences* 7, 629–641.

Santos, J.F., Vareiro, L., Remoaldo, P. and Ribeiro, J.C. (2015) *Mega Cultural Events: Does Attendance Affect Residents' Perceptions of a City's Identity?* Universidade do Minho, Guimaraes, Portugal.

Simon, N. (2010) *The Participatory Museum.* Museum 2.0, Santa Cruz, CA.

Tilden, F. (1957) *Interpreting Our Heritage.* University of North Carolina Press, Chapel Hill, North Carolina.

Tuan, Y.-F. (2001) *Space and Place: The Perspective of Experience.* University of Minnesota Press, Minneapolis, Minnesota.

TVR.RO (2015) Cenaclul Flacăra: a fost sau n-a fost un fenomen cultural unic? [Cenaclul Flacăra: was it or not a unique cultural phenomenon?]. *TVR.RO* [Bucharest] 30 May (in Romanian). Available at: http://www.tvr.ro/cenaclul-flacara-a-fost-sau-nu-un-fenomen-cultural-unic_12658.html#view (accessed 11 September 2015).

Visit Berlin (2015) *Events Calendar.* Visit Berlin, Berlin. Available at: http://www.visitberlin.de/en/experience/events/event-calendar (accessed 11 August 2016).

Webber, D. (2004) Understanding charity fundraising events. *International Journal of Nonprofit and Voluntary Sector Marketing* 9, 122–134.

Žižek, S. (2014) *Event: Philosophy in Transit.* Penguin, New York, NY.

20 The Power of the Web: Blogging Destination Image in Bucharest and Sofia

Alexandru Gavriş[1]* and Ioan Ianoş[2]

[1]*Faculty of Business and Tourism, Bucharest University of Economic Studies, Romania; [2]Faculty of Geography, University of Bucharest, Romania*

20.1 Introduction

The increasing competition of cities for tourism emphasises the importance of destination image as one of the most valuable features in tourism marketing and promotion. It is an element that is prominent in the study and practice of tourism (Pike, 2002), and it can possess a transformative power over tourism space and the actors within it. The significance of destination images has risen to new heights with the development of cyberspace, which now represents an important source of power for articulating and reinforcing such images. Information and communication technologies have redefined the tourist gaze, becoming powerful tools of image formation that can enhance the fortunes of some destinations and diminish the image of less competitive places. Despite a substantial literature on city image formation, several authors (e.g. Lee *et al.*, 2005; Tasci and Gartner, 2007; Lepp *et al.*, 2011) have stressed the need to explore the potential of and understand better the image formation processes of lesser-studied destinations.

In the former communist countries of Central and Eastern Europe (CEE), a new context has emerged in the competitive market where tourism is strongly promoted and re-evaluated as an essential added value to the economy. Capital cities have been prominent in this process, and they provide particularly fruitful environments for tourist behaviour research; but current knowledge is highly uneven. Bucharest (Romania) and Sofia (Bulgaria) remain among the capital cities that have been little explored in tourism research, despite the need to understand the image formation of 'newer' tourism destinations better.

This chapter, therefore, continues to fill a gap identified in the literature (Kolbe, 2007; Maitland and Ritchie, 2009). It does this by addressing the links between two of the region's 'marginal' capital cities and the shift of power relations promoted by the Western world as expressed in the online representation of destination images. The popularity of travel blogs offers the opportunity to analyse images framed by tourists, both before and after EU accession in 2007, and to examine the extent to which they may possess the power to influence the images of these two cities significantly.

To reveal some of the geopolitical power of cyberspace, we investigate the representation of online content as part of a narrative process. Our aim is to understand the images and impressions communicated by tourists and to highlight the power of blogs in the evolution of the destination image in post-socialist urban space. The research draws on data from Travelpod.com to frame the components that create a destination image and to discuss the emerging power produced

*Corresponding author. E-mail: alexandru.gavris@rei.ase.ro

through blogs. Content analysis and text mining are the methods used to identify the images of the cities as revealed by the blogging experience of travellers. The findings are further employed to interrogate the power that blogs can exert in the tourism context.

20.2   Literature Review

This chapter is based on the assumption that people's narrative practice can offer a detailed image of the spaces visited, and that storytelling in the form of blogs has the ability to emphasise hidden characteristics of the tourists' experience. This represents a valuable contribution to understand the power that blogs possess in image formation. Much has been written on the value of destination image (Chon, 1990; Baloglu and McCleary, 1999; Pike, 2002; Cai *et al.*, 2003; Beerli and Martin, 2004), its nature and the formative influence that it has on tourists (Echtner and Ritchie, 1993; Gallarza *et al.*, 2002; del Bosque and San Martín, 2008; San Martín and del Bosque, 2008). Image formation is a mental construct that can be transmitted with fresher and deeper meaning in the form of a blog narrative, and this medium may suffer less from the influence of classical image formation agents. As with many concepts, a standard form of destination image is yet to be fully accepted, but it is clearly concerned with 'impression' and 'perception' (San Martín and del Bosque, 2008). Since these words express subjectivity, the cumulative force of tourists' narration shapes the destination image and creates the tourist product in complex ways, emphasising personal experience (Tasci and Gartner, 2007), which is well encapsulated in blogs. Thus, image formation narrated by blogs is shaped by an interaction between destination attributes and tourists'/bloggers' feelings (Prayag, 2009).

20.2.1   Image formation and information sources

The conceptual evolution of this area of study has taken place around three main stages of destination image research (Tseng *et al.*, 2015). The first of these has contributed to theorisation of the field; the second has involved behavioural research in which attitude theory has gained the attention of researchers and facilitated measurement and the identification of components. The third stage has involved a greater focus on the qualitative aspects of the destination image and its interaction with other concepts. Throughout these stages, several models of destination image formation have emerged (Gunn, 1988; Echtner and Ritchie, 1993; Baloglu and Mc-Cleary, 1999; Tasci and Gartner, 2007; Kim and Chen, 2016) discussing sources of image formation agents. Among these, blogs in particular have brought a different perspective to the ways tourists perceive destinations and are involved in their (re)construction.

The role of information is critical in tourism, and for its dissemination, a number of frameworks have shifted towards social media platforms. In a comprehensive study, Zeng and Gerritsen (2014) scrutinise this direction, discussing the power shift that social media has brought to tourism, and its resulting challenges. They articulate the aggregated characteristics of social media as 'social networking sites, consumer review sites, content community sites, *wikis*, Internet forums and location-based social media' (Zeng and Gerritsen, 2014: 28). Such tools have empowered tourists (Neuhofer *et al.*, 2014) to communicate their experiences, and have created new ways of mediating image formation that complement (Jacobsen and Munar, 2012) and enhance tourism. Therefore, online content plays an important role in influencing tourist behaviour (de Valck *et al.*, 2009), and research suggests that social media exert a major impact on the tourism sector (Gretzel *et al.*, 2008). It can be said that social platforms have 'reinvented' communication in tourism (Volo, 2012) and have (re)activated the role of tourists.

With the advent and development of the Internet and its tools of analysis, destination images are recreated continuously on the Web, such that the actors traditionally involved in these images' 'official' construction now hold diminished power: their level of control is challenged by Web interaction and social media, emphasising the importance of virtual space. Thus, using travel blogs becomes salient to gain new insights into image formation (Choi *et al.*, 2007).

20.2.2 Understanding blogs in tourism

Among applications that have enhanced tourism, travel blogs are identified as asynchronous and electronic word-of-mouth channels. They involve many categories of agents related to the tourism sector (Litvin *et al.*, 2008) whose communication develops horizontally as opposed to the traditional, vertical mode of communication, and even mixes the two modes (Castells, 2007). Travel blog sites allow tourists to share their trips and experiences, and to exchange information during the planning process. The quality of the posts that appear at the top of the page are managed through a ranking system, and through the bloggers' involvement.

The popularity of blogs has expanded among travellers seeking prior knowledge of sites of interest. After early anticipation of a high potential for blogs as a tourist information source (Crotts, 1999), research into electronic narration and tourists' storytelling emerged rapidly. The potential of blogging overlaps many fields of research (Volo, 2010), and can provide a powerful experience for readers affiliated with the blogger (Volo, 2009).

Although volatile and appearing in many forms, blogs represent a significant part of tourists' communication and travel-planning strategies that help to articulate the destination image. Yet the Web 2.0 sources appear to act only as a complement to tourist decision making (Jacobsen and Munar, 2012), and may be viewed as actually hindering image formation processes in the way they encourage contestation. The credibility of Internet sources has often been questioned in relation to the quality and expertise of content generators (Mack *et al.*, 2008). But for members of the same community, as in the case of travel blogs, credibility is generally high (Buhalis and Law, 2008), especially since online communities have become more selective and experienced. Therefore, travel blogs are now regarded as highly valued social media (del Chiappa, 2011). However, the role of blogs as image formation agents has not yet been incorporated into Gartner's (1994) original model, despite appeals for its inclusion (Choi *et al.*, 2007) and subsequent modifications (Tasci and Gartner, 2007; Kim and Chen, 2016).

The content of travel blogs has been scrutinised to provide support for marketing and management (Pan *et al.*, 2007; Pudliner, 2007; Woodside *et al.*, 2007; Carson, 2008; Tussyadiah and Fesenmaier, 2008; Volo, 2009) and to identify strategies that assist economic entities (Schmallegger and Carson, 2008). Moreover, travel blogs express an alternative way to obtain data for research, facilitating the exploration of tourists' experiences (Schmallegger and Carson, 2008; Volo, 2010). As such, user-generated content activities and travel blog studies have increased in recent years as the importance of blogs has matured (Douglas and Mills, 2006; Karlsson, 2006; Lin and Huang, 2006; Choi *et al.*, 2007; Thevenot, 2007; Mack *et al.*, 2008; Tussyadiah and Fesenmaier, 2008; Wenger, 2008; Stepchenkova *et al.*, 2009; Xiang and Gretzel, 2010; Tseng *et al.*, 2015). Akehurst (2009) has suggested further directions for travel blog analysis in the form of artificial intelligence and 'opinion mining' or a blog visualisation system.

Despite challenges to blogs being fully utilised in the tourism sector (Akehurst, 2009), their advantages over other social media content can be exhibited (Schmallegger and Carson, 2008). The depth of information found in studies analysing travel blogs has motivated administrators to consider them in the strategic development of the destination image at different levels: national (Wenger, 2008; Lepp *et al.*, 2011; Li and Wang, 2011; Tseng *et al.*, 2015), capital city (considered to have a unique image) (Huang and Lee, 2009), urban (Choi *et al.*, 2007; Hsu *et al.*, 2009; Law and Cheung, 2010), regional (Douglas and Mills, 2006; Pan *et al.*, 2007; Carson, 2008) and micro-level (Banyai, 2010). The focus varies from reporting tourist activities, their characteristics and the involvement of authorities, to differences between the expectations and requirements of the bloggers within the space travelled. Therefore, the potential of travel blogs and other social media is high and is acknowledged by researchers, tourists and marketers (Yoo and Gretzel, 2012). One constraint is the fact that the different social media tools receive unequal attention, and are being embedded differently within the strategies of various national tourism organisations (Hays *et al.*, 2013).

The growing interest in tourist blogs and content analysis has triggered a critical evaluation of the methodologies employed (Banyai and Glover, 2012). Various methods of conducting research on blogs reveal a bias towards quantitative approaches, with an under-representation of qualitative research in destination image analysis (Pike, 2002). Because of this, Banyai and Havitz (2013) have suggested the need for more profound qualitative research of blog content that targets travel activities.

20.2.3 Tourism image in transition

For almost 50 years, the Cold War maintained a geopolitical balance that constrained tourism between the ideological blocs within Europe. But from the 1990s, the power that the Western world had generated allowed their tourists to influence image formation by communicating their experiences of former communist countries. The knowledge and spectacle that previously had been reproduced through television programmes and guidebooks evolved to Web 2.0, where travel blogs and tourists' narratives could add variety to the discourse about tourism in former communist societies and the little-explored spaces of CEE countries. As post-communist countries have re-entered the global tourism market, they have experienced two stages in the development of destination images: first, immediately after the shift to the Western political and economic system and then, second, for some of them, following EU accession.

During communism, capital cities were the focus of the projected image of the regimes. But little information was obtained from actual tourists about the destination and how they perceived it. After economic and political change, some capital cities struggled to maintain their leading characteristics. To reclaim regional power and to attract investments, former communist cities followed different paths. While the more Western cities faced easier adaptation, the 'marginal' capital cities such as Bucharest and Sofia lagged behind. Their countries invested a great deal in tourism redevelopment and employed these capitals as hubs for other destinations within the country. During the 1990s, the main attractions that interested tourists involved 'red' and dark tourism, a development that contrasted and conflicted with the authorities' plans to promote the cities' renewed image. The new regimes largely ignored tourists' interests in communist heritage and artefacts of the revolution. The official priority was to recreate the mythical image

of the inter-war period (for Bucharest), and to avoid relics of communism, to promote an alternative to neighbouring countries' capital cities (for Sofia).

This seemed little more than a continuation of old ideological practices aiming to fit into a Western/European projection (Light, 2006). In fact, it was a privatisation of power (Hall, 2000) used to reconstruct old interests. At the same time, through various publicity and promotion campaigns, the authorities attempted to produce official country images to reaffirm historic ties to the Western world (see Chapter 3, this volume). But the challenges of post-communist development and the contested nature of tourism pressured the authorities to prioritise other regions and projects. As such, official concern for developing and implementing a coherent image of the capital city was low.

However, Western travel guidebooks and tourism operators responded to the interests of tourists wishing to experience 'new exotic destinations' that had been part of communism (Light, 2007). Bucharest and Sofia appeared to be overlooked by tourists, who were focused on seaside and ski resorts, rural tourism and heritage. There was also a mismatched strategy to promote the cities and not their surroundings as a whole destination. This is more obvious in Sofia, where the city tourism relies on its urban forms, neglecting the potential of the nearby Vitosha mountains and their natural springs, whose popularity now appears to be in decline (Petkova and Marinov, 2014). Overall, in both cases, tourism was of secondary importance and tourism administration was being constantly restructured, reducing the effectiveness of any attempts to project a coherent image.

After the EU accession of both Bulgaria and Romania in 2007, their capital cities faced radical changes, which also affected tourism. Communist heritage was now seen as an important asset that could be used to enhance the development of the city. Bucharest and Sofia embarked on promoting flagship projects (including football arena redevelopment, the hosting of major sports competitions, cultural festivals and the redevelopment of key central areas), which were regarded as important in diversifying their tourism attractions. But this strategy met with limited success in both cases. The cities' tourism development processes remained heavily politicised, many of the decisions being criticised because too much importance was given to unsustainable projects.

Alongside these issues, extensive areas of the cities received investment for their rehabilitation and promotion. Tour operators and hotel chains gained confidence to invest and enhance the potential for these cities' tourism facilities, accommodation quality and variety of gastronomy. Connected to the new liberalisation of life, clubs and bars in the main tourist spots organised specifically themed parties, which assisted in the development of the cities as important destinations for weekend tourism. Yet, overall, tourism development in Bucharest and Sofia has looked like a sideways step, with misguided strategies that do not connect key tourist attractions and areas, thereby producing fragmented experiences and images. It is a mix of old communist practices with a particular understanding of capitalism, in which the power of national and local actors shapes image formation and strives to attract tourists to help raise once again the country/region/city to the firmament of a 'tourism destination'.

20.3 Methodology

The use of content analysis has allowed improved research (Pritchard and Morgan, 2001) and has become common in destination image studies (Choi *et al.*, 2007; Pan *et al.*, 2007; Carson, 2008; Wenger, 2008; Stepchenkova, 2012; Tseng *et al.*, 2015). Krippendorff (2013) has shown the importance of content analysis, and Sebastiani (2002) improved automatic text categorisation, arguing that it may be more effective than human decision. The approach based on text information and content analysis in tourism finds support in previous studies (Fennell, 2001; Choi *et al.*, 2007; Stepchenkova *et al.*, 2009; Shuang *et al.*, 2013). It emerges that travel blogs are among the best candidates for such analysis because tourists' power to produce the image is based on attributes and themes, offering a targeted description of parts of the destination visited, easing the collection of data, comparing evolution over time, limiting the biased elements and thus enhancing trust. But what is more relevant in travel blog posts is that authenticity emerges more strongly, as people write about their travel experience and compare it with other channels of information.

The research for this chapter used the texts of travel blogs relating to Bucharest and Sofia to analyse their tourist images. This was undertaken in three stages. First, text-mining techniques were employed to extract the data, to clean it from the fuzziness of the blog structure and to include it in a corpus for further data exploration. Second, a drill-down analysis extracted and highlighted the themes related to the research topic. The last stage comprised the analysis of each resulting corpus within a quantitative content analysis framework. Each resulting corpus, corresponding to each city, allowed an enquiry into the greatest frequency of words and the co-occurrence networks, which were explored to define themes and develop codes for a dictionary. Statistical procedures and semi-automatic coding were used to assist the data analysis (the coding involved procedures described in the KH Coder manual: Higuchi, 2016). In other words, the importance of text mining and content analysis is to use 'public knowledge' in the learning and discovery of new features about destination images and tourists' perceptions, while the themes' evolution suggests changes in the influence of the blogs.

KH Coder (Higuchi, 2016) assisted the analysis of texts of the travel posts and their mining, providing options similar to established software used in the field. Its use in tourism research has been to analyse tourist travel behaviour (Sasaki and Nishii, 2012) and to evaluate historical districts as tourism destinations (Naoi *et al.*, 2011). Its advantages rely on the fact that it combines Perl language with a forefront for R software environment on given packages that involve text mining and computational linguistics. This mix allows superior interoperability, facilitating the analysis, testing of data and achieving results through different well-documented procedures (Higuchi, 2016). The words reveal that the concepts and the co-occurrence maps augment the visual exploration of word associations. The interpretation of maps depends on the location of circles inside the diagram, the thickness of the lines and the proximity on the diagram. Location shows the importance of the words, the most central ones representing critical information, while thickness represents the strength of association among key words. The tones represent the communities based on random walks,[1] which allow a better structuring of the clusters (Aggarwal, 2011), but the role of tones is not essential, only adding insight to the analysis (Higuchi, 2016).

20.3.1 Data

The variety and number of blogs necessitate extensive processing capabilities. This limited the analysis to one public travel blog site hosting individual stories and comments: Travelpod.com. This was chosen because it hosts a sufficient number of posts with details about experiences in Bucharest and Sofia. It is the oldest functional site of its kind that facilitates free registration and hosting for writing, posting and uploading data on the Web. Other travel sites were considered, but were seen to be inferior by virtue of their lack of relevance, limited nature, inactivity or direct commercial interests.

The blogs were collected in December 2014. After removing the redundant ones, the blogs' content comprised 14,000 sentences for Bucharest from 542 valid posts, and 15,000 sentences encountered through 573 posts for Sofia. To preserve the unity of analysis, we examined only the English language posts. Although translations from other languages were possible, they posed the risk of deforming the authenticity transmitted by tourists.

20.4 Findings

The posts on Travelpod.com involved mainly travellers from English-speaking countries (Fig. 20.1) before and after 2007, documenting different impressions of the tourism experience. Information posted by travellers involved sending reassurance to relatives about their status, describing the historical and political context of the cities and their sightseeing experiences, while others just remarked on their travel destinations, providing scarce details. All the blogs assessed contributed to the results, out of which several themes emerged (Fig. 20.2a and b) reflecting the changes produced by cities' integration into the EU.

20.4.1 Contrasting image

The two cities were compared for the periods before and after EU accession in 2007, for each

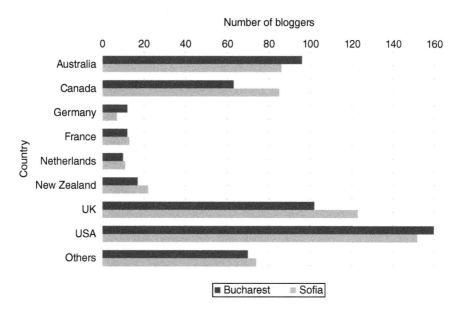

Fig. 20.1. Bloggers' country of origin. (From authors' analysis of Travelpod.com postings.)

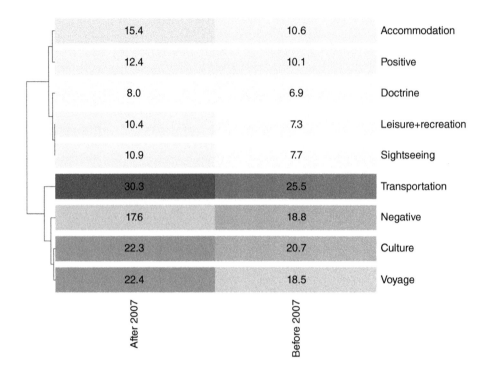

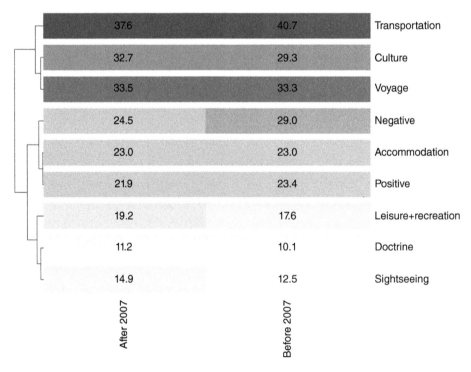

Fig. 20.2. (a) Blog themes: crosstab for Bucharest; (b) blog themes: crosstab for Sofia. (From authors' analysis of Travelpod.com postings.)

year throughout the discourse of the bloggers. The travel experiences comprised many details, and we could identify both positive and negative elements in image creation. Before 2007, the two cities were seen in profoundly negative terms – 'not worth a visit at all' –, with tourists highlighting in detail every unfriendly experience and its attributes. It was for many 'the first culture shock ... since Africa' or, later, 'it felt like a historical city from a parallel universe'. The negative aspects emerged from attributes related to traffic and transportation issues, crime environment perceptions, the presence of Roma people, dogs, and decaying buildings that have 'that stereotypical Eastern European look, dark and gloomy'. Situations discussed in 2001 for Bucharest found the city to be '... dirty, crazy, insanely unsafe for driving and infested with wild rabies infected dogs and shady looking people just waiting to rip you off', while 'Sofia's not the safest of places once darkness falls'.

Any positive features of the two cities were eclipsed by feelings of insecurity and the lack of confidence in the attractiveness of the cities, even by the country's inhabitants, as revealed in their interactions with tourists. This was emphasised by a blogger asking a guest house manager about Sofia, who:

> ... gave a disappointed sigh. 'If you must go there, I strongly suggest only staying one night'.

Reflecting the insipid images of the two cities, negative descriptions persisted after EU accession, but their intensity was diminished and transformed into a more puzzling experience. Discussed by many of the pre-2007 blogs, the bleak atmosphere of Bucharest and Sofia was gradually replaced by a different perspective of positive discovery. It was a contrasting city image that challenged the dark one that had been previously communicated to bloggers by third parties, where:

> everybody that I have met so far ... told me that Sofia was terrible, ... that I shouldn't go there ... [but] ... I find Sofia really cool.

Or,

> thoroughly un-recommended by most guide books, we actually really liked Bucharest.

So despite a previous negative image and warnings from other image-formation agents, the two cities became attractive, but their images

remained blurred into microgeographies where tourists did not know what they were seeing or how they should react to different encounters. This happened because, according to at least one blogger,

> opening *Lonely Planet Romania* they make Bucharest like a very fancy, newly trendy place: 'Forget Prague, forget Budapest ... Bucharest is where travellers are heading. This is Eastern Europe's secret – but it's about to get out',[2]

thereby misleading tourists into expecting too much or becoming apprehensive. This dissonance is reflected in the messages of the bloggers, who 'can't really explain why' there is such a contrast and how the cities occupy a place in the '"underrated European city" category'.

Positive images came from the fact the cities were cheap ('God, how I love that exchange rate!'), the gastronomy was appealing ('our dinner in Bucharest was quite notable', 'had a delicious meal at an authentic Bulgarian restaurant') and from a fascination with dark and communist elements, which perpetuated intriguing and contradictory elements:

> It [Bucharest's Parliament Palace] makes Buckingham Palace look a little on the dinky side.

Or,

> it offers beauty in unexpected places, and in unusual forms ... Sofia still manages to offer up many of the same pleasantries as Europe's great, and more famous capitals ... Sofia still has something to offer those that are looking for something different.

20.4.2   Image of a regional transport hub

Both cities recorded a large number of posts about arriving or departing for other destinations from their respective countries or nearby ones. This underlines the fact that Bucharest and Sofia are perceived by many as cities to be visited for a short time only:

> Looking at the tour itinerary from Budapest to Istanbul I can't help that think the stops in Romania only serve to break up the trip a bit.

More important areas to visit are considered to be elsewhere in the country, away from the capital city. This is why numerous bloggers contribute to the image of Bucharest and Sofia by referring to transportation experiences that mark the whole journey:

> we had some troubles with the public transport ...

in Bucharest, and

> the more common form of transport ... is the long orange trolley cars that creek through the city ...

in Sofia.

The terminal infrastructure also plays an important role in highlighting travel perceptions:

> Every other train station ... had either English signs or at least little pictures. Not Sofia, everything was written entirely in Bulgarian and the Cyrillic alphabet ...

or,

> I walked around the train station for about thirty minutes and couldn't find the ticket counter. I also wanted to find the bus stop. There was a stop, but no signs on it so I had no idea if it was right or not.

20.4.3 History and ideological perspective

The discourse on ideology is embedded strongly in many blogs. While discussing cities and their attributes, many bloggers' references created an image anchored to the past and to the political changes. It is a perspective that emerges from the inevitable references to the Parliament Palace, the country's 'transition' period or integration into the EU. The repetition of these elements produces a mythical image, which is seen with compassion. Communist relics or cultural heritage affected by communism stimulate detailed discussion, with many examples and 'lessons of history' in both Sofia and Bucharest. Also, it shows the power of tourists in assessing the transformation faced by cities during communism and in the new relations with capitalism.

> Bucharest itself is best described as a city undergoing a painful and awkward adolescence. Stripped of its original beauty ... by the Communist dictatorship, it is now struggling to

find itself and find an identity in the midst of the relics of past eras and the encroachment of capitalism and modern technology. Like many adolescents rebelling against oppressive rules, it has turned largely to easy pleasures of the kind forbidden under the former regime. Casinos and strip clubs have sprouted up like acne alongside fast food joints and clothing chains. There is beauty here, but you have to hunt for it.

> You can see that the years of a Communist regime have really taken their toll on the city [Sofia] and the older people in the city. They are doing all that they can though to embrace Capitalism and improve the city's infrastructure.

20.4.4 City cultural experience/ identity

Cultural identity is reflected in the large number of blog references to different heritage components of the cities. In Bucharest, the cultural experience is overwhelmed by the 'House of the People' (Parliament Palace), which triggers many references to the past and to other cultural objects within the city. It is the magnet that attracts almost all the other cultural experiences. Despite this attraction, tourists interested in a broader experience manage to discover 'hidden gems', which comprise churches, architecture, food, human interaction. These are concepts that Sofia reveals, given the fact that its main attractions concentrate on churches (Saint Aleksander Nevski, Saint George, Saint Nedelya). But, as in Bucharest, the main disappointment of tourists is that some of the cultural heritage, belonging to the past or to communism, was destroyed during wars or ideological shifts:

> it's unfortunate that relics of that era were destroyed so wantonly.

The cultural experience emphasises once again a sense of contrast and fragmentation which is everywhere:

> I already felt the clashing styles of architecture.

Or,

> people too seem divided between those embracing new business models and others seemingly intent on developing their own counter-culture.

20.4.5 Word frequency and co-occurrence network map

Terms used in the analysis comprise less than 14,000 unique words (not counting the stop words) for Bucharest, and almost 15,000 in the case of Sofia. The selection of the most frequent ten words revealed expected elements in both cases (Table 20.1), reflecting the strong connections of the cities within the travel experience.

Co-occurrence network analysis was used to identify a map of the tourists' image. The procedure involved selecting the filter edges at the top 75 with a minimum 125 words frequency, where words used in the filtering were only common nouns, proper nouns and verbs. Circles (nodes) represent key words based on their importance and lines show how strong the edges are. These highlight a structure of the more important clusters in relation to the number of nodes and their position in the map.

The results for Bucharest show five clusters related to city image formation (Fig. 20.3a). The main elements, which are present in the narrative experience of tourists, focus on travel experience in general and visits to the Parliament Palace building in particular. We note that tourists' blogs record an overwhelming presence at the Parliament building, while their second major experience is to prepare for further destinations. Other clusters indicate details about the trip, among which the accommodation and the travel experience reveal preferences for specific elements (hostels and trains).[3] The overall results indicate that the tourist image of Bucharest is well defined, but only through a few elements; tourists talk less about other sights. It shows a lack of perceived complementarity between the Parliament Palace complex and the historic centre of Bucharest (inferred from the night cluster that connects accommodation and eating).

Sofia's map (Fig. 20.3b) emphasises the dynamic of the trip, with many words indicating a short trip and an image with many 'things' to be found. The main cluster contains most of the words encountered in the map of Bucharest, but with a slightly modified structure. The important sights are dominated by churches or unnamed buildings. Another cluster reveals the importance of accommodation, which is expanded further

Table 20.1. Word frequency.

City	Noun	Frequency of word	Proper noun	Frequency of word	Verb	Frequency of word
Sofia	City	606	Istanbul	147	find	537
	People	597	English	100	look	432
	Day	570	Bulgarian people	97	come	408
	Train	455	Belgrade	92	walk	396
	Place	449	Turkey	77	leave	389
	Bus	426	Europe	75	arrive	287
	Night	383	Plovdiv	70	start	263
	Hostel	351	Alexander Nevsky Church	69	meet	242
	Hotel	330	Orthodox	68	spend	227
	Church	305	Serbia	61	feel	218
Bucharest	Building	567	Nicolae Ceaușescu	231	find	488
	City	519	Parliament Palace	209	walk	387
	People	486	Brașov	132	look	384
	Day	477	Romanian	124	leave	376
	Train	475	Old Town	107	come	361
	Night	434	English	98	arrive	266
	Place	334	Budapest	86	head	228
	Hostel	317	Istanbul	85	start	211
	Room	292	Romanian people	82	spend	206
	Hotel	266	Dracula	76	meet	198

towards the cluster where tourists talk about restaurants and food. A last cluster indicates some problems about travel experiences at the Turkish border.

20.5 Discussion

The study endeavoured to understand the power of blogs in relation to image formation in Bucharest and Sofia, two cities with similar pasts for the past 70 years. Discussing the image of the two cities, the bloggers exposed a blurring and a tension between the meaning of positive and negative attributes. It is this negotiation about what is good or bad for tourists, what is real and what has been communicated differently by other agents that creates the power of blogs. It reveals

that power is brought by the authenticity of the posts and the credibility given to bloggers who have the explored unknown facets of the cities within their posts.

In focusing on the details of their trip, travel bloggers did not hesitate to emphasise the worst elements encountered, while the best experiences appeared to be communicated in a comparative sense, associated with visits elsewhere, as alluded to in such comparisons as, 'Bucharest/Sofia and their parts are better than x', '... look so much like y', 'it is amazing to find how much w looks like z', and so on. As revealed in this way, during the trip, tourists discovered little things that contributed to a broader experience, making the minor influential. They exposed elements hidden or ignored by other sources. The blogs therefore emphasised an important

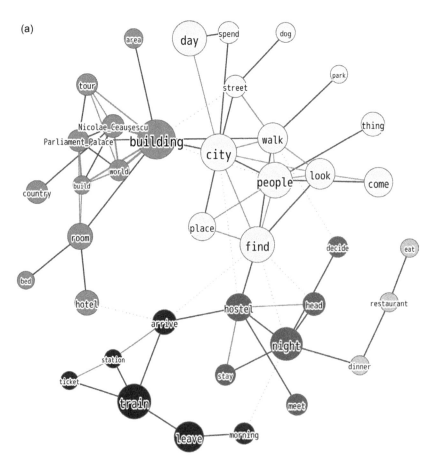

Fig. 20.3. (a) Co-occurrence network map: Bucharest; (b) co-occurrence network map: Sofia. (From authors' analysis of Travelpod.com postings.)

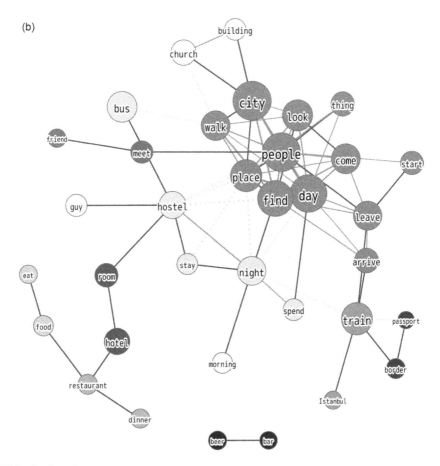

Fig. 20.3. Continued.

element in the focus of Web interaction – making things visible.

Therefore, within the networks of travel blogs, tourists' actions are not passive. Tourists are seen to possess the power to influence image formation, and thus the behaviour of future visitors, by communicating their knowledge about the travel experience to the world with the help of blogs and other Internet-related tools. Tourists produce knowledge and normalise the discourse about such tourist sites as Bucharest and Sofia, thereby exerting their power (Cheong and Miller, 2000) over the destinations and the actors (stakeholders) involved. This appears more pronounced in tourist spaces that are still developing, such as in CEE, where the communication of knowledge–power relations can reveal the influence of tourists.

In the case of Bucharest and Sofia, the power of the posts manifests itself by maintaining a

confusing image, one that is discordant with the image transmitted by classical image-formation agents. It is the attribute searched for by tourists who long for intrigue and different experiences (Urry, 2002). Once bloggers have visited the tourist sites, they emphasise that the image to be found there can be different to conventional wisdom, and tourists need to detach themselves from the limits imposed by traditional image generators. Indeed, the overall aspect of the cities is considered dull, but this is opposed by other bloggers who talk about the valuable hidden tourist sights found during their travels. The tourist value of the city is therefore not obvious and has to be discovered. Travel guides and other information sources highlight attractions and activities that may lag behind recent developments in tourist places. These are the details that empower tourists with the help of blogs. Because the speed of changing identity is high in the two cities, bloggers are faster than other agents in promoting more relevant images to potential visitors.

It can be inferred that blogs are helping the democratisation of travelling by exposing different views on little-explored sites, thereby increasing the strength and importance of these networks and the communication made through them. This is because when bloggers are writing about their travel experiences, they do not have a vested interest or wish to express a show of power over the destination visited. The interest of tourists is about writing and socialisation in a different space. But because blogging creates an unbiased collective image of the destination, tourists' communication can trigger new policies and actions from agents that try to respond and adapt to new ways of producing tourism.

While posts on individual blogs do not impose an authoritative view of shared experiences, travel blogs have developed a way to standardise the narratives of individuals and transform them into a tool important for understanding the power relations of the communicated image. This happens through blogging activities because, overall, the image is being produced and reproduced continuously, although fragmented at the individual level. But the collective blog image is significant enough for future tourists who are interested in comparing subjective experiences to analyse and share it further. Still, this process is slow and depends on being able to be transmitted towards more popular channels of media communication and active communities. In this way, the power of tourists with their individual posts wrapped up in travel blogs can attain a superior power when taken up by long-established agents. The latter have the resources to render the image more generally visible and to make use of it through standardisation and ranking displays, mediating tourists' activity on blogs.

We further suggest that the findings of the study have revealed an explicit correspondence between tourists' feelings expressed in their blogs and structural changes within the cities. As Bucharest and Sofia represent former communist cities struggling to reconstruct their images in a post-communist context, tourists' blog commentaries, especially those from Western countries, can be considered a barometer for measuring progress in unfolding the cities' attractiveness.

Indeed, tourism blogging can be harnessed as an important tool for urban planning, taking into account the information derived from blogs expressing the expectations of tourists: to know where and how to improve services and infrastructure and, not least, how to organise better accessibility to major tourist objectives. Thus, the multiple replication of tourists' positive points of view can be connected to an improvement in tourism services, urban infrastructures and leisure facilities. This was revealed in several interviews with local authority officials in Bucharest, who affirmed that strong support from the municipality for business and public investments was a result of the high number of tourists now visiting the city and blogging about it.

The former mayor of Bucharest, when interviewed, emphasised the pressure exerted by weekend tourists, a situation that encouraged the city administration to redevelop the historical centre. In interview, Bucharest's Chief Architect also acknowledged that the high number of comments on different blogs targeting tourism and business motivated the municipality to hasten restoration of the city's historic centre. The rehabilitation of historical urban areas, connected with new and modernised airports, and with the improvements to individual security within the cities, have represented an important way in which the image of Bucharest and Sofia have become more attractive.

This has also been achieved through the relatively inexpensive nature of tourism here (prices of hostels and restaurants) and from low-cost airline companies that have eased the integration of the cities, both literally and metaphorically, with the European urban network. Such realities, seen through tourists' eyes and experienced by them, improve the credibility and power of attraction of the cities.

20.6 Conclusions

This chapter has explored and highlighted, within a less-visited CEE context, the virtual power of social media platforms and of the actual collective power of tourists in contributing to the production and reproduction of destination city image through their travel blogs. In the context of Bucharest and Sofia, the analysis has bridged some links between marginal capitals of the EU and travellers interested in exploring the eastern, 'other' side of Europe. Through this, it has also added insights into the contemporary reimaging of Europe (Light and Young, 2009) through the lens of tourists.

Overall, the analysis has exposed that there is much to consider about image formation derived from and generated by travel blogs. The study has provided additional empirical support to the growing base of academic tourism research focused on blogs, and contextualises it for an area that is less researched – capital city tourism in less-visited urban spaces. Further, it has extended the research into capital city tourism through a text-mining framework, uncovering image production influenced by EU accession.

The analysis has suggested that the power of blogging has brought a process of democratisation to tourism. Social media in general, and travel blogs in particular, have heralded a significant power shift within the realm of tourism and its imagery. The power held by the classical agents of tourism and marketing has now been challenged by individual tourists through sharing their authentic experiences in a free environment.

None the less, while blogs now possess power to bring positive or negative value to the destination image, this is counter-challenged by the organising structures in which blogs are embedded: the power that tourists possess by blogging is diluted in the web of the Internet. Image formation still comprises a mix of media and agents, in which blogs play their role, but not the main one. What counts is the scale of bloggers' perceptions and their will to narrate their travel experiences without restraint. Their images and behaviours are particularly powerful for small-scale locations and sites, while for larger-scale destinations, the power of the blog aggregation is 'flattened' by the technicalities of the blog reviewing process. This suggests that while blogs

may encourage a fragmentation of image, the travel blog infrastructure standardises it. The power emerges from the way places are chosen and produced within the travel blogs' structure, allowing tourists to anticipate what they seek: a different sense of the quotidian upon which they can gaze (Urry, 2002).

These are some of the elements that contribute to the power of travel blogs and articulate the importance of Internet communication. Further, through blogging narratives, tourists participate twice in their destination image formation. The actual visit responds to their need to gaze at the destination, while through the narrative participation they revisit the destination and impart a transformative power. This can happen because bloggers are now part of a structure – the travel blog community – that is gradually shaping destination images, and even their own lives. Travel knowledge and experience may no longer be about being informed about a destination, but about producing an image destination 2.0, the power of which the tourism industry needs to recognise better. The intimate geopolitics of online communities and bloggers' interactions, coupled to the wider geopolitical power of collective blogs and their online platforms, are forces that cannot be ignored.

Acknowledgements

We wish to address our kindest appreciation to Mircea Gherghina and Adele Youmans, whose suggestions have motivated continuous improvement of this work. We acknowledge the support of Iuliana Armaş, who participated in a previous version of this chapter presented to the IGU Kraków 2014 conference (grant PCE-PN-II-ID-PCE-2011-3-0175; nr. 285/5.10.2011). The authors would also like to thank the editor of this book for his energy and contribution to make this work a much better one.

Endnotes

[1] This is the way nodes are ranked within a cluster. It has evolved from Markov random walks. KH Coder uses the algorithm developed by Pons and Latapy (2005).

[2] The blogger cited page 51 for this source, which features in the guide's 3rd edition (Kokker and Kemp, 2004), but does not appear in the 5th edition (Pettersen and Baker, 2010).

[3] While this might suggest a sample bias towards younger travellers, the age breakdown of bloggers on Bucharest, for example, was: 15–19 = 21 (3.9%); 20–39 = 345 (63.6%); 40–59 = 112 (20.8%); 60–79 = 25 (4.6%); n/a = 39 (7.2%). This pattern is similar to previous blog-related research.

References

Aggarwal, C.C. (2011) An introduction to social network data analytics. In: Aggarwal, C.C. (ed.) *Social Network Data Analytics*. Springer, New York, pp. 1–15.

Akehurst, G. (2009) User generated content: the use of blogs for tourism organisations and tourism consumers. *Service Business* 3, 51–61.

Baloglu, S. and McCleary, K.W. (1999) A model of destination image formation. *Annals of Tourism Research* 26, 868–897.

Banyai, M. (2010) Dracula's image in tourism: western bloggers versus tour guides. *European Journal of Tourism Research* 3, 5–22.

Banyai, M. and Glover, T.D. (2012) Evaluating research methods on travel blogs. *Journal of Travel Research* 51, 267–277.

Banyai, M. and Havitz, M.E. (2013) Analyzing travel blogs using a realist evaluation approach. *Journal of Hospitality Marketing and Management* 22, 229–241.

Beerli, A. and Martin, J.D. (2004) Factors influencing destination image. *Annals of Tourism Research* 31, 657–681.

Buhalis, D. and Law, R. (2008) Progress in information technology and tourism management: 20 years on and 10 years after the Internet – the state of eTourism research. *Tourism Management* 29, 609–623.

Cai, L.A., Wu, B.T., and Bai, B. (2003) Destination image and loyalty. *Tourism Review International* 7, 153–162.

Carson, D. (2008) The blogosphere as a market research tool for tourism destinations: a case study of Australia's Northern Territory. *Journal of Vacation Marketing* 14, 111–119.

Castells, M. (2007) Communication, power and counter-power in the network society. *International Journal of Communication* 1, 238–266.

Cheong, S.-M. and Miller, M.L. (2000) Power and tourism: a Foucauldian observation. *Annals of Tourism Research* 27, 371–390.

Choi, S., Lehto, X.Y. and Morrison, A.M. (2007) Destination image representation on the web: content analysis of Macau travel related websites. *Tourism Management* 28, 118–129.

Chon, K.-S. (1990) The role of destination image in tourism: a review and discussion. *Tourism Review* 45, 2–9.

Crotts, J. (1999) Consumer decision-making and prepurchase information search. In: Pizam, A. and Mansfeld, Y. (eds) *Consumer Behavior in Travel and Tourism*. Haworth Hospitality Press, New York, pp. 149–168.

de Valck, K., van Bruggen, G.H. and Wierenga, B. (2009) Virtual communities: a marketing perspective. *Decision Support Systems* 47, 185–203.

del Bosque, I.A.R. and San Martín, H. (2008) Tourist satisfaction a cognitive-affective model. *Annals of Tourism Research* 35, 551–573.

del Chiappa, G. (2011) Trustworthiness of Travel 2.0 applications and their influence on tourist behaviour: an empirical investigation in Italy. In: Law, R., Fuchs, M. and Ricci, F. (eds) *Information and Communication Technologies in Tourism 2011*. Springer, New York, pp. 331–342.

Douglas, A. and Mills, J.E. (2006) Logging brand personality online: website content analysis of Middle Eastern and North African destinations. In: Hitz, M., Sigala, M. and Murphy, J. (eds) *Information and Communication Technologies in Tourism 2006*. Springer, Vienna, pp. 345–346.

Echtner, C.M. and Ritchie, J.B. (1993) The meaning and measurement of destination image. *Journal of Tourism Studies* 2, 3–13.

Fennell, D.A. (2001) A content analysis of ecotourism definitions. *Current Issues in Tourism* 4, 403–421.

Gallarza, M.G., Saura, I.G. and Garcia, H.C. (2002) Destination image: towards a conceptual framework. *Annals of Tourism Research* 29, 56–78.

Gartner, W.C. (1994) Image formation process. *Journal of Travel and Tourism Marketing* 2, 191–216.

Gretzel, U., Kang, M. and Lee, W. (2008) Differences in consumer-generated media adoption and use: a cross-national perspective. *Journal of Hospitality and Leisure Marketing* 17, 99–120.

Gunn, C.A. (1988) *Vacationscape: Designing Tourist Regions*. Van Nostrand Reinhold, New York.

Hall, D. (2000) Sustainable tourism development and transformation in Central and Eastern Europe. *Journal of Sustainable Tourism* 8(6), 441–457.

Hays, S., Page, S.J. and Buhalis, D. (2013) Social media as a destination marketing tool: its use by national tourism organisations. *Current Issues in Tourism* 16, 211–239.

Higuchi, K. (2016) *Shakai chōsa no tame no keiryō tekisuto bunseki.* [*Quantitative Text Analysis for Social Research.*] Nakanishiya shuppan, Kyoto, Japan (in Japanese). English version available at: https://sourceforge.net/p/khc/wiki/KH%20Coder%20Reference%20Manual/ (Version 3) (accessed 23 August 2016).

Hsu, S.-Y., Dehuang, N. and Woodside, A.G. (2009) Storytelling research of consumers' self-reports of urban tourism experiences in China. *Journal of Business Research* 62, 1223–1254.

Huang, W.-J. and Lee, B.C. (2009) Capital city tourism: online destination image of Washington, DC. In: Höpken, W., Gretzel, U. and Law, R. (eds) *Information and Communication Technologies in Tourism 2009.* Springer, Vienna, pp. 355–367.

Jacobsen, J.K.S. and Munar, A.M. (2012) Tourist information search and destination choice in a digital age. *Tourism Management Perspectives* 1, 39–47.

Karlsson, L. (2006) The diary weblog and the travelling tales of diasporic tourists. *Journal of Intercultural Studies* 27, 299–312.

Kim, H. and Chen, J.S. (2016) Destination image formation process. A holistic model. *Journal of Vacation Marketing* 22(2), 1–13.

Kokker, S. and Kemp, C. (2004) *Romania & Moldova.* Lonely Planet, Footscray, Victoria, Australia.

Kolbe, L. (2007) Central and Eastern European capital cities: interpreting www-pages–history, symbols and identity. *Planning Perspectives* 22, 79–111.

Krippendorff, K. (2013) *Content Analysis: An Introduction to Its Methodology*, 3rd edn. Sage, Thousand Oaks, California.

Law, R. and Cheung, S. (2010) The perceived destination image of Hong Kong as revealed in the travel blogs of mainland Chinese tourists. *International Journal of Hospitality and Tourism Administration* 11, 303–327.

Lee, C.-K., Lee, Y.-K. and Lee, B. (2005) Korea's destination image formed by the 2002 World Cup. *Annals of Tourism Research* 32, 839–858.

Lepp, A., Gibson, H. and Lane, C. (2011) Image and perceived risk: a study of Uganda and its official tourism website. *Tourism Management* 32, 675–684.

Li, X. and Wang, Y. (2011) China in the eyes of Western travelers as represented in travel blogs. *Journal of Travel and Tourism Marketing* 28, 689–719.

Light, D. (2006) Romania: national identity, tourism promotion and European integration. In: Hall, D., Smith, M. and Marciszewska, B. (eds) *Tourism in the New Europe: The Challenges and Opportunities of EU Enlargement.* CAB International, Wallingford, UK, pp. 256–269.

Light, D. (2007) Dracula tourism in Romania: cultural identity and the state. *Annals of Tourism Research* 34, 746–765.

Light, D. and Young, C. (2009) European Union enlargement, post-accession migration and imaginative geographies of the 'New Europe': media discourses in Romania and the United Kingdom. *Journal of Cultural Geography* 26, 281–303.

Lin, Y.-S. and Huang, J.-Y. (2006) Internet blogs as a tourism marketing medium: a case study. *Journal of Business Research* 59, 1201–1205.

Litvin, S.W., Goldsmith, R.E. and Pan, B. (2008) Electronic word-of-mouth in hospitality and tourism management. *Tourism Management* 29, 458–468.

Mack, R.W., Blose, J.E., and Pan, B. (2008) Believe it or not: credibility of blogs in tourism. *Journal of Vacation Marketing* 14, 133–144.

Maitland, R. and Ritchie, B. W. (eds) (2009) *City Tourism: National Capital Perspectives.* CAB International, Wallingford, UK.

Naoi, T., Yamada, T., Iijima, S. and Kumazawa, T. (2011) Applying the caption evaluation method to studies of visitors' evaluation of historical districts. *Tourism Management* 32, 1061–1074.

Neuhofer, B., Buhalis, D. and Ladkin, A. (2014) A typology of technology-enhanced tourism experiences. *International Journal of Tourism Research* 16, 340–350.

Pan, B., MacLaurin, T. and Crotts, J.C. (2007) Travel blogs and the implications for destination marketing. *Journal of Travel Research* 46, 35–45.

Petkova, E. and Marinov, V. (2014) Development of diversified tourism destination products – a case study of tourism destination, Municipality of Sofia, Bulgaria. *Journal of Environmental and Tourism Analyses* 2, 33–47.

Pettersen, L. and Baker, M. (2010) *Romania*, 5th edn. Lonely Planet, Footscray, Victoria, Australia.

Pike, S. (2002) Destination image analysis – a review of 142 papers from 1973 to 2000. *Tourism Management* 23, 541–549.

Pons, P. and Latapy, M. (2005) Computing communities in large networks using random walks. In: Proceedings of the 20th International Symposium Computer and Information Sciences (ISCIS 2005). Springer, Berlin, pp. 284–293.

Prayag, G. (2009) Tourists' evaluations of destination image, satisfaction, and future behavioral intentions – the case of Mauritius. *Journal of Travel and Tourism Marketing* 26, 836–853.

Pritchard, A. and Morgan, N.J. (2001) Culture, identity and tourism representation: marketing Cymru or Wales? *Tourism Management* 22, 167–179.

Pudliner, B.A. (2007) Alternative literature and tourist experience: travel and tourist weblogs. *Journal of Tourism and Cultural Change* 5, 46–59.

San Martín, H.S. and del Bosque, I.R. (2008) Exploring the cognitive–affective nature of destination image and the role of psychological factors in its formation. *Tourism Management* 29, 263–277.

Sasaki, K. and Nishii, K. (2012) Study of blog mining for examination of tourist travel behavior in Japan. *Transportation Research Record: Journal of the Transportation Research Board* 2285, 119–125.

Schmallegger, D. and Carson, D. (2008) Blogs in tourism: changing approaches to information exchange. *Journal of Vacation Marketing* 14(2), 99–110.

Sebastiani, F. (2002) Machine learning in automated text categorization. *ACM Computing Surveys (CSUR)* 34, 1–47.

Shuang, X., Tribe, J. and Chambers, D. (2013) Conceptual research in tourism. *Annals of Tourism Research* 41, 66–88.

Stepchenkova, S. (2012) Content analysis. In: Dwyer, L., Gill, A. and Seetaram, N. (eds) *Handbook of Research Methods in Tourism: Quantitative and Qualitative Approaches*. Edward Elgar, Cheltenham, UK, pp. 443–458.

Stepchenkova, S., Kirilenko, A.P. and Morrison, A.M. (2009) Facilitating content analysis in tourism research. *Journal of Travel Research* 47, 454–469.

Tasci, A.D. and Gartner, W.C. (2007) Destination image and its functional relationships. *Journal of Travel Research* 45, 413–425.

Thevenot, G. (2007) Blogging as a social media. *Tourism and Hospitality Research* 7, 287–289.

Tseng, C., Wu, B., Morrison, A.M., Zhang, J. and Chen, Y.-C. (2015) Travel blogs on China as a destination image formation agent: a qualitative analysis using Leximancer. *Tourism Management* 46, 347–358.

Tussyadiah, I.P. and Fesenmaier, D.R. (2008) Marketing places through first-person stories – an analysis of Pennsylvania Roadtripper Blog. *Journal of Travel and Tourism Marketing* 25, 299–311.

Urry, J. (2002) *The Tourist Gaze*, 2nd edn. Sage, London.

Volo, S. (2009) Conceptualizing experience: a tourist based approach. *Journal of Hospitality Marketing and Management* 18, 111–126.

Volo, S. (2010) Bloggers' reported tourist experiences: their utility as a tourism data source and their effect on prospective tourists. *Journal of Vacation Marketing* 16, 297–311.

Volo, S. (2012) Blogs: 're-inventing' tourism. In: Sigala, M., Christou, E. and Gretzel, U. (eds) *Web 2.0 in Travel Tourism and Hospitality Theory Practice and Cases*. Ashgate, Farnham, UK, pp. 149–163.

Wenger, A. (2008) Analysis of travel bloggers' characteristics and their communication about Austria as a tourism destination. *Journal of Vacation Marketing* 14, 169–176.

Woodside, A.G., Cruickshank, B.F. and Dehuang, N. (2007) Stories visitors tell about Italian cities as destination icons. *Tourism Management* 28, 162–174.

Xiang, Z. and Gretzel, U. (2010) Role of social media in online travel information search. *Tourism Management* 31, 179–188.

Yoo, K.-H. and Gretzel, U. (2012) Use and creation of social media by travellers. In: Sigala, M., Christou, E. and Gretzel, U. (eds) *Social Media in Travel, Tourism and Hospitality: Theory, Practice and Cases*. Ashgate, Farnham, UK, pp. 189–206.

Zeng, B. and Gerritsen, R. (2014) What do we know about social media in tourism? A review. *Tourism Management Perspectives* 10, 27–36.

Part VI:

Mobilities

_____

Referred to in the UK press as a 'travel-industry guru' (Calder, 2005: 3), Neil Taylor, as a founding director, employs the UK travel firm Regent Holidays in Chapter 21 to exemplify some of the geopolitics behind the role of a select few Western tour companies who, operating on the periphery of business logic, managed to open doors into Central and Eastern Europe and influence Western tourists' perceptions of 'the other side' during the worst excesses of the 'Cold War'. While such companies that still exist have both revised and diversified their portfolio of destinations, Regent's 'Cold War' mediating role continues with its escorted tours to North Korea.

Although Regent Holidays tends not to use them, 'no-frills' airlines – low-cost carriers (LCCs) – have played an arguably crucial facilitating role in opening up more marginal regions of Central and Eastern Europe to Western tourism and travel markets. In Chapter 22, Edyta Pijet-Migoń examines some of the processes and consequences of this, and of the political and economic power such airlines wield. Indeed, it could be argued that as important geopolitical players, such companies' choice of routes and operational procedures influence considerably the spatiality of ('low cost') tourism and travel in Europe, and impact significantly on the socio-economic well-being of those who live and work in their destination areas.

But, while LCCs have facilitated a massive growth of west to east tourism and of east to west labour migration, Pijet-Migoń points out that they seem to have largely failed to improve

air connectivity significantly within CEE itself. Have they therefore been complicit in reinforcing a mobilities-led dependency relationship, one level of which is represented by the vulnerable position that some regional airports and their regions have been held to by the default monopolistic role of some larger LCCs?

Chapter 23 addresses the interrelated issues of tourism development, national identity and the apparent hegemony of anti-corruption ideology, as expressed in processes of connectivity within south-eastern Europe. It identifies the problematic nature of such interrelationships at a time when the role of Albania within Euro–Atlantic processes is viewed as a source of stability and security in the otherwise pejoratively signified 'Western Balkans', not least because of its co-ethnic relationships in Kosovo, the Former Yugoslav Republic of Macedonia (FYROM) and Montenegro, and the mobilities that connect them. The chapter highlights the 'West's' ambivalent attitude towards development processes in this European semi-periphery.

By contrast, Piotr Trzepacz and Derek Hall, in Chapter 24, broaden the geographical canvas by examining the nature and significance of international association football player mobilities. In a growing area of research characterised by theoretical debate and contestation and growing gender awareness, Trzepacz and Hall draw on the concepts of core–periphery relationships and semi-colonialism to address the nature and significance of asymmetrical flows from generally less developed to more developed countries. The chapter highlights the European ubiquity of Serbian players and the changing political stances taken towards foreign player employment in Russia in advance of hosting the 2018 World Cup.

Completing Part VI, and to conclude the contributors' chapters, Kevin Hannam reviews, in Chapter 25, aspects of tourism and critical geopolitics. Examining the development of research into tourism mobilities, he goes on to look at aspects of critical geopolitics from a mobilities perspective before discussing the geopolitics of erasure in relation to refugees and migrants transiting through CEE. In particular, Hannam examines how tourists 'on the spot' sought to disengage from the events of the 2015/16 refugee/migrant crisis in Europe by finding ways to avoid the spaces of the migrant.

Marschall (2015) has raised the concept of erasure in relation to earlier forced migration and refugee experiences in CEE, and draws on recent scholarship in the field of memory studies. She also invokes the phenomenon of 'homesick tourism' within diasporas, well known in the German literature, and a far broader concept that, she argues, has gone largely unrecognised by Anglophone tourism authorities and scholars (but see Baraniecki, 2001).

In response to the 2015/16 refugee/migrant crisis, a geopolitics of erasure, or at least of denial, certainly appeared to permeate the political elites of a number of CEE EU member states. Poland's president, Andrzej Duda, complained about 'dictates' from Brussels to accept migrants

from the Middle East and Africa. Slovakia's prime minister, Robert Fico, declared that his country would accept only Christian refugees, as it would be 'false solidarity' to force Muslims to settle in a country without a single mosque.

Viktor Orban, Hungary's prime minister, argued that 'we come from a region where the tradition of accepting culturally different refugees is very weak'. The dubious claim that the former Soviet bloc states have no history of colonialism was meant to justify the attitude that:

> We didn't meddle in these countries that are now sending the refugees, like other nations did, and so we have no sense of guilt about our obligation to deal with them.
>
> (Lyman, 2015)

In contrast to tourists and politicians in denial, the large number of young volunteers who travelled to refugee reception centres to assist efforts there not only presented a countervailing spatial pattern of mobilities that appeared to symbolise the best European values, but also reportedly saw such volunteers becoming radicalised in the face of apparent higher-level political hypocrisy and inaction (Smith, 2016).

Critical of the EU core prior to such events, Carr (2015) found the 'gated continent' to be dysfunctional, counterproductive and contrary to the principles on which the EU was founded. But he could see grounds for optimism in the borderland, where a new Europe was coming into being and where 'borders can still turn into bridges'. Perhaps a third edition of his book will require some revision.

References

Baraniecki, L. (2001) Politics and tourism: 'sentimental tourism' development in East-Central Europe. *Geographica Slovenica* 34(1), 105–113.

Calder, S. (2005) Country or commodity? *The Independent Traveller* [London] 18 July, p. 3.

Carr, M. (2015) *Fortress Europe: Inside the War Against Immigration*, 2nd edn. Hurst, London.

Lyman, R. (2015) Eastern bloc's resistance to refugees highlights Europe's cultural and political divisions. *New York Times* [New York] 12 September. Available at: http://www.nytimes.com/2015/09/13/world/europe/eastern-europe-migrant-refugee-crisis.html?_r=0 (accessed 15 August 2016).

Marschall, S. (2015) Tourism memories of the erased city: memory, tourism and notions of 'home'. *Tourism Geographies* 17(3), 332–349.

Smith, H. (2016) Pope follows thousands of volunteers to Greek island at frontline of migrant crisis. *The Guardian* [London] 16 April, p. 23.

21 The Role of Pioneering Tour Companies

Neil Taylor*

Independent Travel Consultant

By the late 1960s, the major UK tour operators such as Clarkson, Thomson and Cosmos were well established, so could take over many smaller companies still concentrating on beach holidays around the Mediterranean. Their holding companies were often involved in other businesses too; Thomson, for instance, owned *The Times* and a chain of regional newspapers and, like Clarkson, had its own in-house airline. They were all members of ABTA, the Association of British Travel Agents, which had been founded in 1950 to link tour operators and retail travel agents.

Their tourism product was straightforward, varying little between Spain, Italy and Greece. In fact, many tourists probably only knew the name of their resort, and not the country where it was situated. They travelled for guaranteed sunshine and for a product and price that British seaside resorts were increasingly unable to match. Full board was the norm, as clients were reluctant to explore local venues, and excursions sold by the tour operators' representatives were a crucial source of revenue. These again took advantage of the fact that the clientele was largely unadventurous, so were unlikely to use local transport or to hire a car. In the 1970s, Tunisia and Turkey also became mass-market destinations, having the advantage of their particular appeal during the winter months.

Those who had travelled in their own cars to France in the 1930s had started to do so again

in the 1950s, but were a small element of the total market. Currency restrictions[1] would limit them until the late 1970s, when it became possible to purchase property abroad, and a whole new market was born. Currency restrictions probably encouraged some families to take an inclusive package holiday who otherwise would have travelled independently, as the cost savings gave them more spending money or the chance to take a second holiday within a year.

Against this background, it was inevitable that a variety of entrepreneurs would arise offering something very different from seaside family holidays. The battle for market share in the mass market did not encourage new competitors, but the uncharted waters of many different destinations and specialisations certainly did. Few entered this side of the travel business to make money, and probably could not have done so in the early days given their lack of any relevant training; they mostly wanted to earn a basic living from their particular passion and would have been incredulous at the thought of selling out for millions of pounds, as several did, 30–40 years later. In 1975, a number of these entrepreneurs formed the Association of Independent Tour Operators (AITO), as they saw a need for smaller, often family businesses to lobby government and to present collectively their products as very different from those of the mass-market operators.

---

*E-mail: neiltaylor90@hotmail.com

Tours for birdwatching, military campaigns, pilgrimages, scuba diving, steam railways and trekking were among the themes developed by these operators. Maybe skiing should be included here, although it has a much broader appeal and perhaps cannot be seen as specialist. Winter sports holiday operators had in fact started before World War II, with the most successful in this field being two people who would give their names (and their souls) to their companies and who would remain friendly rivals for decades – Erna Low and Walter Ingham.

City breaks have to be mentioned, too, although from a 21st century perspective they might seem to be a surprising inclusion in the category of 'pioneering'. Roland Castro, with his company Time Off, was one of the first in this field. He would book a train or flight with a hotel and send a map to his clients, together with details of taxis and public transport. It would never have occurred to him to suggest a private transfer or that a client would not be able to speak sufficient French or German to get around the destination with ease.

Companies in either field could operate well in business environments that were little different from those in the UK, even before the advent of the European Union (EU). They had to deal both with nationalised industries such as the airlines and rail companies, as well as with hotels and coach companies in the private sector. Probably dealing with national airlines brought them closest to the experiences of operators to the eastern side of Europe, since the duopolies that operated on so many routes, which fixed fares, capacity, catering and luggage allowances, gave little scope for initiative. It would only be in the 1990s, when all relevant countries were in the EU, that airlines were largely privatised and had to compete (see Chapter 22, this volume).

Those tour operators who decided to concentrate on what was then simply called 'Eastern Europe' should probably be called 'destination' specialists. There was clearly not a sufficient market to warrant specialising in just one destination, and they had to manage the general Western perception that, because these countries were referred to as being 'communist', they could be regarded as all offering an identical product. It was also wise to be ready for the occasional political event that would greatly harm bookings, such as the building of the Berlin Wall

in 1961, the crushing of the Prague Spring in 1968 and the opposition of many Western countries to the Olympic Games in Moscow in 1980 in the wake of the Soviet invasion of Afghanistan. Given the nature of the political regimes involved, such events actually occurred far less frequently than in many other holiday destinations.

To succeed in 'Communist Eastern Europe' required patience, tolerance and minimal exuberance, just the qualities lacking in the buccaneers who were so successful in the businesses referred to earlier. The state tourism organisations in each country, such as Intourist in the USSR or the Reisebüro in East Germany, had a clear role in extracting foreign ('hard') currency from tourists without allowing them to interfere with the political infrastructure or having too close a contact with the local population. Prices were set to undercut those in the West. The lack of tasteful souvenirs, together with the fully inclusive nature of the tours, brought a regular clientele concerned more with saving money than with pursuing any particular interest. The communist state organisations did not appear to show any obvious favours towards those companies that clearly promoted visits out of political motives, such as Progressive Tours, which was linked to the British Communist Party. In fact, the state bureaux probably found commercial businesses easier to deal with, partly because the vast majority of tourists from the UK who took holidays behind the 'Iron Curtain' were mildly politically curious, but certainly not politically committed to the way policies were being carried out in the region.[2]

Occasionally, a mass-market operator would come up with a novel idea which would break the cosy relationship that regular Western operators enjoyed with their suppliers. Thomson Holidays did this with Intourist in 1972, when they negotiated for winter weekend breaks in Moscow, offering a lead price of £29 (approximately €35), including flights, transfers and meals. Probably equivalent to £300 (€360) in 2016, this price, and many a little higher, immediately attracted thousands of bookings, both from a new market that never would have considered travelling to Russia except under the auspices of a well-known operator, and also from those who previously had no choice but to accept the longer tours and higher prices offered by regular Intourist agents.[3]

One of the more precarious tour operations in the 1970s and 1980s was Yorkshire Tours, run from their home by Laurie and Ida Shaw. While they were personally very political, most of their travellers simply wanted an adventurous coach tour that took them vaguely to 'Eastern Europe' and which from time to time would offer beds in proper accommodation to relieve the discomfort of spending every night on the coach. Tea was brewed in the aisle of the coach, to save the expense of using cafes and to take advantage of an era when health and safety legislation was only in its infancy. Both Shaws died in 1990, conveniently, when legislation was becoming too much of a burden, and also just when their destinations ceased to have any political significance.

It was not easy to establish the right to represent any of the communist bloc state bodies involved in tourism and travel. A haphazard contact, perhaps through an embassy, might start the ball rolling. An approach could be made when another company was closing or had clearly lost serious interest in the area. Small companies could rightly claim that they were more likely to show long-term commitment to an area than a large one that might operate well one year and then abandon the destination entirely the next. Regent Holidays, the company of which I was a co-director from 1975 to 2001, was lucky that it approached Albturist in 1971, after two British companies, firstly Lord Brothers and then Horizon, both attempted (and failed) to operate conventional seaside holidays there. The Albanians needed to claim international links, and more than ever they needed hard currency following the withdrawal of Soviet aid in the early 1960s, which is why they opened the Adriatic seaside resort near Durrës to Westerners.[4] Regent was able to satisfy this need together with bringing a clientele willing to accept the state's restrictions on individual travel, the need for men to have short hair and the ban on all public religious observance.

Until the end of the 1970s, when a new hotel was built in Tirana, all groups had to stay at the seaside resort a couple of kilometres outside Durrës, except when they took the 3-day tour to the south of the country. Albturist seem to become reconciled to the fact that the moment tourists were told they should not walk along the beach to Durrës, this is exactly what they would do. The resort was built deliberately at a distance from the town so that neither the earlier Soviet tourists nor the later Western ones would have much contact with local people.

On a Tirana excursion, local guides would become nervous if a coach stopped in the town centre, as this could in theory lead to fraternisation with local people. They were much happier if the group was forced to linger at the Martyrs' Cemetery, a safe distance from the town centre, or at the Albania Today exhibition, modelled on (albeit no comparison with) the Moscow Exhibition of Economic Achievements. Both Tirana attractions were, of course, deserted, as local people only visited as part of a collective school group or factory outing. In the town centre, the coach would keep moving, not difficult in a country with so few cars and with wide roads, which only came into their own on 1 May and 28 November (National Day).

Once established, relationships between operators in the West and state tourism organisations in the East tended to continue and potential competitors could often be persuaded to book through the representative companies already active in the area. While Regent produced brochures each year and dealt with passengers both directly and through retail agents, most of its business was wholesaling to organisations and other operators wanting one-off group tours to 'Eastern Europe'. In some ways, the most stimulating, but in other ways the most frustrating tours to operate were those for special interest groups. If one could obtain an itinerary sufficiently specialist to satisfy dedicated birdwatchers or botanists, this was a great achievement, given that such activity could easily be viewed locally as espionage and having nothing to do with tourism.

Regent was both working with and competing against its principals in many of the communist bloc countries. Intourist in the USSR, the Reisebüro in East Germany, Ibusz in Hungary, Čedok in Czechoslovakia and Polorbis in Poland all had lavish London offices, with generous promotional budgets. They would have preferred to have monopolised travel to their respective destinations but their head offices fortunately saw the need for additional outlets, in the same way that their national airlines, equally well provided for in London's West End, had to seek out varying outlets to sell their flights. While the directors of these state-run offices were usually approachable and knowledgeable, their staff tended to be the complete opposite, with no interest in customer care. It was thus not difficult for Regent to find clients dissatisfied with these offices who were relieved to be able to book elsewhere. Some of these clients became regular, as having had a satisfactory tour in say the USSR, they were then happy to entrust Regent with a similar programme elsewhere in the communist bloc. Tour operators based in the UK (and other West European countries) could also operate tours that included Western destinations, which of course these state tourism offices could not do. Itineraries such as West and East Berlin or Helsinki combined with Leningrad come to mind in this context. Regent could exploit the Sino–Soviet rift to offer tours using the trans-Siberian railway from Moscow through Mongolia to Beijing, which Intourist had no desire to promote.

A major problem faced by operators to the USSR was never knowing in advance which hotel would be used; only a certain category was promised.[5] This effectively prevented any contact from abroad being made with tourists while they were travelling in the country. The UK operator could send a telex to Intourist in Moscow (numbers for local branches were never divulged) and just hope that it would be passed on. And of course, this practice particularly made contact between local people and tourists more difficult.

There were also limitations on the time that could be spent in many of the smaller towns. For the general tourist, this did not matter too much but for the various diasporas who had to use Intourist itineraries to visit their relatives, in particular those linked to the Baltics or to the Caucasian Republics, a three-night limit prevented much contact, which was presumably the aim of such a policy. At a time when few people had direct access to a telephone, and all letters would be censored, any contact would be rendered very difficult. On many routes, such as those from Leningrad to the Baltic capitals, trains could only be taken at night, or the route flown, to prevent the local countryside (and whatever it may have contained) from being seen. While plenty of worthwhile towns were included in Intourist itineraries, most of the Soviet Union remained closed to foreigners from the mid-1920s until the end of the regime in 1991. Apart from Albania, the other communist countries were more liberal in their travel policies, with the whole country being open and there being no need to

book the itinerary in advance. Visa procedures were also easier and there was no division between hotels used by hard currency tourists and those for the local population or visitors from elsewhere in the communist bloc.

Black markets, particularly in foreign currency, would hit tourists in all major towns behind the 'Iron Curtain'. Westerners would be offered seemingly wonderful exchange rates in comparison with the official ones. While the authorities clearly turned a blind eye to small-scale activity in this field, they took a number of steps to prevent large sums of foreign currency reaching local people in this way. Sometimes, as in the USSR, all hotel bookings had to be made in advance at the official exchange rate before a visa would be granted. Most of the bars in the hotels used by foreigners only took foreign currency, and excursions out of town could only be booked through Intourist, again not using roubles. East Germany had a minimum daily exchange from hard currency that tourists had to make. Inevitably, some tourists taken in by hustlers, or even hotel staff, found themselves with far more local currency than they could possibly use, which then had to be thrown away before departure to prevent its discovery by customs officers.[6] A few visitors with special interests could dispose of these funds. Books were cheap to buy and to post home, records were often of a high standard and certain shops, such as the *Delikat* chain in East Germany, had goods for sale in local currency at prices that were high for the local population but not for tourists with an abundance of black-market banknotes.

The legal environment that governed tour operating until 1992 was very gentle towards operators and made complaints from passengers difficult to pursue. It therefore did not matter much if, for example, an itinerary was suddenly changed without apparent reason, which could always happen in an environment where customer care was not taken seriously. The Package Travel Regulations 1992, applicable to all businesses operating in the then EU, completely altered the legal framework in the client's favour. One sentence in these regulations says it all:

> The other party to the contract is liable to the consumer for any damage caused to him by the failure to perform the contract or the improper performance of the contract unless the failure or the improper performance is due neither to any

fault of that other party nor to that of another supplier of services.

What was crucial in this sentence was the responsibility imposed on the tour operator for the entire operation of the holiday, even though supervision of suppliers and of safety standards was totally unrealistic for small operators. Previously, many complaints by clients could be dismissed on the basis that the responsibility for any supposed failing lay with a local supplier and not with the UK operator. The client in theory could, of course, pursue action against such a supplier, but in most cases that would have been an unrealistic proposition, particularly beyond the 'Iron Curtain', where any attempt to challenge a governmental organisation was doomed to failure from the start. While insurance could be taken out to cover the risk of major claims following, for example, a coach crash or a hotel fire, from the operators' point of view it gave little scope for flexibility once a brochure had been printed with a specific itinerary. There could be many reasons for making changes during the year or so that might pass between the printing of the brochure and the tour taking place; however, to avoid legal disputes, it was easier to stick to an itinerary than to risk a litigious client picking holes with changes that might be made. It is doubtful whether this legislation improved the quality of adventure tourism – competition and bad publicity soon saw off operators who were incompetent or dishonest – but it certainly curtailed the passion for innovation and exploration so prevalent in the 1980s.

The year 1992 was, of course, just after the political changes that led to the demise of the USSR and the end of its influence in Central and Eastern Europe (CEE). It is fortunate that this change in Western European legislation took place then and no earlier, since it would have been very difficult for operators to take on legal responsibility for a product over which they had no control. This was in complete contrast to the major operators to Mediterranean beach resorts who had representatives and contract managers constantly in touch with local suppliers and who could regularly see safety reports for any hotel they planned to use.

The early 1990s were the most difficult time for operators in the West to provide a reliable CEE 'product' to sell. The former state organisations reacted in different ways and at different times. Most names, such as Intourist, Čedok and Polorbis, were retained, together with offices abroad, although these had to move out of city centres to keep them financially viable. Inevitably, many of the original staff defected to set up their own companies, and local hotels, just as much as tour operators abroad, were bombarded with requests for cooperation and assurances about the level of service that would be offered by these 'restructured' entrepreneurs. Large hotels in resorts in the former USSR suffered the most from geopolitical change, as previously they had hosted trade union groups from the bloc countries, who took the same number of rooms over the same period every year. After the sudden collapse of the USSR, the unions, and therefore these groups, disappeared, leaving no obvious alternative source of clients for the hotels. Marketing was therefore a totally new concept for them, particularly as the staff would not have travelled elsewhere so would have no idea of appropriate standards and charges. They also would never have dealt with foreigners unable to speak a word of Russian.

With the prevalence of fax communication, and the continuing reduction in telephone costs, tour operators could also begin to deal directly with hotels, guides and coach companies if they wished to do so. Even before consumers had general access to the Internet, many in Western Europe would make direct bookings with airlines, hotels and car hire companies. This would be a further challenge to operators, albeit a longer-term one in relation to CEE. Even now, writing in 2016, the vast majority of bookings to this area for anything but the simplest of arrangements, such as a weekend in one hotel, will be made through the travel trade; clients want the financial and legal security that only booking through a bonded tour operator or retailer will provide, whereas if they travel in Western Europe, this seems to be far less of a concern. Although many of the former communist countries are now fully integrated into the EU – most for more than a decade – for potential visitors from the West (or at least the UK), they are still seen as somewhat different and therefore should be visited in an appropriately different manner (see Chapter 1, this volume).

In the former Soviet Union, the situation was the most complicated, as not only did the country cease to exist but also 15 countries took its place, each eager to promote its tourism companies and products on an individual basis. The transition in the Baltic area was the smoothest: a group of former Intourist staff in all three countries set up independent companies that cooperated closely with each other. The three governments implemented a joint visa, and exempted British passport holders from this requirement. Visas for others could be obtained on arrival at seaports and airports. Elsewhere, in many respects, the situation became more complicated, as several visa applications had to be made where previously one Soviet document had been sufficient. The currency situation was also fluid for several years, as each new country broke away at a different time and in a different manner from the Russian rouble.

Once currency and visa issues were clarified, there was no specific need for any destination specialists to continue operating to this area. Tour operators in the West could contact whomever they wished in these countries to establish cooperation, and there was no need for any formal accreditation. The 'ultra-specialists' were perhaps the first to take advantage of this in fields such as birdwatching and steam railway tours. These hobbyists had understandably resented having to work through intermediaries who had little knowledge or understanding of their interest and so they were initially happy that experts in these fields from the former communist countries could now work directly with contacts in the West. But in the early post-communist days, results were often far from satisfactory. A passionate Soviet birdwatcher previously on a government salary could not always convert to the rigours of the cowboy economy that characterised the Yeltsin era. He or she probably would have had no previous contact with foreigners, and definitely no business experience outside local barter deals that had kept day-to-day life going during the Soviet era. In an era of wild inflation, he or she certainly could not fix prices 18 months in advance, which is what tour operators abroad would require. Insurance was another novel concept: what would happen in the case of an accident involving tourists from abroad? How would business relationships be started with coach companies and with hotels outside the nature reserve? Seventy per cent of new businesses fail in the UK each year, even though their owners will have lived in a capitalist

environment. It is therefore no surprise that so many people whose knowledge of capitalism was restricted to black-market recordings of *Dallas* or *Dynasty* should likewise come to grief.

Regent had to reinvent its business model by quickly taking advantage of its destination knowledge to offer itineraries that had been impossible in Soviet times, and above all by offering tours that no longer needed to involve stays in Moscow and what was by now once again St Petersburg (Leningrad in Soviet times). The company would be most successful in the Baltics, where the term 'pioneering' could still just about be used. Scandinavian Airlines and Finnair had started services to Tallinn, Riga and Vilnius in the late Soviet era, and by the mid-1990s, local airlines would offer services to most Western capitals. SAS and Finnair would continue to take most of the business, as they offered so many regional connections in Britain and Germany, as well as several services each day. For Regent, the countries offered the novelty of its long-haul destinations such as North Korea and Vietnam, but at a much cheaper cost and with a much more predictable product. Fortunately, for several years, Regent had no serious UK competitor for this area and its knowledge of St Petersburg enabled it to combine a traditional visit there with tours in the newly opened Baltic countries. The Caucasus and Central Asian areas were problematical during the 1990s because of civil war in some areas (Georgia and Tajikistan) and border disputes in others (Armenia and Azerbaijan). While none of these issues have been fully resolved, tourism is now established on a regular basis in all 15 former Soviet Republics. Clients who want a flavour of life prior to 1991 tend to choose Belarus or Turkmenistan, as these two countries have changed the least since then.

Because close links had been established with Finland in the late 1980s, Estonia was able to offer a totally Western product very quickly after the re-establishment of independence in August 1991. Having been independent from 1920 to 1940, the country's government was keen to part company from anything Soviet as quickly as possible. A hard currency tied to the Deutschmark was introduced in June 1992, and international telephone links followed soon afterwards, breaking the total control that Moscow had previously imposed on contacts abroad. English soon replaced Russian as the first foreign language taught in schools and colleges. Three million Finns would visit Estonia in 1992, and this figure has remained consistent since then. Finns' interest in this neighbour from whom they had been largely excluded for 50 years, plus the closeness of the languages, ensured that hard currency and long-term investment poured in from the beginning. It took Latvia and Lithuania a little longer to be seen as 'Western', and in some isolated areas perhaps this description is still inappropriate, but it certainly applies to any town visited by tourists. Tourists would often first book a city break in one of the three capitals and then return to see the rest of the country, having been reassured by the standards and interest that Tallinn, Riga or Vilnius could offer.[7]

Seasonal pricing was the issue that took longest to resolve through the 1990s. In Soviet times, there were probably high-season and low-season prices for most hotels, with perhaps a 25% difference between them. This is clearly an unrealistic model almost anywhere, but certainly in cities that in February have little to offer beyond short days, endless rain and closed attractions. Few hotels had thought about additional sources of revenue and remained too concerned with the basic rate. However, in winter there was great scope for using the room rate as a loss leader to bring in clients, who would inevitably take more meals and drinks in the hotel than in the summer, when hundreds of other restaurants provided attractive alternatives. Hotels needed to think about introducing or upgrading their spa services, and at that time telecommunications were also potentially lucrative: this was a time before mobile phones and laptops became standard and when it was necessary to use computers in a business centre. It was probably only around 2000 that a 75% reduction was seen as sensible to ensure a reasonable year-round occupancy rate.

In the first decade of the 21st century, speculation about the future of the travel industry echoed the pessimism that swirled around the book industry. What role was there for tour operators and retail agents, not to mention printed brochures, when potential customers could arrange everything online? Probably niche operators have suffered less here than some larger companies. After all, their product and their expertise cannot be replaced easily with online research. There is also the security of dealing with a bonded operator, and potential clients are more willing to pay for such services than those wanting something more straightforward. Interestingly, 2014 saw an increase in the number of books bought in UK shops and an increase in tours sold through UK retail agents. This trend should boost the numbers of visits to CEE, since agents are likely to recommend the area to clients looking for something different, whereas vague searches on the Internet may not reach that far. While there is no longer any need for destination specialists, the region should benefit from more mainstream operators looking to the region for new products.

When ten mostly CEE countries joined the EU in April 2004, low-cost carriers (LCCs), particularly Ryanair and Wizzair, took advantage of the deregulation of air services within the EU to start flights from the UK to all of these countries, given that surface transport offered little competition. However, these flights have been largely geared to the ethnic market of migrant workers and their families rather than to tourists. Birmingham to Bydgoszcz in Poland and Doncaster to Kosice in Slovakia are routes unlikely to sell in any serious quantity to other markets.[8] In this respect, the business model is the complete reverse of many routes in Western Europe, such as Bristol to Bergerac or Liverpool to Lanzarote, which are geared purely to UK holidaymakers (see Chapter 22, this volume).

There are, of course, LCC services from airports near London, such as Luton and Stansted, to many of the CEE capitals. But these have failed to have much impact on British Airways' practice of flying more frequently and more conveniently from Heathrow.

If the general tenor of this chapter has been about change, perhaps it is appropriate to end with a note on North Korea, the Democratic People's Republic of Korea (DPRK). Although now desperate for foreign currency, in terms of tourism hospitality, the country has gone into reverse. When Western tourists first visited the DPRK in the mid-1980s, they could obtain local currency and walk outside the hotel unaccompanied. Neither of these activities was permitted in 2016. The country's fate remains as difficult to predict as always. It is easy to think that it will collapse, but was the same fate not allocated to Cuba half a century ago? And certainly, in every year since the 1980s, tourists have been encouraged to visit Cuba before it changes. North Korea, like Cuba, survived the collapse of the USSR, although it suffered massive famine a few years later. Unlike Cuba, it has not made peace with the USA[9] and so remains largely isolated from change elsewhere. For those travellers who want to relive the ambience of the Chinese Cultural Revolution during the late 1960s, North Korea is an ideal place to go.

In contrast, from a West European travel industry perspective, it is no longer possible to write about 'Eastern European' tourism as a separate entity. Given the Schengen commitment to open borders, it is often difficult to tell where the 'Iron Curtain' used to run.[10] Travel arrangements to Warsaw or Prague are no different from those to Munich or Madrid, so the same companies can and do offer both.

As most of the countries on both sides of this former divide are now in the EU, perhaps the greatest accolade one can accord to the former Soviet bloc countries is to quote what the erstwhile President Ilves of Estonia has frequently said about his country, but which applies equally to the others. 'Estonia is now normal' is the sentence he often likes to quote, and few of its citizens would want anything else,[11] nor would most members of the travel trade.

Endnotes

[1] In the summer of 1966, the UK government introduced the '£50 limit' to help reduce the balance of payments. Flight, rail and coach travel were excluded from this, but £50 per person per year had to cover accommodation, food and all incidentals, whether paid directly or through a tour operator. This became a greater restriction following the devaluation of the pound by 15% in November 1967. Gradually, the limit was increased, during the early 1970s, to £300 for each trip, equivalent to about £2500 in 2016. All UK currency controls were completely abolished in 1979.

[2] There were official student travel organisations, such as Sputnik in the USSR, whose Western clients were obliged to participate in ideological meetings and to adjust their sightseeing to an unnecessary number of war memorials. The turnover of such organisations was, however, minimal compared to that of Intourist and its equivalents in the other bloc countries, so they have little significance in an overview of tourism in that region.

[3] Another new market was attracted to this Thomson programme, as luggage was treated in a much more cursory manner by Soviet customs than was usually the case for those travelling on scheduled flights. This enabled dissident communities to import and export banned literature much more easily than previously, and also to meet their supporters in the West, who could travel unnoticed in such a large group of tourists.

[4] This beach complex had originally been built with Soviet tourists in mind.

[5] The Chinese tourist authorities, when they began to accept Western tourist groups in the mid-1970s, did the same and also would not book single-occupancy rooms.

[6] Currencies were inconvertible and in theory it was illegal to take them out or to bring them (back) into the country. Notoriously, one or two bureaux at Berlin Zoo station thrived on exchanging them, and they could also be obtained in certain quarters of some Western ports frequented by communist bloc seafarers.

[7] Although Ryanair have operated to Kaunus, Lithuania's second city, for some time, from a number of UK and other airports, few Western tourists take weekends there. There is a direct bus from the airport to Vilnius and most passengers, who will in any case be largely Lithuanians, take that. Ryanair sometimes operates to both airports, and at other times just to one of them, obviously playing them off against each other.

[8] Travel journalist Tom Chesshyre writes amusingly about some of the Ryanair destinations in *How low can you go? Round Europe for 1p return (+ tax)* (Hodder & Stoughton, London, 2007).

[9] A peace treaty has never been signed to end the Korean War (1950–1953) formally in which NATO (including UK and US) forces opposed armies from North Korea and China, in support of the South Korean government. Arguably, this was one of the hottest spots of the 'Cold War', and its legacy persists.

[10] Although, in fact, the author now leads 'Iron Curtain' route tours from the Baltic to the Adriatic (editor's note).

[11] Such a sentiment may not have been the case in the 1990s, when the significant proportion of ethnic Russians in the country enjoyed rights that seemed to be somewhat less than equal. But now the standard of social care, and the level of pensions and salaries available, is so much higher in the Baltic countries that very few ethnic Russians would seem to have any desire to leave. For the younger ones, there is the appeal of an EU passport, enabling them to work elsewhere if they wish to do so. As conditions deteriorate in Russia over the next few years, these differences will be accentuated even more. Russians happily take holidays in the Baltics, as their language is understood and travel costs are low. The Baltics certainly benefitted in early 2016 from the downturn in travel to Turkey as Russian tourists sought an alternative within the budget of what a Turkish holiday would have cost.

22 The Geopolitics of Low-cost Carriers in Central and Eastern Europe

Edyta Pijet-Migoń*

Institute of Tourism, Wrocław School of Banking, Wrocław, Poland

22.1 Introduction

The European Union (EU) enlargements of 2004 and 2007 brought a range of political, economic and social transformations to the new member states that included profound changes in the civil aviation market. The new EU countries were required to accept an 'open skies' policy and to adjust their aviation laws. Such neoliberal policies could be seen as early symbols and embodiments of 'Europeanness', facilitating some dramatic transformations in tourism and employment mobility, and in business practice, across the new member states.

Prior to these accessions, the aviation market in Central and Eastern Europe (CEE) had been strictly regulated. Capital city airports and national (flag) carriers held a dominant position. Regional airports had a limited number of regular international connections (charter flights notwithstanding), mainly to major European hubs such as Frankfurt, Munich, Copenhagen or Vienna. The level of passenger traffic was generally low. Only three capital airports – Prague, Budapest and Warsaw – served more than 5 million passengers annually, and only two regional ones – Varna and Burgas in Bulgaria – had more than 1 million passengers, while Kraków, Gdańsk and Timişoara each recorded between 0.3 and 0.6 million (Fig. 22.1).

Liberalisation of air transport in the 'old' EU had been implemented in phases: the first 'liberalisation package' was introduced in January 1988, followed by a second in November 1990 and the third in January 1993, with a 4-year transition period. The final opening of the EU passenger aviation market thus took place in April 1997, when remaining regulations concerning stand-alone cabotage were lifted (Dobruszkes, 2014).

In the new EU countries of CEE, liberalisation of air transport was almost revolutionary, preceded by a short preparatory phase. Among the most evident consequences was the expansion of low-cost carriers (LCCs) in and to the region. These companies clearly recognised that the emerging markets of the new member states presented a growth opportunity.

In this chapter, the expansion of LCCs into CEE and the power they can wield – both implicit and explicit – will be examined, along with a discussion of some of the consequences of these developments, not least the impact on tourism and related mobilities. The important question concerning the extent to which the growth of LCC connection networks resulted in an increase in tourists' interest in less popular destinations, cities and regions will be addressed.

*E-mail: edyta.migon@wsb.wroclaw.pl

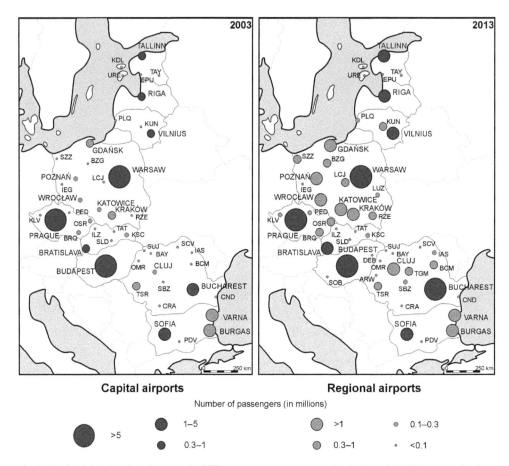

Fig. 22.1. Capital and regional airports in CEE countries: passenger traffic, 2003 and 2013. (From author's compilation.)

Note: IATA (International Air Transport Association) codes are used for smaller regional airports. Estonia: TAY – Tartu, KDL – Kärdla, URE – Kuressaare, EPU – Pärnu. Lithuania: PLQ – Palanga, KUN – Kaunas. Poland: BZG – Bydgoszcz, LCJ – Łódź, SZZ – Szczecin, IEG – Zielona Góra, RZE – Rzeszów, LUZ – Lublin. Czech Republic: BRQ – Brno, KLV – Karlovy Vary, OSR – Ostrava, PED – Pardubice. Slovakia: KSC – Košice. Hungary: DEB – Debrecen, SOB –Sármellek (Héviz). Romania: ARW – Arad, BAY – Baia Mare, BCM – Bacău, CND – Constanţa, CRA – Craiova, IAS – Iaşi, OMR – Oradea, SBZ – Sibiu, TSR – Timişoara, TGM – Târgu Mureş. Bulgaria: PDV – Plovdiv.

22.2 Expansion of Low-cost Carriers in CEE

Liberalisation of air transport and the adoption of an 'open skies' policy resulted in new opportunities for airlines. Any airline with a licence in one of the EU countries, in a member country of the European Economic Area (EEA) (Norway, Iceland, Liechtenstein), or in Switzerland, was entitled to start business in the new member countries, offering connections on any route, for any price and with unregulated frequency,

although it had to respect the principles of a free market economy. These circumstances allowed Western European LCCs to expand, but more established legacy carriers from Western Europe were also interested in the new markets (Bjelicic, 2007; Gross and Lück, 2013). The new regulations also acted as a catalyst for the expansion of fledgling local airlines in the new member states, by whom the low-cost business model was generally adopted (Table 22.1). In Poland, such a new airline was Air Polonia, and later Central-wings, which operated within the structure of

Table 22.1. Low-cost carriers established in new EU member countries. (From author's compilation, based on airline websites.)

Name of carrier	Country of origin	Commenced operations	Ceased operations
Sky Europe	Slovakia	February 2002	September 2009
Smart Wings	Czech Republic	May 2004	
Air Polonia	Poland	December 2003	December 2004
Centralwings	Poland	December 2004 (as a brand of LOT)	March 2009
Wizzair	Hungary	May 2004	
Blue Air	Romania	December 2004	
Air Baltic	Latvia	Established in 1995, as an LCC from 2004	

LOT Polish Airlines. Similar developments in other countries included the launching of Smart Wings in the Czech Republic, Sky Europe in Slovakia, Wizzair in Hungary and Blue Air in Romania. In Latvia, the local carrier Air Baltic changed its business model, initially towards a hybrid, and then to entirely low cost.

In the increasingly competitive post-accession market, as outlined in Table 22.2, not all LCCs survived. Air Polonia and Sky Europe were bankrupted, while LOT suspended indefinitely flights operated by Centralwings.

For Slovakia, growth in 2004 was 72.7%, while for the Baltic States, Latvia experienced a 68.7% increase, Estonia 39.5% and Lithuania 37.7%. These levels persisted until 2007. The highest annual growth, of 77.3%, was recorded for Latvia in 2006. Considerable increase in passenger traffic typified the Romanian market as well. Annual growth rates there were 35% in 2005 and 47% in 2006. Hungary experienced more modest annual growth: 28% in 2004 and 25% in 2005, but a mere 4% in the next 2 years. Political and economic crisis in 2008 brought a reduction in passenger traffic across the region.

22.3 Impact of LCC Expansion on the Air Passenger Market

22.3.1 Growth in passenger numbers

Low fares offered by LCCs, followed by significant price reductions from traditional legacy carriers struggling to survive LCC competition, resulted in a substantial increase in demand for flying (Franke, 2004; Doganis, 2006; Dennis, 2007). Simultaneously, the opening of EU employment markets resulted in considerable labour migration from CEE. This was particularly evident in the first years after accession, when LCCs responded by opening many connections with Western Europe, and notably with the UK, Ireland and Norway (Burrell, 2011; Pijet-Migoń, 2012).

Consequently, 2004–2007 witnessed particularly high growth in passenger traffic (Fig. 22.2). In Poland, the number of passengers in 2004 increased by 24% over those of 2003, and in 2005–2006, annual growth exceeded 30%.

22.3.2 Network expansion

The arrival of low-cost airlines in CEE brought a major network reorientation. In particular, the number of 'point-to-point' connections to various European destinations increased significantly, especially from regional airports. But Western legacy carriers expanded too, mainly in Poland and Romania, and provided more flights to their hub airports, also opening new connections from cities not previously included in their networks. This applied particularly to Lufthansa (Frankfurt and Munich) and Austrian Airlines (Vienna), although the latter reduced its network of feeder links after 2008.

Five years after the 2004 accession, Ryanair, easyJet and Wizzair had the most extensive LCC networks in the new EU countries (Dobruszkes, 2009). Strong competition and a gradual polarisation of their presence in different markets has since been exhibited. In Poland, Wizzair

Table 22.2. Early expansion phases of LCCs in CEE. (From author's compilation, with additional information from Királová, 2006; Puczkó and Rátz, 2006.)

Country	Year	LCC developments
Czech Republic	1999	First LCC, GO (British Airways subsidiary), initiated a London Stansted–Prague route (sold to easyJet in 2002, which continued flying to Prague).
	May 2004 (EU accession)	LCCs flying to Prague increased to 11: Bmi Baby, Flybe, Germanwings, Jet2.com, Sky Europe, Snowflakes, Smart Wings, Wizzair, Sterling and Helvetic Airways.
		The Czech Smart Wings started flights to Paris, Zurich, Madrid, Amsterdam and Copenhagen; subsequently also to Vienna, Rome and London.
	2005	Ryanair connected Brno with London Stansted.
Poland	December 2003	Air Polonia – first LCC, operating before the expected arrival of West European carriers – inaugurated Warsaw to Wrocław and Gdańsk, Warsaw to London Stansted.
		Subsequently, connections to London from other Polish airports (e.g. Katowice, Gdańsk and Poznań), to Paris from Katowice and Wrocław, to Brussels Charleroi from Warsaw and Katowice, to Köln/Bonn from Katowice, and to Rome, Athens and Madrid from Warsaw.
		For a time, Volare offered code-share flights.
		Although popular, Air Polonia was declared bankrupt: all flights were suspended from December 2004.
	May 2004 (EU accession)	Hungarian Wizzair opened operations in Poland, based at Katowice, quickly followed by Slovakian carrier Sky Europe flying to/from a base in Kraków. Air Berlin and Niki offered flights to their main hubs in Berlin and Vienna, and then to various south-western Europe destinations. Both suspended operations in March 2005. Air Berlin resumed operations in Poland, in April 2009, flying from Kraków and Gdańsk.
		For the 2004 summer season, Germanwings launched flights from Warsaw and Kraków; the second largest European LCC, easyJet, soon followed suit.
	February 2005	Centralwings – second Polish LCC – began operations, offering regular, charter and semi-charter flights.
	March 2005	Ryanair inaugurated a Wrocław–London Stansted service, and several more routes serving Polish regional airports quickly followed.
	Also 2005	Norwegian Air Shuttle started connecting Warsaw and Kraków with Oslo.
		For the summer season, barely a year after EU accession, eight LCCs were operating in the Polish market.
	2006	Ryanair served eight regional airports: six routes from Wrocław and Kraków, three from Gdańsk, Poznań and Łódź, and one (London Stansted) from Bydgoszcz, Rzeszów and Szczecin. Most destinations were British or Irish.
	2006-7	New airlines at Polish airports included Sterling and Jet2 (2006), Blue 1, Iceland Express, Clicair and Transavia (2007).
		Fifteen LCCs were present in Poland in 2007, at 10 airports.
Hungary	Pre-accession	Two LCCs were flying to Budapest in 2003.
	May 2004 (EU accession)	Eight LCCs operating; ten for the 2005 summer season.

Continued

Table 22.2. Continued.

Country	Year	LCC developments
Baltic States	October 2004	Ryanair started from Riga, the capital of Latvia, with flights to London Stansted, Frankfurt Hahn and Tampere (Finland). Subsequently opened a base at Kaunas in Lithuania, 100 km from the capital, Vilnius.
Slovakia	2002	Indigenous LCC Sky Europe initially dominated its home market.
	2004	easyJet opened connections to London Luton and Berlin Schönefeld.
	2005	Ryanair started flying from Bratislava, which was promoted as an LCC airport for nearby (60 km) Vienna. Ryanair also connected Poprad with London Stansted.
	2009	Sky Europe was declared bankrupt.
Romania and Bulgaria	Pre-accession	LCC connections began prior to EU accession in 2007 as restrictive regulations in air transport were removed. In Romania, Blue Air was established in 2004 and chose Bucharest Băneasa (Aurel Vlaicu) – traditionally the domestic airport – as its base.

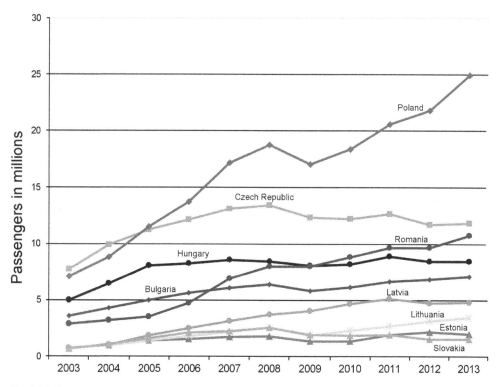

Fig. 22.2. Increase in the number of passengers in CEE countries, 2003–2013. (From author's compilation, based on Eurostat data.)

was for long the dominant LCC, but then lost its leading position to Ryanair, although its share in the market is still substantial (19.3%). The latter expanded so much that, in 2013, more passengers flew Ryanair than the flag carrier, LOT Polish Airlines. Ryanair is also strong in Lithuania and Latvia, whereas Wizzair has expanded considerably in the Romanian market. Such polarisation can also be seen within countries. For example, two busy regional airports in southern Poland, Kraków and Katowice, are separated by less than 100 km. The former is served by Ryanair, with no Wizzair flights, while the latter is the major base of Wizzair and is connected to 26 other airports, with only a marginal presence of Ryanair (five destinations in 2015).

Since the early days of LCC expansion, connections to/from British airports have dominated (Bjelicic, 2013). In addition, Latvia and Estonia have had frequent links to Scandinavian cities, while Romania has seen flights to Italy and Spain (Gabor, 2010). After accession, the popularity of the newly established network reflected mainly the opening of job markets for citizens of the new EU countries. Labour migration rates were often spectacular (half a million Poles into the UK, for example), generating significant numbers of two-way family visits (Burrell, 2011). Business links also played a part. Subsequently, flights aimed at tourism and leisure trips were added, with outbound seasonal Mediterranean routes to Spain (e.g. Alicante, Malaga), Italy (e.g. Cagliari, Trapani), Malta and Greece (e.g. Chania).

The share of LCCs in the structure of passenger traffic in the new EU countries is a clear indicator of their rapid expansion, although there are marked differences between countries. In Slovakia, LCCs served 49% of total passenger traffic as early as 2004, increasing their presence to 65% in 2005 and to 90% in 2008. The reasons for this extreme growth were complex and included price sensitivity of the local market, but also the weak position and financial problems of the relatively new flag carrier, Slovak Airlines, which was bankrupted in 2007. In Poland, too, LCCs had quickly acquired a dominant position in the market, taking 52.7% of the total traffic in 2008, increasing this share to 61.5% in 2013 (Dziedzic, 2008, 2014). A considerable presence of LCCs was also noted in Romania and Bulgaria (around 35% each).

Significantly, very few connections were established between the new EU countries themselves. In certain years, Wizzair operated from Katowice to Budapest, and Sky Europe flew from Kraków to Prague. Latterly, Wizzair and Smart Wings have included Burgas and Varna in Bulgaria as typical holiday destinations. But these tend to be exceptions.

In spring 2014, Ryanair took advantage of the 9th freedom of the air and the right to stand-alone cabotage,[1] opening internal connections within Poland. Flights from Warsaw Modlin airport (low-cost airport for Warsaw) to Gdańsk and Wrocław were launched and soon proved successful.

22.3.3 Development of regional airports in CEE

Low-cost carriers often choose cheaper and less congested airports in smaller cities, or secondary (additional) airports serving large urban agglomerations. Therefore, they may become engines of regional growth, and this can be observed in CEE, especially in Poland and Romania (Fig. 22.3). Both these countries are large, geographically complex, with many important urban centres located far away from capital airports, offering clear opportunities for LCCs to expand. Indeed, Pancer-Cybulska *et al.* (2012) recognise that the growing number of flights from regional airports has helped regions to improve transport accessibility and territorial cohesion, thereby encouraging economic development.

Case study of Poland

In 2003, the year prior to EU accession, Poland had ten regional airports. Among them, five were served by international flights (Kraków, Gdańsk, Wrocław, Poznań, Katowice), but international traffic in general was clearly focused on the capital airport in Warsaw. In 2003, the share of Warsaw airport in total passenger traffic in the country was 73%. In the following years, the relative role of the capital airport declined in favour of regional ones, being 69% in 2004, 62% in 2005, while in 2007, for the first time, it fell below 50%. In 2014, Polish regional airports served 54.6% of the country's total number of passengers (ULC, 2015).

After accession, nearly all regional airports became internationally connected, the only exception being a small airport near Zielona Góra in westernmost Poland (Huderek-Glapska, 2010). There was a marked increase in both the number of carriers flying to Poland (see Table 22.2) and the number of cities that could be reached by direct flights (Table 22.3). However, there was also considerable instability in the network (Fig. 22.4).

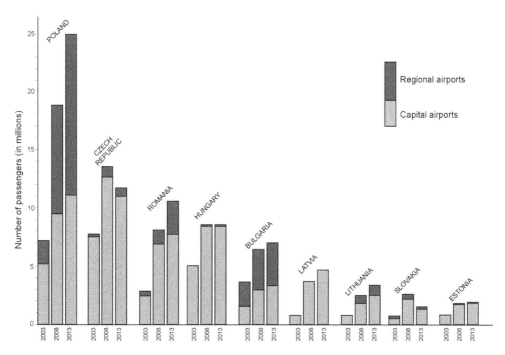

Fig. 22.3. Changes in market share of capital and regional airports in CEE countries. (From author's compilation, based on Eurostat data.)

The position of LCCs becomes evident if their share in the structure of passenger traffic at regional airports is considered. As early as 2005, low-cost airlines served the majority of passengers in Kraków (52.75%), Katowice (84.9%) and Łódź (97.5%). In 2007, their share was above 50% in all regional airports from which they flew, including 82.4% in Katowice, 87% in Bydgoszcz and 98% in Łódź. They dominated at two new airports, with a 93% share at Lublin and 99.7% at Warsaw Modlin for 2013. The latter is intended to be an LCC airport and an alternative for the increasingly busy capital airport at Okęcie but, by 2015, only Ryanair was operating out of Modlin, other LCCs continuing to use Okęcie.

Case study of Romania

In 2006, just prior to EU accession, as many as 15 airports, including two in the capital, were served by regular flights within the country (see Fig. 22.5). However, as much as 74% of passenger traffic passed through the international airport of Bucharest, Otopeni (now named Henri Coandă airport). Otopeni was served mainly by legacy carriers, although several LCCs were also present (Aer Lingus,[2] easy-Jet, Alpi Eagle, Clicair and Wind Jet). But it was Bucharest Băneasa, the former domestic airport, that became the main LCC airport and the base of Blue Air, until closure of the airport in 2012. Flights were offered by Germanwings, Myair, Oneair, Sky Europe and Wizzair. Italian destinations dominated: Milan, Rome, Venice, Florence, Bari, Bologna, Naples, Catania and Treviso.

The biggest regional airport in 2006 was Timişoara, which served 753,000 passengers (15.9% of the total). It was selected as a main hub by the regional carrier, Carpatair, and was also served by Austrian Airlines, Lufthansa, Malév, Tarom and LCCs such as Volare, Blue Air and Alpi Eagles. Traffic in Timişoara grew in absolute terms, up to 1.2 million in 2011, although its share in the national market declined to 11.5%, due largely to the doubling of passenger traffic in Romania. After 2011, certain routes were closed and traffic declined, until, in 2013, Carpatair suspended its business. The total number of passengers through the airport fell back to 757,000: just 7% of the national market.

Table 22.3. The number of air carriers operating from Polish airports and the number of summer-season destinations. (From author's compilation, based on airline timetables.)

Airport	2003 Number of carriers	2003 Number of destinations	2008 Number of carriers	2008 Number of destinations	2013 Number of carriers	2013 Number of destinations	2014 Number of carriers	2014 Number of destinations
Warsaw	21	54	32	80	32	90	33	86
Kraków	6	10	19	40	13	51	14	52
Katowice	2	3	4	23	4	31	5	26
Gdańsk	2	4	8	26	8	41	8	47
Wrocław	3	4	8	21	6	32	7	29
Poznań	4	5	7	17	6	25	7	21
Łódź	1	1	3	8	2	8	2	5
Rzeszów	1	1	2	5	4	14	4	10
Szczecin	2	2	3	8	4	7	4	6
Bydgoszcz	1	1	3	12	2	7	2	4
Zielona G.	1	1	1	1	1	1	1	1
Lublin	–	–	–	–	3	5	4	6
Warsaw Modlin	–	–	–	–	1	26	1	26

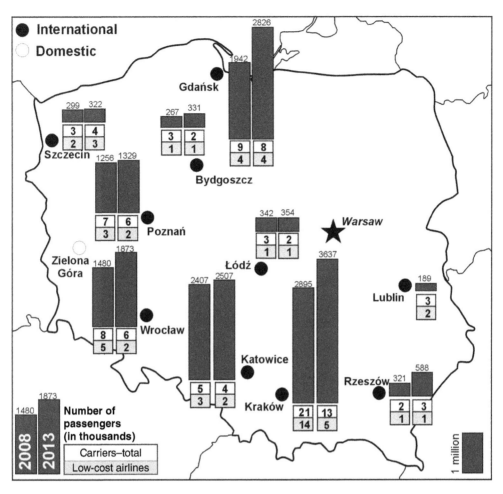

Fig. 22.4. Polish regional airports: numbers of passengers and carriers, 2008 and 2013. (From author's compilation, based on airports statistics and timetables.)

The second most important regional airport is Cluj Napoca. In 2006, it was served by Tarom, Carpatair and Austrian Airlines, and 244,000 passengers (5.2%) used it. Subsequent years have witnessed a steady growth, accelerated after Wizzair opened its base there. The number of passengers exceeded 1 million in 2010, and reached 1.2 million (10.3%) in 2014. In the same year, more than 200,000 passengers were recorded at airports in Târgu Mureş (343,000), Bacău (313,000), Iaşi (273,000) and Sibiu (215,000). Constanta, Craiova and Arad also had a few international flights.

As in Poland, the patterns of connectivity from Romanian regional airports are not stable. Routes are often suspended due to carrier withdrawal and bankruptcy, although the most popular links are quickly taken over by other carriers. Among LCCs, Wizzair has been most expansive in building its network, and in 2015 the airline offered flights from Bucharest and eight other Romanian airports.

Other countries

In the remaining, smaller EU countries of CEE, changes in the role of regional airports were less pronounced, relating to the rather compact size of these countries, smaller populations and shorter distances/easy access to main airports. In the Czech Republic, the busiest regional airport is at Brno (486,000 passengers in 2014, but only 4%

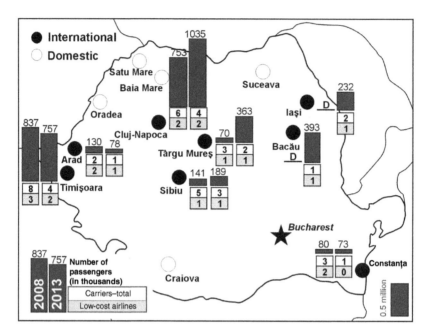

Fig. 22.5. Romanian regional airports: numbers of passengers and carriers, 2008 and 2013. (From author's compilation, based on airports' statistics and timetables.)

of the country total), served by Ryanair, Wizzair and Smart Wings. Considerably fewer passengers were recorded in Ostrava (282,000), Pardubice (184,000) and Karlovy Vary (103,000), where charter flights and infrequent legacy carrier flights take most of the traffic.

In Slovakia, the airport at Košice in the far east, developed rapidly, serving 590,000 passengers in 2008. However, the bankruptcy of Sky Europe and the withdrawal of Ryanair resulted in a steady decline of passenger traffic in the following years, reaching a low of 234,000 in 2013. Since then, some growth has taken place, with new connections opened by Wizzair.

In Hungary, traffic at airports other than the capital is very limited. Debrecen held the leading position in 2014 with 146,000 passengers, whereas the local airport in Héviz served fewer than 30,000, mainly by charter and seasonal flights.

Among the Baltic States, only in Lithuania has a regional airport experienced significant growth. Kaunas, the country's second largest city, was incorporated into Ryanair's network in 2005 when the airline opened a base there, and added a number of new destinations in subsequent years. Peak traffic (873,000) was recorded

in 2011, when the share of Kaunas in the national market reached 25%. By contrast, in Latvia and Estonia, air passenger traffic is concentrated in the capital airports of Riga and Tallinn. Small regional airports in Estonia, in Tartu, Parnu, Kuressaare and Kärdla, see fewer than 20,000 passengers each.

LCC policy and regional airports

Low-cost airlines, particularly the larger ones, are often criticised for their policy towards smaller regional airports. Realising how valuable air connections are and what opportunities for business growth may locally emerge, they are tough negotiators with local governments and airport authorities regarding the launch of new connections. LCCs often decide to expand their network from an airport under the condition of receiving financial incentives from either airport authorities or local/regional governments, or both, presented as marketing support. Smaller airports, which have recently opened or upgraded their infrastructure, are particularly interested to attract new carriers and establish new routes, hoping for returns on investment; local authorities realise the potential positive effects for regional development with increased transport accessibility and new job opportunities, both at the airport itself as well as in related services (Pancer-Cybulska *et al.*, 2014). In Poland, it has been demonstrated that transport accessibility, including the number of direct flights, influences the decisions of foreign investors concerning the location of greenfield production investments, accountancy services and call centres (Huderek-Glapska, 2011; Pancer-Cybulska *et al.*, 2014). Financial incentives take different forms, including the reduction of, or even exemption from, landing and handling charges, coverage of certain operational costs (e.g. pilot training, hotel accommodation) and contributions to promotional activities (Echevarne, 2008; Olipra, 2015).

These financial incentives offered to LCCs might be considered as unlawful state aid, and several cases have been subject to investigation by the European Commission (e.g. Echevarne, 2008). In CEE, these have included allegations against Bratislava airport in respect of Ryanair, Timişoara airport regarding Wizzair and Cluj-Napoca and Craiova for their programmes to support airlines intending to establish new routes from their airports (Olipra, 2015).

At certain regional airports, clear domination or even monopoly of one carrier may be observed. This is the case of Kaunas (Lithuania), where nearly 100% of traffic is by Ryanair. Such a degree of dependence on one commercial operator may have considerable negative consequences for the airport if the carrier withdraws or suspends operations.

22.3.4 Modernisation and expansion of infrastructure

One of the consequences of air traffic growth, especially at regional airports, has been the need to upgrade the capacity of old terminal buildings and other infrastructure. Alongside such improvements, in many cases, change in airport ownership has taken place. Local governments acquired shares in airports and became interested in their development, assuming – generally correctly – that a well-connected airport might be a stimulator of economic growth in the entire region (Huderek-Glapska, 2011; Pancer-Cybulska *et al.*, 2014). New, modern terminals have been built in capital cities (Warsaw, Prague), as well

as at regional airports (Brno, Wrocław, Katowice, Gdańsk, Rzeszów, Kaunas). Others have been considerably modernised and enlarged, with significant improvements in infrastructure crucial for the safety of landing/take-off operations.

In order to improve access to airports, railway lines have been extended to airports in Warsaw, Kraków and Gdańsk. Hoping for a further development of air traffic, several decisions to build brand new airports have been made, or to convert existing military airports into civil ones. In Poland, a new airport was built in Lublin in the east, and opened in December 2012. In Romania, construction of an airport in Braşov commenced in 2008, but due to shortage of funds and legal complications, it still had not been completed by mid-2016. Former military airports in Gdynia and Radom in Poland have been expanded to handle passenger traffic, but neither case has yet proved to be successful. Radom, located less than 100 km from Warsaw, struggles to attract air carriers, and flights are sporadic, while the airport in Gdynia filed for bankruptcy after the European Commission decided that some financial support had been spent incorrectly.

22.4 New Trends in Regional Tourism Related to the Growth of Air Transport

An increase in the number of passengers travelling by air in CEE countries is among the most evident consequences of air transport liberalisation. Affordable prices have enabled air travel for people who did not consider flying previously (Brilha, 2008; Castillo-Manzano *et al.*, 2011). At the same time, labour migration, and subsequent family visits, have contributed to increasing demand for air travel, encouraged by EU mobility policies. In CEE countries, the notion of a 'global family', with its members working or studying in different countries, and hence using air transport on a scale unknown before, has become a striking feature of contemporary life. Such mobility stands in stark contrast to the previous restrictions placed on travel under the communists. This CEE diaspora, and the LCCs' ability to facilitate and exploit it, is foreseen to grow further (Henley Centre HeadlightVision and Amadeus, 2010; Oxford Economics and Amadeus, 2010).

The number and frequency of short-term trips have increased markedly, largely as the result of LCC operations (Barrett, 2008). In inbound and outbound tourism alike, city breaks and short breaks have become popular as a result of the availability of direct and more frequent air connections and lower prices. Point-to-point flights, from a regional airport to the final destination, without the necessity to travel via a capital airport or international hub, have reduced flying times significantly, encouraging people to travel more frequently (Olipra, 2012).

Expanded networks at regional airports have offered more options to choose destinations for leisure trips (Pijet-Migoń, 2008). In inbound tourism, short-term sightseeing visits to capital cities (Prague, Budapest, Riga) and to other well-known destinations, such as Kraków, have become common, but other large cities, such as Gdańsk or Wrocław in Poland, have also been discovered by foreign tourists. In Prague, the number of foreign visitors in 2011 was 70% higher than in 2003. In Budapest, an analogous value was 43% (Dumbrovska and Fialova, 2014). The number of foreign tourists in Kraków in 1988, before the political changes, was 335,000, doubling by 2003 to approximately 680,000. Immediately after EU accession, and concurrent with LCC expansion, this figure grew to 1.5 million in 2004, and to 2.1 million in the following year. A peak occurred in 2007, when nearly 2.5 million visitors were attracted to the city. The pan-European economic crisis caused a decline in the period 2008–2009 (to 1.95 million), but in subsequent years, growth has again been recorded, reaching 2.45 million in 2014 (EU Consult, 2014).

The concurrent growth of city tourism and LCC networks has contributed to significant season extension and low-season visits, a previously much less familiar phenomenon.

It has been estimated that the number of foreign visitors flying low-cost into CEE reached about 30% on selected routes (Echevarne, 2008). A popular phenomenon has been to seek new and cheap foreign destinations to have a party, to celebrate birthdays, bachelor stag and hen parties and the like. New EU countries quickly became popular among young British, Irish and Scandinavian tourists (Iwanicki and Dłużewska,

2015). However, promotion of this particular form of tourism generated objections, both from the residents of cities favoured by party tourists (e.g. Kraków, Riga, Vilnius, Bratislava, Gdańsk) as well as from representatives of local tourist enterprises, arguing that negative stereotypes about CEE were being reinforced. In addition, the shocking behaviour of some 'partying' tourists caused dissatisfaction among other visitors, generating a negative destination image (Thurnell-Read, 2011, 2012).

Low-cost connections have contributed to the development of event and sport tourism. This was particularly evident during football EURO 2012 in Poland, when a marked increase in traffic to cities hosting games was recorded (Bartoszewicz and Skalska, 2013).

Better accessibility of cities with airports increases their attractiveness as business tourism destinations, especially as venues of congresses and conferences. Anticipating rising demand, large conference centres have been built in a number of Polish cities, such as Gdańsk, Wrocław, Katowice and Kraków (Poland Convention Bureau, 2015).

The development of low-cost airlines has also had an impact on the behaviour of consumers. Since LCCs encourage people to use the Internet for transactions, potential passengers have become accustomed to search for information, and to purchase products and services via Web distribution channels. New technological solutions make it possible to build individual holiday packages, and the preparation of a trip is now much simpler and more convenient than it was previously. Some decisions to undertake a holiday or sightseeing travel are made spontaneously. Seeking cheap flight offers and opportunities to travel cheaply are trends observed not only among the younger generation. For those who prefer to fly cheaply, price is often a more important factor for choosing a destination than the destination itself (Graham, 2008).

Increasing interest in low-cost travel has not been ignored by the authorities of airports located close to attractive holiday, recreation and spa destinations. To increase visibility and underline the proximity to the area of interest, several airports have modified their official names. Thus, the airport in Poprad, Slovakia was renamed Tatra Airport, and the airport in

Héviz, Hungary, temporarily used the name Fly Balaton Airport, after the biggest lake in the country and a popular tourist spot. A small regional airport in Szymany in northern Poland, scheduled to open in 2016, will be branded Olsztyn–Mazury to emphasise that the Masurian Lakeland – one of the most acclaimed tourist regions of Poland – is close by.

22.5 Summary and Conclusions

The expansion of low-cost airlines in CEE following the liberalisation of air transport consequent on EU membership brought about dramatic changes in the mobilities of the region. Price affordability extended the market to a new range of customers, resulting in a massive growth in the number of passengers travelling by this mode. Labour mobility in and from CEE increased markedly with EU accession and employment opportunities in Western Europe. Such economic and social transformation was reflected in new destinations launched by LCCs, responding quickly to employment market trends and mobilities. In particular, the number of connections to British and Irish cities from CEE countries grew rapidly. For Romania, destinations in Italy and Spain became important. In the north, Nordic countries became popular destinations from Riga and Tallinn.

LCC growth in the region was most dynamic in the first few years after EU accession. Regional airports boomed, especially in Poland and Romania. To cope with increasing traffic and the projected rise in demand, considerable upgrades were made at many airports and decisions were enforced to build new airports, although the latter moves experienced mixed success.

In 2009–2010, in many CEE countries, growth slowed or reversed and levels of passenger traffic reflected the economic crisis throughout Europe. Competition between carriers increased, and some did not survive. Since 2011, growth in most countries has resumed, but a parallel process of market consolidation has taken place. While the number of carriers operating in national markets is declining, the number of destinations is growing as a result of further expansion of the major LCCs, notably Ryanair and Wizzair.

Regional airports have benefitted most from the development of LCCs, acting as facilitators for regional development diffusion processes. Typically, low-cost carriers did not open connections on established routes operated by legacy airlines, but launched new routes between European regions not previously served by direct flights. In this way, they contributed significantly to the improved accessibility of regions hitherto considered peripheral. Notably, in LCC networks from CEE, regional airports mostly connect with 'old' EU member states. By contrast, routes between CEE states have developed only to a limited degree.

The improved accessibility of these regional destinations to Western Europe has carried implications for the host cities and their surrounding regions. The growth of inbound tourism has embraced 'city breaks', sightseeing tours, business tourism and party tourism, helping to offset seasonality effects. Many regions, poorly accessible before, are now readily available as holiday and health tourism destinations.

In the period 2004–2015, the number of foreign tourists grew significantly in the capital cities of the new EU countries (particularly Prague, Budapest, Warsaw and Riga), in popular tourist centres outside the capitals (Kraków, Gdańsk) and also in less internationally recognised destinations such as Wrocław, Poznań and Timişoara. In terms of outbound mobility, LCCs have encouraged an increasing readiness for pursuing individualised holiday planning and package building.

In conclusion, therefore, the geopolitical impacts of the neoliberal business model and practices of LCCs in CEE can be summarised in terms of: (i) greatly broadening and extending the market for air travel; (ii) opening hitherto less accessible regional centres to inbound tourism, FDI (foreign direct investment) and possible regional development diffusion effects; (iii) facilitating increased and varied types of inbound tourism to capital cities; (iv) generating new images of known and less well-known destinations for tourism, investment and residence; (v) facilitating substantial labour migration across the EU, most notably from east to west; (vi) facilitating easier and more affordable outbound tourism and leisure opportunities; and (vii) stimulating indigenous business practices, not least in travel and tourism.

Endnotes

[1] Ninth freedom – full cabotage is the operation by an airline of services that originate and terminate wholly within a single foreign country (Holloway, 2008).
[2] Aer Lingus – previously Ireland's legacy flag carrier, now a hybrid airline that has changed its business model to low-cost on European flights, but still operates as a traditional airline on transatlantic routes.

References

Barrett, S. (2008) The emergence of the low-cost carriers sector. In: Graham, A., Papatheodorou, A. and Forsyth, P. (eds) *Aviation and Tourism. Implications for Leisure Travel*. Ashgate, Aldershot, UK, pp. 103–118.

Bartoszewicz, W. and Skalska, T. (2013) *Zagraniczna turystyka przyjazdowa do Polski, w 2012 roku. [International inbound tourism to Poland in 2012.]* Instytut Turystyki, Szkoła Główna Turystyki i Rekreacji, Warsaw (in Polish).

Bjelicic, B. (2007) The business model of low-cost airlines – past, present, future. In: Gross, S. and Schröder, A. (ed.) *Handbook of Low-cost Airlines*. Erich Schmidt, Berlin, pp. 11–31.

Bjelicic, B. (2013) Low cost carriers in Eastern Europe. In: Gross, S. and Lück, M. (ed.) *The Low-cost Carrier Worldwide*. Ashgate, Farnham, UK, pp. 39–58.

Brilha, N.M. (2008) Airport requirements for leisure travellers. In: Graham, A., Papatheodorou, A. and Forsyth, P. (eds) *Aviation and Tourism Implications for Leisure Travel*. Ashgate, Aldershot, UK, pp. 167–176.

Burrell, K. (2011) Going steerage on Ryanair: culture of migrant air travel between Poland and the UK. *Journal of Transport Geography* 19(5), 1023–1030.

Castillo-Manzano, J.C., Lopez-Valpuesta, L. and Gonzalez-Laxe, F. (2011) The effect of the LCC boom on the urban fabric. The viewpoint of tourism management. *Tourism Management* 32, 1085–1095.

Dennis, N. (2007) End of the free lunch? The response of traditional European airlines to the low-cost carrier threat. *Journal of Air Travel Management* 13, 311–321.

Dobruszkes, F. (2009) New Europe, new low-cost services. *Journal of Transport Geography* 17, 423–432.

Dobruszkes, F. (2014) Geographies of European air transport. In: Goetz, A.R and Budd, L. (eds) *The Geographies of Air Transport*. Ashgate, Farnham, UK, pp. 167–186.

Doganis, R. (2006) *The Airline Business*. Routledge, London.

Dumbrovska, V. and Fialova, D. (2014) Tourism industry in capital cities in Central Europe: comparative analysis of tourism in Prague, Vienna and Budapest. *Czech Journal of Tourism* 3(1), 5–26.

Dziedzic, T. (2008) *Rynek lotniczy 2008. [Air transport market 2008.]* Instytut Turystyki, Wiadomości Turystyczne, Warsaw (in Polish).

Dziedzic, T. (2014) *Rynek lotniczy 2014. [Air transport market 2014.]* Instytut Turystyki, Szkoła Głowna Turystyki i Rekreacji, Warsaw (in Polish).

Echevarne, R. (2008) The impact of attracting low cost carriers to airports. In: Graham, A., Papatheodorou, A. and Forsyth, P. (eds) *Aviation and Tourism. Implications for Leisure Travel*. Ashgate, Aldershot, UK, pp. 177–193.

EU Consult (2014) *Badanie ruchu turystycznego w województwie małopolskim w 2014 roku. [The research of tourism in Malopolska Province in 2014.]* EU Consult, Gdańsk, Poland (in Polish). Available at: http://www.malopolskie.pl/Pliki/2015/RAPORT_badania_ruchu_turystycznego2014.pdf (accessed 17 August 2016).

Franke M. (2004) Competition between network carriers and low-cost carriers – retreat battle or breakthrough to a new level of efficiency? *Journal of Air Transport Management* 10, 15–21.

Gabor, D. (2010) Low-cost airlines in Europe: network structures after the enlargement of the European Union. *Geographica Pannonica* 14(2), 49–58.

Graham, A. (2008) Trends and characteristics of leisure travel demand. In: Graham, A., Papatheodorou, A. and Forsyth, P. (eds) *Aviation and Tourism. Implications for Leisure Travel*. Ashgate, Aldershot, UK, pp. 21–33.

Gross, S. and Lück, M. (eds) (2013) *The Low-cost Carrier Worldwide*. Ashgate, Farnham, UK.

Henley Centre HeadlightVision and Amadeus (2010) *Future Traveller Tribes 2020*. Amadeus, Gatwick, UK. Available at: www.amadeus.com (accessed 18 September 2015).

Holloway, S. (2008) *Straight and Level. Practical Airline Economics.* Ashgate, Aldershot, UK.

Huderek-Glapska, S. (2010) Economic benefits of market liberalization. Evidence from air transport in Poland. *Journal of International Studies* 3, 49–58.

Huderek-Glapska, S. (2011) Wpływ portu lotniczego na gospodarkę regionu. [The influence of airport on regional economy.] In: Rekowski, M. (ed.) *Regionalne porty lotnicze w Polsce – charakterystyka i tendencje rozwojowe. [Regional airports in Poland – characteristics and trends in development.]* Wydawnictwo Uniwersytetu Ekonomicznego w Poznaniu, Poznań, Poland, pp. 193–236 (in Polish).

Iwanicki, G. and Dłużewska, A. (2015) Potential of city break clubbing tourism in Wroclaw. *Bulletin of Geography, Socio-Economic Series* 28, 77–89.

Királova, A. (2006) Tourism in the Czech Republic. In: Hall, D., Smith, M. and Marciszewska, B. (eds) *Tourism in the New Europe. The Challenges and Opportunities of EU Enlargement.* CAB International, Wallingford, UK, pp. 104–115.

Olipra, Ł. (2012) The impact of low-cost carriers on tourism development in less famous destinations. *Sinergie Journal. Refereed Conference Proceedings, Cittaslow: The Value of Slowness for the Tourism of the Future.* Perugia, Italy, pp. 41–56.

Olipra, Ł. (2015) Wspieranie połączeń tanich linii lotniczych ze środków publicznych. [Supporting low cost airlines connections from public funds.] *Studia ekonomiczne* 209, Uniwersytet Ekonomiczny w Katowicach, Katowice, Poland, pp. 146–157 (in Polish).

Oxford Economics and Amadeus (2010) *The Travel Gold Rush 2020. Pioneering Growth and Profitability Trends in the Travel Sector.* Amadeus, Gatwick, UK. Available at: www.amadeus.com (accessed 23 October 2015).

Pancer-Cybulska, E., Szostak, E. and Olipra, Ł. (2012) The impact of the migration process on the low cost airlines' routes between EU countries and Poland after the accession to the EU, and on the territorial cohesion of Polish regions. *Studia Regionalia* 33, 115–131.

Pancer-Cybulska, E., Olipra, Ł., Cybulski, L. and Surówka, A. (2014) *The Impact of Air Transport on Regional Labour Market in Poland.* Wydawnictwo Uniwersytetu Ekonomicznego we Wrocławiu, Wrocław, Poland.

Pijet-Migoń, E. (2008) The development of regional airports in Central and Eastern Europe as an opportunity for inbound tourism. In: *Conditions of the Foreign Tourism Development in Central and Eastern Europe,* Vol 10. Institute of Geography and Regional Development, University of Wrocław, Wrocław Poland, pp. 345–356.

Pijet-Migoń, E. (2012) *Zmiany rynku lotniczych przewozów pasażerskich w Polsce po akcesji do Unii Europejskiej. [Changes in passenger air transport in Poland after the accession to the European Union.]* Rozprawy Naukowe Instytutu Geografii i Rozwoju Regionalnego 25, Uniwersytet Wrocławski, Wrocław, Poland (in Polish).

Poland Convention Bureau (2015) *Poland Meeting and Events Industry Report 2015.* Polish Tourist Organisation, Warsaw. Available at: www.poland-convention.pl (accessed 23 October 2015).

Puczkó, L. and Rátz, T. (2006) Product development and diversification in Hungary. In: Hall, D., Smith, M. and Marciszewska, B. (eds) *Tourism in the New Europe. The Challenges and Opportunities of EU Enlargement.* CAB International, Wallingford, UK, pp. 116–126.

Thurnell-Read, T. (2011) 'Common-sense' research: senses, emotion and embodiment in researching stag tourism in Eastern Europe. *Methodological Innovation Online* 6(3), 39–49. Available at: http://mio.sagepub.com/content/6/3/39.full.pdf+html (accessed 23 August 2016).

Thurnell-Read, T. (2012) Tourism place and space: British stag tourism in Poland. *Annals of Tourism Research* 39, 801–819.

ULC (2015) *Urząd Lotnictwa Cywilnego. [Civil Aviation Authority of Poland.]* ULC, Warsaw (in Polish). Available at: www.ulc.gov.pl (accessed 17 August 2016).

23 Tourism and a Geopolitics of Connectivity: The Albanian Nexus

Derek Hall*

Seabank Associates, Maidens, Scotland, UK

Past a certain threshold of energy consumption for the fastest passenger, a worldwide class structure of speed capitalists is created ... Beyond a critical speed, no one can save time without forcing another to lose it.

(Illich, 1974: 41–42)

23.1 Introduction

Central to the European project is connectivity, both virtual and physical, to which tourism may be an adjunct or critically central. In the previous chapter, however, Edyta Pijet-Migoń pointed to the relatively poor development of low-cost carrier (LCC) air connections within Central and Eastern Europe (CEE), certainly compared to the myriad links established with Western Europe. This chapter examines the geopolitics of connectivity surrounding the development of an intra-Balkan highway – partly justified in terms of facilitating and generating tourism – that has been pursued in the face of opposition from supranational institutions. The chapter articulates, through this contentious development, the ambivalence of 'the West' and its widely proclaimed anti-corruption ideology towards 'Balkanism'.

Although often perceived as, at best, peripheral, currently beyond the European Union's (EU) external borders, Albania commands an important physical and symbolic bridging position. Located on the fault line between Catholic and Orthodox Christianity (see Chapter 4, this volume), it was during the 14th and 15th centuries that the Ottoman Turks incorporated Albanian lands into their Islamic empire for the best part of half a millennium.

Denied access to Western technology and know-how under the Ottomans, and for half of the 20th century under a Stalinist regime, since 1991 this country of 3 million people has embraced the neoliberal cornucopia while becoming (not for the first time) the object of hegemonic competition of an economic, spiritual and geopolitical nature.

Central to Albania's role is its close, if dynamic, relationship with a newly emergent country of co-ethnics. This Kosovo heartland of Albanians' 19th century struggle for national recognition was excluded from an independent Albanian state established in the early 20th century by representatives of the then major powers (Hall, 1994).

After the fall of communism, when the rigid border that had for so long separated Albania from Kosovo was (re)opened, ethnic Albanians in the former Yugoslav landlocked territory gained access – first as refugees from a vicious conflict (see Chapter 18, this volume), and subsequently as tourists – to Albania and its coastline.

These dynamics have advanced as 'Europeanisation' (or rather Euro-Atlantic)[1] processes have rolled south-eastwards, and have drawn Albania and Albanians not only into grand

*E-mail: derekhall@seabankscotland.co.uk

plans for consolidating a continent-wide connectivity programme – and its potential for furthering tourism aspirations – but also into an ideological project that imposes a range of norms and values that include the rhetoric of anti-corruption ideology.

This chapter therefore addresses the interrelated issues of tourism development, national identity and the apparent hegemony of anti-corruption ideology, as expressed in the processes of connectivity within south-eastern Europe. It identifies the problematic nature of such interrelationships at a time when the role of Albania within Euro–Atlantic processes is viewed as a source of stability and security, in the otherwise pejoratively signified 'Western Balkans', not least because of its co-ethnic relationships in Kosovo, as well as in Montenegro and the Former Yugoslav Republic of Macedonia (FYROM) (e.g. Reszczynski, 2010; Tamminem, 2012; Metushaj, 2015). This co-ethnicity (and the expectations arising from it) may itself impose an element of path dependency on Albania's geoeconomic and geopolitical trajectory.

The roles of tourism within and resulting from geopolitical relations can be played out on a number of levels. In the case of Albania, tourism has acted as an (not necessarily positive) instrument of identity and imagery, as a tool of ideology and, most recently, as an expression of such co-ethnicity.

23.2 Tourism as a Geopolitical Instrument

In 1974, when Europe was on the cusp of sweeping away its last fascist dictatorships, and Stalinist Albania was about to sever its close relationship with China, the list of proscriptions of and on foreign tourists seeking the privilege of visiting the country embodied the geopolitical significance of international tourism for this paranoid south-east European regime (Table 23.1).

> Thus, the 'foreign body' came to represent compliance with official Albanian norms while the prescriptions were explicitly gendered: hair, beard, trousers for men, skirt length, neckline, heel shape and size for women.
> (Ateljevic and Hall, 2007: 146–147)

If such rigidly enforced proscriptions were aimed at protecting Albanian citizens from alien influences, this was not the first time that the role of travel in Albanian lands had embraced the geopolitical (or the symbolically embodied). In their diverse ways, 19th and earlier 20th century author-travellers such as Byron, Edward Lear (1851) and Edith Durham (1905, 1909, 1928) had tended to emphasise the 'otherness' of their experiences, depicting Albanians and Albanian lands as exotic and romantic, even 'Oriental' (cf. Said, 1978).

Consolidating its economic hegemony through military occupation in 1939, Fascist Italy was to become, ironically, long associated with subsequent communist Albania's only premier class hotel (until well into the 1980s). The *Dajti* in central Tirana was built during the occupation as part of a new administrative district laid out to the south of the capital's centre. The hotel's post-war role included being a meeting ground for diplomats, businessmen, selected foreign tourists, clandestine journalists and those whose careers were based on observing all the others.

But for almost half a century following World War II, Albania's ideal physical conditions for international tourism – clear, warm seas, long, sandy beaches, spectacular uplands, material heritage from several cultures – were

Table 23.1. Tourism as an embodied instrument: Albania's foreign tourist proscriptions in the early 1970s. (From Regent Holidays' information for tourists to Albania, 1974; Albanian customs declaration form, 1974.)

Passports	Greece, Israel, Portugal, South Africa, Spain, USA, USSR, Yugoslavia
Women	Short skirts, very long skirts, wedge heels, décolletage
Men	Flared trousers, tight trousers, long hair, full beards
Accompanying luggage	Anything of a religious, political or pornographic nature (terms 'liberally' interpreted to encompass certain Western guidebooks to the country and virtually all foreign newspapers), radio transmitters and receivers, arms and explosives

neutralised by an inhospitable, rigid and paranoid communist political environment and inadequate infrastructure. Such foreign tourism that was developed in Albania offered a model of prescription matched only by North Korean practice. Honed from the Intourist blueprint, it was collective, rigidly timetabled and segregated, and closely 'guided' (Hall, 1984, 1990).

Until the later 1980s, such national identity that was conveyed through tourism experiences was of austerity, impenetrability and potential hostility. When the structures of communism were dismantled in 1991, Albania assumed, or rather returned to, a role of viewing itself as a bridge between East and West: starkly expressed in large-scale emigration in both directions and in the Albanian diaspora, which was thereby substantially expanded.

With the opening of Albania's borders, and especially after landlocked Kosovo's self-declared independence in 2008, Kosovars (and co-ethnics in FYROM and in Montenegro) could travel to and take holidays in Albania. In 2010, 1.18 million Kosovars were recorded entering Albania (more than double the figure for the previous year). This figure rose to 1.71 million in 2012, fell back in 2013, before rising to 1.38 million in 2014, representing a market share of 37.55% (Table 23.2) (UNWTO, 2015).[2] Road access across often difficult terrain has been critical in this process.

In their interview survey of tourists from Kosovo, Zoto and Vangjeli (2013) found that 83% of visitors arrived in Albania by private car.

More than half travelled directly to their sole destination, while a quarter opted for circuit tourism. Some 80% visit during June, July and August (Tavanxhiu and Gaspari, 2011).

Table 23.2 suggests that the international tourism market in Albania is skewed heavily towards immediate neighbours – the top five source countries being either contiguous or, in the case of Italy, near contiguous – with Kosovo being dominant. Encouraged by nationalism and improved connectivity (see below), current Kosovar demand might, nevertheless, be considered 'albatross tourism', in the sense that, along with domestic demand, it skews structurally the Albanian tourism product and image heavily towards low-spending (albeit in euros), high-season beach holidays, exerting environmental pressures on coastal locations and becoming a considerable weight around the neck of those who seek to diversify Albania's tourism attractions and its cultural image. Such tourism trajectory tensions are likely to persist.[4]

23.3   The Connectivity of Albanian Lands

Albanian lands acted as part of an important through route in Roman times, when the *Via Egnatia* bifurcated the area on its passage between Eastern and Western capitals (O'Sullivan, 1972; Raven, 1993). Following Ottoman conquest (via the Roman *Via*) from the 14th century onwards,

Table 23.2. Main sources of non-resident visitors to Albania, 2014. (From UNWTO, 2015.)

Country	Visitor numbers (thousands)	Market share (%)
1. Kosovo	1379	37.55
2. Former Yugoslav Republic of Macedonia	514	14.01
3. Greece	370	10.07
4. Montenegro	239	6.50
5. Italy	196	5.35
(Total for 'Central and Eastern Europe' category[3]	163	4.44)
6. UK	91	2.48
7. Germany	89	2.44
8. Turkey	59	1.61
9. Serbia	55	1.49
10. Switzerland	41	1.11
11. France	37	1.02
Total: all non-resident visitors	3673	100

the area was largely isolated from Western cultural and technological developments. None the less, connectivity within the wider Ottoman Empire offered opportunities for trade, migration and individual advancement.

Modern road building was introduced during World War I by Austrians and Italians, largely for strategic reasons. Between the wars, Italy provided increasing financial assistance and technical aid for transport and communications development, preparing the country for its 1939 occupation. The Azienda Strado Albania (ASA) was established to develop and maintain the road system (Mason *et al.*, 1945).

In the earlier 1930s, every Albanian over the age of 16 had been bound by law to provide 10 days' free labour to the state every year. This largely entailed road construction (the *corvée* system). If a person did not wish to undertake the work, they could pay someone else to take their place. The Italians inherited and exploited this 'gift' of free labour and put it to work for the ASA.

The post-war communist regime reinvigorated this 'tradition' (Pollo and Puto, 1981: 249). A 1949 law required all adult men up to the age of 45 to work 'voluntarily' in road maintenance and construction (Dalakoglou, 2012). This requirement persisted throughout the communist period, extending to railway and other construction projects. But, by the 1980s, ideological enthusiasm for such work, and thus its efficiency and effectiveness, seemed to have waned (Dalakoglou, 2010).

By 1990, total road length was 7450 km, with connections, albeit sometimes tenuous, to the more remote villages of the northern highlands and southern uplands. This was complemented by the communist authorities' virtual monopoly on the use of motorised transport, prohibiting its private ownership. Personal mobility was severely limited by additional stringent internal security measures: travel of any distance required appropriate authority. Internal, especially rural to urban, migration had been virtually extinguished, and foreign travel was the preserve of a small elite: little traffic passed through the country's land borders with Yugoslavia (Montenegro, Kosovo, Macedonia) and Greece.

One of the culture shocks of political change in 1991 was the leap to the private ownership of motor vehicles: 1500 motor cars per month were imported during the early 1990s (Pojani, 2011). Not only were many families now considerably more mobile (albeit often without any formal driving instruction) but also, in the absence of political constraint, the rush to build new or extend existing residential dwellings saw their construction often removed from locations accessible by public transport (Pojani and Pojani, 2011). These processes were reinforced by programmes with high investment priority for road building at the expense of public transport.

23.4 Dependency, Connectivity and Anti-corruption Ideology

The World Bank, European Bank for Reconstruction and Development (EBRD) and the European Investment Bank (EIB) have been the most important sources of development funding for Albania, although the finance received is mostly in the form of loans (usually with stringent conditions attached) rather than grants. In this way, Albania has been rendered dependent through its requirement for long-term debt repayment. Much funding is returned to donor countries through fee repatriation, and is often wasted through duplication and the inappropriate knowledge of foreign consultants acting on the donors' behalf (see Simpson and Roberts, 2000).

Pojani (2010) highlights the fact that over the 20-year period 1991–2010, foreign 'donors' funded no less than ten transport plans and studies for Tirana, which often reiterated previous reports. Usually, funding was secured only to prepare the studies themselves, with no provision for their actual implementation. Such plans have not been widely circulated nor easily obtained, often being treated as confidential, and not even translated into Albanian.

Three national tourism strategies were funded between 1993 and 2007, the third being an analysis of the first two, with a focus on developing cultural tourism, up to 2013 (Vladi, 2014). A culture marketing strategy produced by Irish consultants was published in 2010 (TDI, 2010).

The trade-offs involved in Albania's path towards potential EU accession (candidate status was awarded in 2014) have included transport infrastructure commitments that the country has been hard pressed to meet. Successive European Commission reports have pointed to little progress being made in the country's transport policy, alignment with the transport *acquis*, or in strengthening administrative and technical capacity (e.g. European Commission, 2015). Regional neighbours have also commented on Albania's apparent tardiness in plugging gaps in the putative Pan-European Corridor system (e.g. Grimaldi, 2009).

Prior to these perceived shortcomings, and perhaps the cause of them, a 2003 World Bank feasibility study for upgrading the single-carriage road to the Kosovo border (Brunwasser, 2015) was seized upon by the political elite intent on establishing a legacy project that would also embody national support for Kosovar co-ethnics. A fast-track process was put in train by the Albanian government in 2006 to build a four-lane highway – far in excess of what the World Bank study had indicated – connecting the capitals of Tirana and Prishtina. Such a highway had not been prioritised in any pan-European plans, and it raised fears, not least in Serbia and Greece, of being a step towards creating a 'Greater Albania' (Koleka and Buza, 2007).

Other observers were more concerned with the subsequent political processes associated with the highway's construction.

Corruption became a high-profile concern with the development of international state-building practices by Western governments and institutions in the 1990s. By placing anti-corruption at the core of its good governance initiatives, the 'international community' (in Kosovo and Bosnia) indicated that it viewed corruption as the central barrier to its project. The Stability Pact for South Eastern Europe in 1999 proclaimed the 'fight' against corruption to be a top priority, and a Stability Pact Anti-Corruption Initiative (SPAI), designed to play a leading coordinating role in the state-building process (IAACA, 2012), was established the following year. This defined, and saw the ills of, corruption within a broad-brush perspective, with little apparent analytical or evidence-based support (Chandler, 2006).

Conventional wisdom suggests that corruption in transport projects can account for between 5% and 20% of transaction costs, resulting in significant diseconomies whose scale impacts tend to be inversely proportional to a country's wealth. The end result represents a significant informal shift of resources from poor to richer countries (and from poorer to richer within countries) that, by definition, tends to be unrecorded (World Bank, 2009; Sieber, 2011).

Albanian citizens have ranked corruption as the country's second most important problem after unemployment (UNODC, 2011), while business representatives have cited corruption as the second most significant obstacle to doing business, after high taxes (UNODC, 2013).[5] On taking office in 2013, new prime minister, Edi Rama, declared tackling corruption a priority (just as his predecessor, Sali Berisha, had done). He was supported in this by the United Nations Development Programme (UNDP) (Bloomer, 2015).

But anti-corruption campaigns can be counterproductive by disrupting too much local economic fabric too quickly, particularly where they are organised from the centre for application at the periphery. They can echo neocolonialism and be portrayed as the product of 'Western' double standards in reinforcing the idea that problems in the periphery are the result of policies made by local elites, when it is the decisions of international capital that generate dependency relationships between 'rapacious suppliers of corruption' from the core and weak governments and private institutions of the periphery, who can become addicted to the graft and debt on offer (Kennedy, 1999: 458).

Articulations of nationalism and co-ethnicity (nominally embracing tourism development aspirations), set against international institution hegemony and anti-corruption rhetoric, provide the context for the following section.

23.5 Dependency Redefined?

Few geopolitical studies have paid attention to such aspects of transport infrastructure as the construction and operation of motorways (Grubišić Šeba, 2015). Transport and transport infrastructure are, of course, essential components of the tourism process, linking source markets with host destinations and providing mobility and access within a destination area or region. Geopolitically, they are essential for providing fixed links with international traffic and trade and for state-building processes, integrating outlying, difficult and peripheral regions with the core. With the need to consolidate new state systems, relationships and identities, as in the case of the Yugoslav successor states, transport and transport infrastructure can express important geopolitical orientations and aspirations (e.g. Hall, 1993).

The construction of the four-lane 'Patriotic Highway'/'Dr Ibrahim Rugova Highway',[6] which now slices its way through one of the poorest and most remote corners of Europe, connecting the Albanian and Kosovar capitals, Tirana and Prishtina (Figs 23.1 and 23.2), was justified on the premise of creating wealth from the generation of increased trade and tourism, not least permitting easy access for tourists from neighbouring landlocked countries and beyond to travel to Albania's Adriatic and Ionian beaches and to the ferry port of Durrës. The highway superseded a narrow, slow, and in parts dangerous, road that wound around hill- and mountainsides.

The name 'Patriotic Highway' popularly accorded to the four-lane road in Albania, articulates the rhetoric that accompanied its development as a costly (Box 23.1) symbol of nationalism and/or political vanity. At a total length of 234 km, its construction became Albania's largest public works project in several decades.[7] One Albanian analyst referred to it as 'pharaonic' (Mentor Nazarko quoted in Koleka and Buza, 2007).

In the early stages of development, the Albanian highway narrative was outwardly tourism and trade driven, albeit within a nationalistic frame: linking the port and beaches of Durrës with emergent Kosovo to 'ease travel for the hundreds of thousands of Kosovars who cross the border on summer holidays' (Likmeta, 2008).[8]

One former prime minister even suggested that the highway would

> ... crystallize a year-round tourism industry and double the size of the Albanian market.
> (Pandeli Majko quoted in Koleka and Buza, 2007)

Following Kosovo's self-declared independence, political emphasis was placed on a highway that would link the two countries' capitals, and the adoption of 'Patriotic Highway' in Albania as explicit nationalist rhetoric reflected this. Notably absent in the road's justification was the question of raising the prospects of those living in impoverished, mountainous northern Albania, through which the road slices. But there was an overriding domestic political imperative in this project: the road was required to be completed in 2009 as a centrepiece of Prime Minister Sali Berisha's re-election campaign.

> The World Bank had offered to help Albania finance and prepare a tender procedure for local contractors to build a two-lane road....(it) would have cost about one third the price ... But Berisha insisted on a four-lane motorway, and he wanted it fast. Bechtel was happy to help.
> (Brunwasser, 2015)

At the opening ceremony of the second stage of the road, from the Albanian border to Prishtina, in November 2013, Kosovo President Atifete Jahjaga, described it as 'a national dream ... now a national reality' (Collaku *et al.*, 2014). It would contribute to the country's future economic and social growth, and would cut driving times from Prishtina to the Albanian coast from 9 h to 4 h. Yet by 2013, only one in seven Kosovars owned a car, one of the lowest rates in Europe (Brunwasser, 2015). Subsequently, several officials would suggest that the road was working at just 10% capacity (e.g. Koleka and Bytyci, 2014).

Despite the huge investment, trade between the two countries has not thus far strengthened markedly, and economic benefits have yet to be made manifest. This is particularly significant, as recession in Europe has resulted in a serious decline in the level of remittances sent home by Albanian and Kosovar émigrés (Hoti, 2009).

According to Kosovo's Agency of Statistics (KAS, 2014), 10.3% by value of all Kosovo exports went to Albania in 2005, a figure that had risen to 14.6% in 2012 and to rank second in 2014, albeit with a value of just €44,011. Imports from Albania accounted for just 1.6% of Kosovo's 2005 total, rising to 4.4% in 2012, and by 2014 ranking only eighth, with a total value of €133,702 (Table 23.3). The improved high rankings for China and Italy in Table 23.3 might suggest Kosovo's increasing use of the port of Durrës for transhipment.[9] However, only one-third of Kosovo's seaborne imports arrives via

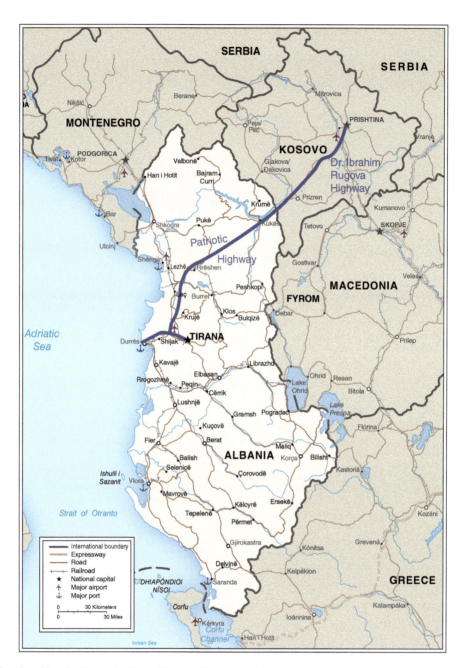

Fig. 23.1. Albania–Kosovo highway. (Redrawn from author's compilation.)

Albania; most come through Montenegro's port of Bar and from Thessaloniki in Greece via FYROM (Koleka and Bytyci, 2014) (see Fig. 23.1). Serbia remains by far the most important (official) source of Kosovo's imports.

As noted earlier in the chapter, the number of Kosovar visitors to Albania peaked in 2012 and then fell back, suggesting that the highway has also fallen short of its objective in encouraging tourism.

Box 23.1. Key elements in the development of the Albania–Kosovo highway

Albania: The Patriotic Highway (*Rruga e Kombit*): Durrës/Tirana to the Kosovo border

2006: construction contract awarded in a 'fast-track' procurement process. No feasibility study on economic returns. The only Albanian appointed to assess the highway bids resigned after 1 day, believing the tender process to be flawed. US construction giant Bechtel, with Turkish partner Enka, won the contract to build the 61 km mountainous section (Rreshen–Kalimash) for an initial price of €418 million, but without set price limits or construction plans. (Contractors working on the remaining portions of the highway were Albanian- and Austrian-based companies). Costs escalated, with Tirana eventually paying €950 million for the road.	The World Bank, International Monetary Fund (IMF) and others claimed the procurement process was uncompetitive and unlawful. They refused to support the project or help Tirana fund it. The US embassy helped override these concerns, arguing that the road would boost both the Kosovar and Albanian economies. 2008: almost 89% of Albania's capital expenditure was consumed by the road. When the transport minister from 2005 to 2007 was indicted for corruption (the case was later dropped), employing rhetoric that would be appreciated by Kosovars, he accused opposition politicians of working on behalf of Serbia to sabotage the road and, echoing the darkest of Stalinist days, called the opposition leader (Edi Rama) the political heir of Koci Xoxe.[10]

Kosovo: *Rruga Dr Ibrahim Rugova*: Albanian border to Prishtina

April 2010: contract to build this section again awarded to Bechtel–Enka, following lobbying by the US embassy, just as the Albanian highway was being completed. Again, it was signed without set price limits or construction plans. Costs in Kosovo escalated – the government failed to heed its own legal advice to set a fixed price for the road – from €400 million for 102 km of highway to €838 milion for 77 km. Kosovo's total budget for 2012 was €1.5 billion. Other infrastructure projects were postponed as budget expenditures were cut by 48% for 3 successive years.	The IMF, World Bank, EU and NGOs expressed concerns over lack of transparency in the bidding process and subsequent negotiations, the lavishness of the project and its likely damage to the Kosovo economy. Prishtina's legal advisers, UK firm Eversheds, warned that signing the contract would be 'extremely dangerous'. They identified areas where the standard contract for major infrastructure projects – the Federation of Consulting Engineers' Red Book – had been amended 'in a completely one-sided way'. At the time of writing, the Kosovo contract was being investigated by prosecutors at the EU rule-of-law mission in Kosovo, EULEX.[11]

(From Anon., 2008a,b; Likmeta, 2008; World Bank, 2010, 2013; Capussela, 2011; Marzouk, 2011; IMF, 2012; Collaku *et al.*, 2014; Marzouk *et al.*, 2014; Brunwasser, 2015.)

23.6   Subverting Neoliberal Hegemony?

Economic integration between Albania and Kosovo will inevitably grow, and for Kosovo the route through Albania, unlike those through Serbia and Macedonia, faces fewer geopolitical uncertainties. The four-lane highway must now be connected to other regional routes and wait for sufficient growth in trade and traffic.

The transport planning concept of predict and provide in this case appears, critically, to have dispensed with the first of its two components. According to one blogger,

... politicians from both Albania and Kosovo used nationalist rhetoric to cloud the minds of the regular people and avoided scrutiny of the costs. Any rational opposition to the road was attacked as unpatriotic by those few who profited most from the inflated cost.

(*Gjon Shpataj* in Marzouk *et al.*, 2014)

Fig. 23.2. The 'Patriotic Highway' in northern Albania. (Photograph courtesy of Derek Hall.)

Over both sections of highway, the World Bank found itself opposing US government-supported projects, and also in both cases, governments ignored the misgivings of international financial institutions (IFIs) and other international representatives. Bechtel–Enka subsequently won a further large infrastructure project, in Kosovo, to build a '€600m' Prishtina to Skopje (FYROM) highway. Tourism was again invoked as a potential beneficiary.

Political change in Tirana in 2013 saw the Albanian and Kosovo governments meet in Prizren in Kosovo – a town intimately associated with the Albanian national awakening in the 19th century – to pursue areas of potential cooperation. Almost as a post hoc justification, an Albanian government representative was quoted as saying that the countries' economic cooperation had to be stepped up to make the highway serve the country's (sic) economy (Koleka and Bytyci, 2014). Subsequent agreements on joint tourism development and promotion have sustained this trajectory (MFA, 2015).

23.7 Conclusion

The roles of tourism within and resulting from geopolitical relations can be played out at a number of levels. In the case of Albania, tourism has acted as a (not necessarily positive) instrument of identity and imagery, as a tool of ideology and, most recently, as an expression of co-ethnicity. Such co-ethnicity is the basis of claims that Albania plays an important role in maintaining stability in the Balkans by virtue of its influence in Kosovo, FYROM and Montenegro. But in terms of its path-dependent demands, this role is not unproblematic.

First, it raises fears (however unrealistic) among a number of neighbouring countries of an irredentist 'Greater Albania'. Second, the tourism characteristically pursued by Kosovars (and Macedonians) in Albania tends to be low cost and beach focused, acting as a constraint on the requirement to diversify and upgrade the country's tourism image and market base. Third, the questionable justification for and financial circumstances surrounding much of the Tirana/Durrës to Prishtina highway, for which encouraging tourism was cited as a significant factor, have been heightened by the road's underuse and the still relatively low level of recorded trade between Kosovo and Albania. This in its turn has raised critical regional core–periphery issues. By early 2016, the highway appeared not to have generated significant benefits for the impoverished

Table 23.3. Kosovo's main trading partners. (From KAS, 2014, 2015).

Country	Imports into Kosovo 2005		Imports into Kosovo 2014		Exports from Kosovo 2005		Exports from Kosovo 2014	
	Value €000s	Rank	Value €000s	Rank	Value €000s	Rank	Value €000s	Rank
Albania	18.1	15	133.7	8	5.8	4	44.0	2
Austria	20.7	11	36.7	15	1.0	10	6.4	10
Bosnia-Herzegovina	18.4	13	64.8	10	3.4	7	3.81	13
Bulgaria	37.8	9	47.2	14	0.97	11	3.82	12
China	54.9	6	204.8	4	0.01	25	42.2	3
Croatia	25.0	10	62.9	11	0.92	12	2.4	14
France	19.4	12	29.2	17	0.5	15	1.2	16
FYR Macedonia	220.2	1	139.7	6	10.8	1	36.0	4
Germany	123.8	3	273.0	2	6.0	3	11.3	7
Greece	44.0	8	137.5	7	5.5	6	0.9	17
Hungary	16.2	18	24.9	18	0.1	19	0.1	20
Italy	49.6	7	203.1	5	5.7	5	49.7	1
Montenegro	6.4	26	13.8	19	0.7	13	16.1	5
Poland	14.8	19	55.8	13	0.1	18	5.8	11
Serbia	152.3	2	368.2	1	8.6	2	14.5[a]	6
Slovenia	55.0	5	66.7	9	1.2	8	0.6	18
Switzerland	18.4	14	30.1	16	0.7	14	10.0	9
Turkey	85.4	4	238.3	3	1.0	9	10.4	8
UK	7.5	25	13.6	20	0.07	20	1.3	15
USA	17.7	16	62.7	12	0.2	16	0.5	19

Note: [a]Figure for 2013.

marginal regions through which it passes. But such upland areas of northern Albania and adjacent Kosovo, with their rich (but diminishing) biodiversity, would appear to offer strong potential for joint, sustainably managed tourism-related development and promotion that the highway could help facilitate (see Chapter 18, this volume).

In the meantime, Albania has signed up to the EU-sponsored Blue Corridor project,[12] aimed at establishing an Adriatic–Ionian coastal highway from Trieste in north-east Italy to Kallamata in Greece (Anon., 2015), with significant implications for both tourism development and environmental impacts.

Endnotes

[1] Albania was the first country in the region to establish contacts with the North Atlantic Treaty Organization (NATO) and the first post-communist country to join the Partnership for Peace programme in 1994. The country formally joined NATO, alongside Croatia, in 2009 (Reszczynski, 2010).

[2] Within United Nations World Tourism Organization (UNWTO) statistics, Kosovo is not named, as it is not universally recognised as a sovereign state. Given that all other European states are included by name in the statistical yearbook, the category 'Other countries of Southern Europe' would appear to be Kosovo's exclusive domain.

[3] Countries of south-eastern Europe are entered in the 'Southern Europe' category.

[4] The competing Montenegrin resort of Ulcinj reported record numbers of tourists from Kosovo and Macedonia for summer 2015 (Ulcinj English Online, 2015) (see also Chapter 7, this volume).

[5] 'Foreign assistance to combat corruption may elevate public expectations...' (Kurtoglu Eskisar and Komsuoglu, 2015: 301).

[6] Dr Ibrahim Rugova, president of Kosovo's Writers' Union from 1988, emerged as the then province's Albanian national leader, advocating peace. He was de facto president 1992–2000 and 2002–2006, until his death.

[7] Possibly since Enver Hoxha's paranoid construction of 600,000 defensive concrete bunkers in the 1970s.

[8] In 2009, Albanian Prime Minister Sali Berisha declared that newly independent Kosovo could take over the running and enlargement of the Adriatic port of Shengjin as its own outlet to the sea, some 125 km from its border (Koleka and Bytyci, 2014). But neither government took this further, and in 2013, the new Rama government in Tirana sought Chinese support for a comprehensive upgrade of the port (Anon., 2013; Zogjani, 2014), with the possibilities of a Trans-Adriatic gas pipeline in mind (Metushaj, 2015). In the meantime, Shengjin has become one of most popular beach holiday destinations for Kosovars (Kosova Press, 2014), as a consequence of the new highway permitting a greater dispersion of Kosovar tourists along the Albanian coast away from the congested Durrës area (Tavanxhiu and Gaspari, 2011).

[9] The highway to Durrës is meant to be an alternative to the route leading to Thessaloniki, yet Durrës is a much smaller and less efficient port. Albania's securing Chinese concessions to upgrade the port of Shengjin could be significant here (see Endnote 10).

[10] The minister executed as a Yugoslav spy in 1949 as part of a series of show trials following Yugoslavia's expulsion from the Soviet bloc in 1948.

[11] Fully operational from April 2009, EULEX is deemed to monitor, mentor and advise (MMA) local authorities and law enforcement agencies in the wider rule of law, while exercising some executive responsibilities. For critiques of its role, see Greiçevci (2011) and Radin (2014).

[12] As a priority within the Instrument of Pre-Accession (IPA) programme. (This is not to be confused with the EU 7th RTD Framework Blue Corridors programme concerning innovative technologies in liquefied natural gas (LNG) transport and infrastructure).

References

Anon. (2008a) Albania €230 million new loan for highway. *BalkanInsight* [Belgrade] 24 April. Available at: http://www.balkaninsight.com/en/article/albania-23-million-new-loan-for-highway (accessed 18 August 2016).

Anon. (2008b) Albania-Kosovo road costs 'over €1 billion'. *BalkanInsight* [Belgrade] 11 December. Available at: http://www.balkaninsight.com/en/article/albania-kosovo-road-costs-over-aa-billion (accessed 30 December 2015).

Anon. (2013) China is offered the strategic port of Shengjin in Albania, after roads in FYROM and Montenegro. *Independent Balkan News Agency* [Thessaloniki, Greece] 27 November. Available at: http://www.balkaneu.com/china-offered-strategic-port-shengjin-albania-roads-fyrom-montenegro/#sthash.ISFSN11O.dpuf (accessed 18 August 2016).

Anon. (2015) The project of the Blue Highway starts, it links the West Balkan countries. *Independent Balkan News Agency* [Thessaloniki, Greece] 25 March. Available at: http://www.balkaneu.com/project-blue-highway-starts-links-west-balkan-countries/ (accessed 18 August 2016).

Ateljevic, I. and Hall, D. (2007) The embodiment of the macho gaze in South-eastern Europe: performing femininity and masculinity in Albania and Croatia. In: Pritchard, A., Morgan, N., Ateljevic, I. and Harris, C. (eds) *Tourism and Gender: Embodiment, Sensuality and Experience*. CAB International, Wallingford, UK, pp. 138–157.

Bloomer, N. (2015) Albania makes headway in battle to beat corruption and improve its image. *The Guardian* [London] 26 June. Available at: http://www.theguardian.com/global-development/2015/jun/26/albania-battle-against-corruption-organised-crime (accessed 28 February 2016).

Brunwasser, M. (2015) Steamrolled. *Foreign Policy* [Washington, DC] 30 January. Available at: http://foreignpolicy.com/2015/01/30/steamrolled-investigation-bechtel-highway-business-kosovo/ (accessed 28 February 2016).

Capussela, A.L. (2011) Kosovo: the unnecessary highway that could bankrupt Europe's poorest state. *Osservatorio Balcani e Caucasa* [Rovereto, Italy] 2 December. Available at: http://www.balcanicaucaso.org/eng/Regions-and-countries/Kosovo/Kosovo-the-unnecessary-highway-that-could-bankrupt-Europe-s-poorest-state-108430 (accessed 28 February 2016).

Chandler, D. (2006) *Empire in Denial: The Politics of State-building*. Pluto Press, London.

Collaku, P., Rusi, E., Likmeta, B. and Marzouk, L. (2014) Albania–Kosovo highway costs soar to 2 billion Euros. *BalkanInsight* [Belgrade] 23 April. Available at: http://www.balkaninsight.com/en/article/albania-kosovo-highway-costs-soar-to-2-billion-euro (accessed 30 December 2015).

Dalakoglou, D. (2010) The road: an ethnography of the Albanian–Greek cross-border motorway. *American Ethnologist* 37(1), 132–149.

Dalakoglou, D. (2012) 'The road from capitalism to capitalism': infrastructures of (post)socialism in Albania. *Mobilities* 7(4), 571–586.

Durham, M.E. (1905) *The Burden of the Balkans*. Nelson, London.

Durham, M.E. (1909) *High Albania*. Edward Arnold, London.

Durham, M.E. (1928) *Some Tribal Origins, Laws and Customs of the Balkans*. Allen and Unwin, London.

European Commission (2015) *Albania 2015 Progress Report*. European Commission Staff Working Document SWD (2015) 213, Brussels.

Greiçevci, L. (2011) EU actorness in international affairs: the case of EULEX mission in Kosovo. *Perspectives on European Politics and Society* 12(3), 283–303.

Grimaldi, M. (2009) Corridor VIII development: cross-border issues and cooperation in the transport sector. Paper presented at ITF/UNECE/WB joint seminar *Overcoming Border Crossing Obstacles*, Paris, 5–6 March. Available at: http://www.internationaltransportforum.org/Proceedings/Border2009/09Grimaldi2.pdf (accessed 8 August 2015).

Grubišić Šeba, M. (2015) Transport infrastructure construction in Croatia: an analysis of public–private partnerships. *Southeast European and Black Sea Studies* 15(3), 327–360.

Hall, D.R. (1984) Foreign tourism under socialism: the Albanian 'Stalinist' model. *Annals of Tourism Research* 11(4), 539–555.

Hall, D.R. (1990) Stalinism and tourism: a comparative study of Albania and North Korea. *Annals of Tourism Research* 12(1), 36–54.

Hall, D.R. (ed.) (1993) *Transport and Economic Development in the New Central and Eastern Europe*. Belhaven, London.

Hall, D.R. (1994) *Albania and the Albanians*. Pinter, London.

Hoti, E. (2009) *Remittances and Poverty in Albania*. Department of Economics at the University of Lund No 192, Lund, Sweden.

IAACA (International Association of Anti-corruption Authorities) (2012) Stability Pact Anti-Corruption Initiative (SPAI). *iaaca.com* [Vienna] 15 February. Available at: http://www.iaaca.org/AntiCorruptionAuthorities/ByInternationalOrganizations/NonGovernmentalOrganization/201202/t20120215_805503.shtml (accessed 15 December 2015).

Illich, I. (1974) *Energy and Equity*. Marion Boyars, London.

IMF (International Monetary Fund) (2012) *Republic of Kosovo: Second Review under the Stand-by Arrangement, Request for Rephasing of Purchases and Modification of Performance Criterion. IMF Country Report No 345*. IMF, Washington, DC.

KAS (Kosovo Agency of Statistics) (2014) *Statistical Yearbook of the Republic of Kosovo 2014*. KAS, Prishtina.

KAS (2015) External Trade Statistics. KAS, Prishtina. Available at: http://ask.rks-gov.net/eng/external-trade (accessed 2 March 2016).

Kennedy, D. (1999) The international anti-corruption campaign. *Connecticut Journal of International Law* 14, 455–465.

Koleka, B. and Buza, S. (2007) Highway set to bring Albania and Kosovo closer. *Reuters* [London] 28 June. Available at: http://www.reuters.com/article/us-albania-kosovo-link-idUSL261003820070628 (accessed 3 May 2016).

Koleka, B. and Bytyci, F. (2014) After slow start, Albania and Kosovo look to potential as partners. *Reuters* [London] 17 February. Available at: http://uk.reuters.com/article/kosovo-albania-integration-idUKL6N0LM26120140217 (accessed 1 March 2016).

Kosova Press (2014) Tourists from Kosova choose Shengjin for cleanness and cheap prices. *Kosova Press* [Prishtina] 30 July. Available at: http://www.kosovapress.com/en/region/tourists-from-kosova-choose-shengjin-for-cleanness-and-cheap-prices-22314/ (accessed 28 February 2016).

Kurtoglu Eskisar, G.M. and Komsuoglu, A. (2015) A critical assessment of the transformative power of EU reforms on reducing corruption in the Balkans. *Southeast European and Black Sea Studies* 15(3), 301–326.

Lear, E. (1851) *Journals of a Landscape Painter in Greece and Albania*. Hutchinson, London.

Likmeta, B. (2008) Albania's 'Patriotic Highway' scandal. *Bloomberg Business* [New York] 22 December. Available at: http://www.bloomberg.com/bw/stories/2008-12-22/albanias-patriotic-highway-scandalbusiness-week-business-news-stock-market-and-financial-advice (accessed 28 February 2016).

Marzouk, L. (2011) Kosovo spurned legal advice on 'dangerous' highway deal. *BalkanInsight* [Belgrade] 23 May. Available at: http://www.balkaninsight.com/en/article/kosovo-spurned-legal-advice-on-dangerous-highway-deal (accessed 30 December 2015).

Marzouk, L., Collaku, P., Rusi, E., Likmeta, B. and Lewis, P. (2014) US Ambassador to Kosovo hired by construction firm he lobbied for. *BalkanInsight* [Belgrade] 14 April. Available at: http://www.balkaninsight.com/en/article/bechtel-hires-us-diplomat-amid-kosovo-contract-controversy (accessed 30 December 2015).

Mason, K., Myres, J., Winterbotham, H.S.L., Longland, F., Davidson, C.P., *et al.* (1945) *Albania*. Naval Intelligence Division, London.

Metushaj, M. (2015) Geopolitics of Albania in the Balkans after NATO membership. *Academic Journal of Interdisciplinary Studies* 4(3)[S1], 400–402.

MFA (Ministry of Foreign Affairs, Republic of Albania) (2015) Second joint meeting of the governments of Albania and Kosovo takes place in Tirana. *Telegram Diplomatik: Albanian MFA Newsletter* 9, 31 March.

O'Sullivan, J. (1972) *The Egnatian Way*. David and Charles, Newton Abbott, UK.

Pojani, D. (2010) *Albania in transition: international assistance for roads but not public transport*. Proceedings of REAL CORP 2010, Vienna, pp. 57–64.

Pojani, D. (2011) From carfree to carfull: the environmental and health impacts of growing private motorization in Albania. *Journal of Environmental Planning and Management* 54(3), 319–335.

Pojani, D. and Pojani, E. (2011) Urban sprawl and weak regional transport in 'Durana'. Presented at *Stable Local Development: Challenges and Opportunities* conference, Peja (Peć), Kosovo, 3–4 June.

Pollo, S. and Puto, A. (1981) *The History of Albania*. Routledge and Kegan Paul, London.

Radin, A. (2014) Analysis of current events: 'towards the rule of law in Kosovo: EULEX should go'. *Nationalities Papers: The Journal of Nationalism and Ethnicity* 42(2), 181–194.

Raven, S. (1993) The road to empire. *Geographical Magazine* 65(6), 21–24.

Reszczynski, L. (2010) Albania – the geopolitical reactivation. *Nova Srpska Politička Misao* [Belgrade] 22 June. Available at: http://www.nspm.rs/pdf/nspm-in-english/albania-%E2%80%94-the-geopolitical-reactivation.pdf (accessed 26 February 2016).

Said, E.W. (1978) *Orientalism*. Routledge and Kegan Paul, London.

Sieber, N. (2011) *Fighting Corruption in the Road Transport Sector, Lessons for Developing Countries. Sustainable Urban Transport Technical Document #10*. GIZ (Deutsche Gesellschaft für Internationale Zusammenarbeit), Bonn, Germany.

Simpson, F. and Roberts, L. (2000) Help or hindrance? Sustainable approaches to tourism consultancy in Central and Eastern Europe. *Journal of Sustainable Tourism* 8(6), 491–509.

Tamminem, T. (2012) Re-establishing cross-border cooperation between Montenegro, Kosovo and Albania: the Balkan Peace Park and local ownership. *Slavica Helsingiensa* 41, 125–151.

Tavanxhiu, M. and Gaspari, A. (2011) The Durres–Kukes highway construction impact on Albanian and Kosovo economic development. Presented at *Stable Local Development Challenges and Opportunities* conference, Peja (Peć), Kosovo, 3–4 June. Available at: http://www.dukagjinicollege.eu/libri/ (accessed 18 August 2016).

TDI (Tourism Development International) (2010) *Albania Culture Marketing Strategy*. TDI/UNDP MDG Achievement Fund, Dún Laoghaire, Ireland. Available at: http://www.undp.org/content/dam/albania/docs/Final%20CULTURE%20MARKETING%20STRATEGY-July1.pdf (accessed 2 March 2016).

Ulcinj English Online (2015) Ulcinj tourism boom. *Ulcinj English Online* 13 September. Available at: http://ulqinenglishonline1.weebly.com/ulcinj/ulcinj-tourism-boom (accessed 18 August 2016).

UNODC (United Nations Office on Drugs and Crime) (2011) *Corruption in Albania: Bribery as Experienced by the Population*. UNODC, Vienna.

UNODC (2013) *Business Corruption and Crime in Albania: The Impact of Bribery and Other Crime on Private Enterprise*. UNODC, Vienna.

UNWTO (World Tourism Organization) (2015) *Yearbook of Tourism Statistics*. UNWTO, Madrid.

Vladi, E. (2014) Tourism development strategies, SWOT analysis and improvement of Albania's image. *European Journal of Sustainable Development* 3(1), 167–178.

World Bank (2009) *Deterring Corruption and Improving Governance in Road Construction and Maintenance. Transport Papers TP 27*. World Bank, Washington, DC.

World Bank (2010) *Kosovo Public Expenditure Review*. World Bank, Washington, DC.

World Bank (2013) *Albania: Transport Infrastructure*. World Bank Policy Brief, Washington, DC.

Zogjani, N. (2014) Kosovo loses hope of getting Adriatic sea port. *Balkan Insight* [Belgrade] 9 September. Available at: http://www.balkaninsight.com/en/article/kosovo-lose-hope-to-get-adriatic-sea-access (accessed 8 March 2016).

Zoto, S. and Vangjeli, E. (2013) An analysis of Kosovar tourists visiting Albania. Comparison with Macedonian touristic demand. Presented at *Research and Education Challenges Towards the Future* conference, Shkodra, Albania, 24–25 May. Available at: www.konferenca.unishk.edu.al/icrae2013/icraecd2013/doc/496.pdf (accessed 28 February 2016).

24 Heroes or 'Others'? A Geopolitics of International Footballer Mobility

Piotr Trzepacz[1]* and Derek Hall[2]

[1]*Institute of Geography and Spatial Management, Jagiellonian University, Kraków, Poland;* [2]*Seabank Associates, Maidens, Scotland, UK*

> ... as FIFA President it gives me great joy to see the FIFA World Cup spread to new geographical regions and cultures such as Eastern Europe ...
> (Sepp Blatter quoted in Carter, 2013: 70)

24.1 Introduction

The role of sport in the construction of national imagery and identity has long been the subject of research (e.g. Bale, 1986; Bairner, 2001; Jarvie, 2003; Thorpe, 2014), and the relationship between leisure sports mega-events and soft power was discussed briefly in Chapter 1, this volume. Sport mobilities is an area that has received increasing attention since the 1990s, and Maguire and Falcous (2011: 1) identified a number of pathways along which sports labour migration research has developed. These include: migratory influences and consequences, migrants' experiences, the spatial patterns of such mobilities and their implications for sport policy and for domestic and foreign policies of nation states affected.

Complementing debates within tourism concerning its role in enhancing mutual understanding across cultures and contributing to peace, the literature on whether international footballer migration has generated 'an array of more cosmopolitan emotions' or has increased prejudice and resentment is inconclusive.

While highly asymmetrical, the globalisation of elite sport participation and power is perhaps less dominated by the West/North than other spheres of transnationalism. This can be seen in the role of Latin America in world football and in global cricket's power shift to the Indian subcontinent (Maguire and Falcous, 2011: 5). Or perhaps the latter is reflective of a broader transfer of global economic power.

Global sport, of which sport migration is an increasingly important part, is a highly contested, structured process that is contoured by power dynamics that enable and constrain opportunities for social advancement and the reinforcement of exploitation and inequality: processes that range from establishing and encouraging intercontinental 'talent pipelines', to pejorative aspects of national stereotyping. With the growing commodification of European football as part of the wider sports industrial complex, the rewards for success and the costs of failure can be considerable (Maguire and Falcous, 2011: 5–7), and can be articulated in a footballer's migratory trajectory.

Within Central and Eastern Europe (CEE), it has been argued (Doupona Topič, 2015) that sports-related research has been constrained by economic factors, and the question has been posed as to how non-English-speaking scholars can gain a more meaningful voice in this arena (Földesi, 2015).

---

*Corresponding author. E-mail: piotr.trzepacz@uj.edu.pl

This chapter explores, from a largely Polish perspective, some of the geopolitical dimensions and tensions of elite footballer mobilities.

24.2 Elite Sport and Migration

Miller *et al.* (2011) locate sporting migrants within the context of an aggressively globalising (sporting) capitalism that seeks comparatively cheap labour in countries that can provide skilled workers to supplement costly local labour. Within this view, 'production' in football is increasingly 'outsourced', while control over content remains at the 'centre'. The resulting 'system' may reveal imbalance and profound inequity.

This sits with the tradition of viewing processes of international footballer mobility as semi-colonial expressions of core–periphery relationships. Poli (2006a; Poli and Besson, 2011) for example, has contended that sport migration necessarily involves structural inequalities between countries, and that these unequal relations offer an analytical framework. Carter's (2013) concern has been to shift theoretical premise from global institutional structures to one centred on the experiences of people and the spaces through which they move. Immigration policies, labour law and international governing bodies' regulations all play significant roles in shaping these patterns, as Poli (2006b, 2010) recognises.

But Carter (2013) suggests that a more thorough understanding of the vagaries of transnational sport migration can be produced if greater attention is paid to individual experiences and the (microgeo)politics of their mobility (see Elliott, 2015).

Gendered critiques of sport represent a growing body of work (e.g. Messner, 2007), while the role of women per se in sport is receiving belated attention, both in the published literature (e.g. Pfister, 2015) and in the popular media (e.g. Shephard, 2016), in a hitherto male-dominated, governed and portrayed arena (Hoffman *et al.*, 2006; Selmer and Süzle, 2010). Gender-aware analyses of sport migration have embraced women's football in recent years, both within a framework of globalisation and in more nuanced studies of migration motivation (Botelho and Agergaard, 2011; Agergaard *et al.*, 2013; Haugaa Engh and Agergaard, 2015; also Agergaard and Botelho, 2011; Agergaard, 2015; Agergaard and Tiesler, 2015).

According to data gathered by the first author, the premier leagues of UEFA (the Union of European Football Associations) members were home to representatives of 157 countries in 2011. Darby and Solberg (2010) describe the migration of footballers to play for European clubs as a 'muscle drain' – in reference to the 'brain drain' phenomenon, which characterises the migration of educated, especially young individuals, from poorer to wealthier regions and countries. A common locational profile for foreign players is participation in the leagues of old colonial metropolises, which also tend to be the best European leagues. Relatively few players in these leagues come from a neighbouring country (whose leagues are also robust and share a similar profile). The two main origins of incoming players are strong South American leagues and countries that used to be under the colonial rule of the host country.

An example of such a relationship may be found in the characteristics of footballers playing in France, where countries of origin from the former French North Africa and French West Africa dominate, and notably footballers from Algeria, Mali, Senegal and Cameroon. In French league football, Serbs and Montenegrins are also notable migrants, as well as, exceptionally, players from Belgium.

The consequences of 'muscle drain' have been observed on source countries. Alvito (2007) found, in the case of the Brazilian league, an overall decline in the quality of games and a drop in attendance figures, with lower investment in players and infrastructure: thus setting in motion a downward spiral.

The scale of footballer migration from the African continent is perceived there as a serious problem contributing to a weakening of national leagues (Darby, 2011). But core–periphery processes are also at work *within* the continent. A convergence of players on clubs in the Republic of South Africa is considered to be particularly harmful (Cornelissen and Solberg, 2007). The impacts on migration of South Africa's hosting the 2010 World Cup tended to exacerbate such processes. Although the country set a quota on foreign-born players allowed to play in local leagues, such quotas were circumvented through the acquisition of dual citizenship, a loophole exploited by each club in the South African premier soccer league.

Darby (2010) suggests that there exists a significant correlation between player status and the role of football in their country of origin. He points to the example of Ghana, which, by investing in the development of football infrastructure since it gained independence in 1956, has competed successfully in World Cup tournaments (surviving into the last 16 in 2006 and to the quarter finals in 2010).

While many migrant players from the global periphery retain citizenship of the country they were born in, which potentially allows them to play for the national team, it is becoming a common practice to adopt the nationality of their host country, thereby both denying their country of origin talent for the national team and of role models for young aspirants, while suppressing demand and opportunity for home talent within the destination country.

Eliasson (2009) identified the strength of European footballing countries in terms of centres, semi-centres and peripheries. According to her assessment, the first group consists of countries with leagues strong enough for their players to consider termination of contracts that are disadvantageous to them. At the same time, the clubs constituting those leagues are a desired goal for the best players in other leagues. From the perspective of migration dynamics, those countries may be considered as being football player immigration destinations. The second group, the semi-centres, among which she counts her native Sweden, are countries that lose their best players to top-of-the-chart leagues but which are still attractive as a transfer destination for players from lower leagues. Football peripheries are those weakest leagues within the continent, including several in CEE.

Footballer migration studies have been undertaken in Europe in relation to the four most popular destination countries (Maguire and Pearton, 2000) and regarding the 'big five' football leagues (Littlewood *et al.*, 2011). In both cases the focus is, by definition, on Western Europe. The latter authors refer to the big five becoming 'dependent development' states in the sense of their dependency on the in-migration flow of talent and a failure to invest in home-grown player development programmes.

Within UEFA, it is possible to see clear disproportions in the levels of internationalisation of league players. The share of players who trace their origins to other countries possessing their own national leagues varies from just a few to a majority. European countries form monolithic areas characterised by a similar scale of this

phenomenon (Fig. 24.1). Its dominance is most evident in the English, Portuguese, Cypriot and Luxembourg premier leagues. In these, more than 50% of footballers playing in the premier league are from another country (or, more precisely, from a territory with its own national level representation). Each of these leagues has their own specifics, however. In the case of the English premier league, a significant proportion of players are natives of Wales, Scotland or Northern Ireland, and therefore still from within the UK. Part of the reason for the large share of foreign-born players in Luxembourg's league is simply the fact that it is a small country. And while also a relatively small country (countries?), the geopolitical circumstances of Cyprus strongly influence representation there. Reflecting its colonial inheritance, Portugal draws heavily on Brazil.

The large proportion of players from areas that belong to other national football federations is in line with the overall character of the strength of European leagues: German, Italian and Dutch being among the strongest. While interpreting the diversity of the phenomenon among various European countries, it has to be said that the standing of a league is, at least in part, due to the players' ability to adopt the citizenship of a host country. In countries that facilitate the switch from the status of immigrant-player to citizen-player, the share of foreign players may be statistically lower. Herein lies the explanation for the relatively low percentage of foreign players in the make-up of Scandinavian leagues. There have also clearly been opportunities for the offspring of immigrants from CEE to nurture their talents here. A prime example of this is the Swedish national player, Zlatan Ibrahimović (at one time ranked third best in the world: Taylor *et al.*, 2013), whose Bosnian father and Croat mother migrated to Sweden, where they met, in the 1970s (Ibrahimović and Lagerkrantz, 2016). The large share of such naturalised players is also characteristic for the Russian league, in contrast to the leagues of neighbouring states.

By contrast, the Balkan countries, especially Serbia and Macedonia, demonstrate some of the lowest proportions of foreign players in Europe. In this case, an outflow effect can be demonstrated, as Serb players (along with Montenegrins) make up the numerically most represented nationality on European football fields. Reasons for this may not be entirely clear, but the long existence of a global Serbian diaspora, escape

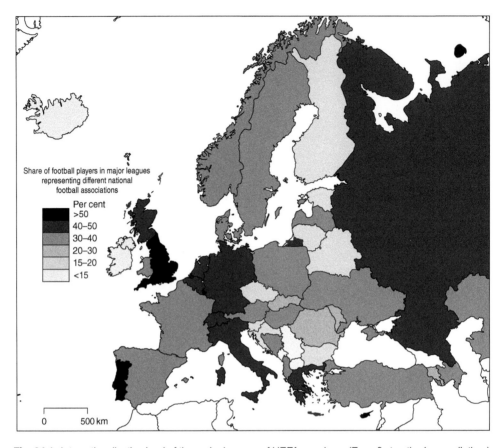

Fig. 24.1. Internationalisation level of the major leagues of UEFA members. (From first author's compilation.)

from Balkan events in the 1990s and the location of Serbs in a range of former Yugoslav states after independence have all contributed to this phenomenon. Ironically, Zec and Paunović (2015) emphasised how football proved to be a positive influence in rebuilding trust and mutual cooperation in the former Yugoslavia in the turbulent periods after World Wars I and II.

24.3 Mobilities, Power and 'Others': Footballer Migration in CEE Countries

Overall, relatively low proportions of foreign-born players can be found in most of CEE. Several CEE countries' leagues – for example, those of Poland and Romania – fall significantly below the standards of Western or south European counterparts, and could be considered by African

players as an exile from the top leagues. This was highlighted with the death, while playing for Dinamo Bucharest, of 26-year-old Cameroon midfielder, Patrick Ekeng, who had previously played for Le Mans, Lausanne and Cordoba before joining the 18-times Romanian champions as a free agent in January 2016 (Anon., 2016).

The 2012 European championships, jointly hosted by Poland and Ukraine, were said to offer a 'watershed moment' for football in CEE (Elliott and Bania, 2014), and began to draw more attention to the region's sport in general and to football in particular. Poland's top division, Ekstraklasa, while not within Europe's core, is, none the less, seen to offer much as a migration destination for certain kinds of players (Elliott and Bania, 2014), although the functioning of the Polish Football Association has been the focus of some recent critical attention for its perceived policy of 'exclusion' (Pezdek and Michaluk, 2016).

The role of Africa as a resource for Polish league teams has fluctuated over the past two decades (Elliott, 2013), perhaps reflecting the 'crumbs from the table' situation of less well-placed European leagues. Poli's (2006a,b, 2010) research on players of African descent found that they frequently arrived at major European football clubs with significant potential and high expectations, but could soon be forced to accept a contract in a lower league, either in the same country or in that of a less prestigious football-ing nation.

Research on the in-migration of footballers to Hungary identified migration 'pipelines', rep-licating the mechanics of often informally sus-tained mobility streams connecting source and host within push–pull migratory processes (Mol-nar, 2006, 2011). Elliott's (2014) work on foot-baller migration into Hungarian leagues reveals the transitory and dynamic nature of migration experiences.

Leagues in CEE countries tend not to nurture European or world champions, but as transfer destinations they may serve – as bookends – either to provide a gateway function for players moving on to stronger leagues or as a symbol of a failed or waning career profile (Molnar, 2015).

Polish (Fig. 24.2) and Russian leagues (Fig. 24.3), between which some parallels may be drawn, tend to attract players from neighbouring coun-tries. In the case of Poland, these may be from the Czech Republic, Slovakia and the Baltics, while Russia draws in players from former Soviet re-publics and from the Balkans. Religious and cul-tural ties with Russia may serve as a pull factor for Serb (and Montenegrin and Macedonian) players in this respect. However, the imposition of tighter quotas on foreign players in Russian football, interacting with other changing geo-political circumstances, has impacted on this pattern.

In the 2014 World Cup, Russia was elimin-ated in the group stage of the competition, the national team having not progressed beyond this stage of a major international competition since 2008. With Russia's hosting the World Cup in 2018, an event being personally over-seen by the president, any comparable failure would, at best, result in political embarrass-ment. After the country's sports minister, Vitaly Mutko, argued that the performance of home-grown players was suffering by being 'crowded out' by expensive foreign talent (Reevell, 2015), for the subsequent 2015/16 football season, the Russian Football Union tightened the quota on players not carrying Russian passports to six per team on the field. The big-ger clubs, including Zenit St Petersburg (main backer Gazprom), Lokomotiv Moscow (Russian Railways) and Dinamo Moscow (state bank VTB) were not in favour of the proposals (Anon., 2015). Such an apparent resistance

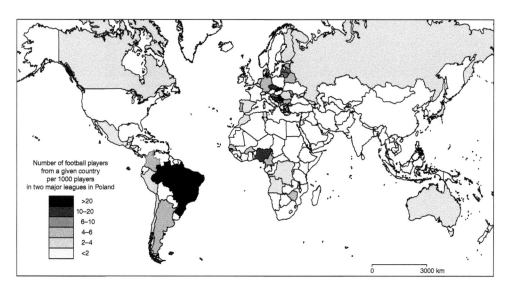

Fig. 24.2. The origin of football players in the two major leagues in Poland. (From first author's compilation.)

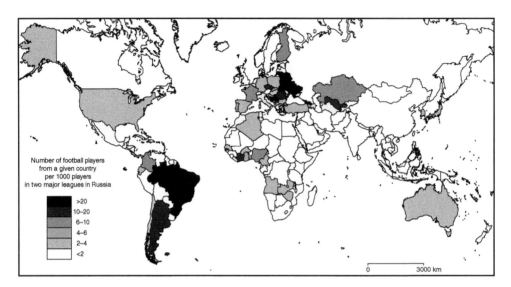

Fig. 24.3. The origin of football players in the two major leagues in Russia. (From first author's compilation.)

was soon followed by Mutko suggesting that the State *Duma* (parliament) would be introducing a draft law to prevent state monopolies using their money to buy foreign players (Reuters, 2015). This move was partly justified on the grounds that the rouble had lost half of its value against major global currencies within a year. One observable knock-on effect of these interventions was a slowing down in the growth of match attendance and of the commercial value of Russian football (Charyev, 2016).

Russian clubs had begun enthusiastically importing foreign players (called 'legionnaires') after the Soviet Union collapsed. But only in recent years have Russian league teams been able to afford more significant international talent, as a result of finance from their state-company sponsors (Reevell, 2015).

Following increased restrictions on foreign players, just after the start of the 2015/16 season, the Russian sports ministry signed off a document banning all foreign head coaches from the Russian league, at a time when six of the sixteen clubs in the premier league were run by foreign managers. As the ban did not apply either to the national team or to assistant coaches, how such a market intervention would be played out was unclear at the time of writing. But it appeared to reflect a wider attitude towards (inter)nationalism emanating from the Kremlin.

24.4 Consequences of the Internationalisation of Football Leagues in UEFA Member States

The internationalisation of league players has been present in football since the moment the first professional organisational frameworks were created (Lanfranchi, 1994). Regrettably, as foreigners joined, some antipathy among fans also became visible. Within the French context, Lanfranchi (1994) tried to rationalise such reactions as a show of concern for the heritage of football, noting the alleged danger incoming players posed to national qualities and style of play, which were perceived as having been distinct to specific countries. According to this argument, the presence of foreign footballers blurs differences in game techniques, robbing football of depth. However, studies by Wilson and Ying (2003), conducted among the strongest European leagues, demonstrated that both the results achieved by individual clubs and match attendance figures were correlated positively with the increasing number of foreign-born players. The authors went on to claim that the most positive influences related to the involvement of players native to former Yugoslavia and Brazil.

The absence of racist incidents at the 2006 Football World Cup hosted in Germany was considered a success (Kassimeris, 2009) when considering the scale such phenomena had achieved following German reunification. Mega-events such as World Cup finals can be employed to popularise actions by anti-xenophobia organisations striving for racism-free sport. Kassimeris (2008) quoted the results of studies on the scale of xenophobic phenomena on the Internet, with 10% of Web pages related to football containing such content. The author noted that racism was a universal problem, regardless of the actual proportion of foreign-born players in the sport's structure. Kassimeris also claimed that 'pathological behaviour' relating to the diversity of some players did not stop at ethnicity, and he examined reactions to players' religious affiliation. The latter has the added dimension that, in some instances, entire clubs have been the targets of attacks because of their religious associations (e.g. AS Roma, Austria Wien, Bayern Munich).

This is an issue present in Polish football reality. In the inter-war period, such Polish clubs as Hasmonea Lwów, Jutrzenka Kraków or Makkabi Kraków were established by members of the Jewish community. Confrontations on the field were often called 'the holy war' because entrenched Zionist and anti-Zionist views were expressed. More recently, Dmowski (2013) has examined fan rivalry based on race and ethnicity in CEE and the Caucasus. Sexual orientation has also been the subject of debate in recent years, especially with the de facto outlawed status of homosexuality in Russia.

Vrcan (2002) explored relationships between football and politics in Croatia, and particularly the fandom–nationalism nexus. He focused on an internal conflict in the 1990s that 'began as a family quarrel in the same Croatian nationalist ideological and political family' (Vrcan, 2002: 59) concerning an imposed name change of a football club, but gradually became the first public political challenge to the then president, Franjo Tudjman, a challenge that was to gain wider momentum. Also in Croatia, Hodges

(2014) examined fan behaviour in relation to stereotypes of 'Balkan mentality' and 'primitive behaviour'. He argues that such associations may be explored in terms of a nesting intra-orientalism, whereby non-European 'Others' are constructed at different levels within a state, rather than projected as outsiders. Kossakowski (2015) has recognised a transformation – or at least a locational shift – in fan behaviour, contending that in the Polish context acts of 'hooliganism' have been pushed out of stadiums to function as a niche activity outside the immediate context of football.

In terms of other forms of mobility, the ways in which soccer may play a role in identity formation and a sense of belonging in the host country for those seeking asylum has been explored by Woodhouse and Conricode (2016). The authors examine the potential of football participation in alleviating pressures that the status of being an 'asylum seeker' brings. This would seem to possess limited application in some CEE countries given their political elites' response of denial to the 2015/16 refugee/migrant crisis (see the introduction to Part V Mobilities and Chapter 25, this volume).

24.5 Conclusions

The study of elite footballer international migration can add to our knowledge of European mobilities, of the sources of wealth, power and inequalities influencing such mobilities, and what such migrants' spatialised trajectories tell us about European cores, peripheries and semi-peripheries in different forms of mobility practices. That the top soccer leagues in CEE tend not to be part of the migratory destination core does not reduce the significance of the region's roles in both generating and hosting migrant footballers, and in reflecting the geopolitical dimensions of the attitudes adopted towards the consequences of such mobility processes by both political elites and soccer 'fans'.

References

Agergaard, S. (2015) Current patterns and tendencies in women's football migration: outsourcing or national protectionism as the way forward? In: Elliott, R. and Harris, J. (eds) *Football and Migration: Perspectives, Places and Players*. Routledge, Abingdon, UK, pp. 127–143.

Agergaard, S. and Botelho, V. (2011) Female football migration: motivational factors for early migratory pro-
    cesses. In: Maguire, J. and Falcous, M. (eds) *Sport and Migration: Borders, Boundaries and Crossings.*
    Routledge, Abingdon, UK, pp. 157–171.
Agergaard, S. and Tiesler, N.C. (eds.) (2015) *Women, Soccer and Transnational Migration.* Routledge,
    Abingdon, UK.
Agergaard, S., Andersson, T., Carlsson, B. and Skogvang, B.O. (2013) Scandinavian women's football in a
    global world: migration, management and mixed identity. *Soccer & Society* 14(6), 769–780.
Alvito, M. (2007) Our piece of the pie: Brazilian football and globalization. *Soccer & Society* 8(4),
    524–544.
Anon. (2015) Russia introduces new limit on foreign footballers. *ENCA* [Johannesburg, South Africa] 14 July.
    Available at: https://www.enca.com/sport/soccer/russia-introduces-new-limit-foreign-players (accessed
    9 May 2016).
Anon. (2016) Inquiry opens into death of Cameroon star Ekeng. *The Observer* [London] 8 May, *Sport*, p. 9.
Bairner, A. (2001) *Sport, Nationalism and Globalization.* SUNY Press, Albany, New York.
Bale, J. (1986) Sport and national identity: a geographical view. *International Journal of the History of Sport*
    3(1), 18–41.
Botelho, V.L. and Agergaard, S. (2011) Moving for the love of the game? International migration of female
    footballers into Scandinavian countries. *Soccer & Society* 12(6), 806–819.
Carter, T.F. (2013) Re-placing sport migrants: moving beyond the institutional structures informing inter-
    national sport migration. *International Review for the Sociology of Sport* 48(1), 66–82.
Charyev, G. (2016) Consequences of the limit on foreign players in Russian football. *Soccer & Society*
    17(4), 571–587.
Cornelissen, S. and Solberg, E. (2007) Sport mobility and circuits of power: the dynamics of football migra-
    tion in Africa and the 2010 World Cup. *Politikon* 34(3), 295–314.
Darby, P. (2010) Go outside: the history, economics and geography of Ghanaian football labour migration.
    African Historical Review 42 (1), 19–41.
Darby, P. (2011) Out of Africa: the exodus of elite African football talent to Europe. In: Maguire, J. and
    Falcous, M. (eds) *Sport and Migration: Borders, Boundaries and Crossings.* Routledge, Abingdon,
    UK, pp. 245–258.
Darby, P. and Solberg, E. (2010) Differing trajectories: football development and patterns of player migration
    in South Africa and Ghana. *Soccer & Society* 11(1), 118–130.
Dmowski, S. (2013) Geographical typology of European football rivalries. *Soccer & Society* 14(3),
    331–343.
Doupona Topič, M. (2015) Assessing the sociology of sport: on sport and the challenges of post-socialist
    countries. *International Review for the Sociology of Sport* 40(4–5), 424–429.
Eliasson, A. (2009) The European football market, globalization and mobility among players. *Soccer & Society*
    10(3), 386–397.
Elliott, R. (2013) New Europe new chances? The migration of professional footballers to Poland's Ekstraklasa.
    International Review for the Sociology of Sport 48(6), 736–750.
Elliott, R. (2014) Brits abroad: a case study analysis of three British footballers migrating to the Hungarian
    Soproni Liga. *Soccer & Society* 15(4), 517–534.
Elliott, R. (2015) Chasing the ball: the motivations, experiences and effects of migrant professional footballers.
    In: Elliott, R. and Harris, J. (eds) *Football and Migration: Perspectives, Places and Players.* Routledge,
    Abingdon, UK, pp. 21–35.
Elliott, R. and Bania, K. (2014) Poles apart: foreign players, Polish football and Euro 2012. *Soccer & Society*
    15(2), 256–271.
Földesi, G.S. (2015) Assessing the sociology of sport: on world inequalities and unequal development.
    International Review for the Sociology of Sport 50(4–5), 442–447.
Haugaa Engh, M. and Agergaard, S. (2015) Producing mobility through locality and visibility: developing a
    transnational perspective on sports labour migration. *International Review for the Sociology of Sport*
    50(8), 974–992.
Hodges, A. (2016) The hooligan as 'internal' other? Football fans, ultras culture and nesting intra-orientalisms.
    International Review for the Sociology of Sport 51(4), 410–427.
Hoffmann, R., Chew Ging, L., Matheson, V. and Ramasamy, B. (2006) International women's football and
    gender inequality. *Applied Economic Letters* 13(15), 999–1001.
Ibrahimović, Z. and Lagerkrantz, D. (2016) *I am Zlatan Ibrahimović* (trans. Urbom, R.). Penguin, London.

Jarvie, G. (2003) Internationalism and sport in the making of nations. *Identities: Global Studies in Culture and Power* 10, 537–551.

Kassimeris, C. (2008) *European Football in Black and White: Tackling Racism in Football*. Lexington Books, Lanham, Maryland.

Kassimeris, C. (2009) Deutschland über Alles: discrimination in German football. *Soccer & Society* 10(6), 754–765.

Kossakowski, R. (2015) Where are the hooligans? Dimensions of football fandom in Poland. *International Review for the Sociology of Sport* DOI: 10.1177/1012690215612458.

Lanfranchi, P. (1994) The migration of footballers: the case of France 1932–1982. In: Bale, J. and Maguire, J. (eds) *The Global Sport Arena: Athletic Talent Migration in an Interdependent World*. Frank Cass, London, pp. 63–77.

Littlewood, M., Mullen, C. and Richardson, D. (2011) Football labour migration: an examination of the player recruitment strategies of the 'big five' European football leagues 2004–5 to 2008–9. *Soccer & Society* 12(6), 788–805.

Maguire, J. and Falcous, M. (2011) Introduction: borders, boundaries and crossings: sport, migration and identities. In: Maguire, J. and Falcous, M. (eds) *Sport and Migration: Borders, Boundaries and Crossings*. Routledge, Abingdon, UK, pp. 1–12.

Maguire, J. and Pearton, R. (2000) The impact of elite labour migration on the identification, selection and development of European soccer players. *Journal of Sports Sciences* 18(9), 759–769.

Messner, M.A. (2007) *Out of Play. Critical Essays on Gender and Sport*. SUNY Press, Albany, New York.

Miller, T., Rowe, D. and Lawrence, G. (2011) The new international division of cultural labour. In: Maguire, J. and Falcous, M. (eds) *Sport and Migration: Borders, Boundaries and Crossings*. Routledge, Abingdon, UK, pp. 217–229.

Molnar, G. (2006) Mapping migrations: Hungary-related migrations of professional footballers after the collapse of communism. *Soccer & Society* 7(4), 463–485.

Molnar, G. (2011) From the Soviet bloc to the European Community: migrating professional footballers in and out of Hungary. In: Maguire, J. and Falcous, M. (eds) *Sport and Migration: Borders, Boundaries and Crossings*. Routledge, Abingdon, UK, pp. 56–70.

Molnar, G. (2015) League of retirees: foreigners in Hungarian professional football. In: Elliott, R. and Harris, J. (eds) *Football and Migration: Perspectives, Places and Players*. Routledge, Abingdon, UK, pp. 106–124.

Pezdek, K. and Michaluk, T. (2016) The functioning of the Polish Football Association from the perspective of Michel Foucault's conception of exclusion. *Soccer & Society* 17(4), 450–463.

Pfister, G. (2015) Assessing the sociology of sport: on women and football. *International Review for the Sociology of Sport* 50(4–5), 563–569.

Poli, R. (2006a) Africans' status in the European football players' labour market. *Soccer & Society* 7(2–3), 278–291.

Poli, R. (2006b) Migrations and trade of African football players: historic, geographical and cultural aspects. *Afrika Spectrum* 41(3), 393–414.

Poli, R. (2010) African migrants in Asian and European football: hopes and realities. *Sport in Society* 13(6), 1001–1011.

Poli, R. and Besson, R. (2011) Football and migration: a contemporary geographical analysis. In: Elliott, R. and Harris, J. (eds) *Football and Migration: Perspectives, Places and Players*. Routledge, Abingdon, UK, pp. 36–44.

Reevell, P. (2015) Russian league to cut back on foreign soccer players. *New York Times* 29 April. Available at: http://www.nytimes.com/2015/04/30/sports/soccer/russian-league-to-cut-back-on-foreign-soccer-players.html?_r=0 (accessed 22 August 2016).

Reuters (2015) Russia plans to ban state monopolies from purchasing foreign players. *The Guardian* [London] 19 November. Available at: http://www.theguardian.com/football/2015/nov/19/ruissa-ban-state-monopolies-foreign-players (accessed 23 August 2016).

Selmer, N. and Süzle, A. (2010) (En)gendering the European football family: the changing discourse on women and gender at EURO 2008. *Soccer & Society* 11(6), 803–814.

Shephard, S. (2016) *Kicking Off: How Women in Sport are Changing the Game*. Bloomsbury, London.

Taylor, D., Christenson, M., Ronay, B., Lowe, S., Bandini, P., *et al*. (2013) The hundred best footballers in the world 2013. *The Guardian* [London, UK] 20 December. Available at: http://www.theguardian.com/football/ng-interactive/2013/dec/100-greatest-footballers-2013 (accessed 22 August 2016).

Thorpe, H. (2014) *Transnational Mobilities in Action Sport Cultures*. Palgrave Macmillan, London.

Vrcan, S. (2002) The curious drama of the president of a republic versus a football fan tribe: a symptomatic case in the post-communist transition in Croatia. *International Review for the Sociology of Sport* 37(1), 59–77.

Wilson, D.P. and Ying, Y.-H. (2003) Nationality preferences for labour in the international football industry. *Applied Economics* 35(14), 1551–1559.

Woodhouse, D. and Conricode, D. (2016) In-ger-land, In-ger-land, In-ger-land! Exploring the impact of soccer on the sense of belonging of those seeking asylum in the UK. *International Review for the Sociology of Sport* DOI: 10.1177/1012690216637630.

Zec, D. and Paunović, M. (2015) Football's positive influence on integration in diverse societies: the case study of Yugoslavia. *Soccer & Society* 16(2–3), 232–244.

25 Tourism, Mobilities and the Geopolitics of Erasure

Kevin Hannam*

The Business School, Edinburgh Napier University, UK

25.1 Introduction

On 6 September 2015, I was browsing posts on *Facebook* and came across one from a friend on holiday in Budapest, who noted the fabulous views of the city. She did not mention the migrant crisis down the road, however, and this struck me as a somewhat odd erasure. Moreover, it made me think again about the relations between tourism and geopolitics, particularly in the context of Central and Eastern Europe (CEE), where countries have become transit zones for migrants and refugees from Syria, Afghanistan and elsewhere. In this chapter, I thus want to examine how tourists have sought to disengage from the events of the migrant crisis by finding ways to avoid the spaces of the migrant, leading to the geopolitics of erasure.

The chapter is organised as follows. First, I review some aspects of tourism and critical geopolitics. Next, I examine the development of research into what has been called tourism mobilities. I then sketch out aspects of a critical approach to the geopolitics of events from a mobilities perspective before discussing the geopolitics of erasure in the case of migrants transiting through CEE.

25.2 Tourism Geopolitics

Geopolitics has been defined in terms of the ways in which we view the world; how the global landscape is structured into various nation states and how this informs and is informed by the various foreign policy agendas of different governments (Dodds, 2007). Geopolitical discourses or 'scripts', as shown in a variety of institutional and popular media, are thus powerful and, as they divide up the world, can lead to conflicts over space and resources (O'Tuathail, 2002), leading to various mobilities and immobilities (Hannam *et al.*, 2006). Such discourses make their way into everyday practice through the media, and, indeed, tourism. In the media, we can see various representations of different countries in maps, books, films, television programmes, cartoons and, increasingly, websites that portray stereotypes of different countries for various geopolitical purposes (see Tzanelli, 2013). And websites have become increasingly powerful actors on the contemporary geopolitical scene (Hannam, 2013).

In terms of tourism, geopolitical discourses can also have profound effects on when, who and for what reason people are able to move freely across international borders. Hazbun has

---

*E-mail: k.hannam@napier.ac.uk

been at the forefront of conceptualising tourism geopolitics, arguing that:

> While international tourism remains an overlooked topic in the vast political economy literature on globalisation, the expansion and transformation of international tourism has long exhibited many of the core features of what has come to be characterised as globalisation. Tourism drives transnational flows of people, commodities and capital which circulate in globally coordinated production networks governed by large transnational firms such as airlines, tour operators and hotel management companies. International tourism also operates literally on the leading edge of globalisation by continually transferring consumer tastes, cultural practices, business people and capital across the globe.
>
> (Hazbun, 2004: 313)

Bianchi, meanwhile, has analysed the relationships between tourism, the freedom to travel and the geopolitics of security. He argues that implicit in much of contemporary geopolitics is a Western liberal ideal discourse of tourism as freedom (for some but not for others):

> While places such as hotels, motels and airports may signify a liberating sense of 'freedom' and 'cosmopolitanism' for some, where the boundaries of nationality are temporarily suspended the geographies of travel remain striated by gender, sexuality, ethnicity, class and increasingly, religion.
>
> (Bianchi, 2007: 68)

Moreover, '[w]here perhaps tourism becomes even more closely intertwined with global geopolitics is in the mapping of global risk and threats to security through the mechanism of state travel advisories' (Bianchi, 2007: 70). Advisories such as those produced by the Foreign and Commonwealth Office (FCO) in the UK are extremely powerful in portraying a dominant Western world view through information given on (in this case) the FCO's website (Hannam, 2013; see also Chapter 1, this volume). However, it is perhaps through the lens of what has become called tourism mobilities research that we get a better understanding of the changing relationships between tourism and geopolitical concerns.

25.3 Tourism Mobilities

The concept of mobilities arguably helps us to understand further how geopolitical concerns are spatially connected with people's daily lives, including the geopolitics that drive (and hinder) the movement of people as well as objects, information and non-human things (Hannam *et al.*, 2006). Cresswell (2010) suggests that when mobility is thought of as constellations of movement, representation and practice, we can think through a more finely developed geopolitics of mobility, so as to deduce particular facets, such as force, speed, rhythm, route, experience and friction. This framework thus provides new ways of thinking about the interconnectivity of mobilities at different spatial scales: '[n]ot only does a mobilities perspective lead us to discard our usual notions of spatiality and scale, but it also undermines existing linear assumptions about temporality and timing, which often assume that actors are able to do only one thing at a time, and that events follow each other in a linear order' (Hannam, 2009: 109).

The 'mobilities turn' has, therefore, brought about a renewed interest in the concept of scale. As Baerenholdt and Granas (2008: 2) note, '[c]onnections and encounters crucial to people's lives are often much more complex and dynamic [...]. Contexts are thus not predetermined at any scalar level, but only emerge with the practices of making and becoming places and mobilities.' In this regard, it is unsurprising that scholars have developed new concepts to deal with the multi-scalar and multidimensional fluidity of their objects of study. Concepts such as assemblage (Cresswell and Martin, 2012) are increasingly being used to describe the complexity of what can never be perfectly understood. The attention to scales of movement not only is concerned with human movements (bodily movements, daily circulation, diasporas) but also recognises how the world is composed of all kinds of movement – objects and ideas move as well (Hannam *et al.*, 2014).

In particular, a mobilities approach to tourism and leisure encourages us to think beyond the various mobilities of tourists to ways in which tourism and leisure experiences bring other mobilities into sync, or disorder, and as a result reconceptualises social theory (Rickly *et al.*, 2016). Mobilities research advances an agenda that thinks relationally about the geopolitics that hinder, encourage, regulate and inform mobilities at various scales, from the microbiological to the bodily to the national, as well as the mobility of information and non-human objects. Researching leisure and tourism mobilities involves an understanding of the complex combinations of movement and stillness, realities and fantasies, play and work (Sheller and Urry, 2004; Hannam *et al.*, 2006, 2014; Rickly *et al.*, 2016). In short, proponents of the mobilities paradigm argue that the concept of mobilities is concerned with simultaneously mapping the assemblages of the large-scale movements of people, objects, capital and information across the world with the more everyday processes of transportation, movement through public space and the travel of material things within everyday life (Hannam *et al.*, 2006).

Studies of leisure and tourism mobilities have examined the experience of the different modes of travel that tourists undertake, seeing these modes in part as forms of material and sociable dwelling-in-motion and dwelling-in-tourism (Obrador, 2003), places of and for various activities and how these can become politicised. Conceptualising tourism mobilities thus entails an attention to distinct social spaces or 'moorings' that orchestrate new forms of social and cultural life; for example, stations, hotels, motorways, resorts, airports, leisure complexes, beaches and so on (Hannam *et al.*, 2006). Places are thus significant for understanding the geopolitics of the forms of hospitality involved in mobilities in this context (Fregonese and Ramadan, 2015). Germann Molz *et al.* have also noted how the proliferation of digital devices and online social media and networking technologies has altered the practices of travel in recent years, such that people 'are now able to stay in continuous touch with friends, family and other travellers while on the move' (Germann Molz *et al.*, 2015: 173). This has led to new identities and a 'new sociality: virtual mooring, following, collaborating, and (dis)connecting'. Events, too, have become increasingly significant for people's identities, socialities and the wider geopolitical contexts in which they are situated (Hannam *et al.*, 2016; see also Chapter 19, this volume).

25.4 The Geopolitics of Event Mobilities

As a number of philosophers have noted, events and the acquisition of them have become a defining feature of contemporary life, bound up with our identities (Badiou, 2013; Žižek, 2014). The amount of events, as well as the different scales of them, also leads to various stresses: in terms of transport systems through congestion, in terms of security through geopolitical systems of control, as well as in terms of an individual's abilities to cope with attending multiple events at the same time (should I attend my son's birthday party or go on a protest march through London).

These stresses then also problematise our understandings of what it means to be free (Freudendal-Pedersen, 2009). Sager has further argued that: '[f]reedom as mobility is composed both of opportunities to travel when and where one pleases and of the feasibility of the choice not to travel' (Sager, 2006: 465). Engaging with the freedom to do something, as Bauman (1988) has noted, ultimately leads us into various unfreedoms (Freudendal-Pedersen, 2009). For example, we can go to an event, but the social nature of this event may lead us to become obligated to attend further events that we may not (really) want to attend (such as another political meeting). Tourism, events and mobilities coexist in various foldings and unfoldings through time and space that are difficult to control through contemporary scheduling as much as they are subject to national and international geopolitical structures (Freudendal-Pedersen, 2009). Events may also serve as contexts that provide meanings and purpose to a distinct action – from frantically leaving one's home to escape from a mudslide, to embarking on a protest march (Lamond and Spracklen, 2014; Cook and Butz, 2015).

Theoretically, Slavoj Žižek argues that:

> An 'Event' can refer to a devastating natural disaster or to the latest celebrity scandal, the triumph of the people or a brutal political change, an intense experience of a work of art or an intimate decision.
>
> (Žižek, 2014: 1)

An event, he contends, is, first, commonly understood at its most minimal level as something out of place, something shocking that interrupts the normal flow of things that comes somewhat unexpected, such as the events that led to the transition of the countries of CEE from communism to capitalism. Events like these can take hold of the imagination, such that:

> An event is thus the effect that seems to exceed its causes – and the space of an event is that which opens up by the gap that separates an effect from its causes.
>
> (Žižek, 2014: 3)

Events can also be considered as traumatic, as the 'intrusion of something New which remains unacceptable for the predominant view' (Žižek, 2014: 77). Indeed, Ferron and Massa have argued that:

> Studying how collective memories are formed, particularly in the case of trauma, is important because they persist for entire generations and they play a crucial social role, in that the interaction of the cultural elements involved can influence attitudes not only toward the past but also toward the present of current societies.
>
> (Ferron and Massa, 2014: 23)

A deeply traumatic event such as the disaster at Chernobyl can lead to a multitude of subsequent events, both unplanned and planned, as well as contested memories (Yankovska and Hannam, 2014).

Second, an event can also be conceived as a change: a change in terms of the ways in which reality may appear to us, as well as a transformation of the self. An event thus produces something new and heralds a symbolic transition, as many social anthropologists have recognised in terms of progression through the human life course in different societies (Turner, 1969). Voluntary work and educational mobilities are a good example of this as students embark on gap years and study abroad activities (Hannam et al., 2016).

Third, Žižek considers the motion of events as 'a change of the very frame through which we perceive the world and engage in it' (Žižek, 2014: 10). This alludes to the ways in which films and other social media commonly frame our understandings of events and the places of events. Fundamentally, fiction and reality thus become blurred in events. Tzanelli and Yar, for example, explore the 'intersections between the consumption of mediated popular culture and the real and imagined topographies within which those representations are framed' (Tzanelli and Yar, 2014: 1).

Fourth, we might also conceptualise events as 'extremely fragile moments' that may be initially memorable but which can be easily forgotten – hence, an emphasis on the materialities of events through which we attempt to remember them. Time, in terms of past, present and future, then, are important aspects of events, such that many governments and communities now think of their material legacies as much as the events themselves when planning them.

Fifth, events may also consist of everyday, mundane mobilities (Edensor, 2007). For example, the packing of luggage for an event involves various technologies, while producing worries of loss. The timing of mobility for events is equally informed by more routine moves. How and when people go to work, whether they work from home and how they use their time while commuting are all 'kinds of event-in-progress' (Adey et al., 2013). In the discussion below, I highlight how some of these aspects of events are co-constructed by participants and framed by the media in terms of the everyday understandings of geopolitics.

25.5 Migrants in Transit and the Geopolitics of Erasure

Let us return to the conundrum of the 'migrant crisis' in CEE. Since September 2015, the issue of refugees and/or migrants has entered centre stage in terms of the geopolitics between Western and Eastern Europe, with the centre being reimagined as a space of transit for those seeking a new life away from the fragility of becoming human in Syria, Afghanistan and elsewhere (Fig. 25.1). However, the complexity of the reception was frequently portrayed in the media as a division between those that welcomed these new arrivals and those that expected their government to enforce the borders and prevent so-called abuse of the European Union's (EU) system of asylum. This became focused on the 'mooring' for many potential migrants at the main train station in Budapest, Hungary – a geopolitical space that was subsequently framed and reframed by both the international media and international tourists as either a place to avoid or, conversely, a place to visit and offer voluntary help.

For example, Charles Hebbert, wrote an article in the UK *Daily Telegraph* on 7 September

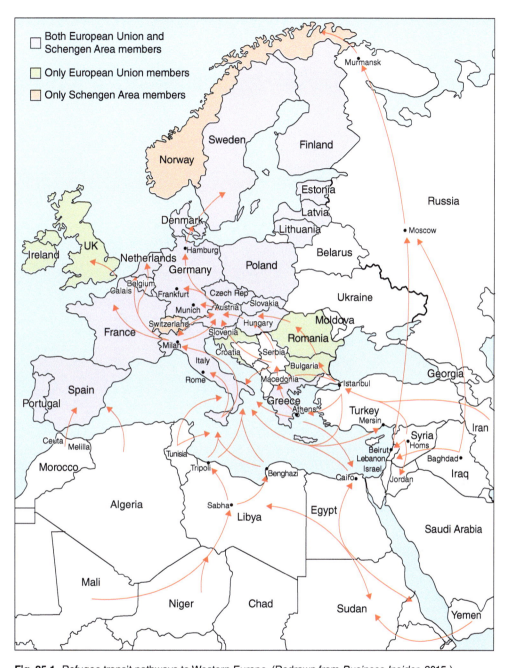

Fig. 25.1. Refugee transit pathways to Western Europe. (Redrawn from *Business Insider*, 2015.)

2015, entitled: 'Migrant crisis: advice for city breaks in Budapest', where he argued that:

> In the city itself, travellers are unlikely to notice the refugee crisis unless they go near the railway stations. Since most refugees see Hungary as a step towards the north and west,

they are keeping close to the stations in the hope that they can move on as quickly as possible.

(Hebbert, 2015)

This advice was further updated in the *Daily Telegraph* on 18 September by travel correspondent,

Natalie Paris, who quoted directly from the UK Foreign Office website's advice:

> 'Disruption and delays are possible at rail and road border crossings with Serbia, Hungary and Slovenia, as a result of significant numbers of people seeking to transit Croatia', advice from the Foreign Office states. 'The situation can change quickly. Air traffic has not been affected so far. The Croatian coast is also unaffected.'
>
> (Paris, 2015)

In Hungary, the newspaper *Hungary Today* similarly sought to reassure tourists that Budapest was a safe destination to visit:

> A top tourism official has issued reassurances that Hungary remains safe and that local authorities can guarantee the security of all tourists who arrive in the country. Deputy state secretary for tourism Ádám Ruszinkó told reporters in front of Saint Stephen's Basilica, in the city centre, that Budapest's tourist attractions are far from areas affected by the refugee crisis. There have been no tensions around the capital's main sites, he added. ... He said the main problem is the constant presence of 'shocking images' in the foreign press, which is scaring away foreign tourists...
>
> (*Hungary Today*, 2015)

The above quotations seek to separate the events of migration spatially from the events of tourism. Travel websites such as TripAdvisor similarly provided a platform for advice that was provided by locals, expatriates and other tourists under the heading: 'Is the refugee crisis affecting tourists in Budapest?' Answers to this question led to the following correspondence:

> Bez: The downtown area is 'business as usual' with no signs of the influx, although the Keleti train station is a different story. Many refugees – that make it to Budapest (which is a small % of the total), go there to take the trains either east to the refugee camps or west headed out of the country. I have not been on the trains lately so I have no experience there.
>
> Gill: I have booked accommodation about 4 km from the train station, so hopefully all will be well.
>
> Cat: Walked a large part of the Pest central district today, did not see a single refugee.
>
> (TripAdvisor, 2015)

Another travel website, www.hungarybudapest-guide.com, pointed out that:

> Is it safe to visit Budapest now?

The answer to this question is definitely yes! In most parts of Budapest you will not really even notice that there is a refugee issue at the moment, and if you should see some migrants here and there, they will not cause any problems or any harm. It is therefore just to come for you and enjoy Budapest!

> There might however be some things you should check out! If you have booked a hotel near the Keleti Railway station you might want to change that, at least if you want to forget about the migrant issue while in Budapest. If you do not mind, and in fact would like to see whats [sic] going on and maybe even bring some refugee something to eat, then don't think about this, but if you want to stay away from this, then you should maybe change your hotel if you have booked yourself in near the Keleti railway station.
>
> (Budapest Guide, 2015)

While these websites again emphasise the spatial separation of refugee from tourist, they also highlight that the tourist can move in the sense of finding 'alternative' accommodation. Here, we see the differential mobility empowerments at play for these two categories of people, with the tourist able to exercise both freedom to travel and freedom of choice in terms of accommodation, and time of travel. Although the latter website also suggests that some tourists may wish to visit the situation and bring some food, the majority of comments emphasise that the international media has exaggerated events and that tourists would have to go out of their way to find refugees. In this sense, what we find in these accounts is a geopolitics of erasure at work (see Aitken, 2016), where the figure of the refugee becomes hidden from the tourist, as the latter is encouraged to seek out 'alternative' sanitised spaces to perform tourism.

Conversely, both locals and international volunteers did seek to actively engage with the refugee crisis in Budapest. An international social media campaign, 'Volunteers for Refugees at Budapest', was organised via Facebook as part of a wider initiative by the Inter-European Human Aid Association, an NGO based in Austria and Germany. This NGO, founded in September 2015, was funded solely by member donations, and sought to coordinate the provision of basic hygiene facilities in Budapest using volunteers. Such efforts can also be viewed as part of the extension of a post-modern discourse of travel philanthropy, whereby individuals become more intensely involved compared with more traditional modes of aid and giving-at-a-distance (Mostafanezhad, 2013; Novelli *et al.*, 2015). In his account of the impact of the refugee crisis in Greece, Papataxiarchis describes how the complexity of the encounters between locals, volunteers, professional humanitarian workers and refugees on the 'front-line' beaches involves symbolic hierarchies – even for those academically trained volunteers who despise such hierarchies, such that:

> At the top of the symbolic hierarchy ... are the fishermen, the lifeguards and the (often professional) lifeboat crews, particularly those who have earned the marks of distinction on the 'battlefield'. For them, the flip side to altruistic behaviour is the power and pain of having to decide on crucial matters of life and death.
>
> (Papataxiarchis, 2016: 6)

These encounters have a profound impact on social spaces, which become 'knotted' together in camps for both refugees and indeed the volunteers and humanitarians themselves. Papataxiarchis (2016) further notes the emergence of 'e-volunteers' who send various performative signifiers, in the form of words and photos online, leaving electronic traces as markers of their identities, as well as other humanitarian 'pilgrims' in search of 'journalistic' intelligence.

25.6 Conclusions

On 4 September 2015, large numbers of refugees who had been attempting to board trains to Austria and Germany at the Keleti Railway Station in Budapest decided to walk instead. The depiction of the mass movement of people marching down motorways led to further political debate about the EU 'migrant crisis', with countries beginning to agree on 'quotas' of refugees. The EU itself has been much criticised for not doing more to prepare Europe for a refugee crisis, with chaos on the ground, as one European country after another has built fences and reintroduced border controls across the continent's supposedly border-free Schengen area, in an attempt to maintain national security. Adler noted that:

> The proposed fix is not only to form a European coastguard and border guard but also to give them the power to intervene at the borders of a country judged not to be doing the job properly itself. Europe's small and under-funded border patrol body, Frontex, until now had to wait to intervene at sovereign borders until invited to do so by the EU country in question.
>
> (Adler, 2015)

Furthermore, following the Paris attacks on 13 November 2015, people throughout Europe feel more exposed and at risk, caught between concern for refugees and fears for their own safety. People and policy makers do not want restrictions on European mobilities, yet the borders will become less porous and subject to more scrutiny in the future.

At the time of writing, the problem had yet to be resolved adequately, as these events painfully illustrated the playing out of geopolitics through the bodies of the migrants and refugees as they attempted to exercise their mobilities through walking. Walking has long been characterised as an inherently political and spatial act that has transformational agency (Edensor, 2010; Pinder, 2011), from Gandhi's walking tours (*padayatra*) to the Jarrow marches in the 1920s.[1] In this latter case, the powerful images conveyed also brought about a swift change in policy through everyday activism, leading to a 'solution' whereby Turkey 'keeps' the refugees in exchange for various concessions towards EU membership, including the movement (ironically) of its citizens through Europe without visa constraints.

Nevertheless, people attempting to reach Europe continue to die on a daily basis, and there is a rise in anti-refugee discourses in the popular media throughout Europe. The discourses of conventional tourism, meanwhile, reveal an attempted disengagement from the events of the 'migrant crisis' – an erasure of the geopolitical by the tourist. Conversely, we also have significant involvement in these geopolitical events due to the democratisation of humanitarianism and the further extension of types of volunteer (tourism).

Future studies of the critical geopolitics of tourism will need to understand the intersection of these different forms of tourism and event mobilities in the context of wider moral concerns (Mostafanezhad and Hannam, 2014).

Žižek's (2014) typology helps us to conceptualise these mobilities in terms of being traumatic and life changing while being framed and reframed within both the international media and wider geopolitical discourses (Hannam *et al.*, 2016). For the refugees themselves, their own mobilities may be extremely fragile and caught up with the everyday mundane tasks of finding food and shelter while being encountered by the media, volunteers, locals and tourists.

Endnote

[1] One might add: and to contemporary protest marches in Western political heartlands disowning military action being undertaken in just those places from which migrants/refugees are fleeing [Editor].

References

Adey, P., Bissell, D., Hannam, K., Merriman, P. and Sheller, M. (eds) (2013) *The Routledge Handbook of Mobilities.* Routledge, London.

Adler, K. (2015) Migrants crisis: embattled Brussels' 'comeback'. *BBC News Online* 15 December. Available at: http://www.bbc.com/news/world-europe-35099068 (accessed 22 August 2016).

Aitken, S. (2016) Locked in place: young people's immobilities and the Slovenian erasure. *Annals of the American Association of Geographers* 106(2), 358–365.

Badiou, A. (2013) *Philosophy and the Event.* Polity, New York.

Baerenholdt, J.O. and Granas, B. (2008) *Mobility and Place: Enacting Northern European Peripheries.* Ashgate, Aldershot, UK.

Bauman, Z. (1988) *Freedom.* Open University Press, Berkeley, California.

Bianchi, R. (2007) Tourism and the globalisation of fear: analysing the politics of risk and (in)security in global travel. *Tourism and Hospitality Research* 7, 64–74.

Budapest Guide (2015) Migrants, tourists, Budapest. *Hungarybudapestguide.com* 3 September. Available at: http://www.hungarybudapestguide.com/migrants-tourists-budapest/ (accessed 22 August 2016).

Business Insider (2015) Map of Europe's refugee crisis. Available at: http://uk.businessinsider.com/map-of-europe-refugee-crisis-2015-9?r=US&IR=T (accessed 22 August 2016).

Cook, N. and Butz, D. (2015) Mobility justice in the context of disaster. *Mobilities*, DOI: 10.1080/17450101.2015. 1047613.

Cresswell, T. (2010) Towards a politics of mobility. *Environment and Planning D: Society and Space* 28, 17–31.

Cresswell, T. and Martin, C. (2012) On turbulence: entanglements of disorder and order on a Devon beach. *Tijdschrift voor Economische en Sociale Geografie* 105, 516–529.

Dodds, K. (2007) *Geopolitics: A Very Short Introduction.* Oxford University Press, Oxford, UK.

Edensor, T. (2007) Mundane mobilities, performances and spaces of tourism. *Social & Cultural Geography* 8(2), 199–215.

Edensor, T. (2010) Walking in rhythms: place, regulation, style and the flow of experience. *Visual Studies* 25(1), 69–79.

Ferron, M. and Massa, P. (2014) Beyond the encyclopedia: collective memories in Wikipedia. *Memory Studies* 7(1), 22–45.

Fregonese, S. and Ramadan, A. (2015) Hotel geopolitics: a research agenda. *Geopolitics* 20(4), 793–813.

Freudendal-Pedersen, M. (2009) *Mobility in Daily Life: Between Freedom and Unfreedom.* Ashgate, Aldershot, UK.

Germann Molz, J. and Paris, C.M. (2015) The social affordances of flashpacking: exploring the mobility nexus of travel and communication. *Mobilities* 10(2), 173–192.

Hannam, K. (2009) The end of tourism? Nomadology and the mobilities paradigm. In: Tribe, J. (ed.) *Philosophical Issues in Tourism.* Channel View, Bristol, UK, pp. 101–113.

Hannam, K. (2013) 'Shangri-La' and the new 'Great Game': exploring tourism geopolitics between China and India. *Tourism, Planning and Development* 10(2), 178–186.

Hannam, K., Sheller, M. and Urry, J. (2006) Editorial: mobilities, immobilities and moorings. *Mobilities* 1(1), 1–32.

Hannam, K., Butler, G. and Paris, C.M. (2014) Developments and key issues in tourism mobilities. *Annals of Tourism Research* 44, 171–185.

Hannam, K., Rickly, J. and Mostafanezhad, M. (eds) (2016) *Event Mobilities*. Routledge, London.

Hazbun, W. (2004) Globalisation, reterritorialisation and the political economy of tourism development in the Middle East. *Geopolitics* 9(2), 310–341.

Hebbert, C. (2015) Migrant crisis: advice for city breaks in Budapest. *The Daily Telegraph Online* [London] 7 September. Available at: http://www.telegraph.co.uk/travel/destinations/europe/hungary/budapest/11848662/Migrant-crisis-advice-for-city-breaks-in-Budapest.html (accessed 5 January 2016).

Hungary Today (2015) Government official plays down impact of migrant crisis on Hungary's tourism sector. *Hungary Today* 7 September. Available at: http://hungarytoday.hu/news/government-official-plays-impact-migrant-crisis-hungarys-tourism-sector-29809 (accessed 5 January 2016).

Lamond, I. and Spracklen, K. (eds) (2014) *Protests as Events: Politics, Activism and Leisure*. Rowman and Littlefield, London.

Mostafanezhad, M. (2013) 'Getting in touch with your inner Angelina': celebrity humanitarianism and the cultural politics of gendered generosity in volunteer tourism. *Third World Quarterly* 34(3), 485–499.

Mostafanezhad, M. and Hannam, K. (eds) (2014) *Moral Encounters in Tourism*. Ashgate, Aldershot, UK.

Novelli, M., Morgan, N., Mitchell, G. and Ivanov, K. (2016) Travel philanthropy and sustainable development: the case of the Plymouth-Banjul Challenge. *Journal of Sustainable Tourism* 24(6), 824–845.

Obrador, P. (2003) 'Being-on-holiday': tourist dwelling, bodies and place. *Tourist Studies* 3, 47–66.

O'Tuathail, G. (2002) Post-Cold War geopolitics: contrasting superpowers in a world of global dangers. In: Johnson, R.J., Taylor, P. and Watts, M. (eds) *Geographies of global change*, 2nd edn. Blackwell, Oxford, UK, pp. 174–190.

Papataxiarchis, E. (2016) Being 'there': at the front line of the 'European refugee crisis' – part 1. *Anthropology Today* 32(2), 3–9.

Paris, N. (2015) Migrant crisis: advice for tourists in Europe. *The Daily Telegraph Online* [London] 18 September. Available at: http://www.telegraph.co.uk/travel/destinations/europe/croatia_/11875241/Migrant-crisis-advice-for-tourists-in-Europe.html (accessed 5 January 2016).

Pinder, D. (2011) Errant paths: the poetics and politics of walking. *Environment and Planning D: Society and Space* 29, 672–692.

Rickly, J., Hannam, K. and Mostafanezhad, M. (eds) (2016) *Tourism and Leisure Mobilities*. Routledge, London.

Sager, T. (2006) Freedom as mobility: implications of the distinction between actual and potential travelling. *Mobilities* 1(3), 465–488.

Sheller, M. and Urry, J. (eds) (2004) *Tourism Mobilities*. Routledge, London.

Tripadvisor (2015) Is the refugee crisis affecting tourists in Budapest? Trip Advisor 26 August–3 September. Available at: http://www.tripadvisor.co.uk/ShowTopic-g274887-i263-k8807515-Is_the_refugee_crisis_affecting_tourists_in_Budapest-Budapest_Central_Hungary.html (accessed 5 January 2016).

Turner, V. (1969) *The Ritual Process: Structure and Anti-Structure*. Aldine, London.

Tzanelli, R. (2013) *Heritage in a Digital Era*. Routledge, London.

Tzanelli, R. and Yar, M. (2014) Breaking bad, making good: notes on a televisual tourist industry. *Mobilities* DOI: 10.1080/17450101.2014.929256.

Yankovska, G. and Hannam, K. (2014) Dark and toxic tourism in the Chernobyl exclusion zone. *Current Issues in Tourism* 17(10), 929–939.

Žižek, S. (2014) *Event: Philosophy in Transit*. Penguin, Harmondsworth, UK.

Part VII:

Conclusions

_____

26 In Conclusion

Derek Hall*
Seabank Associates, Maidens,Scotland, UK

26.1 Where We Have Been

This volume has drawn on a wealth of scholarship and experience to emphasise that tourism possesses inherently geopolitical dimensions and implications that have been significantly under-researched in tourism scholarship. Through a diversity of critical lenses, albeit focused on a particular diverse and dynamic area of the globe, the foregoing chapters have drawn upon a range of conceptual and empirical methodologies, and have addressed issues and concepts articulating numerous facets of the tourism–geopolitics nexus.

As a collected body of work, highly valuable within itself, this volume offers a jumping-off point for further methodological reflection, thematic expansion and theoretical consolidation. Although focused on places, people and processes in Central and Eastern Europe (CEE), the conceptual frameworks, arguments and questions posed possess far wider relevance.

The six main thematic, yet overlapping, sections have highlighted areas of common interest, while recognising multiple interrelationships and the blurring of boundaries between them.

In the first section, geopolitics as a concept – or series of concepts and attitudes – and its relationships with tourism, were evaluated. The changing emphases in the study of both were examined, and theoretical frameworks that would be taken up in subsequent chapters were addressed. The strategic place of CEE in (neo) classical geopolitical thought was juxtaposed with post-communist reformulations of both the nature and relevance of regional ascription and of the geopolitical orientation of CEE countries in relation to European Union (EU) enlargement and transnational economic power. The relationship between tourism and transnational power – first that of the communist state/bloc and subsequently of capitalist corporations and the EU – was a theme that would subsequently preoccupy a number of chapters. Conceptualisation required to raise the rigour of analytical debate within tourism scholarship – often coming from outside of the subject, and notably from geography – was identified.

Part II, while taking largely traditional approaches to geopolitics and international relations, and to tourism's position within Europe's dynamic core and peripheries, highlighted issues of historical change and continuity, and of imagery, identity and the role of tourism in spaces deformed by the mobility of global capital, conflict and geopolitical contestation. It emphasised a need to reconceptualise the dynamic realities of conflict spaces in Europe at different scales and levels, and to appreciate their consequences for the quotidian, not least for tourism.

*E-mail: derekhall@seabankscotland.co.uk

In Part III, the nature and implications of tourism- and leisure-related transnationalism within the wider processes of globalisation were examined in relation to Central and south-eastern Europe, with a range of critiques of neoliberal hegemony and the spatial expressions of capitalist development in core peripheries and peripheral cores.

The palimpsestuous nature of borderlands and their functions as places of cooperation and interaction, of bordering and rebordering, were addressed in Part IV. Notably, the varying and dynamic relationships between 'high politics' at state and supranational levels, and tourism-related action involving border communities at the local level, were examined in contrasting contexts.

The dissonant and contested heritage arising from almost half a century of communism and of post-communist conflict were seen to be resonant in the identity and imagery expressed in the chapters comprising Part V. Looking forward, the role of cyberspace in the construction of destination imagery emphasised opportunities for changing the nature and source of power and influence within place representation, regional identity, tourism 'governance' and global connectivity.

The final main section of the volume, Part VI, addressed the changing nature of tourism- and leisure-related mobilities and their impacts from a number of perspectives. Contextualising the conjunctions of tourism and migration/refugee flight emphasised the contemporary and dynamic nature of such issues at a number of levels and scales.

26.2   Where We Are

Tourism will not be able to ignore the pressures of climate change and resource access, which will stimulate increasing migration and refugee flight around the world. And, if the events of 2015/16 are indicative, much land and sea-borne flight will be aimed at Europe, which, at the time of completing this volume, has been found wanting in seriously addressing such issues.

Indeed, what has emerged from a number of chapters is a sense of avoidance, perhaps denial, even erasure (Chapter 25). Chapters 17 and 18 emphasised the 'avoidance', even repulsion

function of contested heritage and mutually exclusive cultural tourism sites for 'Other' communities in Bosnia–Herzegovina and Kosovo. Chapter 16 identified the notable absence of cuisine from other CEE countries in the restaurants of central Warsaw, while Italian and Japanese food was readily available. Chapter 22 highlighted that while there had been massive growth in low-cost flights between CEE and Western/northern Europe, relatively little additional route development had taken place between CEE countries themselves. Is this simply a reflection of 'market conditions'? The same could be asked of the limited penetration of transnational hotel chains in Bulgaria examined in Chapter 10. And in Chapter 23, a prestige highway project linking co-ethnic capital cities remains significantly underused, perhaps even avoided, because of its perceived nationalist symbolism.

Then again, chapters 12, 14 and 15 emphasised efforts to reduce or even eliminate the barrier effects of international borders to encourage interaction and cooperation, not least in tourism. In Chapter 4, the reunifying role of the Adriatic space was emphasised. How less pejorative is 'Eastern Adriatic' compared to 'Western Balkans' as a signifier?

Part of the CEE neoliberal hegemonic package, with implicit EU and NATO (North Atlantic Treaty Organization) encouragement, has been to reorient mentalities firmly westwards, to relocate identities more centrally within Europe, and to turn backs on the large power to the East. Tourism's agency role in this process is inherently ambivalent, encouraging images of the reassuringly familiar while also offering frissons of the exotic 'Other'. And while Chapters 14 and 15 highlighted work at a local and regional level in stimulating cooperation and overcoming the physical and psychological barriers between 'Europe' and Russia, a contemptuous disregard for the latter's historic role has resulted in the geopolitical contestation whose tourism outcomes were addressed in Chapters 5 and 6.[1] And the local impacts of high-level (geo)politics were clearly exemplified in relation to mobilities across the Finnish–Russian border (Chapter 13) and in the role of Russian tourism-related investment in Montenegro (Chapter 7).

If one of the avenues of critical geopolitics concerns the political dimensions of ways of representing the world and the different modes of knowledge and understanding that inform such representation (Chapter 2), the contributors to this volume have succeeded in articulating such critical concerns in relation to tourism in CEE. If the employment of a regional framework for this volume should be thought of as an anachronism, perhaps even perpetuating Cold War mentalities, the contributors have confounded any such conception.

26.3   Where Are We Going?

A wide range of themes and frameworks for further research agendas, as exemplified in Box 26.1, can be identified as emerging from, or inspired by, the foregoing chapters.

There is clearly much potential in the field of (critical) geopolitical studies of tourism (and indeed of tourism informing geopolitical studies). In the business of anticipating and mitigating the future of tourism and likely impacts upon it (Gössling *et al.*, 2008; Webster *et al.*,

2012; Postma *et al.*, 2013; Webster and Ivanov, 2014), the role of political instability is a common theme. Alongside other drivers of uncertainty, notably climate change and technology shift, the dynamics, 'fuzzy' boundaries and unpredictability of political futures render analytical crystal ball gazing in this arena, and the role and nature of tourism within it, particularly precarious.

Indeed, in the looming shadow of an elephant in the editorial room, these final words were being written just one month before the holding of a UK referendum on whether to continue membership of the EU. The public discourse preceding the vote embraced a hybridity of spurious and depressingly mendacious arguments, articulating geopolitical imaginaries at a number of levels. The mobilities of 'Others', issues of identity and reconceptualisations of 'Europe' were all invoked to sustain or undermine such arguments, emphasising only too well the need for volumes such as this to better inform debate and critical thinking.

Box 26.1   Themes for further research agendas

---

1. Tourism as an activity subordinate to the consequences of higher (geo)politics:
   - tourism-related consequences of spatially expressed contestation (e.g. Isaac *et al.*, 2016)
   - sources of contestation focused on the practices and spaces of tourism development (e.g. Fregonese and Ramadan, 2015)
   - the dysfunction of different levels of governance impacting on transborder cooperation in/constraints on tourism-related mobilities
   - tourist source governments' advisories and popular media imagery, especially following a negative event (natural disaster, terrorism) at a destination
   - the survival and attraction of (the changing nature of?) 'Otherness' (e.g. Verschaeve and Wadle, 2014).
2. Tourism as an agent of/surrogate for geopolitical processes:
   - as the embodiment and diffusion agent of neoliberal hegemony
   - as a vehicle for cross-border, intercommunity cooperation (and economic development)
   - as a signifier and promoter (or conversely as a destroyer) of identity
   - as a vehicle for organised criminality (including money laundering and terrorism)
   - as a symbol of nationalism/potential irredentism and the imposition of unwanted political authority
   - in the power and control exercised over the behaviour of outbound tourists
   - in the soft power role and identity value of international leisure-related events (e.g. Giulianotti, 2015)
   - in the commoditisation of nature for tourism-related purposes and the ecosystem disconnects of neoliberalism (e.g. Duffy, 2015).
3. Critical geopolitical evaluations of tourism processes:
   - evaluations of unequal relationships between stakeholders, such as regional tourism organisations' weak positions in relation to the power of tour operators and airlines (e.g. Farmaki, 2015), or the politics of the quotidian in host–guest relations of hospitality

Continued

Box 26.1 Continued.

- tourism stakeholder responses to geopolitical events: such as terrorism or refugee arrival at tourism destinations
- processes and outcomes of supranational sports institutions' (such as the International Olympic Committee (IOC), *Fédération Internationale de Football Association* (FIFA)) decisions and power
- changing geopolitical influences on popular constructions of 'Otherness'
- sources of oppression or elevation of marginalised peoples as a result of the pursuit of international tourism development (e.g. Xue *et al.*, 2015)
- hospitality as performance (e.g. Craggs, 2012, 2014).

4. Tourism as a means of ameliorating (past) geopolitical processes:
- more nuanced studies on the role of tourism as one potential element of post-conflict 'reconciliation' and reconstruction.

5. Tourism and the changing geopolitics of cyberspace:
- the dynamics of power and control of destination imagery and regional identity, particularly of less visited places
- real space contestation in residential locations impacted by cyberspace tourism accommodation facilitators
- Web 2.0 facilitated peer-to-peer networks extending the sharing economy into tourism performances (e.g. Karlsson and Dolnicar, 2016)
- longitudinal studies of Web-based tourism information (e.g. Bronner and de Hoog, 2016).

6. Critical microgeopolitics
- the construction of tourist behaviour and perceptions from intimate sources of identity and destination imagery, such as ethnic restaurants (e.g. Min and Lee, 2014), cinematic film or televisual experiences (e.g. Fu *et al.*, 2016)
- evaluations of the gatekeepers of 'accessible' tourism
- nuanced studies of the relative power of control and mobility held by differently abled tourists, and in relation to able-bodied guides and other facilitators (e.g. Small, 2015)
- more rigorously gender-aware evaluations of the role of emotion and intimacy in power relationships within tourism-related processes
- embodied interactions between tourists and 'Others' such as refugees or beggars (e.g. Andriotis, 2016).

Endnote

[1] But surely military 'solutions' should have no place in 21st century Europe.

References

Andriotis, K. (2016) Beggars-tourists' interactions: an unobtrusive typological approach. *Tourism Management* 52, 64–73.

Bronner, F. and de Hoog, R. (2016) Travel websites: changing visits, evaluations and posts. *Annals of Tourism Research* 57, 94–112.

Craggs, R. (2012) Towards a political geography of hotels: Southern Rhodesia, 1958–1962. *Political Geography* 31, 215–224.

Craggs, R. (2014) Hospitality in geopolitics and the making of Commonwealth international relations. *Geoforum* 52, 90–100.

Duffy, R. (2015) Nature-based tourism and neoliberalism: concealing contradictions. *Tourism Geographies* 17(4), 529–543.

Farmaki, A. (2015) Regional network governance and sustainable tourism. *Tourism Geographies* 17(3), 385–407.

Fregonese, S. and Ramadan, A. (2015) Hotel geopolitics: a research agenda. *Geopolitics* 20(4), 793–813.

Fu, H., Haobin Ye, B. and Xiang, J. (2016) Reality TV, audience travel intentions and destination image. *Tourism Management* 55, 37–48.

Giulianotti, R. (2015) The Beijing 2008 Olympics: examining the interrelations of China, globalization, and soft power. *European Review* 23(2), 286–296.

Gössling, S., Hall, C.M. and Weaver, D. (eds) (2008) *Sustainable Tourism Futures: Perspectives on Systems, Restructuring and Innovation*. Routledge, Abingdon, UK.

Isaac, R., Hall, C.M. and Higgins-Desboilles, F. (eds) (2016) *The Politics and Power of Tourism in Palestine*. Routledge, Abingdon, UK.

Karlsson, L. and Dolnicar, S. (2016) Someone's been sleeping in my bed. *Annals of Tourism Research* 58, 156–170.

Min, K.-H. and Lee, T.J. (2014) Customer satisfaction with Korean restaurants in Australia and their role as ambassadors for tourism marketing. *Journal of Travel and Tourism Marketing* 31(4), 493–506.

Postma, A., Yeoman, I. and Oskam, J. (eds) (2013) *The Future of European Tourism*. European Tourism Futures Institute, Leeuwarden, the Netherlands.

Small, J. (2015) Interconnecting mobilities on tour: tourists with vision impairment partnered with sighted tourists. *Tourism Geographies* 17(1), 76–90.

Verschaeve, M. and Wadle, H.C. (2014) Tourism and post-socialist heterotopias – Eastern Europe as an imagined rural past. In: Picard, D. and di Giovine, M.A. (eds) *Tourism and the Power of Otherness: Seductions of Difference*. Channel View, Bristol, UK, pp. 74–92.

Webster, C. and Ivanov, S. (2014) Geopolitical drivers of future tourist flows. *Journal of Tourism Futures* 1, 61–71.

Webster, C., Leigh, J. and Ivanov, S. (eds) (2012) *Future Tourism: Political, Social and Economic Challenges*. Routledge, Abingdon, UK.

Xue, L., Kerstetter, D. and Buzinde, C.N. (2015) Residents' experiences with tourism development and resettlement in Luoyang, China. *Tourism Management* 46, 444–453.

Index

Note: bold page numbers indicate figures and tables; numbers in brackets preceded by *n* are chapter endnote numbers.